P9-DMC-950

WITHDRAWN

WITHDRAWN

PSYCHOLOGY IN EDUCATION

PSYCHOLOGY IN EDUCATION

FOURTH EDITION

Herbert Sorenson / University of Kentucky

WITHDRAWN

McGRAW-HILL BOOK COMPANY

NEW YORK   SAN FRANCISCO   TORONTO   LONDON

PSYCHOLOGY IN EDUCATION

Copyright © 1964 by McGraw-Hill, Inc. All Rights Reserved.

Copyright 1940, 1948, 1954 by McGraw-Hill, Inc. All Rights Reserved.
Printed in the United States of America. This book, or parts thereof, may not be reproduced in any form without permission of the publishers. **Library of Congress Catalog Card Number 64-23117**

59685

PREFACE

In the past ten years, man has brought about a revolution in almost every sphere of existence by means of new materials, new machines, and new concepts. But there have been disappointingly few corresponding upheavals in education and psychology since the third edition of this book was published. The schools have been examined a little more critically of late, but the development of the individual remains essentially the same. What we know of the process of education is expanding gradually and education is improving in general. Still, we have achieved no miracles in aiding the learning and behavior of human beings. While we have made fabulous progress in producing *things*, we have been less effective in educating man in certain aspects of his group behavior, as the ominous increases of such social maladies as alcoholism, delinquency, and crime indicate.

Yet, in examining the development of the behavioral sciences over the past decade, we can be encouraged by the solid research that has been done. If we have made no signal discoveries, we certainly have achieved a more comprehensive understanding of the structural and behavioral development of man.

In this fourth edition of *Psychology in Education* much of this recent research has been utilized to clarify the educational processes as we understand them, and, hopefully, to advance our understanding of those processes. A text, such as this, in applied psychology is concerned with understanding human capabilities and the means to bring about their most favorable growth and development. Theory without experimental support serves little use, however, and to correct this common imbalance, the present text has been interlarded with an abundance of experimental data, much of it recent. The objective here is to present substantial content validated in every possible particular.

Another tenet of this text is that the classroom is only one part of the proper sphere of educational psychology. Because man is also a social creature, his behavior is affected in a number of areas—the home, the school, the community, even the larger aspects of the social milieu. The problems of educating the individual are treated here in terms of this larger context.

The first section, devoted to the physical, mental, and social growth and development of the individual, provides a basis for understanding the capacities of the learner and, thus, his readiness for learning. This section also takes up the effects of nature and nurture on growth and development. Because this book is for practicing as well as prospective teachers, a chapter on the personal and professional development of the teacher is included.

Educationally and socially, individual differences can create many problems. The second section of this book, dealing with individual differences and their effects on adjustment in school and post-school life, discusses extensively what the school can and should do for its differing students. Socio-economic class, which contributes greatly to variations among individuals, is treated here as well.

The third section discusses human needs and motives, developmental tasks, mental health, attitudes and behavior, and personal adjustment. This section centers around the school's objective to help the student to become an emotionally healthy and effective human being.

The last section deals directly with learning. A great deal of material about learning and the development of abilities has already been introduced. These several chapters summarize and develop most of what is known about the processes and the enhancement of learning, including a discussion in the last chapter of the evaluation and reporting of growth, development, and the learning of students.

This new edition of *Psychology in Education* is intended to bring together such new information in the field as seems germane with the best of what was previously known and thought. The writer trusts that his material has not been influenced by recent fads and fancies in education and psychology. He has tried to steer a straight course, guided by sound facts and valid principles abstracted largely from recent research, but also from reliable findings of the past several decades.

A book should be interesting and teachable. Several new features are conducive to this objective. Among these are picture groupings or photo quizzes which are planned to help the student to comprehend more clearly various concepts and principles. At strategic places in each chapter are "Exhibits," and "Consider the Data" and "Reflect and Review" sections which encourage the student to enlarge his knowledge and clarify his thinking. These features require the application of knowledge to actual situations and thereby encourage transfer. In addition the many charts, diagrams, and tables are designed to facilitate the development of understanding.

In compiling a new edition of a previous work, a writer, in checking permissions, quotations, and footnotes, may become suddenly overwhelmed by the generosity of the intellectual and scientific world. This writer wishes to thank the many publishers and authors who have granted permission to quote their materials. He feels a great debt, too, to the scholars whose work is indispensable in writing a book in educational psychology: D. P. Ausubel, Nancy Baily, J. I. Goodlad, J. C. Gowan, N. E. Gronlund, R. J. Havighurst, S. L. Pressey, D. G. Ryans, L. W. Sontag, J .B. Stroud, Percival Symonds, L. M. Terman, E. L. Thorndike, and many others.

James Hurst has worked extensively on the manuscript and helped materially in the treatment and development of many topics. The author owes him many thanks. And finally, the writer wishes to thank his wife, Mrs. Mabel Sorenson, for her faithful work on this edition, as on previous ones, for her performance of the many duties that are necessary for the development of a manuscript from its beginning until its publication.

Herbert Sorenson

CONTENTS

PART I
HUMAN DEVELOPMENT

CHAPTER 1
PHYSICAL STRUCTURE
AND FUNCTION

Man's physical life, like that of many living things, is a process of gradual flowering, followed by a period of maturity, and then gradual decline; and school students are at various periods of the developmental processes. Their bodies are maturing and their physical capabilities are developing rapidly. Furthermore, these changes are predisposing them to certain interests and activities. Indeed, youth illustrates beautifully how the human body and the human mind are inexorably linked. Thus, study of the progress of young people toward physical maturity would seem to be strongly related to the study of psychology in education, and experience and reflection show the relationship to be close—so close that we may well begin by considering the physical aspects of human development.

NORMAL BODY CHANGE

The term "physical growth" refers to becoming larger and heavier and indicates increases and changes that are both additive and augmentative. Physical growth can be measured quantitatively in inches, pounds, or other units. The heart becomes bigger; the bones become longer, thicker, and heavier. In general, the body grows by adding more inches in height and circumference and more pounds in weight.

"Physical development," on the other hand, indicates progressive change and advancement toward maturity. Development connotes a process of maturing and functional improvement which takes place because of qualitative as well as quantitative changes in structure and form. Development indicates more specifically than growth the change in character that takes place. Bones grow larger, but they also develop as a result of changes in their material composition and structural form. After birth, the brain cells of an individual do not change in number, but they do grow larger, undergo chemical change, form medullary sheaths, and become more complex individually. Most physical development, of course, is dependent on physical growth; and because of this basic relationship, the terms growth and development are used in close association.

H. V. Meredith has listed five ways in which growth and development are manifested [Meredith, 1957]. The simplest and most evident is change in *size;* for example, the whole organism changes from just a speck to the adult male or female. A second index of growth and development is change in *number:* From the union of two cells—sperm and ovum—comes an adult body of 20 trillion cells. Another aspect of growth and development is change in *kind,* simply illustrated by the change of cartilage to bone—a specific change the progress of which, incidentally, is a good index of physical maturation. A change in *position* takes place as the heart, intestines, and limbs change angles and location. Also there is a change in *relative size;* for example, the head becomes relatively smaller and the legs relatively longer.

Growth does not always contribute to development. A child or adult may grow very fat and heavy, but such growth can hardly be considered development in the sense of advancement to a higher level of maturity. Actually, a person has developed if he is physically healthier and/or has more sensorimotor skills, so that his physical condition is conducive to greater personal effectiveness. Thus, by improving his sensorimotor skills and thereby utilizing better the capacities he has received from about two decades of growth, a person can develop even after physical growth stops.

Course of the Life Process. Life begins with the union of two germ cells, the male sperm and the female ovum. The germ cell of the father fertilizes the germ cell of the mother, and a new life is on its way—from the union of two cellular specks a hitherto nonexistent human being begins his growth and development in the body of his mother.

The growth and development that occur during the 9 months of prenatal life are astounding, especially when one considers that the prenatal period constitutes only about one per cent of a person's life span. Following conception, the embryo grows very rapidly, but it is so minute originally that it is not until the second half of pregnancy that the unborn child experiences a rapid measurable gain in weight. About six times as much weight growth takes place during the second half of gestation as takes place during the first half. A little over half the growth in length takes place during the first half of pregnancy. At birth the infant has reached a relatively advanced stage of development. He possesses all the organic parts he will ever have—toes, feet, legs, genitals, visceral organs, fingers, hands, arms, the nervous system, the various sense organs, the vascular system, endocrine glands, bone and

3

muscular structures. The teeth, which started to form about two months after conception, begin to make their appearance several months after birth. At birth all the sense organs—eyes, ears, nose, skin, and mouth—are ready to function and actually do so shortly after birth. The nervous system, which is one-tenth of the newborn's total weight, transmits some of the stimuli which reach the senses. Indeed, postnatal growth and development cause enlargement and change—in composition and form and, importantly, in function—of the organic parts that the child possesses at birth.

The child grows most rapidly the first year, at a declining rate the second year, and then at a slower but steady pace for about a decade. When childhood merges into adolescence, there is again a period of faster growth. Adolescence slowly becomes adulthood and the prime of life; then follow progressive deterioration, old age, and death. This is the certain march from conception to old age, though many drop out along the way. Yet for all the certainty of this time-bound process, the mysteries of life and of growth and development are much more complex, and challenge the imagination more, than stratospheric rockets and atomic energy.

Common and Individual Patterns of Growth. The statement is sometimes made that the physical growth of the individual child is unique—that each child grows in his own way. This statement, if taken literally, is very misleading since the growth of each child follows a common general pattern, with rare, usually pathological, exceptions.

Increases in height and weight are greatest for nearly all children during the first year of life. The later growth spurt in pounds and inches comes for nearly all just before and during the early teen ages. There is little increase in height after the age of twenty and rarely any after twenty-five. Brain growth is greatest in infancy and early childhood, not in adolescence. The great increase in genital size takes place during the teen ages.

There are, of course, some normal variations in rate and amount of growth. For instance, the smoothed curves (shown in the figure in Exhibit 1) of the height growth of three girls included in a study by Nancy Bayley show that the amount of height change per year varies from person to person during the growing years. The differences are apparent at all ages, but, as with a horse race, which is most decisive in the "homestretch," are most obvious toward the end of the period of growth. Actually, the smoothed curves differ very little from the curves based on the obtained measurements.

Contrasting Development Schedules within the Body. A good way to understand the social and educational problems of human beings is to compare the development of the lymphoid system, the nervous system, the genital system,

Exhibit 1   Height growth pattern of three girls

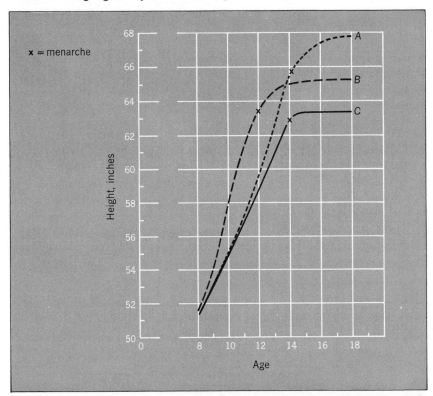

Three girls—*A*, *B*, and *C*—had generally similar patterns of growth in height, but there were differences, with *A* differing most. She was of average height until about the age of 12½, but then grew more rapidly than the average girl does after that age—continuing to grow until about eighteen—and became a tall woman. *B* was a tall girl up to the age of twelve, but grew slowly thereafter— and very little after fourteen—and reached average adult height. If *C*, who was the shortest, had had a little above average growth after fourteen, she would have been about average in height. Most girls can be expected to gain a little over an inch after fifteen; *C*'s growth, however, was very slight after fourteen and stopped at fifteen, and she became a shorter-than-average woman. It will be noted that *A* passed and drew away from *B* before the age of fourteen. *C* gained a little on *B*, but ended 2 inches shorter. (Nancy Bayley, "Individual Patterns of Development," *Child Development,* 27:45–74, 1956. Figure is on page 52.)

and the body as a whole. Much information fundamental for understanding human nature and human development can be gained from such a comparison. (See and study carefully Figure 1, which contains curves showing the course of development in these four aspects from birth to the age of twenty.)

Development of the lymphoid system (Figure 1, curve *A*) is greatest at the end of childhood and in early adolescence when physical growth is very rapid. The lymphatic system consists of its fluid, vessels, and nodes or glands which function to protect the body from disease. The lymph nodes are located under the arms and knees, in the neck, and in several other places. The lymph nodes form lymphocytes which destroy disease-producing bacteria. The lymph nodes filter out these bacteria, and they also filter out cancer cells.

Since the main function of this system is to protect the body against infections, it is interesting to note that its development is at its peak at about the age of eleven, when the death rate is about the lowest, though cause-and-

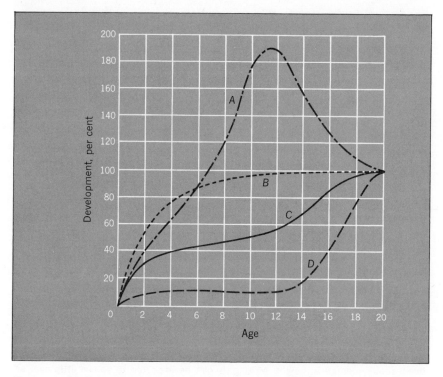

Figure 1 Postnatal development of body parts and organs *The major types of postnatal development of the various parts and organs of the body are shown by four curves. These are drawn to a common percentage scale; that is, the development reached at twenty, essentially the age of physical maturity, is shown in the four curves as 100 per cent. The curves indicate for each type the percentage of twenty-year-old development which is reached at successive ages from birth to twenty.*

A, lymphoid type: thymus, lymph nodes, intestinal lymphoid masses. B, neural type: brain and its parts, dura, spinal cord, optic apparatus, various head dimensions. C, general type: body as a whole, including external dimensions (with exception of head and neck), respiratory and digestive organs, kidneys, aorta and pulmonary trunks, spleen, musculature as a whole, skeleton as a whole, blood volume. D, genital type: testis, ovary, epididymis, uterine tube, prostate, prostatic urethra, seminal vesicles. (J. A. Harris, C. M. Jackson, D. G. Paterson, and R. E. Scammon, Measurement of Man, The University of Minnesota Press, Minneapolis, 1930).

effect relationship between the two statistics is not certain. It seems that the lymphatic system has been designed to aid survival by protecting against disease during childhood and that after reaching its highest development, this protective system declines but continues to do its work well.

Nature hurries to give us high mental power early in life by providing very rapid neural development during the first few years and establishes the full anatomical basis (the nervous system) for intelligence by the age of twenty or within a very few years thereafter (Figure 1, curve B). Thus the brain itself (Figure 2) grows very rapidly preceding and following birth, as if determined to achieve its full weight as soon as possible, and by the age of four attains much the greater portion of its mature weight. Its growth continues at a decreasing rate, and nearly if not quite all the brain's weight is attained by the age of twenty.

It should be emphasized that we are speaking here only of the weight growth of the brain. Tests of mental development indicate that in the very young years mental power and ability do not increase as rapidly as the weight of the brain, that there is more mental growth and development after the age of four than before. Thus later changes that occur in the brain are more important psychologically than the small increase in weight might indicate. It is even likely that growth and arrangement of the fine fibers of the brain, such as the dendrites, continue throughout the early twenties. This development causes little change in weight but probably increases intellectual potential considerably.

The body as a whole (Figure 1, curve C) has a characteristic growth curve which differs from the lymphoid, neural, and genital growth curves in that there are two periods of rapid general growth. The first takes place during the first year of life, with the head and trunk growth being the most rapid; the body becomes longer and broader. At the end of the first year the legs start to grow more rapidly than the trunk and the child appears more slender and even long-legged. This growth ratio continues until the second growth spurt at puberty, when the trunk growth again exceeds the growth of the legs.

There tends to be an increase in fatness during the puberty years but during the following few years of rapid growth, a thinning or loss of chubbiness takes place. Boys grow wider and thicker at the shoulders and chest and develop rapidly in musculature during the teens. Girls do not increase much in musculature during the teens, but round out and become broader in the pelvic region. An aesthetic distribution of fat also takes place to give the girl in her late teens the body characteristics of a young woman.

The second or adolescent growth spurt is the period of maximum growth of the skeletal and muscular systems, which in large part is responsible for the accompanying substantial increase in height and weight. The stomach, heart, liver, and other visceral organs grow faster than they did previously,

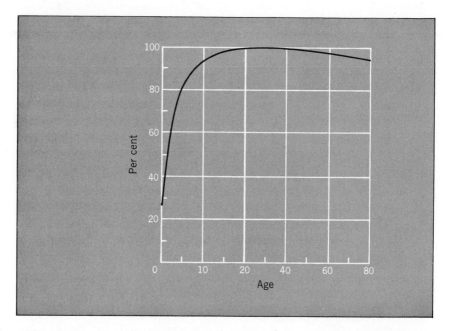

Figure 2 Growth of the human brain *The curve shows the percentage of the brain's growth in weight from birth to physical maturity about age twenty, as well as the slight general decline of later years. (Note that the horizontal scale is condensed after age twenty.)*

At four, nearly 80 per cent of the total brain growth has occurred. At eight, 90 per cent has occurred; from eight to twenty the remaining 10 per cent is achieved.

as do the thyroid, adrenal, and pituitary glands and the islands of Langerhans. An exception here is the thymus, an endocrine gland in the chest, which declines after the teen ages are reached. The function of the thymus is not known. Other systems that do not share in the adolescent growth spurt are the lymphoid system, whose development declines after the age of eleven, and the nervous system, which grows steadily but at a slow and declining rate during adolescence.

The genital pattern of growth (Figure 1, curve *D*) is almost the exact opposite of the pattern of growth of the brain. When the brain is growing most rapidly, the genitals, or sex organs, are growing least rapidly; when the brain is growing least rapidly, there is a rapid growth of the genitals.

At the age of twelve only about 10 per cent of genital growth has occurred. The rate of growth begins then to increase rapidly. Between the ages of twelve and fourteen, 10 per cent of genital growth occurs; and between the ages of fourteen and twenty, 80 per cent takes place. Thus the beginning of this rapid growth corresponds closely with the start of the adolescent's increased general growth; but the growth of the genitals is much more pronounced than general body growth and lasts longer. The genitals are growing very rapidly in the later teens, at which time the rate of general body growth is declining rapidly. It is possible that the maturation of the sex glands and organs and the chemicals (hormones) that they give off stimulate physical growth and therefore account in part, at least, for the acceleration of body growth. The pituitary is without doubt involved, as it governs the growth processes.

The age when both the general and the genital growth spurts start, that is, the beginning of adolescence, is called puberty and occurs at the age of twelve or thirteen, on the average. But individuals within each sex vary here, and girls are generally earlier than boys. Most girls reach puberty, which is marked for them by the first menstruation, between the ages of ten and sixteen, the average being about twelve. About the time of puberty, a girl's breasts grow rapidly, and in general she acquires the body of the woman she is becoming. Boys reach puberty, on the average, at thirteen—occasionally earlier, sometimes later. A boy's voice deepens, and on his face appears tender down which, before adolescence is over, has become whiskers. Hair appears on the bodies of both boys and girls at puberty.

Puberty is sometimes referred to as marking the beginning of a stage of development when boys and girls are capable of reproduction, but some evidence—deduced from the age at which pregnancies occur in girls in those cultures in which children marry before they reach puberty—indicates that this capacity is reached a year or two after puberty, when more sexual maturity is reached.

The Shift in Body Proportions and Other Changes. An adult is not merely a child grown to adult size. The varying rates at which growth takes place in different parts of the body result in a shift in body proportions; thus infants, children, adolescents, and adults are shaped differently (see Figure 3). As the child grows older, the proportion of the head to total body height decreases, and the proportion of the legs increases correspondingly. All the body areas grow larger, of course, but the legs grow comparatively more than the head. The arms also become proportionately longer in adulthood.

The adult body that results is better adapted to the demands made upon it than it would be if it had the proportions of an infant. The adult legs are better adapted for standing and walking; if they were as proportionately small and short as they were in infancy, the adult would be greatly handicapped in maintaining his balance and moving about with ease. The comparatively longer and stronger adult arms are needed for the work and other activities of adults.

J. M. Tanner has reported that by the age of ten, the human head has reached 96 per cent of its adult breadth, length, and circumference [Tanner, 1962]. This relatively early development corresponds to the previously dis-

9

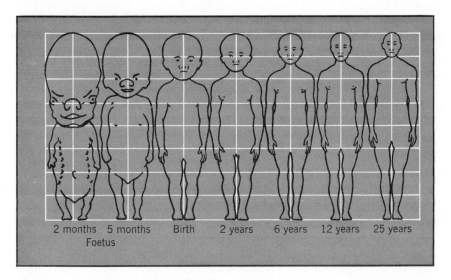

2 months   5 months   Birth   2 years   6 years   12 years   25 years
Foetus

Figure 3   Changes in body proportions   *These figures show the changes in body proportion from the two-month fetus to the twenty-five-year-old adult. At birth the head constitutes about one-fourth the length, or height, of the human body. Never again is it proportionately so large. At maturity it is only one-eighth the total height, half as large proportionately as at birth.*

The legs are only about three-eighths the total height at birth, but in adulthood they are one-half the total height. The torso is three-eighths the body height at birth and also in adulthood; that is, its proportional length remains unchanged. (The figures of the fetus are adapted from C. M. Jackson, ed., Human Anatomy, 7th ed., P. Blakiston's Son & Company, Philadelphia, 1923; *and the figures from birth to adulthood are adapted from* Civa Symposium, vol. 5, April-May, 1943, after Stratz.)

cussed early growth of the brain. The face changes during adolescence, losing its childish appearance and taking on the features of a young adult. The greatest change involves the nose and jaw: both increase in size, and the jaw protrudes more.

The musculature of the body increases from about twenty-five per cent of the total weight in infancy to about forty-five per cent in adulthood. The skeletal structure stays about the same proportion, 15 to 20 per cent of the weight, from infancy to adulthood. The skeletal system of an infant contains considerable cartilage and is relatively soft and flexible. However, the bone development or ossification processes begin in the early embryonic stage and continue until the early twenties.

The bones are bound together with connective tissue to form the framework of the skeleton. With its ligaments and muscles, the skeleton gives the body its shape and both supports and protects the internal organs.

The rate of bone maturation or development varies between the sexes and also within the sexes. The skeletal growth of the female is generally ahead of that of the male. About the age of six the skeletal development of girls is about one year ahead of that of the boys; and by the age of fourteen, girls are about two years ahead of the boys. For both sexes the maturation status of the bones is a useful index to the status of general maturation.

Boys experience an increase in both shoulder and hip width during the ages from thirteen to fifteen. Girls have a smaller increase in shoulder width but a larger increase in hip width during the ages from eleven to thirteen. Both boys and girls have an increase in chest depth and width that corresponds with the period of rapid general growth.

The growth of fat does not correlate closely with the adolescent growth jump. Fat growth cannot be simply described, because it varies with the parts of the body and is clearly different for boys and girls. Boys generally experience an increase in growth of fat from the ages of seven to eleven, after which there is a decline in rate. Increased growth of fat resumes at about fourteen and continues for about two years; this second increase improves the appearance of the bodies of most youths in their late teens. In general there is an increase in fat growth for girls from the ages of six to fifteen, which helps to round out the feminine body and give it its characteristic curvaceous quality.

🍁   *Reflect and Review*

Seventeen-year-old Paul was chatting with some other high school students: "Mr. Edwards said in psychology class today that my brain has about three or four more years to grow. He said the brain is growing slowly when you're seventeen and stops growing when you're about twenty or twenty-one."

"I guess when we're twenty we'll know how much intelligence we'll have for the rest of our lives, won't we?" asked Clarence, another senior from the psychology class.

"I wish my brain would speed up a little. I failed the last psychology quiz!" said Paul.

Were the boys essentially correct in their facts?

Is it true that at the age of twenty one has received most if not all his neurological growth basic to intelligence?

PHYSICAL SIZE

So many conditions influence the height and weight of children and youth that it is difficult to arrive at precise height and weight norms for ages from birth to twenty, essentially the age of physical maturity. The people of some national origins in the United States are larger than the people of others; poorly fed children of the low socioeconomic level tend to be smaller than the well-fed children of the upper levels; and sometimes the children measured are not a good cross section of all children of their ages. The fact that during

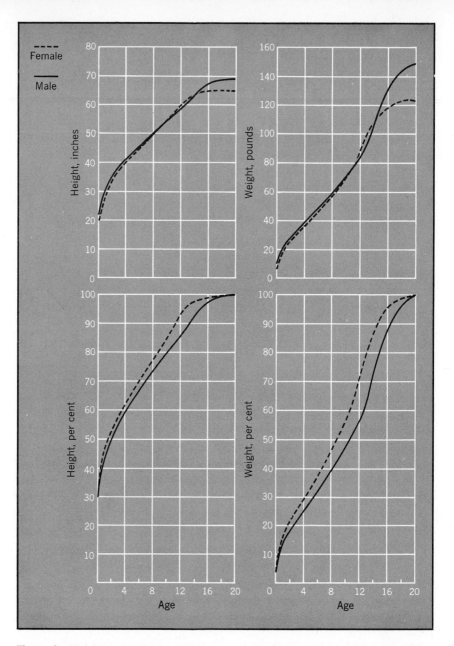

Figure 4 Height and weight of the human body from birth to age twenty *The upper graphs present the height and weight of the average person from birth to age twenty; at twenty the average male is 69 inches (5 feet 9 inches) tall and weighs 150 pounds, and the average female is 65 inches (5 feet 5 inches) tall and weighs 125 pounds.*

The lower graphs present the percentages of adult height and weight ordinarily achieved at particular ages. This information can be used to calculate probable adult height and weight. Thus, boys of twelve have normally achieved 85.5 per cent of their height. If, then, a boy of twelve is 65 inches (5 feet 5 inches) tall, divide 65 by 0.855, obtaining 76. The boy, tall for his age, will grow to 76 inches (6 feet 4 inches) and be a tall adult, if he continues to grow at the normal average percentage rate. Probable adult weight is found in the same way.

this century the height and weight of children have been increasing has reduced the usability of statistics developed a generation or more ago.

On the other hand, the age norms for height and weight presented here (see Figure 4 and Table 1) have been developed by careful evaluation of extensive height and weight data from a considerable number of investigations, and it is believed that the norms given for ages from birth to twenty are acceptably accurate for today's children and youth. Of course, there is a fairly

Table 1   Weight and Height Norms for Boys and Girls

Age	Weight				Height			
	Pounds		Per Cent of Adult Wt.*		Inches		Per Cent of Adult Ht.*	
	Boys	Girls	Boys	Girls	Boys	Girls	Boys	Girls
Birth	7.5	7.0	5.0	5.6	21.0	20.0	30.4	30.8
1	22	21	14.7	16.8	30.0	29.0	43.5	44.6
2	28	27	18.7	21.6	34.5	34.0	50.0	52.3
3	33	32	22.0	25.6	38.0	37.5	55.1	57.7
4	38	37	25.3	29.6	41.0	40.5	59.4	62.3
5	43	42	28.7	33.6	43.5	43.0	63.0	66.1
6	48	47	32.0	37.6	46.0	45.5	66.7	70.0
7	54	53	36.0	42.4	48.5	48.0	70.3	73.8
8	60	59	40.0	47.2	51.0	50.5	73.9	77.7
9	66	65	44.0	52.0	53.0	52.5	76.8	80.8
10	72	71	48.0	56.8	55.0	55.0	79.7	84.6
11	78	78	52.0	62.4	57.0	57.5	82.6	88.5
12	84	88	56.0	70.4	59.0	60.5	85.5	93.1
13	94	100	62.7	80.0	61.0	62.5	88.4	96.2
14	108	109	72.0	87.2	64.0	63.5	92.8	97.7
15	121	115	80.7	92.0	66.0	64.2	95.7	98.8
16	131	119	87.3	95.2	67.5	64.6	97.8	99.4
17	139	122	92.7	97.6	68.4	64.8	99.1	99.7
18	144	124	96.0	99.2	68.7	64.9	99.6	99.8
19	148	125	98.7	100.0	68.9	65.0	99.9	100.0
20	150	125	100.0	100.0	69.0	65.0	100.0	100.0

* At age twenty.
Source: Based on studies by Nancy Bayley, Edith Boyd, E. M. Meredith, H. V. Meredith, F. K. Shuttleworth, K. Simmons, M. M. Snyder, H. C. Stuart, R. D. Tuddenham, Y. S. Vickers, Ruth Wallis, and others (see References).

wide range in individual height and weight at each age, but the averages give the best single general picture of growth in height and weight.

A plotting of the annual height and weight gains—in inches and pounds and in percentages of height and weight at age twenty—yields curves that show the amounts and proportions of annual growth for boys and girls (see Figures 5 to 8). The general patterns of the increases in height and weight are essentially the same. The major difference is the amount.

The two periods of greatest increase are the first year of life and adolescence. For about an eight- or nine-year childhood period between infancy and the beginning of the adolescent growth spurt, the actual or proportionate gains are, on the average, fairly constant. Individuals of course vary and fluctuate more in their growth than is indicated by the curves, which have been smoothed. It will be observed that in terms of the percentages of weight and height at age twenty, girls grow faster than boys to approximately the age of thirteen, after which boys grow considerably faster.

Physical Size Yesterday and Today. The idea is sometimes encountered that today we are shrimpish in comparison with the tall and sturdy people of previous centuries. Is this true or a romantic notion of the past?

We can get one clue to the size of our ancestors by examining the size of the armor they wore. It is quite probable that the armor was worn by men who in general were above average in size. Still, the armor of previous centuries is usually too small for today's average-size young man, who, when he stands alongside a set of armor, is likely to comment, "How small it is!"

To the question of physical size in the more immediate past we can get a more reliable answer by turning to actual measurements. Fortunately, some measurements date back about seventy-five years, which consistently show that children and youth are larger now than they were 50 to 75 years ago.

A specific comparison of the measurements shows that five-year-olds are about two inches taller and about five pounds heavier today than five-year-olds of 50 to 75 years ago. Present-day girls and boys in the age range from ten to thirteen are about four inches taller and weigh fully 10 pounds more. College-age youths today also are larger than their precursors.

Why is this so? The increased height and weight of today's children is attributable to a generally better standard of living. Today's diet is more nutritious—it contains the essential food elements. Children are sheltered by better houses, enjoy more healthful play through improved recreational facilities, and are not stunted by child labor. Immunization, better medical care, and public health practices, have greatly reduced such contagious diseases as diphtheria, scarlet fever, smallpox, tuberculosis, and infantile paralysis. All these advances encourage fuller physical growth and development.

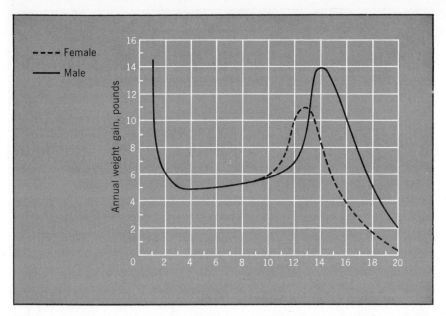

Figure 5 Annual weight gain, in pounds *Boys and girls gain about the same number of pounds per year until about the age of ten, after which the girls gain more in weight for a period of 2 to 3 years; but after the age of thirteen the boys gain more per year and achieve an average of 25 pounds' more weight at twenty than the girls.*

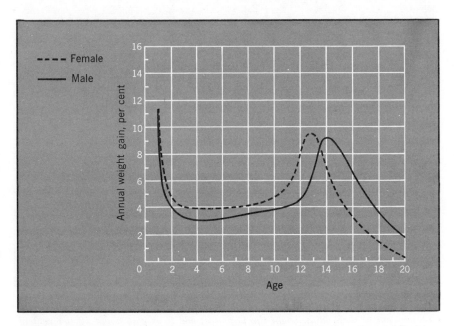

Figure 6 Annual weight gain, in per cent of weight at twenty *During the pre-teen years the girls gain proportionately more than the boys, but during the teens the boys gain more.*

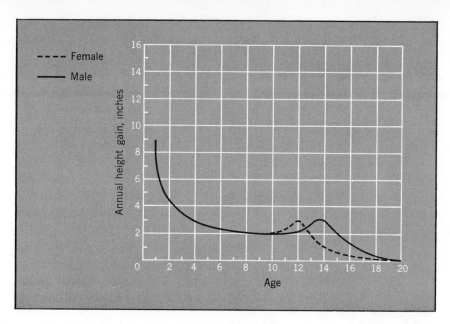

Figure 7   Annual height gain, in inches   *Both boys and girls gain, on the average, 9 inches the first year, 4.5 inches the second year, etc., as shown on the graph. It will be observed that about the tenth year the girls start to gain more in height but by the thirteenth year the boys are clearly gaining more, and they will continue to do so until they achieve a height about 4 inches greater, on the average, than that of the girls.*

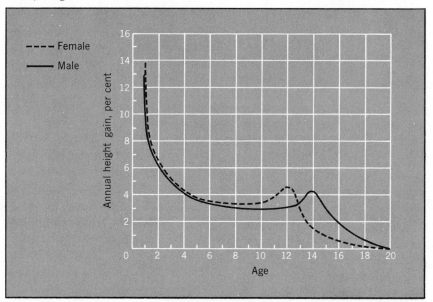

Figure 8   Annual height gain, in per cent of height at twenty   *Girls gain nearly 14 per cent of their adult height the first year, and boys gain about 13 per cent of theirs. During the second year the gains are 6.9 and 6.5 per cent, respectively. The girls gain a larger percentage until about the age of thirteen, after which the boys gain proportionately more.*

☯ *Consider the Data*

Based on Figures 4 through 7

At all ages before twenty, girls have evidently achieved a greater percentage of their adult height and weight than have boys (see Figure 4). Is this fact related to the fact that teen-age girls are more mature than boys of the same age? If so, how?

Do girls actually weigh more than boys at certain ages? If so, what are those ages (see Figure 5)?

Which sex gains more weight after the age of fourteen (see Figure 6)?

What are the two periods of most rapid growth in height (see Figure 7)?

Speculate about how the relative size of boys and girls at various ages affects their play interests and their social and personal relationships.

Prediction of Individual Adult Height. It is impossible to predict adult height of individual children precisely; there are sure to be exceptions to every general phenomenon. Nevertheless, there are bases for prediction which, when used separately or in combination, are far more accurate than sheer guesses. Does the short child become a short adult, the average child an average adult, and the tall child a tall adult? In general, this is the case— height in childhood indicates adult height. However, once in five times a short child will become an adult of average height, a child of average height a short or tall adult, and a tall child an adult of average height. Seldom, though, does a child move two categories, that is, from short to tall or from tall to short, when he grows up.

A second indication of what a child's adult height will be is the age at which his adolescent growth spurt begins. Children who begin their increased adolescent growth early tend to grow less from then until maturity is reached than those who reach the adolescent growth spurt at a later age. For example, imagine two equally tall eleven-year-old girls, one of whom begins the adolescent growth spurt at eleven and the other at the late age of fourteen. The second girl will probably be the taller adult.

Another way of predicting how tall a child will be is to take into account the height of the parents. A son's adult height, for example, can be expected to be approximately midway between his father's height and 110 per cent of his mother's. Thus if the father's height is 5 feet 10 inches (70 inches) and the mother's is 5 feet 5 inches (65 inches) the son will probably be

$$\frac{70 \text{ inches} + (1.10 \times 65 \text{ inches})}{2} = 5 \text{ feet 11 inches (71 inches).}$$

In predicting a daughter's height, the mother's height and 92 per cent of the father's height are averaged. Thus if the mother's height is 5 feet 6 inches (66 inches) and the father is 6 feet tall (72 inches), the daughter will probably be

$$\frac{66 \text{ inches} + (0.92 \times 72 \text{ inches})}{2} = 5 \text{ feet } 6 \text{ inches (66 inches).}$$

In this case the predicted height of the daughter is the same as the mother's height.

The state of maturity of the wristbones as revealed by X-ray pictures also serves in prediction of height. Children whose bones are immature for their age will grow a little more from then until maturity is reached than those whose bones are more mature at the same age.

Most, though not all, very tall children are not quite so relatively tall as adults. Similarly, most children who are very short for their ages are not quite so relatively short as adults. This tendency, called regression toward the mean, also works from generation to generation. Thus, if both parents are considerably under average height one can expect the children to become a few inches, taller than their parents but below average. Correspondingly, if both parents are very tall, their children will probably not be so tall as their parents, but clearly above average.

Generally, predictions of adult height of children in the preteen years can be expected to contain considerable error, probably about two inches in the average case. Predictions for children in their teens, when boys have only about twelve per cent and girls less than five per cent of height left to be achieved, are relatively accurate. In short, the more years that remain until adulthood is reached, the larger will be the error of prediction; and the fewer the years, the smaller the error.

Individual Body Patterns and Health. Two principal features of body patterns are height and weight. If a child is too heavy for his height, he is overweight; and if too light for his height, he is underweight. There is not much that can be done ordinarily to promote or retard the growth of height, but the weight of an individual can be increased or decreased through dietary control, exercise, and rest.

For each age and height there are tables of standard weight ranges, which should be available in every school and to every teacher. There is no true standard weight for any child or youth of a given age and height; but if a student is in the lightest 10 or 15 per cent or in the heaviest 10 or 15 per cent of the range for his height, he should be carefully examined by a doctor to ascertain the condition of his health and to plan for increasing or reducing his weight if required. Ordinarily, the very thin or very fat will experience an improvement in physical health from being brought nearer the average weight.

The teacher should observe the thin and the fat in order to determine also whether or not their physical conditions affect their personalities. Clearly, not only physical but also mental and emotional health may be involved. For instance, a very thin person may, because of poor food habits, be poorly nourished, lack energy, and have emotional problems; and the same may be true of a very heavy person because of poor although very different food habits. Each may be improved physically, mentally, and emotionally by having his weight brought nearer the norm.

But it cannot be emphasized too much that not everyone should be expected to have average or near-average weight. Some will be a lot lighter than average because of a small skeletal frame or because of a general constitutional slenderness; others will far exceed the norm because they are constitutionally sturdy and heavy. Both types can be in good health and have plenty of energy, because their physical growth and development are natural for them.

PHYSICAL ACTION

When a child wants to saw a board, when he fails to throw a basketball, or when a teacher plans to have a youngster sharpen his own pencils, one often hears it said, "That child just is not big enough yet to do that" or, alternatively, "It's time he learned to do that now." Such comments refer to readiness for acquiring sensorimotor skills.

Writing requires various skills in handling pencil and pen; the teacher should recognize the readiness of children and should not expect more than their little, unskilled hands can do; for instance, he should introduce pen and ink only when the children are ready for them. The same applies to the use of scissors, crayons, and brush in artwork; to the use of tools in shopwork; and to the use of needle and thread in sewing. In games and sports, the levels of capacity needed are usually determined largely by size, strength, and previous activities.

A child is ready for learning any new process when he has been equipped by growth, development, and experience to acquire the needed skills easily enough to be pleased as he does so. A child is not ready when, no matter how hard he tries, he is able to make only very meager progress, so that frustration discourages him and kills interest. When this happens, the learner needs to have rich, fruitful experiences which will prepare him for acquiring later the skills which are too difficult for him now; or the now arduous tasks can be postponed until more natural growth and development have made the child able to learn those tasks readily.

Cultivating the Body and Protecting Its Health. Physical and health education must be geared to the course of growth and development of the student, and we should be especially concerned about the program provided for the young child. The nearer the beginning of life, the more important are good nutrition, good medical and dental care, play, and exercise. As our schools now operate, the older the children get, the more emphasis is placed on their athletic and physical training. But games, play, and physical and health education are more beneficial when a person is in earlier phases of his growth. "As the twig is bent . . ." applies particularly to physical development. Consequently, we should plan more for the younger child than we do.

In the kindergarten and grades, the children need the help of teachers who are prepared in health and physical education. Such teachers can help the pupils develop healthfully by conducting social and play activities and by the use of developmental and corrective exercises. Not only children but also adolescents need the services of physical education teachers who understand how to promote the social and physical development of their students and who are socially and physically mature themselves.

Table 2   Age Norms for a Number of Physical Abilities

Physical Abilities	Age							
	10	11	12	13	14	15	16	17
Boys:								
Sit-ups, number	26	26	31	35	39	40	44	44
Standing broad jump	4'6''	4'10''	5'1''	5'5''	5'10''	6'2''	6'8''	6'11''
50-yard dash, seconds	8.8	8.5	8.0	7.8	7.5	7.1	7.0	6.8
Softball throw, feet	87	99	110	121	139	156	165	176
Girls:								
Sit-ups, number	19	20	20	20	18	18	19	16
Standing broad jump	4'3''	4'6''	4'6''	4'8''	4'9''	4'10''	5'0''	5'0''
50-yard dash, seconds	9.1	8.9	8.7	8.5	8.5	8.6	8.4	8.6
Softball throw, feet	41	51	60	69	70	74	76	79

Source: Selected from tables in Paul A. Hunsicker, *Youth Fitness Test Manual,* American Association for Health, Physical Education and Recreation, National Education Association, Washington, D.C., 1958.

The period of the adolescent growth spurt, which takes place for most students during the junior and early senior high school years, should also receive special recognition and attention in any school system's program of physical and health education. In this highly formative period when the bones and muscles are developing at a rapid rate, the individual needs guidance in the use and enjoyment of his changing physical powers (see Table 2).

☯ *Consider the Data*

Based on Table 2

The physical-ability norms generally reflect the physical growth and development that take place from ages ten to seventeen. In all activities the boys improve every year, with a minor exception in sit-ups, where scores for ages ten and eleven are the same, as are scores for ages sixteen and seventeen. The number of sit-ups is the average number each age group can do. An associate holds the ankles while each person pulls himself up from a lying to a sitting position with hands behind his head and continues until he is no longer able to do so.

For the girls some physical abilities do not improve consistently with increase in age; for example, the seventeen-year-old girls are not superior in all four abilities listed. Only in the distance that a softball can be thrown is there a steady annual increase for the girls.

The girls show little overall increase in performance after the age of fifteen, and this is understandable. Many girls grow very little in height and muscle after that age. Also, they usually become more interested in social activities and less motivated to participate in sports; and therefore do not build up their physical skills. The opposite is true for boys, who are intensely interested in athletics during their high school years.

The values, of course, are averages, and there are wide ranges among individuals at each age. In fact, the best ten-year-olds are superior to the poorest seventeen-year-olds; they can run faster, jump farther, and throw a ball a greater distance. This is true for both girls and boys. In this variation for each age lie the superiorities and inferiorities that cause personal problems which the school can help to solve by providing a wide variety of activities.

Refer to Table 2. In what physical abilities do the girls show no improvement or even actual decline after the age of thirteen?

Observe whether or not the boys show improvement after thirteen in the activities listed.

Give reasons for the differences in the development of physical abilities of boys and girls.

For this reason, young people in junior and senior high school should be active in a supervised program of physical activities and training. But their health can be harmed by competitive sports which are not carefully controlled, especially in junior high. Consider the results of two studies of physical training for junior high students:

A group of students who had controlled physical education in a gymnasium was compared with a group which did not. The results indicated slightly better physical development for those who went to the gymnasium than for those who did not.

But in a comparative study by F. A. Rowe a group of junior high school students who participated in competitive athletics was compared with a group of nonparticipants, first when the members of both groups were an average 13 years 6 months old and then again 2 years later at 15 years 6 months [Rowe, 1950]. The nonathletic group gained more than twice as much in height and in lung capacity and a little more in weight, suggesting that the competitive athletics were in some measure harmful.

Adolescents are not yet fully physically mature or at the prime of their physical power and skill. Specifically, the heart of a rapidly growing teenager is still far from its ultimate development, and the strain imposed on it by strenuous and fatiguing competitive sports may do injury in some cases. Moreover, to the unfavorable effects of pure physical wear and tear on the participants must be added physical repercussions from the excitement and tensions which young athletes feel before games—effects including the loss of appetite, diarrhea, frequent urination, and dry mouth which many athletes report experiencing before the game.

From all this it is clear that young teen-agers should not carry the physically and psychologically serious responsibility of enhancing through athletic prowess "the honor of good old Junior High."

At the very best, junior high schools should not play a schedule of games in basketball and football with each other; their activity in these sports should be limited to intramural games and incidental play. If, however, junior high schools do have competitive football and basketball, the youngsters should not play as heavy a schedule as senior high school students do.

Even in the case of senior high school students, who are, of course, still adolescents, there is a well-grounded suspicion that long, crowded schedules of football and basketball are not good for physical growth and development. The highly competitive organization—especially of basketball—in most districts, regions, and states keeps the young students playing often and hard, possibly too hard.

The direct ill effects of school competitive athletics are on the boys and girls who compete strenuously. But senior high school athletics indirectly causes a general ill effect on noncompeting students. In many high schools, a program of physical and health education is crowded out by the time and money spent on competitive sports. Money is spent for a coach, not for a teacher of physical and health education. The boys selected for the competitive sports are the healthiest and strongest of the student body but nevertheless receive most of the staff effort. The result is that the great majority of boys and girls who need physical and health education do not get it. This is not good for the personal and physical development of the students.

In defense of high school athletics it can be said that the well-trained and understanding coach pays careful attention to the welfare of his boys. He builds them up gradually so that they will be conditioned for strenuous play; he checks on their weight and demands that they "keep training" and live healthfully; he makes frequent substitutions during a game. In other words, he does what he can to minimize the bad effects of overstrenuous sports. But how much better it would be if all students—in both junior and senior high school—got comparable expert help toward the best possible physical development.

☯ Reflect and Review

H. Douglas Whittle tested the effects of a good physical education program by comparing two groups of twelve-year-old boys on tests of strength and flexibility of legs, arms, and back [Whittle, 1961]. The twelve-year-old boys were equal in height, weight, and skeletal age. One group of boys attended elementary schools where they participated in good physical education programs, and the other group attended schools that did not have good programs. A good program consists of regularly scheduled play and physical exercises under the guidance of a competent physical education teacher.

The test results showed that the boys participating in a good physical education program were significantly ahead in leg, back, and arm strength and flexibility. Other research has indicated that children who participate in a well-organized program of moderate play and physical training experience better lung development and greater increases in height and weight than do comparable students who participate heavily in strenuous sports.

What is the importance, if any, of being strong and flexible physically?

What should be the purpose of a good physical education program? Health and recreation? Social? Physical strength and skills (athletic abilities)? Physical growth? Any others?

What do you consider a good physical education program for children and adolescents?

Relationships among Athletic and Other Physical Abilities. If a person is a good basketball player, will he also play baseball well? Will a good athlete be skillful at doing heavy manual work with tools in a manual-training shop? Will the good athlete excel at intricate handwork? In general, to what extent are various physical, or motor, abilities interrelated?

There is a positive correlation among the physical skills involved in athletics. In any ordinary group of youngsters, those who are best in one such skill are not best in all, but they are above average in all or most. Those who are average in some skills, say running or catching, are usually average in others such as throwing or jumping; and those who are poor in one are generally poor in others. These generalizations, it should be noted, apply to innate capacity, not to development of ability. Thus an athlete who has equal potentiality in basketball and baseball may, in reality, be a much better basketball player than baseball player simply because he has made a specialty of basketball.

There is a common core among, on the one hand, the motor skills used in football, basketball, baseball, boxing, tennis, and wrestling and, on the other hand, the motor skills which involve the whole body in heavy work activity. But it should be recognized that motor skills range from those required for rigorous activity to those used in intricate hand and finger work involving delicate eye-hand coordinations; and the latter skills—including, for example, those involved in shuffling cards, repairing watches, hand sewing, and certain work with silver and jewelry—show little correlation with heavy-activity skills. Of course, the keenness and sensitivity of the eye, as well as the ear, affect many of our physical activities.

Handedness and Development. In this right-handed world, about 1 adult in 15 is left-handed, and about 1 in 15 is more or less ambidextrous, or right-handed for some activities and left-handed for others. A considerable number of children with a tendency to be left-handed have been trained to be right-handed.

There is disagreement on the genesis of handedness. Some students of the problem claim that the left-handed and the right-handed are born that way because of determining structures in the brain. They contend that in the case of the left-handed the right side of the brain, which controls the left side of the body, is more dominant, and vice versa. Others claim that the left-handed have had early experiences which caused them to be so. The likelihood is that the latter students are right—that during early childhood, accident or circumstances caused the left-handed person to prefer using the left hand, although some children possibly have a natural tendency to be left-handed because of certain patterns of the nervous system.

At any rate, handedness can be and is trained into children. Thus, because it is conventional to be right-handed, most children are so trained; but some are trained to be left-handed, and use of the left hand then becomes a habit. For example, an athletic coach trained his son to be left-handed because he felt that it would be to the son's advantage when he participated in sports. Incidentally, the father was left-handed.

How and when should this be done? Handedness, either left or right, develops by stages in infancy and early childhood, and this is the time the child can best be trained in the firm establishment of the handedness that is desired, by controlling his grasping and manipulation of objects. It is quite probable that if we started in infancy we could train most children to be either left- or right-handed.

What should be done about retraining handedness? For example, if a person is left-handed, should efforts be directed to making him right-handed? This, in fact, is the most important question related to handedness. Emotional disturbances, even personality disorders, may be produced in a child by coercive attempts to change his handedness. Indeed, any attempt to change handedness after habits in the use of the hands are well established can severely disturb a child. Some investigators contend that stuttering is the result of trying to change the handedness of a child, though others disagree. Here, then, are some of the principles to observe when retraining efforts are made:

If a child is to be retrained to use another hand, this should be done early in life, preferably before he starts school. There is seldom a favorable change of handedness after the age of seven or eight; by that time, the handedness habit is well fixed. Thus the correction of handedness should hardly be a school problem at all.

The training should be done thoughtfully so that the child will not be upset emotionally. For instance, little games involving the use of the preferred hand may prove helpful. The problem should never be considered so important that the parent, by force and vigorous control, tries to "break" the handedness. If it is very hard to change handedness, it is best not to try but to accept the handedness that persists.

The problem does invade the classroom necessarily in one of its aspects: the teacher usually has special trouble with the writing, or penmanship, of left-handers. When writing paper is in a good position for the right-hander, the hand of the left-hander is above the line he is writing on. This is a poor position for easy finger and hand movement, and the hand runs over the lines which have been written and smears the ink if it is being used. The paper should be turned for the left-hander so that his writing hand is under the line he is writing. This is less awkward for the left-hander and enables him to read the lines as they are written.

THE BODY, THE MIND, AND PERSONALITY

A number of terms are used by scientists to express developmental status in terms of norms for given chronological ages. Thus, they say a boy has a height age of ten if he is as tall as the average ten-year-old boy, that is, about fifty-five inches tall, regardless of his own chronological age. Other developmental ages are weight age, skeletal—or carpal—age, and dental age. There are also strength ages for pulling, pushing, lifting, and gripping and, in the area of athletic performance, for running, jumping, and throwing.

As children grow older, they develop and grow mentally as well as physically. Thus, children who are 55 inches tall can work more difficult arithmetic problems, in general, than can children who are 45 inches tall; and children who weigh 70 pounds read better, in general, than those who weigh 45 pounds. The taller and heavier children have more intelligence because, being older, they have had more years of mental growth and development.

If, however, we consider children of any one given age, there is only a very low correlation between physical and mental status. To illustrate this, we may consider any large, unselected group of children all of whom are nine years old chronologically.

In this group of nine-year-olds will be found a wide range of mental ability. It is likely that the range in mental age will be as much as from three to sixteen. Probably only a very few of the children will have the mental ability either of an average three-year-old or of the typical sixteen-year-old. Most of these nine-year-olds can be expected to be at the nine-year-old level of intelligence. The others will deviate downward to mental ages of eight, seven, six, etc., or upward to mental ages of ten, eleven, twelve, etc. But as the amount of deviation increases, the number of children involved will decrease. For instance, this nine-year-old group will contain fewer children at six than at eight in mental age. There will, of course, be comparable physical variation among our nine-year-olds. A few will be of the size of average children considerably younger, and some will have the height and weight typical of children much older.

When the mental age and physical size of these nine-year-old children are studied together, a low correlation of about .05 to .15 can be expected to emerge. A child who is large for his age is almost equally likely to be advanced, average, or retarded mentally. Similarly, if a person is retarded mentally, his chances of being advanced, average, or retarded physically are about the same. One cannot judge accurately a child's physical size from knowing that he is bright or slow, nor his mental capacity from knowing that he is small or large.

On the other hand, the slight correlation that does exist between mental and physical status means that high mentality, a little more often than not, accompanies good physical development. There is a likelihood of finding more large, well-developed children among a group of bright children than among a group of children who are mentally retarded. On the average, the bright children will be about two to three inches taller and five to ten pounds heavier. Of course, the differences are less for young children than for older ones. Similarly, one can expect to find slightly more children above average intellectually among a group of physically advanced children than among a group of physically underdeveloped children of the same age. The relationship between mental and physical status of children of the same age is very low; nevertheless, it is sufficiently definite to substantiate in this area of comparison the principle that desirable qualities tend to accompany each other.

Physical Appearance and Personality. In the process of physical development, some boys and girls deviate unfavorably from the norm. They have become very tall, very short, very fat, very thin, or very unattractive of face and figure. Correspondingly, there are those whose growth and development have been very favorable so that they are very attractive.

Extreme thinness, for example, gives the impression of frailty and implies weakness. Actually the thin child or adolescent is usually handicapped in participating in the activities of his age-mates. He is usually unable to compete in sports. His physical appearance excites various unpleasant comments and nicknames. The self-concepts developed by very thin people from their actual physical condition and their experiences tend to be saturated with feelings of inadequacy. Thus thinness may have a negative influence on emotional health and personality development.

What has been said about thinness applies in principle to the other large deviations which have been mentioned. The extreme deviates tend to be sensitive about their large differences from other people. Obesity is a basic health problem and involves so many personality factors that it will be treated rather extensively.

For all young people, fat provides protection for the body; and for adolescents and young adults the growth of fat "fills in" the body, making it appear more attractive. In these respects the body fat is both physiologically and psychologically healthful. Thus, up to the age of thirty, being a little above the average in weight is generally associated with better digestion and greater resistance to colds and tuberculosis. After the age of thirty, it is probably more healthful to be slightly under the average in weight. Thus also, from the standpoint of physical and mental health, as well as of aesthetics, adolescent girls and women in their twenties are simply making a mistake when they eat sparingly in an attempt to "substitute angles for curves."

However, if the accumulations of fat are excessive at any age, the personality may be affected adversely. There is no simple explanation of how obesity, or excessive overweight, comes about, but the best knowledge of the problem indicates that for most people its cause is poor emotional health. Many people, in periods of loneliness, depression, or anxiety, turn to food to relieve their stress, whatever its cause. Grief or shock that comes from a death in the family, breakup of an engagement, or disappointing failure may be alleviated by eating. But when emotional difficulty is deep and persistent, obesity may become a serious problem. For instance, a child who has been overprotected by his mother and consequently has not dealt with his developmental tasks successfully may find comfort in eating. His mother observes her child's desire for food and sees in it an opportunity to provide more care and protection and to gain or keep her child's favor. So she tries to please her child by preparing for him in large quantities "the food he likes best."

There are, in many classrooms, boys and girls who are too fat, who exceed healthy plumpness, who are so fat that they are clumsy and are teased by their peers. These young people need to be observed carefully by their teachers.

A number of characteristics and behavior patterns should be looked for. Are there signs that the fat child is overprotected by his parents? Does the obese youth work up to capacity? Being an underachiever may be evidence of serious maladjustment. Does a fat student enjoy participating in games and sports? Does he have friends, or is he an isolate? Being relatively friendless and alone is very serious. Does he frequently show feelings of hostility? It is also likely that the fat child or youth has a nickname such as "Fats" or "Tubby," which he resents very much because it reminds him of his unhappy condition—and indeed has a right to resent because it is unkind.

But what can the teacher, knowing that obesity is probably the result of poor emotional health and that it surely worsens the mental condition, do about it? The answer is simply stated. If a teacher understands the effect of obesity on the personality and behavior of a student, he is in a better position to deal more wisely and sympathetically with him, and so can give the obese student the guidance and emotional support he needs. The teacher cannot expect to bring about a cure of the obesity—caused by emotional difficulty—but he can at least, by being sympathetic and understanding, alleviate some of the tensions of the overfat student.

The teacher cannot just tell the fat student, "You should reduce"; that might be one of the worst things he could do. Reducing is an extremely difficult thing for a maladjusted overweight person because his overeating is interwoven with his basic personality pattern. He has developed a dependency on food which is strongly motivated by his feelings and needs. When some fat people begin to diet, their initial feeling of joy over the thought of overcoming their dependency on food turns to anxiety and then, in turn, to depression. The teacher should not meddle with the serious problem of losing weight by either starting or supervising individual reducing programs. That should be done under the guidance of a doctor who understands the psychology, as well as the physiology, of obesity. In order for any program of weight reduction to be effective, it is essential but not sufficient that the obese student want and be encouraged to lose weight; and he must also receive professional help with his personality problems from the school counselor or family physician.

☯ *Reflect and Review*

Martha, a college sophomore, was so big horizontally that two girls of normal size standing side by side behind her would be hidden from view. She was of average height but was overweight by more than 100 pounds. She was an unhappy girl; and it is certain that her obesity made her unhappy, even though her condition may have been caused by tensions that she tried to lessen by eating.

Her size attracted the attention of her classmates, and she was aware of the students' negative attitudes toward her. Her clumsiness in sitting down, getting up, and moving about attracted more unfavorable attention to her. Most of the time she was alone and, of course, she had no dates.

Unhappiness generally results in being ineffective in one's work. This was true of Martha. She would start classes and drop some of them before they were finished. She was usually behind in her work and received low marks. Failing to get off probation, she was finally dropped from school.

It is not certain to what extent obesity was the cause or symptom of Martha's troubles because it is also true that some people of attractive bodily proportions have few friends, are lonesome, and fail in their work. Still it is unfortunate that Martha, with the help of a physician, was not able to lose over 100 pounds, become attractive, improve in emotional health, and succeed in her school work. The fact is that her condition remained unchanged and she continued to stay at home, drearily passing the time away.

What do you think were the causes of Martha's difficulties?
What should have been done for Martha?

Physical Development and Personality

> Let me have men about me that are fat,
> Sleek-headed men and such as sleep o' nights.
> Yond Cassius has a lean and hungry look,
> He thinks too much; such men are dangerous.

Shakespeare, *Julius Caesar*

For centuries body type, or somatotype, and personality have been associated by students of human nature. That the thin are intellectual; that chubbiness is accompanied by jollity, that the big-framed, well-muscled man likes adventure and command—all these are old and popular beliefs. The following more recent but fallacious classification of corresponding body types and personalities is itself in accord with these stereotypes:

Body Type	Personality
Ectomorph: skinny, poor musculature, thin, lanky.	Intellectual and tends to be introverted.
Endomorph: heavy, soft, fat, round, bulging.	Likes fun and pleasure. Is relaxed and friendly.
Mesomorph: heavy, thick-set, big frame, muscular.	Likes action and adventure, being in control. Extroverted.
Balanced, or average type.	Balanced interests.

Other designations, used in attempts to associate body types, with psychoses and also with crime, are leptosome, pyknic, and athletic. The leptosome resembles the ectomorph, the pyknic resembles the endomorph, and the athletic corresponds to the mesomorph.

Attempts have also been made to relate body type to personality indirectly, by relating body type to physical fitness as evaluated by strength and endurance tests. As would be expected, on the average the mesomorphs scored highest in physical fitness, the thin and angular ectomorphs ranged next, and the endomorphs averaged the lowest, with considerable overlap between members of these types. Body type was shown to be related to physical fitness and thus an indirect factor in personality if physical fitness is a factor in personality, which it probably is. But this statement is obviously inconclusive; indeed, perhaps all these studies and like studies should be regarded with some suspicion. Thus, the mesomorph is built for physical action, and football players tend to be of this body type; in football, the frail ectomorph might not survive the first rush unhurt. Still it is not safe to extend too far the idea that mesomorphs are adventurous because they are physically equipped for rugged sports.

In short, the problem of relating body types and personalities is very difficult and complex, and one should be very reluctant to accept the idea that there is a dependable relationship between body types and personality. The pattern of evidence hardly supports such a view. Specifically, the ectomorphic people have not been found to be the "mental types" even though there are intellectuals among the thin. Broader, thicker people are found among the literary and scientific leaders of a country. Clearly, corpulent people do not consistently have the joyous, buoyant, and happy characteristics that are attributed to them.

Probably the soundest generalization in this area is that the physique, body characteristics, and sensorimotor abilities of a person affect his personality according to the adequacy of his physical equipment for effective living and also according to how his physical status and powers are regarded by himself and by others. Being weak or strong, attractive or unattractive, skillful or awkward, healthy or sick influences a person's attitudes, interests, and activities. In that sense there is a relationship between physical development, if not body type, and personality.

Still, there is no rule which explains how every individual will react to his physical characteristics. For instance, some who are unattractive and have obvious physical defects become shy, unfriendly, and oversensitive; but others become friendly, helpful, and charming. Inadequacies may more often than not cause and support other inadequacies; on the other hand, a person may develop compensatory strengths. In the classroom, it will be evident that the personalities of some students are partly shaped either favorably or unfavorably by their physical development. Having an understanding of that relationship, the teacher can proceed to assist those pupils who need help in learning to accept their physical characteristics and in making good adjustments.

Physical Development, Adolescence, and Personal Problems. Of all teachers, perhaps the teacher of adolescent boys and girls must be most sensitive to his students' physical development, because of the effects of the physical changes of adolescence on young persons' development as social beings.

Adolescents have various personal problems related to their physical development. First of all, they worry about physical deficiencies or liabilities which invite unfavorable attention or comment:

Not having well-developed chest and shoulders, or enough muscle (boys usually)

Having too large hips or legs (girls usually)

Having too flat a bust (girls)

Being too fat or too thin, too short or too tall

Having a poor complexion, unattractive teeth, or too big a nose

Wearing glasses

Or the adolescent may develop sensitivity about some problem indirectly related to physical changes, such as the rapid outgrowing of his clothes. At the same time, driven by enlarged and more active sex glands whose hormones spark new drives and desires, boys want girls and girls want boys, and they are troubled about how to deal with each other and sometimes frustrated by failing to attract the ones they want. Some boys are not reaching their ideal of manliness, and are shy and self-conscious. Some girls are troubled by not being so attractive as they want to be or by being left out of the social life of their peers.

Underlying all is the basic need to outgrow childhood psychologically. Yesteryear's children are becoming adults in size but still cling to the immature habits and attitudes of childhood. They feel a new need for freedom and see adult liberty ahead of them, but there is conflict with inner restrictions of their childhood as well as with real dependence on their parents. Sometimes suppressed ebullience of energy breaks out in a struggle for freedom against the restraining hand of adult authority that sees the teen-ager in the image of the child he was some years ago.

Of course, the adolescent years of life are usually happy years, as can be appreciated by observing high school students. They are, by and large, developing well and meeting their problems successfully. Like people of all ages, they experience frustration and failures; but on the whole, they get along well.

Still, there are adolescents who need the special help of understanding teachers who, by dealing patiently and kindly with present physical and related problems, can guide these teen-agers into interesting activities and mature solutions of their life problems—preparing for a vocation; having good relationships with peers, parents, and others; observing a good moral code; dealing effectively with members of the opposite sex; having enough money to finance their personal needs.

❢ *Reflect and Review*

Kelley Watters was a fourteen-year-old boy of average physical and mental development. He participated in the games and social activities of the school only reluctantly if at all. His sensorimotor and social skills were as good as those of most boys, but he usually escaped from the folk dancing and other boy-girl activities. Miss Hale, the physical education teacher, was an attractive young lady who had noticed during the first physical education class that Kelley was perfunctory about participating and pulled away when he could. She discussed the problem with Kelley's other teachers, who had also noticed that he tended to stay on the periphery of group work or go off by himself.

Their plan was to begin by being friendly to Kelley—greet him, call him by name, and praise his efforts. After they had gotten his trust, they planned to bring him into more and more group activity and encourage him to take leadership roles occasionally. During the physical education class Miss Hale invited Kelley to be her partner, and she skillfully transferred him to girl partners with whom he learned to feel at ease. He was also given a chance to do the selecting when sides were chosen.

Explain how this procedure helped Kelley to gain social and intellectual insight.

Do you have any suggestions about additional procedures that might be helpful?

Will Kelley's greatest gains be physical, social, or intellectual?

What roles should adolescents in the early teens learn to take?

SUMMARY

Physical growth is quantitative in nature and is usually measured in inches and pounds or their equivalents.

Physical development is both qualitative and quantitative and implies increasing capacities and abilities, maturing, functional improvement, and progress toward higher levels of potentiality and effectiveness.

Growth and development are evidenced by changes in size, number, kind, position, and relative size. The prenatal period is only 1 per cent of the average life span, but during that time the fetus achieves the anatomy of a functioning human being.

About six times as much weight growth takes place during the second half of gestation as takes place during the first half. A little over half the growth in length takes place during the first half of pregnancy.

Except for pathological cases, all individuals follow the general pattern of very rapid physical growth in both pounds and inches during the first year of life, then settle down to a steady but smaller increase in pounds and inches until about ages ten or eleven at which time there is a sharp increase in height and weight until about ages fourteen and fifteen, followed by a fast-declining rate in growth to the early twenties. Height reaches its maximum by twenty for most boys and by sixteen or seventeen for most girls; but weight for both sexes does not have such maxima, as most people gain weight during adulthood.

Even though the general pattern of growth is the same for nearly all, the rate of growth differs considerably from individual to individual.

The lymphoid system grows very rapidly to about the age of eleven, after which it declines.

At birth the nervous system has achieved about 25 per cent of its weight and grows rapidly during infancy but at a declining rate. During the teens the growth of the brain is slow; however, the development of the brain may exceed its growth during those years. The brain is in its prime during the twenties and thirties and usually deteriorates during old age.

The genital system achieves 80 per cent of its growth during the teens.

Puberty, or the beginning of adolescence, is roughly equivalent to the teen ages. For boys the age of puberty is about thirteen and for girls, about a year earlier.

During growth from infancy to adulthood all body parts become bigger; but proportionately the head is only one-half as large in adulthood as in infancy, the torso remains about the same, and the legs increase in proportion from about three-eighths the total body height in infancy to about one-half the total height in adulthood. The arms become proportionately a little longer in adulthood.

Girls have achieved a higher percentage of their adult height and weight at every age than have boys.

Boys, girls, and young adults are larger today than they were several generations ago, probably as a result of more healthful conditions involving nutrition, housing, recreation, and child labor.

Girls and boys at birth are about 20 and 21 inches long and weigh about 7 and 7½ pounds, respectively.

Boys and girls differ very little in height and weight until after the middle teens, when the boys grow more rapidly and become on the average about four inches taller and twenty-five pounds heavier than the girls.

From about age eleven to almost fourteen the girls are actually taller and heavier on the average than the boys.

On the basis of three height categories—short, average, and tall—four out of five children will be in the same categories when they become adults. One out of five will change from his childhood category to one higher or lower, but rarely is there a jump or drop of two categories, such as from tall to short or vice versa.

Other bases for estimating adult height are the percentages given in Table 1 and the heights of the parents. Factors to observe are maturity of bones, age at puberty, and regression.

Most children and teen-agers do not deviate excessively from the weight and height averages of their ages. Those who are very large or small for their ages need to be studied to ascertain the reasons for and the emotional effects of their large deviations from their norms.

Obesity and excessive thinness are serious problems involving both physical and emotional health. Either condition but particularly obesity not only may be caused by emotional health but also worsens the emotional health.

Growth, development, and experience that accompany growing older give a child the maturity level and the readiness for acquiring needed motor skills.

Boys increase in physical power and abilities during the growing years, but girls ordinarily show little or no such increase after the age of fourteen or fifteen. Teen-age boys have a large increase in muscle when their weight increases rapidly.

Children and teen-agers may be harmed physically as well as emotionally by too much participation in strenuous sports like basketball and football.

A wide range of physical abilities characterizes the members of each age group.

It seems that various physical and athletic skills which require speed, strength, and accuracy have much in common.

The causes of left-handedness are not definitely known, but right-handedness is usually developed by favoring that hand and giving it the most use. If left-handedness persists during the preschool years, it is best to accept it. The left-hander should be taught to hold his pen and place his paper so he writes normally and not awkwardly.

Larger children are only slightly superior mentally to smaller children of the same age. Averaging or combining various physical and mental ages is not sound.

Associating various personality traits with ectomorphy, endomorphy, or mesomorphy has not been supported by research. One's physical appearance may affect one's attitude, feelings, and self-concepts according to how favorably or unfavorably it influences others.

Girls and boys are concerned about the features of their physical appearance as it is influenced by their shoulders, chest (bust), hips, legs, thinness, fatness, height, and complexion.

In general, adolescent years are happy years, and the main problem is to make a successful transition from childhood to adulthood.

SUGGESTED READING

Bayer, Leona M., and Nancy Bayley: *Growth Diagnosis*, The University of Chicago Press, Chicago, 1959. Detailed study of physical growth with many pictures and illustrations. Rich in data and information.

Clarke, H. H., and B. W. Jarmon: "Scholastic Achievement of Boys Nine,

Twelve and Fifteen Years of Age, Related to Various Strength and Growth Measures," *American Association Health and Physical Education Research Quarterly*, 32:155–162, 1961. Focuses attention on the relationship of scholastic achievement to measures of strength and growth.

Harris, Dale B. (ed.); *The Concept of Development*, The University of Minnesota Press, Minneapolis, 1957. Contains sections by a number of authorities who discuss growth and development from various points of view. Rich in facts and concepts.

Tanner, J. M.: *Education and Physical Growth*, University of London Press, Ltd., London, 1961, 144 pp. Contains a good discussion of physical development and abilities and points up how readiness emerges from maturing. Excellent discussion of brain growth and mental capacities.

CHAPTER 2
HOW THE MIND MATURES
AND HOW MINDS DIFFER

From conception to adulthood, as the body grows and develops, the mind grows and develops. This mental change is indeed partially dependent upon physical change: The growth of the brain and the rest of the nervous system provides the structural basis for this process of mental maturing. But the individual experiences that parallel the physical processes are also important. Both growth and experience must reach particular levels before a child is ready to attempt certain achievements. In this chapter, we shall turn our attention first to this unfolding of the mind and then to the great differences in mental capacity that exist among individuals.

THE COURSE OF MENTAL GROWTH

We know that just as a child can run faster as his muscles become bigger and stronger, he can read faster and solve harder arithmetic problems as his nervous system grows and develops; that is, mental powers increase with the neural growth and development that accompany an increase in age. The brain and the nerves that lead to it are well on their way toward maturity at birth; and they mature very rapidly after birth, their billions of cells and fibers growing and developing by changing in chemical composition, in size, and in complexity. This maturing brings about an increase of mental power.

Also, as the child grows older, he has more and more experience in using his mind—talking, reading, doing arithmetic problems, asking and answering questions, and taking part in countless other activities. This increasing use of the mind is also an important factor in the mind's maturation; indeed, this is necessary if it is to mature fully.

Does the mind actually need to be nourished by stimulating experiences if it is to develop up to its potentiality? Is it possible that organic development of the nervous system could even be stunted if a child lived in a very impoverished environment for a considerable period such as 10 to 15 years?

Some children are in homes where the cultural-educational level is high. They are involved in conversation which employs a rich vocabulary, and they travel, play extensively with other children, and in general live culturally rich and interesting lives. They react in many ways to the different facets of their environment.

Other children are confined largely to the environment of their barren homes. There are few experiences which stimulate them intellectually and exhilarate them emotionally. Their parents function mentally at about the fourth-grade level and do very little if anything that gives their children information or encourages them to think. Their situation is dull and boring.

Suppose children of equal mental potentiality were in these contrasting environments. How would their mental growth and development be affected?

Signs of Growth and the Teacher's Role. There are many actual evidences of the mental growth that takes place during the years of physical growth. There is an increase in the power to understand directions and comprehend complex meanings. The number of words used per remark or statement increases with age, as do the difficulty of the words and the complexity of the sentence structures. In reading, the sweep of the eye increases; thus the number of fixations decreases and reading comprehension improves. In drawing, ideas are represented more accurately as well as more artistically. The growth of such mental powers as perception, memory, reasoning, and imagination can be observed, reflected in increased ability to deal with academic school subjects such as arithmetic, geography, history, and language. The teacher will see these changes as they happen in the classroom.

But beyond day-to-day observation, a theoretical knowledge of the course of mental growth—of how mental powers increase because of the maturing of the bodily structures (primarily the nervous system) and because of experience—can be used to advantage by the teacher to understand his students and plan their educational progress. Such knowledge can help the teacher to use in learning situations the concept of readiness, already discussed in relation to the acquisition of sensorimotor skills.

The concept of readiness—of the capacity to make good and gratifying progress when a task is undertaken—is applied extensively in connection with learning to read, working arithmetic problems, and so on. At six a child may have no interest in a book because it is too hard, but at eight he may find it interesting because he has reached a higher mental level and it is comparatively easy for him. Thus he is given the book at eight, not at six. But there are many learning tasks to be planned for and coordinated;

and the teacher can do this best if he knows how and when the processes of mental growth can be expected to produce and increase the potential for each and every kind of learning.

☻ *Reflect and Review*

Imagine that the following events are possible and actually occur:

A child is kept in a state of deep hypnotic sleep for 2 years. He is absolutely inert, that is, without active experiences, although he is given nourishment and grows physically at the usual rate. At the end of the 2-year period he is awakened. Naturally, he lacks the abilities he would have acquired had he been normally active during the 2 years he has been in bed. But:

1. Is his mental capacity less than, the same as, or greater than it was before the state of inertness began?

2. How does his mental capacity compare with the mental capacity he would have now if he had been normally active during the period of sleep?

3. If he begins a program of training to learn what he has missed during the 2 years, will his rate of learning be slower than, the same as, or faster than the rate at which he would have learned if he had been learning at all during the 2-year lapse?

In view of the unusual nature of this Reflect and Review, the following brief answers are given:

1. His mental capacity is greater because of the neural growth which has taken place.

2. His mental capacity is probably a little less; growth and learning actually produce more capacity than just growth alone.

3. Because his abilities did not increase during the 2-year lapse, his learning is slower when he resumes. However, he will soon be learning more rapidly than he did 2 years before, because his capacities continued to increase during the lapse.

Growth of Verbal Abilities. At birth, a child is able to make vocal noises in the form of babbling and crying. Soon the sounds begin to differentiate a little into "da da," "de de," and others. By the age of one year or a little later a simple word or two may be spoken. After this happens, the vocabulary increases rapidly.

A person's vocabulary may be thought of as comprised of two parts: the words he uses in speech or in writing and the words he does not use but whose meanings he understands when he sees and hears the words. The number of words a person understands is generally several times as large as the number of words he actually uses. Both parts of a person's vocabulary grow rapidly during approximately the first decade of life; growth then slows down and approaches a leveling off at twenty or in the early twenties. This curve, incidentally, is typical of growth curves of mental abilities. The growth of vocabulary is dependent on the growth of intelligence because the learning of words involves the mental processes of perception, remembering, and thinking.

As is also the case with most mental abilities, there is not much change in knowledge of words during the adult years, though the trend varies with individuals. Adults who read and study a great deal increase their knowledge of words during their adult lives. Adults whose experiences do not expose them much to the use of words tend to have smaller vocabularies as they grow older.

In the Terman-Merrill 1960 revision of the Stanford-Binet Intelligence Scale, there is a vocabulary test consisting of 45 words [Terman, 1960]. The minimum number of words the subjects at various age and developmental levels must define to pass is as follows:

Level	Minimum Number of Words
Age VI	6
Age VIII	8
Age X	11
Age XII	15
Age XIV	17
Average adult	20
Superior adult (I)	23
Superior adult (II)	26
Superior adult (III)	30

Compiled from L. M. Terman and Maude Merrill, *Stanford-Binet Intelligence Scale*, Houghton Mifflin Company, Boston, 1960.

The test standards reflect a continuous development of vocabulary ability from age VI up to adulthood. The standards also reflect the differences between adults, placing the average adult much closer to the fourteen-year-old than to the most superior (III-level) adult.

The pattern of growth in children's word knowledge can also be revealed by testing children of various successive ages and recording the percentage of each age group that can define any one given word. It will be discovered that this percentage increases with age. A larger percentage of seven-year-olds than of six-year-olds will be able to define a given word, a larger percentage of eight-year-olds than of seven-year-olds will be able to define it, and so on up through the ages.

Of course, the vocabulary growth rate is different for each person; usually, the brighter the child, the more words he acquires per year. At the same time, because the pattern of vocabulary growth is consistent with the growth patterns of other mental abilities, the extent of an individual child's vocabulary is a fairly good index of his mental growth. In fact, there is a substantial correlation between the scores made on a vocabulary test and those made on a mental test. These statements about vocabulary and mental growth are based on the assumption that children are in a verbal milieu that is normal. In an intellectually impoverished environment, children of average and above-average capacities, especially, do not have opportunities to learn as many words as they are able to.

Growth of the Capacity to Remember. Memory is a basic ingredient of intelligence and learning. Without it there could hardly be either. If we did not remember any of the general information we acquire from the words we hear, the faces we see, the places we are in, and so forth, we should be in a hopelessly stupid condition.

A young infant does not have a memory of his experiences because he is not sufficiently aware of them. Memory develops as an integral part of general mental capacities, which in turn develop from birth to adulthood. A child cannot have verbal memory until he has sufficient language skill to describe past events.

Still, a young child's emotional reactions to experiences indicate that he remembers them. For example, children who are inoculated before the age of six months will rarely cry just as they are exposed to a repetition of the inoculation process. According to D. M. Levy there is memory cry by only 1 per cent of six-month-old children, while at the age of twelve months, 20 per cent of the children have memory cries. [Levy, 1960]. The interval between the injections influences the memory cries; and the shorter the interval, the more the memory cries. This fact is of course consistent with our knowledge of forgetting.

At birth there is little memory; it grows from birth to adulthood. For instance, there is an increase in memory span from year to year during childhood which is evidenced by growth of the capacity to repeat digits. Indeed, one of the tests of memory is a test of digit memory span, in which the examiner reads digits to the subject at the rate of about one a second and asks the subject to repeat the digits after they have been given. The memory of a child can be tested by this method as soon as he is old enough to talk.

For example, for the aforementioned 1960 revision of the Stanford-Binet Intelligence Scale, Terman and Merrill tested the digit span of persons at widely different age and developmental levels and arrived at these norms, or standards:

Repeating Digits in Order Given		Repeating Digits in Reverse Order	
Level	Number of Digits	Level	Number of Digits
Age II-6	2	Age VII	3
Age III	3	Age IX	4
Age VII	5	Age XII	5
Age X	6	Superior adult (I)	6

Compiled from L. M. Terman and Maude Merrill, *Stanford-Binet Intelligence Scale*, Houghton Mifflin Company, Boston, 1960.

In considering them, it should be kept in mind that some children have a digit span smaller than standard for their ages and some have a greater span and that adults also vary greatly in their digit spans.

Memory is also tested by this scale with the use of objects, designs, sentences, and stories.

Development of Thinking Processes. The ability to think also develops with increasing age, passing through three general stages: (1) enumeration, (2) description, and (3) interpretation. A person's ability to think may be tested by asking him to tell what he sees in a picture; his answers will reflect one or more of these stages. Suppose that children of various ages are shown a picture of a woman running out of a cabin into the woods and are asked to talk about the picture.

The youngest children will enumerate. One may say, "House, woman, trees!" and another, "Trees, woman, house!" "Ground," "Leaves," or whatever else each subject sees in the picture will be added. This naming of the parts of the picture, or enumeration, represents a relatively low level of thinking ability.

Children somewhat older may say that the woman left the cabin in a hurry, that she is running into the woods, that there is smoke coming out of the chimney, that the cabin is made of logs and is located in the woods. That is, they will describe what they see in the picture. Description is a higher type of response and represents a higher level of mental maturity than mere enumeration.

As intelligence grows still further, the ability to interpret develops, so that among the oldest children who see the picture one may say that the woman is running to a neighbor for help because her husband or child has become suddenly ill. Another may take the picture to mean that a bear or a stranger has gotten into the cabin and that the woman is trying to escape by running to a neighbor. "Her husband has come home drunk, and she is trying to escape a beating at his hands," will be the interpretation of a third. The smoke in the chimney may indicate to some that the day is a cool one, to others that the woman was cooking and baking and therefore had a fire in the stove. Such responses indicate that through interpretation each subject has arrived at a comprehension of the situation represented by the picture. The meaning of the picture has been observed; or, more exactly, meanings have been given to the picture.

These stages of thought—enumeration, description, and interpretation—are not separate and distinct in the sense that a child is at one level for a time and then jumps to the next. A child grows steadily and gradually to the next level, and there are progressively different combinations of the thinking processes. For example, there can be a mixture of enumeration and description at one time, and a mixture of description and interpretation later on. As a child matures further, the power of interpretation increases and mere description becomes less prominent.

Three, six, and twelve are the ages at which average children enumerate, describe, and interpret, respectively; but these should be taken just as indications of average mental development, not as definite standards.

These three general stages of thought have important implications for teaching, even with children in the lower grades, who, though not very mature mentally, can be guided into elementary habits of interpreting. When a teacher and his pupils are discussing a topic, the teacher can control the pupils' thinking so that they merely recite facts, that is, enumerate, and the teaching and learning will not be on a very high intellectual plane. A better level of teaching is one on which the pupils and teacher describe what is being discussed, and better yet is to bring in interpretation. This matter is the teacher's responsibility: As a rule, he will get from his pupils the level of response that he stimulates.

History, geography, sociology, arithmetic, language, grammar—indeed, almost every subject—can be taught at any or all of the three levels. In class-work on the development of the great American cities, for example, facts about different cities can be drilled and drilled until the pupils learn to recite these facts—to list or to enumerate them. The development of the cities can be described also, and an interesting picture will emerge. But best of all is to deal with the reasons why New York, Chicago, Los Angeles, Detroit, and other cities have grown so large—to show the influences of location on oceans, rivers, and lakes; of surrounding territory; of natural resources for manufacturing, etc. The teacher should encourage his pupils to think of city growth in terms of its relationship to economic and social forces, as well as results. In other words, he should lead his pupils in the processes of interpreting, so that they will acquire a lively vision of the meaning of what the great cities have been and are.

Mental development is also evidenced by the increasing capacity to solve problems. In other words, the ability to reason and to arrive at correct solutions improves with the growth of intelligence. Problems may be of all kinds: problems in mathematics and science, planning a house, making a bid in bridge or a move in chess, investing in stocks and bonds, selecting employees, repairing a motor, or estimating the age of skeletal remains. Effective reasoning in problem situations of varying difficulty indicates the level of mental maturity.

Originality, creativeness, or imaginative thinking indicates one of the highest levels of mental activity. Such thinking has been designated as divergent thinking as contrasted to convergent thinking, which is more typical or traditional in nature. Inventiveness, new ideas, improvements, formulation of principles, and discovering new knowledge indicate the highest level of thinking. In the classroom, creative, problem-solving methods encourage the children to be imaginative and original.

The teacher who asks "What do you think?" or commends the student for emerging with good answers arrived at by his own methods encourages high-level mental activity. All school subjects present situations that encourage individual responses. The procedures of teachers are changing from emphasis on rote memorizing and recitation to the encouragement of productive thinking.

The Age of Mental Maturity. Just as there is an age when a person stops growing taller and stronger, so there is an age when a person's mental capacity stops increasing. This is the age when mental maturity is reached, the age when the curves representing mental growth level out. In terms of measurement, it is reached when a person is unable to improve his performance on intelligence tests, when mental-growth curves reach their maximum height.

Various ages ranging from thirteen to the early twenties have been called the age after which there is no further mental growth. For instance, during the First World War the mental abilities of American soldiers, as measured by mental tests, were found to be equivalent, on the average, to the abilities of American school children a little over thirteen years old. On the basis of this finding, it was concluded that, on the average, mental maturity is reached at thirteen, that is, that no mental growth takes place after this age. On the other hand, some psychologists have found that experimental groups given other mental tests have not increased their scores after the ages of fourteen, fifteen, and sixteen. As a consequence, these psychologists have concluded that mental growth stops at those ages.

We now know that these early ages are erroneous. Tests have shown that there is considerable growth beyond thirteen. Also, the research evidence is clear that there usually is some mental growth in the late teens and suggests that there is some in the early twenties for most people, indeed, the studies of mental growth and of adult mental abilities have yielded strong support of this statement. It is probably safe to conclude, then, that the average person reaches his maximum mental level about the age of twenty or slightly thereafter. This indicates that mental maturity is reached about, or slightly after, the time when the brain and the nerves leading to and from it cease to grow (see Figure 9).

It is true that on the average there is only a little mental growth during the late teens, as measured by tests and shown by growth curves; for instance, the measured growth from seventeen to eighteen is less than that from seven to eight. Nevertheless, this small amount may be very important. A little growth in the late teens may be just enough to enable a person to perform certain tasks, say in college or on the job, that otherwise he could not do.

Another important thing to realize is that even though mental growth stops at twenty or thereabouts, it does not follow that educational growth need stop at that age. In fact, it is after a person has obtained his maximum basic mental power that he is best equipped for learning. It is then that a person is ready to study for law or medicine; it is then that he can master his craft or learn a business well.

Patterns of Individual Growth. Curves for any individual's growth would tend to have the same general shape as the curves shown in Figure 9, but would show irregularities. Such irregularities tend to balance out when many are tested to produce representative curves like these.

At birth, not all children are equal potentially. Although infants can hardly be distinguished according to mental ability, the curves diverge. For all three representative persons, there is a little more mental growth in the first 5 years than between the ages of five and ten. There is less between ten and fifteen than between five and ten, and even less between fifteen and twenty. Mental growth thus tends to have the general pattern of, but to lag behind, the physical growth of the brain (see Figure 9). The trend of growth for every intelligence quotient (IQ) is essentially the same, except that the child with the highest IQ has a longer period of development than the duller child, though the differences in the age when mental maturity is reached are not very great.

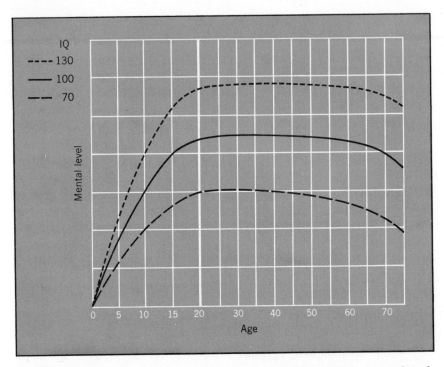

Figure 9 **Growth and decline of general mental ability** *Patterns of growth and decline of mental ability, as measured by general intelligence tests, are shown for a span of 75 years. Note that the horizontal scale is condensed after age twenty.*

The curves show the average course of change in mental level of three representative persons whose intelligence quotients (IQs) differ. The three have IQs of 70, 100, and 130, respectively. Seventy is the upper IQ limit of the least-retarded category; 100 is average; and 130 is the lower limit of the very superior classification.

TESTING THE CONSTANCY OF MENTAL GROWTH AND IQ

The IQ is calculated by dividing the mental age (MA) by the chronological age (CA) and is defined as an index of brightness and as an indication of the rate of mental growth. Mental age is determined by the scores made on intelligence tests in terms of age norms. The IQs of elementary school and junior high school pupils are more reliable than the IQs of preschool children; and for students in their late teens and twenties, the IQ is not an indication of the rate of mental growth, as mental growth has slowed down greatly in the late teens. A fuller discussion of IQ and MA is given in Chapter 6, pages 163 to 166.

Testing children mentally every year over a period of years not only will indicate the course of mental growth but also will give some information about the constancy of the IQ.

Exhibit 2   Mental-growth rates of four different people

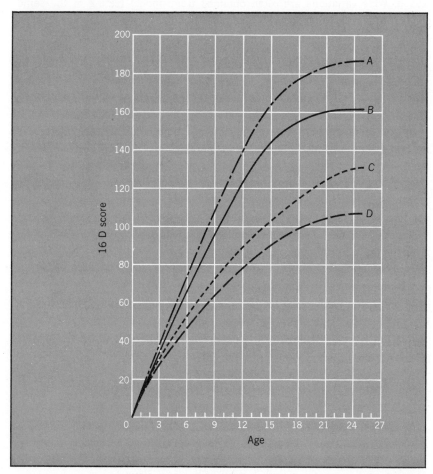

These smoothed curves depict the mental growth of four individuals. *A* is the brightest, *D* the dullest. The scores obtained on intelligence tests given the four persons were converted into units of deviation from the mean (see Appendix) at age sixteen and so are called 16 D scores. The standard deviation at age sixteen was used as the deviation unit. This attempt to convert the scores at each age into comparable units has much to recommend it. The scores for 3-year intervals were taken and smoothed by calculating a moving mean. Thus the score for age six was the mean of 16 D scores for ages three, six, and nine. The method yields relatively realistic curves by removing unreliabilities caused by testing errors and fluctuations. (Nancy Bayley, "Individual Patterns of Development," *Child Development*, 27:45–74, 1956. Figure is on page 67.)

How such testing is done is very important, however, for the following reason: Wide variations are often obtained from annual testing of the same child over a period of years. For example: In some cases the IQ variation is 45 points or even higher. Such large changes are fortuitous, and few if any educational psychologists would claim that the true intelligence of a person varies as much as 45 points during the childhood years. Such fluctuations in the recorded IQ of any given individual, except in the case of injury or deterioration of the nervous system, are caused by:

Erratic or fluctuating performance of the subject due to such factors as interest, effort, health, fatigue, and enriched or impoverished environment.

Normal deviations in performance due to actual individual variations in growth. Nature follows a definite general course for almost every individual but does allow some fluctuation from it.

Variation in the correctness and effectiveness with which the examiner gives the tests.

Unreliability in the mental tests themselves. Hence such large fluctuations do not represent changes in true intelligence.

In short, the intelligence testing must be well and carefully done, and the results must be smoothed, or averaged out, so that wide fluctuations do not distort the IQ and mental-growth curves of the child (see Exhibit 2 on the previous page).

☯ *Consider the Data*

Based on Exhibit 2

Is the course of growth essentially the same for all four persons?
How do the courses of growth compare after the age of twenty?
At what ages is mental growth fastest? When is it slowest?
Comment on the mental growth of person *C* after the age of eighteen.

The excellent work of A. H. Hilden, who tested 30 children over a period of more than a decade, is illustrative of both the rate of mental growth and IQ changes from a little after the age of five to the middle teens (see Exhibit 3).

In a more recent study of the mental growth and personalities of 140 children, L. W. Sontag, C. T. Baker, and Virginia Nelson have provided interesting material with which to compare children whose IQs increase, remain fairly constant, or decrease from early childhood to age twelve (see Exhibit 4).

Exhibit 3 Mental age and intelligence quotient from childhood to age fifteen

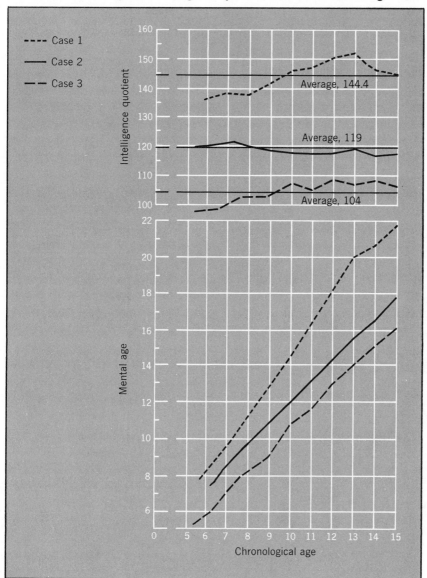

The person whose intelligence quotients and mental growth are represented as case 1 is very bright, and shows a greater range in IQ and MA than cases 2 and 3. Thus case 1's lowest IQ is 136, and his highest is 153, giving a range of 17. His largest deviation below his average IQ of 144.4 is 8.4, and his largest positive IQ deviation is 8.6. This peak variation above average considerably exceeds that of either case 1 or case 2. Yet, the curve representing case 1's mental growth is for the most part steady.

Case 2 has above-average intelligence. He also has a very constant IQ, the largest variations from his average 119 being only about two points. The curve of mental growth for case 2 has only very small fluctuations and represents a steady growth.

Case 3's intelligence is about average. The range of his IQ is from 97 to 108, with the largest deviation being seven downward from his average 104. The curve of mental growth for case 3 fluctuates more than the other two curves. Note that the IQs and MAs of these three persons do not overlap.

In order to obtain accurate intelligence quotients and a true course of mental growth for each person, his IQs were smoothed over the years. For example, the IQ for age six was calculated from the average IQ for ages six and seven. (Adapted from A. H. Hilden, "Longitudinal Study of Intellectual Development," *Journal of Psychology*, 28:187–214, 1949.)

Exhibit 4   Stanford-Binet intelligence quotients of six children

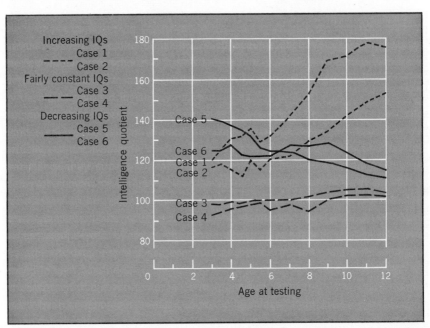

The intelligence quotients of six children are shown from age three to age twelve.

In case 1 the increase in IQ after school entrance is about 40 points, from about 130 to 170. Such an increase is very unusual, especially when the increase is above such a high IQ as 130. The increase in IQ in case 2 is about 30, which is very high also. The IQs shown in cases 3 and 4 fall within a range of five; there is little trend in either direction. The variation in IQ in case 5 after the age of six is about 15 points, and the trend is consistently downward. Case 6 moves downward generally, but has an up-and-down pattern. (Lester W. Sontag, Charles T. Baker, and Virginia K. Nelson. *Mental Growth and Personality Development: A Longitudinal Study*, Monograph XXIII (2), Society for Research in Child Development, National Research Council, Washington, D.C., 1958, pp. 57–81.)

☯ *Consider the Data*

Based on Exhibit 4

Unfortunately, no information on achievements and interests was reported for these cases to validate the reported large increases and decreases in the intelligence quotient. Judging from the charts alone, what answers do you think we might expect to the following questions:

What achievements and interests would you expect to find reported in the school and home history of the child depicted in case 1 who had such a large increase in IQ? Would you expect that over the years his abilities to do schoolwork showed a large increase? That his intellectual interests expanded? Do you suppose that at home he may have developed hobbies or engaged in activities that reflected greater mental dynamics?

Would you expect some of the same achievements and interests to be reported in the school and home history of the child depicted in case 2? Why or why not?

Might the opposite be true in case 5?

Would you say that the child depicted in case 6 probably showed a consistent performance in mental output and personal adjustment or that he fluctuated?

Do you agree that in cases 3 and 4 the children were probably quite consistent in their performance and interests?

In their study, Sontag, Baker, and Nelson also separated from the 140 students the 25 who experienced the greatest increase in IQ and the 25 who had the greatest decline, to provide comparative data on the IQ increases and decreases, including differences between the sexes (see Exhibit 5).

Conclusions from Testing. What conclusions can be drawn from these and comparable tests? Neither the rate of mental growth nor the IQ is ever constant in the absolute sense, of course. No human growth, ability, or behavior is that. But can it be said that IQ is at all constant?

For most students, careful testing over the period of the school years will establish dependable IQ levels. The IQs for each person for a given year are not free of deviations from his average, but the level is so constant or becomes so constant that it can be depended upon. Most of the Sontag-Baker-Nelson subjects were found to have fairly constant levels of intelligence from ages eight to twelve.

A few students will show fairly large increases and decreases in IQ. Furthermore, there is evidence suggesting that some have more favorable mental development in the late teens than others. Usually, however, if a school child has been tested four or five times in as many years, especially from the fourth- to the eighth-grade ages, the results will indicate dependably his

Exhibit 5   Mean IQ points gained by extreme ascending and descending groups in a study of mental growth

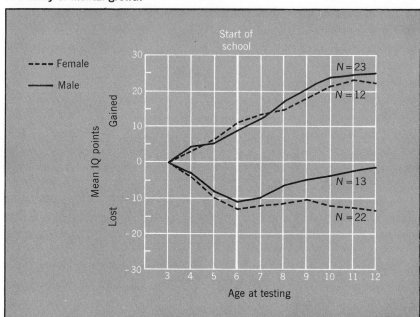

In the group of 35 students who experienced increases in IQ, there were nearly twice as many boys as girls, and the boys' IQs went up a little more than the girls'. *In toto* this group achieved half their IQ increase of about 24 points before the age of 6½, or near the time of starting school, and the other half after that age. In the group of 35 students who experienced decreases in IQ, there were nearly twice as many girls as boys, and the overall decline for the boys was considerably less than that for the girls. In fact, by the age of twelve the boys were almost at their starting level and were continuing an upward trend which had started at the age of 6½.

The four curves suggest that after children have been in school three or four years their IQs become fairly stable, and this is substantiated by many of the individual charts for the 140 children studied. (Lester W. Sontag, Charles T. Baker, and Virginia L. Nelson, *Mental Growth and Personality Development: A Longitudinal Study*, Monograph XXIII (2), Society for Research in Child Development, 1958, 143 pp.

mental level. For the larger increases or decreases, validating evidence should be provided in the form of better or poorer performance in school or increased or decreased intellectual interests. If there is no such evidence, the cases which purport to show large increases or decreases in IQ are in doubt and should be carefully examined again.

Causes of Demonstrated IQ Changes. Finally, what of the causes of noticeable changes in IQ or rate of mental growth over a span of years when they

do occur? Sontag, Baker, and Nelson report that general physical growth was not associated with increase or decrease in IQ. They did find that certain personality factors were related to change in IQ. Those who gained in IQ showed independence, aggressiveness, initiative, problem-solving ability, and competitiveness, according to these authors. They stated that the achievement motive was a characteristic common to those who gained most in IQ. In other words, they possessed strong motivation to do well. It is possible, too, that the increase in mental capacity had a dynamic effect which manifested itself in greater drive to achieve.

Does an increase in IQ usually result from a better-than-average growth and maturation of the nervous system? Is the opposite, poorer-than-average neural development, responsible when IQs go down appreciably? We have no direct evidence that individual children differ in the growth and development of their nervous systems, but inasmuch as the measured rate of physical growth of children varies in many particulars, there probably is a difference in the rate of growth of the nervous system. This varied growth and development may well be reflected in increases and decreases in IQ. In a few exceptional cases there may be changes in the apparent rate of mental growth or in the IQ because the environment changes so sharply that it is much more or much less stimulating. Also, in the case of some individuals there may be organic reasons for either a dying down in general interest or a much more vigorous and extensive response to their situations.

THE RANGE OF HUMAN INTELLIGENCE AND THE TEACHER'S RESPONSIBILITY

Those early statesmen of the United States who said that everyone was created equal clearly were not referring to mental capacity, but rather were expressing the ideal of equality before the law. Today we speak of equal opportunity; but even if it did exist it would not be equally made use of, simply because of the great and basic differences in individual mental capacity.

At the bottom of this wide range in human intelligence are those classified as mentally retarded or mentally deficient, some of whom have IQs just a little above zero. The mentally retarded are also called feebleminded, a term which is not favored at present by those who work with children of low mental capacity. At the top of the distribution are those very exceptional persons called very superior, with IQs approaching 200. Each of these two groups constitutes about two per cent of the population. The largest group— the 50 per cent of the people regarded as average—includes persons with IQs between 90 and 110 (see Figure 10). The IQs of a representative group of persons—children or adults—distribute according to the curve for the whole population, or approximately so. Indeed, almost everywhere people gather there will be a wide range in mental capacity.

Like anyone else dealing with human beings, a teacher should be keenly conscious of this tremendous range in human brightness. As he surveys his class, he may at one moment be looking at a student with a mind that seems to "soak up everything," a mind far beyond its years, and at the next moment at a student who fails to understand most of what is taking place in the room. While the former speaks to the point, reads well, and is enthusiastic about many of his studies, the latter expresses himself poorly, comprehends little of what he tries to read, and tends not to like any of his subjects. The teacher cannot see these differences between the two persons by looking at them casually; but he can see it by careful observation of the pair, supplemented by knowledge of their performance on intelligence tests and in their subjects. All this observational groundwork on the part of the teacher is very important, for he will always find it necessary to make many adjustments to the differences between the two, as well as among the other students distributed between these extremes.

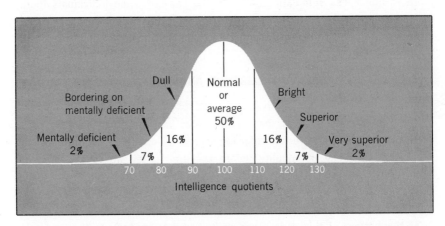

Figure 10 Distribution of intelligence quotients *The curve is divided to indicate the proportion of the various classifications of mental capacity in the population or in any true sample of the population. Opposing categories contain equal percentages of the people.*

Note that the curve does not show the long "tails," or "ends," which should approach 0 to the left and 200 to the right. In a curve of this size the tails, reaching extreme mental retardation to the left and the highest intelligence quotient to the right, would extend beyond the edges of the page. Also, the curve is a smoothed composite of the many data that have accumulated up to this time. Curves representing actual findings of specific studies each have the same general shape as this curve but are not so regular.

Mental Retardation. As indicated previously, the 2 per cent of the population with IQs below 70 are regarded as mentally retarded or deficient. As children, they develop mentally at a rate that is less than 70 per cent of the average rate. Some of these children who are mentally weak in terms of the intelligence-test standards for their ages become vocationally adequate if employed to do the simplest of unskilled work and if sympathetically supervised until they become fairly well established in their vocational routines. None of them can do really well in school subjects, and they will be failed consistently if their teachers judge them by the usual standards of achievement.

But this is a general statement and not quite complete, for actually, a person with an IQ of 70 or less is not classified as mentally deficient on the basis of mental-test results alone. If he can hold a job, can get along with people, and does not require the supervision of the social worker or probation officer, he is not classified as mentally deficient. Conversely, a person who tests 75 or 80 but who requires almost constant supervision and guidance may warrant classification as mentally retarded.

Some academic material can be successfully taught to the mentally retarded if the timing is carefully related to their social and mental maturity. The mentally retarded child's adjustment is more important than his academic achievement. Generally, he will acquire the few arithmetic or reading skills within his ability much more readily and happily if the teacher waits until he has social bearings and has matured, at an older-than-usual age, to the mental level at which these skills are usually learned.

The mentally retarded have a wide range of IQs, and have been classified into three groups. Those with IQs up to 25 have been classified as "idiots," or low-grade defectives. Those with IQs from 25 to 50 have been called "imbeciles," or middle-grade defectives. The highest order of the mentally retarded have been termed "morons," or high-grade defectives. They have IQs from 50 to 70 and are, of course, least distinguishable from the normal group. There is a tendency today to abandon the terms idiot, imbecile, and moron and instead refer to them respectively as severely retarded, or custodial; less severely retarded, or trainable; and least retarded, or educable.

Fortunately, the relative number of custodials, trainables, and educables in the population corresponds to their IQ levels; there are fewest of the severely retarded (custodials) and most of the least retarded (educables). Yet in one sense, this is unfortunate, for it is the educables and those with intelligence just above and below the educable level who, as adults, usually have large families and thereby perpetuate and even aggravate the problem of the mentally and socially inadequate. The most severely retarded rarely have offspring.

⦿ *Reflect and Review*

A school boy had an IQ of only 70, but fortunately he was disposed to be helpful and was a diligent worker. The academic subjects were difficult for him; but by continuing in school, he managed to obtain a minimum elementary school education. His teachers were sympathetic and understanding and did not press him unduly. He was allowed to be a handyman for the school building. The result was that he had a feeling of personal worth, he adjusted well to the school, and the school adjusted well to him. His school experience fostered his industry and initiative. In the summer months when jobs were hard to get, he created a position for himself by pointing out to a local storekeeper various little jobs which needed doing and which he could do in the store.

What elements of this boy's environment contributed to his better-than-average success, considering his mental capacity?

How did his teachers develop his capabilities and minimize the effects of his deficiencies?

What are this boy's prospects for economic and social success as an adult, again considering his mental capacity?

How strong a possibility is there that the special treatment he received during his school years will have built up in him a false sense of his own capabilities which will be roughly contradicted in the adult world?

What specific things should a teacher do to encourage the successful adjustment of a boy like this?

The Very Superior. There is also a great range in the intelligence of the very superior—the upper 2 per cent of the population, whose IQs are 130 and above. If, as is generally done, we consider the maximum IQ to be 200, then we have a range of 70 for the upper 2 per cent; and this also is essentially the range for the lowest 2 per cent, the mentally deficient. In a typical community of 5,000 school children, for instance, the child with an IQ of 130 will be included among the brightest 100. A child with an IQ of 170 will probably be the brightest of all the 5,000 children.

The big range in the upper 2 per cent of the population is made more meaningful by comparing the mental ages of children within it—children with IQs of 130 and 180, for example. At the chronological age of six, the usual age of school entrance, the child with an IQ of 130 has a mental age of 7 years 10 months, while the child with an IQ of 180 has a mental age of 10 years 10 months—a difference of 3 years in mental age. At the chronological age of ten years, the respective mental ages of these two children are thirteen and eighteen—a difference of 5 years in mental age. If we had used an IQ of 200, these differences would have been still greater, but the value of the comparison would have been largely theoretical because such high IQs are extremely rare. Even the number of children with IQs of 180 is small, and an investigator would have to pursue his inquiry for some time in order to locate several of them.

Mental-performance Variations and the Schools. With the wide extremes of intelligence just discussed, the children of any given grade in school would be expected to vary greatly in subject-matter abilities and knowledge; and the actual variation is very wide, as shown by test results in science (see Exhibit 6), language, arithmetic, geography, history, and other subjects.

Exhibit 6   Range in science knowledge among seventh-graders

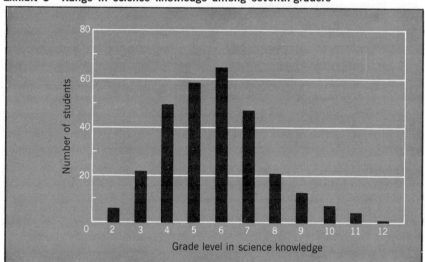

Tested science knowledge among the 296 seventh-grade students of a county school system ranges in level from grade 2 through grade 12, with the mode (see Appendix) at grade 6. Almost inconceivably, these students cover nearly the whole range of grade and high school in levels of science knowledge. The six students at the second-grade level form 2 per cent of the class; the twenty-six students at the high school level (grades 9 through 12) comprise nearly 9 per cent of the class.

Note that the majority of the seventh-grades have fourth-, fifth-, or sixth-grade knowledge in science; the average level of these 296 students in the subject is 1.5 grades under the national average. (Courtesy of Paul Street, Director, Bureau of School Service, University of Kentucky, Lexington, Kentucky.)

Thus the problem posed in education by range of intelligence goes beyond the province of the individual teacher, who, after all, can usually make only limited allowance for the extremely different students he teaches in an ordinary class. The problem must be tackled at a school administration level.

Those students who test four or five grades below standard should be placed in special classes for greatly retarded students of low mental capacity. Students who are three, four, and five grades ahead of themselves are very capable intellectually, and should be in special sections for the most advanced or should be given special guidance and provided opportunities to finish high school at the age of sixteen or seventeen.

MENTAL CAPACITY DURING THE ADULT YEARS

The course of mental capacity during the adult years has been the subject of many inquiries. Mental tests, including tests of learning ability, have been used to investigate the mental capacity of adults over a wide age range. Careful inquiries have been made about the ages when the best books are written, when the most important scientific discoveries are made, when chess players become champions, when men are most inventive—in general—all based on the hope that if the ages of greatest mental achievement were known, we should have important clues to the understanding of the course of the mental powers through life.

Much has yet to be learned on the subject, but from disagreement some valuable hypotheses have emerged. Thus, some psychologists believe that mental capacity begins a slow decline after the early twenties which continues until old age is reached, when the decline becomes rapid; but this contention is hardly consistent with many important facts. Recent research indicates that mental powers hold up during the adult years much better than this.

Another important consideration here is that just as effective physical power does not reach its maximum as soon as a person reaches his full stature, so is it likely that full effective mental power is not reached in the early twenties when the nervous system has reached its maximum growth. On the basis of the research findings on mental capacity and adult learning it can be stated with considerable confidence that effective mental capacity probably reaches its maximum in the thirties. This is not to imply that after twenty or thereabouts there is any organic growth of the central nervous system which causes an increase in basic intelligence or mental capacity. Whatever increase in the ability to use the mind occurs between the early twenties and forty seems to come from the addition of educative experience to basic mental maturity.

Obviously, if an adult, on leaving formal education behind, abandons intellectual and learning practices and lives a dormant mental life, tests of his mental powers will show a steady decline beginning in the twenties. Thus, the statements about continued effective mental growth in the twenties and thirties, it should be emphasized, are based on the assumption that adults equip their minds through sustained mental activity——that they exercise mentally by using the imagination, by reasoning, and by studying new sources of information as much as a student in school does.

There is considerable evidence that, with such activity, mental powers are maintained throughout the adult years quite well. But even for those who keep their minds vigorously active, there is hardly any doubt that some time during the adult years, probably in the forties and fifties, certain changes in the central nervous system and in the senses take effect and cause decline in mental capacity to set in. The course of decline is not sharp, but very gradual during most of later life. In fact, the vocabulary and fund of general information may even increase up to the last of adult life; and the decline in most mental powers becomes rapid only during the very advanced years when the infirmities of old age have set in.

SUMMARY

Improved functioning of the mind depends on the growth of physical structures and on experience.

The growth of functioning intelligence depends greatly on the richness of the environment and the extensiveness of experiences. Conceivably the higher areas of the nervous system grow and develop better too if stimulated by much mental activity.

Evidence of the growth of mental capacity is the ability to do more mental tasks, as well as more complex and difficult ones.

Mental growth gives the pupil an increased readiness for tasks which formerly were too difficult.

The growth of vocabulary accompanies the course of general mental growth except that it takes a year or two after birth before a child begins using words. The growth of vocabulary is a general indication of the growth of mental capacity because the learning of words depends on the mental processes of perception, remembering, and thinking.

Memory is evidenced by the ability to reinstate or repeat previous experiences and learning. As an integral part of mental capacity, it increases according to the general pattern of mental growth.

Mental growth is more rapid for the brighter than for the duller and continues a little longer and declines later and more slowly than the mental abilities of those with low IQs.

The acme of mental development, or the period of mental maturity, is the first half of adulthood, or the years from the early twenties to the early forties.

Mental decline is usually slow until the last years of life, when it speeds up, especially if sight and hearing weaken greatly and if there is much other physical deterioration.

Mental abilities maintain themselves very well for adults who use their minds fruitfully and are in good health.

The intelligence quotient (IQ) is an index of brightness and indicates the rate of mental growth.

Testing of children during the grade and high school years yields the most dependable intelligence levels. Testing of preschool children, especially two- and three-year-olds, does not yield very dependable results.

The IQ or rate of mental growth is reasonably constant, as determined by periodic testing during the age range from seven to fifteen, for example. Wide fluctuations in the IQ of an individual from one testing to the next do not represent a true change in IQ.

The IQ levels of most children are reasonably constant. A few tend to increase, a few tend to decrease, and a few vary up and down. Large changes occur infrequently. If an increase or decrease in IQ is very large, it should be accompanied by validating evidence in the form of greatly increased or decreased intellectual interests and performance in school. Particularly the students' out-of-school activities will reflect the levels of their intellectual functioning. If such evidence or validation is missing, there probably has been no large change in IQ.

Increases or decreases in IQ may be caused by increase or decrease in the rate with which the nervous system develops or, rarely, by environmental influences which have differential effects on the development of intellectual ability.

Children and adults differ greatly in mental capacity, the distribution of which is represented by a normal curve (Figure 10). The wide range in capacity is reflected in the classroom by the great differences in the abilities of the students.

About two per cent of the people are mentally deficient and are classed as educable or least retarded, trainable or moderately retarded, and custodial or severely retarded. Some of the mentally retarded are employable for simple work, handle their responsibilities well, and get along independently.

The very superior constitute 2 per cent of the total population, and balance the mentally retarded numerically. There is a range of about 70 points in IQ among the very superior.

There is a very wide range in the knowledge or educational abilities of the children of a given grade—a range caused largely by the great differences in mental capacities and the environment.

SUGGESTED READING

Birren, James F., Henry A. Imus, and William F. Windle (eds.): *Process of Aging in the Nervous System,* Charles C Thomas, Publisher, Springfield, Ill., 1959. Much information about the maturity and deterioration of the nervous system during the adult years is presented. Provides an excellent anatomical basis for understanding intelligence over the wide span of adulthood.

Symonds, P. M.: "What Education Has to Learn from Psychology: Individual Differences," *Teachers College Record,* 61:86–98, 1959. In this article the reader will learn about the differences in the learning capacities of students and how to cope with those differences.

Terman, Lewis M., and Maud A. Merrill: *Stanford-Binet Intelligence Scale,* Houghton Mifflin Company, Boston, 1960. A perusal of this book will acquaint the reader with a widely used individual mental examination and with the psychology of mental abilities.

CHAPTER 3
MATURING SOCIALLY

We all realize that man's life is, among other things, a constantly unfolding pattern of social learning and change. This chapter examines this aspect of development—this ever-changing relation of the individual to the other social beings around him. It is very important for a teacher who wishes to understand and work efficiently with his students to know something of their experiences with social living and their patterns of friendships and antipathies; he must learn ways of helping them to mature socially and thereby to achieve richer and more successful social relationships.

Social maturity is evidenced by an individual's capacity for making and keeping friends. To be effective in his social relations, a person needs to acquire the social skills that enable him to deal with people tactfully and with understanding. He must be conscious of the interests of others, appreciative of their goals, and supportive of their feelings of personal worth.

All this applies to most personal relationships, but there are times in the life of every individual when social maturity expresses itself in other ways. There will be conflicts among people over their goals and over moral issues. Then when people take a courageous stand, they will make enemies. Still, in crucial situations, social maturity is evinced by poise, courtesy, and a well-controlled temper.

THE SOCIALIZATION OF THE INDIVIDUAL

A human being gradually evolves from the extreme individualism of the infant and accompanying dependency on a few persons, chiefly the mother and father, to outgoing membership in an adult social group and dependency on its many members.

The infant must be given painstaking care, and "gives out" little if anything in return. He is a little tyrant demanding almost constant attention, as is necessary, of course, because of his helplessness. But the infant soon starts to respond to people by kicking, waving, and holding out his arms and trying to move toward the members of the family who approach him; and he becomes able to recognize individuals when he is three to four months old. He then begins to differentiate his mother, or whoever takes care of him, from others. At six months, when the mother holds her baby, he may reach for her face and smile while he tries to grasp or pat it. These are the beginnings of outgoing behavior.

When nearly a year old, the infant starts paying attention to others of the same age; he will then reach out and take hold of another child's foot, hair, or arm. If there are toys within reach, one-year-olds will often try to pull them toward themselves. Sometimes two children of this age will be tugging on the same toy; there is no evidence of sharing and cooperation at this time.

From this time until they start school, children play together, but the play remains largely individualistic. In this period, one occasionally does say to another, "You may have this," or "You may use this," but there is not yet much cooperation.

There is, however, a strong tendency for some to dominate others; definite evidence of social ascendancy shows itself during these preschool years. Indeed, even in early infancy some individuals are more aggressive and assertive than others.

When children enter school, they enter an environment of play and work activities that tends to socialize them. They work on classroom projects together, and they play games that call for some teamwork. They borrow and share, and they find that antisocial and overindividualistic behavior is reproved by their teachers and frowned upon by fellow students. In other words, they are now members of a defined group, having experiences that cause them to become group-minded.

During the fourth to seventh grades, specialized social groups enter children's lives. They join girl and boy scout troops. Boys, especially, have their little neighborhood gangs and organize themselves into football and baseball teams. Extreme individualism has now been overcome by banding together for work and play.

During high school, boys and girls are still more organized. Boys have well-knit teams for more sports than before, and both sexes carry on the activities of many school-centered but extracurricular organizations. A look at any high school bulletin board will show how much goes on—how the student council, the drama club, the literary organization, the religious group, and so on have scheduled meetings which they are urging members—and sometimes interested observers—to attend.

Importantly present and influential at this adolescent stage of socialization, of course, is increasing personal awareness of sex.

During infancy and the following preschool years and in the primary grades there is not much consciousness of sex. Boys and girls play together on equal terms. Shortly before puberty, boys become more conscious of girls but look down on them. It is "sissy" to play with girls, they feel, for they regard them as being the weaker sex. Girls at the same stage of physical development have a corresponding interest in boys but are apt to hide it by considering them "perfectly stupid." Then, during early adolescence, girls are for a time physically larger than boys their own age and are more mature socially because they reach puberty earlier. Yet these and related differences and difficulties are overcome during adolescence, at least by those boys and girls who are neither shy nor overaggressive, who know how to converse effectively and "get along." A major problem in social maturation is faced; boys and girls seek each other's company, have dates, and begin romances. In doing so, they achieve considerable social maturity.

Both children and adults are gregarious, but adulthood usually brings less social isolation than exists at any earlier time of life. Men and women join in marriage and thus form the family unit. For security, they join or form business corporations and cooperatives, labor unions, and various movements. For other specific social purposes, they join churches, lodges, and clubs and societies of myriad kinds. They like to be together less formally, too, for the simple, elementary purposes of playing and visiting.

In short, in the process of growing up, we become more and more social, finding many advantages and inner rewards in being together in a variety of ways.

The Decline of Egocentricity. All this suggests that as a person matures socially, he becomes less and less egocentric, or self-centered—that his interests, thoughts, and expressions are increasingly centered less on self and more on others and the whole world outside himself. In other words, he is nurturant. This change is, moreover, a necessary inner complement of the increasing outer activity that leads to social maturity. But unfortunately, this gradual loss of egocentricity is not a universal process. It is one in which some individuals go far but others do not. Thus, it may be taken as a reliable index of individual social maturation.

As the necessarily self-centered infant becomes the child, he starts to play with other children; later, at school, he learns to give and take in many ways; and he comes home and does chores for his mother. He is learning to be less self-centered. However, some children always remain very egocentric and consequently remain socially immature. They become those adults whose attitudes toward everything are shaped by the thought "What is there in it for me?" and who, when they are with others, try to attract attention to themselves rather than concentrate on those around them—adults who, in a word, are selfish.

Children, teen-agers, and adults can be socially mature when they have learned to cooperate with and give service to others with little conscious or unconscious thought of "what I can get out of it" or "what I can corner for myself." A person shows social as well as personal maturity when he is so absorbed in his outgoing activities that selfish, egocentric interests are at a minimum.

A person must have intelligent self-interest; not to have it would be most socially immature, for if an individual does not take care of himself, he will be dependent on others. But intelligent self-interest is often based on cooperation with others, and the results are mutually advantageous. The highly egocentric person, moreover, does not usually get along successfully, just because his ego is in the way, preventing him from serving himself by cooperating with others. To overcome that obstruction he must externalize his interests by working and playing with people.

We must, however, distinguish the person who is engaged in much individual activity from the self-centered individual. There are the normal, retiring youths who spend more than the usual amount of time with books, music, tools, and equipment. They may be called introverted but not egocentric; individualistic but not unsocial. Actually they have friends and are not unpopular. They are not shy; but because they find true satisfaction in solitary activities, their participation in peer-group activity is underaverage.

The Body and Mind and Social Maturity. The decline of egocentricity is, of course, only one element of social maturation. A young man of twenty also reacts differently to people than he did when he was a child of two, because of the increased body size and greater mental power he has acquired in growing older; he now has more personal equipment for dealing with people. The social development that goes along with growth in physical and mental stature cannot be simply represented by curves and charts; the best we can do is describe and discuss personal relationships, play interests, social activities, and other aspects of behavior that indicate the social growth and maturation. But measurable facts of physical and mental development are often related to the comparative social maturation of individuals. Thus, a physically large and well-developed child tends to do better socially, for he can cope relatively well physically with people and things. Being bright, or having a mental age in advance of his years, also tends to make a child socially mature, for such a child is more aware of what is happening about him. On the other hand, either physical or mental underdevelopment tends to retard a child socially. Thus undersized children often fail socially by failing at play with their age-mates, and so tend to play with children younger than they are in order to achieve social adjustment. Thus, also, children who have low IQs and therefore learn slowly in school are easily recognized and often rejected by their classmates. The mentally retarded are usually older and larger than their classmates; and if this is so, they are even more likely to be pinpointed as academic failures and therefore to be socially rejected.

The Importance of Early and Late Physical Maturation. Early or late physical maturing is a factor of great importance in the individual's social development as well as one which complicates the overall social situation within any group of adolescent and preadolescent boys and girls.

Status of physical maturity is determined by X-ray examination of the bones in the knees and hand, including the wrist. The early maturers are generally of mesomorphic type (muscular-athletic), and the late maturers more ectomorphic (slender build). At the ages of eleven to fourteen, even though not so much in the late teens, the early maturers are taller and also have more physical strength. They are more attractive physically and in addition groom themselves better than do the late maturers. The late maturers are more eager and uninhibited and try to attract attention; while the early maturers are relaxed, matter-of-fact, and unaffected. In other words, the early maturers have more poise.

When Mary Jones and Nancy Bayley studied boys who were early and late physical maturers, they concluded that early maturers are more popular, display more leadership, and have older friends [Jones and Bayley, 1950]. Of 16 early-maturing boys of high school age, two became class presidents and one the president of the boys' club, four were prominent athletes, and several were on committees. Among 16 late-maturing boys of the same age, there were one vice-president and one athlete. In essence, it was apparent that a relatively high degree of physical maturity was associated with outgoing social and athletic qualities.

When Mary Jones studied 33-year-old men who as teen-agers had been in some cases early and in some cases late maturers, she found that the physical differences had largely disappeared and that, in addition, the later maturers were equal to the early maturers vocationally and socially [Jones, 1957]. Nevertheless, the later maturers were found to have been socially and physically at a disadvantage during their teens.

The findings of both studies point up, incidentally, an important responsibility of the home and school: to help the late-maturing boy through the teen years when he is at a disadvantage. Not yet having attained the same degree of manliness, he should not be placed in competition physically or socially with the boy whose developmental rate has brought him to adolescence sooner. The slow maturer will catch up physically and socially in early adulthood, but the tasks set before him now should be suitable for his development so that he will not suffer from a perception of himself as inadequate and adjust to it in an unfortunate way—for instance, by becoming aggressive and trying to attract attention to himself, as many relatively immature boys do.

With girls, the social implications of the maturation schedule are more complex. Girls who mature early, for example, may be socially hindered or helped by becoming physically adult at an early age; this depends on other than physical circumstances. If she is also advanced mentally, early physical maturation may be an advantage for a girl. She may be fully capable of good social as well as mental adjustment in classes and other groups in which the members are, on the average, about two years older than she is. Such a girl may enter college at sixteen and be at ease with classmates who are even 3 years older than she. On the other hand, dull girls who are early maturers—girls who look older than their age but are mentally behind their age and far behind their appearance—may have extraordinary social problems. Even before the early teens, they may have a more-than-usual interest in boys, an interest not balanced and restrained by the other interests that superior mental qualities lead to. Thus, whether they are rich or poor, college is out of the question for such girls; and especially if of low socioeconomic status, they tend to get married very young. When this happens—when their early-maturing bodies and sexual feelings plunge them into the burdensome responsibilities of wifehood several years too young—they are, as it were, cheated of many normal adolescent experiences.

Special mental conditions apart, if the early-maturing girl is in classes with boys and girls her own age, they will naturally seem young and immature to her, and she will prefer the companionship of older boys and girls. This indicates that there are always problems of social adjustment for these girls; and this is especially true in relation to boys. When of junior and senior high school age, girls are ordinarily one or two years more advanced, both physically and in their social inclinations, than boys; thus an early-maturing girl is three or four years ahead of average boys of her age.

The relation between physical-maturity level and social effectiveness shifts as they pass through the ages and grades, as Margaret S. Faust found in studying 731 girls in grades 6 to 9 [Faust, 1960]. The girls were rated in social prestige, or popularity, by a test in which they identified other girls whom they "thought a lot of," who had much group influence, and so forth. As a whole, the 21 items were related to the prestige factors: friendliness, leadership, assuredness, good looks, and enthusiasm. Negative, as well as positive, reactions were elicited.

In this study it was found that in the sixth grade girls who were average, or at phase, in physical status had most prestige. These girls were prepuberal, that is, had not reached the menarche. The girls who were most mature seemed to be put at a social disadvantage, being physically ahead of their group and yet not able to utilize this fact. In junior high school, where, incidentally, most girls reach puberty, the more physically advanced girls were found to have more prestige.

As the Faust study confirms, by junior high school more womanliness engenders more respect, and more physically advanced girls have more influence on their peers and are more popular than other girls.

Girls who are relatively immature in junior high school tend, in contrast to boys in the same situation, to withdraw and be inconspicuous. It is not known, however, whether this is a conscious or an unconscious adjustment to the situation which finds them behind other girls in the transition from childhood to adolescence.

☯ *Reflect and Review*

Debbie, a fourteen-year-old girl who had reached puberty at the age of twelve, was an attractive young woman. Her home was in the poorer part of town, as her father was a factory worker whose annual income was scarcely adequate for providing the family necessities. Debbie had always been an underaverage student and had had only a few friendships in school. She found that her eighth-grade classmates did not have her social interests, and she got along better with the sophomore and junior boys. To appear sophisticated, she talked to her classmates about having dates and going car riding, dancing, and to the movies.

What developments were likely to take place for Debbie in regard to:

Continuing or dropping out of school
Job experiences
Boy-girl relationships
Marriage and family life
Future socioeconomic status

Personal Traits and Leadership. As previously stated, some very young children are more assertive than their peers and thus gain a certain measure of ascendancy and control; but there is, in early childhood, little formal recognition of the leader. At this time, children are not highly enough organized to need a captain or a president. In later childhood, however, organizations that require a leader begin to crop up. Then it is found, by the person who has been watching a group of children grow, that it is usually those who are socially most able and best adjusted who are selected as leaders of little gangs, captains of teams, and presidents of clubs and of classes.

The specific qualities of a leader vary with the kind of group which selects him. The person selected as captain of a team is generally a player who, if not the best, is one of the best. But in addition to respecting his playing ability, the players generally regard him as being decisive, friendly, and fair—a person who has a plan and acts on it, who is easy to like, and who handles team disputes well and gives each player his chance. Among the important characteristics taken into account in the selection of class presidents and presidents of student councils are intelligence and scholarship. Students who are bright and have good marks are most likely to be selected, and one can be reasonably sure that a dull student will not be. Friendliness toward and the ability to get along with the various kinds of people in the class or school are major considerations, too. Some students show budding administrative and managerial abilities which their classmates recognize by choosing those students for various school offices. The sportsmanship of a team captain and the high intelligence of a good student officer are generally important to leaders. But what other qualities do good leaders tend to have in common?

In childhood the larger (usually older) individuals in social groups tend to be stronger and more assertive and thus to lead, and this size element of leadership continues to be important in adult life. Thus, it is true that business executives, school superintendents, political leaders, and all others in positions of leadership tend to be above average in size. Yet there are many exceptions; size alone is a poor guarantee of leadership.

A much more constant characteristic of leaders—one that is to be expected, since it is close to the very idea of leadership—is extroversion. The person whose thoughts and interests are introverted can hardly be a leader. Leadership falls to persons who have outgoing personalities, that is, persons whose thoughts and interests center in others, who like to be with others. Still, the leader may obtain many of his ideas and plans from introverts whom he is glad to have on his team. The introvert may compensate for the shortcomings and illuminate the blind spots of the extrovert.

Beyond simple extroversion, the effective leader has keen perceptions of how others in and out of his own group think and feel, supplemented by an appreciation of their values. Consequently, he is not negative in his attitudes toward others. Rather, he is cooperative by nature and adjusts his thinking readily to changing conditions and the new leadership requirements they bring. Furthermore, he is able to guide his group in satisfying its needs. He takes various roles. Now he is a listener, now ready with a suggestion. At moments of group decision he can either serve as a guide for the group or take a firm hold on the reins. The good leader delegates authority wisely and maintains strong group cohesiveness and pride. The effect of all this is that the group makes progress in reaching its goals.

The habit of hard work and a willingness to expend extra effort are also very important in leadership. A lazy person is seldom selected as leader in the first place, and leadership in any field is to be kept only at the price of hard work. Talent and good ideas are barren if not nurtured and developed even at the cost of occasionally distasteful effort.

Not only among adults but also among senior high school and even junior high school and grade school children, socioeconomic status is taken into account in choosing a leader. Thus better clothes, more pocket money, better-educated parents, and a nicer home give students who have them prestige that works to their advantage. A person having these advantages at least symbolizes leadership and therefore has a head start over a person of lower socioeconomic status.

Besides the prestige factor, the children in the upper socioeconomic levels have had social experiences with the consequent development of abilities which equip them for leadership, more so than the children of the lower levels. This subject of socioeconomic levels and its influences crops up now and then in this book; however, it is discussed separately in Chapter 9.

The Formation of Friendships. One of the most subtle of human relationships is that of friendship; and its formation and progress, as well as its failure to grow where it might be expected, are sometimes hard to explain. Having an abundance of general social grace and popularity does not always mean a person will be adept at friendship; and conversely, two people who are rather unpopular with the rest of their social group are sometimes very close friends themselves. We cannot hope, of course, to analyze completely the reasons for such seeming mysteries, but a few observations about the conditions that promote friendships will help us to understand such relationships as they generally exist, particularly among young people of school age.

Generally, friendships are formed by people who find mutual association interesting, stimulating, and rewarding. Friends satisfy each other's needs for activity, for pleasure and companionship, and for a feeling of personal worth. But what, more specifically, are the causes of friendships? Why should Bob and Bill, Mary and Jane, Fred and Lillian be friends? Two sets of factors make for friendships: factors of propinquity and of similarity.

Propinquity, or being near, is an obvious spur to the formation of friendships. Of course, not all persons who are together in one place or another become friends, but people cannot become friends unless they get a chance to see each other. Children of the same neighborhood and those who go to the same school, particularly if they are in the same classroom, are very likely to get acquainted; then those who like each other have a chance to become friends. When they do so, the other important factors determining friendships—those of similarity—are involved, as a rule; for, though there is a commonly held theory that opposites attract each other, it is most often the likes who attract each other—friendship is usually based on qualities people have in common.

Bright children tend to associate with bright, average with average, and dull with dull. A bright child and a dull child are rarely companions; they seldom find each other interesting. Consequently there are social advantages in grading and grouping children so those of comparable intellectual and personal interests will be together.

Likewise, persons who have the same recreational interests tend to be friends. We may ask whether people primarily become friends because they play together or play together because they are friends. Undoubtedly, however, similar interests cause people to get together for activities, and playing together at what they like causes them to enjoy each other and thus develop friendships.

Similar age is another basic factor in friendship, especially in childhood. Children of about the same age tend to be companions because they tend to be "birds of a feather"—the same size, in the same grade, with the same interests and the same mental development. Nor do companions usually differ very much in age during the adolescent and early adult years. In the thirties and forties and later, there is greater variation, though even then the ages of friends and companions do not usually differ very much. In romances between the sexes also, the ages are usually about the same in the late teens and twenties. The husband and wife of most young married couples differ by less than four years in age, but husband and wife of couples who marry in middle and old age often differ by 5, 10, and even more years.

Persons with the basic common outlook on the world that exists when they have similar types of personality also tend to become friends. Extroverts—persons who are socially outgoing and who are happiest when engaged with other people—are likely to strike up friendships with each other. Introverts, who are more retiring, will find greater satisfaction in each other than in extroverted persons. Again we must hasten to say that there are many exceptions, as there are people of differing characteristics who enjoy each other's companionship. The members of many married couples, for example, may differ greatly in aggressiveness or in desire for outdoor activities and still get along very well because of a solid core of mutual motives and satisfactions.

Some of the similarity-based factors of friendship are more sociological

Steps to Social Maturity

The physically and mentally developing individual becomes socially mature by stages, at each of which he has and integrates a new kind of experience of the world and of society. Thus, during specific parts of the process of social maturation we can see the start, continuation, or completion of important changes in his close interpersonal relationships, in his interaction with others at work and play, and in his application to social life.

What pictures reflect maturation in close relationships? What pictures most fully reveal the changing structure of peer relations? The development of imagination is best displayed in what pictures? Use the groups of pictures you have chosen to define each of these changes.

1   **2**

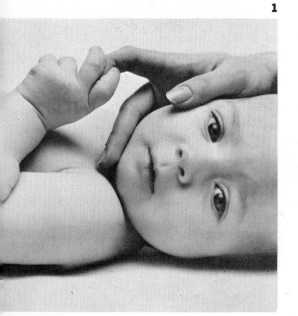   

3

1   Courtesy of Johnson & Johnson.
2   Courtesy of *The New York Times.*
3   William T. Stabler for the California State Department of Education.
4   Courtesy of Boy Scouts of America.
5   Herbert Breuer.
6   Courtesy of Clearasil.
7   Courtesy of *Parents' Magazine.*

4

5

7

6

than personal. Children and adults of the higher socioeconomic levels associate with others of the higher levels, those of the average levels with others of the average levels, and those of the low levels with others of the low levels. There are exceptions, of course; but society, which is not generally friendly to the crossing of classes, is also so alert in observing it as to impose a form of censorship which makes quite rare the mixing of persons who differ socioeconomically. Sharp differences in religious points of view also are not conducive to friendship. Generally, Jews get along best with Jews, Catholics with Catholics, and Protestants with Protestants. Also, those who are conservative and orthodox in religious attitudes tend to befriend each other rather than to become intimate with those who are progressive and modern in their religious points of view.

It is often gratifying, however, when the compelling need for these similarities in entering on friendship is overcome—when people not only become sufficiently mature socially to be sympathetic with and tolerant of conflicting points of view but also occasionally try to make a friend who can give the stimulation and the other view of the world that only a person with a very different background and beliefs can present.

THE SCHOOL AND TEACHER AND SOCIAL MATURATION

In a sense, a child inherits not only his biological potentialities but also the socioeconomic and cultural environment of his parents. Then, consciously and unconsciously, he adopts the ways and attitudes of the members of his family and, to a lesser extent, of the playmates and other adults in his surroundings; and when he enters school, his behavior reflects all this.

Homes vary greatly, from the ideal home—happy, well-managed, and economically secure—to the most miserable home conceivable—unhappy, seriously chaotic, and poverty-ridden. Thus there are great differences in the behavior patterns of the children who come to the schoolroom to be exposed to the same physical environment and discipline. These differences, moreover, are not hidden by the new equalizing surroundings but are revealed by the various ways in which different children adjust to the new situation. Children who have had many and varied socializing experiences will usually adjust well to the school. Children from all types of homes may meet difficult problems of adjustment to the school environment, and the teacher needs tact and understanding for helping these children solve those problems.

Introduction to the School Environment. Most children, regardless of their backgrounds, look forward to beginning school with eagerness and experience a successful start. However, some are not inwardly prepared for their new life and are ill at ease and unhappy their first few days in kindergarten or first grade, as the case may be. Some of this can be prevented by having the child who is preparing to enter school visit there a few times as the guest of a sister or brother. But a more all-inclusive plan is the following: Children who will begin school the following school year can be introduced to it through special visiting days. Members of the first-year class can each have a member of next year's class as a guest, so that the prospective school beginners can spend a day under supervisory control and get some orientation to school life. Both the hosts and the guests will have good social experiences; and the following fall, when the latter walk up to the classroom door, they will have some idea of what to anticipate. Their new world will not be entirely unfamiliar, and so adjustment will be easier.

After attempts to avoid the first day in school's being a traumatic experience with resultant fear, dislike for school, and timidity, the social needs of the children, as they arise, should still be carefully considered. A socially sensitive teacher will be aware of the experiences which children need for maturing socially, and she will help them feel less shy, redirect their aggressiveness, and reward them for being more supportive of others.

In later school years also, a comparably sensible approach to social problems is important. For instance, the social situation should be considered when very bright children are about to be given extra promotion that will put them in grades with children 1 or 2 years older than they are. In a graduate school, a person of twenty-two may easily adjust to being in classes with persons of twenty-five; but this may not be so in the seventh grade if children ten and eleven years old are with children of twelve and thirteen. Very bright younger children may be able to do the schoolwork satisfactorily, but are not large and socially mature enough to cope with the larger, older children of their grade. Consequently, they may develop attitudes of insecurity and inferiority that may handicap them socially as long as they live. However, if children of a given grade are classified according to their abilities, discrepancies in age that tend to cause social problems will be lessened.

At any rate, children soon learn at school to evaluate themselves in relation to their classmates and, as we have already suggested, become motivated to socialize themselves so that they will be accepted by these classmates. They also become very much concerned about how they are getting along with their teachers, and having teachers as well as parents to adjust to sometimes produces conflicts over "who knows best." But adjustment to the other children in the school and understanding oneself are the most pressing social problems for the school child.

In Celia Stendler and Norman Young's study of adjustment in the first grade, 86 per cent of the parents questioned reported a change in the behavior of their children when they started school [Stendler and Young, 1950]. Of these, 78 per cent noted improvement, and 22 per cent felt that the behavior had become worse. Those who improved were said to be more independent and responsible and to show better self-control and work habits. The less desirable behavior reported consisted chiefly in arrogance, whining, aggressiveness, and irritability. According to the first-graders themselves, 92 per cent of them liked school, although there were particular days when they did not. All in all, the socializing effects of the school were favorable.

Teaching Methods and Social Learning. One way to gain insight into the complexity of the long-range socializing effects of the school is to consider the different ways elementary school classrooms are managed by various teachers. Let us consider first a classroom where the teacher is a complete autocrat, then a classroom run by a very democratic teacher, keeping in mind that every teacher fits at some point on a scale that runs from one extreme to the other.

The autocratic, or authoritarian, teacher in effect says to his pupils, "I'm the one who asks the questions, not you," and at recitation time the questions turn out to be very specific questions on the details of the lesson for the day—questions which give no opportunity for intellectual speculation or exploration. This teacher chooses his answers most methodically, and is especially pleased when the exact words of the textbook being used are parroted in answering questions. He tends to foster and rely upon enumeration, the least advanced of the three thought processes discussed in Chapter 2.

During all this, the pupils are forced to sit quietly and are discouraged from showing any evidence of curiosity, initiative, or originality, in a room very nearly barren of any attractive evidence of what they are studying; finally they are given the next day's assignment, which usually consists of "the next 10 pages in the textbook."

When it is time for the children to leave the room, they must first sit in rigid position and then, in response to signals by their formal and unbending teacher, turn, stand, and "pass." In "passing," the children march in step and have to maintain a set distance from each other. If they talk or whisper before they get out of this teacher's area of supervision, they will be punished by having to stay in during recess or after school or by having to write a hundred times, "I shall not talk or whisper when passing."

Now, let us take another classroom, where the teacher is entirely different—informal and relaxed, not formal and unbending, and extremely demo-cratic rather than autocratic.

Instead of giving and taking daily lessons on the next 10 pages in the textbook, this teacher and the children work together—cooperate—in enter-ing various areas of learning. When they take up the topic of American colonization, for example, this teacher and his pupils spend time together in planning how they will study it, during which the teacher welcomes sug-gestions by the pupils. A list of references is prepared by the teacher or under his direction; and when further study and illustrative materials are found by the teacher or a child, they are added to the list.

The children work in planning, discussion, and study groups, several children acting as leaders. They are encouraged to bring to school pictures, art objects, small pieces of furniture, and other material to help them under-stand the colonists and their life. Posters, murals, pictures, and collections are arranged to illustrate how the early American colonists adjusted to their environment. Before the class has finished studying this topic, there are many evidences in the room of their interested work. The pupils consult with persons in the community whose ancestors were colonists, and they take trips to museums. They do extensive reading in reference books, textbooks, and magazines.

In and out of the classroom itself, this teacher and these pupils move about in a natural and informal manner. There are guidance and control, of course, but these are the outgrowth of group planning and organization, not of "strong-arm" methods applied by the teacher (see Figure 11).

As imagining oneself in either situation will suggest, the social climate of each of these two classrooms reflects the personality of its teacher and his methods.

The extremely authoritarian teacher controls his students as if he had each in harness and held all the reins. Thus his classroom furnishes the pupils no experience in exchanging ideas or in group work. Each child sits at his desk; and all intellectual and social traffic, limited as it is, is between the individual pupil and the teacher. Consequently, social development is at a minimum. There are, in fact, negative reactions. Unhealthful competition and self-consciousness are stimulated; at the same time, children become frus-trated, afraid, and recessive and learn to think up artifices for pleasing the teacher.

In the second schoolroom the social situation is excellent. Its democratic and cooperation-oriented teacher guides the students in a group attack on problems so that all work together, each contributing his bit in formulating and solving them. In this process, the children, having an opportunity to confer with each other, have experiences in mental and social give-and-take.

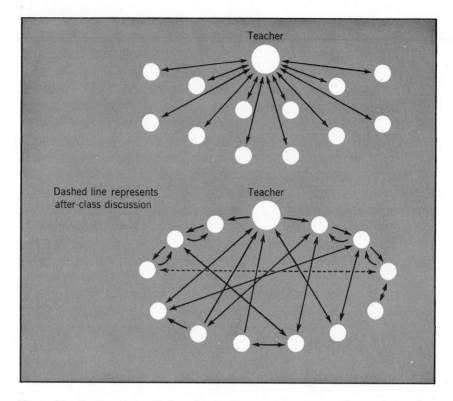

Figure 11 Patterns of verbal exchange in two classrooms *Above, the teacher establishes an unrelentingly formal routine in which he asks the individual students questions in series and each answers him directly. This teacher does not allow the spontaneous development of discussion of the topic being studied.*

Below, the teacher refuses such a dominating role in verbal exchange. Instead, he initiates informal discussion of the topic, allowing information, ideas, questions, and study suggestions to flow freely between himself and the students, as well as among the students themselves. The dotted line indicates an independent after-class exchange between two students who have been stimulated by the class discussion without actually taking part in it.

In addition, children have an opportunity to exercise leadership. In a given situation one child has the most ability and interest and consequently is in the ascendancy, the others responding to his leadership; a new situation develops and someone else starts to lead. And so it goes. The children are making intellectual and emotional contact and are learning to work and play together in many situations. Group concern is being aroused, frustration prevented, and harmony created among the pupils; and these are important to their social development.

Sociodrama and Its Use in Social Conflict. Sociodrama, as its name suggests, is the dramatizing of personal and social problems, including problems of intergroup relations, by persons who are in some way involved in them. This is a technique that can be of much importance in the school and classroom, where such problems can work handicaps on the education, as well as the happiness, of young people. The sociodrama may be used profitably beginning with the lowest grade level where the students have ideas that they can express on the personal problems being considered. Usually this level is the third grade or higher.

Suppose a teacher becomes aware of a strong continuing conflict between one class member and a group of his classmates. They must deal with him, and vice versa, but the dealings are going badly. The teacher—or the students, if they have been familiarized with the idea of sociodrama—may propose that they dramatize the situation. They plan the general structure of the sociodrama and decide on the roles to be played. In such a sociodrama the characters would be the isolated student, the teacher, the other students involved in the conflict, and whoever else the group thinks should be included. The teacher sometimes selects the participants, and class members also volunteer. Then they dramatize the situation, using for scenes various real or hypothetical events related to it. The lines are not written but are spoken spontaneously as various scenes develop which are consistent with the experiences of the students. Sometimes the sociodrama becomes exciting, and at other times it may seem dull; but with experience, it can be made effective in promoting social learning.

After the various relationships among the students involved have been shown, it is desirable to discuss the sociodrama with a view to increasing social understanding—to underscore, as it were, what the sociodrama may have suggested as a socially intelligent resolution of the problematic situation. If the group thinks it desirable, the various roles can be taken by different students and the sociodrama played again. It will be sure to develop differently, and new aspects of the problem will be brought out.

Many problems of young persons can be dramatized in this fashion—problems pertaining to dating, lonesomeness, aggressive behavior, withdrawal, the students' family relationships, and a host of others. Thus the "actors" as well as the observers and discussants gain sympathetic and understanding insights into a variety of events going on around them, the meanings of at least some of which would otherwise escape them.

However, besides the social learning to be had from the sociodrama experience, in frequent instances there is also a direct therapeutic gain for the role player, namely, overcoming the uneasiness which many people have in their personal and social relationships. By expressing himself in a sociodrama closely modeled on a situation where tensions have choked off expression, the actor gains not only social skill but also understanding of himself that can prevent control by these tensions the next time the portrayed situation comes up in his life; and as the tensions relax, better feeling and more sympathy for others are allowed to develop.

☯ *Reflect and Review*

The teacher of a seventh-grade class was disturbed by the way some of his students behaved when they attended the junior high school basketball games, which were a popular school social occasion. Certain students had shouted insulting remarks at the visiting team members; and one or two, on a few occasions, had thrown objects onto the playing floor. After the most recent game, a fist fight had occurred outside the gymnasium between an eighth-grader and a student team manager from the visiting school.

The teacher decided to employ the sociodrama to point up some principles of sportsmanship and interschool rivalry. The class went in a body to the gymnasium and, with the help of the teacher, selected classmates to play the roles of a group of students from its own school who had come to a game together and of a group from the visiting school who were sitting next to them on the bleachers. The teacher, using suggestions from the members of the class, gave each of the "actors" a simple outline of the character he was to play. The class then decided to have three scenes: the first taking place at a moment during the game when the score was tied and the crucial free-point shot was being attempted; the second during the half-time break; and the third after the game, which the visiting team had, according to the chosen plot, won. The teacher took care to make the starting situations and the progress of the action as clear and specific as possible. The students, after some initial self-consciousness, fell into the spirit of the improvisation and acted out the scenes in a lively way, in this case in the very place where the events that had inspired the use of the sociodrama occurred. Then there was discussion of the play.

If one or more of the offenders were in the class, how should the technique of planning and executing the sociodrama take account of this fact?

How could the teacher guide the acting of the sociodrama so it would have point and meaning and would not degenerate into an embarrassing, pointless experience?

How could discussion of the sociodrama best be handled? Should discussion follow each scene? Should the play and its background events both be discussed? If so, which first? Justify your answers in terms of what the class should learn from such an exercise.

SOCIOMETRY AND WHAT IT REVEALS

From an early age some children have much more social ability than others. Some have conspicuous initiative and leadership ability, are aggressive, and take an active part in games and other group activities; others are shy and retiring, fearful of ridicule, and more ready to follow than lead.

It should not be surprising that these differences create a variety of relationships among the members of any one class. On the principle that like is attracted to like, we should expect to find the more aggressive students forming close friendships with each other and the shyer ones finding more pleasure with others like themselves. Add to this simple division, however, the almost infinite gradations between thoroughly outgoing and extremely retiring, the great influence of socioeconomic factors upon social relationships, and a host of other quantities that make up the subtle alchemy of friendship, enmity, and indifference; and it will be obvious that social relationships, even within a small group, are highly complex.

The teacher, of course, does not need to know the last detail of these social patterns within his class, but it is useful for him to have a fairly accurate idea of the social adjustment of the various members and of the ways the various personalities react upon each other. Knowledge of these matters will help him to understand the attitudes of his students on other matters as well as to help his students toward rewarding social experiences.

Probably a good guide in these things is the teacher's own observation; he will usually be able to discern without much difficulty the broader divisions of social groups within the class, for instance. Such observations are necessarily highly subjective, however, and to a large extent will depend for their accuracy upon the teacher's own social sense and sensitivity. A more objective way of gauging social relationships is therefore desirable.

Such a method is provided by the technique of sociometry. Sociometry is the measurement and analysis of social relationships, and as such is an objective, though not completely precise or infallible, tool for social study which gives the teacher a useful check of his own judgments of his students' social patterns.

The social patterns are revealed by gathering and correlating information on their positive and negative feelings, as well as neutral attitudes, toward each other. Any of a variety of tests and questionnaires may be used to elicit the responses—responses which will display wide and enthusiastic social acceptance of certain individuals, total or almost total rejection of others, and the overall pattern of likes and dislikes. We shall be primarily concerned with the general acceptance range here, but it should be noted that students' judgments of each other in regard to very specific qualities may also be revealed by specially designed tests and questionnaires.

Gathering the Data of Sociometry. One method of gathering data for gauging relative popularity and social acceptability is to ask students to list the names of their "best friends" and of other students (they) like, or would like, to work or play with, as well as the names of those they "don't like at all" and of those they would not select as associates in work or play.

A frequently used variation of this is the social-distance question. The psychological basis of this type of question is exemplified when someone is heard to say, "I wish he were out of sight; the farther away he is, the better," or, at the other extreme, "He's a close friend of mine." Not to care for a person but to have no particular objection to having him in the same classroom or on the same team means one wants him at a medium social distance. Social-distance questions are so phrased that a student indicates how close or how far away from him he wishes to have each classmate.

Another way of gaining information on students' social patterns is to use a "guess-who" test, in which students are drawn out on each other's characteristics. A guess-who test consists of pairs of questions seeking identification of people who are opposites—happy and unhappy, friendly and unfriendly, and so on. For example: Who is a big braggart, often telling what he has and what he does? Who is shy and bashful, staying in the background and not saying much about himself?

Classifying the Data. Using the data from sociometric questionnaires, a teacher may classify the students in his class in groupings, each of which involves only part of the class, as well as in their total mutual relations.

The partial groupings include mutual pairs, triangles, and chains of good friends (see Figure 12). A chain is comprised of several students who have chosen each other, (some) of whom have friends outside this group. Sociometric studies may also reveal cliques. A clique consists of a number who choose each other, stick together, and function as a well-insulated group without the occasional outside relationships which chains involve. If these students exercise a great deal of influence in "running things socially," they are a power group.

Such groupings fit into the larger context of the social relationships of the whole class, the members of which are classifiable not only as parts of the groupings but also as individuals with various degrees of social acceptance. There are several systems for classifying individuals in terms of the relative number of classmates who choose each as a friend. One system—the one which we shall use in the ensuing discussion—involves four categories: highly chosen (star), average-chosen, little-chosen, and nonchosen.

Analysis: Use of the Sociogram. Whatever system of classifying individuals is used and whatever groupings are found, the choices and rejections must be carefully analyzed by the teacher if the data are to fulfill their first purpose—to help explain the social behavior in and of the class.

To aid this sort of analysis, results of sociometric studies are usually expressed in sociograms—charts which represent graphically the class social

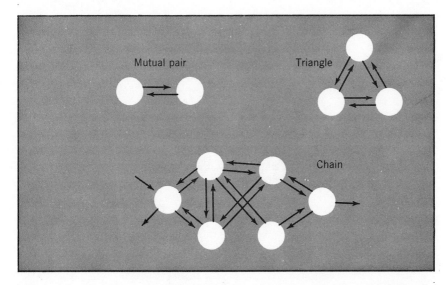

Figure 12 Three forms of social grouping *The circles represent individuals, the arrows their choices of friends. Each member of the mutual pair has chosen the other as his most important friend. Each member of the triangle has chosen its other two members as his two most important friends. Each member of the chain has a close relationship with from two to four of its six members. The two "end" members have close social connections outside the chain; if these outside connections were discontinued, the chain would become a clique. These combinations change with the shifting of choices even though the number of times that individuals are chosen or rejected generally does not change much.*

pattern. Thus all the students may be represented by symbols placed on a background of concentric circles, resembling a target, with the highly chosen in the bull's-eye and the less chosen arranged around them. In such a sociogram, specific, individual choices may be indicated by arrows pointing from one number to the other and mutual choices by arrows pointing in both directions (see Figure 13).

There are, of course, other ways of setting up a sociogram. Parallel rows may be used instead of concentric circles, for instance. Any sociogram, however, should show each student's specific choice or choices, the number of choices received by each student, and the sex of each student.

Pertinent information on the students represented in this sociogram includes the following:

The star girl, a winner of spelling contests, is generally the top student in the class. She smiles readily and is friendly to all. Her parents are above average in socioeconomic status, that is, prosperous and well respected in the community. The girl who received no choices, on the other hand, comes from a poor home; thus she is poorly dressed and has free-lunch status in

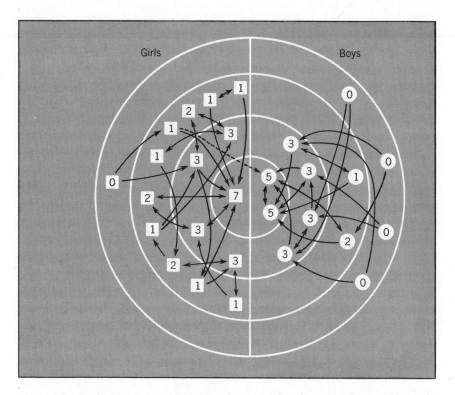

Figure 13 Sociogram for a sixth-grade class   *In this class of 12 boys and 16 girls each student made two choices of best friends. The number within each square or triangle indicates the number of choices made for that student. Additional numbers are ordinarily placed below the symbols to identify each student. The highly chosen occupy the sociogram bull's-eye and are also called stars. The average-chosen occupy the next two circles, the little-chosen the next circle, and the nonchosen the outermost circle. Besides the solid-line single arrows indicating individual choices and double arrows indicating mutual choices, one dotted arrow indicates choice of a boy by a girl.*

school. She has been retained in a grade once. She is the quiet kind, who comes and goes alone usually and speaks only when spoken to—and then only a few indifferent words.

The two star boys are both better-than-average students and on the basketball team as well. Both smile readily and are pleasant to others; one is an outstanding leader in sports and parties. The other, while not a leader, cooperates readily and is known as a good sport. The parents of both these boys have above-average socioeconomic status and are good supporters of the school. Three-fourths of the boys who were not designated as a best friend have repeated a grade. The nonchosen boys are each new to the community, or unfriendly, or shy and thus nonparticipating in activities. As a whole, their parents are of low status in the community and are not interested in school.[1]

☯ Consider the Data

Based on Figure 13

Consider the choices of the highly chosen girl and boys. Which is involved in the most completely integrated small social grouping, and what kind is it? Of the same three stars, whose choices are least reciprocated? Do the relationships of the star boys suggest that there would or would not be strong power groups among the boys in the class?

Did the nonchosen boys as a whole jump more categories in their choices than the nonchosen girl? Did all the nonchosen generally jump more categories than the stars?

If this group of students were to stay together and be the subject of a similarly organized sociometric study every year, what general change might be expected in their choices? How would this change be reflected on such a sociogram?

Personal Characteristics as Reflected by Sociometric Choices. Studies of the characteristics of children and teen-agers in various sociometric categories have shown that the highly chosen tend as a group to have certain consistent personal qualities.

First, they generally are more intelligent than other students. For example, in a study of third-, fourth-, and fifth-grade boys and girls, R. F. Heber found a positive relationship between intelligence and sociometric status determined by a social-distance scale [Heber, 1956]. Of the 19 high-IQ children studied, only 3 were below the average in sociometric status; of the 21 with low IQs, only 1 was above average in sociometric status. Those who were average mentally showed less regularity in sociometric status; some were very high, some were very low, and some were average.

Second, the highly chosen are physically equipped and personally inclined to meet the world well. They tend to be physically attractive and to keep themselves well groomed—these factors, incidentally, are especially important among teen-agers—and they participate more than other students in such school activities as sports, dramatics, and parties.

Third, in meeting other individuals, the highly chosen as a whole are friendly, good-natured, and modest; in a variety of situations they show good

---

[1] Courtesy of Walter Martin, Superintendent of Schools, Buckskin Valley School District, Rusk County, Ohio.

taste, are dependable, and have good manners. They put others at ease; they do not make others feel inadequate.

In personality as in intelligence, the highly rejected generally display qualities which are the opposite of those possessed by the highly chosen. In their relations with the world at large, they tend to be the "no-hit—no-run—no-error" kind of children—recessive young people who attract little attention or listless youths who lack interest or the social skills to participate effectively in what is taking place about them. In their personal relations, the highly rejected are generally highly egocentric and thus indifferent to promoting the interests and activities of others. In dealing with others they are inflexible or chronic complainers. Some of them present behavior problems at times because, while they feel inadequate, they still want to attract attention. These are the bossy and quarrelsome children, the bad-tempered poor sports, and so forth. Of course, the ways these elements operate as factors in sociometric status are most complex. For instance: High intelligence is usually accompanied by other desirable personal qualities, but it also sociometrically self-supporting, as it were. Thus J. J. Gallagher's research has indicated that bright children are more socially perceptive than others and, in particular, are more accurate in judging who will pick them as friends or associates [Gallagher, 1958]. He studied 355 second-, third-, fourth-, and fifth-graders and found that the bright children judged those who selected them with 70 per cent accuracy, while those of average mentality were only 59 per cent accurate. This would seem to give the bright children an initial advantage in achieving high sociometric status.

Yet even if a student is distinctly superior in intelligence, and thus in scholarship, the advantages he has sociometrically may be wiped out by a personality failure. If, say, he lets his superiority show too much by bragging, he may be revealed by a sociometric study as a not-very-popular person because in personal relations he is threatening the status of others instead of making them feel worthy.

Actually, neither all the qualities which characterize the highly chosen nor all those which characterize the nonchosen are often found in one person. The popular simply have many more of the favorable characteristics and the unpopular more of the unfavorable ones, as a rule. Therefore, individual interpretation of the sociometric status of students is often necessary to understand the student and the social pattern in which he fits.

Sociometric Status and the Individual's Future. Is there a high constancy of sociometric choices from year to year? For example, are the most popular fourth-grade children usually still the most popular in the eighth grade, and are the little-chosen high school freshmen ordinarily in the same sociometric position in their senior year? Relatedly, does the sociometric status of a student today suggest whether he can be expected to finish school successfully or drop out along the way?

Results of research have indicated that the answers to these questions are affirmative and thus that sociometric studies have considerable predictive value. K. L. Cannon studied a group of students who made choices in the ninth grade and then again in the twelfth grade and found that the correlations of the choices were in the .70s and .80s, illustrating a strong trend for the choices to be the same and thus for most students to keep about the same sociometric status [Cannon, 1958]. In addition, N. E. Gronlund and W. S. Holmlund found in a study of the same subject that the sociometric status of students in the sixth grade indicated corresponding status in high school [Gronlund and Holmlund, 1958].

The latter researchers also found that sociometric status was related to persistence in school and graduation from high school.

All these findings can be explained on a variety of bases. Thus the fact that those of higher sociometric status participate continually in school activities tends to keep their status high simply by maintaining the interpersonal contact that can lead to their choice by others. Thus also, low sociometric status is an index of the existence of social and personal handicaps that make success in school more difficult, so such status encourages leaving school (see Table 3).

Table 3   The Effect of Sociometric Status* on Success in High School

	High-status Pupils		Low-status Pupils	
	Graduates	Dropouts	Graduates	Dropouts
Boys	25	6	11	13
Girls	21	1	16	9
Total	46	7	27	22

* Note that status here is based on social acceptance.
Source: N. E. Gronlund and W. S. Holmlund, "Value of Elementary School Sociometric Status Scores for Predicting Pupils' Adjustment in High School," *Educational Administration and Supervision*, 44:257, 1958.

⚫ *Reflect and Review*

The following are vignettes of five students. Do you think each would be highly chosen, average-chosen, little-chosen, or nonchosen by his classmates? In each case, why?

Darrell was bright and got good marks. He rarely missed a chance to show that he "had the answer," and he laughed at others when they made mistakes. He never revealed before class time that he had the answers because he did not want to be asked for them by his classmates.

Jane was a girl whose general status and home situation suffered from the background of an alcoholic father whose consequent incompetence kept his family in semipoverty. In spite of these threatening conditions, Jane was very active in school affairs and played her various roles with aplomb and in a friendly, cooperative manner. She was the most attractive girl in her class and her social skills had a corresponding status.

Bill was a big, slow-moving boy who was a good athlete and a fairly good student. He conversed pleasantly but did not talk excessively. He was friendly and usually had a good word for his classmates. If the class had a project, Bill worked hard at his part of it and then helped the others do their work too.

Judy, a seventeen-year-old girl, at school was quiet and attracted little attention. She had had a very strict upbringing and her social activities had been closely supervised by her mother. As a junior in high school, she was frequently in unsupervised groups, where she took the role of a cutup. At parties she would take a few drinks and soon attract a group who laughed at her rowdy antics. Judy enjoyed her reputation of being "some gal."

Randy was a good athlete and was well liked by the boys and girls of the school because he was sincere and generous. He and the coach were very friendly, but the coach was not very successful and was replaced by a new one who was very popular with the student body. Randy would not accept the new coach, and it was apparent to the student body that Randy did not play so well as he had for the former coach. Randy also argued with many of the students, praising the former coach and playing down the new one.

The Teacher and the Best Use of Sociometry. When a teacher rates his students socially, he tends to select and reject the same students that they, as a group, select and reject. In other words, teachers' preferences reflect, in general, the composite choices of their students. Thus students who are stars, or highly chosen by their fellows, are preferred most often by their teachers, although it does occasionally happen that a star is least preferred by a teacher. Research also indicates that teachers rarely prefer the non-chosen, but occasionally they do prefer the little-chosen, and more often the average-chosen. There are variations in the social perceptiveness of teachers, but these statements characterize the typical teacher.

At the same time, and this partly because of the differences that do exist between the preferences of students and teachers, it sometimes happens that teachers are not aware of how extensively certain students are going to be chosen or rejected when a sociometric study is made. Then, as they consider the sociograms, they wonder why certain "good" boys or girls are so low in the popularity scale and why other students are so high. For instance, in investigations of teachers' abilities to predict sociometric choices, teachers have predicted selections for workmates more accurately than they have predicted selections for play or social purposes. This suggests that teachers are more work-oriented than socially oriented; and this is understandable since in the past, great emphasis was put on "doing the lessons." At present, there is again an emphasis on the lessons. However, with a clear awareness of the great value of social development for personal happiness and vocational success, we can now hope to become just as discerning of social relations in the school as of lesson-getting. Sociometry, in the hands of keenly observant teachers, can be an increasingly useful tool for heightened social understanding. But what is to be done with the clearer vision that is to be gained?

As we have seen, sociometry is a test of popularity and unpopularity. As we have also seen, sociometry gives the lie to the frequently encountered idea that there is a superficiality about popularity—that it is achieved by tricks and flashy characteristics. The results of sociometric studies indicate that this is seldom the case—that, rather, popularity is achieved by having highly desirable personal qualities, that those who are not popular generally have low status because of undesirable qualities. Here, then, we arrive at the important final educative purpose of sociometric investigations—quite simply, to aid in guiding students toward a better social life. The students of low sociometric status are greatly handicapped socially and therefore need help; those who are average need some help too; and even those of high status can profit from learning more about interpersonal relations.

Practical applications. What specifically can be done to help students be more effective in their personal relations? By carefully observing his students with the facts of the sociogram in mind, the teacher can learn why each has the social status he has within his class and then set about to deal helpfully with the personality of the individual and to improve the social climate of the group.

There are a variety of ways to do this. For some examples, the excellent work of N. E. Gronlund, H. H. Anderson, and others suggests the following means by which the school can promote social acceptance among students:

Aim to achieve neatness and well-groomed appearance.

Teach social skills and good manners.

Direct socially retarded students into positions of responsibility and opportunities for leadership.

Conduct class discussions on how to be socially effective.

Promote individual counseling of students by teachers.

Encourage students to discuss and evaluate social behavior with a view to learning how to improve social relationships.

Practice mixing up of children in activities, in committees, and in seating for encouraging the acceptance of little-chosen students.

Build up the reputation of individual students by favorable recognition.

Praise students for improving in social development.

Encourage more social activity. Guide students into situations that will stimulate more social interaction.

Promote a big-sister or -brother attitude by which a high-status student helps a low-status one.

Use the sociodrama for advancing personality development by extensive role playing for dramatizing social and interpersonal problems.

Such things, of course, must be carefully done. Thus when committees are formed, it is ordinarily well to put compatibles together, with the addition of just one little-chosen or nonchosen student in order to encourage his being effectively integrated in the group activities. Thus also, children who have tensions in their interpersonal relationships can be discovered and so guided in their associations that many of their tensions will be released; but care must be taken when deep personal difficulties are contributing to the tensions.

In all this, the teacher himself is central. First of all, the teacher is a prestige figure in the eyes of his students so that any favorable, supportive association he makes with a student will give that student a little more prestige. For instance, a social underachiever who is given small responsibilities and opportunities for more interpersonal relationships will usually become more favorably known generally, especially when the teacher makes it evident that he is interested in and looks with favor upon this student.

But the teacher can also, in his direct relationship to any student, help him accept himself as a person who has the potentiality for improving his sociometric status, so that he will become more disposed to work for his personal improvement and less likely to avoid facing his personal weaknesses by rationalizing his situation or by compensating in undesirable ways.

The teacher who has an understanding not only of the sociometric pattern in his class but also of the basis for acceptance, neglect, or rejection of the individual student is in an especially good position for furthering his social development. But there is a further crucial consideration here: In the teacher's relationships with the student, the teacher loses his effectiveness by evaluating or sitting in judgment on the student. To do this is threatening to the student and so puts him on the defensive. The teacher will influence the student more favorably if he is sympathetic. Encouraging the student to talk about his own social problems may make those problems seem less insurmountable; and an empathetic attitude will stimulate the teacher to devise plans for the student's social development. The school can well help such a teacher by arranging for time to be set aside for considering problems of personal relationships.

Limitations of sociometry: basic personality problems. The relationship of the teacher and student impinges, of course, on the basic personality and its development and improvement, and these are not simple matters.

Personality does change, and this is obvious in school. Students improve in their personal relationships by being more friendly and kind, and some become more highly chosen as they improve in personality; on the other hand, some students become less likable (and less popular) by, say, growing quarrelsome and aggressive. Such negative changes are a personal loss; but it would be unfortunate if personality were constant because then there could be no improvement. The good school takes the position that it can improve a student's personal relations and that such endeavor is one of its major functions. Nevertheless, personal characteristics tend to be very persistent. Thus, when a group of babies were studied again 15 years later as teen-agers, Neilon was able to identify with a better-than-chance success several elements of personality which had characterized the 25 as babies, in spite of the difficulty of defining very clearly the personal characteristics of babies [Neilon, 1948]. Beyond such observational findings, moreover, we know that clinicians who work with personality disorders frequently fail to bring about any desirable changes, a particularly sobering fact that must be reflected time and time again in the course of efforts by teachers and schools to improve personality.

The conclusion is clear. As teachers improve their ability to further the social development of their young charges through thoughtful and informed application of such techniques as sociometry, students of personality must progress in research on how and why personality both improves and becomes less desirable. Then we may be able to develop still better methods of bringing about desirable personality changes in the classroom.

⦿ Reflect and Review

A sociogram revealed that a little girl named Mary was not desired for a friend by a single one of her sixth-grade classmates. She was a social isolate who kept near the teacher in order to acquire some social security.

One day the teacher led the class to discuss how anyone "left out of" his or her social group is bound to be unhappy and how everyone has some talent that can enrich the work of the group. A few days later she suggested that Mary care for the classroom flowers during the following week. Mary, who was good in arithmetic, was also encouraged by the teacher to help those classmates who were having difficulty with problems in that subject. Later, Mary was selected for traffic duty. At about the same time, the teacher had an opportunity to discuss with Mary how she could help her classmates while working with them, and laid stress on how to be courteous and friendly.

Thus Mary sensed that for her as for others, there were ways of making friends. Her earlier negativism diminished, and she became cooperative with her fellow students. Because participation had replaced isolation, Mary acquired a feeling of belonging which was missing before. Subsequent sociograms showed that Mary was increasingly accepted by her classmates, and finally she was elected chairman of a committee.

How does Mary's improved behavior illustrate social learning?

If Mary had not been helped by a discerning teacher, what would probably have been her social behavior?

SUMMARY

Socialization is on its way when the infant begins to distinguish between individuals. With increasing age the child becomes more outgoing and engages in cooperative activities, and egocentricity diminishes.

Promoting the processes of socialization and adjustment to the environment is being recognized as an ever more important function of the school, in which valuable experiences are derived from group activities and where effective boy-girl relationships can develop.

Personal responsibility and intelligent self-interest are evidences of social maturity and should not be confused with extreme self-centeredness and selfishness. Some individuals who spend much time in solitary activities pursuing their personal interests are nevertheless socially adequate.

Competence in the form of good physical and mental development for his age equips an individual for greater social effectiveness, while poor physical and mental development tends to handicap him socially. Cognizance of this is seen in the selection of leaders, who generally are chosen for good personal qualities; competence in their fields; and the capacity to play several roles in order to help the groups achieve their goals.

Close companionship among individuals results from satisfying and rewarding experiences. Convenient and frequent contact by children of the same neighborhood or in the same classroom results in many friendships. Large differences in socioeconomic status, religion, and politics tend to prevent friendship.

Early-maturing boys and girls tend to be advanced socially. In junior high school especially, these children have more prestige. Girls of poorer intellect and low socioeconomic status, however, often assume the responsibilities of courtship and marriage too early in life.

The social cultural climate of the home equips the children with social behavior that either prepares or fails to prepare them to get along well in school.

In schools where the procedures are formal and rigid there is so little social and intellectual interchange among the students that little social experience and development occur. In classrooms where the procedures involve the students in cooperative activities and group work, they have many social as well as productive intellectual experiences.

The sociodrama is a method of "playing out" various personal-social problems so that the participants and observers may release their tensions and gain social understanding.

There is a wide range in the feelings of the students of a classroom or school toward each other, as expressed in friendships.

Sociometry is a method of learning about these personal and social attitudes of the students or about their friendships. Sociometric methods involve the expression of preference or choice for various activities, of indicating social distance, and of naming those who fit given descriptions (guess-who). Classification of sociometric data is made into categories: highly chosen, average-chosen, little-chosen, and nonchosen. Special groupings are mutual pairs, triangles, chains, cliques, and power groups.

The sociogram is a graphic method of showing the frequency of choice of each student and thereby the social status of each student within his group. The highly chosen or popular students are friendly, cooperative, modest, successful in school, and of above-average socioeconomic status. They tend to be of high IQ, to have good physical appearance, to be well groomed, and to participate in school activities. The little-chosen and rejected are usually lower in mental capacity and are colorless, quarrelsome, aggressive troublemakers and, in general, are less effective in dealing with others.

Students tend to keep about the same popularity status throughout the grades and high school.

Students of higher sociometric status are more successful in school and drop out less frequently than do less popular students.

The teacher's judgment of the popularity status of his pupils is fairly accurate in general, but is more accurate for predicting who will be chosen for work situations than for predicting who will be chosen for social activities.

Popularity with one's peers is based on highly desirable personal qualities, and unpopular students behave in detrimental ways. A responsibility of the school is to help the students to improve their social behavior.

The teacher can use his prestige position and his knowledge of social development to help students become more effective socially. The teacher will find opportunities for involving the student socially; and by looking for special abilities and interests, the teacher can guide the individual student so he will be an asset to the group.

SUGGESTED READING

Gronlund, N. E.: *Sociometry in the Classroom,* Harper & Row, Publishers, Incorporated, New York, 1959. Gronlund's book contains a wealth of material on the personal relationships of students and their social development. Social competence is evaluated in terms of various abilities and capacities.

Guinovard, D. E., and J. F. Rychlak: "Personality Correlates of Sociometric Popularity in Elementary School Children," *Personnel and Guidance Journal,* 40:438–442, 1962. A study of the personal characteristics of 86 boys and 80 girls in grades 6, 7, and 8. The personal qualities that underlie peer acceptance are set forth.

Kanous, L. E., R. A. Daugherty, and T. S. Cohn: "Relation between Heterosexual Friendship Choices and Socioeconomic Level," *Child Development,* 33:251–255, 1962. The boy-girl and girl-boy choices of grade school children raise some questions about sociobiological influences. The choices of three distinctly different socioeconomic groups were analyzed.

CHAPTER 4
HEREDITY AND ENVIRONMENT
IN HUMAN DEVELOPMENT

Some viewpoint on the relative influence of heredity and of environment on human development is basic to any philosophy of education, for the subject pervades many areas of human experience.

It is a subject on which people often take extreme positions. When a person says, "Insanity runs in that family," or "It's in my blood, so there's nothing I can do about it," or even "His father couldn't get arithmetic either," he is expressing, though often unconsciously, a hereditarian view of human development. Other common statements reflect the opposite: an environmentalistic viewpoint. A parent says, "What else can you expect of a kid from the slum he comes from?" or a teacher confidently declares, "I can teach algebra to any student in my class who is willing to work."

These statements generally reflect grossly oversimplified views of the nature-nurture subject—views which cause discussions of the subject to degenerate too often into debates over whether heredity or environment is "most important." Such arguments are futile and meaningless. The truth is much more complex than this kind of controversy implies, for each person represents a subtle combination of traits, every one of which has been influenced by both heredity and environment.

Heredity seems to be largely responsible for some human characteristics, environment for others. The color of the eyes, width of the head, fingerprint patterns, age of puberty, and stature are believed to be determined chiefly by genetic factors. On the other hand, such psychological matters as temperament and attitudes are probably determined more by environmental influences; the best studies of human behavior indicate that the ethics of a person's behavior and the health of his personality are caused more by his experiences than by heredity. Yet the mixture of environmental and hereditary factors is always important.

The relative influence of environment and heredity may also vary at different ages. For example, consider the problem of longevity. Scientific care during the prenatal period and infancy prevents many deaths, and this is an environmental factor; but after a person has reached middle age, the factors that determine whether or not he will live a long life seem to be largely hereditary in nature.

Teachers, as well as students, can be overdeterministic about their behavior and achievement, that is, view it as out of their control, if they take either an extreme hereditarian or an extreme environmentalistic point of view of human development.

Thus they need some basic knowledge of the nature of the influence of heredity and environment, respectively. To present information on this subject is the purpose of this chapter.

THE LEGACY OF HEREDITY

It would be just as naïve to expect all the children of a couple to be just alike as it would be to believe that no characteristics are transmitted from parent to child. Yet the first of the three general principles of inheritance which can help us to understand human characteristics is that like begets like. In other words, children tend to resemble their parents, in many ways, considerably more than they resemble adults of the same race and age selected at random. Bright parents generally have bright children; average parents, average children; and dull parents, dull children. Mature offspring tend to be physically similar to their parents, and so forth.

To use intelligence as an example, here are some carefully worked-out estimates, based on extensive study of this aspect of parent-child relationship, of the relative numbers of mentally retarded children produced by parents at three separate levels of intelligence:

Parents' IQ Level	Number of Mentally Retarded Children (IQ 70 or below) per 1,000 Offspring
130	1
70	160
40	335

There are, however, many exceptions; and there is this important fact to remember when applying this principle: Children do not inherit the acquired abilities of their parents. As an adult gets older, he may acquire new skills, increase his general efficiency, and add to his store of knowledge, but such improvement is not transmitted to his offspring. The germ cells are independent of such influences. If the values of a parent's experiences were inherited by the children, the younger children in a family would generally be more capable than the older. But this is not the case; there is no positive or negative relationship between order of birth and the various capacities of the offspring.[1]

The second principle of inheritance is that there is variation among offspring. Children are not exact replicas of their parents; like also begets unlike. The reason lies in the characteristics of the germ cells of the parents. Germ cells contain many determiners (chromosomes and genes) which unite in different combinations to form offspring differing among themselves. This principle of variation explains why children in the same family differ in intellect, size, temperament, and so on.

For purposes of illustration, let us assume that two parents could have a much larger number of children than is actually possible. The children would show a wide range of characteristics, though most of their characteristics would be clustered at or near the average of their parents'. The quality of the average offspring would be determined by the average quality of the parents' germ cells, but there would be radical individual differences. The child resulting from the most favorable combination of the parents' genes would be the most superior offspring. The child resulting from the poorest combination would be the least able.

In actuality, inferior parents have some superior offspring, and some superior parents have inferior offspring; for example, very bright parents have a few children bordering on mental retardation. Both these relationships of parents and offspring have to be attributed to the parents' genes and thus to heredity rather than environment; exceptions are birth injuries and congenital influences, which exist, for example, when the pregnant mother contracts certain illnesses and develops complications which inflict permanent injury on the baby.

The third general principle of inheritance is that offspring move from the extremes, which is called regression toward the mean: the tendency for children of unusual parents to be less unusual than their parents. For any trait, whether it lies on a superiority-inferiority scale or not, there is a tendency for the children to regress toward the mean or the average. Not all the offspring will regress; but as a group, they will move toward the average rather than remain as far below it, remain as far above it, or move farther from it in either direction. One form of regression toward the mean—the

[1] A distinction should be made between ability and capacity. Ability is indicated by one's actual performance, skills, and knowledge or by what one is able to do at the present time. Capacity is potentiality, or what one can do with the most favorable learning. Capacities are, in effect, the limits to which one can develop. One has capacities in many areas but has no abilities in those areas because of no corresponding experiencing and learning.

tendency of children of very tall or short parents to be less extreme in height—was discussed in Chapter 1.

For example, usually the children of a very gifted father (or mother) are not so gifted as that parent, though the offspring tend to be decidedly above the average (see Table 4). A great scientist seldom sires so great a son, and rarely does the son of the big-league baseball player reach the big leagues.[2]

There are two principal reasons for such regression. In the first place, the father's outstanding traits represent the product of the most fortunate combination of the determiners in the germ cells of his parents. Therefore, the germ cells that he carries are, on the average, inferior to the particular combination from which he developed. Second, it is likely that he will mate with a woman not so outstanding as he, who will be almost certain not to carry germ cells as good as those which combined at the time of his conception.

Table 4   Distribution of Stanford-Binet IQs of Offspring of Terman's Gifted Subjects

IQ	Boys	Girls	Total
190–199	1	1	2
180–189	3	7	10
170–179	15	9	24
160–169	22	33	55
150–159	82	66	148
140–149	137	125	262
130–139	188	180	368
120–129	181	168	349
110–119	86	83	169
100–109	53	48	101
90–99	13	11	24
80–89	4	2	6
70–79	1	6	7
Total	786	739	1,525
Mean IQ	132.7	132.7	132.7
SD*	17.2	18.0	17.6

* Standard deviation. See Appendix for an explanation of its meaning.
Source: L. M. Terman and Melita H. Oden, *The Gifted Group at Mid-life,* Stanford University Press, Stanford, Calif., 1959, p. 141.

On the other hand, the average germ cells of two middle-grade defectives (IQs of 25 to 49) are likely to be better than the particular combinations from which they sprang. Therefore, most of the offspring of such parents will

[2] Regression, of course, is not limited to human beings. Man o' War, one of the greatest running horses in American racing, produced some great runners, but of his 386 offspring not one was so great a runner as he.

Consider the Data

Based on Table 4

The mean IQ of the parents, the gifted subjects of Terman's study, was 151. The mates of the gifted probably did not average as high. Note the distribution of the IQs for the boys and girls, as well as their mean IQs.

Indicate how the principle that like begets like is illustrated in the table. How is regression illustrated?

Is the concept of variation illustrated?

How many of the children have such low IQs that they probably do not have enough ability to do satisfactory schoolwork (grade school, high school, and college)? Your general estimates based on the figures in the total column will be satisfactory.

have more mental capacity than the father and mother, tending to average at the level of upper-grade defectives (IQs of 50 to 69). However, a child of two middle-grade defectives occasionally even has average mental capacity; on the other hand, sometimes offspring are more deficient than their mentally retarded parents of middle-grade status.

Family Trees and Their Fruit. We have spoken just of parents and children in setting forth the three general principles of inheritance. But in applying these principles, it must be realized that the child's heredity is not determined solely by his immediate parents: he also inherits from his grandparents, his great-grandparents, etc. Thus it is partly because of the heredity from these less immediate forebears that very superior parents generally have less superior children and very inferior parents have children better than themselves.

Most of a person's inheritance comes from his immediate ancestry, and the hereditary determinations from remote ancestry are least influential. One-half of the inheritance is from the parents, one-quarter from the grandparents, one-eighth from the great-grandparents, and so on back through the less and less immediate generations. Yet heredity works strongly enough through the series of generations that, to a conspicuous degree, eminence and distinction of mind and morality are found in some family lineages; and mental deficiency, insanity, criminality, and other social deficiencies are found in others.

If the outstanding men and women in any city or county, say the one outstanding person in every 4,000, were selected and then an equal number of persons were selected at large for comparison, it would be found that the eminent persons had many more eminent relatives of their own or earlier generations than those picked at random. In fact, when Francis Galton, a great English scientist of the nineteenth century, made such a study to select the most eminent person in 4,000, he found that the distinguished persons considered had 134 times as many outstanding relatives as the persons taken at large.

On the other hand, studies of the families of persons committed to prisons, insane asylums, and institutions for the mentally retarded show that as a whole they have many relatives who have or have had the same deficiencies. Two well-studied family lineages, those of the Jukes and the Kallikaks (both fictitious names), have shown a distressingly large number of inadequates. For instance, in the Kallikaks' lineage, which began at the time of the American Revolution, many were mentally retarded or insane persons; many were thieves, indolent persons, or prostitutes. Some were normal and adequate persons, but many inadequates came forth each generation.

Selective Mating. Because they have observed the striking influence of heredity on individual and collective human destiny, thinkers have been intrigued for many centuries by the subject of selective mating. Plato planned for the philosopher-kings in his hypothetical ideal republic to arrange all marriages in the state by mating the most able citizens with each other in order to produce more philosophers. George Bernard Shaw proposed, half in earnest, a human breeding farm.

If the brightest, healthiest people married others like themselves exclusively, would there be more excellent children? And conversely, if persons with retarded minds and poor health wed each other, would numbers of the inadequate increase?

We have observational but no experimental results on human beings, but animal studies have indicated not only that there are true differences in the native learning abilities of children but also that parentage is responsible for the differences. Thus, though there is a long phylogenetic distance from rats to men, there is so much in common in the two species' genetics that it is safe to draw some conclusion about human learning from what has been found for rats—that selective breeding does affect the intelligence of the succeeding generations (see Exhibit 7).

In the fields of animal husbandry and horse racing, there is no question about the dominance of genetic factors. It is through selective mating that the best beef types, the most productive milk cows, the fastest horses, and the hunting dogs of the best physical types, temperaments, and skills are produced.

Yet when we return to consideration of the human being and pursue the evidence that bolsters the hereditarian view of man's development, we find

Exhibit 7 Ability of rats to run a maze: an example of the effect of selective breeding on intelligence

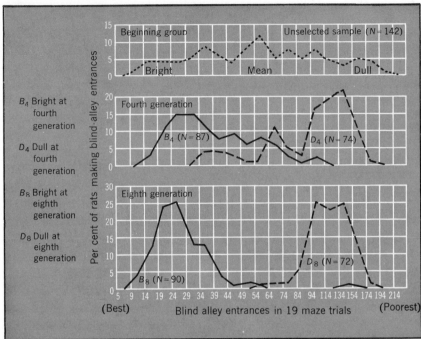

The rats used in these tests were selectively bred, and the graphs show their ability at maze running over eight generations. R. C. Tryon in his well-known study tested a group of rats for ability to run a maze—an ability that measures fairly accurately the intelligence of a rat. Then he bred the most intelligent rats with the most intelligent, and the least intelligent with the least intelligent, through a number of generations in order to determine whether he could establish a bright and a dull family line among the rats.

It will be observed that the parent, or beginning, group had a range such that some made less than 10 entrances into blind alleys in running the maze 19 times, while some made about 225 such entrances. This distribution of abilities is a typical one.

By the fourth generation, the developing of two separate groups of rats progressed to a considerable degree; and by the eighth generation, there was almost complete separation of the two groups. Note that one rat in the eighth generation of the "bright" mating is dull, having made about 150 blind-alley entrances. (Adapted from R. C. Tryon, "Individual Differences," in F. A. Moss (ed.), *Comparative Psychology*, Prentice-Hall, Inc., Englewood Cliffs, N.J., 1934.)

along the way complications, seeming contradictions, and other factors that must give us pause.

Limits of Hereditarianism. Although eminence and distinction, on the one hand, and deficiency and depravity, on the other, characterize some family lineages, we still do not have clear-cut proof that heredity is responsible; for the children of prominent parents have a superior cultural inheritance also, while the children of the very poor and ignorant are born into a very meager and disordered culture. Thus the evidence from family lineages has the weakness of not being able to attribute to either heredity or environment the main responsibility for either distinction or deficiency. Rather, good inheritance and good environment work together to produce distinction, while poor nature and poor nurture work together to produce weakness.

For example, high musical ability tends to run in families; most eminent musicians have, if not a parent, other relatives who have been recognized for their musical abilities. Thus a child gifted musically is born into a musical environment. The appearance of high musical talent early in life also indicates that the gifted child has inherited the right sensori-muscular-neural-skeletal connections for music. Yet there are important exceptions to the presence of high musical talent in the parents and other relatives of great musicians. Toscanini was a musical genius from a family in which there was little musical talent; but like that of other great musicians, his talent was evident in childhood.

Finally, consider the complications of status. Genius and distinction appear among all levels of people except possibly the very lowest, but by far the largest proportion of the gifted are born to the upper socioeconomic groups, even though such groups constitute only about ten per cent of the population. Still, greatness will show up in comparatively common quarters. Benjamin Franklin came from reasonably humble circumstances, and Mark Twain was born of pioneer parents who were good but in no way outstanding. John Burroughs, the famous author-naturalist, was born on an ordinary farm in New York State of parents who were opposed to schooling.

Correlation of Characteristics and Capacities among Relatives. The most closely related individuals are identical twins, who develop from a division of the same cell. Next in degree of relationship are fraternal twins, who develop simultaneously from two separate cells. Next are other children of the same parents, then cousins. Parents and children are more closely related than grandparents and grandchildren.

The correlations[3] of physical and mental traits and thus capacities are well enough known for these degrees of blood relationship to indicate that they correspond to nearness of kinship. Correlations of tallness, weight, mental-test ability, achievement in school subjects, and other characteristics and capacities vary a little from investigator to investigator; but as compiled

---

[3] The reader should consult the Appendix, p. 539, for a discussion of the meaning of correlation.

below, the correlations for the various degrees of blood relationship are reasonably accurate in indicating this general trend.

Relationship	Correlation
Identical twins	.80 — .95
Fraternal, or nonidentical, twins	.65 — .75
Other brothers and sisters (siblings)	.45 — .50
Cousins	.20 — .35
Unrelated children	.00
Parents and children	.40 — .45
Grandparents and grandchildren	.10 — .20

This is not necessarily proof that characteristics and capacities are inherited according to the degree of blood relationship. For it is likewise true that the closer the degree of blood relationship, the more nearly alike the environment. For twins, prenatal environment is more similar than for nontwins. Brothers and sisters experience a more similar environment than do cousins. And yet again, the fact that sisters and brothers differ is just as valid an argument that traits and capacities are inherited as the fact that they correspond to a degree represented by a correlation of .45 to .50.

Studies show that a tendency toward mental illness also accompanies blood relationship. Less than 1 per cent of the population becomes ill with schizophrenia, a severe form of mental illness, but about one-sixth of the children of parents who are schizophrenic become afflicted. Furthermore, if one identical twin is schizophrenic, the probability is that in seven out of eight pairs, the other twin will also become schizophrenic, astounding as this seems.

The record for manic-depressive psychosis has a comparable pattern. Where one fraternal twin becomes manic-depressive, so will the other twin in one out of four cases. If single members of sets of identical twins become manic-depressive, the probability is that about twenty-four out of twenty-five of the other identical twins will also do so.

This would seem to be strong evidence for the hereditary transmission of weaknesses which dispose the offspring to mental illness. The evidence, however, is complicated by the fact that the closer the offspring are environmentally, the greater the correspondence in occurrence of mental illness. For example, identical twins have more nearly identical environments than do fraternal twins, who in turn have more similar environments than do other related children. Moreover, it has been found that when children of mentally ill or alcoholic parents are placed in foster homes, most of them do not become mentally ill or alcoholic. This also indicates that their surroundings influence children strongly, since in such cases the emotional climate of the foster home is usually far better than that of the original home.

On the basis of these facts it is difficult to ascribe the cause of mental illness to nature or nurture. It seems that a person inherits the neural, glandular, and sensorimotor structures that make him more or less susceptible to various degrees of personality disorder and instability. Yet since the circumstances which surround a child clearly influence him emotionally, the environment helps determine how much disorder develops.

☯ *Reflect and Review*

Workers in state institutions for the mentally retarded frequently discover that a number of their wards have come from several generations of the same families. Justice Oliver Wendell Holmes was cognizant of that fact when he wrote, in his famous decision favoring the legal control of mental deficiency, "Three generations of imbeciles are enough."

What do you think about this persistence of mental deficiency in the same families?

A cliché about marriages is that they are made in heaven, and it has been added that college campuses are branch offices. There is evidence indicating that marriages resulting from college romances are in general very good marriages.

Sociologically, psychologically, and genetically, why should these marriages on the whole turn out well?

It has been reported that when George Bernard Shaw and Isadora Duncan, the great dancer, were visiting, she said in an idealistic vein that they could have remarkable children if they would get "my beauty and your brains," to which Mr. Shaw replied with catastrophic implications, "But suppose they inherited my beauty and your brains."

Discuss what parents can expect their children to be in terms of what the parents are. Think about this from the genetic and congenital standpoint and in terms of the home environment which the parents provide their children. It will be helpful to consider such categories as mental health, attitudes, mental capacity, physical health and development, delinquency, and amount of education.

ENVIRONMENT: BOON OR BURDEN

Our discussion of heredity has shown that heredity and environment can seldom be separated—that it is extremely difficult to say whether a certain characteristic of an individual is due to what he inherited or what he has experienced. Yet, as with heredity, it is valuable to consider separately a few important points about environment and its effect upon human development, again keeping in mind that the separation is primarily an organizational convenience.

Congenital Influences. Certain events during the congenital period of life— the child's embryonic and fetal period, the mother's period of pregnancy, or gestation—may influence the physical or mental development of the child. Unfortunately, we know relatively little about the exact nature and extent of these influences, but we do know enough to say that a good environment for the miraculous growth and development that take place during these 9 months is very important.

Thus certain conditions of the mother during the gestation period can have an effect on the embryo and fetus. We know that venereal diseases can be contracted congenitally and that the "Rh factor" sometimes sets up serious reactions in the infant's blood. The mother is Rh negative when she lacks a protein element in the red corpuscles, and the fetus is Rh positive when it has that protein. The mother may develop antibodies which attack the red corpuscles of the fetus, thus causing the newborn child to become anemic. A yellow pigment, a breakdown product of the red corpuscles, may also develop which deposits in the brain, interferes with normal neurological development, and thereby reduces the intellectual capacity of the child. German measles has also been identified as a cause of injury to the embryo. If the mother contracts German measles during the first three months of pregnancy, there appears to be about a 1 to 5 chance that she will give birth to a defective child. The abnormality may be a cleft palate, a malformed heart or other organ, or possibly a damaged brain. Prolonged inhalation of automobile fumes and lack of oxygen associated with mountain climbing appear sometimes to cause fetal abnormalities.

Little is known about the effects congenital injuries may have upon intelligence, although it is possible that many mental deficiencies which have been hastily called hereditary in the past may in fact result from congenital conditions. It is, understandably, difficult to gather precise information on this subject since the injuries which may cause such deficiencies occur during gestation and are usually impossible to diagnose even after birth.

Surely, little needs to be said about the transmission to the embryo and fetus of the experiences and thoughts of the mother during pregnancy. The prospective mother who watches crime movies will not therefore give birth to an incipient juvenile delinquent; and a mother may spend hours viewing masterpieces of painting with the wish that her offspring will become a distinguished artist, but all her hopes and visions will have absolutely no effect on the embryo or fetus.

This is not to say that the pregnant woman should not try to stay calm, happy, and mentally healthy, for there is some slight evidence that the unhealthy emotions of the mother can have disturbing effects on the fetus and predispose it to later instability. The conditions of the birth itself, which ends the gestation period, are important because some children may undergo physical injuries at birth that affect them mentally or physically. Some cerebral palsy may be caused during birth by abnormal pressures or chemical conditions that cause bleeding inside the baby's head. At this time also, small hemorrhages and nerve injuries may have effects, either serious or trivial, which become apparent later.

Medical Care as an Environmental Influence. Another important aspect of environment is the medical care a person receives from birth on through his life. This is an especially interesting subject because it illustrates how the environment of our whole society is changing.

Great improvement in medical care has taken place in this country since the beginning of the century. A brief summary of some facts about the conquest of some illnesses and the increase of others suggests what scientific health care can and cannot do at the present time. Deaths from tuberculosis, influenza, and pneumonia have been reduced a little over 80 per cent; and some diseases, such as diphtheria, have been almost entirely wiped out. The death rate for all causes has been reduced by nearly one-half.

Still, some causes of death have increased. During this century, deaths from cardiovascular and renal diseases have increased about 40 per cent, and deaths from various forms of cancer have increased about 115 per cent. The explanation is probably to be found in the great reduction of death rates for infants, children, and youth: many more people are reaching middle and old age—times of life when heart and kidney diseases and cancer are the more typical diseases. The great progress in keeping the young alive saves them to be afflicted by these ailments later.

To date very little progress has been made in prolonging the lives of people who reach their fifties and beyond. Possibly the longevity potentials set by inheritance will defy such efforts. Should it happen, however, that medicine becomes as successful with these degenerative diseases as it has been with infectious diseases, there will be a substantial increase in the percentage and number of persons who reach the advanced age of seventy-five and beyond.

THE COMBINED FORCES OF HEREDITY AND ENVIRONMENT

In the very process of considering heredity and environment discretely, we have seen repeatedly how the two elements encroach upon each other in the study of development. How, then, do scientists unify the study of heredity and environment, and what more can their efforts teach us?

Most scientific studies need a control, which must be similar to the experimental subject except for one difference which forms the point of the experiment. This difference is called the variable; the similarity is called the constant. Finding a suitable control is sometimes a very difficult problem, particularly when human beings, who are so full of variety and complexity, are being studied. In studies of the effect of environment and heredity upon human development, generally the problem is this: to find two people with exactly the same heredity (the constant) but with different environments (the variable). The natural solution to this problem lies in the use of identical twins. Such twins are genetically alike and thus the environment becomes the variable to which resultant differences can be attributed.

Studies of Identical Twins Reared Apart. Identical twins have been studied to see how much alike they are in physical characteristics and in mental and educational abilities. Studies have shown that for twins reared together these characteristics have an overall correlation of about .94, which is very high. This means that it can be expected that if one of a pair of identical twins is tall, the other is also tall—indeed, the same or very nearly the same height. If one has an IQ of 120, the other has about the same. If one has a low standing in his knowledge of school subjects as determined by standardized educational tests, then the other has about the same standing. All this is true if the identical twins have been reared in the same home, which, of course, is not always the case. It does sometimes happen that identical twins are separated at birth or early in life, one being placed with one family and the other with another. The homes sometimes differ greatly. In addition, they are sometimes in separate, very different communities. On the assumption that the heredity of identical twins is virtually the same, scientists can attribute the differences found in their personalities, intelligence, health, and physical development to the effects of their different experiences.

The general pattern of such studies of identical twins consists in the description and evaluation of the environment in which each twin of each pair has been living and of the abilities and characteristics of each twin. Then the characteristics of each twin are related to the environment in which he has lived so that the effect of the environment can be understood better. Since identical twins have the same heredity, great strength of hereditary processes is indicated if they remain the same even though they have lived in different environments.

A recent study by the English researcher, James Shields, involved 38 pairs of identical twins who had been separated during the first few years of life—most of them during the early part of their first year—and had lived apart ever since [Shields, 1958]. Personal history, questionnaires, and direct observations were used to identify various characteristics. It is in this area of personal qualities that this study is most useful. Following are some of the findings:

Six pairs of the thirty-eight pairs of twins were strikingly alike in interests and activities; twins brought up together were not more alike.

Fifteen pairs had striking resemblances but some differences; resemblances were stronger than differences.

Ten pairs had similarities and differences which were about equally balanced.

Seven pairs had very evident differences and only minor similarities.

Obviously, hereditary determinations remained most evident in the first cases, and environment had the most marked effect in the last.

The following selections from Shields's observations present some of the nature and nurture effects in specific cases. In considering them, it should be remembered that in some cases the subjects did not know they were members of a pair of twins.

Both members of one pair were bright, both were teachers, both were writers, and both were good organizers.

Both members of one pair had been advised to enter a mental hospital because of anxiety and depression.

Both members of one pair showed sharp tempers.

Both members of one pair had low energy.

Some twins said they were most alike "in our mannerisms, our voices, the way we think, our tastes and interests."

Other pairs were alike in shyness, talkativeness, sociability, musical abilities, and tastes.

In the case of one pair of twins, both had had considerably better jobs than their present ones. Their vocational status was comparable before and after the decline.

Both members of one pair were restless and anxious.

Both members of one pair had duodenal ulcers.

These similarities, which are evident even though the environments have been different, indicate the dominance of hereditary factors. For other twins, different environments had strong influence on their experiences and personalities, as the following indicates.

Of 12 pairs in which one twin was more neurotic than another, 9 of the more neurotic were reared in socioeconomically poorer homes.

A twin boy raised by a cruel and nagging stepmother had many fears and eventually ran away from home. As a thirty-seven-year-old adult he was clearly more sensitive and anxious than his twin brother, who had not had such painful and unhappy home experiences.

A twin girl had an unhappy relationship with her foster mother who, for instance, showed preference for this girl's younger brother. At the age of twenty-seven, this girl was diagnosed by a psychiatrist as suffering from neurotic depression. Her twin sister, who was raised in an emotionally healthful home, manifested no neurotic tendencies.

Twins raised in homes of the higher socioeconomic levels tended to marry those who were well off more often than did twins raised in homes of the lower socioeconomic levels.

One twin, reared in a very protective and sheltered environment, was more quiet and reserved than the other twin, who was reared in a normal environment.

The Shields study was fairly consistent in indicating that "sweetness or bitterness" of the environment has the effects on the personality that might be expected. Bitter and cruel environments generally seemed to produce anxiety, depression, shyness, and neurotic tendencies. Those who were badly treated were often in poor mental health, and those who were well treated were generally in good mental health.

In a comparable investigation—one of the best such studies, incidentally— 20 pairs of identical twins who had been separated at birth were carefully examined as to their health, physical development, intelligence, and subject-matter abilities, as measured by educational tests. This was the famous study by H. H. Newman, F. N. Freeman, and K. J. Holzinger [Newman et al., 1937]. The following are examples of the differences related to different modes of living.

One twin girl, who was raised on a farm, developed a sturdy body and weighed nearly 30 pounds more than her sister, who had been raised in the city and did little hard work. On the other hand, one twin who had lived on a farm as a struggling farmer's wife weighed nearly 10 pounds less than her twin, who had had a more comfortable married life. The one who had lived well had perfect teeth, while the twin sister who had fought poverty on a farm had teeth missing and decayed.

One twin had been raised in the "goiter belt," while the other was raised where she had plenty of antigoiter foods. The former had a goiter, and the latter did not; the former was also heavier and less alert in moving around.

There were also differences in educational achievement and mental age between some of the twins studied, reflecting differences in the number of years of schooling. Some twins had had only some grade school education, while their twin sisters or brothers had had high school education. There were differences of as much as 3 years in both mental and educational age, as determined by tests.

Generally, the study confirmed that certain differences in the environment influence the human body either favorably or unfavorably, and that additional years of education are reflected in higher mental development.

Other Studies of Twins. Other very important studies of twins have aimed to show the strength of heredity as well as the powerful influences of environment through comparing various categories of twins.

Comparative study of identical twins reared together and apart and of fraternal, or nonidentical, twins reared together has shown that environment has very little effect on certain basic physical characteristics but more effect on measured intelligence and knowledge acquired (see Table 5).

Table 5   Correlations of Physical Traits and Mental-test Scores for Three Classes of Twins

	Identical, Reared Together	Fraternal, Reared Together	Identical, Reared Apart
Standing height	.98	.93	.97
Sitting height	.96	.90	.96
Weight	.97	.90	.89
Head length	.91	.69	.92
Head width	.91	.65	.88
Average	.95	.81	.92
Binet mental age	.92	.83	.64
Binet intelligence quotient	.91	.64	.67
Otis intelligence quotient	.92	.62	.73
Stanford achievement	.96	.88	.51
Average	.93	.74	.64

Source: After Horatio H. Newman, Frank N. Freeman, and Karl J. Holzinger, *Twins: A Study of Heredity and Environment,* The University of Chicago Press, Chicago, 1937.

☯ *Consider the Data*

Based on Table 5

Correlations in the high .90s indicate that the twins are very much alike; correlations in the .50s and .60s indicate some fairly large differences. Note that in physical measurements identical twins tend to be very much alike. The degrees of similarity, moreover, are about the same for the identical twins reared apart as for those reared together, with weight most affected by differences in environment.

The greatest influence of the environment here is on mental and educational abilities or abilities in school subjects. Identical twins raised in the same homes show a high degree of similarity in mental and educational tests: the average correlation is about .93, which is nearly the same as that for physical qualities. But for identical twins raised in different environments this correlation is about .64—less, even, than the correlation for fraternal twins, which is .74. It is thus apparent that being raised in different environments with their different intellectual stimulation and educational opportunities makes identical twins more unlike than if they had been raised together. Yet even though identical twins have been separated, they still are more alike intellectually and educationally than are ordinary brothers and sisters reared together in the same families, going to the same schools, and in general having the same environment, the usual correlation of intellectual and educational abilities of ordinary siblings being about .50. Fraternal twins reared together are more alike in mental-test abilities and in educational-test scores than are identical twins reared apart.

A number of studies have been made of delinquency and adult crime records for the following classes of twins: (1) identical twins, (2) nonidentical twins of the same sex, and (3) nonidentical twins of opposite sexes.

Analysis of a number of such studies of adult crime among twins reveals that the classes of twins vary in the proportion of cases where if one twin has a criminal arrest record, the other does also, as shown in the following table.

Classes of Twins	One Twin Only, Per Cent	Both Twins, Per Cent
Identical	33	67
Nonidentical, same sex	65	35
Nonidentical, opposite sex	90	10

If one identical twin was a criminal, the other was also in two out of three pairs, but only one out of three pairs of nonidentical twins of the same sex were both criminals. There is almost an exact reversal of the percentages.

In the case of nonidentical twins of opposite sexes, the proportion of pairs in which a twin sister and her twin brother both had a criminal record was 1 in 10. In most of the other 9 out of 10 times, the one criminal was the boy twin and the girl twin did not pursue a criminal life. Women are much less likely to become criminals than are men.

The data for juvenile delinquency among the three classes of twins resemble the data for adult crime in that it is most likely for both identical twins to be delinquent and least likely for both nonidentical twins of opposite sexes to be so, as shown in the following table. The tendency for both members of a pair to be delinquent is, of course, greater in all classes of twins than the tendency for both to become adult criminals, because adult crime is for any individual a more serious and dangerous activity.

Classes of Twins	One Twin Only, Per Cent	Both Twins, Per Cent
Identical	10	90
Nonidentical, same sex	46	54
Nonidentical, opposite sexes	77	23

Nine times out of ten, both identical twins were delinquent if one was, as against two times out of three for adult crime. A little more often than not, both nonidentical twins of the same sex were delinquent if one was, whereas this happened about one out of three times with crime. Finally, in nearly one-fourth of the cases studied, both nonidentical twins of opposite sexes were delinquent, while both such twins became criminals in only one-tenth of the cases.

As mentioned earlier in this chapter, data on personality maladjustments and mental illness of twin pairs reflect a larger percentage of cases where both members of identical twins develop a mental affliction when one does than is the case with nonidentical twins. Thus the data on mental illness correspond with the above crime and delinquency data in this respect.

The interpretation of data from studies using this combination of twin types varies greatly, as far as the relative influences of nature and nurture are involved. Identical twins are more alike genetically than are fraternal twins who fit between identical twins and siblings genetically. It is therefore assumed by some that since their crime and mental-illness records are in turn considerably more alike than are those of nonidentical twins, hereditary factors may predispose any person toward antisocial behavior and mental illness. It is contended by others that identical twins live closer to each other than do nonidentical twins and therefore are influenced more by the same environment and that this makes environment the basic factor in mutual tendencies to crime and mental illness. This point of view sometimes includes the contention that identical twins influence each other more than do other twins. (It is because of various interpretations like these that twins reared apart furnish such a good experimental situation.) There is, of course, no doubt that a comparison of these different classifications of twins furnishes valuable facts.

Studies of Foster Children. Apart from special studies of separated twins, studies of adopted, or foster, children have also been made for the particular purpose of discovering what effect various kinds of foster homes have on their intelligence, school progress, and behavior. In such studies, the true parents and general background of the foster children are known and the foster homes in which they live are evaluated. Also, their intelligence is measured carefully by intelligence tests, their progress in school is carefully checked, and their behavior is carefully evaluated. Thus the behavior and development of foster children can be evaluated in terms of the quality of the foster home.

A home is rated high if the parents are of high standing in the community; if they are well educated; if they have good financial means; if they have a home with good books, television, and a telephone; and if the house is an ample, well-built attractive one in a neighborhood where the other children are intelligent and well behaved. In such homes the foster children generally have maximum opportunities for self-development.

A home is rated low if it is in a poor district and if the parents are of poor character, are poorly educated, and have small incomes. The influences in these homes make for poor school attendance, lack of ambition, and delinquency.

These two types represent the extremes at which the various foster homes can be classified, but there must also be consideration of the following elements:

Nutrition and mental care available to foster children range from superior quality to the bare minimum.

The communities themselves range from prosperous ones with good schools and other institutions to poverty-stricken places with meager facilities.

Foster parents range from warm, kindly, sympathetic, and loving to severe, dominating, neglectful, and indifferent.

Intellectual climates range from those which emphasize learning, culture, and wholesome leisure-time activities to those which ignore these things completely or are actively hostile to them.

Various studies indicate that intelligence develops more in the better than in the poorer homes; and the longer a foster child is in a good home, or the earlier the child is adopted, the greater the increase in IQ. Part of this may be due to the tendency of parents from better homes to choose children who appear to be healthier and more alert. Being abler persons, they would be expected to select children who show more promise. But basically the IQ increases because of the more favorable circumstances the child finds in such a foster home. The positive influence of the better home is not very great, however, bringing about an increase of about five to eight points in IQ, on the average. In some individual cases this is as high as 15 to 20 points, but individual cases do not constitute very reliable evidence. Such exceptional individuals might have increased in intelligence under average circumstances.

The reason that this increase is not large, is that the increase in the abilities measured by intelligence tests soon encounters the limits set by underlying capacities. (Later we shall show the opposite of this—that when children are deprived of normal schooling, their IQs go down because their developed mental abilities fall considerably below their mental capacities.) Thus foster children sometimes make good or better-than-average progress in elementary school; but in high school, this is often not the case. Many foster children have poor heredity, so that when they attend high school their hereditary limitations set in and the work becomes too hard for them. In grade school, through their own efforts and guidance of their foster parents, such foster children can do the work satisfactorily; but in high school the comparatively difficult algebra, foreign languages, history, English, and science are too hard for them to master.

The behavior of foster children is very favorable in relation to family background. Foster children generally have much better behavior records than their true parents had, and probably better than they would have had if left in the environments of their true homes. It seems, indeed, that the greatest favorable influence of foster homes on foster children is on their behavior. This is very important and encouraging, as it shows that children reared in a good environment generally do not become behavior problems.

Harmony between Capacity and Environment. Before the turn of the century, a boy tending cattle on the grassy slopes of Sweden found his situation was not satisfying or rewarding, so he left it. He emigrated to the United States—in a sense, made this country his foster nation—and earned a Ph.D. degree. Possessing curiosity and drive, he found just meeting classes and performing routine activities lacking in intellectual vitality. After tedious labor and some opposition to his experimental adventures, he perceived research opportunities in his field and went on to become a world-famous physiologist—a leader in his field of science.

This true story illustrates two things. People tend to seek an environment which is compatible with their capacities and interests, or they utilize their situation in a way that is compatible with their capacities and interests. Those with musical capacity seek out musical training, those with good healthy bodies and sensorimotor skills participate in sports, and those of limited abilities are found doing simple work and living in humble circumstances. Within the normal environments of the United States, certainly, the way a person lives—including his interests, activities, and achievements—is fairly good evidence of the dimensions of that person; in other words, his situation and his capacities and drives are in reasonable harmony.

Very unfavorable environments affect children growing up in them very negatively. Such children usually are penalized both by poor heredity and by poor environment. Still, a few who are raised in a poor environment have average or, occasionally, even high capacities; and these persons sometimes extricate themselves from the grip of their childhood circumstances through education. Enduring low status in childhood motivates some to work exceptionally hard to escape it.

On the other hand, there are those who are so limited that no matter how advantageous the environmental stimuli, they gravitate to a low status. (If such persons are relocated by being put in a housing project, their living quarters soon become a mess.) Though such persons are given any number of jobs, they fail in all of them. If closely controlled, some of them seem to get along a little better; but as soon as the props of active guidance are removed, they revert to ineffectiveness. Many of them become delinquents and thus produce social problems in spite of controls and restraints. Such persons are so heavily laden with hereditary and acquired liabilities that they gravitate to the lowest environmental levels, in contrast to those so richly endowed that they rise to the highest. It is also true, however, that many persons relocated in better housing and community environments respond by living up to the improved situation.

Contributions of Nature and Nurture Generalized. Out of the large amount of evidence provided by such studies and life observations, it is possible to compare the relative contributions of heredity and environment in four areas of growth and development as general guides for our understanding. (See Table 6.)

🜚 *Reflect and Review*

Let us assume that we have 500 children from 100 families, an average of five brothers and sisters from each family, who vary normally in their mental and physical capacities. We shall assume that each child is put in one of 500 different homes before he is one month old and that these 500 homes offer the widest possible range of environmental factors.

In this way a girl, for example, might have the best possible environment for her physical, emotional, and educational development, while her sister has the poorest possible.

Describe the probable effects of these varied environments upon the following aspects of the children's lives: health, happiness, progress in school, delinquency, and vocational and social status as adults.

Table 6 Relative Contributions of Heredity and Environment to Growth and Development

	Heredity	Environment
A. In the area of physical growth and development:	Height, bodily frame, and structure of the bodily organs are probably determined by the growth potentials in the genes; the structure of the nervous system also is probably determined genetically. The limits of sensorimotor development are set genetically, and these limits vary widely. Thus, the great differences in the motor skills and athletic abilities of children, youth, and adults are caused largely by heredity.	These hereditary influences all can be distorted by abnormal environment. Moreover, physical health and survival itself depends on good care. Good medical skills, including public health practices, and good nutrition are essential. Deficiencies and deprivation inflict huge penalties on the human body.
B. In mental growth and development:	The evidence indicates that children are born with a very wide range of general mental potential and with different potentialities for music, painting, the other arts, public speaking, and so forth, for which limits are set genetically.	Good environments are needed for developing abilities to levels close to capacity levels.
C. In mental and emotional health and personality:	Though, in this area, the circumstances of life have dominant influences, people seem to be born with physical structures—nervous system, glands and organs—on which emotional stability depends and to differ more greatly in their potential stability as a result; that is, some people are much more disposed by heredity to mental instability than others.	If children are raised in a healthful home where the blood or foster parents live in love and harmony and are kind and supportive to the children, there is a high probability that the children will have good mental and emotional health and thus good personality development. In protective environments, fewer of the unstable in the population will become mentally and emotionally ill than in severe and insulting environments.
D. In attitudes, beliefs, and values:	Position in life depends a great deal on capacities, which are set, to a considerable extent, by inheritance. Attitudes, beliefs, and values are affected by one's position in life, so, indirectly at least, heredity has some influence.	Attitudes, beliefs, and values develop largely from the culture into which one is born, and are influenced greatly by ego, or personal, involvement.

Suppose that when the children become young adults, they are again classified in their original family groupings and correlations are then calculated for the educational, intellectual, and physical measurements of brothers and sisters. Would these correlations be higher or lower than they would have been if the children had grown up in the homes of their own parents? Explain your answer.

Home I The husband and wife are thirty-five and twenty-five years old, respectively. Both are college graduates and had a standing in the top 10 per cent of their classes. Both were reared in upper socioeconomic homes. The family income permits a high standard of living and there is money left over for saving. On a marital scale, this family would rate only average because the degree of love and affection required for a highly happy marriage does not exist. There is little open conflict, and reasonably good routines have been established. The couple is childless and adopts a girl infant who turns out, when tested several times, to have low-average mental abilities and who is a slow learner in school. The child has good health and is physically attractive. What will probably be the influences of this home on the foster child, and what are the prospects for this child as an adult?

Home II Both parents are high school graduates with average academic standing. The father is a bricklayer who is in great demand because of his excellent work and pleasing personality. The emotional climate of the home reflects the happy relationship that exists between husband and wife. Being childless, they adopt an infant boy who turns out to be a quick learner in school and consistently is one of the best students in school as well as a very good athlete. What will the parents probably succeed in doing for this child? What are the prospects for this child (1) as to personality and social abilities and (2) vocationally? Will the child move above or below his parents socioeconomically?

HEREDITY AND ENVIRONMENT IN THE CLASSROOM

A human being is always most effective if he is realistic in what he does, that is, if his action is based on facts and evidence (on the truth); and for the teacher who wishes to excel, this necessarily means learning some of the basic facts about how mental development is controlled by nature and influenced by nurture. More specifically, the relative influence of heredity and environment on the mental development of children and adolescents is of particular concern to the teacher, because the teacher himself is one of the principal influences in a child's environment; and the good teacher is concerned about using his situation to help children in various ways.

If a teacher takes an extreme hereditarian point of view on development, his attitude is fatalistic; he feels that there is little to be done to stimulate mental and social development because the behavior of a person is largely the predetermined unfolding of the potentials that the person has inherited.

If, on the other hand, the teacher takes an extreme environmentalistic point of view, he maintains that the differences in children are largely due to environmental conditions. He believes that children can be greatly molded by the teaching they receive and by their other experiences. In Russia, for example, this point of view prevails. There it is believed that differences in people, except for the mentally deficient, are largely the results of opportunity and experiences. Heredity plays a minor role, according to the official doctrine. T. D. Lysenko, the principal Communist geneticist, even teaches that acquired characteristics are transmitted through the genes. This concept was rejected by geneticists elsewhere decades ago; its acceptance in Russia shows a very strong commitment to the environmentalistic point of view.

Both points of view are oversimplifications. The teacher must know this and also must know the complex truth that lies between, in order to do the most possible for his students. It can be very important to a student who as a first-grader seems very slow to learn, and continues to be slow in the second and successive grades, for the teacher to recognize that he has a low inherent mental level and should not be treated like the most capable children in the class. It could be most unfortunate for a bright child who learned faster than his classmates to have a teacher who thought he would wilt later by learning a lot now because bright minds are fragile and deteriorate with use. It is desirable for every child to have a teacher who knows in what areas he, as a vital force in the environment, can be most effective.

Let us illustrate the importance first of heredity and then of environment to educability. In a class in which there is a fairly wide range in chronological age because of promotional and selective policies, it will be found that the oldest children are less capable than the youngest. The oldest pupils have lived longer and have had several years more of instruction and usually a great deal of special help. But inherited limitations which are never overcome have caused them to be surpassed by younger, brighter children who have inherited greater capacities.

Compare the average chronological age, the average number of years of schooling, and the average mental age of the 15 youngest and 15 oldest boys in a freshman high school class which exemplified this a few years ago. (See table at top of p. 119.)

Mental age was determined by the scores that the students obtained on general intelligence tests. The older group was, on the average, 4.1 years older than the younger and had had 3.7 more years of schooling but still was 1.6 years below the younger group in mental age. Additional education

	Average Age, Years	Average Number of Years of Schooling	Average MA
15 youngest	11.7	5.7	16.7
15 oldest	15.8	9.4	15.1

All data were provided the author by Royal Embree, Jr.

and more years of living failed to overcome what no doubt was a basic inferiority of the older group, that is, an inferiority due to poorer inherent qualities. This difference in mental age continued to increase; and when adulthood was reached, the two groups were further apart than they had ever been. This kind of analysis of any grade would have obtained similar results.

These are important ideas for the teacher. He must realize that there are these true differences in the capacities of children to learn—that some will grow educationally and intellectually much faster and much more than others. The teacher must learn to recognize these constitutional differences in the particular children he works with, being very patient with the dull and the slow and guiding the bright into interesting and stimulating activities. He must realize that he cannot overcome basic limits but must work with those limits for the maximum development of all children.

Now let us consider a situation which illustrates the power of environment to affect the mental development of children, whatever hereditary endowments they may have. When, some years back, the children living in a group of isolated mountain pockets were given mental tests, it was discovered that their mental-performance abilities were decidedly below average. When the children of these same areas were tested a number of years later, the mental levels were significantly higher. What had happened? Good roads had reached these pockets, causing them to become more integrated with other communities and causing school attendance to improve. The schools the mountain children attended had been greatly improved also. In essence, the environment had become more stimulating to the children.

All the evidence we have substantiates this case by indicating that improvement in school attendance and improved schools are accompanied by increases in the abilities measured by mental tests. An improved environment does not produce an increase in basic mental capacity, but with better teaching and more intellectual experiences the mental abilities of the students come nearer to approximating their hereditary mental capacities.

Apart from the quality of the schools, if children stay out of school a goodly portion of the time, the development of their mental abilities will suffer, and the discrepancy between their mental-performance abilities and their underlying mental capacities will increase; and the poorer the school attendance, the greater this discrepancy. When children miss school a great deal, their loss of mental abilities, whether measured by comprehensive educational tests or by general mental-ability tests, corresponds to the amount of school lost (see Exhibit 8).

This assumes, of course, that the home does not provide instruction or stimulate extensive reading to compensate for losses from nonattendance. The assumption, sadly, is usually a correct one, for the homes of children whose school attendance is very poor are usually quite barren culturally.

Besides having favorable effects on the emotional development, mental health, and personality of students, good teaching in good schools develops the mental abilities of the students to a level close to their capacity levels. Importantly, full (as contrasted with limited) educational opportunities make a tremendous difference in the lives of those who have high capacity to learn. Through good education such students become prepared for and win

Exhibit 8   Decline in intelligence quotient as a result of very poor school attendance

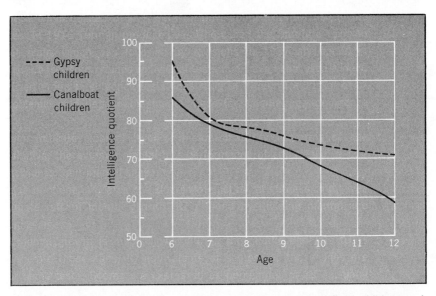

These curves show how the intelligence quotients of canalboat children and gypsy children decrease with increasing age. The canalboat children attended school an estimated 5 per cent of the time, or 1 day in 20, because of the modes of living of their families. The decline in IQ indicates that because these children are missing so much schooling, their mental abilities are not increasing normally. (Based on data given on p. 54 of Hugh Gordon, *Mental and Scholastic Tests among Retarded Children*, Educational Pamphlet 44, Board of Education, London, 1923.)

important positions as professional men and executives in various endeavors. They then enjoy high status in positions which equip them to help others.

If persons of high capacity and willingness to work are benumbed by poor schools or do not have opportunities to finish school, they usually find themselves at vocational levels considerably below those of their intellectual equals who were able to obtain adequate education.

SUMMARY

The genetic inheritance of a child, largely responsible for the structural makeup and its limitations, and the environmental forces—prenatal, home, and community—interact to determine the characteristics of the child and even the adult.

In trying to understand children in terms of their parents it will help to remember that children tend to resemble their parents, that there is variation in the capacities of the children of a family, and that the potentialities of the children of the extremely capable and the extremely incapable parents tend to regress toward the average.

Some family lineages contain comparatively many important people, and in other family lineages there are extensive records of deficiency. Both heredity and environment work positively in the first situation and negatively in the second.

When the ablest are mated with the ablest and the poorest with the poorest throughout several generations, there will develop a wide separation in the capacities of the offspring.

The closer the blood relationship, the larger the correlation of abilities and characteristics; but the closer the blood relationship, the more nearly alike are the environments also.

It seems that weaknesses of the physical structures are inherited; and, to a considerable extent, the degree to which the environment is severe, the weaknesses develop into various illnesses.

Good health practices have during this century practically eliminated a number of lethal diseases of children and youth. But for middle-aged people, some mortal illnesses are increasing, and there is essentially no prolongation of life after middle age.

From the studies of twins reared apart it does seem that in spite of different environmental influences the twins develop similarly in a number of respects. On the other hand, mental health and personality, educational abilities, and general health can be affected considerably by particular environmental situations.

Identical twins tend to have similar criminal records and similar psychotic afflictions. For fraternal twins there is considerably less similarity, and for twins of unlike sex there is least similarity, both in delinquency and in psychosis.

The intellectual abilities of children in good foster homes improve enough to register an average increase of five to eight points in IQ. Generally children raised in such homes are nondelinquent, and conceivably the greatest contribution of the foster home is in the area of socially accepted behavior.

To a considerable extent, people with high capacities seek out environments that provide opportunities to utilize their capacities. People of inferior capacities gravitate to corresponding environments.

It may help to evaluate the differential effects of nature and nurture on physical and on mental development, on emotional health, and on attitudes and beliefs.

Bright children will outstrip dull children even if the dull children have had considerably more years of education.

SUGGESTED READING

Burt, Cyril L.: "Inheritance of Mental Ability," *The Eugenics Review,* 49:137–139, 1957. It is true that like begets like, but it is also true that like begets unlike. Sir Cyril Burt's penetrating analysis presents some fresh ideas about inheritance.

————: "On D. H. Stott's Article: Interaction of Heredity and Environment in Regard to Measured Intelligence," *British Journal of Educational Psychology,* 30:273–275, 1960. Sir Cyril Burt replies to Dr. Stott. The reader will be exposed to some high-level thinking when he reads these exchanges of ideas.

Hardin, Garrett: *Biology and Individual Differences,* National Society for the Study of Education Yearbook, part I, pp. 11–24, 1961. Presents a number of problems involving heredity and environment and discriminating analyses of them. A good orientation to this complex and important topic.

Stott, D. H.: "The Interaction of Heredity and Environment in Regard to Measured Intelligence," *British Journal of Educational Psychology,* 30:95–102, 275–276, 1960. Dr. Stott discusses prenatal influences and various other influences on mental development. Shows how complicated it is to understand the influences of heredity and environment.

CHAPTER 5
THE PERSONAL
AND PROFESSIONAL
DEVELOPMENT OF THE TEACHER

Let us apply the relationship between heredity and environment to the teacher himself. To say, "Teachers are born, not made" is to err. The basic qualities of mind and personality that predispose an individual to success in teaching are influenced greatly by the home and community in which he is reared; also, such qualities can be cultivated. Therefore a knowledge of desirable and undesirable qualities will help the teacher or prospective teacher to set his goals for, and to understand the problems of, becoming an effective professional person.

WHO WILL BE GOOD TEACHERS?

College students who prepare to become teachers go on to experience notably different degrees of success in their teaching careers. As a result, many studies have been conducted in order to discover what types of students become good teachers and what types become poor teachers. The best of these studies have furnished some surprises and thus explained why predictions of success or failure have not been very accurate in the past.

One might expect, for instance, a primary correlation[1] between measured intelligence and comparative success in teaching, but actually this correlation is not crucial. This does not mean that intelligence is not an important qualification for teaching; but because most college students are clearly above average in intelligence and therefore have enough for teaching, other personal qualities are the deciding factors in determining success. Furthermore, the wide range in teaching positions provides opportunities for teachers of special abilities and various aptitudes to be successful.

[1] See Appendix for a discussion of correlation.

Recognizing the Best Teachers of Tomorrow

A good teacher loves knowledge and imparting it; beyond this he is especially capable of setting goals for learning, selecting the right materials for reaching them, presenting these materials in such a way as to foster the development of all his various students, and observing and guiding his students, both singly and as a class. Some students show such love and such capacity and so reveal themselves as the potentially outstanding teachers of the future.

Which two or three of the students shown here seem to display clearly one or more of these desirable qualities of a teacher? In each of these cases, how would knowing the student's emotional reaction to the situation in which he or she was photographed help you to judge better that student's potential teaching ability? Of the student teachers, which would you suppose to be the better one?

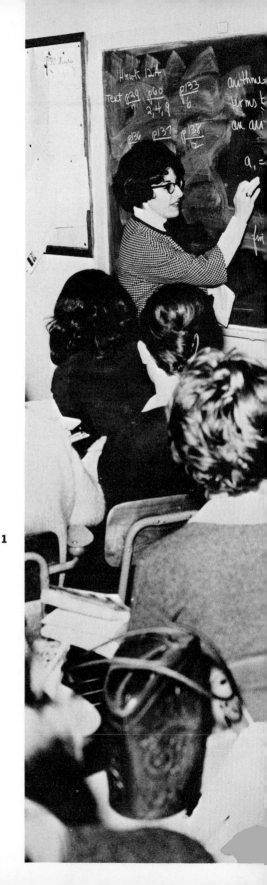

1

1 Courtesy of Hunter College High School.
2 Courtesy of Boys' Athletic League.
3 Courtesy of Eastern Fine Paper and Pulp Division, Standard Packaging Corporation.
4 Courtesy of Scholastic Magazines.

2

3

4

Marks earned in practice teaching have not been accurate indications of subsequent success in teaching, either. In the first place, there are inaccuracies in rating college students' success in practice teaching. Secondly, the degree of apparent success in practice-teaching situations is not prognostic of success or failure on the job, because of big differences in these situations. Often the practice teaching is done under conditions which are artificial and not so difficult as those which will be experienced when the beginning teacher takes his first position. The practice teaching may be done for single periods with the supervising teacher present or close at hand. The student teacher does not have responsibility for establishing and carrying out the classwork. Rather, he steps into a going situation. Consequently, practice teaching frequently does not test or reveal the professional and personal qualities that are needed for teaching successfully. Then, too, the mark in practice teaching is based in part on conferences and the lesson plans, which, of course, are not actual teaching.

Personal appearance, scores on teacher attitude scales, and health do not seem to serve as useful standards with which to differentiate good and poor teachers. Teacher attitude scales require that the person answering the questions indicate what he thinks about pupils and how they should be dealt with; and a person's attitude apparently does not indicate very accurately how well he actually handles his students. Health is a poor standard, because practically all college graduates are in good health. Similarly, most graduates have adequate personal appearance.

What qualities, then, should a prospective teacher have in order to succeed? H. T. Olander and H. M. Kleyle, in their study of this problem, carefully rated 108 elementary school teachers with 2 to 5 years of teaching experience [Olander and Kleyle, 1959]. Many data were available on these teachers from the time when they were college students. These men found, as have other investigators, the following qualities and abilities to be prognostic of success as a teacher:

Sociability and Emotional Maturity. He is active socially, works and plays effectively with people, is friendly and makes friends. He is in good mental health.

Scholarship and Mental Capacity. He has done well on the National Teacher Examinations, reading tests, English tests, and tests of general mental capacity. His scholarship, as indicated by point standing in college, is high.

It was found that a considerably greater number of successful teachers were in the top quarter in a composite of ratings and measurements based on these two categories than in the lowest quarter.

In spite of such findings as these, it is often thought that if a person is high in scholarship, he will be a poor teacher. Some believe that teachers with especially good personalities are not likely to be good scholars. In colleges and universities it is frequently claimed that teaching suffers because of the emphasis placed on research with its consequent writing of articles and books. For these and many other related claims, there are counterclaims. In short, there is much disagreement about the relations between scholarship, personality, and teaching.

In order to get the most dependable answers available to the questions involved in the various points of view, let us turn again to research—specifically, to an excellent study by A. H. Maslow and W. Zimmerman, in which 86 teachers were rated by their students and their colleagues for (1) teaching ability; (2) scholarship, including creativeness; and (3) personality [Maslow and Zimmerman, 1956]. Each teacher was rated by at least three colleagues and by a median number of 35 students. Though these were college teachers, the results of this study seem to apply to teachers at high school and grade school levels, since the same abilities and qualities are needed there.

These researchers discovered that the correlations between personality and teaching ability, between scholarship and teaching ability, and between scholarship and personality range from the .50s to the .70s, showing a dependable relationship between all these qualities. In other words, those teachers who were high in one quality tended to be high in the other; those low in one tended to be low in the other. For example, the correlation of students' ratings of personality and teaching was .76, and the colleagues' ratings of teachers for scholarship and teaching ability correlated .77.

Correlations do not permit one to draw conclusions about cause and effect. Thus we cannot say that high teaching ability causes high scholarship or vice versa. These correlations do indicate, however, that teachers with the best scholarly abilities tend to be the best teachers, as well as that good personality is also associated with good teaching.

Also of importance is the fact that ratings of teaching by fellow teachers and the ratings of the same teachers by their students correlated .69. This rather remarkable correlation shows considerable agreement between students and teachers in their opinions of teaching ability.

Taken together, these two studies furnish strong evidence that outstanding personal and intellectual qualities enable a teacher to manage his work efficiently and to guide and instruct his students effectively. This idea is developed in the ensuing discussion.

THE TEACHER'S PERSONALITY

We are so concerned about the behavior of the students that we often overlook the personality and behavior of the teacher. But the teacher spends most of the school day in close association with his students; and as a result, his basic attitudes and actions, his tastes and mannerisms have great influence on them. The teacher creates the emotional climate in the classroom just by being friendly or unfriendly, tolerant or overcritical, generous or severe, calm or nervous.

This directly affects the children themselves because children learn attitudes and behavior by example. Emotional tensions, for instance, are contagious; a teacher who is fearful, tense, and generally hostile can induce fear, worry, and insecurity in his students. The learning situation is also affected by the personality and behavior of the teacher, for the student's response to what is being taught is determined largely by his response to the teacher. This is important because one of the major objectives of education is to instill in students a love of learning. Specifically, the teacher strives to interest his students in the subject he teaches. Effective or ineffective teachers with correspondingly good or poor personalities, moreover, often determine not only the response to their own courses but also the students' future attitude toward the entire subject. When people are asked to recall which courses they liked and disliked in school, it is found not only that the most popular courses were taught by the teachers who were best informed and most stimulating but also that college students seldom continue study in subjects which were taught in high school by unpopular teachers but do continue study of subjects which were taught by popular teachers. Thus a teacher of a required college course can, because of his personality problems, be so ineffective in his teaching that his students are negatively influenced, and none will major in his field in graduate school.

The personality of the teacher is important outside as well as inside the classroom proper. Teachers are continually in contact with each other; they share offices and teach the same students, so they must be able to plan and work together well. Work with principals and other school officials is also part of the professional situation; and teachers' personality patterns must not make it difficult for them to accept the amount of authority and guidance that is required in a school system. The quality of these teacher relationships with equals and superiors determines to a considerable extent the morale of the school; thus it is important to the success of the school.

Students' Reactions to the Teacher's Personality. Teachers differ in their ability to establish good student relationships because they differ in self-assurance, personal vitality, and capacity for dealing with people in general. There are certain specific kinds of teacher behavior, also, that students respond to favorably. Let us consider some of these:

Being courteous, friendly, and approachable; recognizing a student and speaking on meeting; really liking the students

Possessing a sense of humor; being willing to smile, laugh, and enjoy a good joke

Showing interest in all students; appreciating and being sympathetic with their study efforts

Giving help kindly, sincerely, and patiently

Keeping good order

Most of this behavior is manifest in a wholesome, friendly personality. Opposed to it is the following list of characteristics which students dislike:

Being grouchy or irritable; having fits of temper which end in shouting and yelling

Being overcritical; scolding sarcastically

Having "pets" and disliking or "picking on" other students; being unfair

Being dull, inanimate

Taking a negative approach to teaching and learning problems by maintaining poor discipline

These are not separate traits; rather, they are phases of a single pattern of behavior that does not influence people favorably in any area of work. In general, it is symptomatic of an unhealthy personality and of the lack of adequate social and professional skills; as such, it does not go with effective teaching.

Various annoying habits, in addition to these behavior patterns, reduce the effectiveness of the teacher. For example, J. E. Moore learned from students that they disliked such mannerisms as pacing the floor, fiddling with watch chain and keys, staring out the window, and putting feet on the desk— that, in general, they wanted their teachers to concentrate on their work in a dignified manner without any show of physical nervousness [Moore, 1940]. Poor grooming also arouses negative feelings.

Students dislike having their teachers employ favorite expressions over and over or stray off the subject, say to dwell on their personal affairs. They do not like old, stale jokes. Monotonous or shrill voices, voices that are notably loud or low, frequent clearing of the throat, "ahing" and "aheming"— all these trouble or distract students.

In studies of best elementary teachers by J. C. Gowan and of best and poorest teachers by D. G. Ryans, certain practices and abilities were evident [Gowan, 1957; Ryans, 1960]. Out of a group of 3,000 elementary teachers, 20 of the best ones—according to the judgment of trained investigators who observed their teaching—were selected and studied by Gowan. They ranged in age from 22 to 56, with a median age of 39. While growing up, 14 of the 20 had been active as members of groups; 12 had been superior students,

5 had been average, and 3 had been below average. Their main satisfactions in teaching were being with children and observing them grow and develop. They were particularly concerned with helping the children personally and socially so they would develop healthy personalities. A most remarkable fact is that of these 20 superior elementary teachers, 4 had written and published children's books and 3 had published poetry.

Most had good family backgrounds where education and doing well in school were highly regarded. Nearly all of them liked very much to go to school. Most of them had had music and dancing lessons and annual family vacations.

All these 20 teachers were warm and friendly in their personal relations. They were trustful, not suspicious. They did not blame others, but assumed responsibility for their own difficulties and failures.

These 20 very successful teachers liked best their teachers who were genteel, emotionally mature, democratic, friendly, permissive, definite, and fair.

They disliked the teachers who were unfair, arrogant, ignorant, intolerant, and sarcastic and who habitually blamed others and yelled at students.

Ryans picked 67 best teachers and 37 poorest teachers out of a large number on the basis of being (1) friendly and understanding versus aloof and egocentric; (2) responsible, systematic, and businesslike versus evasive, unplanned, and slipshod; and (3) stimulating and imaginative versus dull and routine.

These best teachers had the following characteristics, interests, and abilities:

Generous opinions of people
Strong interest in reading and in literary fields
Interest in music, painting, and the arts in general
Participation in social groups
Superior verbal abilities
Enjoyment of their pupils
Preference for nondirective classroom methods
Good emotional health and adjustment

These are the characteristics and abilities of well-educated people of good cultural and professional standing.

The poor teachers were consistently the opposite. For example, while the superior teachers had a good social life and had friendly relationships and fraternized with their peers, the poor teachers had a restricted social life and poor personal relationships.

Learning the Students' Reactions. Teachers, like anyone else, cannot correct their ineffective behavior until they know what it is; but there is a simple, workable way to learn this. If a teacher wants to know what his students like or dislike about him, say what distracting habits he might have, he can ask to be rated by his students on a simple evaluation scale including space for comments on the particular strengths and weaknesses of the teacher (see Figure 14).

In order to secure objective ratings, a teacher should give his students the opportunity to rate him anonymously and with complete impunity. Any feeling on the part of a student that there may be an attempt to discover his identity as a rater will, of course, influence his rating and thus defeat the entire purpose of the procedure. In order to prevent the handwriting from revealing the individual students, the comments should be typed. Single, isolated comments may reflect a student's weakness, rather than the teacher's; but when the same comment turns up a number of times, it is likely to be a good indication of the teacher's behavior. Many research studies have indicated that students' opinions of their teachers' behavior in the classroom are competent. Even children in the lower grades seem to "know what they are talking about" when they comment on their teachers.

Whether the rating is done under the direction of the individual teacher or the administration, the teacher should have full opportunity to study the comments about him. Then it is very important that he not be offended by unfavorable ratings and comments or sensitive about learning that his teaching is not totally effective. On the contrary, any such evaluation should be regarded as an opportunity to improve his professional skills. The teacher then can set about to overcome or substantially lessen whatever faults make his teaching less effective than it could be.

The Teacher outside School. Personality, of course, is not a veneer that can be applied to a person by himself or by anyone else, nor something he can turn on or off like an electric current. Rather, personality has its roots in physical health, emotions, intelligence, knowledge, and ideals. It is the sum of a person's total capacities and developed abilities. Thus, it is not only the school life of the teacher that is involved in his personal and professional development, but his out-of-school existence as well. Studies have shown that well-adjusted teachers have more hobbies and out-of-school activities than poorly adjusted teachers. W. S. Phillips and J. E. Green discovered, for example, that about four times as many well-adjusted teachers as teachers with neurotic symptoms were engaged in outdoor sports and were active socially in other ways [Phillips and Green, 1939]. On the other hand, six neurotic teachers spent their "recreational" time in activities that

Look over all of this scale before you begin to rate the teacher. Then check the appropriate place on the scale.

I. The Effectiveness of the Teaching. Rate the teacher, considering his helpfulness, his ability to communicate in explanations, guidance of learning activities, his knowledge and general wisdom.

5	4	3	2	1

Excellent:
teaches very well,
is interesting and
stimulating

Average:
fairly
effective

Very poor:
dull,
ineffective

Comments:

What should the teacher do to improve?

II. Personality of the Teacher. Rate the teacher in terms of courtesy, friendliness, patience, fairness, sense of humor, and appreciation of you as a student.

5	4	3	2	1

Very likable and
pleasing: has a
good emotional
effect on you.

Average:
has a reasonably
good effect
on you

Disagreeable:
has a bad
effect on you

Comments:

What should the teacher do to improve?

III. General Rating. Rate the teacher in comparison to the other teachers you have and have had.

5	4	3	2	1

The best or one
of the best

Average:
typical

The poorest
or about
the poorest

Comments and recommendations:

Your standing in the class. Please check:

1st quarter (highest) _____

2d quarter _____

3d quarter _____

4th quarter (lowest) _____

Figure 14   A scale for student evaluation of the teacher and his teaching

resembled their teaching activities or in routine work activities for every well-adjusted teacher who did.

No one can be sure of a cause-and-effect relationship between personal leisure activities and mental health, but it seems clear that teachers need the enjoyment and relaxation that come from physical and other social activities. A sedentary, socially isolated life neither indicates nor promises good mental health.

Thus developing an interest in and a flair for social activities is an important facet of preparation for teaching. The person who leads a reasonably active personal social life in addition to succeeding in his intellectual activities has the best potential for teaching.

Mental Illness among Teachers. Serious personality disorders are no more prevalent among teachers than among any other group of adults. Evidence even indicates that the proportion of teachers in hospitals for the mentally ill is smaller than the proportion of the population as a whole. Yet, a distressingly large proportion of teachers have personality problems which, although they are not severe enough to warrant hospitalization, are a serious handicap in their work. It is almost certain that a student will have at least one teacher before he graduates from high school whose deficiencies of personality have troubling effects on him.

That mental illness should ever hospitalize a teacher is in itself a tragedy, but it is a greater tragedy that some teachers who are clearly mentally ill continue in the classroom year after year, in a position to influence the children in their charge. Thus we shall not dwell on cases serious enough to warrant isolation and extensive treatment, but shall consider those teachers with psychological difficulties serious enough to lessen their teaching competence, to prevent them from dealing effectively with their students and with other adults. Such difficulties take many forms. For just one instance, there are the neurotic perfectionists—teachers who insist that everything must be done "just so"; who are overfastidious and very formal; who try to compress themselves, as well as their students, into a rigid, set form.

Not just a few teachers, moreover, have serious emotional problems. Data indicate that one teacher in ten has had a nervous breakdown. This means that one teacher in ten has, over a long period, become progressively and then crucially unable to cope with the reality or the idea of failure, stress, unhappiness, or difficulty in getting along with others. More inclusively, the National Educational Association has reported that 37.5 per cent of teachers have stated that they are so troubled over such matters as keeping order, conflicts with other teachers, and loneliness that their sleep, health, and efficiency are affected [National Education Association, 1950]. Thus more than three out of ten teachers are emotionally and socially maladjusted to a recognizable degree.

Other evidence indicates that from one-third to one-half of the illnesses which necessitate long absences of teachers from school are primarily emotional in origin.

What characteristics contribute to such distress among teachers? An analysis of teachers who had been hospitalized for mental illness may be of value in determining this by highlighting the causes of the less severe mental illness with which we are primarily concerned; maladjustment is only a matter of degree.

Characteristically, the hospitalized teachers were found to have been:

Introverted, quiet, and retiring
Overambitious and selfish
Anxious, irritable, and hyperactive
Eccentric in behavior

Introversion, as used here, indicates abnormal preoccupation with one's self, and is associated with a strong tendency to engage in solitary activities rather than in activities involving others. Extreme social isolation and withdrawal from others are often associated with maladjustment.

Though it may be surprising that the teachers who became severely ill tended to be overambitious, it is true that excessive ambition may be a symptom of deep-seated insecurities. Moreover, since the overambitious person is constantly frustrated, he is continuously under great strain, which only aggravates his maladjustment.

Anxiety, irritability, and hyperactivity are a constellation of conditions that create additional strain. A person who is under such tension finds it difficult to deal satisfactorily with others. Misunderstandings and conflicts are frequent; and these, in turn, increase his tensions and thus make his troubles worse.

Unsuccessful attempts to deal with the anxieties and conflicts aroused by maladjustment frequently result in behavior patterns that are odd, or eccentric. This eccentric behavior may, in turn, increase the difficulty of social relationships and thus cause more stress and strain. The difficulty of improving these behavior patterns is evidenced by the fact that a number of teachers who have them become seriously ill. However, an awareness of these problems may stimulate the affected individual and those about him to contend with such problems more intelligently. The individual can try to be more social, less selfish, more accepting, and less individualistic in his behavior. Those who deal with him can be more patient, sympathetic, and understanding.

☯ *Reflect and Review*

Miss A., who had just graduated from college, was employed to teach in junior high school. Although she could not be numbered with the best students, her scholarship was clearly satisfactory; and she was highly recommended by her professors as a serious, dutiful girl.

One of her professors was doubtful about Miss A. He appreciated her qualifications, but he wondered how effective she would be as a teacher. He had observed that she did not communicate much with her classmates; when she came and went, she was usually alone. He had never seen her at any of the college social affairs. She had no enemies, but she had no close friends either. The professor feared that her poor social adjustment had given her so little experience in dealing with people that she might not know how to deal successfully with her students and colleagues.

This neophyte proved a dismal failure. She was unable to control her students, and conditions became so chaotic in her classroom that she could not finish the term. If this girl had had normal social experiences since early childhood and had learned to be socially adequate, she might well have been a successful teacher from the beginning and a healthy, happy one throughout her whole career. It was evident in college that she did not integrate socially with the other students, and she could have been guided by the dean of women and faculty members into social participation. Because a student is more likely to fail in a job because of social inadequacies than because of inadequacies in scholarship, it is reasonable for a college or high school to require that its students "pass" socially before they are graduated; thus it is the responsibility of the student to learn social skills.

Miss B., a second-grade teacher, had a difficult problem. She seemed to work endlessly over the details of her teaching, spending long hours after school and during the weekends going over and over lesson plans and the written work of the student teachers assigned to her. She was deeply entangled in the meshes of minutiae.

She regimented her pupils with small tasks which could only be called busywork instead of relating her teaching to their development in the fullest sense. Indeed, she failed to sense their feelings and wants. All the classwork, down to the smallest point, had to be executed according to precise and constricted forms; there was no plan for imagination, creativeness, and expansiveness. This caused unhealthful tensions in her pupils which in turn tightened the tensions of this inflexible person. Yet she carried on in the belief that she was teaching well.

Miss B. had very little social life. She rarely left the area marked by her classroom, her apartment, and the route she walked between these two places. She said she was glad when she could close the door of her apartment and be alone. In reality she lived a very restricted and prosaic life.

What similarity do you find in the lives of Miss A. and Miss B.?

Does Miss A. or Miss B. seem to have a deeper psychological problem as a teacher? Why? What is ironic about what happens to Miss A. as compared with the course of Miss B.'s school life?

What psychological phrase is used to describe such a person as Miss B.? What causes her to affect her pupils' attitudes and feelings as she does?

When a teacher seems most concerned that "every *t* be crossed and every *i* be dotted," what educational procedures and values are usually overlooked?

THE PROFESSIONAL GROWTH OF THE TEACHER

As teachers grow in competence, they become increasingly successful and feel more wanted and worthy, and their personalities are favorably affected. But some teachers, like some other professional people, stagnate; and by the time they are forty or forty-five they reach a condition in which they oppose improvements in their field of education, are overcritical of their associates, and seem helpless in a profession and world that are moving forward.

What can a teacher do to grow professionally? What are the evidences of professional growth on the basis of which a teacher can evaluate himself?

It is sometimes said that degrees do not make a teacher; then, to clinch the argument, a teacher is mentioned who has advanced degrees but does his work poorly. It is true, of course, that graduate work does not make a good teacher out of a person who lacks the basic qualities needed for success in teaching. Still, most teachers are improved by graduate work; and, all in all, the teaching profession is improved when the standards of education of teachers are raised.

In the education of teachers, certain studies besides general academic and professional courses[2] are highly desirable.

First, all teachers, at all levels, should be thoroughly competent in the subjects they teach. They should acquire from advanced study a much wider and deeper knowledge of the subject matter than is directly needed in class. One cannot teach what he does not know, nor can he teach with enthusiasm unless he knows so much about his field of learning that he is confident and enthusiastic about his specific subject. Facts, ideas, and inspiration flow from a mind that is full.

One of the worst effects of not knowing the subject is the influence of this

[2] Courses in school administration, supervision, curriculum, methods, and educational psychology are professional education courses.

deficiency on the personality of the teacher. Some teachers become harsh and uncompromising, while others are sensitive and overcritical.

Suppose, for example, someone has been a lazy, uninterested, and thus weak student in college, but has gone on to various graduate schools, finally obtained the doctor's degree with minimum marks, and started teaching in college. Such a person's teaching will not be inspired. He is likely to waste a good deal of time on trivia or to be irritable and fault-finding with his students, or both. Not succeeding himself because he does not have the capacity for what he is doing, he can be expected to be jealous of fellow teachers who do well. He may ultimately have a very serious, even debilitating emotional reaction—perhaps the psychophysiologic reaction of ulcers of the stomach, perhaps something else. Sadly, such experiences are typical at all grade levels.

Teachers must also understand the children and youths they teach. They must have a sound body of knowledge about the students' physiology and psychology. And to this understanding must be added a theoretical knowledge of how material can be efficiently and effectively presented to students. Thus, good scholarship in several areas is a first requirement.

The teacher can also improve his professional abilities by attending clinics, workshops, and conferences whenever possible. These are usually arranged for the purpose of taking up some special topic, such as the teaching of reading, the core curriculum, the growth and development of children, or teaching through activities. Teachers generally help in planning these meetings. Usually the procedures are informal and the groups small enough that problems of the individual teacher can be taken up. All who attend these sessions have opportunities to learn better ways of helping their students. In addition, there are teachers' conventions which are county-, state-, and nationwide which serve to stimulate the teachers personally and professionally.

Finally, a basic requirement for keeping one's teaching vital and stimulating is experimentation. There are, of course, teachers who have taught 30, 40, or 50 years without changing their methods who may be reasonably good teachers. But if they had broadened their teaching experience by giving new and different techniques serious trials, they very likely would have been more effective in their teaching. Some teachers initiate their own experiments, and others participate in large projects involving several or many teachers.

Experimentation of this kind carried out by a teacher in his field of work is called action research, and by means of it the teacher contributes to our growing knowledge of education and psychology. Also, the teacher will develop personally and professionally from the fun and work of doing research and of reporting it.

Keeping Intellectually Alert. A teacher should have daily association with magazines and books—professional and recreational—and, in addition, should hold discussions with friends and colleagues to enliven his intellectual interests and deepen his thinking. Benjamin Franklin gathered often with a few associates to exchange books and to discuss various ideas he found in and outside them. Out of this interest in books and learning he organized a method of exchanging books which was the prototype of our present-day lending libraries. Thomas Edison gloried in obtaining the books on electricity by the leading scientists of his time because such books furnished ideas which helped him with his experiments. If a person who is entering any profession quits studying when he learns that he has finished his courses and accumulated enough credits for final graduation from academic pursuits, he will start to wither intellectually. Thus the graduate should continue study, but the bulk of his studying should be done on his own.

Such activities indirectly stimulate a teacher in his work. Other independent activities directly help him keep interested in his field. One of the best of these is writing. A teacher has more opportunities to write magazine and scholarly journal articles and even books than most other persons. This writing is generally based on extensive reading and also involves careful thought about the writer's own experiences. Thus there is probably no activity that keeps up one's interest and scholarship so much as this.

Teachers are also enriched both personally and professionally by travel. Traveling is enjoyable and often rejuvenating, and one learns many things— applied psychology, geography, history, sociology, languages, art, and economics. A teacher who has visited places that are discussed in his lessons puts more vitality into the lessons by sharing his experiences with his students.

Evaluation of the Teacher. The purpose of a system of teacher evaluation should be to help the teacher improve himself. He needs to know what his status is in terms of his fellow teachers and the reasons for his relative standing. The scheme illustrated in Figure 15 includes seven criteria which are believed to indicate the vitality and worth of the individual teacher. Records are kept of each teacher for the seven items given; and on the basis of such data each teacher can be ranked from highest to lowest and given a position, as illustrated in Figure 15. Data for items VI and VII can be obtained from the use of a rating scale of the kind illustrated in Figure 14. Ratings can be made of the teacher anonymously by the students, supervisor, principal, and possibly by fellow teachers, and the teacher should have an opportunity to study such ratings.

The standing of the teacher reported in Figure 15 indicates the following:

His 24 semester credits beyond the master's degree place him in the middle of the top quarter (item I).

He is in the middle of the second quarter in professional activities such as workshops and conventions (item II).

He ranks essentially at the top of the highest quarter in effective cooperation with colleagues and parents (item III).

His scholarship as indicated by his studying and writing places him essentially at the top of his group (item IV).

In extensiveness of traveling, he is just a little above the average for his group (item V).

He is a very superior teacher of subject matter, as indicated by a rating that places him at the top of the highest quarter of his group (item VI).

He has a top rating also as a teacher of students, as indicated by his personal qualities and their effects (item VII).

Items III, VI, and VII are the most fundamental ones, with the others being more or less supporting or supplementary ones. If this teacher has been appraised accurately, his standing in the various items indicates that

First quarter (highest)	Second quarter	Third quarter	Fourth quarter (lowest)		
X				I	Formal education: degrees and credits
	X			II	Attendance and participation: workshops, conventions, etc.
X				III	Working effectively with fellow teachers, administration, and parents
X				IV	Individual reading, studying, and writing
		X		V	Travel
X				VI	Effectiveness in terms of knowing the subject and methods of teaching
X				VII	Good personal qualities: having wholesome effect on pupils

Figure 15 A teacher's ranking by fellow teachers *This chart shows how one teacher was ranked by his fellow teachers on the basis of seven criteria.*

he is a superior teacher—probably the best, or surely one of the best, in the school system.

It will be discovered that teachers vary in their standing, as evidenced by their being in different quarters of each item. Generally a teacher is consistently above or below average. The pattern of a teacher's rating is also fairly consistent; and on the basis of the general pattern and with most emphasis on items of personality value, teaching effectiveness, and cooperativeness, a teacher's position or quarter in the group can be determined.

INCENTIVES AND REWARDS FOR TEACHERS

We shall consider the socioeconomic status of the teacher in general terms in Chapter 9. But the status-related topics of incentives and rewards of teaching should be touched upon here as closely related to the personal and professional development of the teacher.

Does the teacher get special rewards for being superior? Does not a poor teacher get as much pay as a good one, and sometimes even more? Is it actually worthwhile for a teacher to try to grow personally and professionally?

Practically all the larger school systems have a salary scale, and a considerable number of them have a tenure system. The salary scale usually provides a minimum starting salary with annual increments until a maximum is reached, as well as more pay for those with more degrees or with specified numbers of credits beyond the bachelor's degree. Usually there is a three-year probationary period during which a teacher can be dropped merely by notification that he will not be reemployed; then a teacher receives tenure and can be dropped only after charges are made and full open hearing is held on them. Rarely is a teacher on tenure discharged.

The provision of more pay for more education does induce many teachers to work for the master's degree and beyond. Generally, though, the increase in pay is hardly commensurate with the amount of time and money a teacher spends in going to the university for this work. There are few if any financial rewards, moreover, for simply being a truly outstanding teacher. All in all, the individual teacher is paid pretty much according to the amount of formal schooling he has had and the length of time he has been in a school system.

There is a wide range in the competence and effectiveness of the teachers of any given staff. In schools with tenure and a salary scale it is not uncommon to have in adjoining classrooms a teacher who is clearly outstanding in guiding the activities of his students and a teacher who does very badly in dealing with his. In such cases, it also commonly happens that, because the inferior teacher has been in the system longer than the superior teacher, he is paid more.

The second teacher is a liability, and it is unfortunate for the school and the students that he has a teaching position. The worthy teacher is usually aware of the comparative merits of the other teacher; and this awareness, at least when a basically unfair salary situation is involved, lessens his motivation to do his very best. "What is the use? A liability gets as much pay or even more than an asset!" Without pay for merit, the superior teacher is not rewarded more than the mediocre teacher is, and the resulting tendency is to produce a common denominator of teaching proficiency.

Fortunately, there are other rewards than financial which motivate a teacher to do as well as he possibly can. The teacher wants the esteem of his colleagues and the reputation of being a good teacher. Then, too, even though the usual systems of tenure and salary scales work against the teacher's desire to develop personally and professionally, the minute-to-minute situations in his workday can stimulate him to do well. For instance, the good teacher enjoys the friendship and appreciation of his students. For 5 or 6 hours a day the teacher associates with his students; for the good teacher this contact is pleasant and gratifying, but for the unsuccessful teacher it is a source of strain.

A special reward that the good teacher receives is the satisfaction—the feeling of self-respect—that comes from having developed to a high level both personally and professionally. Such development is, indeed, one of any well-minded person's highest ideals.

An inquiry into the experiences and attitudes of teachers who had the reputation of being unusually successful indicated that the resolution of most difficulties and frustrations of teachers lies within themselves rather than in the school and the community. It was discovered that these successful teachers valued their schools and communities highly and were enthusiastic about them; nor were these teachers ambitious for other jobs. The elementary school teacher was not trying to become a high school teacher, the high school teacher a principal, the principal a superintendent. Each was happily and successfully concentrating his energies on his work rather than setting up frustrations by continuously trying to get a "better position."

COUNSELING FOR TEACHERS

The general indication was that if a teacher is clearly successful, many of the conditions that are considered oppressive and therefore damaging to mental health will be overcome.

The teacher must assume the responsibility for his own success and well-being. He needs to realize that he must adjust to financial rewards that fall within a fairly definite range. If the community is not friendly, possibly this is because he is not friendly. If he does not get along successfully in school, perhaps his own personal inadequacies are the cause. In some instances good friends can aid in overcoming such personal inadequacies. Discussing a problem often clarifies it, suggests solutions for it, or at least enables a friend to give helpful advice.

Sometimes, however, professional help may be required. When one lives with his troubles, he has mischievous companions which, although seemingly dormant, will cause distress and discomfort. A professional counselor not only can help in reaching the root of the trouble but can give the temporary support a troubled person needs. At some time or other, everyone needs someone to lean on.

By participating in group clinics, teachers often get the needed help for solving their personal and professional problems. Such group conferences ought to be guided by a psychologist, psychiatrist, or counselor who is skilled at group work and is aware of the problems of the teacher and his pupils. At these clinics, problems of personal relations are frankly discussed with an attempt to get at the dynamics of interpersonal strains and anxieties.

In the smaller communities, professional counselors may not be available, and then a trusted pastor or a physician should be consulted. In other instances group therapy might be tried. The difficulty about group procedures is to get the troubled teachers together. Who will initiate the meetings, and which teachers will join? Conceivably, as teachers gain more knowledge about personality they will understand better what to do. Group therapy is very tricky; but if teachers make a special study of it and proceed experimentally, they may be able to help each other.

Asyra L. Kadis describes a situation in which a teacher was frequently upset over one of her boy student's teasing of one of the girls in class and tells of her frustrations in trying to improve the relationships of those two students [Kadis, 1960]. In the clinic discussion, it was brought out that this teacher had been teased by her brother and that she had often become angry at him. Out of the discussion, understanding emerged which helped her to sublimate the unpleasant feelings and to cope with the teasing.

Generally many of the teacher's emotional reactions to problems have their roots in the background of her own experiences and frustrations. People need to understand their hostilities, guilt feelings, and traumatic experiences. Discussion may reveal the relationship between the teacher's own ego involvements and the situations she faces. Furthermore, consideration may be given to an effective mode of present-day living.

Many teachers, and especially single teachers, drift into a mode of living which is conducive to personality problems and ill health. These single teachers, by the time they have reached early middle age, have established a routine life characterized by withdrawal, monotony, and loneliness. Discussion groups of the kind mentioned can take up the problem of how one can program his living so it will be interesting and stimulating. Many teachers let intellectual rigor mortis set in; at these clinics they can discuss activities that will keep them mentally alive and, correspondingly, can suggest social programs. They can also outline the steps to take in order to achieve a better pattern of living. Many teachers need help to put more life into their years.

An annual health examination by school physicians or by private physicians who are sensitive to the physical and mental health problems of the teachers or of their "occupational hazards" will often catch health difficulties in their incipient stages. Many teachers, like a large number of other adults, develop organic and functional disorders which usually can be helped—or even prevented—by early detection and treatment.

☯ Reflect and Review

The following are short descriptions of some activities or practices of teachers. Evaluate them in terms of the personal and professional growth of the teacher.

Mr. Henry is a high school physics teacher who obtained a master's degree in physics before he was twenty-two years old. He has been teaching physics for 5 years and spends several hours a day experimenting and studying. He is working with one of his former college professors in preparing a high school physics text.

Mr. Jones belongs to the local Kiwanis Club. He is active in helping arrange the programs, and occasionally he and a few other members develop stunts or surprise activities which are highly entertaining. Mr. Jones participates in some community activities, especially in directing youth activities, such as scouts and sports.

Miss Leonard has been teaching English for 10 years. She probably does more reading than any other faculty member. She reads the significant literature in her field but does considerable general reading also. She is becoming recognized as an authority on Mark Twain and occasionally she writes an article for one of the English journals.

Miss Wright is usually present at school events—parties, plays, musicals, and athletic contests. She makes a point of speaking to the students, helping them with their problems, and praising them for their efforts. She probably knows more students than any other teacher.

Mr. Graves seems quietly busy and keeps his interests to himself. He does not share his ideas, experiences, or books with anyone. He takes the attitude that his ideas and ways of teaching are better than those of his colleagues. In fact, he shows little respect for the efforts of his fellow teachers and is critical of them.

Mrs. Hamilton is a real progressive. If there is something new in education, she wants to know about it. She therefore frequently requests the librarian to get new books, and as a consequence the professional library of the school has almost every book that Mrs. Hamilton can use. She goes to summer school at different universities about every fourth year and occasionally takes an evening course. She selects her courses very carefully. She puts her learning into practice, and in her teaching she tries this and that. Her students have been known to say, "There is no knowing what Mrs. Hamilton will do next, but it is exciting." Mrs. Hamilton says, "If I don't move ahead I'll get bumped off my intellectual feet and become a has-been."

What is good about the activities of these teachers?
What is not good about them?

SUMMARY

Teachers are both born and made, as their effectiveness depends on their inborn capacities plus the experiences they have had which are responsible for their personal and professional development.

The largest percentage of successful teachers will develop from students who are in the top quarter in both scholarship and social maturity, and the fewest from students in the lowest quarter in these respects.

In general, good scholarship, good personality, and good teaching go together; and the opposite is equally true.

Teachers need to be socially effective because they deal so extensively with people—students, their professional associates, and the public.

A teacher-rating scale can be used to determine how effective the individual teacher is and also to indicate to the teacher his strengths and weaknesses so he will learn what to do for self-improvement.

Most successful teachers have healthful social and recreational interests, but few neurotic and ineffective teachers do. The latter usually spend their out-of-school time on routine duties of one kind or another.

Being socially and intellectually effective is directly influenced by emotional and physical health. A fairly high proportion of teachers, ranging up to nearly one-half, at some time or another are handicapped by poor emotional health and consequent physical illness.

Behavior which is characteristic of maladjustment and predisposes a teacher to increasingly serious trouble is characterized by loneliness, extreme egocentricity, anxiety, impatience, and eccentricity.

There are a number of things a teacher can do to grow professionally and thereby personally too. He can take graduate courses, both academic and professional, and earn advanced degrees. He can attend and participate in conferences, conventions, and clinics. Probably of first importance is that he be an omnivorous reader. Teachers advance personally and professionally if they experiment and if they do professional and literary writing. Travel is usually invigorating and enlivening.

Teachers can be evaluated in terms of various criteria of professional vitality and effectiveness as a teacher.

In many situations there is little formal incentive to be a superior teacher, as pay is usually based on amount of formal education and years of service. However, rewards in the form of satisfied students, gratifying personal relationships, and a sense of worth from being successful are experienced by the good but not the poor teacher.

SUGGESTED READING

Buck, Roy C.: "The Extent of Social Participation among Public School Teachers," *Journal of Educational Sociology,* 33:311–319, 1960. Buck's study indicates that teachers participate extensively in community activities. Good discussion of the teacher's role as a social participant.

Goodacre, E. J.: "Teachers and the Socioeconomic Factor," *Educational Research,* 4:56–61, 1961. The periodical *Educational Research* is published in England. It is of interest to get an English point of view. The material of this article is of special interest and value to teachers in general.

Ryans, David G.: *Characteristics of Teachers,* American Council on Education, Washington, D.C., 1960. An extensive, sophisticated study of teacher behavior. Contains a wealth of material for understanding the effectiveness of teaching.

PART II
INDIVIDUAL DIFFERENCES

CHAPTER 6
INTELLIGENCE:
MEANING AND MEASUREMENT

"Joe made all A's this term. He is really smart. But I wouldn't have his personality for the world."

"Liz doesn't do well in school, but she takes a good commonsense view of things."

"George flunked algebra, but when it comes to tinkering with cars, he's a real professional."

All these remarks imply some judgment of mental capacity, but do they reflect sound concepts of what constitutes intelligence? What exactly do we mean when we say that a person is intelligent? Can we reasonably call Joe intelligent on the basis of his school grades and ignore the fact that his capacities for social skills seem to be of a low order? Is Liz really the intelligent one? Can we logically say that George is intelligent in mechanics but unintelligent in algebra?

Intelligence is such a complex subject that there is little agreement even among psychologists on its definition. Some definitions center on the effectiveness of the intellectual processes—perception, memory, reasoning, and imagination. Thus intelligence has been defined as the ability to do abstract thinking, as the capacity to learn, and as the ability to respond in terms of truth and fact. But it has also been called the ability to adjust to one's environment and has been given numerous other definitions.

In earlier chapters we have implicitly relied upon certain generally recognized standards of intelligence, for example, the idea that the child who learns quickly and who senses implications not obvious to everyone is bright and the child who fails in these regards is dull.

Now we must explore more fully the meaning of intelligence. In addition, we shall be centrally concerned in this chapter with how intelligence is measured—with the ways we have of making our appraisals of intelligence more precise through mental tests as the child becomes older and is confronted with school situations.

TOWARD A DEFINITION OF INTELLIGENCE

When Florence Brumbaugh asked the sixth-graders in the Hunter College Elementary School in New York to describe the brightest child in class, the following were some of the replies:[1]

"Is good at almost anything."
"Manages to finish what most of us can't."
"Most of his answers are right."
"Remembers easily."
"Thinks faster than the rest of us."
"Thinks out things logically."
"Can figure out examples that I do not know how to start."
"Remembers everything she hears."

It will be observed that the answers emphasized, by implication, the mental processes of comprehending (or perceiving), remembering, and reasoning. Imagination was left out. "Good at almost anything" and "know how" suggest wide general mental capacity. "Answers are right" corresponds with the concept that intelligence is indicated by responses in terms of truth and fact. "Finishes tasks" and "figures out examples" indicate power of mentality; "thinks fast" is indicative of the high speed associated with high mental power. "Remembers" refers, of course, to memory and implies comprehension. The children did very well in describing high academic capacity; they included most of the major features we shall discuss.

Most definitions of intelligence, like these children's, center on facility with ideas and concepts, most of which have an academic orientation and therefore involve words, numbers, formulas, and their meanings in the various fields of learning. Accordingly, intelligence is evaluated in terms of the facility of the mental processes in dealing with such abstract symbols.

Yet facility with the academic and abstract is not the whole of what can be defined as intelligence. Body skills, as well as facility with concrete materials, are included as standards of broader definitions; and some definitions emphasize any adjustment to new conditions or facility in solving new problems. All these considerations permit an interpretation of intelligence as including more of a person's behavior than that which involves only words and other abstract symbols.

A still more comprehensive definition of intelligence holds that a person is intelligent according to the effectiveness with which he relates to all the elements in his environment; a person's intelligence is evaluated according to how he deals generally with people, things, and ideas. Thus the element of social—or, more properly, social-emotional—intelligence is added.

[1] Florence Brumbaugh, "What Is an I.Q.?," *Journal of Experimental Education*, 23:359–363, 1955.

Often, the good qualities that comprise these definitions go together; for instance, often an individual with good abstract intelligence also has good social understanding, and a person with high mechanical intelligence is likely to be above average in abstract intelligence. But a person may be intelligent in some respects and not in others, of course. He may be very intelligent in mathematics but be a fool with money or a dullard with tools. If a brilliant architect is so egocentric that he alienates his friends, his behavior is certainly not very intelligent. A child may be a good student but be so full of unreasonable anxiety and conflicts that he is unhappy and ineffective much of the time. No matter how intelligent they may be in some respects, such persons are not uniformly so. At the same time, it is impossible, in studying how an individual functions, to separate the mental, social, and other elements of his behavior. Therefore it is useful to evaluate all of a person's behavior to determine the nature and extent of his intelligence.

Accordingly, the term intelligence applies to all behavior, and a person's intelligence is determined by how effectively he deals with situations. Thus there will be little reluctance in granting that postwar economic policies in West Germany were the products of very intelligent minds or that anyone who can write as well as Shakespeare is exceptionally intelligent; but if a batter scores four runs by hitting a home run with three on base and wins the game and some one says, "That was a very intelligent thing to do," those who hear the remark may wonder about that use of the term "intelligent." Nevertheless, such a statement is reasonable, given a broad view of intelligence. At present, however it is very unlikely that anyone will develop a single test for assessing the principal areas of human behavior. We shall continue to use tests for specific abilities and on the basis of these tests shall judge academic, musical, social, clerical, typing, athletic, and other aptitudes.

Adjustment. Let us insert a word of caution here—a word of caution necessitated by taking a broad definition of intelligence as our study base. As we have seen, some descriptions of intelligence include the idea that it may be judged by how effectively a person adjusts to his environment. But what does adjustment mean here?

Some think adjustment means adapting oneself to, and getting along in, the situation as it is. But a broader, more comprehensive concept is required, one which includes the adjusting or improving of the situation in which a person finds himself. In other words, adjustment requires that people do all they can to make a favorable environment for themselves and that they control themselves in order to be more effective in their environment. To the degree that people do both, adjustment indicates intelligence.

All through history people have lived as best they could under tyranny and poverty, but they have struggled to obtain greater freedom and more material welfare. In places where there is little rainfall, the farmers have raised sheep rather than plant corn, but they also have built dams and irrigated semiarid lands. Both students and teachers try to live with any bad situation they may have in the classroom, but they work cooperatively to develop better situations. Intelligent people are ingenious both in fitting themselves to their situations and in improving their circumstances.

Classifying Our Capacities and Abilities. In describing intelligence as involving effective behavior in several areas, it is not valid to make complete distinctions between the areas, for they are interrelated. Thus there is an abstract thought component in most motor, mechanical, and social activities. But it is useful to speak discretely of capacities and abilities in each of the areas of intelligence.

Capacity or any of its equivalent terms—aptitude, talent, and potential—indicates the promise a person has in any field of activity. We speak of academic potential, mechanical aptitude, musical talent, social capacity, and so forth. Ability, on the other hand, is manifested by actual performance. A person's baseball abilities are indicated by what he can actually do in baseball: catch, bat, throw, run bases, etc. A person's abilities in a language are indicated by his actual abilities to read, write, and speak that language. Also a person may have capacities but no abilities because he has not learned. The boys and girls of Louisiana probably have as much capacity for ice skating as the boys and girls of Canada, but they do not have the ability to ice-skate that the Canadians have because they have not learned how.

There is no one test that is satisfactory for indicating individual capacity in all these various areas. What has been called the general intelligence test is actually an aptitude test for the various academic subjects and thus for capacity with abstract materials. A great many unnecessary difficulties in the field of education might have been avoided if such "general intelligence" tests had been called academic or school aptitude tests, incidentally. But various aptitude and ability tests have been devised which do measure other capacities, and there are other means of determining these.

A person is said to have little capacity, aptitude, talent, or potential for a given activity when, after earnest effort, he has acquired few abilities in that activity. For example, every boy, with very few exceptions, has had a number of opportunities to play baseball, basketball, and other games. Some continue to be poor in these games because they have little aptitude for athletics; others make rapid progress and become good players because they have high aptitude. Similarly, quick success in academic subjects indicates a student's aptitudes for them. Prime indication of capacity, of course, is the age at which a child shows his abilities. Children who learn to walk early, who know how to read before they start school, who do anything at younger-than-average age are demonstrating high capacity.

Let us, then, appraise the various areas of intelligence through considering the various capacities and abilities which comprise or contribute to them.

Facility with the Abstract. The capacity required for dealing with the materials generally found in the academic curriculum is termed "abstract intelligence." It is an aptitude for learning to read; for working problems expressed in words, numbers, and other symbols, including symbols of spatial relations; and for memorizing verbal content. In general, abstract intelligence is the capacity that expresses itself in effective behavior with such abstract materials.

The first evidence of such functioning of the mind is that it perceives or comprehends. Since the mind also remembers what it perceives, memory is also an essential factor of intelligence. The active processes of intelligence then consist in the use of the abstract materials in reasoning. Thus intelligence varies from person to person with the capacity to perceive, and remember, and with the effective use of the abstract materials involved in reasoning and in creative thinking.

This type of intelligence, also sometimes called "verbal" intelligence, is important for doing well in school, for it is necessary for success in arithmetic, geography, history, and the other academic subjects; and it is most essential for those entering occupations requiring extended formal schooling. Thus it is possessed in abundance by the successful professor and scholar, the fluent writer and speaker; and in general, those who are best endowed with abstract intelligence usually move toward the top of the vocational hierarchy, while the poorest endowed find themselves at the bottom. But beyond vocational considerations, during all of adult life abstract intelligence provides fundamental personal capital used by us all almost constantly in handling our own affairs.

In this area, the intelligence of a person can be measured by the difficulty of the academic tasks that he can do; and the difficulty of tasks is determined by the percentage of people in a specified group who can do them. For instance, in the case of twelve-year-old children, the easiest arithmetic problems, are those which all can solve, and the hardest are those which none or very few can solve. The relative degrees of difficulty of the hard items can be determined by giving them to older children and to adults. Thus the child who can do the most of the tasks in which his peers generally fail is the most intelligent.

The altitude, or power, of a person's abstract intelligence, or intellect, is determined by the most difficult tasks that he can do; its width, or range, is determined by the number of tasks that he can perform at each level of difficulty. The area, or spaciousness, of the intellect is then determined by its altitude and its width.

There is a close correspondence between altitude and width; the person who can reach a high altitude of performance can usually do more at each level than a person who cannot. For example, the twelve-year-old who can work arithmetic problems missed by 95 per cent of twelve-year-olds can do more than his average age-mate can of the easier arithmetic problems that are missed by only a few twelve-year-olds.

This outstanding twelve-year-old can also do the easier tasks faster. Indeed, at the low levels of difficulty, tasks do not satisfactorily differentiate the dull from the bright children unless the speed of performance is measured.

Let us refine our definition of altitude, or power, in order to relate it to this other very important intellectual factor—speed. Power is determined by the difficulty or complexity of the task a person can do when he is given all the time he needs. Power indicates the ability to perform mental tasks such as following directions, solving problems, memorizing, defining words, seeing relationships, and integrating a whole out of parts when plenty of time is given. Speed refers to the quickness with which one can do these things. The tasks and exercises used to determine power generally range from relatively easy to very difficult; the tasks which test speed are only moderately difficult for the person being tested.

Power and speed are related in that a person is ordinarily quick in accomplishing tasks because of his high mental power. A person of high intellectual power can do most tasks easily and therefore rapidly, although he will do much more slowly the tasks of a difficulty near the limit of his intellectual power. An exception to this general relationship of speed and power exists in some children and adults of high mental capacity who are deliberative in their nature and are so constituted emotionally that when they are put under pressure to work rapidly they do so very poorly. Speed tests, which are often used in school, are harassing to pupils of this nature. These are the students who on first look may seem less capable than the flashy speedster but who on the job work deliberately and in the end do more work and do it better.

Tests seem to engender anxiety in some students and thereby cut down their efficiency. Irwin G. Sarason took an inventory of college students' anxieties and correlated anxiety scores with results on intelligence and achievement tests [Sarason, 1957]. Small but consistent negative correlations of −.09 to −.30 between test scores and anxiety scores were obtained, thus indicating either that those who had less capacity tended to be more anxious and those who had more capacity tended to be less anxious or that being anxious reduced individual effectiveness in taking the test.

Mechanical and Motor Intelligence. Two closely related aspects of intelligence are reflected in the capacity for dealing with situations involving palpable external objects and the aptitude for efficient and strong use of one's own body—the mechanical and motor capacities, respectively.

The boy who is apt at handling tools, taking a clock apart and putting the parts together, or repairing an automobile, radio, or television set has a high order of mechanical intelligence. He is successful in solving problems involving concrete, or objective, materials. The person who can execute difficult dance steps, do acrobatic stunts, juggle balls, throw and catch a ball skillfully, dodge quickly and play several physical games well, or generally handle his body with grace and skill has a high order of motor intelligence. In the field of physical education, such a person is said to have outstanding motor abilities, that is, physical or athletic skills.

At the other extreme is the very awkward person who seems to be all thumbs, as we say. Since he has very little aptitude for athletics and other physical activities, he usually has no interest in taking part in them, although he may have great admiration for those who do. Most people fall roughly midway between the extremes in motor abilities, as they do in most measurable human characteristics.

As we saw in Chapter 1, tests have been devised for measuring motor capacity. There are also tests of mechanical aptitude. The latter generally involve assembling the parts of a mechanical device, such as a mousetrap, doorbell, three-piece clothespin, or bicycle bell. Mechanical-assembly tests have been used extensively with school children in connection with industrial courses.

The correlation between the capacity measured by mechanical-assembly tests and abstract intelligence is comparatively low, although certain mechanical abilities involve a large component of abstract knowledge, as is evidenced by the achievements of engineers, inventors, surgeons, dentists, and some other professional men. Some motor skills do not require much abstract ability. A person may be an outstanding athlete, for example, and yet underaverage in abstract abilities, thus illustrating that the ability to manage one's body skillfully may be distinct from abstract intelligence.

The correlation between abstract mental abilities as measured by the usual mental tests and the abilities measured by mechanical-assembly tests usually is found within the range from .20 to .35. Correlation between abstract intelligence and mechanical knowledge and mechanical reasoning will be higher—usually between .40 and .60. When mechanical abilities involve the perception of form and relationships (as found in gears, levers, and cylinders), a large symbol component is involved and then the correlation with general mental abilities will be higher—sometimes as high as .60 or .65.

The correlation between the simpler motor abilities, as indicated by dexterity of the fingers and hand, and general mental ability is typically about zero, sometimes slightly positive and sometimes slightly negative, depending on the tests used and the group tested. In general, however, those who are above or below the average in general mental ability are about equal in the simpler motor skills, as indicated by quickness, accuracy, and steadiness of fingers and hand.

The Socially Intelligent Person. A person who can deal well, or behave effectively, with people has good social intelligence. The small-town businessman who is cordial, helpful, and friendly and whom the people like and therefore trade with has a high capacity for social relationships. The teacher whom students have confidence in and are fond of and who gets along well with his fellow teachers is well developed socially. The student who works and plays well with others and is a leader in school activities has good social qualities. On the other hand, many persons fail in life because of poor social intelligence—probably more than the number who fail because of inadequate abstract intelligence. A person of high abstract intelligence has the mental capacity for knowing how to deal effectively with others but still may not do so. There are many inconsistencies between social and abstract intelligence because there are a number of elements in social abilities that are not abstract in nature. Personal traits are more closely related to, if not an integral part of, social intelligence. A person's temperament and attitudes, honesty, judgment, humor, friendliness, and degree of freedom from jealousy are all important factors in determining how well he will get along with others. Finally, a person of high social ability is usually in good physical health. People in poor physical health usually lack the vitality for participating effectively in social activities. Also a person who does not feel good is so preoccupied with his health problems that he is not companionable.

A study of 1,015 school children of grades 4 through 6 yielded striking information about social characteristics. The top 10 per cent in social leadership, artistic talent, and intellectual ability as well as the top 10 per cent for aggressive maladjustment and withdrawn maladjustment were given special study. Gordon Liddle, who conducted the study, used sociometric methods whereby teachers and students chose both the most maladjusted and those highest in leadership ability [Liddle, 1958]. Artistic talent was determined by having professional artists judge four drawings of each of the pupils. Intellectual abilities were determined by a number of intelligence tests.

Those who were maladjusted were low in social abilities, and those high in social leadership were low in maladjustment. Of 104 students who were in the top 10 per cent for social leadership, 45 were also in the highest 10 per cent intellectually, 31 were in the highest 10 per cent in artistic talent, and none was found in the two maladjusted areas. Social leadership is incompatible with maladjustment but compatible with high intellectual and artistic abilities.

Of the 107 who were in approximately the top 10 per cent in mental ability, 78 were found in the top 10 per cent in either social leadership or artistic ability and 6 were found among the 10 per cent who were most maladjusted. Thus there are among the brightest thirteen times as many who are social leaders and artistically able as are judged to be the most maladjusted of the students.

Of the 102 who were in approximately the top 10 per cent in artistic talent, 64 were in the top 10 per cent in either social leadership or mental ability. There were 12 of these top artistic-ability students among the most maladjusted. The ratio here is over 5 to 1 in favor of the best artists' being tops in either social leadership or mental ability rather than being among the most maladjusted 10 per cent of their group. Thus it seems that being desirably high in one respect is much more often associated with being high in another desirable respect and reduces greatly the probability of being maladjusted.

☯ Reflect and Review

Young John J. has a very good mind, as his colleagues on a college teaching staff put it. For advanced students, he is regarded as one of the most stimulating teachers in the college. He is very alert mentally, his fund of knowledge is unusually large, and the ideas he expresses in and out of his classes show that he has the power of penetrating deeply into his subject.

But socially he is a different man. At times he is charming; but if crossed a bit, he becomes disagreeable; often he loses his temper. He does not have the capacity to meet people with consistent cordiality. His circle of friends is small, and its members change often; hardly anyone remains a friend very long.

John's mechanical and motor abilities are poor. He has engaged in sports very little. He handles his automobile so poorly that it often needs mechanical attention, and he cannot then make even the simplest repairs and adjustments.

Next door to John lives William S., whose neighbors think of him as a good all-round fellow; they say he understands what is going on. William, who is the head of a department in a large store, did excellent scholastic work in his student days and also learned to play several musical instruments. These abilities, of course, call for both abstract and motor skills since abstract intelligence is required in order to understand and interpret the written music, and motor and mechanical abilities are involved in manipulating the keys or strings. William also knows how to deal with motors. When, on a fishing trip, his outboard motor was not working very well, he took it apart and cleaned, reassembled, and adjusted it, after which it operated perfectly. He is a good shot with both rifle and shotgun, and he can play a good game of tennis, baseball, or basketball.

William has many friends who visit him at his home and whom he calls on. Those who work under his supervision at the store have better morale than exists in most of its departments.

What is John J.'s strong area of capacity? Which of his two areas of weakness is more destructive of his personal happiness? How does this weak area frustrate other persons in his case?

Is William S. a man of many dimensions?

How would you expect these two men to feel toward each other? In activities related to which area of capacity might they find the best grounds for friendship? Explain your answer.

Imagination, Creativeness, and Originality. Probably the highest aspect of abstract intelligence is to be found in imaginative, original, and creative work; the lowest, in the mere imitation of simple activities. The musician who composes masterpieces is much more intelligent than the person who beats out a simple rhythm on the drum. The man who can discover important chemical reactions is more intelligent than the person who can understand simple formulas. Of course, it takes high intelligence just to understand advanced science, but the scholars who discovered and developed its concepts had even higher intelligence.

The term "genius" is used to designate the people who exhibit creativeness, inventiveness, and originality in various forms of productivity and outstanding performance in music, literature, science, mechanics, and other areas of knowledge. There is a range of genius from minor ones to those who are world-famous for what they have done.

It should be pointed out that people with very high standing on intelligence tests and consequently with high intelligence quotients are not necessarily geniuses, because they are not necessarily creative. Still, people who are original and inventive have high intelligence quotients. In addition, they have that special intellectual capacity for creativeness which is not measured by mental tests. In fact, there are no accepted tests for measuring creativeness. Efforts are being made to develop them, but the probabilities of being successful are small simply because people of genius are extremely rare. Special interest also centers on how to develop originality and creativeness at various intellectual levels. Only a few will reach the genius level, but many can learn to be original in an effective way if the emotional climate and intellectual stimulation are conducive to it. Instead of rewarding students for conforming intellectually and thereby regimenting them, the schools can encourage the students to try multiple methods and solutions. Many students show special mechanical, collecting, and exploratory interests; and if these activities are reinforced, they can lead to individual creativity.

That this is evidently not done in many cases has been shown (see Table 7) by J. L. Holland, who studied the traits and the high school grades of 984 students who reached the finals of the National Merit Scholarship Qualifying Test and who had shown concrete evidence of high scientific or artistic achievement on the high school level [Holland, 1961]. Awards, prizes, or publications were considered to be evidence of productive achievement. The students were evaluated according to 72 criteria, on the basis of several tests, self-ratings, and teacher ratings.

Holland found that on this level there was a negligible relationship between academic aptitude and creative performance (but that was to be expected because all this group had very high capacity). However, it further appeared that the creativeness of many of these students was actually a liability in school. Curiosity, for example, which is an important element in creativity, was negatively correlated with high school grades. Holland concluded that

Table 7 Correlations* between Academic and Creative Performance and Aptitude, Personality, and Background Variables for Boys†

Variable		Creative Performance		High School Grades
		Scientific	Artistic	
1. Initiative	Ghiselli Self-description Inventory	.11‡	.07	−.02
2. Self-assurance		.09§	.12‡	.11‡
3. Physical activity		.18‡	−.04	.02
4. Intellectuality	Vocational	.23‡	.03	.07
5. Responsibility	Preference	−.17‡	.20‡	.05
6. Verbal activity	Inventory	−.10§	.11‡	.00
7. Emotionality		−.05	.31‡	.02
8. Independence		.15§	.20‡	.06
9. Self-confidence	Self-ratings	.10§	.23‡	.13‡
10. Perseverance		.11‡	.15‡	.27‡
11. Citizenship		.00	.09§	.26‡
12. Popularity	Teacher ratings	.01	.05	.17‡
13. Social leadership		.00	.10§	.19‡

* It is suggested that the reader consult the Appendix for the meanings of correlation and significance.
† $N = 649$.
‡ Significant at the .01 level.
§ Significant at the .05 level.
Source: Adapted from J. L. Holland, "Creative and Academic Performance among Talented Adolescents," *Journal of Educational Psychology*, 52:136–147, 1961.

creative high school students tend to be independent, intellectual, expressive, asocial, consciously original, and ambitious, in contrast to high academic achievers, who tend to be more persevering, sociable, responsible, and governed by authoritarian parents. Holland also suggested that efforts should be made to construct measures of creativity, in view of the fact that current achievement tests tend to penalize the creative student.

The person who is original and creative has high basic capacities which it is doubtful that education or training can give. Still, a large proportion of very bright people do not manifest much originality and creativeness. Conceivably, more of them would be productive if their experiences had encouraged them toward this rather than led them to learn in given ways and to fit their intelligence into restricted patterns and procedures.

☯ Consider the Data

Based on Table 7

This table shows a few of the results from a study by J. L. Holland of the traits of 984 national merit finalists who showed concrete evidence of outstanding scientific or artistic creative activity while in high school. Holland studied both boys and girls and drew up correlations for 72 variables; Table 7 is merely a sampling of some of the more significant correlations.

Which traits are significantly correlated with high school marks but of only slight importance to creativity?

Which traits are important elements in creativity but evidently not important for obtaining good high school marks?

What are the differences in the traits required for scientific and artistic achievement? (Note particularly items 5 and 7.)

MEASURING THE MIND

In turning to a consideration of mental testing we must realize that by the very nature of their work, teachers must be aware of the development of their students' abstract intelligence and so must have a special concern with how their students differ in it.

Therefore we shall follow, in two ways, the lead of psychologists who have tested for educational purposes: Our study of the testing of the mind will center on measurement of facility with abstract materials; and when we say "mental capacity," "mental test," or "intelligence," we shall primarily mean "the mind's capacity for dealing with symbols," "test of abstract intelligence," and "abstract intelligence," respectively.

Development of Individual Intelligence Tests. Differences in the abstract mental capacities of students, and problems arising from these differences, have always confronted the teacher; thus psychologists and educators recognized the need for accurate mental tests even before the beginning of this century. They have had enough success in measuring people's mental capacities that it has become a common practice. Many applicants for positions in the government service and in private industry are given intelligence tests. However, these tests are used most extensively in the schools, where they serve as a very helpful basis for student guidance as well as teaching.

The distinguished American psychologist James McKeen Cattell in the 1890s developed a series of exercises by means of which he hoped to test mental capacity, including tests of quickness in naming 10 colors, strength of grip, ability to bisect a 50-centimeter line, and speed of arm movement. These exercises, however, mostly tested sensorimotor abilities and generally failed to measure the abstract mental processes such as perception, memory, and reasoning. Cattell discovered that there was no relationship between the abilities of college students as demonstrated by these tests and their academic success in college. He assumed that ability to learn in school is a general indication of mental capacity and concluded that because the measured abilities did not correlate with school ability, these tests did not measure intelligence.

It remained for the Frenchman Alfred Binet to develop a scale that was actually a mental test—the first successful individual examination of mental abilities and thus indirectly of mental capacities.

Binet was asked by the school authorities of Paris to work out a method for identifying the dull pupils. The schools were troubled by problems connected with the failures of retarded children to do schoolwork, and a system of judging their capacities for it was needed.

Alfred Binet, with the help of his colleague Theodore Simon, worked for over a decade at this problem. He set out to test the complex mental powers rather than the sensorimotor abilities which others, particularly in the newly established psychology laboratories of that time, had tested. He devised problems and exercises to test comprehension, memory, power of making comparisons, ability to draw conclusions, and other mental abilities.

Binet also made use of the fact that mental growth accompanies increasing age, showing itself in the ability to do more difficult tasks or in greater success with the same tasks. He arranged his tests in a scale of age levels, determining difficulty of the tests by the percentages of children of various given ages who passed each one.

In 1905 the examination, which consisted of 30 separate test items, was published. But Binet continued to rework his scale, bringing forth a revision in 1908 and another in 1911, the year of his death. This last revision, which included more tests than the earlier versions, could be used for testing subjects ranging in age from three years to adulthood. The test exercises were also graded according to age, and the mental-age concept was introduced with this revision. Passing all the tests of any given year level gave one year of mental age; thus the mental age credited depended on the number of tests passed at the various age levels. Inasmuch as the tests were graded according to difficulty, if a child could pass all the tests of year seven, for example, he was given credit for all the previous years. In testing a child, effort was made to start at the highest year level where the child could pass all the tests.

The Binet-Simon Scale was introduced to the United States by H. H. Goddard, who translated and adapted the 1908 scale and the 1911 revision for use at the institution for the mentally retarded at Vineland Training School, Vineland, New Jersey. Here, again, the test was first used on the retarded— a fact that may account for some of the prejudice that has existed against mental examinations in general.

Individual Intelligence Scales in the United States. The individual mental examination that has been used most in the United States is the Stanford revision of the Binet scale originally formulated by the late Lewis M. Terman, then a professor at Stanford University. His first test was published in 1916. Terman and M. A. Merrill published a revision consisting of two tests, or comparable forms, in 1937 and a new single-form revision in 1960. This is essentially the same as the 1937 revision, but a number of refinements have been made on the basis of the extensive experience with the 1937 version. Both are designed to test downward to the age level of two and upward to the most superior adult. The problems are assigned to children's age and adult's superiority levels according to difficulty.

The subject matter of the 1960 revision by Terman and Merrill calls for identifying objects (for young children), defining words, repeating digits, extracting the thought of passages, working arithmetic problems, seeing similarities and differences, detecting absurdities, interpreting proverbs, and giving general information.

Two other widely used individual tests, the Wechsler Intelligence Scale for Children and the Wechsler Adult Intelligence Scale, contain verbal materials not very different from those in the Terman-Merrill tests. But Wechsler makes more extensive use of nonverbal material. Such activities as completing and arranging pictures, organizing blocks according to designs, and assembling objects such as manikins, faces, and animals from their parts (as in jigsaw puzzles) are included in the Wechsler scales. Wechsler has also developed a method for scoring the tests that is different from the Terman-Merrill method and has introduced an improved method of calculating the IQs of older subjects.

Group Tests. The Binet-Simon, Terman-Merrill, and Wechsler tests are all individual tests; that is, they can be given to only one person at a time. As such, they pose practical problems. The individual examination is a satisfactory test of mental capacity, but it usually takes more than an hour to test a child, score his answers, and calculate his mental age and intelligence quotient. Therefore, it has long seemed highly desirable to have reliable intelligence tests that can be taken by a roomful of students at one time, and much work has been done in developing such tests, which are known as group tests. The usual group intelligence test consists of a booklet with several sections, each devoted to a different kind of exercise such as word meaning, sentence meaning, verbal analogies, space relations, arithmetic problems, and others. Each section is usually headed by directions and practice exercises. The person administering the tests can guide an auditorium full of students, each of whom has a test booklet, by giving general directions and specific ones for each part of the test, which is carefully timed. It is obvious that group tests cannot be used with students until they are old enough to read the directions and the various test exercises.

When the United States entered the First World War in 1917, a number of American psychologists were already working on developing group intelligence tests. War caused them to utilize these efforts in preparing group tests known as the Army Alpha and Army Beta, which were used for discovering the mental abilities of American soldiers. Results stimulated the construction of other tests, so that within a few years after the close of the war many group tests for children and youth had been prepared. During the 1920s, torrents of group mental tests poured from the presses, and the psychological and educational journals contained hundreds of articles based on their use. These were prolific years for standardized tests.

The use of group mental tests has persisted, and a considerable number of them have come to be used extensively. During the period of the Second World War, for instance, the Army General Classification Test, AGCT, was given to over 10 million members of the Armed Forces. A revised form is now being used. The general classification test, like the Army Alpha before it, has proved very useful for making a quick and fairly dependable assessment of the mental capacities of those tested. The results have been used, along with other information, for assigning members of the Armed Forces to the training and responsibilities for which they are most suited.

Group intelligence tests include exercises for measuring the following:

extent of vocabulary, reading ability, ability to solve arithmetical problems, ability to complete sentences, and knowledge of general information. Thus they test comprehension, ability to perceive differences and similarities, ability to think in terms of space and form, ability to see logical relationships, judgment, common sense, memory, etc. Most of the items are verbal in nature, although numbers, figures, geometrical forms, and pictures are used.

Mental Age and Intelligence Quotient. In developing an intelligence test, the test maker assembles and arranges the materials that he wants to include in his test, but he does not have a dependable instrument until he establishes norms, or standards, for it. To do this, he must administer his test to many representative children of the ages for which it is designed in order to discover the average scores for children of these different ages. These average scores are the norms for these ages. The average score for six-year-olds will represent a mental age (MA) of six; that for seven-year-olds, a mental age of seven. Indeed, the developer of a mental test generally provides a manual containing norms expressed in years and months, such as 6 years 1 month, 6 years 2 months, and so forth.

These average scores, or norms, are used to determine any tested child's mental age. Then his intelligence quotient (IQ) is calculated. Specifically, his mental age, revealed by the manual of norms for the intelligence test, is divided by his chronological age (CA) to give his IQ.

Let us illustrate this: A boy 8 years 1 month old who is given an intelligence test obtains a score that is the average score for children 10 years 2 months old. Thus this child has an MA of 10 years 2 months. Knowing his CA and his MA, we can determine his brightness, which is expressed in terms of the IQ. The formula for IQ is:

$$IQ = \frac{MA}{CA} \times 100$$

In this example,

$$IQ = \frac{10 \text{ years 2 months}}{8 \text{ years 1 month}} \times 100$$

$$IQ = \frac{122 \text{ months}}{97 \text{ months}} \times 100 = 126$$

The IQ indicates the rate of mental growth of a child. An IQ of 126 indicates that this child has grown mentally at the average rate of 1.26 years for each calendar year. Thus the mental growth of this child has been more rapid than normal. The purpose of the 100 in the formula is to get rid of the decimal point. If this child's rate of mental growth had been just average, the mental age would have equaled the chronological age and the IQ would have been 100. To use this example in a slightly different way, if we had started by knowing just this child's IQ and CA, we could have obtained his MA as follows:

$$MA = \frac{IQ \times CA}{100}$$

$$MA = \frac{126 \times 97 \text{ months}}{100}$$

$$MA = 122 \text{ months}$$

We can, of course, make similar calculations for a child whose mentality is lower than average. For example, take a girl who is 12 years 4 months (148 months) old but whose performance on a mental test is equal to that of the average of children 8 years 10 months (106 months) old, so that her MA is 106 months.

$$IQ = \frac{106}{148} \times 100 = 72$$

This child has grown mentally at a rate that is only about 72 per cent of the average for all children. It has taken her 12 years 4 months to reach a mental level of 8 years 10 months. By indicating the rate of mental growth, the IQ provides a convenient index of the relative brightness of age-mates. An eight-year-old child, for instance, whose mental growth is characterized by an IQ of 125 is obviously brighter than one with an IQ of 75. The former eight-year-old has reached the mental level of an average ten-year-old, whereas the latter eight-year-old is equal to the average six-year-old.

For senior high school and college students, however, there are complications in determining mental ages and intelligence quotients from scores on mental tests. The problem arises principally out of the difficulty of deciding what CA to use in the denominator. During the late teens, mental capacity increases much more slowly than it has previously, and thus the ratio between MA and CA is violently altered. The concept of MA is thus not useful for normal adults. Some tests use fifteen and sixteen as the CA for those past these ages, but better than trying to obtain an IQ in the usual way is to refer to the student's percentile standing on the national norms of college aptitude tests. The percentile standing of a student indicates the percentage of students who established the norms who are below him. If an IQ score is wanted for high school and college students, an earlier IQ score can be obtained from their permanent grade and junior high school records. Comparison of these records with percentile standing enables an experienced mental tester to judge the present IQs of the older youths and adults fairly accurately. For some tests the IQ equivalent of the scores which late teenagers and adults obtain have been worked out. Thus the scores of teen-agers of eighteen, for example, have their IQ equivalent which can be looked up in a booklet of norms. Therefore the IQs of adults and near-adults is obtainable in this way.

Children may have the same IQ but differ in their MA because they vary in CA. Obviously, two children eight and twelve years old, each with an IQ of 100, are not equal mentally. The older child can comprehend more than the younger, not because he is brighter, but because in living longer he has reached a higher mental age. In 4 years, the eight-year-old child will have reached the mental age that the twelve-year-old now has, that is, he will have essentially the same mental capacity. Potentially they are equal; and when both of them reach maturity, they will have essentially the same capacity for learning. It is assumed, of course, that their IQ, or rate of mental growth, will remain essentially as it is, which is a reasonable assumption for most students. Two bright children of the same IQ but different CAs differ more in MA than in CA. Thus two children with IQs of 135 whose respective ages are eight and twelve years have mental ages of 10 years 10 months ($1.35 \times$ 96 months) and 16 years 2 months (1.35×144 months), respectively. This MA difference, 5 years 4 months, exceeds the CA difference. But if the children had IQs of 60, the mental ages would be 4 years 10 months ($0.60 \times$ 96 months) and 7 years 2 months (0.60×144 months), respectively. The two children would differ 4 years chronologically but only 2 years 4 months in mental age. Children who vary in both CA and IQ may be found, when measured by the same intelligence test, to be of the same MA; their scores on the mental test are the same. The younger pupils in this instance are brighter; the older are duller. For example, an eight-year-old boy with an IQ of 125 and a twelve-year-old boy with an IQ of $83\frac{1}{3}$ both have the MA of ten; in other words, both do as well on the intelligence test as the average child who is ten years old.

Will these students of the same MA achieve equally well if placed in the same grade? The likelihood is that for a short time the older pupil will probably do slightly better in the academic subjects though he is duller, because he has been in school more years and consequently has had more teaching. Furthermore, teaching is usually adjusted to the average and below-average rather than to the bright. In the nonacademic activities such as manual training, sewing, and penmanship, moreover, the older pupil with the lower IQs definitely can be expected to show greater skill than the younger brighter pupil with the same MA. The implications of these facts as they relate to ability grouping will be discussed more fully in Chapter 8.

❂ *Reflect and Review*

Six children live together in a foster home: Bill, who is exactly 18 years old; Alex, exactly 11 years old; Ronnie, 10 years 8 months old; Marie, 10 years 3 months; Tom, 9 years 9 months; and Joan, 9 years 4 months.

Their foster parents need to establish their respective IQs. The five youngest children are given the same intelligence test.

Marie's score is the one which is average for children twelve years old. What is her IQ?

Alex makes the same score on the test as Marie. What is his IQ?

Ronnie's score is also the same as Marie's. What is his mental age?

Joan and Tom make identical scores on the test. Which one has the higher IQ? Can you determine whether Tom's mental age is lower than, higher than, or the same as Marie's?

How should Bill's IQ be determined? Assuming his mental capacity to be developing normally, how might his IQ rating be distorted if he took an IQ test and his real chronological age were used in calculating his IQ?

Validity of Intelligence Tests. Although psychologists use the term intelligence to designate the capacities that are measured by the use of intelligence tests, these tests do not measure capacity or aptitude directly. Rather, they do so by measuring extremely important mental abilities which reflect the effectiveness of the mental processes. The devisers of intelligence tests assume that these various mental abilities are an index to a person's general mental capacity.

How good an assumption is this? How valid are intelligence tests?

Some evidence of the validity of intelligence tests is to be found in the fact that success in these tests corresponds fairly strongly with success in school. The correlation between intelligence-test scores and school marks is usually about .50. Moreover, those who have most ability, according to these tests, tend to continue longest in school; and those who show the lowest ability tend to drop out earliest in their school careers. Incidentally, there is also a positive correlation between teachers' estimates of the brightness of their pupils and the IQs of the students, as determined by these mental tests. The correlation is about .50.

But why is there not a perfect correlation between intelligence test scores and academic success?

The answer is that, although these tests measure students' potential for doing schoolwork, they do not completely show what the individual student will do. For many reasons, some students do not do as well in school as they are able to; the most common one is lack of motivation and of conscientious effort. On the other hand, some pupils who have low capacity according to the tests achieve fairly well or better than might be expected because of unusual diligence and application.

These inconsistencies do not mean that intelligence tests indicate little or nothing. The tests indicate fairly well the mental potentialities of the individual children. The important thing is just to realize that mental tests cannot be expected to indicate the degree to which children are industrious and utilize their capacities. Because of their differing experiences, children, like adults, vary greatly in their drives and ambitions. The problem of the school here is not with the tests. Rather, the tests can be used to reveal differences between potentiality and performance and thus to help stimulate and guide children to perform and achieve. Our schools will doubtless always fail with some children; some will always be underachievers, but if the schools try in many ways to adapt their educational methods and content to the differences in the aptitudes of individual children, they will succeed much better than they do at present.

Finally, the fact that, among adults, vocational status and ability in these tests are closely related suggests the tests have validity. Empirically, we know that the professions call for a much higher order of mental ability than does unskilled labor. In general, occupations are classified with the professions at one end of the scale and unskilled labor at the other according to the amount of intelligence needed by the members of these occupations.

The Army General Classification Test, which is in effect a general mental ability test, was used extensively in the Second World War to test the United States soldiers. The scores for 227 occupations were analyzed and found to show a wide range for each occupation. Exhibit 9 illustrates the hierarchy of occupations according to average scores on the AGCT.

Achievement Tests and Academic Aptitude. After children have been in school a few years, a comprehensive standardized achievement, or educational, test seems to be as good a test of their academic, or "general," intelligence and thus of their capacity to learn, as the usual intelligence test. Such a comprehensive test measures the students' abilities in reading, arithmetic, geography, history, language and grammar, and spelling. Through such a test, children of the same age who have the same number of years of schooling can be compared, moreover, in order to determine their relative potentiality for learning. The educational quotient (EQ), described in Chapter 18, which is found by dividing educational age (EA) by chronological age and multiplying by 100, is thus probably as good an index of brightness as the IQ.

THEORIES OF THE ORGANIZATION OF INTELLIGENCE

There are three rather distinct theories about the organization of intelligence—each with its correlate in learning theory also. As we have mentioned before, intelligence may be defined, broadly, as the sum of all one's abilities

Exhibit 9   AGCT test scores of occupational groups

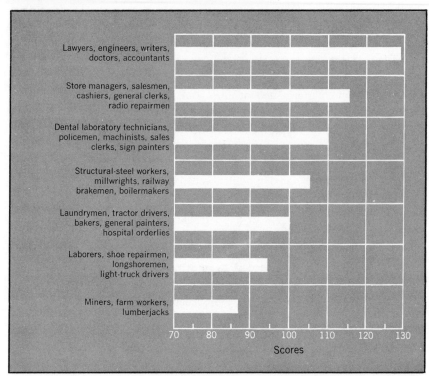

The bar graphs show the approximate average Army General Classification Test scores of occupational groups in the Second World War. There was a very wide range of scores for each occupation, and the striking fact is that the best 10 per cent of the lowest-scoring occupations such as the lumberjacks and the farm workers were as high as the lowest 10 per cent of the highest-scoring occupations such as lawyers, engineers, and accountants. Thus there was an overlap of the scores of lowest- and highest-scoring occupations to that extent. (Based on data in Naomi Stewart, "AGCT Scores of Army Personnel Grouped by Occupation," *Occupations*, 26:5–51, 1947.)

or, narrowly, strictly as the ability to deal with the abstract. These two possible views should be kept in mind while considering these three theories, and distinctions should be made about which aspects of each theory are applicable to each definition.

Thorndike's Neural Bonds. E. L. Thorndike assumes a specific neurological basis of intelligence in the form of connections between stimulus and response. According to his theory, specific neural bonds, or connections, underlie behavior. If a person knows a name or can define a word, recite a poem, give the product of two numbers, recognize a face, juggle balls, or carve meat with skill, he can do so because of connections established in the nervous system through learning and practice. The human being possesses an estimated 13 billion neurons, so the potential number of neural bonds is very great.

Thorndike's theory, moreover, allows for all sorts of combinations of connections in extensive and very complicated patterns as bases of skills and learning of all degrees of complexity and comprehensiveness. In other words, it is a mistake to think of the connection as a simple, direct line sequence of neural connections.

Intelligence, according to this theory, is basically the sum of the actual and potential connections and bonds in the nervous system.

Two Kinds of Factors: Charles Spearman. The English psychologist, a contemporary of Thorndike, advanced a theory of intelligence based on a general mental factor which is designated as "g" and specific factors designated as "s." The g factor represents the general mental energy or power that functions in all a person's mental performances. Above the limit set by the size of a person's g factor, his performance depends on s factors.

Let us consider first the g factor. Think of a student who is very good in a wide variety of studies: mathematics, science, philosophy, literature, languages, and others. He deals effectively with ideas in all fields that he studies and also with various abstract symbols such as words, mathematical and scientific symbols, and pictorial forms. This student has a large g factor. Another person, whose g is only average, will tend to be only average in his fields of study. A student whose general mental capacities are very limited has a small g.

The concept of the s factors explains the special capacities a person may have which are evidently above his general capacity. When a person is especially good in languages, music, mathematics, or building design, that is, when his capacity in it extends above his g factor, this capacity is accounted for by an s factor.

After the announcement of these two factors, Spearman decided that s factors are sometimes interrelated sufficiently to constitute what he called a group factor. However, the basis of Spearman's theory is his concept of the g and s factors.

As a rule, the generally weak and mediocre do not have high special abilities; in other words, large s factors do not accompany small g factors. However, this is not always the case. Sometimes, for example, good musical ability is shown by people of very moderate general capacity. A more extreme, even slightly bizarre, illustration is afforded by a person of limited mental capacity who could read the numbers of the cars of a passing freight train and give the sum of these numbers when the caboose passed by him. He had, of course, a very extraordinary s factor.

In psychology textbook discussions it is sometimes said that a certain kind of genius is occasionally found among the mentally deficient. This is misleading, because what is found is a highly specialized mechanical skill—such as one for carving figures or ships, for example. It is a reproductive type of skill and does not involve the higher mental processes or a big g. The perceiving, reasoning, and imagination of the mentally retarded are rudimentary. If the idiot savant is asked to give a speech or write a paper on his specialty, it will be found that he cannot do it. His power for abstract thinking is very limited, and his particular specialty is based on a very small g.

Yet a person who has a high special capacity usually has high general capacity. The superior composer or performer of music is usually a person of much more than ordinary general intelligence. The best bridge and chess players usually have high capacities in a number of other fields. Excellent inventors, mathematicians, and scientists generally have spacious minds—large foundations for their high special capacities.

The theory of the g factor is that the brain, to a considerable extent, functions as a unit, or as one mass, and that the size of g is largely determined by this functioning of the brain as a whole. The s factor is based on the idea that a brain function depends on the presence or absence of certain especially favorable structures and connections; the size of s, then, reflects that particular or specific function of the brain. The concept of the s factor must not be confused with the idea that certain parts of the brain are equipped for special mental activities. In explaining s, it is not indicated or implied that s factors depend on a given locale in the brain; rather, they depend on a neurological organization which is favorable to specific abilities but contributes little to general capacity if at all. This concept relates to Thorndike's theory that responses and abilities depend on specific neurological connections and their various combinations. In other words, functions depend on correlate neural structures, but Thorndike's theory assumes greater specificity of that dependency than does the g factor theory.

☻ Reflect and Review

A young man of college age but not a college student visited a college and demonstrated to the mathematics professors that he could multiply numbers of several digits mentally and get the correct answer quickly. Also without the use of paper and pencil, he could give almost instantly the square roots of large numbers. In short, his mental arithmetic was phenomenal.

The professors asked him some questions about his interests and abilities in algebra, geometry, and trigonometry and found that he did not have any general interest in mathematics. Indeed, he had low general capacity for mathematics and for the other subjects of college education.

What does this indicate about the size of his *g*?

How do you explain his exceptional ability to calculate?

Thurstone's Primary Mental Abilities. An attempt to explain the organization of abstract intelligence has been made by L. L. Thurstone. He used mental tests and special statistical techniques to divide intelligence into seven primary abilities:[2]

1. Numerical ability
2. Verbal fluency and facility
3. Spatial visualization or thinking
4. Word relations
5. Inductive and deductive reasoning
6. Perceptual ability
7. Memory

According to the Thurstone theory, intelligence manifests itself in these seven independent mental abilities; moreover, these abilities are nearly or completely separate and distinct functions of the mind.

This is not strictly true, however; there is considerable functional relationship among numerical, verbal, and spatial abilities and also among the mental processes of visualization, reasoning, perception, and memory. These abilities and processes are not independent of each other but are organically integrated. A further weakness in this list of primary mental abilities is that they are not simply coordinate in function. For example, memory is listed separately; but there would be no numerical, verbal, and spatial abilities without memory, as memory "holds" the numerical, verbal, and other symbolic material one works with. Similarly, in visualizing and thinking spatially, that is, in terms of forms and shapes, the processes of perception and reasoning are fully in play.

These weaknesses suggest the basic error of the exponents of the primary mental abilities theory: that they designate mental abilities according to the kind of test materials—the substance of the tests used in developing the theory.

There are, of course, verbal, numerical, and spatial abilities just as there are linguistic, mathematical, and various engineering and architectural abilities. Also there are many phases and aspects of abilities evidenced in reading, sociology, economics, physics, chemistry, and many other fields of

[2] Lists of primary mental abilities sometimes vary slightly from this one, but it includes the essentials.

learning. Each has its more or less specialized symbols and concepts; but all stimulate the mental processes of perceiving, remembering, reasoning, and creating. Still we find that any given individual differs in his interest and abilities in the many areas of learning or fields of intellectual activity.

It is useful, of course, to measure the facility of the mental processes with tests containing various symbols—numbers, words, pictures, formulas, and so forth. Such tests show the symbols with which an individual's mental processes are most effective. There are mentalities that are especially effective with words and related ideas and therefore have aptitude in fields such as languages and literature. Other mentalities may function best with spatial concepts and their various forms and figures and therefore may have special talent for art and design, architecture, or certain mechanical pursuits. Facility with numbers and other mathematical and scientific symbols indicates talent for mathematics, chemistry, physics, and engineering.

Yet the results obtained from testing individuals suggest again the weakness of the idea that primary mental abilities are unrelated. Though everyone varies in his capacities, a person whose mental processes are good with one form of symbol is likely to be adept with others also. It is rare that a student tests high in mathematics and low in verbal material, for example. It should also be remembered that thinking with several types of symbols has been necessary for the very development of our civilization. Thus the various branches of medicine require a high order of verbal ability as well as facility with numerical, space, and form symbols. To become a doctor the student must learn and remember hundreds of technical names and meanings; without high verbal abilities, his advancement will be blocked.

SUMMARY

Intelligence may be regarded as the functional effectiveness of a person's abilities: the effectiveness of the mental processes of perceiving, remembering, reasoning, and imagining or the extent of adjustment in the comprehensive sense.

A teacher needs to be cognizant of those abilities and capacities of students which are designated as abstract, social, mechanical, musical, athletic, speech, and others.

Abstract abilities involve words, numbers, mathematical and scientific symbols, musical notes, diagrams, and images.

The human mind can be characterized by its power and speed of functioning; also by its altitude or reach and its breadth, and thereby its spaciousness.

Mechanical and motor abilities involve tools, machines, and other mechanical devices, the human hand, the other bodily parts, and the body as a whole.

Social abilities involve interpersonal behavior, and a person is socially intelligent according to the skill he possesses in dealing with others.

The various human abilities correlate to the degree that they have elements in common. For example, there is a moderately high correlation among the abstract abilities but low between abstract and athletic abilities.

Few school children who are high in intellectual, artistic, and leadership abilities are found among the most maladjusted.

A genius is a person who is creative and is recognized for distinguished productiveness and performance. The synonyms for creativity are originality, imagination, inventiveness, and productiveness.

Geniuses have high intelligence, but people of high intelligence are not necessarily geniuses.

The school can encourage imaginative and original behavior rather than restrict the mental processes and regiment the students.

Tests of physical or sensorimotor reactions do not yield valid measurements of mental abilities, but when Alfred Binet at the beginning of this century prepared problems which required that the examinee compare, discriminate, remember, see relationships, or, in short, think and reason, a successful test of mental abilities was devised.

Several Americans utilized Binet's work for developing tests for use in the United States. In 1916 Terman produced what he called the Stanford revision of the Binet scale, which was followed by revisions in 1937 and again in 1960. Wechsler has also produced individual tests that have been used widely.

Standardized group intelligence tests consisting of different kinds of exercises or problems yield dependable mental ages for calculating intelligence quotients.

Mental age indicates mental level or mental maturity in terms of age standards; that is, the average mental-test performance of children of a certain age determines their mental ages.

Intelligence quotient indicates the degree of mental brightness and gives the approximate rate of mental growth. It is found by dividing mental age by chronological age.

Because mental growth is much slower during the middle and late teens than it was before those ages, IQ equivalents of scores for those ages are available for some tests. Scores are expressed as percentiles or as so many plus or minus standard deviations.

If an older and younger child have the same IQ, the older child has more mental ability because he is older and has a higher mental age.

A younger child will have more mental ability than an older child if his IQ is high enough.

Intelligence or mental-ability tests indicate fairly well a pupil's capacity to succeed in school, but it must be borne in mind that achievement depends on motivation and industry as well as mental ability.

A comprehensive achievement test of educational abilities is a fairly good mental test because the amount that has been learned indicates fairly well the mental capacity to learn.

There are three prevailing theories about the functioning and organization of intelligence: (1) individual neural connectors, (2) general and specific factors, and (3) primary mental abilities.

According to the first-named theory, one's intelligence depends on the number and combinations of neural pathways and how they function. The general-factor theory assumes mass action of the brain and that favorable neural structures and their organization underlie the specific factors. The primary mental factor theory is named according to the kind of content in the tests used and in that sense is fallacious, as it is not based on how the brain functions but rather on the content with which it functions. We have only rudimentary knowledge about how the brain functions, but it is generally accepted that mental capacity depends on the neural structures.

SUGGESTED READING

Blosser, G. H.: "Group Intelligence Tests as Screening Devices in Locating Gifted and Superior Students in the Ninth Grade," *Exceptional Children*, 29:282–286, 1963. Shows how various intelligence tests were used to identify superior students. A number of problems in the use of mental tests are discussed.

Harsh, Richard: "Intelligence: Its Nature and Measurement," *National Elementary Principal*, 41:23–28, 1961. Harsh discusses in a lucid manner a number of topics related to intelligence, such as the meaning of IQ, viewpoints on intelligence, and differences in performance.

Scott, C. M.: "Relationship between Intelligence Quotients and Gain in Reading Achievement with Arithmetic Reasoning, Social Studies and Science," *Journal of Educational Research*, 56:322–326, 1963. Scott shows a number of relationships not only between intellectual status and learning the school subjects but also between the subjects. Various implications about how the minds of students function are evident in this article.

CHAPTER 7
MENTAL CAPACITY,
PROGRESS IN SCHOOL,
AND PERSONAL SUCCESS

As we have seen, the capacities and attitudes of students are varied enough to cause some in a classroom to learn quickly and show interest and alertness, while their neighbors have difficulty in reaching the minimum class standard and show little or no enthusiasm for their work. As we have also seen, mental-test scores are related to success in school. But how close is this correlation? Is it possible to test a child in, say, the fourth grade and use the results to predict with any degree of accuracy how he will do in his freshman year of college?

Further questions arise. How does the superior student in the small rural high school compare with his opposite number in the gleaming new big-city school? Exactly how much more mental capacity is needed for successful completion of college than is needed to graduate from high school? And for that matter, does a student need the same capacity to attend his local community college that he would need to attend Harvard or Yale? Do high capacity and high academic achievement provide a better-than-average chance of achieving personal happiness in later life? Is the academic success of the student of exceptionally high capacity, as measured by intelligence tests, ensured? Or is he likely to be a failure in his academic life as well as neurotic and maladjusted in his personal life?

Most thinking on the subject of intelligence revolves around high academic achievement. There are too few sound opinions about the relationships between mental capacity, school success, and personal success; few people have much evidence for their points of view on this controversial topic.

This chapter will explore facets of these relationships, providing objective evidence which may suggest answers to some of the above questions and related ones.

USING MENTAL TESTS AND SCHOOL MARKS TO PREDICT EDUCATIONAL SUCCESS

An important problem for teachers, particularly when they are confronted by counseling situations, is how much weight should be given, in predicting the probability of academic success, to mental-test scores and how much to school marks already achieved. Parents of even very small children often want to know what the intelligence test can tell them about how their young ones can be expected to do in school. All through school, teachers use both marks and tests in planning their students' education. Finally, once they are in high school, students want to know not only what marks and tests can tell them about which courses they should take but also whether they have the capacity for going to college or should make other vocational plans. Knowledge of the relationship between mental tests, marks, and future academic success is therefore desirable for the teacher who wants to extend his helpfulness to his students beyond the day-to-day classroom activity of imparting knowledge.

Intelligence-test Scores and Standings in School Subjects. As stated in our previous discussion of the validity of intelligence tests, correlation of intelligence-test scores with success in school subjects sometimes reaches .60. But the large amount of experimental work that has been done to determine this has shown that the correlations vary for individual subjects.

In general, these correlations are highest—typically about .40 or .50—for the academic subjects in which the verbal and other symbolic elements predominate, such as reading, composition, history, foreign languages, and mathematics. Furthermore, intelligence tests indicate the student's success in the abstract portions of particular courses more accurately than they indicate his success in the mechanical portions. For example, test scores predict success in solving reasoning problems in arithmetic more accurately than they predict success in computational skills.

The correlation is much lower between intelligence-test scores and subjects in which skills other than symbolic are frequently required, which is understandable since intelligence tests call primarily for verbal and other symbolic abilities. Thus correlation in subjects such as drawing and penmanship is only about .20, and it is the same for subjects such as woodworking, mechanical drawing, sewing, and cooking. On the basis of such a low correlation, a teacher can hardly predict success in these studies. If, of course, teachers of these primarily nonsymbolic subjects stress learning of definite content as well as the exercise of concrete skills, the correlation is considerably higher and predictability more accurate.

The intelligence-test correlation with spelling ability is midway between those with academic and concrete-skill subjects. It generally falls between .30 and .40, indicating a recognizable relationship between abstract intelligence and the ability to spell words correctly.

Of course, the reliability of the intelligence tests and the achievement tests is an important factor in determining the relationship between the test results and subject-matter achievement. When especially carefully devised intelligence tests are used along with reliable tests of achievement, the correlations are generally higher than otherwise. From the results of such testing, the teacher can judge with considerable accuracy what school success can be expected of a child.

Uses of Testing in the Early School Years. Carefully testing the intelligence of a child when he begins school is especially valuable. Then it is advisable to retest occasionally—every other year or even more often, depending on the specific educational purpose involved. Subsequent tests may offset a part of the unreliability inherent in the testing of a child before he has had school experience. Also, standardized achievement tests will give information on how well each child who has been in school awhile is learning. By using these in conjunction with intelligence-test results, the teacher can have a wider base for judging how well each child can be expected to achieve. We shall see repeatedly in this chapter how achievement tests can be used to supplement marks and other tests.

In some school systems the kindergarten teacher tests the beginning kindergarten pupils, thus gaining almost on first acquaintance a fairly accurate knowledge of the mental maturity and alertness of each child. He learns in an hour or two as much about a child's mental capacities as he might otherwise learn in a year.

In the first grade, testing is useful in determining readiness for learning specific subjects. If, for example, a teacher knows the IQs and MAs of his pupils when they enter the first grade, he has data that will help him anticipate what they will do in reading and arithmetic, though those who did best in the intelligence test will not necessarily be highest in these subjects, and those who scored lowest will not necessarily be poorest.

Thus experience and experimentation have demonstrated that a child with a mental age of five is hardly developed enough mentally for learning how to read. Time thus spent would be wasted, for the child cannot learn to understand enough of the printed words to make more than discouraging progress. With a mental age of six, on the other hand, he may enjoy learning to read and may make good progress; and a child with a mental age of 6½ or 7 can usually learn quickly.

Specific reading-readiness tests will prove a good supplement to intelligence tests, incidentally, for the teacher who needs to judge when a child is ready to take up reading. Such tests use pictures to test the child's oral vocabulary, require the child to identify rhyming or matching sounds or to match letters and words visually, or even ask him to learn a few words during the test. They indicate a little better than intelligence tests what progress a child in the first grade will make in reading.

Mental age is an index to arithmetic readiness also. It has been discovered that for arithmetic, as for reading, time is wasted and bad attitudes are formed if children study the subject before they are ready for it. It is really best if number work is taught only incidentally before a child reaches a mental age of eight or nine, when it can be taken up systematically. Up to that time, the teacher can help get him ready for arithmetic by using some of the terminology of numbers and simple measurements. There are definite methods for thus developing arithmetic readiness.

Determining Aptitudes. Special tests, called *aptitude tests*, have been devised for judging capacity for particular subjects and special fields. The readiness tests for reading are actually aptitude tests, as are the readiness tests given for algebra. Thus, what a pupil has done in arithmetic is a fair indication of what he will do in algebra, but algebra-readiness tests are a little better indication because they are designed to test specifically the aptitude for algebra. Readiness tests in other academic subjects seek, much as special tests of artistic and athletic capacities do, to determine capacity as well as possible apart from practice and experience. Clerical, musical, and mechanical aptitude tests give valuable information about a person's potentiality in these special areas which is not yielded by the use of intelligence tests.

The pattern of a student's school marks is a fairly good indication, too, of where his stronger and weaker aptitudes lie; and a combination of a student's school record and the results of aptitude tests indicates better than either standard alone the areas of activity in which a student will probably be most or least successful.

Predicting Success in College; College Aptitude Tests. Special concern surrounds the method of predicting success in college. It usually costs a considerable amount of money to go to college, and often the high school graduate leaves home to enroll in a college many miles away. In a sense, many a college student cannot afford to fail. Thus, if a student can be rightly told that he probably will not succeed in college, he can be greatly helped to avoid costly and often humiliating failure. How can mental tests and school marks help here?

To begin with, there is generally a correlation of .40 to .50 between scores on college aptitude tests and achievement in college. This is about the same correlation as that existing between IQ and high school achievement in the academic subjects and, in turn, between IQ and ability in the academic subjects all through school.

College aptitude tests, as distinct from the aptitude tests already discussed, are divided into sections for testing different abstract abilities. Such tests provide problems which test a person's processes of perception, memory, reasoning, and imagination in using spatial, numerical, verbal, and other symbols. Some widely used college aptitude tests are devised to measure verbal and quantitative abilities (V and Q) specifically.

The scores from the different sections indicate relative strengths and weaknesses which should be considered in guiding the student so that he will take the courses for which he has most aptitude. For example, high verbal abilities may indicate aptitude for, and particular interest in, courses in literature, philosophy, languages, history and other social studies, journalism, and library work. Numerical, mechanical, and spatial-thought abilities determine whether or not the student is well fitted for courses in mathematics, science, engineering, architecture, and probably dentistry. A high level in a variety of ability areas, of course, represents added equipment for any field of activity; in this case the student can be guided more by his immediate interests than if he were not widely endowed.

Thus college aptitude or general mental tests are a workable tool of prediction. But the marks that a student has earned should also be considered in predicting success. A high school student's marks in arithmetic, algebra, geometry, chemistry, and physics are a good index of his aptitude for college mathematics, science, and engineering. Similarly, good marks in English, Latin, and other languages indicate interests and aptitudes for continuing in fields which require verbal facility. Indeed, high school marks are a slightly better indication than these aptitude tests of what a student will do in college. Though it must be borne in mind that standards of achievement are higher in college than in high school, marks show what the student has done and therefore indicate what he is likely to do, while aptitude tests provide only an abstract indication of what he should be able to do. Again, the best solution is a combination of marks and tests; this provides a good basis for prediction.

Thus very few students who have a record of poor marks and who also score low in college aptitude tests succeed in college. On the other hand, those who have both a very good high school record and a high rating on these tests succeed in college, with only a few exceptions.

It has been found that few students who graduate from high school with

Table 8   Percentages of High School Pupils of Particular IQ Levels Who Attained to Various Stages of School Progress

Progress Beyond High School:	Intelligence Quotients					
	70–84 (N=40)	85–94 (N=130)	95–104 (N=280)	105–119 (N=451)	120–139 (N=202)	140–150 (N=99)
No additional schooling	67.5	51.5	40.7	30.8	21.3	
Transferred to junior colleges, business schools, and other non-degree-granting institutions	32.5	38.5	36.1	25.1	17.8	
Sent transcripts to degree-granting institutions, but did not enter the University of California		5.4	9.3	12.4	13.4	33.3
Entered the University of California		4.6	13.9	31.7	47.5	66.7
	100.0	100.0	100.0	100.0	100.0	100.0
Through the University of California:						
Did not obtain junior certificate		3.1	7.9	10.2	9.4	11.1
Obtained the junior certificate but no degree			1.4	6.2	5.9	
Graduated without honors		1.5	4.3	14.0	28.2	11.1
Graduated with honors			0.4	1.3	4.0	44.4

Source: Noel Keys, "The Value of Group Test I.Q.'s for Prediction of Progress beyond High School," *Journal of Educational Psychology,* 31:81–93, 1940.

a composite ranking in scholarship and college aptitude tests that places them in the lowest fourth of high school graduates should attempt to attend colleges in which students are generally average or higher in capacity; because, for such low-ranking students, failures there are many, and even moderate successes are extremely few. At the other end of the range, those students who are in the highest fourth, according to a combined ranking of their aptitude tests and high school marks, will almost all do satisfactory work in these colleges. In fact, at every point in the range of scholarship and aptitude standing, there is a dependable relationship to college success. The higher the composite standing, the greater the chances of success, and vice versa.

It is, of course, relatively harder to predict success or failure for those individuals who are high in one respect and low in another than it is for those who are consistently high or low in both respects. If a high school graduate is high in mental capacity, as shown by a college aptitude test, but has achieved poorly, as reflected by low marks, it is likely that his achievement will be no better in college. Possibly he may start utilizing his mental powers, but the likelihood is that he will have the same problems of achievement—usually, poor study habits and general indifference—that he had in high school. A person's habits are very stubborn, and it is with discouraging infrequency that a student substitutes good study habits for the poor ones that he has had for many years. However, if a high school graduate has a very good record in his subjects but an aptitude test score that is only average for high school graduates, it is likely that he will do well in college.

☯ *Consider the Data*

Based on Table 8

Noel Keys, observing that attempts to predict college success are usually based on tests of specific college aptitudes administered just before the student enters college, determined to investigate the possibility of predicting college success from IQs obtained when students were in junior high school [Keys, 1940]. He considered this valuable not only because of the subject's inherent interest but also because group intelligence test scores are generally available to the high school counselor, while other scores are not always available. He therefore examined the records of 1,112 students who had left Oakland (California) High School in a five-year period, securing first their recorded IQs and then information about whether or not they had attended college and, if so, their degree of success. Most of those who had attended college had gone to the University of California, which is only a few miles from Oakland.

He found that the IQs arranged themselves in a steady upward progression when the students were ranked by academic success beyond high school. He was able, moreover, on the basis of percentages of students of particular IQs who attained particular levels of academic success, to make several generalizations about the probability that students of similar IQs and from a similar population would succeed at various levels of academic attainment. For children with IQs of 70 to 84, he found the chances to be 68 in 100 that they would not continue schooling beyond high school. The chances were 40 in 100 that children with IQs from 95 to 104 would not continue beyond high school; one in four gained admission to a degree-granting institution of higher learning. Three out of ten of the group with IQs between 105 and 119 will not proceed beyond high school, while only one out of five of the group with IQs between 120 to 139 will not progress beyond high school. Forty-four per cent of the students with IQs over 140 graduated from the University of California with honors.

Since the University of California is only 8 miles from Oakland, students at this high school had a good chance to go there. Does this help to account for the high overall proportion of the students who went on to college?

If the students had gone to a greater variety of colleges and universities, is it likely that their chances of success on various IQ levels would have been different?

On the basis of these data, would you advise an Oakland student with an IQ of 102 to attend the University of California? What additional facts would you have to have in order to answer the question satisfactorily?

High School Subjects and College Success. Do the patterns of subjects taken by students in high school have any relationship to the degree of subsequent success in college?

The high school graduate who has had 4 years of Latin, 3 years of mathematics, 3 years of science, 3 years of French, and 3 years of English usually can be expected to have good potentiality for college. Ordinarily, the student who takes this pattern of courses, or one closely resembling it, has much higher than average capacity. Also, if he were not a persistent worker, he would not work through a sequence of such courses. Finally, he usually comes from a home that is college-oriented—a home where plans are carefully made for each child's higher education.

The high school graduate with three credits in English, two in history, one in journalism, one in psychology, one in music, and the rest in shop training and agriculture probably does not have so much potentiality for college. Students who take vocational courses and a large variety of courses generally do not have so high academic intelligence as those who select and survive the mathematics, science, and language courses.

Yet the courses a student takes in high school generally have little to do per se with his subsequent success in college. Research has shown that most important is the mental capacity of the student and his motivation as shown by his work habits. Having had chemistry or physics in high school, for example, gives a student little or no advantage when he takes science in college. Many boys and girls who have had little or no science in high school do better in college science courses than some of those who have had several courses in high school science. Students who have had high school science seem to have an initial advantage, but it is soon evident that capacity and hard work determine success.

This means, incidentally, that in selecting high school graduates to recommend for college entrance, teachers should place less emphasis on the specific courses a student had in high school than on how he ranked in his class in marks or comprehensive achievement-test scores, his performance in college aptitude tests, and his ways of working. Those who rank highest in all are the best prospects, of course, particularly when they also have a record of effective participation in extracurricular activities in the high school.

In this connection, there is one pattern of work that seems in itself to indicate high capacity and thus to be prognostic of success in college. The evidence indicates that the student who has taken an extraordinarily heavy load of any subjects with high success and is ready for college a year or two earlier than the average student will do very well in college. This student has demonstrated both that he will work hard and, by being very successful in his courses, that he has high capacity.

All this is not to say, of course, that the student who is preparing for college should not be selective in the courses he chooses. If, for example, a student plans to major in music in college, he should have taken music in grade and high school and should have achieved as much competence on his instrument as he can; or if he expects to major in languages, he should have a comparable background in them; for these are fields where early time well spent counts heavily in being able to take maximum advantage of opportunities offered in college.

The high school student should, moreover, pay close attention to his degree of success in various fields. If he takes several courses in a field and is mediocre in them, he will probably be mediocre or even poorer in that field in college; on the other hand, if he is good in a field in high school, he will usually be successful in it in college.

Are Sex Differences Related to Educational Capacity? Some students of sex differences claim to have found evidence that girls of primary-school age are so mentally superior to boys that boys should be 3 to 6 months older than girls when entering school. This notion has persisted over a number of years; and recommendations that the age of school entrance be regulated accordingly make a regular appearance in the educational literature.

The difficulty with such recommendations is that many other sex differences also would have to be taken into account. For example, the fact that girls reach puberty earlier than boys do is probably of more educational import than are the fairly minor differences at school-entrance age. The more rapid physical development of girls from about age eleven to age fourteen, the comparatively greater aggressiveness of boys at all ages, the phenomenon of boys' voices changing (important in school music programs): all these factors probably are more important than sex differences in mental ability at age six. Moreover, the amount of difference is by no means certain, anyway, because the major intelligence tests have been deliberately constructed so as to eliminate the influence of sex differences.

Before administrators adopt a plan of different school-admission ages for boys and girls, we should have more reliable evidence that girls have greater capacity than boys do. Results of intelligence testing indicate that boys and girls of the same age are, throughout the school years, essentially equal in mental capacity. When analysis is made of particular abilities, it is usually found that girls are superior in the early grades in penmanship and English courses, going on in high school and college to be ahead in foreign languages and in verbal understanding and expression generally. Boys are usually ahead throughout their educational careers in arithmetic, algebra, geometry, and the sciences. But the ability differences among the members of one sex in any given grade are very much greater than the differences between the averages of the two sexes.

The fact that males and females have been differentiated mentally in their verbal and mathematical abilities, furthermore, may not even mean there is a real difference in their capacities for verbal and numerical materials; apparent differences may be due to different average experiences.

Thus when Robert Sommer tested college students on quantitative items (see Table 9), girls apparently had more knowledge of such measures as pints, quarts, teaspoons, and tablespoons [Sommer, 1958]. In other words, girls had superior knowledge of quantities in which they had interest and with which they had had experience.

On the other hand, when a memory test was given to the same men and women on a passage which contained several large numbers and some proper names, the men remembered the large numbers better than the women, who tended to get mixed up on them. In this case, it is likely that the men had had more experiences with large numbers and therefore could comprehend and recall them better. On the nonquantitative material, there were no differences in the average memory abilities of the men and women.

It is, of course, possible that men have neural structures that give them more basic capacity for dealing with numbers. But it is hard to imagine that such specialized brain patterns would enable them to be superior with numbers and not with names, in view of what is known about the functioning of the brain—meager as that knowledge is.

This speculation about the importance of cultural factors in such measurable sex differences as have been identified has been confirmed by several studies. One such study is that of H. Barry, M. K. Bacon, and I. L. Child, who studied sex differentiation in 110 different cultures of the world [Barry

Table 9 Percentage of Correct Responses to Quantitative Items

Items	United States Students			Canadian Students		
	Male ($N=61$)	Female ($N=34$)	P.*	Male ($N=89$)	Female ($N=65$)	P.*
Population (U.S. or Canada†)	64	47	0.08	95	55	0.01
Distance (N.Y. to Paris)	54	59	N.S.‡	54	25	0.01
Pints in a quart	72	91	0.02	83	86	N.S.‡
Teaspoons in a tablespoon	13	70	0.001	20	48	0.01
Population (college or university town)	51	28	0.05	89	52	0.01

* Probability that the differences between males and females are not significant. The decimal 0.08, for example, indicates that there are 8 chances in 100 that the differences are not significant. Thus the smaller the decimal values the fewer the chances that the differences are not significant. See Appendix, p. 538.
† Students in college in the United States were asked to give the population of the United States; Canadian students were asked to give the population of Canada. The same questions were asked concerning the population of the city in which their colleges or universities were located.
‡ Not significant.
Source: Adapted from Tables 1 and 2 of p. 188 of Robert Sommer, "Sex Differences in the Retention of Quantitative Information," *Journal of Educational Psychology*, 49:187–192, 1958.

et al., 1952]. They concluded that cultural considerations—what the culture "expects" of a man or woman—are the major factor in sex differences. L. M. Terman and L. E. Tyler add that, in our own society specifically, biologically based differences are reinforced and strengthened by cultural forces [Terman and Tyler, 1954].

Most psychological sex differences, then, appear to be the product of both biological and cultural forces. Within our own culture, as we have said, boys appear to be more commonly oriented toward mathematical and scientific skills, while girls seem more likely to excel in verbal and linguistic skills. In a study by Walter J. Pauk, 150 boys and 150 girls in the ninth grade were given reading comprehension tests; and approximately the lowest quarters and the highest quarters of the boys and girls in reading ability were selected and given a battery of tests, which included those listed in Table 10.

Scores on the tests were studied to discover correlations between scores and skill in reading. The relative importance of each ability in differentiating between good and poor readers of each sex was expressed in terms of a percentage. This percentage indicated the relative degree to which a specific skill contributed to reading ability.

The abilities which contributed most to differentiating good and poor girl readers were the verbal abilities, as indicated by the L (linguistic) score, spelling score, and sentence-interpretation score. These three scores ac-

Table 10   Relative Contributions of Seven Like Variables to Reading Abilities

Test	Relative Contribution in Differentiating Good and Poor Readers	
	Girls, Per Cent	Boys, Per Cent
L Score (ACE)*	46.05	29.71
Spelling (DAT)†	17.23	7.11
Sentences (DAT)†	17.62	.67
Abstract Reasoning (DAT)†	6.45	19.59
Numerical Ability (DAT)†	5.12	33.69
Study Habits (Brown-Holtzman)‡	3.77	6.90
Reflective (Thurstone)§	3.76	2.33
	100.00	100.00

* The *L* score is the linguistic or verbal score on the American Council on Education (ACE) Psychological Examination for College Freshmen, which is a college aptitude test.
† Differential Aptitude Test, which is also a college aptitude test.
‡ Brown-Holtzman Survey of Study Habits and Attitudes.
§ The term reflective refers to one type of score of the Thurstone Temperament Schedule.
Source: Walter J. Pauk, "Are Present Reading Tests Valid for Girls and Boys?" *Journal of Educational Research*, 53:280, 1960.

counted for 81 per cent of the grounds for differentiation of good and poor girl readers. On the other hand, the good and poor boy readers were differentiated best by their scores on the tests in abstract reasoning and numerical ability. These two scores made up 53 per cent of the total difference between scores of good and poor boy readers.

It should be noted that the abilities which best differentiate good and poor readers of each sex are those in which that sex is most commonly thought to be superior: verbal ability for the girls and numerical ability for the boys. Judging from this study, girls who read best are high in verbal ability and boys who read well are high in numerical ability. This seems to indicate a persistent sex difference, which is probably due to a combination of biological and cultural factors.

These findings on sex differences in ability are substantiated consistently by other studies. P. J. Stinson and Mildred M. Morrison tested 36 boys and 33 girls chosen at random from a large senior class [Stinson and Morrison, 1959]. The boys were superior in numerical and mechanical abilities and the girls in word knowledge (verbal) and in clerical skills. As usual, the girls had higher school marks than the boys. Other studies have consistently shown that girls are better spellers on the average.

As Pauk's study demonstrates, however, these differences do not necessarily result in widely varying levels of achievement in such skills as reading, since reading skill is not determined by verbal ability alone. When they start school, boys tend to be a little slower than the girls in reading, but above-average and top-level boys in a year or two develop faster and will equal and may even surpass the girls by the sixth grade or later. Willis W. Clark tested 69,354 pupils in 341 school systems of 48 states and, on the basis of samples for grades 3, 5, and 8, concluded that there are no fundamental sex differences in the reading abilities of boys and girls, although there are small differences in phases of reading such as reading vocabulary and reading comprehension [Clark, 1959]. Clark expresses the opinion that no cognizance need be taken of sex differences in reading abilities in admitting pupils and that the entrance age should be the same for both boys and girls.

The general belief that boys tend to be poorer readers than girls is probably the result not of fundamental differences in capacity but of cultural attitudes toward school achievement. There is almost certainly more pressure upon girls to excel in the lower grades than there is upon boys. Moreover, such differences in reading achievement as do exist are only part of the same forces which produce, on the junior and senior high school levels, a higher proportion of underachievement, retardation, and delinquency among boys than among girls. The values of our culture, the emotional impact of adolescence, and the relatively greater independence of boys' personal lives are probably all more important than basic abilities are in determining levels of achievement in reading, as in other subjects.

SELECTIVITY IN THE EDUCATIONAL PROCESS

Why may a child who ranked among the top pupils in the third grade be only a mediocre student in high school? Why does a student who transfers from a school in one part of the country to a school in another part sometimes find his class standing radically different thereafter? Answering this question involves the important principle of selectivity and thus school standards, for these determine to a large extent the degree of selectivity at work in any given school situation.

The Intelligence Quotient as Selector. The average intelligence quotient of students in high school is higher than that of grade school pupils; and that of college or university students is, in turn, higher than that of high school students. The main reason for this is the retardation and dropping out of the less capable students. The more capable tend to finish high school; the still more capable finish college. The most capable students of all are generally those who work for advanced degrees. Another way of putting this is to say that those who finish high school are a more selected group, according to aptitude, than are those who finish grade school; those who finish college are a more selected group than those who finish high school; and those who work for advanced degrees are a still more selected group than college graduates.

However, by adulthood the mental-test standard is no longer the sole standard of capability. Psychologists are concerned with mental abilities (such as original and inventive capacities) not measured by college aptitude tests, that is, with qualities of high-ability level. Individuals with such special talents sometimes are not uniformly good students, and the school processes do not encourage them to seek the highest academic degrees.

This selection that takes place from the lowest step in the educational ladder to the highest is clearly shown by a comparison of the intelligence-test scores of Terman's gifted subjects (whom we shall consider in detail later in this chapter) with the scores made by the candidates for the Ph.D. degree in psychology at Stanford University (Terman's study was conducted at Stanford). Such candidates probably represent the very highest selection of students. The average score of the candidates for the Ph.D. degree was slightly above that of college students who were selected because they had IQs of 140 or more, which itself represents a selection of about the best 1 in at least 400. It is thus apparent that in the academic progress from kindergarten up to the highest reaches of graduate school, the competition gets harder and harder along the way; and only the very ablest, a small percentage of those who started, are still in the running at the advanced graduate level.

It is this selective character of education that helps to explain why some children who seem superior in the lower grades prove to be only average or slightly better in high school, and poor or failures in college. For example, a first-grade child with an IQ around 115 may seem to be the brightest child in his class; but when this child reaches high school, there will probably be in his classes some students considerably brighter than he. In turn, the student who seemed so bright in high school may not have such an impressive relative standing in college. He may be only average or even less, for he will be competing with the best students from many high schools; that is, the average intellectual quality of his classmates will be higher than that of his high school classmates.

It is true, however, that education is not so selective now as it was, say, before the Second World War. More and more students are found in high school; and because of this tremendous increase in enrollment, there is a larger percentage of low IQs than there was in prewar years. College enrollments also have increased greatly since 1945, so that more of the less able students are also found in college. The best students in high school and college are as capable as were the best students in the prewar years, but many more of the less able students continue in school than formerly.

Owing to these conditions, it is more difficult now to show what IQ is necessary for success in high school and in college than it used to be. Many high schools have enlarged their curricula to offer so many different types of courses that students can now obtain a high school diploma even if their strictly academic abilities are low.

Such adjustment to individual differences is desirable, for the schools should serve students of all potentials, offering work suitable for children of all degrees of brightness and interest and all kinds of capacities. It is not the purpose of the schools to serve only the brighter youth—to offer such a limited program of courses that the academically duller students drop out. But the adjustment to individual differences does mean that high school diplomas may not represent the same kind and quality of scholarship that they did years ago.

It is believed, however, that high school students should ordinarily have IQs of at least 105 in order to grasp the content of the traditional high school subjects in schools with fairly high standards. Higher degrees of brightness are desirable, of course; students with higher intelligence acquire a better-than-passing comprehension of their subjects. But it is doubtful that less bright children can well understand the use of formulas in algebra, interpret the facts in history, or acquire the vocabulary in Latin or the principles of physics; that is, it is doubtful, in general, that they can comprehend the abstract and symbolic elements in their subjects. High school students with IQs of about 105 can do passable work in subjects with a great deal of abstract content but cannot progress very far in them. Still, they can profit from such courses as citizenship, physical training, manual arts, music, and typing; in these they are likely to have adequate capacity. Thus the high school can furnish these students valuable educational, as well as personal, experiences.

The minimum IQ for doing acceptable work in a college with fairly high standards is higher than that for high schools—approximately 110; and in order to be able really to comprehend college instruction, to integrate the subject matter, and to react in a somewhat imaginative way to it, a higher IQ is needed—preferably 125, 130, or even more.

Exceptions to the seeming rule. To be arbitrary about minimum IQs is wrong, for there are always the exceptions who achieve surprisingly well in spite of mediocre intellectual equipment, as well as those whose abilities have been inaccurately measured by tests. When the success of a group of college students is compared with their college aptitude test scores, it is usually found that some whose scores are below the usual "cutoff" point—or so low that failure is expected for them—graduate from college and that an occasional low-scoring student graduates with distinction. Every college and university that uses college aptitude tests or intelligence tests, for that matter, has had some very low-testing students who have earned a degree.

There are two basic reasons for this. In the first place, there are a few low-capacity students who, because of effective work habits and tenaciousness, are overachievers in relation to their mental endowments. These students generally have had good or fair high school records. It is doubtful, however, that any of these "pluggers" who utilize their low capacities to the maximum degree do superior work in college. In the second place, better endowed students will sometimes "fall down" when they take the college aptitude test. Actual capacity may be considerably higher than that indicated by a single test score, so that, if they were tested several times, such students would show substantially more potentiality. To the extent that this happens, judging students' potentiality for college on the basis of one college aptitude test is a rather precarious procedure which makes selectivity appear less important than it really is. Thus is emphasized the need for educational administrators to consult also a student's high school scholastic record along with his record of other aptitude tests taken in high school. Comprehensive achievement tests are also useful. If students test low on college aptitude tests, they will generally test low on comprehensive achievement tests too; that is, the tests tend to verify each other.

Selectivity within Individual Colleges and Universities. There is selectivity among university and college departments too. The average mental aptitude of students in the various departments differs, depending on the difficulty of the courses offered by the departments, the selection which the departments exercise in accepting students, and the varying department standards that determine the percentages of students who are failed.

Engineering, law, and medical students have relatively high average aptitudes, although there is a wide range of scholastic aptitudes among them. These students are ordinarily a highly selected group, for the courses require a high order of the abstract capacity which is measured most adequately by the aptitude tests.

Students majoring in music schools, agricultural departments, home economics courses, physical education, elementary education, and schools of dentistry tend, on the average, to have lower mental capacity than the students in other departments; nor should this be surprising. Students are in a music school because of their musical talents first and their academic abilities second. Also, although the training of a dentist involves a considerable amount of theoretical learning, much of his success depends on skill and dexterity with his hands and with tools, so that dental students are selected in part on the basis of capacities other than those measured by mental tests.

All these students, incidentally, probably have special capacities, comparable to those of the dental student, that are higher than those of academic students. This is not to say that they are not better students in their chosen fields if their academic aptitudes are high. Indeed, it is those who rise above the average in academic aptitude who are the brilliant and exceptional students in these fields and go on to the greatest vocational success in them later.

Not only is there a tremendous range in the mental abilities of students of any one college or university, but there are very large differences in the average mental abilities of college student bodies. Exhibit 10, adapted from the work of Paul Heist, demonstrates these ranges and differences.

Exhibit 10   Aptitude scores showing the range in mental ability of students in colleges of the United States

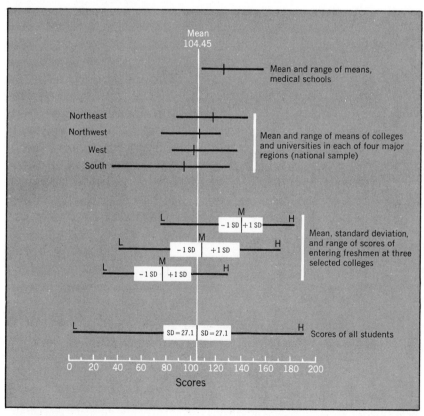

The base line gives the scale of scores for the American Council on Education (ACE) Psychological Examination for College Freshmen, a college aptitude test that has been used very extensively.

Directly above it are the scores for all college students. They range from a low (L) of 1 to a high (H) of 190, and the mean score is 104.45 with a standard deviation (SD) of 27.1.

The mean (M), standard deviation (SD), and range scores for three colleges are presented next. These three colleges differ greatly in the average mental abilities of their students; the range for each institution is also very large. Observe that the best student in the college with the lowest average score scored about 10 points lower than the average score of the highest-scoring college of these three.

The four horizontal lines grouped above these three represent the mean, or average, ACE scores of colleges in the four sections of the United States. The college with the lowest mean score has one of only 36, and the college with the highest mean score has one of 143. Thus there is a tremendous difference between them.

The top line indicates the range of the mean scores of the senior students of the nation's medical schools. The lowest average is only slightly higher than the average for all entering freshmen of American colleges; Heist states in his report that 16 per cent of the seniors in medical schools are under that average. The highest-average medical school has a substantially higher mean than that of the highest college in the United States.

The data indicate that there is a great range in the quality of the student bodies of American colleges as well as a wide range within each college. The various courses, departments, and areas of learning within a college or university attract students of different interests and abilities. (Adapted from Fig. 1, Paul Heist, "Diversity in College Characteristics," *Journal of Educational Sociology*, 33:279–291, 1960.)

Socioeconomic Classes and the Average Capacities of Student Bodies. The average levels of mental capacity of the student bodies in schools in various districts in any town or city, especially a large city, differ substantially for a simply stated reason: The school aptitudes of children follow consistently the socioeconomic levels of their families. Though we shall discuss socioeconomic class in detail in Chapter 9, it is relevant to our treatment of selectivity in education to note that the schools situated in upper-class residential districts have more capable student bodies than schools which draw from the middle-class districts, and the schools situated in areas of shacks or dilapidated tenements have students who on the average are the lowest in capacity. Thus the socioeconomic status of a district becomes a general index to the average mental capacities of the students from it.

These differences in capacities of the pupils of schools situated in the richest and poorest districts are large and are educationally very discernible. For children of the age of twelve, the difference in average educational achievement is as much as two grades. Over 80 per cent of the children in some individual schools are above the city mental-age medians or norms, while less than 10 per cent are above those medians in some other schools. Relatedly, there are big differences in the amount of retardation, truancy, delinquency, and dropping out of high school before finishing.

The teachers in a school located in a depressed neighborhood may try as hard as they can, but it is doubtful that their students will, on the average, reach the city educational age norms; and it will be practically impossible for the teachers in this school to bring their children's performance up to the levels of performance of a school in a fine residential area, which is almost certain to be above the city norms no matter how poor the teaching. Supervisors may commend the one school for its fine achievement and point out to the other that it is not up to standard; yet if they take into account the average mental capacity at the two schools, they should not expect the poorer school to match the richer in average student achievement.

Variation of Capacities within and between States. School administrators also have found that the average mental capacities of school children vary greatly from area to area within whole states. For example, the average mental-test scores of high school seniors from schools in city, town, mountain, and other rural areas within a state may show a great variation, as indicated in Table 11, which gives the results of a study of a particular state.

Table 11 Comparative Percentile Standings of High School Seniors in One State and in the Nation on a College Qualification Test

Nation	State	Sections of the State			
		Mountain	Other Rural	Town	Metropolitan
75	91	97	94	86	85
50	78	90	83	69	64
25	55	71	61	44	38

☯ *Consider the Data*

Based on Table 11

The 75th percentile for the nation is the 91st percentile for this particular state as a whole, the 97th percentile of the mountain section of the state, the 94th percentile for the other rural sections, etc. This means that whereas 75 per cent of tested students in the nation as a whole fell below a certain score, 91 per cent of the tested students in this state fell below it, 97 per cent of the tested students in the mountain section fell below it, 94 per cent of the tested students in other rural areas of the state fell below it, etc. In other words, 25 per cent of the tested students of the nation exceeded this score, only 9 per cent of the state students exceeded it, only 3 per cent of the mountain students of the state did so, only 6 per cent of the other rural students of the state did so, etc. The national 50th and 25th percentiles are comparably related to the state percentiles, as will be seen.

Taken together, all the percentiles indicate two things:

Sizably larger percentages of high school seniors in the state failed to achieve given scores than did seniors in the nation as a whole. The seniors of this state thus seem to have considerably less college aptitude than those of the nation as a whole. This is strikingly exemplified by the fact that the 78th percentile of the state equals the 50th percentile for the nation and that thus only 22 per cent of the high school seniors of this state are above the national median.

It is also apparent that within the state there are fairly large differences in the scores, and thus the average capacities, of the seniors in the high schools of the different sections of the state. The metropolitan sections have the most capable; the towns are next; then come the rural sections, generally; and lowest is the mountain section. Thus the score that determined the 50th percentile for the nation as a whole determined the 90th percentile for the mountainous section, 83rd for the other rural sections, 69th for the towns, and 64th for the metropolitan sections. This means that in the mountainous section only 10 per cent of the students exceeded the score which was exceeded by half the tested students in the nation. This 40 per cent is a very large difference.

Do these figures justify a conclusion that city children are more intelligent than country children in this state? What are the other possibilities?

Note that the difference between the national and state standing is greater at the 25th percentile level than that at the 75th percentile level. What generalization can be made from this fact?

B. S. Bloom has found strong indications of state-to-state differences in students' mental abilities by administering to high school students, during the last 2 months of their senior year in representative high schools in all the states of this country, the Tests of General Educational Development, or GED [Bloom, 1956]. These are tests of education and intellectual effectiveness and can be regarded as good general educational and mental tests. Developed for use in the Army, they have been used extensively for educational and vocational purposes.

Included are sections in English, social studies, natural sciences, literary materials, and mathematics. Thus state-by-state comparisons of the GED scores taken by Bloom reveal how widely students differed in these school abilities. The figures in Table 12, based on Bloom's data, show the percentages of students in two states with scores large enough to be in the high-scoring half of all those tested over the nation. The states are those whose students as a group made the highest and lowest scores, respectively.

Table 12 Percentages of High School Seniors above the National Median in GED Scores

	Social Studies	Natural Sciences	Literary Materials	English	Mathematics
Highest state	70	72	78	65	70
Lowest state	29	30	35	33	42
Ratio	2.41	2.40	2.23	1.97	1.67

Source: Based on data in B. S. Bloom, "The 1955 Normative Study of the Tests of General Educational Development," *School Review*, 64:110–124, 1956.

Note that for every subject the high-score state has from 1.67 to 2.41 times as many students in the upper half of the national distribution as the low-score state. These facts show what a very large difference there is in the quality of the seniors in the states in this country, that is, in the educational products of the high schools of the different states.

How are we to explain the considerable differences between the quality of students in different states and the quality of those in different parts of the same state? All that we have said about the interrelationships of intelligence and socioeconomic factors is relevant here. In the first place, it is clear that certain states and certain areas within states are populated predominantly by members of certain socioeconomic levels. The proportions of the various classes from I to V are obviously different in, say, the "exurban" areas of Pennsylvania than they are in the coal-mining areas of West Virginia. If average IQs are higher for Class I than for the classes lower on the scale, an area with a high proportion of Class I inhabitants will produce students of higher average capacity (provided, of course, that the other classes remain relatively balanced).

Secondly, we must point out that the tests used by Bloom are tests not of IQ but of educational development. Variations in the quality of schools therefore are important. That such variations exist can hardly be doubted, and they are certain to be reflected in the quality of students which the schools turn out. It is logical to assume that, if all students tested had attended schools of equal quality, the differences would be smaller.

The differences in the capacities of students from various geographical locations—different parts of the same city, state, and nation—have been gone into in some detail not only because of the subject's inherent interest but also because these differences illustrate the impact of socioeconomic forces upon the task of the schools on many levels. The American schools are faced by the challenge of educating children from all levels and classes of environment and capacity. Only by understanding that challenge can the schools meet it effectively.

Capacity Levels in Colleges. Clearly, large differences exist in the average capacities of student bodies in various colleges throughout the land. The dullest of high school graduates with adequate resources to pay his tuition and support himself could likely discover some college where he would be able to obtain a degree (see Exhibit 10). On the other hand, some colleges select only students who have superior high school records and rank very high on entrance examinations.

On the basis of extensive testing, it is reliably estimated that the average IQ of the students at the poorest colleges in the United States is about 90, while at the best colleges it is at least 130. This tremendous difference means that most students in the best colleges are superior to the best students in the poorest colleges. Many students in the poorest colleges are no more capable than ordinary ninth-graders.

The standard of work in the colleges with very superior students is very high, while in colleges with the lowest-testing students the work can hardly be better than that of average high schools. Yet colleges whose students are so different in their abilities are similarly accredited and give the same degree. The degree cannot, under such conditions, represent the same levels of achievement. In fact, good scholarship in the colleges with the poorest students would be considered failure or, at best, just passing in the colleges that attract the best students.

☯ *Reflect and Review*

Bill M. and Joe L. are both seniors in a moderately large city high school. Bill has an IQ of about 90. He was a slow learner during grade and high school, but is about to graduate at eighteen with a C+ average. He is a likable boy who works hard in order to please his parents, who are ambitious for him. He is not enthusiastic about going to college for its own sake, but wants to go in order to please his parents, who want to send him, and because he knows it will help him get a better job.

Joe L., on the other hand, has an IQ of 139. He has earned very good marks in grade and high school and he has just scored in the top 5 per cent on the national scholarship examination which he took in his senior year. He took part in several activities in high school and wants to go to college to study mathematics, in which he is very much interested. He works hard and is willing to work part-time in order to help pay his college expenses, though his parents are fairly well off and willing to finance his education.

What do these boys' respective mental capacities indicate about whether each should go to college? Explain your answer.

What kind of college should each boy choose? Might both be successful in the same college? What factors should they take into account, and what kinds of courses should each study?

Do you think it likely that Bill could continue to overcome his poor mental capacity through hard work in college? Upon what circumstances would this depend?

CHARACTERISTICS OF THE SUPERIOR STUDENT: THE TERMAN STUDY

In recent years, as we have become increasingly aware of the need for education, more and more concern has been expressed over the fact that many of the abler high school graduates do not go to college. Yet the current idea that many geniuses have been allowed to do nothing with their gifts is misleading in several ways.

First, this idea makes the doubtful assumption that most students in the upper half of their high school graduating class want to go to college, whereas in truth a number of them have little or no interest in such a course and have, in fact, better opportunities elsewhere. College is by no means the only place where the promise of high capacity can be fulfilled. In the arts, particularly, professional schools such as conservatories and apprentice theaters can fulfill certain needs more efficiently.

In the second place, there are many students who are in the upper half of their high school graduating class but are not good college material. Those who are in the next-to-the-highest quarter, especially those just a little above average, are far from being as capable as those who are at the top of their classes. In other words, there are very wide ranges in the capacities and abilities of students in the upper half of their high school graduating class.

In the third place, the fact is that most very superior students do go to college. A much larger percentage of the high school graduates who were at the top of their class than of those who were near the average is found in our colleges. The few with IQs over 140, for example, who do not go to college generally lack the emotional qualities that result in ambition and drive and have not achieved well in high school, in spite of the fact that a student with an IQ of 140 or over is one of the two brightest in about one thousand unselected students. It is true that a considerable proportion of students from the low socioeconomic classes who do satisfactory or superior work in high school fail to go to college, and the high school staff and community should always try especially hard to guide these students into institutions of higher learning. It is, however, doubtful that the highly gifted students even in the low socioeconomic classes do not have opportunities to attend college.

All these valid points must lead us to deeper considerations. Take the fallacy that all the more able students are intellectually very curious, that they have an almost unquenchable thirst for learning. It is, of course, important to know that this is not typical of all or even most of the superior students— that there are just a few whose capacities seem to drive them to study, to write, to play musical instruments, to work with electrical and mechanical devices, or to develop botanical or zoological interests. But it is more important to realize that the majority of clearly above average students need to be guided and stimulated. They need to be stimulated by effective teaching and by incentives such as honors and other special recognition. For one thing, a lack of motivation in school can carry over into the vocational lives of the mentally superior with the result that they function far below their potentiality.

It should be the purpose of education and psychology to do the best for those at all points within the wide range of human capacity. In the past, the American home and school have not developed in some gifted children the feelings, interests, and attitudes that are the core of motivation to learn; and during the last 20 years, even though we have gained valid and comprehensive knowledge about individual differences, we have done even less, until very recently, for the gifted than we did before. In short, the classwork and teaching have been geared to the average and the dull. There is now, however, more concern for the most favorable development of those with top capacities; in this desirable sense, the era of the "common man" has passed, in part.

Educating superior grade and high school students is neither difficult nor expensive, because they are capable of working independently. The principal need is to understand the gifted child and to give him a chance to do more and to do it faster than other children.

Fortunately, we have a monumental study by L. M. Terman and his associates which gives us much information about a group of intellectually superior individuals who were studied as children, as young adults, and as middle-aged adults [Terman et al., 1959]. The study of these gifted subjects has been in progress for over 40 years; even now it is continuing toward another report to be made on the group when its members will have been studied for about fifty years. Many other studies of mentally advanced children support the findings of Terman's—the most extensive study of very intelligent people.

This study will be presented here in considerable detail because it demonstrates the role of mental capacity and other factors in the personal progress not just of its subjects, who have very high mental capacities and abilities, but of other people as well. The Terman studies and others of a similar nature bring out certain principles or generalizations about human abilities and personal qualities in their relation to achievement and adjustment that are helpful in understanding what people can do and what they are likely to do.

Terman's study of the mentally gifted began in 1921 with the selection of 1,528 children, of whom 857 were boys and 671 were girls. The average age was eleven years. A few had IQs between 133 and 139; most had IQs of at least 140; and the average for the 1,528 subjects was 151. On the average, the mental powers of the subjects were of the high order which is found only once in over 500 typical schoolchildren. There were 77 subjects with IQs of 170 or above.

In the first investigation, reported in 1925, the physical, social, moral, and emotional characteristics of the gifted children were studied. Their educational experiences and progress were also studied, and the socioeconomic status of their families was determined. All levels of socioeconomic class were represented, although there was a considerable preponderance of upper-class homes.

Three other reports of the group followed—in 1930, in 1947, and in 1959. Since these reports present no important contradictions, a short survey of the first (1925) and last (1959) reports will suffice for our purposes [Terman et al., 1925–1959].

Gifted Children as Grade and High School Students. Here is a summary of the first study, made when the subjects were grade and high school students.

Physique and health. Measurements indicated that these very bright children were a little taller and a few pounds heavier and were better developed physically than were unselected children of their ages. This does not mean that none of the gifted children were underdeveloped physically; nevertheless, the typical gifted child seemed to be better off physically than the typical child of average mental capacity.

The Terman gifted children also had better health histories than the generality of children. Headaches and defective hearing were about one-half as common as among the nongifted. Physical and organic defects of the lungs, heart, and kidneys were also less frequent. Colds, worrying, and nervousness were about as frequent among the gifted as among children at large. Although more of these intellectually gifted children than average children wore glasses, the principal explanation lies in the much greater use of their eyes in reading and studying, not in any inherent weakness. For comparable reasons, accountants, architects, and professors wear glasses much more frequently than do farmers, longshoremen, or factory workers.

Inasmuch as these results were first reported in 1925 and have been confirmed by subsequent studies, we have known for several decades that gifted boys and girls are not weak physical specimens as they have often been depicted. On the whole, they are not bigheaded, sunken-chested, spindly, awkward, and pale youngsters; rather, they are generally larger and healthier than children of only average mental capacity.

Of course, some of the physical superiority of the gifted children can be attributed to the fact that a higher-than-average proportion of them came from upper-class homes and thus probably had better physical care than the average child does. Terman concluded, however, on the basis of comparisons with unselected children, that the physical superiority of the gifted children surpassed what could be accounted for by better care alone.

Interests and play activities. It has been customary to think of exceptionally bright children as engaging in lonely pursuits and not joining other children of their ages in games and sports. This point of view logically followed the once generally accepted idea that bright children are too backward physically to participate in competition with other children.

Terman's gifted boys were not less masculine than a control group of mentally average children with whom they were compared in game participation; and in knowledge about sports and games, the gifted children—girls and boys—were far ahead of average children. These control children were slightly more interested in social participation than were the gifted; this was judged to be a result of the greater capacity of the intellectually superior to find satisfaction in reading and other solitary activities.

Such intellectual interests showed up in the reading habits of these very bright youngsters. They read over twice as many books as did a control group of children, and the books they read were generally of higher quality. Correspondingly, they had more interest, as a group, in the academic and abstract school subjects and less in vocational subjects. But the very bright brought their intellectual interests out, so to speak: they had more interest in public speaking, dramatics, and debate than average children. All this is consistent with their orientation toward professional occupations rather than toward those in the middle or lower part of the vocational scale.

Moral, emotional, and social qualities. The gifted children, when compared with a control group, had better scores on overstatement (lying), cheating, emotional stability, and social attitudes and characteristics (see Exhibit 11). This finding, as we shall see, later was substantiated by the adult record of the gifted, which is almost free of crime and delinquency. The gifted children were decidedly more truthful and conscientious. Other research indicated that

Exhibit 11 Percentage of gifted subjects who equaled or surpassed the mean of control subjects in each of seven character tests and in total score

Tests	Boys	Girls
1. Overstatement A	57	59
2. Overstatement B	63	73
3. Book preferences	74	76
4. Character preferences	77	81
5. Social attitudes	86	83
6. Cheating tests	68	61
7. Emotional stability	67	75
Total score	86	84

This table shows the results of a battery of seven character tests Terman administered to 532 of his gifted subjects when they were seven to fourteen years old and to 533 unselected children ten to fourteen years old. The tests were from batteries designed by V. M. Cady and by A. S. Raubenheimer. The first two both tested tendency to overstate or lie in reporting experience or knowledge, the next three tested presumed "wholesomeness" of tastes and preferences, and the last two tested tendency to cheat under tempting circumstances as well as emotional stability. (L. M. Terman and Melita H. Oden, *Genetic Studies of Genius,* vol. V, *The Gifted Group at Mid-life,* Stanford University Press, Stanford, Calif., 1959, p. 12. Reprinted in the 1959 volume in recalling the finding of the first study reported in 1925.)

they were clearly ahead in leadership, though only a little above the average in social acceptance by their peers.

The gifted children were regarded by their teachers as being distinctly superior in the power to persevere and the drive to excel. They also had more general comprehension, more ability to anticipate what would happen, more confidence, more cheerfulness, and better sense of humor than the non-gifted, according to their teachers. Morally, socially, emotionally, and volitionally the gifted children were clearly—and, in some instances, substantially—above average.

Educational status and progress. The superiority of the intellectually gifted children, however, was most evident in their educational achievements. This was to be expected, as the abilities needed for educational achievement are more closely related to intelligence than are moral, social, emotional, and physical qualities. Intellect and educational achievement are as closely linked as physical skill and athletic prowess, for example.

The gifted grade schoolchildren were given the Stanford Achievement Test in reading (nearly half of them had been able to read before they started school), arithmetic, and language usage, as well as for information in various fields. Their average achievement quotient (see page 520) was 144, and many of them demonstrated achievement up to three and even four grades above the grade they were in. The educational achievements of the gifted children were, in a word, consistent with their very high intelligence quotients.

Gifted Subjects as Middle-aged Adults. Just as this report of the first Terman investigation corrected many erroneous notions about gifted children, the 1959 report cleared up the basic question of the success of gifted children, relative to others, in later life.

The 1959 report, by Terman and Melita H. Oden, was based on an investigation made of the original group of gifted children when they had reached an average age of 44. Remarkably, only 28, or less than 2 per cent, of the original group of 1,528 had been lost track of by 1955. Another 104, or nearly seven per cent, had died.

The 1959 report verified the previous reports on the gifted group by describing a record of high success experienced by a large majority of the subjects.

Abstract intelligence. Terman's gifted children were selected, as has been explained, for their very high IQs. Were the subjects, about 34 years later in mid-adulthood, as superior in abstract intelligence as they were when children? Terman and Oden's data make it clear that extremely high abstract intelligence in childhood is followed by equally high abstract intelligence in adulthood.

The Terman adults were measured by a test called the Concept Mastery Test. It consists of 120 pairs of words which the subjects mark as having either the same or opposite meanings, along with 70 analogies which test reasoning power and knowledge in science, mathematics, geography, sports, music, and other fields. The test was especially constructed in 1939 for Terman's subjects because existing intelligence tests were not so satisfactory for adults as the experimenters wished. The reliability of the test was carefully established, and it has since been published and enjoyed a wide use. Its results can be correlated with Stanford-Binet IQs for purposes of comparison.

The Terman adults' scores on the Concept Mastery Test were compared with those of various student groups in order to have a basis for judging their intellectual levels as adults. These groups included Ph.D. candidates, M.D. candidates, and applicants for graduate fellowships. The average of the Terman adults was clearly higher than the averages of these various superior student groups. The results showed that these one-time gifted children had maintained their high intellectual endowments into middle adulthood and were, on the average, at the time of the test, in the top 1 per cent of the population at large in intellectual abilities. There was a wide range in the scores the Terman adults made on the Concept Mastery Test, but even the lowest scores were above the average of the general public.

Yet Terman's 1959 report of the gifted subjects revealed not a single famous genius in the group. Though they had written novels, short stories, poetry, plays, and scientific articles, taken out patents, and composed music, not one of these gifted persons seemed to have produced work of the very highest creative order. Theirs, apparently, is a story of success and distinction, but not of genius. Thus they suggest that the occasional designation of any person with an IQ of 140 or over as a genius is an unfortunate one—that genius is a very special creative capacity that should not be attributed to IQ.

Educational progress. At the time of the last research done in 1955, four years before it was published, the education of the gifted children of 1921 had been practically completed. An occasional gifted adult of this study may have taken a few courses or may even have gotten an advanced degree at a later date. But the 1955 findings on the educational records of the gifted subjects are practically the final score.

In educational progress, the gifted dramatically exceeded the average. Of the 1,528 included in the study, only 2 men and 9 women had not earned a high school diploma, but 4 of these had taken business or trade courses and 4 others had studied in schools of dramatics, dancing, or music. Of the gifted men, 70 per cent earned bachelor's degrees; of the gifted women, 67 per cent did so. At the time of the first Terman investigation, only about eight per cent of all students finished college; the record of his gifted group was more than eight times as high.

In addition, 56 per cent of the men and 33 per cent of the women had earned advanced degrees; and one-fourth of the men had earned the doctor of philosophy degree, the medical degree, or the law degree. These figures contrast sharply with those for the college population in general, of whom, in 1953, only about seventeen per cent continued to the master's degree and only about two per cent to the doctorate. These strikingly high proportions, incidentally, help to explain why many of the gifted achieved high socioeconomic status as professional people. Of course, many of the gifted children came originally from homes high on the socioeconomic scale; education, however, helped them to maintain or raise their positions.

The careers of the gifted. The careers of the gifted correlate in a general way with their education and mental capacities. When investigated in 1955, not all the men had reached the high socioeconomic levels of which they were capable, but not one of them was in the lowest occupational group classified as unskilled. About one per cent of the gifted (two of whom were bartenders and managers of bars) were in the semiskilled occupations (see Table 13). It will be observed that nearly 90 per cent of the gifted men had achieved high vocational status. A higher proportion of all gifted men (even including noncollege graduates) than of college graduates as a general group are in the top occupational class.

About one-half of the gifted women were housewives with no outside-the-home employment. However, 41.5 per cent were employed full time. They included doctors, lawyers, members of college faculties, schoolteachers, social workers, authors, librarians, secretaries, stenographers, executives, and real estate dealers. Many were doing well occupationally; as a group, these women were far more active and successful than women of their ages in general.

The median family income of the gifted subjects in 1954 was $10,866. Since the median income for urban white families in the United States in 1955 was $5,069, the median for the gifted subjects was comfortably above the United States median. Ten per cent of the gifted men had annual incomes of $25,000 or over.

The 1954 median income of the fully employed women of this study was $4,875, with 6 per cent of the women making $10,000 or more. The highest income, that of a woman physician, was $24,000.

On the whole, the gifted men and women were well adjusted vocationally. Nearly half the men and a little over half the women were highly interested in and very satisfied with their vocations. A little over a third of both sexes were fairly content with their vocations. A little over 10 per cent of the men

Table 13 Comparison of Occupations of Gifted Men and College Graduates in the United States

Occupational Classification	College Graduates, Per Cent		All Gifted Men, Per Cent
	All	Gifted	
1. Professional of all types, proprietors, managers, executives	84	93.7	86.3
2. Clerical, sales, and kindred workers	10	4.3	10.9
3. Skilled, semiskilled, and unskilled workers	5	0.5	1.2
4. Farmers and farm workers	1	1.5	1.6

Source: L. M. Terman and Melita H. Oden, *Genetic Studies of Genius*, vol. V, *The Gifted Group at Mid-life*, Stanford University Press, Stanford, Calif., 1959, p. 80.

and a little less than 10 per cent of the women were discontented or not particularly happy with their vocations; only about one per cent were strongly dissatisfied and wished to change work.

Politics. In political and social outlook, these gifted adults were, on the whole, moderate. Only a little over 1 per cent of the gifted men and women held political views on the radical left; slightly over 5 per cent of the gifted adults classified themselves as extremely conservative. Thus, a relatively small percentage of these gifted middle-agers took a strong view on maintaining their *status quo* and keeping what they had. Most of the gifted adults tended to be average in their political views.

This was to be expected, of course. It is natural that adults who have very good positions and incomes will not become very radical. They do not have the vocational and personal frustrations that are likely to breed the social hostility and aggressiveness that often express themselves in radicalism. Troubled and failing people often rationalize their situations by blaming the political and/or economic situation and becoming exponents of communistic ideologies or advocates of sweeping changes. The gifted adults had been under few of the frustration pressures that cradle radicals.

Not many members of the gifted group had aspired for political office, and not one had been elected to high state or national office such as governor or congressman. One gifted man who had run for United States representative had been defeated.

Although the group as a whole was judged, on the basis of total rankings, as "slightly right of center," the most conservative were found to be the older men, those who had entered but not completed college, businessmen, and those with the lowest scores on the Concept Mastery Test. Surprisingly, there was little relationship between income and degree of conservatism.

Death rate, health, and emotional and social adjustment. As previously stated, 104, or nearly 7 per cent, of the gifted had died by 1955. When we compare this death rate with that of the population at large, we find that, for the subjects Terman studied, the death rate was lower by 1.1 per cent.

The physical health of the gifted subjects, moreover, was better than average. At the average age of forty-four, about 90 per cent were in good or very good health, and only about 2 per cent were in poor or very poor health.

But what about their mental health, and what about their relations to the world at large? Very bright people are often characterized as tending to fail in emotional and social adjustment. One evidence of such failure is mental illness. The percentage of Terman's subjects who were hospitalized for mental disorders between the ages of ten and forty-five was almost exactly the same as that for the general population (3 per cent). Moreover, the high socioeconomic status of the group as a whole would indicate that more cases were detected and treated than are likely to be treated in the general population. If figures were available for comparable socioeconomic groups, Terman's group might well be under the average for such groups.

Another stereotype links brilliance with alcoholism. Only about 1 per cent of Terman's adults were experiencing serious trouble with liquor in 1955. Another 1 per cent had been alcoholics but had overcome their difficulty. This figure is much lower than that for the United States adult population, which is 3 to 4 per cent.

Still another stereotype pictures very bright people as hard to get along with; if this were true, there would be a high divorce rate among the gifted. The divorce rate of the gifted adults (one in five) was also a little less than that of married people in general in 1955 (one in four). Of special interest here is the fact that within the whole group, relative degrees of education were related to marriage success. There had been twice as many divorces among the gifted men who had not finished college as among those who had finished. The percentages were 35 and 15.8. The gifted men and women who did not go to college had had a still larger percentage of divorces. The suggestion is that going to college and finishing require the same persistence and capacity for adjustment which are needed for marital success.

Finally, Terman's subjects have shown little sign of the maladjustment which manifests itself in crime and delinquency. Three of the gifted boys had been sent to reformatories. One adult man had spent several years in prison for forgery. One woman had served a jail sentence for vagrancy. At the time of the last study, however, none of the gifted adults was imprisoned, and the five who once had been were getting along well personally and vocationally. The gifted had proved to be superior in various degrees in every characteristic which had been evaluated, but their superiority was probably most marked in their low criminal records.

Those Who Did Not Fulfill Their Promise. In the Biblical parable of the talents it was the person with only one talent who buried his; those with the most utilized them. Yet in the case of Terman's gifted, as we have seen, a few fell far short of what could be expected of them—a few of these most fortunate persons did bury their talents.

Why did a number of these gifted persons progress no further? Why did several not finish high school, and why did a larger number start in college but not graduate? How could some, in 1955, be in vocations that are considered far below the level of people with superior intellects? Why were some of these gifted persons fated to go on only to status achievement that can be expected, indeed, of boys and girls with IQs of 100? And why did those few we have mentioned as failing in personal adjustment to life do so badly?

The nature of these questions prohibits answers in terms of statistics or percentages. The reasons for failure to achieve one's promise are usually complex and elusive. Terman's study did not attempt to identify the reasons for the relative lack of achievement by some of his subjects, but the questions are so intriguing that it may be useful to suggest a few plausible answers.

Of central importance is the fact that other qualities besides intellect account for progress and adjustment. A person with superior intellect needs to choose suitably high goals and to possess the perseverance that will carry him to their achievement, and he needs feelings which will serve as motivating forces as well as facilitate good day-to-day personal adjustment. The gifted children who as adults failed to live up to their promise apparently lacked these emotional and volitional qualities. In other words, probably there was an inadequate integration of feelings and intellect.

One explanation for this might be found in home situations of these few during early childhood. Were the parents in disagreement? Were these gifted children rejected by their parents? Did they learn from their home situations to feel unsafe and unsure? It is quite possible that their home experiences caused them to develop attitudes or feelings which inhibited them, diffused their interests, and rendered them less effective.

Probably, too, some gifted children who did not live up to expectations were affected negatively by the school situation. Their teachers may not have understood that they were extra bright and so may have given them work that was deadening for them. If the gifted were then scolded and reprimanded for not working hard on their lessons, they were conditioned by the school to avoid work or against sustaining their efforts to reach their goals. In school situations where the work was unsuitable for their abilities, they had few if any goals to work for. Any such failure to understand or appreciate very bright children would tend to build up negative feelings toward school and its responsibilities. Possibly if the school had understood some of these gifted children better and adapted their work to their capacities, more of them would have developed effective habits while in school, so that even fewer of them would have been ineffective as adults.

Some of the gifted who did not do very well vocationally possibly had a constitutional weakness. Could it be that in the structural makeup of some—nervous system, glands, organs, etc.—there was some deficiency which resulted in various degrees of ineffectiveness? This might be the case in some instances, although such an explanation should be advanced only tentatively.

Indeed, for most of the failures, any one cause is probably not a sufficient explanation. It is more likely that most of the individual cases of under-achievement would have to be explained by complex combinations of these external and internal influences—the home, the school, and the individual's organism.

☯ *Reflect and Review*

Gary has an IQ of 155. He has a superior mind, but received only average marks in school. He wanted to spend his time as he pleased, did not care to do the assignments, and got through high school without showing any interest in his work. The teachers said that it was a pity he did not use his capacities. He did not participate much in the school activities and was not popular with the other students.

After he started college, he was called into the counselor's office frequently; and he dropped out of college in the first semester of his sophomore year.

What are his prospects vocationally?

Describe what his future is to be in terms of the discussed aspects of the lives of the middle-aged adults who had been Terman's gifted children.

What one word describes best what a person like Gary needs very much in school?

How good a husband is Gary likely to be?

SUMMARY

Factors basic to effective learning and personal success, such as achievement drive, emotional health, cultural background, and curiosity, should be kept in mind even when the factor of mental capacity is given primary consideration.

Standings on intelligence tests correlate only moderately with marks in the academic subjects because of differences in the students' industriousness, inaccuracies in marking, and unreliability of test scores.

Correlations between intelligence-test standings and special subjects such as art, sewing, woodworking, and other skill subjects are low.

Intelligence quotients and mental ages obtained for school entrants by means of individual mental examinations are helpful for guiding the child and for predicting his progress in learning.

Results from special aptitude tests are often a useful basis for guiding students into areas where they have the greatest capacities and thus are most likely to succeed.

Intelligence-test standing indicates what a student should be able to do, and school marks indicate what he has done and therefore will probably do again. Students who are high in both intelligence-test standing and school marks usually progress up the educational ladder. Dropouts are generally lacking in both capacity and achievement.

As students progress from first grade up to higher and higher educational levels, the decreasing number of survivors have correspondingly higher mental capacities, and the dropouts tend to have less capacity. The earlier they drop out the less their capacity. This is correspondingly true of the ambition and industry of the students.

Ordinarily the more difficult subjects are no better preparation for college than the easier subjects. Most important are the mental capacity, motivation, and study habits of the high school graduate. Nevertheless it is desirable to gain as much competence and develop as much interest in a needed subject or area as one can.

Even though there appear to be differences in the mental abilities of boys and girls, conceivably such differences are caused by custom and interest rather than by differences in the nervous system. It should also be remembered that the sex differences in mental abilities are in terms of averages and that there are many of each sex who are superior to members of the other sex in all mental abilities. In terms of educability, boys and girls may be considered as being essentially equal on the average.

Even though girls tend to be better readers in the primary grades and more boys are problem readers in those grades, the average differences in the two sexes are not large enough to warrant the girls' starting school younger than the boys.

Sex differences also show themselves in the school marks received. Girls receive better marks for their schoolwork than do the boys, even though on comprehensive, objective examinations the boys tend to score higher than the girls.

There is a very wide range in the mental capacities of the students of a given class, department, school, or college.

Even though there is a positive correlation between years of school attendance and mental capacities, high school and college are not so selective as they once were. Still there are some colleges which select only students of high capacities and high achievement.

There are substantial differences in the average mental capacities of students in individual schools, in sections of a city or of a state, and among the states themselves. The differences can be attributed largely· to the vocational-economic-educational status of the people in the various sections.

Pupils of high mental capacity come largely from homes of above-average socioeconomic status. In personal qualities and equipment they tend to be above average—in physical size, health, ethical sense, emotional stability, and recreational interests.

As adults, Terman's gifted are still very superior in general intelligence; approximately nine times as many of them have finished college and obtained advanced degrees as a comparable age population; they have achieved high vocational status, are exceptionally free of crime, are in better-than-average health, and have lower-than-average death rates. The stability of their marriages also is probably a little better than average.

The gifted who did not live up to their promise were usually under-achievers in school and dropped out before finishing college. They lacked the emotional, volitional qualities necessary for the utilization of their capacities.

SUGGESTED READING

Dinger, J. C.: "Post-school Adjustment of Former Educable Pupils," *Exceptional Children*, 27:353–360, 1961. Dinger made a careful follow-up study of 100 subjects with IQ's ranging from 50 to 85 and with an average of 70.5. He discusses their post-school record according to (1) educational experiences, (2) military experiences, (3) occupational history, (4) marital history, (5) financial history, (6) community participation, and (7) leisure-time activities. The reader will probably be surprised by the successful experiences they have had.

Dugon, Ruth: "Investigation of the Personal, Social, Educational, and Economic Reasons for Success and Lack of Success in School as Experienced by 105 Tenth Grade Biology Students," *Journal of Educational Research*, 55:544–553, 1962. A comprehensive overview of the problem of withdrawing from school. Much information is presented about the attitudes and abilities of students in terms of both persistence in school and dropping out.

Mannino, F. V.: "Family Factors Related to School Persistence," *Journal of Educational Sociology*, 35:193–202, 1962. This research brings out some ideas about the mothers' attitudes toward education and persistence in school. Shows how complex the whole problem of school dropouts really is.

CHAPTER 8
ADAPTING THE SCHOOL
TO ITS
DIFFERING STUDENTS

Most children and youths want to be successful at their various school tasks and are happy when they are able to do them well; though they want to be challenged by their tasks, they do not want the tasks to be so difficult that they set up feelings of frustration and defeat. At the same time, every ordinary group of students is comprised of individuals who differ very widely in their capacities and abilities and, relatedly, in their motivations. Thus tasks that are easy for some students will be too difficult for others, and some will grasp lessons much faster than others.

Children will therefore be happiest and do their best work in classes where the experiences are suited to them as individuals, and the school must guide each child so that his experiences will satisfy his needs. There are a number of ways the school can do so; and these adjustments of the school to the student are discussed in this chapter.

CLASS PROJECTS, ENRICHMENT, AND INDIVIDUALIZED INSTRUCTION

Class projects provide a wealth of opportunities for adapting instruction to the variations among students. In addition, the individual student can be helped by what is called enrichment of his normal curriculum. And third, a school can use some form of individualized instruction in order to ensure that each child is given work that will enable him to achieve success with his schoolwork, on the one hand, and to widen the range of his interests and abilities, on the other.

Let us consider separately these three ways of adapting the learning situation to the varying needs of students.

The project method of teaching and several variations (known as activity, progressive, or student-centered methods) allow for the wide variety of individual differences within heterogeneous groups of students through introduction of class projects related to subjects of study. The activities needed for carrying out such projects are diverse and so call on various aptitudes and inclinations. Thus academically bright children get a chance to work independently by looking up and studying special references on which they then report to the class. Duller students too can do special work in areas where they have a particular talent and interest.

The child who has a special talent, say, in acting or painting is provided with needed chances to develop it through projects. He can direct and present a little play based on a historic event or can do a mural depicting it, for example.

Also, the less academically and artistically able may find enough to do that they may be stimulated too. Thus a boy who normally is a marginal member of a class may be right in the center of a certain activity because of his ability to construct things with his hands.

This boy is particularly illustrative of the value of the project method of teaching. Suppose he is chosen to build a model of a historical object. He may have to do a considerable amount of figuring and, because he has a special stake in doing so, may learn more arithmetic than in almost any number of formal lessons. Then he may have to express himself orally by explaining the model to the class, and he will probably do so much better than might be expected, again because he is highly interested.

Probably best of all, this boy will be getting social experiences that he would not get if his manual flair, which the other children do not have but are intrigued by, were not called forth. Children learn more when their present skills and interests lead to developing additional ones, and they have better social experiences when this learning process is closely related to the activities of their peers.

Special abilities can also be cultivated by supplementing the study resources within particular fields of learning. Such inclusion of additional materials and activities, so that those who can do more than the average amount of work in a field can have more profitable experiences, is called enrichment.

Thus, through enrichment, the brighter students, particularly, can be given opportunities to pursue an especially interesting topic far beyond the sometimes pedestrian limits of classwork and thus to explore the limits of their own capacities. Thus, when a geography class is studying the state of New York, the brighter student may read books on the state for which others cannot find the time, gather and arrange graphic materials illustrative of its contrasting environments, and interview persons who have lived in and are well informed about New York, that is, they may engage in activities that will give them a more comprehensive understanding of the state.

Enrichment also takes other forms. There can be special periods in which the school librarian helps students explore books in various fields—biography, psychology, art, to name a few. The reading may be supplementary to courses, or independent of them, or both. Thus, the students are encouraged to expand their knowledge in familiar fields and also to explore new areas. Enrichment can be provided in a slightly different way by offering advanced work in various academic subjects to groups of especially qualified students. Here the teaching is geared to a higher-than-usual level. Special consideration is given to principles, theories, and generalizations; in other words, the work is made more abstract and less concrete. The students react to ideas and evaluate them.

Sometimes enrichment is achieved by encouraging abler students to take such courses as typewriting, painting, and woodwork, or to participate in such extra activities as dramatics, playing a musical instrument, and gardening. This can enlarge the range of interests possessed by such students, who tend to do extended and intensive work on just a few academic subjects. Even activities with questionable academic value—gardening, for instance— may enrich such a student's later life immeasurably by providing him with a stimulating hobby.

Enrichment is provided for some children outside the school; some parents introduce special training in music, dancing, dramatics, or art early in the lives of their children and continue it as long as their children are in school. If students are spending some of their out-of-school hours in such activities, the teacher should not, of course, load them with special work in order to achieve enrichment. They are already experiencing desirable forms of it, and the teacher may concern himself primarily with enrichment of the subjects and activities regarded as the more essential elements in the curriculum.

J. M. Dunlap reports a striking effect of enrichment for bright children who met with "enrichment teachers" in groups of 8 to 10 twice each week for 40- to 50-minute periods [Dunlap, 1955]. During these enrichment periods the students worked on topics which interested them, such as history of the wheel, children in other lands, prehistoric times, and great inventions. It was discovered that among the seventh-graders 14 members of the honor roll's 62 members came from the enrichment group of 23 members while only 4 came from the control group of 23 members having similar IQs.

It seems that membership in the enrichment group motivated the members to work more effectively. This is consistent with the general findings, especially for the brightest students, that experimentation or activities of various kinds stirred up new drives which increased accomplishments. Special interest in the pupils and their activities, variations in teaching procedures, acceleration, ability grouping, and the departures from the usual routines affected many students favorably by giving them confidence and new interests.

Individualized instruction is a method of teaching that enables the student to learn at his own rate. This system requires specially prepared materials— instructional materials arranged in units so that the child can master the contents with a minimum of help from the teacher, accompanied by self-testing exercises which enable the student to determine how well he has mastered the part of the subject that he has studied. When he passes an examination on one unit, he is permitted to begin another unit. The progress of students under this plan thus depends even more than usual on their industry and learning ability.

Incidentally, there has recently been much interesting use of teaching machines to facilitate individualized instruction. The machines are designed to allow the bright student to master quickly what might bore him if a great deal of time were spent on it and, at the same time, to let the dull student progress without being harried by the speed of those quicker at learning than he is. Observers have reported that students are often eager to use the machines. The brighter students enjoy being able to forge ahead, while the duller students are freed from the anxiety of a competitive situation and therefore can better enjoy learning.

The term "teaching machine" is not, perhaps, a fortunate one, since it implies to many people a sensational, robotlike device that is to "replace human beings." This, however, is a misconception. A teaching machine, or auto-instructional device, is merely a recently developed means of applying learning principles which not only are very old but also are universally used by good teachers no matter what their particular methods are. These principles are basically those of the tutorial system, in which a tutor works with an individual student, constantly explaining, questioning, and encouraging the student to progress. Thus the student is presented with material in small units which he can grasp quickly; he is immediately tested and immediately rewarded if he responds correctly or is immediately helped if he does not.

How can a machine do this? There are many different types of teaching machines, but they have certain elements in common. A typical machine looks like a box (about the size of a small television set) with an opening in the top, sometimes partially covered by glass. A long roll of paper upon which the material is printed is moved past this window, and the student can answer the questions which he is asked by writing directly on the roll of paper through an opening provided for that purpose. Some method of advancing the roll is provided, either a button or a lever which the student operates. A very early teaching machine was designed in the 1920s by S. L. Pressey, but the man most responsible for the reinvention and development of teaching machines is B. F. Skinner, of Harvard University.

Several special terms are used in connection with teaching machines. The material is called a "program"; the portion which appears at any one time in the window is a "frame." The technique in general is called "programmed learning" and need not be confined to machine use; indeed, some programs are now published in book form.

One great virtue of the best programs is the surprisingly efficient way they can adapt to individual responses. The goal is to elicit only correct responses from the student, thus positively reinforcing the learning. If a student makes a wrong response, however, he is given additional explanation, instructed to repeat certain frames, and (in the best programs) given detailed analyses of how he went astray.

The use of the term teaching machines and their sensational treatment in the press when they were first introduced have led to a great deal of controversy over their implications for education. Much of the controversy is a result of misinformation or distortion of facts and of attempted mis-applications of the concept of programmed learning. Some of the doubts, however, are well founded, and indeed are a matter of concern among those who are most in favor of the machines' use. The chief points of controversy are (1) the machines' apparent primary orientation toward objective, factual material; and (2) the danger that the machine-taught learners may not be exposed to enough opportunities for social learning. Certainly these are valid objections, but they actually imply only what is already obvious: that the method cannot relieve the individual teacher of responsibility for their wise use. The study of the potentialities of teaching machines is by no means complete. It is progressing, as a matter of fact, rather slowly, because of the length of time required to write and test a good program. For the teacher who is genuinely concerned with exploiting every possible method to help his students develop their own individual potentialities to the fullest extent, however, programmed learning holds exciting promise.

Teaching machines may be used just as a supplement to the usual teaching in a course. The best results seem to occur, however, when the machine is regarded as a device which can substitute, in certain cases, for the regular classroom instruction. This keeps the student who completes a machine program and demonstrates that he has really mastered its content, for instance, from having to rehash his knowledge in the slower-moving regular class.

The individualized method of instruction emphasizes acquisition of the basic facts and skills in the various subjects; and it is doubtful that, by this system alone, the student gets adequate opportunity to apply these facts and skills, as he might if he were learning through activities or in a social situation. There are schools, however, where individualized instruction is used but not allowed to dominate the program. Such a school is that of the Winnetka,

Illinois, public school system, which in the 1920s was developing a pioneer program in individualized instruction. At Winnetka, half the day is spent in group activities and the other half in individual work. Groups of children engage in pageants and plays, group singing, excursions, the arts and handicrafts, and creative writing. In addition, having their own government helps teach the students social skills. The combined program gives the children an opportunity to relate their instruction to group living.

Spending Time on Weaknesses. Individualized instruction allows students to strengthen themselves in their weaker subjects by spending more time on them and less time on their stronger subjects. Thus it suggests the important general question: Is it wise for a student with one or more particular abilities and one or several weak points to neglect the former in order to strengthen the latter? For example, should a student who is an excellent musician but is failing mathematics spend less time practicing music and more time working with numbers?

For the most part, teachers do make a practice of drilling students on their weak subjects at the expense of time available for strong ones. Thus teachers in effect espouse the idea of an educational system directed toward uniform development.

Is this generally wise? Let Amos Dolbear suggest our answer.[1]

> In Antediluvian times, while the animal kingdom was being differentiated into swimmers, climbers, runners, and fliers, there was a school for the development of the animal.
>
> The theory of the school was that the best animals should be able to do one thing as well as another.
>
> If an animal had short legs and good wings, attention should be devoted to running so as to even up the qualities as far as possible.
>
> So the duck was kept waddling instead of swimming. The pelican was kept wagging his short wings in the attempt to fly. The eagle was made to run and allowed to fly only for recreation.
>
> All this in the name of education. Nature was not to be trusted, for individuals should be symmetrically developed and similar for their own welfare as well as for the welfare of the community. The animals that would not submit to such training, but persisted in developing the best gifts they had, were dishonored and humiliated in many ways. They were stigmatized as being narrow-minded specialists, and special difficulties were placed in their way when they attempted to ignore the theory of education recognized in the school.
>
> No one was allowed to graduate from the school unless he could climb, swim, run, and fly at certain prescribed rates; so it happened that the time wasted by the duck in the attempt to run had so hindered him from swimming

[1] Amos E. Dolbear, "Antediluvian Education," *Journal of Education*, 68:424, 1908.

that his swimming muscles had atrophied, and so he was hardly able to swim at all; and in addition he had been scolded, punished, and ill-treated in many ways so as to make his life a burden. He left school humiliated, and the ornithorhynchus could beat him both running and swimming. Indeed, the latter was awarded a prize in two departments.

The eagle could make no headway in climbing to the top of a tree, and although he showed he could get there just the same, the performance was counted a demerit since it had not been done in the prescribed way.

An abnormal eel with large pectoral fins proved he could run, fly, climb trees, and swim a little. He was made valedictorian.

As should have been the policy for these unfortunate animals, a student should not be forced to neglect his strength or strengths in order to cultivate his weaknesses. More growth results from time spent in cultivating and perfecting one's greater talents than from the same time given to attempting to develop one's weaker powers. If a student has a special interest in a subject, especially if he also has more ability in it than in others, he should work at it more rather than less. The teacher and librarian should provide him with extra books in the field and should be alert in calling his attention to lectures, motion pictures, exhibits, and other opportunities for sharpening his interest, widening his knowledge, and developing his critical attitude toward this field of his special ability. Thus he may develop a proficiency in a field of study that he will pursue all his life.

Conversely, much extra time devoted to a student's weaknesses is probably not well spent because it may prevent him from such development and may even dull him in the drilled subject. A better plan is to develop children into adults who are strong in some fields of knowledge and weak in others rather than uniformly mediocre in all.

This idea, it should be noted, is not so applicable to specific weaknesses within a given subject as it is to larger areas of ability. If, for example, a pupil is weak in certain basic steps in arithmetic, there should be drill on that weakness so that it will not remain to prevent growth in that subject. On the other hand, if a student is particularly good in the manual arts and poor and uninterested in certain required academic subjects, emphasis should be placed on learning those vocational subjects. If there are subjects for which a student has an aptitude, schools should never be arbitrary about requiring other subjects that, for him, are extremely distressing.

Almost every teacher, especially those in high school and college, can recall the effects of instances where students have had to repeat a subject several times. Some students have been driven from school because of their inability to pass a certain course after two or three attempts. Others have survived academically, but in doing so have suffered an ordeal that has left a scar on their personality. In cases where students do well or reasonably well in all but one or two subjects which seem, for one reason or another, to be insurmountable obstacles, it is good educational procedure to substitute other subjects for the overtroublesome ones. In other instances, the difficulty of the student can be overcome by giving him a change of teacher. At any rate, adjustment of one kind or another should be made so that failure in one or two subjects will not have the chance to destroy a student's whole educational career.

Adults are not required to be uniformly proficient in many abilities; after all, there are scores of languages and hundreds of fields of learning of which many well-educated people have no knowledge whatever. In other words, adult life does not call for symmetrical development. Much less does child life, and only in school do we work for it. In adulthood, we are most successful when we do the work in which we are most interested and when we capitalize on our greatest capacities. In education, we tend too much to neglect this fact; the Greek ideal of harmonious all-round development is still too much with us.

There are, of course, personal and not directly academic weaknesses that should be given considerable attention when a student manifests them. For example, if a child stutters, special and even extended effort should be devoted to overcoming his speech defect, for such a defect is a serious handicap in all personal relationships. Similarly, if a child is very shy, uncommunicative, fearful, and suspicious, the teachers must pay special attention to him and try to develop him into a pleasant, personable child who plays and works happily with his fellows. The physical education teacher tries to overcome physical defects in a child and improve his bearing so that he will have fewer difficulties both in childhood and in adulthood; likewise, time should be devoted by other teachers to the kind of handicaps mentioned here until they have been entirely overcome or are no longer serious threats to development.

● Reflect and Review

Suppose there is a boy named Andrew in your seventh-grade class who has a great deal of difficulty with history, which "bores" him, he says. His IQ is about 115; in classes other than history, although he does not distinguish himself by any means, he does reasonably well. Although he does not have the antipathy toward his other classes that he has toward history, his work is perfunctory and seemingly directed only toward satisfying the minimum requirements. You find out that his hobby is electronics and that he has a surprisingly wide knowledge of the field. He subscribes to several technical magazines and has built several complex radios, as well as other electronic equipment. He is looking forward to high school science and shop courses, although he dreads the other classes he will have to take.

Would it be wise to allow Andrew to neglect history and take some special work in science and electronics? Why or why not?

Could Andrew's special interest be used to increase his efforts in his history class? Describe a class situation in which this might be possible.

If you succeed in awakening Andrew's interest in history, should the same techniques be used to increase his interest in, say, English and mathematics? Is it likely that increased enthusiasm for history will be transferred, to some extent, to his other classes?

ABILITY GROUPING

The modern techniques of project teaching, enrichment, and individualized instruction seek to adapt the educational process to differences among the students found in a given classroom. In addition, schools may employ ability grouping as a means of placing students in the classrooms where they can learn best. Indeed, many schools have practiced ability grouping for years to the satisfaction of both teachers and students.

This method of classifying students ignores, to a large extent, the traditional rigid grouping by age and adopts, as a more relevant standard, the relative abilities of students. Because ability grouping, in spite of extensive use, is widely misunderstood and because particular applications of it differ greatly, considerable attention will be given here to its theory and practical uses.

The Grade System versus Classification by Mental Ability. Attempts to divide children into homogeneous groups have been made as long as we have had group instruction. Our present system of organizing children into grades—first, second, third, etc.—based on chronological age is such an attempt. This system assumes that children of the same chronological age are likely to be of the same mental age also; this is, of course, true only for children of similar IQs. The present grade system has several obvious weaknesses, particularly in respect to nonaverage children—children whose IQs are higher or lower than those within an "average" range.

As we know, children of the same age differ in physique, in ability to adjust socially, and in the capacity to comprehend the instruction that they receive. This last is a very important area of difference, educationally speaking, and it is here that the grade system falls down most glaringly in achieving homogeneity. For instance, some fourth-graders have a greater total of skills and knowledge than some eighth-graders in the average school, and there are first- and second-graders who in this regard surpass a few fourth-

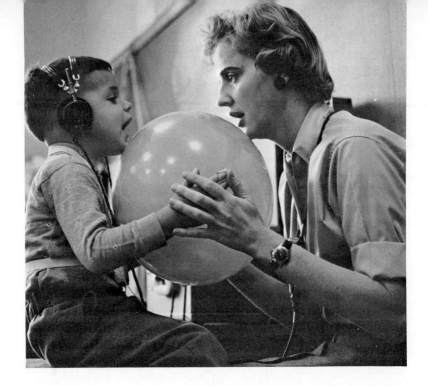

1 An exceptional youngster learns to sound words through touch.

How the School Confronts Individual Differences

The best possible education for each individual is an old and basic idea in our society; but as the behavioral sciences have taught us more and more about how people differ in capacity, personal background, and interests, fulfillment of this idea has become a more and more complex undertaking for the school. Widely various subject material methods and tools of teaching, and student groupings must be provided, experimented with, and correlated.

Define the relationship between teaching method and size of student group in each of the learning situations presented here. Where is this most important? Which situation most clearly encourages the development of individual differences? In which situation is the teacher's role most important to the total learning process of the individual? How else does this situation essentially differ from the others? Which situation most clearly involves educational experimentation?

1 Courtesy of *Parents' Magazine.*
2 Robert J. Smith from Black Star, courtesy of *Friends Magazine.*
3 Courtesy of *Parents' Magazine.*
4 Courtesy of Hunter College High School.

At least the brightest young children can handle math concepts traditionally considered advanced.

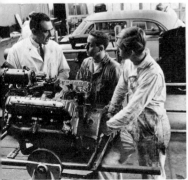

These skilled mechanics-in-the-making will be on the job next year.

4 An enrichment group in chemistry.

graders. Relatedly, the general achievement of the best one-fourth of any grade in the average school is distinctly better than that of the poorest one-fourth of the grade above it; and in the upper grades, the general achievement of the best one-fourth of the students of a grade is better than that of the poorest one-fourth of the class even two or more grades above it.

Miss Virginia Mitchell, in a recent study which linked school achievement to home environment, found that achievement levels in the fourth grade she studied ranged from second- to eighth-grade norms [Mitchell, 1959]. In the fifth grade she studied, some children were still at second-grade achievement levels, while others had reached ninth-grade levels; the sixth grade, too, had the same wide span of individual achievement levels.

Let us see how ability grouping can be used to do away with just such situations: situations in which the teaching must always fail to serve the brighter and the duller students equally well.

To group together children similar in chronological and mental ages is, to begin with, a basic general goal of ability grouping. But how is this to be practically achieved?

Children of essentially the same IQ and CA—that is, of about the same degree of brightness and about the same chronological age—will by definition be quite similar in MA. Thus one way to make sure that the children in a group will be homogeneous in MA is to select those of the same CA and the same IQ. It is, of course, impossible in a practical situation to choose children of exactly the same CA and the same IQ, so it is a good practice to begin the grouping by selecting those children who fall between given points on both IQ and CA scales, for example, children eleven and twelve years old with IQs between 90 and 110. The next step is to group together the brighter younger children and the less bright older children. Thus a twelve-year-old child with an IQ of 100 will fit fairly well in a group with an eleven-year-old child with an IQ of 110, for both have an MA of about 12.

Depending on practical consideration, such as the number of students to be classified, children of a given age can be divided in this way into as few as two or as many as five or six groups. Theoretically, all the students of each group should then be able to learn with about equal facility, for their intellectual progress should be nearly uniform. There will, of course, always be a small MA variation within any group organized to be homogeneous, but this will provide a stimulating variety in achievements.

In this connection, it should be noted that in ability grouping as in scholastic placement generally, teachers' marks and achievement-test results should supplement the MA shown by intelligence tests as standards of classification, as the ensuing discussion of specific applications of ability grouping will show.

There are, of course, many schools where it is almost impossible to group the students according to their measured mental abilities. In the many schools with very few students, it is especially impracticable to do so. Yet there are also schools where ability grouping might seem impossible to a casual observer but actually is not. In the single-room rural schools where the enrollments are comparatively small but eight grades are included, for instance, effective reclassification into more homogeneous groups can be achieved.

We have gone into considerable detail in describing the techniques of grouping by mental ability because this system seems more generally desirable than systems of grouping by chronological age. This does not mean, however, that grouping by mental ability is without its pitfalls and limitations. Some of these were suggested in Chapter 6, where the nature of intelligence was described.

One danger in grouping by general mental ability occurs primarily when the resulting grouping is maintained over a long period of time. Let us consider what happens when children beginning school are classified by mental age, for example. Such classification is better than the arbitrary chronological grouping that occurs when six-year-old children enter the first grade, but whatever homogeneity of ability is obtained by it does not last long. Let us assume that a few with MAs of six have IQs of 120 and that some have IQs of 86. Thus the brighter children are five years old and the duller are seven. For a time they will probably be about equally apt as pupils. However, as they grow older, they will grow apart in their mental capacity. Thus at the end of four years the mental age of any one of the younger students will be about $1\frac{1}{3}$ years more than that of any older one: the brighter student will have an MA of 10.8 years [$1.20 \times (5 + 4)$], and the duller one will have an MA of 9.46 years [$0.86 \times (7 + 4)$].[2]

Yet, if two children with IQs of 120 and 86, respectively, are admitted to school at the age of six, they differ by 2 years in MA when they begin school; at the age of six the child with an IQ of 120 has an MA of 7.2 years, and the child with an IQ of 86 has an MA of 5.2 years. Four years later, they differ mentally by 3.4 years, having MAs of 12 and 8.6, respectively.

It should be emphasized again that, although homogeneity in MA is a consideration in ability grouping, MA alone is not a good determinant. If children of the same MA were grouped irrespective of other factors, they would differ widely in CA and IQ, and thus would probably not be homogeneous in physical and social development. Instead, children within a narrow range of CAs and IQs should be grouped to obtain a fair degree of homoge-

[2] $IQ = \dfrac{MA}{CA} \times 100.$

neity not only in MA but also in physical and social development. Such ability grouping may be carried out within conventional grade divisions (intraclass grouping) as opposed to systems which completely eliminate grades or which overlap grade divisions (interclass grouping).

Ability Grouping for Specific Subjects. If students are classified on the basis of general mental ability and school achievement, they are classified according to the sum of their mental abilities. It will be found, however, that students classified on this general basis are not uniform in their ability to learn each particular school subject. A few in the usual brightest group, for example, are not so apt in arithmetic as in other subjects and would profit more by the arithmetic instructional methods used in a group where the general run of abstract intelligence is not so high. By contrast, a child of a dull group who has a special ability that enables him to be particularly strong in, say, history would profit by taking instruction in that subject with a brighter group.

If the grouping is done separately for each subject on the basis of marks and specialized tests, such variations in ability may be taken into account. Classes that result from such grouping allow for suitable and effective educational programs geared to each child's abilities in each subject. As with generalized grouping by mental ability, there is some unavoidable variation, but the range can be made narrow enough to permit effective teaching.

Table 14   Ability Grouping and Gains in Arithmetic

IQ Level	Experimental Groups			Control Groups			Excess Gain†
	No.	Average IQ	Gain*	No.	Average IQ	Gain*	
High	110	120	22.2	71	120	12.3	9.9
Middle	106	111	14.2	70	110	12.3	1.9
Low	66	105	11.7	71	106	13.0	−1.3
All	282	113	16.7	212	112	12.5	4.2

* Increase in raw scores on arithmetic test.
† The difference of 4.2 at all levels is significant at the .01 level of confidence (see Appendix), and the difference of 9 9 of the high-level groups is still more significant. The differences of 1.9 and −1.3 are not large enough to be significant.
Source: Adapted from Malcolm M. Provus, "Ability Grouping in Arithmetic," *Elementary School Journal*, 60:393, 1960.

 Consider the Data

Based on Table 14

Malcolm M. Provus reports an experiment in ability grouping in arithmetic conducted in Homewood, a suburb of Chicago [Provus, 1960]. The experiment involved 19 intermediate classrooms. Eleven classes formed the experimental group: they were divided into ability groups on the basis of their performance on a special adaptation of the arithmetic concepts subtest of the Iowa Tests of Basic Skills. The classes were on the fourth-, fifth-, and sixth-grade levels. Eight other classes in which no grouping or other changes were introduced formed the control group. Teachers of both the experimental and the control group allowed students to advance as quickly as possible through a well-defined curriculum without regard for grade divisions. At the end of the school year, all 494 students were reexamined to determine their growth in arithmetic achievement.

The results of this comparison are given in Table 14. The divisions into high, middle, and low levels refer to grouping by IQ, which was done for the control group after the experiment was concluded in order that gains might be compared for different levels of general capacity. Note that the IQs of the experimental and control groups were approximately the same. The figures representing amounts of gain are amounts of increase in the scores on the arithmetic test. Their significance is explained by the figures in the excess-gain column. Note that only the differences in gain of the groups as a whole and of the high levels are significant.

When the experiment was over, the teachers who took part in it favored ability grouping. They recognized the problem of providing, and aimed to provide, instruction suitable for each group. The teachers found that new pupil leaders developed in each group.

The ablest students gained most when taught in an ability group. When ablest students were taught in a typical class as members of the control group, how did their gains compare with those of the students of lower abilities in the control group?

The least able students in the experimental group gained least of all; the difference in their gain and that of the least able in the control group was too small to be significant. How do you explain the apparent fact that ability grouping did not help them? Is it possible that they were already achieving close to their capacities in their previous traditional class and hence did not have the potential for accelerated learning that the more able students did?

On the whole, the test scores of the students who were classified into ability groups rose 4.2 more points than did those of the control group. This is a significant difference, statistically. What, then, do the results of the experiment suggest about the value of ability grouping for this academic subject?

Ability grouping for individual subjects also achieves more distribution and a greater mobility of the students, both of which are beneficial to them. Classes are not always made up of the same students, which keeps the students from feeling that they are stratified in any given group. Students may be transferred from group to group for given subjects in accordance with their achievement, which motivates them to work hard in order to improve or maintain their classification in each subject.

A student's abilities for such special subjects as art, music, and physical education, it should be noted, do not correspond so closely to his general mental level as do his abilities for academic subjects. Thus homogeneous grouping on the basis of abstract mental ability does not classify students so effectively for special as for traditional academic subjects. Even for special subjects, however, it is better than no classification at all. If classification is desired in the special subjects such as art, music, dramatics, public speaking, and physical education, it can be accomplished on the basis of demonstrated abilities in each of those subjects.

Making Ability Grouping Work. Ability grouping, then, is a potential means for bringing about effective instruction for children of all abilities in a wide variety of learning situations—a system designed for educating students according to the valid principle that instruction directed to the dull is not suitable for the average and the bright and that instruction directed to the bright is not suitable for the average and the dull. But there is no point in classifying children according to their abilities if educators do not plan beforehand how they will adjust their methods of instruction and curricula to the characteristics of the groups. Teachers, principals, and other supervisory personnel must do their part to make instruction with ability grouping most effective.

First, it is important to select and assign teachers according to their qualifications for instructing the children of the various ability groups. Thus some are best fitted for teaching dull children—that is, they are outstandingly able to work patiently and gently with such children—while others have imaginative qualities and sweep of mind that comprise a special capacity for stimulating bright children.

Secondly, when children are classified into ability groups, the content of the courses and the method of instruction have to be adapted to their learning capacities in order to take advantage of the homogeneous groupings. Bright children have to have study materials and teaching that lead them to work independently, exercising their own initiative and originality, and then to interpret and coordinate what they learn. Dull children have to be supplied with more direct help from the teacher, who must, further, be able to adjust his teaching methods to both the degree of dullness of his students and the nature of the subject matter. Despite what has been said about the doubtful value of intensive drilling on weak subjects, it is certainly true that certain subjects require more memorization and, hence, more drill than others. Moreover, differences in capacity for memory work necessitate varying amounts of drill for various students. Thus drill and frequent reviews and testing, though deadening to the bright pupils, are sometimes effective for the dull, but there are phases of arithmetic that require more drill and review than are necessary in history or geography. Or, there may be more need for intensive work in teaching a subject in its initial stages than later on. The teachers of the dull also need special study materials.

Finally, even when ability grouping has been established, continuous study of the arrangement should be maintained so that beneficial adjustments can be made. Indeed, only if an experimental attitude is maintained and adjustments are made as the need arises can the effectiveness of any ability-grouping project be truly determined, much less made as great as possible. For instance, some students will usually have to be transferred from one group to another, and, no doubt, some teachers can well be shifted occasionally so that they will find by experience the groups for which they are best adapted. In the case of students' being transferred, moreover, the problems may be somewhat complex.

In view of the fact that actual achievement does not always correspond to capacity to learn, the question may be raised as to whether or not children should be transferred to other groups according to their achievement. Thus, should a student who achieves especially well for his capacity be shifted to an abler group, and should one who achieves poorly in terms of his capacity be transferred to a less able group?

To solve this particular kind of problem, the following procedure might prove helpful. In determining actual achievement, it is necessary to check or validate the teachers' marks against comprehensive achievement tests. Standard achievement tests may show that a dull child getting fairly good marks really does not have the knowledge to justify these marks and that a bright child who really has more knowledge than most of his classmates still has been receiving only average or poorer marks.

Thus a high school student with an IQ of about 160 who is getting A in everything but, say, mathematics, in which he regularly receives only C, may in fact be more able in mathematics than in any other subject, that is, he may be exceedingly alert in comprehending the problems and in making original applications in order to reach the answers in his own way. But if his teachers of mathematics are unimaginative, this bright student may have lost interest and become satisfied to "get by." A student like this should be in the ablest group in mathematics even though his marks are only average. On the other hand, a dull child with average achievement should probably be kept in the dull group, where instruction is geared to his ability to comprehend the subject. If, however, a child in the dull group has excellent achievement, he should be tested again, for it may be found that he has been incorrectly classified. If this turns out to be so, he should be placed in an abler group and kept there if his achievement continues to be excellent.

All the above processes of instituting and carrying out an ability-grouping program are essential to its success. Let an example of good classification but poor subsequent control show what even partial failure can do to an ability-grouping program.

In a junior high school of over 1,000 pupils the children were classified into five ability groups on the basis of IQ and MA. The groupings were worked out by the school psychologist, after which the principal assigned the teachers to the respective groups. The teachers followed the same course of study as before and taught much as they had previously, except in some cases where the new circumstances forced them to make some adjustments. The teachers of the brightest groups found it easy to cover the material, and the achievement of their pupils was high. But those who had the poor groups labored hard to cover the course of study for their grade, and the achievement of their pupils was low.

The principal and many of the teachers in this school were not satisfied with ability grouping. They felt that the former heterogeneous classification, which, of course, saved the work of organizing the students into homogeneous groups, was probably just as satisfactory. Yet actually, it was not the principle of homogeneous grouping that was at fault but the psychologist, the principal, and the teachers, who failed to function in such a way as to fulfill the opportunities offered by ability grouping.

In the first place, the psychologist should have explained to the principal and teachers just how the children had been grouped and just what he thought should be done, in the way of changes in teaching methods and curriculum; to make the most efficient use of such grouping. After this, the principal should have supervised the teachers and the psychologist in planning both kinds of changes as needed to fit the abilities of the different groups. The teachers would then have been ready to make the most of the situation when they began their work with the different ability groups.

But what essentially happens to the learning situation when ability grouping is carried out well?

Ability Grouping, Motivation, and Social Atmosphere in the Classroom. Often, in the adult world, the fast worker on the job soon becomes unpopular with the other workers, and a pressure develops to bring his performance down to the norm which they have established. This works as a sort of collective protection.

Likewise in groups of students with a wide spread of abilities, the able and ambitious are looked upon with disfavor, and there is pressure to bring the better-than-average students down toward a common denominator. In some classes, therefore, the superior student "takes it easy" so he will give the impression of being "one of the fellows."

One of the advantages of ability grouping is the avoidance of such situations. Quite simply, each group has its own norm, or standard, to act as prime influence on the morale of the group and its achievement motive. The top ability group sets its own norm higher than that of the middle group, which in turn has a higher standard than the lower group. With norms thus corresponding to ability levels, the members of each group have more realistic aspiration levels than when all are thrown together.

Some of these generalizations have been confirmed by Elizabeth M. Drews in a preliminary report of a study of the effects of homogeneous and heterogeneous grouping on (1) student achievement, (2) skill development, and (3) attitudes [Drews, 1960]. Sixteen classes were studied, containing a total of 593 ninth-grade students. Four of the classes were homogeneous bright, four were homogeneous average, four were homogeneous slow, and four were heterogeneous. Tests included written examinations and ratings by trained observers, teachers, and students.

Drews found that slow students in homogeneous groups did more reading, recited more, liked school better, felt more confident, and were better accepted socially than slow students in heterogeneous groups, though there was no acknowledgeable difference in reading and language skills. The volitional and social gains expectably reflected the fact that these underaverage students were not being reminded hourly of their inferiority by the much better performance of the above-average student.

Drews also found that bright children conducted more mature discussions and used more difficult words—in general, did more complex and abstract thinking—in homogeneous groups. Bright children in homogeneous groups had a stronger desire to learn than did equally bright children who were in classes with average and dull children. Also, the bright children who were in homogeneous classes were more modest in their self-rating than were bright children in classes where most children were less capable than they— a most desirable and gratifying outcome of the ability grouping.

The ability groups Drews studied had been classified on the basis of reading and intelligence test standings, school marks, and teacher recommendations; but her evaluations of the effectiveness of the groupings were made by means of achievement test results, tests of attitudes and special interests, and teacher and peer ratings. In other words, study was made of the feelings of the students and the dynamics of the classes, as well as the levels of intellectual activity. This made it possible to gauge the social, as well as the intellectual, results of the grouping.

This is important because objections have been raised against ability grouping on the grounds that it is not democratic per se and that it tends to have effects often associated with undemocratic processes—specifically, that it tends to make the students in the better groups snobbish and to give those in the poorer groups feelings of inferiority. In Drews' groups such was not the case. But what of other cases?

It is true, of course, that the students know which group is which, no matter how the groups are designated. The teacher was a bit naïve who said that her calling one group the "rabbits" and the other the "turtles" kept the students from knowing. In one situation a child suggested that the groups be called the squirrels and the nuts.

Robert C. Wilson has studied the attitudes of students who take part in special programs for the bright [Wilson, 1955]. As research director for the Gifted Child Project of the Portland public school system, in 1952 he helped set up a number of special classes for gifted children. The program was an extensive one involving 19 schools. The staff was curious to find out whether participation in the classes had affected the students' relationships with other students. In response to a question on this matter, 52 per cent of the elementary school students replied that they got along better than they had before with their classmates. Among high school students, 80 per cent reported no change. Twenty per cent said they had gained prestige, and none felt that their relationships had been damaged. Wilson reports that some of the bright children learned in the special classes that there were others just as bright as they or brighter; tendencies toward conceit were thus actually curbed. Others, who had not thought of themselves as bright before, gained in feelings of personal worth.

It seems clear, from this evidence, that ability grouping results in definite social and psychological gains for both bright and dull students. Unfortunately the evidence is less unequivocal on intellectual effects of ability grouping on dull students. Drews found no appreciable difference in the rate at which dull students in homogeneous and heterogeneous groups acquired language skills; her results conform in this respect to those reported by several other investigators. It has been suggested (again without experimental support) that dull students profit from the stimulation of the presence of brighter students in a heterogeneous group. However, the real reason why dull students gain less in educational achievement from ability grouping lies in their being generally better taught in heterogeneous classes than the bright are and so they achieve no better in homogeneous classes. The dull learn about all they are able to learn in heterogeneous classes, but the bright do not.

Daisy M. Jones has more evidence (see Exhibit 12) which confirms the more generally accepted belief that ability grouping, properly administered, results in intellectual (as well as social) gains for both bright and dull students.

Exhibit 12   Achievement when instruction is adapted to individual differences

IQ Level	Number in Each Group	Growth, Years							
		Reading		Arithmetic		Spelling		Average	
		Con.	Exp.	Con.	Exp.	Con.	Exp.	Con.	Exp.
110 and above	24	1.27	1.38	1.60	1.45	1.30	1.65	1.36	1.60
90–109	82	0.66	0.91	1.02	1.17	0.74	1.05	0.81	1.08
Below 90	19	0.27	0.63	0.40	0.72	0.28	0.63	0.36	0.73
Total or average	125	0.73	0.96	1.03	1.19	0.78	1.21	0.87	1.11

This table presents the results of an experiment in the effectiveness of individualized instruction on 250 fourth-grade children. Experimental groups were taught by techniques and materials determined by the individual abilities of the students. Control groups were taught by standard fourth-grade texts and techniques. The figures represent educational growth from September to May in terms of year units (that is, 1.27 represents a growth of 1.27 years). These figures were calculated on the basis of the following tests: Stanford Achievement, Spelling, Form E; Stanford Achievement, Arithmetic, Form E; and Gates Basic Reading, Form 1. It will be noted that on the average the experimental groups gained more in every subject than the control groups and that normal and dull children benefited slightly more from individualized instruction, especially in arithmetic and reading, than did bright children. (Daisy Marvel Jones, "An Experiment in Adaptation to Individual Differences," *Journal of Educational Psychology,* 39:257–272, 1948. Table is on page 264.)

Finally, other studies have suggested that the system of placing students in classes in which they feel inferior and frustrated and which may cause them to fail and drop out of school causes far more undesirable social effects on teen-agers than ability grouping does.

⊘   Reflect and Review

John P. is thirteen years old and is in the seventh grade of a large junior high school. Although his IQ is 145 (and his MA thus almost 19), he does not do particularly well in his schoolwork. Most of his grades are C's, but he has received several D's (particularly in science courses) and one F (in mathematics). When measured by standardized achievement tests, however, his achievement proved to be three or four grades higher than his grade placement in all subjects.

John's school practices ability grouping by subject, and John is in the group of average ability in all subjects except mathematics, in which he is in the slow group. His mathematics teacher and his English teacher have reported him several times as a behavior problem, and in his other classes, too, he is often sullen and uncooperative. All his teachers feel that John is lazy and could do much better, except his mathematics teacher, who says he has no capacity for mathematics. She was surprised to find that his mathematics achievement score was his second highest.

John dislikes school and receives little encouragement at home. He dislikes all his teachers, particularly the mathematics teacher, to whom he is often rude.

Should John be moved to the brightest group? In all subjects? What data did you consider in reaching your answer?

What is the probable relationship between his low classroom achievement and his problem behavior?

Why has John's classroom achievement been unsatisfactory in terms of his capacity?

What kind of teaching and grouping will John respond to best? Abstract, theoretical and advanced? Drill and review? Considerable freedom and independence? Student-centered methods?

SOCIAL VERSUS TRADITIONAL PROMOTION: AN IMPORTANT ISSUE

Completely free ability grouping eliminates, of course, the problem of traditional promotion. Most schools which practice ability grouping, however, combine it with the conventional grade system. For these schools and those who do not use ability grouping at all, the problem of promotion centers on the welfare of the individual student. It demands careful thought and decision about policies which are both psychologically and educationally sound.

In the past the policy of most teachers and most school administrations was to reward those whose achievement in a school year was above the minimum acceptable level by promoting them to the next grade. The students whose achievement was below that minimum level traditionally were failed and required to repeat their grade. There was an element of punishment in failing a child, and it was believed that "giving him what he deserves" would cause him to do better work.

In recent years there has been a great change from this attitude. More and more teachers and administrators have come to feel that many students fail not because of lack of industry but because of emotional trouble and lack of capacity. These educators feel, moreover, that such pupils will not be helped and actually may be harmed by nonpromotion.

This has led to the policy of promoting every student—of having no repeaters—the policy called social promotion. Social promotion allows even scholastically poor children to stay with the class group of their own age and size on the theory that they will consequently develop better educationally, emotionally, and—as the term implies—socially. If students are retarded one, two, three, and more years and thus become progressively older and larger than their classmates, it is said that they will be out of place socially, will develop poor self-concepts, and will be badly frustrated educationally.

There are, however, teachers who assume that failure is generally attributable to laziness and thus fear that the present tendency to promote all students, even the "failing" ones, will produce a generation of students who will not work—who will have the attitude "What is the use of being industrious when everyone will pass?" Others criticize social promotion on the grounds that it causes the weak student to get further and further behind his classmates as he passes from grade and grade until, eventually, he cannot hope to gain anything from his situation. More subtly, it is sometimes claimed that when the poorest students are passed along, they get the notion that they are much more able than they actually are, even as able as most other students in the class. This overrating of self may eventually result in a very painful jolt, it is claimed, when the student meets the realities of adult life and learns that he does not have the capacities he was led to believe he had.

Where does the truth lie? What policies should the school practice in regard to promoting or not promoting its weak students?

The Retained Student as a Type. Let us begin our search for an answer by considering what retained students are like as a group.

Retained students tend to have the following characteristics and backgrounds, which, it will be observed, tend to go together.

Their average intelligence quotient is some 10 to 15 points under the average for their classmates; and the more years the student has been retained, the lower his intelligence quotient tends to be.

Even though older, these students receive the poorest marks in the class. Retained students lack motivation for doing schoolwork, and their efforts to do it are fruitless; as a result, they usually dislike school.

Retained students have poorer-than-average records of attendance. Because their school life is not very rewarding, they miss school and therefore have even less success in school.

Retained children are poorer than average in mental health. Being older, they feel inferior; being duller, they are frustrated; and they almost invariably present the school with many of its worst behavior problems.

The children who are retained come in large proportion from the lower socioeconomic classes. One case of this is children of transient parents; such children are often held back because they have to transfer to different schools so frequently.

Incidentally, students who withdraw from school early, or dropouts, tend to have the same characteristics and to be affected by the same conditions as retained students. For example, although a few are high achievers, a large majority of dropouts are low in achievement; more specifically, more than three times as many poor readers as good readers in American high schools drop out before graduation from high school. But the correspondence is more than casual, for the above characteristics and conditions are descriptive of the typically inadequate student; and in general, the more inadequate a student is, the more likely he is to drop out of school at the first opportunity.

The parallel characteristics of the retained and the dropout suggest the basic conditions underlying the problem of the slow-learning student. That both are likely to be "inadequate students" is only a symptom of the real basis of the relative failure of each. Both the retainee and the dropout are typically haunted by a sense of inadequacy and failure, they feel rejected by their teachers and their classmates, and they are likely to take the attitude "what's the use?" Such conditions are an integral part of the pattern of failure, and they cannot be eliminated by a rigid policy of retarding all those who do not come up to a prescribed standard in a prescribed period of time. The real solution lies in a larger view that regards the real problem of both the retainee and the dropout as being an emotional and psychological one as well as an intellectual one. More on the conditions surrounding the typical dropout has been given in Chapter 3.

Now what do the extensive thinking and research that have been devoted to the problem of promotions, suggest should be done about these students?

Comparative Effects of Promotion and Nonpromotion. First, the idea that when a child takes the same work a second time it will be easier for him and he will do excellent work has been discredited over and over by researchers. A student may be benefited by nonpromotion, but this is by no means usually the case. One reason is that the social stigma of nonpromotion may prevent efficient learning; another is that the basic causes of low achievement may not have been removed. Mere repetition of the same task is seldom a way to learn better. Edna W. McElwee studied 300 children, comparing those who had been retarded with accelerated and normal children [McElwee, 1932]. She found that, on the average, the retarded children were less well adjusted than either of the other groups. It has been experimentally proved repeatedly that, in general, poor students who are promoted actually work more effectively and so learn more subject matter than similar students who repeat the grade.

W. H. Coffield and Paul Blommers, having selected 147 students who had been failed before they reached the seventh grade, used the Iowa Tests of Basic Skills to match them with nonfailed students who were comparable in general academic capacity: reading, language, and arithmetic achievement; and in "study skills" [Coffield and Blommers, 1956]. The resulting matched pairs provided a good basis for studying the effects of nonpromotion.

The comparison showed that:

Failed students typically make only 6 months' educational progress during the repeat year and only 1 year and 3 months' progress in the 2 years following failure. (The results of the Iowa tests are expressed in years and months.)

Failed students seldom achieve the norm for the failed grade by repeating it.

Seventh-grade students who have been failed once are generally on the same level educationally with students of similar ability who have not been failed and who have thus spent 1 year less in school. They are about eight months behind eighth-grade students of similar capacity who have spent the same amount of time in school as they.

Clearly, the failed students were not benefited by nonpromotion. Indeed, this study indicated—consistently with other studies of nonpromotion—that a child who is failed loses about a year of progress in education.

The reasons for the declining use of the policy of nonpromotion in our schools are obvious from the results of studies such as the Coffield-Blommers. These authors estimate that, in 1900, approximately 50 per cent of those who had finished their schooling had been failed at one time or another in their school careers. By the thirties, this figure had declined to about 25 per cent; by 1954, to about 10 per cent. Such a revolution in policy appears to be, on the whole, a gain for our schools.

In a technical sense, the dull student, if promoted regularly, does get progressively further behind in his studies, and a time comes when he must discontinue going to the next higher grade and turn to specialized training pursuits. But—given our modern teachers, flexible in their methods and correspondingly able to make many adaptations for individual students—while he is in grade, junior high, and senior high school, the dull student can take work from which he can profit; adjustments are made in the work so it is suitable for him. Therefore the socially promoted pupil usually gets along fairly well—at least, better than he would if retained several years or if failed out of school several years before he reaches a satisfactory time for discontinuing school.

But what effect does promotion or nonpromotion have on the social and emotional development of students?

Studies of this problem—which have used the methods of sociometric devices, self-ratings, ratings by teachers, and adjustment inventories—have suggested, as a whole, that the socially promoted are personally happier, have more satisfactory relationships with their peers, and have less dislike for school and desire to quit it than nonpromoted students. Relatedly, the evidence seems to indicate that there are fewer behavior problems among nonretained students than among students of equal capacities and abilities who have not been promoted. The evidence, it should be noted, is not entirely against having weak students repeat their grades; but it does indicate that more weak students are helped socially and emotionally by being promoted than by being failed. J. I. Goodlad, for instance, in a study of 55 promoted and 55 nonpromoted children, found that the promoted students were clearly at an advantage in peer-group relationships [Goodlad, 1952]. The promoted students also tended, however, to be more disturbed personally over their school progress and home security than the nonpromoted students were. Such ambivalent results argue against a blanket promotion policy, while indicating clearly the social benefits of promotion.

Finally, the more forward-looking educators do not agree with the idea that denying a child promotion will "prepare him for life and its disappointments." Rather, they take the following point of view: The poorest students experience so much frustration and failure with the lessons and other tasks that test and try them daily that it is not necessary to make them repeat grades to make it clear to them that they are inferior. In other words, there is no danger that if he is passed annually, a dull child will get any euphoric notions about his capacities and consequently aspire to goals he has no chance of reaching. Indeed, he is more likely to be crippled by feelings of inferiority than to overestimate himself.

What, then, should be done?

The Best Policy. Since the evidence indicates that children are usually harmed educationally, socially, and emotionally by having to repeat a grade, clearly there should not be a fixed policy of failing a given percentage or of failing those who do not reach a set standard of subject-matter achievement. It would seem a far better policy for schools to operate on the assumption that every child should be passed except when his own situation strongly suggests that he will profit from repeating a grade. Such may be the case if the child's deficiency could clearly be remedied by more time spent on the subject matter and if it appears that the child would not be seriously harmed socially or emotionally by the retention.

The matter is not a simple one, of course, and no one all-inclusive policy is likely to be completely satisfactory. A policy of rigid adherence to "standards" of promotion and a policy of blanket promotion are both dangerous. As in all educational problems, a flexible, intelligent approach that takes the child's best interests as its prime aim is the most satisfactory solution.

When a child fails in his schoolwork, he should be studied carefully before nonpromotion is decided upon. The child may be shying away from doing classwork, and thus becoming more retarded, because of social insecurity. He may be unable to concentrate on his work because he is in an unhappy emotional state which is keeping him absorbed only in himself and his problems. Understanding teachers can help such students make better and happier social and emotional adjustments to their school situation.

In addition, the curriculum and the teaching methods must be studied with an eye to gearing them to the ability level of the failing child, for he may really be less able than most. If so, he must be protected from unnecessary frustration. We have already said that flexible modern teachers have various ways of doing this. For example, much frustration may be eased in some cases by eliminating the competitive nature of examinations and the usual report card, rather than by denying automatic (social) promotions. This does not mean that the duller children should not take examinations; rather, it means that the results of the examinations should be handled in such a way that the weaker students are not made painfully conscious of their low standing. The examination can be used as an instructional device to help these students become more competent. Such students can be helped and must not simply be relegated to manual workshops and janitorial duties. A grade school and a high school education, even though standards must be lowered, are desirable for their present and future well-being.

In this connection, good educators try especially hard to watch for the potential dropout and then to adjust the work to his capacities and personal situation, reward his efforts, and promote him every year.

☯ *Reflect and Review*

John attended a small country school until he was fourteen years old. School attendance was not enforced rigidly, and he frequently stayed away from school to help on the farm and to earn a little money. His school attendance varied between 90 and 100 days a year. At age fifteen he went to a large consolidated junior high school in a nearby town, where he entered the eighth grade. Tests he took upon entering showed that he had an IQ of 123; he ranked at about the 40th percentile, however, in general achievement. At first John liked the big new school, but he did rather badly in his schoolwork, despite the fact that he attended regularly and studied hard. He had particular difficulty with history and English; he read slowly and his oral English was ungrammatical and full of regionalisms. He became so discouraged over constant corrections and failing grades that his attendance fell off toward the end of the year. His grades in history and English were below passing; he had done fairly well in his other work.

Should John be allowed to enter the ninth grade, or should he be made to repeat the eighth grade? Why?

What do you think John's teachers could do to help him overcome his difficulties?

How would ability grouping help John?

Ungraded Organization. Usually a larger proportion of nonpromotion occurs in the first three grades than in the middle and upper grades, because of the special difficulty which some children have in learning to read and in acquiring the basic skills in arithmetic. In addition, the pass-or-fail problem is generally most psychologically critical, sometimes traumatically so, for a child in the first 3 years of school.

Thus ungraded organization is now being tried in some elementary schools as a means of avoiding promotional problems. Children who would ordinarily be in the first, second, and third grades are not classified into grades at all but are guided into schoolwork and activities according to their varying educational capacities and personal needs. When the pupils have reached adequate levels of educational attainment and personal maturity, they enter the fourth grade. Most do this after three years in the ungraded division; a few get there in a little less and a few in a little more time.

In ungraded organization, the lack of concern about promotion from first to second grade and from second to third grade frees teachers to give more attention to understanding the children and to providing them with maturing school experience suitable for them as individuals. There is, of course, the problem of determining when the children are ready for the fourth grade; but on the other hand, the greater flexibility in the ungraded situation provides more opportunities for helping them. Achievement tests, close observation by the teachers, and general consideration of the child's total development can make the decision on fourth-grade entrance a wise one and one much more closely governed by the child's needs than three yearly decisions on promotion or nonpromotion are likely to be. Three years in an ungraded situation free from the requirements and threats of annual promotion is conducive to many children's making a satisfactory educational and personal adjustment.

RECOGNIZING AND CLASSIFYING THE RETARDED CHILD

Studies have shown that the speech development of mentally retarded children is slower than normal; they use relatively few words, and errors in pronunciation are common. Thus lateness in a child's speech development is often an indication of mental retardation, though the rather wide age range in which normal children learn to talk prevents clear-cut inferences on the state of a very young child's mental development by his speech alone.

However, when the mentally slow child gets to school, the learning experiences he encounters soon reveal his deficiencies, particularly if he is given intelligence or subject-readiness tests on arrival. It is soon discovered that his perception of words is poor and his progress in reading is very slow, that he acquires number concepts very slowly and lags behind his classmates in learning the simple number combinations.

It is also soon found that the retarded child is socially less responsive than normal children. Because of his inability to comprehend much of what is taking place, he is limited in his participation in group activities. Lacking the capacity for active cooperation, let alone leadership, he often becomes stubborn or much more passive than other children in defensive reaction to his mental frustrations. In short, it is soon evident that the dull, slow-learning child is handicapped at every turn.

We have seen in Chapter 2 that the IQ range, though not absolutely reliable, is helpful in classifying degrees of retardation. We have also touched briefly upon problems of educating mentally retarded persons. Let us now traverse the lower parts of the IQ range in order to consider fully the educational meanings of the differences among them.

The group with IQs between the low 70s and the high 80s—the slow learners—will find "regular school" very hard. Though a child with an IQ of 89—a "dull" child—is more teachable than one with an IQ of 71—"bordering on mental retardation"—neither is really equipped for comprehending many abstract or theoretical concepts. They can learn to do simple reading and arithmetic and to express themselves clearly as well as to be pleasant and sociable people. But their vocational futures almost invariably lie not in the use of symbols and ideas but in the use of their hands. Some of the more capable may become semiskilled and possibly skilled laborers; others will join the ranks of the unskilled.

The group of mentally handicapped with IQs below 70 but above 50 is often described as educable, or least retarded. Actually educable in a very limited way, these children make good progress if helped in their preschool years and primary grades through remedial programs and special tutoring. They can learn to read and figure a little; they can also learn a little about their immediate environment: about the seasons, the weather, and the interests and activities of people about them. They are likely to join the ranks of unskilled day laborers, in which group they can often become trusted and capable workers, if they are given careful supervision.

The middle grade of the retarded, or those with IQs generally between 25 and 50, is even less educable (and then only in some cases) but is generally described as trainable. These children must be trained to take care of themselves in such simple activities as eating, going to the toilet, and dressing. They can also learn to take care of their belongings and to do very simple tasks. They have little curiosity and are unlikely to manifest much interest in their environment, except in a direct, elementary way. Some of the more capable may be able to become unskilled laborers.

The most retarded are those with IQs below 25. They need regular attention; they are usually institutionalized and given custodial care. Their outlook is one of minimum development and a life of dependence on others. They have a very limited awareness of their environment, are not educable at all, and are only slightly trainable.

Let it again be said, however, that the IQ classification is only one criterion and that each child should also be evaluated according to his own effectiveness. Success at all levels of capacity depends not only on IQ but also on the individual's motivation, mental health, motor skills, and experiences. The group intelligence test demands that the subject be reasonably confident and that he not have excessive emotional reaction to a test that resembles a school task. Since the mentally retarded have so frequently experienced failure that they fear school-like experiences, the group intelligence test often ranks them at IQ levels lower than they actually have. For this reason, individual tests, supplemented by personal observation, are the best methods for classifying retarded children.

Children whose IQs fall below 70 constitute only about two per cent of the school population. Nevertheless, they deserve a chance for training up to their limited capacities. The special problems which they present to the conscientious teacher, however, often demand attention which exceeds that paid to the problems of average children. Such efforts are well repaid, however, by the knowledge that a human being can be helped to lead a happier and more normal life.

Retarded children may be taught in school either in regular classes or in special classes. Although a homogeneous class is better for a retarded child, he can also achieve in a heterogeneous class if his teacher is aware of his problems and makes adjustments for him.

The most serious objection to training the retarded child within a regular class is that his circumstances make him prone to emotional and psychological pressures that can make learning even more difficult for him. Teachers often describe retarded children as sullen, uncooperative, and rebellious. Their classmates often find them inclined to bullying or fighting. The reason for these manifestations of antisocial behavior is, of course, the frustration caused by intellectual inadequacy and failure.

A second objection to teaching the retarded child in a regular class is that he requires more time to reach a state of readiness for learning than the normal child does. A child with an IQ of, say, 60 reaches a mental age of six only when his chronological age is ten. If he entered school at age six, he has by this time experienced 4 years of failure and frustration. He, his teachers, and his classmates have probably decided that he will never be able to learn to read and do the other tasks he should normally have learned by the age of ten. He therefore sits to one side, ignored and discouraged, and though he is now probably able to learn to read, he does not receive the help he needs.

For these reasons the regular classroom is less than satisfactory for the slow learner. Of course the teacher can do much to overcome these disadvantages, if he keeps himself alert and informed, through tests and observation, of the retarded child's progress and helps the child to feel a part of the school program by giving him tasks within his capabilities. The problem is different, too, for children of different degrees of retardation. The child whose IQ falls between 80 and 89 is obviously much easier to teach satisfactorily within a regular class than one whose IQ falls considerably below that level. Relatively minor provisions can make him a satisfactory member of the class group. The child whose IQ is below 50, on the other hand, probably should not be in a regular class at all, if it can be avoided. He needs training which is more directly related to his needs than he can get in a regular class.

Special classes generally offer a better opportunity for giving retarded children the help they need. Such classes usually are directed toward the "educable" retarded children with IQs between 50 and the low 70s. Usually these classes are part of a regular school and provide the retarded children with as much contact as possible with normal children. Three stages of work are usually provided, which enable them to progress at their own rate, that is, when they become mentally ready for new tasks. From age six to age eight to ten, they study preacademic subjects, learning simple games, personal tasks, etc. When they become ready for reading (as shown by tests), they enter into the second level, in which they spend 5 or 6 years learning to read, to write, and to do arithmetic. By age thirteen or fourteen, they are usually able to join their normal age peers in nonacademic junior high school subjects, such as shop, agriculture, music, and home economics, while still continuing a special program of academic subjects geared to their capabilities.

Such a program ensures that each retarded child be given the chance to learn what he can when he himself becomes capable of learning it. Frustrations are minimized and he is able to experience a feeling of success and achievement within the framework of his capacity. At the same time, he comes in contact with normal children and learns to get along with them as he will have to after he leaves school. Thus the retarded child is given the optimum opportunity to become a useful and self-sufficient member of society.

Goals for the Retarded Learner's Education. Naturally the level of achievement expected of a retarded child must be carefully considered. To be avoided is the attitude that any lapse from the ideal standard of a normal child constitutes failure. What may the retarded child be expected to learn, and what should the teacher try to teach him (see Table 15)?

As was mentioned earlier, the child with an IQ of below 50 is probably only trainable, not educable in any real sense. Usually such children are not in school; their training is handled in special institutions and by specially qualified people.

There are several specific goals for the school to try to attain for the child whose IQ falls between 50 and 70 or 75, however. Various levels of achievement within each category can be reached, of course, depending upon the degree of retardation and the success of the school program.

First of all, the school can help the child to develop a pleasant personality. The "sullenness" and "belligerence" of the retarded child are usually avoidable. He must be made to feel that he is accepted for what he is and that it is possible for him to achieve success in terms of his own capacity. He should not be made to feel rejected; he should be helped to have pleasant social relationships and to get along with other people.

Second, it is highly desirable that the slow learner be able to communicate in a simple, pleasant way. Much of the communication even of capable people consists of greetings, farewells, simple requests such as asking the time of day, and remarks in passing. The slow learner can be trained to express himself adequately at this level and thereby escape giving the impression of "not being all there."

Third, the slow-learning child needs to learn as much reading, writing, and arithmetic as he can. The children at the lower range of the educable

Table 15 Retarded Children's Mental-Age Expectancy* for Increasing Chronological Ages†

IQ	Slow Learner's Chronological Age										
	6	7	8	9	10	11	12	13	14	15	16
70	4–3	4–11	5–7	6–4	7–0	7–9	8–5	9–2	9–10	10–6	11–3
75	4–6	5–3	6–0	6–9	7–6	8–3	9–0	9–9	10–6	11–3	12–0
80	4–10	5–7	6–5	7–2	8–0	8–10	9–7	10–5	11–3	12–0	12–10
85	5–1	6–0	6–10	7–8	8–6	9–4	10–3	11–1	11–11	12–9	13–8
90	5–4	6–4	7–2	8–1	9–0	9–11	10–10	11–9	12–7	13–6	14–5

* In years and months.
† To derive the grade-placement capacity, subtract 5 from the mental age—the rule of 5.
Source: Lloyd M. Dunn, *Journal of the National Education Association*, October, 1959, p. 20.

group can probably attain third- or fourth-grade levels in these skills; those at the upper range may reach sixth- or seventh-grade levels by the time they leave school. Such skills will be invaluable to them in later life, particularly in job situations.

Fourth (and relatedly), the retarded child should acquire some vocational skills. He usually can manage his hands and body much better than his mind and, accordingly, is destined to become an unskilled or semiskilled worker. In some cases, slow learners can even become skilled workers such as bricklayers, plasterers, and carpenters. They should, then, when they reach junior or senior high school age, be given experience in shop training, be taught to handle tools, and so be given a start toward a semiskilled or skilled vocation. The retarded girls should learn some of the household arts so that they will possess some homemaking skills when they marry.

Fifth, a specific part of the retarded student's education for living should be training in taking care of money. He should be taught the principles of thrift and economy and, whenever possible, should be given experience in saving and spending money wisely. If he is to be self-sufficient in later life, this training is highly important; he can generally be taught basic principles of handling money if he can master simple arithmetic.

How effective is such training? If the retarded are destined for lives of dependence upon others anyway, the wisdom of expending care upon their training is questionable. Several studies of post-training careers of low-IQ students, however, have shown that this is not the case. I. N. Wolfson, for example, studied 223 retardants who had been discharged from the Newark State School in 1946 [Wolfson, 1956]. He found that, 8 years after their discharges of 158 less retarded, 61 per cent of the men and 73 per cent of the women had found socially satisfactory and economically independent places in the community. Such returns certainly justify much attention to the needs of those who, through no fault of their own, are unable to compete on an even basis with those of normal intelligence.

ACCELERATING THE BRIGHT STUDENT

The curriculum and class instruction in the average school are geared to average capacity and average progress, and superior children are regularly held back while the teacher directs his attention toward the children of average and underaverage capacities. How can appropriate educational advancement be provided for these bright youngsters, who often are too few in number for organization into a uniform group? They are the retarded ones, in a sense, because their mental ability is ahead of the average for their grade.

One method of adjusting to individual differences is to give extra promotion to students who are capable of doing work one or two grades, or even more, above the grade that is normal for their chronological age. This practice is called acceleration. It is commonly used, and the evidence we have clearly favors its use.

The Results of Acceleration. Studies of accelerated students while they were in school and after they finished school show convincingly that, on the whole, acceleration is profitable for superior students; accelerated students do better than equally bright nonaccelerated students on nearly all, if not all, counts.

Terman found that those of his gifted students who were accelerated got better marks, completed more years of school, obtained better jobs, and were more successful in their personal lives than equally able students who were not accelerated. Conceivably, the accelerated students were the more highly motivated and effective workers and would have outstripped the others even if they had not been accelerated. Thus the causes of their selection for acceleration may have been the principal determiners of subsequent success, rather than the acceleration itself. Still, the bulk of Terman's evidence favors acceleration for students of high capacity, particularly since, as he points out, acceleration, even if it is not a direct cause of success, enables the gifted student to avoid the deadening experience of working far below his capacity.

Marie A. Flesher and S. L. Pressey compared students who finished college in less than the usual 4 years—by means of extra-large course loads, summer school, independent work, and examinations—with an equal number of equally capable nonaccelerates [Flesher and Pressey, 1955]. Of the accelerated group, 32 had earned advanced degrees: 24 master's degrees, 1 LL.B., 1 M.D., 4 Ph.D.'s, and 2 certificates in physical and occupational therapy. Among the nonaccelerates, there were only 12 master's degrees. In addition, when the accelerates were asked to give their opinions about such a program, the large majority spoke favorably of it. Seventy-nine per cent indicated that acceleration was desirable, while only ten per cent reported that acceleration was a drain on the health, interfered with a good social life, and/or prevented them from doing their best schoolwork.

Other studies substantiate these results and have much the same pattern. A large majority of accelerates favor the experience, do better work and progress further in school, and make a better post-school adjustment vocationally and personally. The evidence is so consistent as to warrant saying that, in general, bright, ambitious students should be accelerated and that not to accelerate them is to do them an injustice.

But acceleration is not a simple subject. There are questions of whether, when, and how much—all related to the individual mentality of each bright child. Furthermore, other factors must be considered.

The physical adjustment and social adaptations of the individual child are also important, giving rise as they do to doubts and complications. Several extra promotions that bring the child into a group whose chronological age level is years in advance of his own may lead to physical and social maladjustment. The bright youngster may be able to compete with the older pupils in recitations and examinations but be a misfit in the sports and social activities of his fellows. This sort of thing has happened often enough that one of the clichés in education and psychology is that a student should be "kept in his social group."

On the other hand, a student should have an opportunity to enlarge and shift his social circle. Though the school should guide the students so they become happy members of a social group, it is a mistake to think of the social group as something in which one remains fixed as a permanent member. Students should learn to make new friends while keeping old ones; entering new social groups is a dynamic and developing process; a student should not become too dependent on one social group.

Early School Entry. The easiest way to save time for a capable student is to start him in school a year younger than the age at which he would enter if the general regulations were observed. The usual requirement is that a child be five before some given date of the year he enters the kindergarten, or six before a given date of the year he enters the first grade. The children whose birthdays fall later in the year usually must wait until the next September, although they will then be a number of months over the minimum age for entrance. What happens when, to avoid this delay, bright students are admitted even though they are several months below the usual required minimum age for starting to school?

D. A. Worcester has given us an extensive summary and excellent analysis of several studies of the success of underage children who entered school on the basis of mental age and IQ—children who would have had to wait another year to begin school if they had not been admitted on such a basis [Worcester, 1955].

The early entrants—who were required to have a minimum IQ of about 115 and an MA of about $5\frac{1}{2}$—were evaluated on several bases. Here are the general findings of most of the studies:

1. The early entrants had less emotional difficulty than children who entered school at the regulation age.
2. They were more friendly and got along better with their classmates

than regulation-age children did. In leadership they were as high, or slightly higher.

3. They were as well developed physically as their classmates, were in good health, and had just as good coordination, or a little better.

4. On the whole, their achievement was clearly above average. A few of the early entrants were below average in achievement, but the percentage was not so large as that of regular entrants who were below average in achievement.

5. The attitude toward school of early entrants was more favorable than that of other pupils.

In a study (see Exhibit 13) of 4,275 children, Karl Mueller compared grade school children who had entered school early on the basis of an early-entrance examination with children who had either entered school at the regular time or passed the test but did not enter school early [Mueller, 1955]. He found that the percentage of students who were regarded by their teachers as "liking school" was significantly higher in the group that entered early than the percentage who "liked school" from the other groups. All this evidence is clearly favorable to a policy of admitting to school bright children who are several months under the regulation age.

It is sometimes held that a child may profit by staying home an extra year and thereby being more mentally and emotionally mature when he begins school; this greater maturity, it is believed, will enable the later-entering

Exhibit 13 Early entrance to school in relation to achievement in school subjects and emotional adjustment

Group	Above Average in Achievement, Per Cent	Above Average in Emotional Adjustment, Per Cent
Passed test (early entrants)	41.78	37.97
Failed test (entered next year)	25.81	30.64
Regular (entered on basis of age)	30.10	31.04

The table shows the percentages of students in three categories who were ranked by their teachers as "above average" in achievement and in emotional adjustment. The "passed" group consists of students who passed a prekindergarten test and entered school early. The "failed" group took the test, failed it, and entered the next year. Children in the "regular" group were admitted to school on the basis of age without taking the test. All children from kindergarten through the fifth grade in several school systems in Nebraska (4,275 students) were included in the study. Karl Mueller, who made the study, also obtained teacher evaluations of health, coordination, acceptance, leadership, and attitude. The results shown here are typical of all categories. (Reported more fully in D. A. Worcester, *The Education of Children of Above-average Mentality*, University of Nebraska Press, Lincoln, Nebr., 1955, pp. 21–28.)

child to make a better academic and social adjustment. But comparison of bright children who entered school early with equally bright children who waited until the next fall has shown no advantage gained from staying home. The evidence thus seems to indicate that when a child is mentally mature enough to begin school, he should do so.

It is, of course, hard to speculate about what a child would have achieved if he had not entered school early—no two children are just alike—but a study by Oak-Bruce, as well as that by Mueller, indicates that nothing is gained by one more year at home [Oak-Bruce, 1948].

Various school systems, of course, will have to adopt various specific standards for early entrance according to their own conditions. But generally, it can be recommended that children up to 6 months younger than the minimum age be admitted to the kindergarten if their mental ages are at least five and their IQs at least 115. If there is no kindergarten, the requirement for entrance to the first grade can be a minimum mental age of six and an IQ of 115. On this basis, about one-sixth of all children admitted to first grade or kindergarten would be a year younger than the average.

But what of the dependability of mental tests for determining the IQs of such young children for such a crucially important purpose? It is true that mental tests are more valid for children with two or more years of school experience, but they have proved very useful for evaluating the future success in school of children approaching the school-entrance age. An individual mental examination such as the Terman-Merrill revision of the Stanford-Binet Intelligence Scale or the Wechsler Intelligence Scale for Children will, indeed, do a satisfactory job.

Of course, the tester should also evaluate each child's physical and social development in judging whether he should be admitted. Especially, it is essential to gauge the child's desire to start to school. Generally, the child of enough mental capacity to qualify him for early entrance will be greatly interested in entering into the activities of the kindergarten or the first grade. There are exceptions, however, and certainly the child who wants to go to school is a better prospect than the equally able one who clearly does not. Great care must be used in discovering the wishes of a child, moreover, because he may say he does not wish to go to school when he truly does or may say he does want to go when he does not.

Who Should Be Accelerated Later? And How Much? In order to be considered for acceleration, a student already in school should have high capacity and high achievement, as shown by intelligence or general aptitude tests and by school marks and standardized achievement tests—all of which standards should verify each other. But how high should the student's capacity and achievement be?

It is doubtful that more than the best 10 per cent of students gain by acceleration, generally speaking; and not all these should be accelerated. Only the ones who are highly motivated to learn and want to try acceleration and whose parents favor it should be given the opportunity.

On the other hand, there may be situations where it is advisable to give extra promotion to a student who is less superior than the best 10 per cent in achievement. Such a lower-achieving student should have an IQ of 130 or above, be socially mature, and have a desire to progress rapidly. Thus it is possible that a student with superior potential but low achievement may become industrious and a good achiever if motivated by the opportunity to progress faster than normal. Such cases must be picked with great care and their progress carefully evaluated. Yet an experimental attitude should be taken; students who have high potential, even though they are not doing superior work, should be given an opportunity to progress faster.

In all cases, incidentally—even when the child being considered for skipping a grade is two grades ahead of his own grade in achievement—it is desirable to ascertain whether or not there is, in the grade he is going to skip, any work which he has not had. If there is, he should be given special instruction in it, for example, in particular processes or problems in arithmetic which he might otherwise miss.

In view of the preceding discussion of ways in which acceleration may be accomplished, the question might naturally be asked as to the best time for acceleration. Is a bright child better off if he is admitted to school early, if he skips grades, or if he enters college before graduation from high school (see page 249)? This question is impossible to answer conclusively because so many factors must be taken into account. Early entrance has the advantage of preventing the accelerated child from missing any parts of the normal curriculum. Skipping grades, on the other hand, allows more opportunity for the teacher to identify the bright child. Acceleration at the senior-high-school level has an advantage based on the fact that much of the work of the last two years in high school and the first two years in college overlaps, as G. Hildreth has pointed out [Hildreth, 1952].

Probably the best answer is that all methods should be kept in mind, and those best suited to the needs of the individual student should be used to help him.

To the next question, "How much acceleration?" the answer is even less precise. The answer again depends on the capacity, achievement, and desire of the individual student; but here, his social development becomes an increasingly important factor.

Consider, as an example of this, the college-bound accelerated student. Saving one year and graduating at the age of seventeen rather than eighteen may be preferable for some accelerated students. Others may well save 2 years and graduate at the age of sixteen. Ordinarily, 2 years is considered acceleration enough, because most accelerated students are bound for college, and the age of sixteen is considered about the lowest at which a person can satisfactorily be immersed in a college or university environment, except in a very few cases.

If the college or university to be attended is very near where the young student lives, adjustment to the college situation, including its social aspects, may be fairly untroublesome. The freshman will be living at home and can continue his friendships with his neighbors and high school classmates. He will not have to experience the sometimes serious troubles of leaving home and enrolling in a college many miles away. It is conceivable, therefore, that in some situations an occasional student may be accelerated as much as 3 years and enter college—a college near home, that is—at fifteen.

Ways and Means of Shortening High School and College Careers. In high school the ablest students can easily handle an extra subject each year and, if they have picked up a high school subject at the end of junior high, finish high school one year early. In other cases summer school can provide the opportunity to shorten a high school career.

In addition, some colleges have the policy of accepting distinctly superior high school graduates and giving them a standing as second-semester freshmen or even as beginning sophomores, provided that, besides possessing high intelligence, they demonstrate high superiority on entrance or scholarship examinations.

This departure from the traditional concept that students must attend classes a required number of hours, days, weeks, months, and years before moving up each rung in the educational ladder is a sensible recognition of the great differences that exist in the achievement of students. For an example especially pertinent here, W. S. Learned and B. D. K. Wood discovered by examining a number of college-entrance test scores that the scores of the best 10 per cent of high school seniors on comprehensive subject-matter tests are above the median or middle score of college seniors and also that the scores of the poorest 10 per cent of college seniors are below the median score of high school seniors [Learned and Wood, 1938]. One striking reflection of such differences, incidentally, is that there are a few high school seniors who know more science than some college seniors who have majored in science and plan to teach it.

Thus colleges which accept superior and ambitious high school graduates and give them advanced standing are taking a negligible risk. These students, with rare exceptions, do very good work. The acceleration challenges and motivates these young people to do well in college, while giving them an opportunity to be gainfully employed a year early.

Another way of accelerating superior students is to accept them into college at the age of about sixteen before they have graduated from high school. These students also do well in college; like superior students who have been accelerated in other ways, they are clearly above average in their classwork.

It should be pointed out, however, that a better arrangement for such students would be enough earlier acceleration so that they could graduate from high school at about sixteen. Then such students would be able to get a high school diploma before entering college. Moreover, taking advanced high school work might make transition to college easier for them.

☯ *Reflect and Review*

Dorothy has been the outstanding student in her small-town school ever since she started in the first grade. She has always been hard-working and conscientious, and mental tests have shown her IQ to be 149. She skipped the third grade and so, though she is now a sophomore in high school, is only fourteen years old. Dorothy is an only child; her father is a retired railroad worker, rather old. Though not the most popular girl in her class, Dorothy is well liked and seems happy, though she is quiet and reserved. She does, however, frequently seem embarrassed by her scholastic achievement. Her English teacher suspects that she feels that her high grades prevent her from being "part of the gang."

If Dorothy takes certain courses in her junior year, she will have finished the requirements for entering college before she graduates from high school. She wants to go to the state university, which is about fifty miles from home and which takes ungraduated high school students who meet certain standards. If she enters college early, she will be barely sixteen.

Would you advise Dorothy to take the courses and enter college early?

What other information would help you be surer in your decision?

What other plan for accelerating a student's high school education might be better for Dorothy, and why so in her case?

THE MANCHESTER GRAMMAR SCHOOL

In Manchester, England, is located the famous Manchester Grammar School, which has been in operation since 1515. It will be described here for two related reasons. First, its methods of selection and grouping of students involve educational procedures and psychological principles that are of special interest today. Secondly, the Manchester Grammar School has an enviable reputation for winning scholarships in the leading universities of England—in some years it has won more of the most cherished scholarships than any other secondary school in England; and of its graduates, 85 per cent continue study in some university.

Selection and Grouping of Students. The students of the Manchester Grammar School are selected by examination from the boys who live within a distance about twenty miles from the school—an area with a population of about three million. About two thousand students who are approaching their eleventh birthdays are permitted, on the basis of their school records and recommendations which they receive from their schools, to take the examination. The examination consists of a general aptitude test and achievement tests in English and mathematics.

Of the approximately two thousand boys who take the examination, the 450 who score highest are selected to take a second examination. The 210 who score highest on the second examination are selected for admission. The selection is entirely objective, being determined by scores on the examination and nothing else; that is, the students are selected "without fear or favor." The son of an instructor in Manchester Grammar School will not be admitted unless he is one of the highest 210.

These 210 students represent very high selection, as they are probably most of the brightest and most ambitious eleven-year-old students in a general population of about three million, there being no other comparable school in the area. Yet there is still a fairly large range in the capacities and abilities of these students.

In order to reduce this variation, the students are divided into four ability groups or "streams," as they are called in England. This division is made on the basis of the scores earned by the students on the entrance examinations. The students are aware of which ability group they are in.

After the completion of the first year's work, the students' academic records are carefully studied for the purpose of reassigning some students to different ability groups. Some are shifted upward because of higher-than-expected scholarship, some downward because their work did not meet expectations. About twenty-five per cent of the students are transferred to different ability groups annually.

The Competitive System: Its Workings and Its Value. This educational system is based on competition; both admission and grouping are competitive. Acceptance in and the winning of scholarships to the universities of England are also based on competitive examination. Thus the internal atmosphere of the Manchester Grammar School is in harmony with its objective of gaining entrance and, when possible, scholarships for its graduates to the best English universities.

An educational situation involving so much competition is sure to be criticized by adherents of the school of educational thought that claims that competition brings out selfish striving and causes many to be frustrated and unhappy. Success is bought at too high a price, these persons claim, and tragic failure is the fate of many.

Some leading members of the political parties also hold strongly to such opinions. For example, members of the Labor party and others with socialistic leanings favor the abolishment of schools (like the Manchester Grammar School) for the gifted student and believe that the less competitive modern high school, similar to the typical American high school, is adequate for the educational needs of English youth.

This attitude is understandable, as relatively few of the successful candidates for the grammar schools are from the working classes; instead, they are largely from the higher and less populous socioeconomic levels which are made up of the executive, managerial, proprietary, and professional people. The grammar schools are supported by public funds while the public schools, as they are called and of which Eton is an example, are private schools privately supported. The Socialists may also feel that highly selective schools tend to develop an intellectual and political elite with rightist attitudes.

One educational philosopher in a British university stoutly held that the Manchester Grammar School and its procedures did more to harm education than any other school or practice in the Kingdom. He stated that the school engaged exclusively in "stuffing the students"—that the *only* objective was to prepare the students for the university entrance examinations.

However, firsthand observation has shown that the teaching was not made up of mere drill, memorizing, or stuffing. The teachers encouraged the students to give wide play to their clearly superior alert minds. The students were stimulated to reason and to imagine; individuality and creativeness were fostered.

A broad-minded educator of the John Dewey school of progressive education would have seen much good in the teaching, although the Manchester Grammar School is technically not a progressive school at all.

The Manchester Grammar School also seemed concerned with the healthful physical, emotional, and social development of its students. There were opportunities for memberships in clubs of various kinds. Once every two weeks, each boy was on the playing fields for half a day engaging in directed sports and games. A tolerant atmosphere was indicated in dealing with personality problems. For example, when a boy childishly and compulsively "choo-chooed" about the halls in imitation of a train for several months, the faculty accepted this behavior on the assumption that he would outgrow it (which he did).

Yet, aside from the apparently well-rounded operation of the Manchester Grammar School itself, does the English examination system per se have detrimental effects on the social and emotional development of students?

The grammar schools and public schools of England select their students by examination, and of course many ten- and eleven-year-olds are anxious to pass those examinations. (The public schools are actually private schools.) Actually, because of the importance of these tests, it is felt that education is restricted largely to preparation for the examination.

Philip E. Vernon, a distinguished educational psychologist in the University of London, has the following to say:[3]

> The eleven year selection examinations in England provide a terrible object-lesson; many, though by no means all, primary schools concentrate so exclusively on cramming their fifth and sixth grade pupils for objective tests that any other educational activity, however valuable it might be to children's general growth, tends to get crowded out.

On the other hand, in discussing the question of specific ill effects on the mental health of the individual students, Vernon says:[4]

> A careful survey of child guidance clinic cases has been made and no tendency for an increase in referrals was found around the time of the examination. In only one child in about 500 does the examination appear to contribute to maladjustment and then only in children who were already prone to anxiety through earlier upbringing or constitutional weakness.

It will be observed that Vernon's objection is that concentration on the examinations crowds out of the school program various activities that a child should have.

Certainly, before competitive examinations and assignment to ability groups or streams are condemned as having bad social and emotional effects on the students, more research should be conducted to evaluate their effects. In the interim, with our knowledge of individual differences and our growing appreciation of the opportunity for superior children to develop themselves as fully as possible, there would seem to be a place for schools like the Manchester Grammar School, though it is probable that the highly competitive selective system enters the children's lives too early. The ages of twelve and thirteen would probably be better than eleven for selecting the ablest students for special secondary schools. Postponing the selective tests for 2

[3] Philip E. Vernon "Education and the Psychology of Individual Differences," *Harvard Educational Review*, 28:91–104, 1958. Quotation is on page 99 and permission to quote was kindly granted by the editor.
[4] *Ibid.*, p. 99.

years would give the aspirants a longer childhood. Also, on the basis of what we know of maturing and learning, it can be concluded that by the time these students are seventeen to eighteen years old, they will be as far advanced if they enter a high-level school at thirteen as they would if they entered at eleven.

The formerly dominant belief that all children, except the mentally deficient, have the same potentiality and will all reach high levels of achievement if brought up in a sufficiently stimulating environment is, to a large extent, based on the ideals and principles of democracy. But commendable as this attitude is, it is not supported by facts; the large individual differences in potentialities are so firmly established that their denial reveals ignorance of a large body of knowledge on this subject. Furthermore, if we are actually to be democratic, we must give children of all capacities the opportunities to develop as fully as they can. Therefore, if a highly endowed student wishes to work hard and try to progress to the schools which select students of high capacity and corresponding industry, he should have that opportunity.

SUMMARY

Children of the same age differ so much in their abilities, interests, and general adjustment that it is highly desirable to adapt the school to these individual differences.

Within heterogeneous groups, appeal can be made to the individual child by having him take appropriate parts in class projects, by giving him special or extra work that interests him, or by individualized instruction facilitated by teaching machines and programmed material in text and workbook form.

A pupil has personality, physical, and educational weaknesses and strengths. As a rule a student will profit most by developing his individual talents and interests but should overcome his weaknesses sufficiently so that they will not handicap him. A student should be trained and educated to be personally and vocationally qualified.

Ideally, students of about the same social, intellectual, and educational maturity should be in the same groups and taught according to their needs and ability to learn. The evidence indicates that the students of highest capacity increase their achievements materially when classified into homogeneous groups and that students of all abilities feel better and are more responsive when they are in groups with classmates of approximately equal abilities and similar interests. Classification according to individual subjects has the advantage of taking cognizance of special abilities and also of varying the memberships of the ability groups at each level.

The trend over the past years and at present is away from retaining the students. Instead, the practice is to promote all or nearly all of them. The evidence indicates that students who repeat a grade learn less than students of equal capacity and achievement who are promoted. In addition, retardation is damaging to their social acceptance and mental health.

In the ungraded organization the teachers have more time (generally 3 years) in which to help children in their first years of school to acquire the skills and make the adjustments which are prerequisites for entering the fourth grade without the constrictions of classifications into grades 1, 2, and 3 and the incident threat of nonpromotion at the end of each school year.

Mentally retarded children are very slow in learning to talk; in school they make very slow progress in reading and number comprehension and usually are ineffective in their relations with other children.

The dull child, who is found between the mentally retarded and the normal, will generally not progress through high school; if he does, he will usually have taken vocational training. The retarded but educable will profit most in special classes where the work is fitted to his capacities. The best of the more retarded can be trained to a limited degree, can do simple tasks, and can become dependable, unskilled workers. The lowest levels of the mentally retarded need custodial care.

The bright student who achieves well and wishes to work hard should be accelerated a year or two so he enters college at a correspondingly younger age than average. Acceleration seems to step up the tempo of achievement, as indicated by the superiority of accelerated students over equally capable nonaccelerated ones.

High-achieving bright students generally profit both academically and socially by acceleration. Early school entrance for the bright, well-adjusted young child may serve as a means of acceleration.

Highly motivated, high-achieving students of superior mental capacity are sometimes prepared to enter college with advanced standing and thereby shorten the time for obtaining college degrees.

The practice of the Manchester Grammar School of selecting students solely on the basis of aptitude and achievement tests and classifying them into ability groups illustrates how students can be grouped for effective teaching. The system is highly competitive; and although it may restrict the earlier education of the aspirants for admission to persistent preparation for the examinations, it does not seem to have a deleterious effect on their mental health.

SUGGESTED READING

Byers, L.: "Ability Grouping: Help or Hindrance to Social and Emotional Growth?" *School Review*, 69:449–456, 1961. Byers reviews evidence and raises a number of questions about the social and emotional effects of ability grouping. This article enlarges one's understanding of problems emerging from the grouping of children according to capacity.

Gallagher, J. J., and L. J. Lucito: "Intellectual Patterns of Gifted Compared with Average and Retarded," *Exceptional Child,* 27:479–482, 1961. The gifted, average, and retarded reveal "different patterns of intellectual strengths and weaknesses." On the basis of those differences, appropriate instructional procedures can be developed.

Goldberg, M. L., and A. H. Possow: "Effects of Ability Grouping," *Education,* 82:482–487, 1962. Raises a number of problems about ability grouping and points out that if ability grouping is to be effective the teaching must be adapted to the learning capacities of the groups.

Henry, Nelson B.: *Individualizing Instruction,* The Sixty-first Yearbook of the National Society for the Study of Education, The University of Chicago Press, Chicago, 1962, part I. Various contributors to this volume discuss how to deal with individual differences. This volume provides a broad coverage of this problem.

CHAPTER 9
SOCIOECONOMIC
CLASS AND ITS IMPACT
ON THE SCHOOL

That neatly dressed girl sitting near the teacher's desk lives in a mansion located far back from the sidewalk among tall, branchy elms and oaks. Her father is the president of the community's largest bank and her grandfather is chairman of its board of directors.

The boy in the middle of the side row near the blackboard, whose shirt and blue jeans are soiled and crumpled, lives in a dilapidated house by the railroad track in the industrial end of town. His father does not have a steady job, but occasionally cleans the office of a local contractor and helps local truckers load and unload freight. When work is slack or there has been sickness in the family, he goes on relief.

The teacher realizes that these two students come from widely different homes and that the other children in the classroom are ranged between, in this regard.

In other words, the teacher knows that schoolchildren come from very different socioeconomic classes—that though we are sometimes taught that, in America, all are equal and there are no real distinctions of class, we actually have a socioeconomic hierarchy with top positions, bottom positions, and positions between.

Beyond simple awareness, however, the teacher needs to have a thorough and sensitive understanding of the classes because the capacities, attitudes, ideals, and ambitions of children vary importantly according to class, with profound effects on the teaching situation.

Some of these effects we have already referred to incidentally. In this chapter, we shall go further: We shall first describe the American class structure and then discuss its significance in education.

HOW IS CLASS DETERMINED?

People take positions in the socioeconomic hierarchy, that is, they possess varying degrees of socioeconomic status in accordance with what they do, what they are, and what they have. In other words, the factors which determine the socioeconomic class to which a person belongs do not stand alone but are interrelated and integrated in his way of life. Yet these various factors may be considered separately, first, as the skeletal forms of our socioeconomic hierarchy.

The Prime Factors. The following are the five most essential status factors which determine socioeconomic class:

Vocation. A person's job—his place in the established hierarchy of vocations—is the most important single determiner of his socioeconomic status. The status a vocation gives is, in turn, determined by:

The significance of the work being done
The power and responsibility exercised
Capacities, training, skills, and experience required
Prestige and dignity attached to the vocation
Pay, or income, received

For example, the work of the banker mentioned at the beginning of this chapter is significant because he furnishes means for the economic growth of the community. Relatedly, he has the power to lend money or to withhold it and already holds scores of mortgages on homes and businesses. He has to be capable of understanding economics well, and it has taken him many years of training and experience to achieve his position. He is considered one of the most important and respectable men in town, and his salary and other earnings make him one of the richest.

Of course, high vocational status takes various forms. Thus the doctor has high status because he holds power over people's physical lives; indeed, people go to him and put their lives in his hands. His knowledge and techniques are outstanding and, moreover, not understood by his patients, so that there is a prestigious "mystery" about the doctor's art and science.

On the other hand, the unskilled worker whose little boy is in school with the banker's daughter does work that, until multiplied by that of many other laborers, has nearly no community import. He takes but does not give orders; he has no special skills. His work commands no community prestige; economically, he and his family are engaged in a rudimentary struggle for survival.

Finally, between the top and bottom of the vocation hierarchy are many other levels, varying in job significance, power, capacity and training required, prestige, and pay.

Income and wealth. The annual job income of Americans has an enormous range. At present, some tenant farmers, indifferent laborers, and even small landowners earn only a few hundred dollars a year; a few oil men, manufacturers, and financiers receive annual income of over a million dollars. The median earning per full-time individual male worker is about $5,500 per year; and those men workers who earn $12,000 or more per year are in the top 5 per cent. For full-time, female workers the median income is about $3,500, and those women workers who earn over $6,000 are in the top 5 per cent of their sex. These dollar values change with economic conditions; but the relative size of incomes changes only very slowly.

The latest records of incomes date back to 1959; and since incomes were slightly larger in 1963, an upward adjustment has been made in Table 16. In 1963 about seven per cent of the families in the United States had incomes of $15,000 and over. Thus any family with such an income could lay claim to being in the top income class.

Table 16 shows family incomes in five categories, along with the estimated percentages for each, based on 1959 figures with an adjustment for increased income since then. The percentages and classifications correspond to those for the socioeconomic classes described later in this chapter. On the basis of Table 16 a person can judge what group or class a given family belongs to in terms of income. For example, the middle group, or Class III, ranges in family income from $5,000 to $9,000.

Income is closely related to vocation as a status factor. But the wealth of people is also shown in their nonjob income and material possessions; and the wealthy have economic security and the poor do not. Accordingly, wealth can be considered as a separate element of status. Thus being a member of one of the richest families in an area does not ensure high socioeconomic

Table 16 Estimated Family Income by Groups

Income	Per Cent	Class or Group
$15,000 and over	7	I
9,000–14,999	21	II
5,000–8,999	35	III
2,500–4,999	22	IV
2,499 and under	15	V

Source: Based on data reported in U.S. Bureau of the Census, *Statistical Abstracts of the United States,* 1961, p. 317.

status, but it contributes greatly to its possibility; and being poor does not automatically place a person on or near the bottom in status, but that is certainly the tendency.

There are, of course, important refinements to be made on such statements. New wealth ordinarily does not have the status of old wealth, primarily because old wealth has been on show for a longer time. On the other hand, people of old wealth sometimes lose status because they have deteriorated in personal effectiveness and declined in community influence. People of new wealth gain it because they are dynamic. Wealth gained by gambling and racketeering does not have the prestige of wealth from manufacturing, merchandising, finance, inventions, and the professions; there are rural areas where "cattle looks down on oil."

Despite these reservations, we may say that wealth tends to group people on a scale that ranges from those with old and unimpeachably solid financial standing and the financial power to surround themselves with status-giving material goods to those whose credit is nonexistent and whose meager material possessions label their owners as failures and paupers.

Home and location. The home and its location comprise such an important reflection of the status given by various degrees of wealth that they may be considered as a discrete status factor.

The banker's mansion and the casual laborer's shack are the extremes in houses as status indicators; between these are houses of all degrees of attractiveness and desirability, with the well-kept two-bedroom house of no easily definable architectural design midway between. The highest-status houses tend to be on the largest lots, the shacks on the smallest.

The homes of each class, moreover, tend to be clustered together. Thus every community, whether large or small, has a range of classes not only of homes but also of residential sections; and a drive through any community will make one quickly aware of the different socioeconomic levels which they represent.

There are, comparably, very wide distinctions among farms and farm areas, where the land itself is a crucial status symbol. There are big, fertile farms on rich, flat land, and there are little, gullied, hillside farms; the houses range from pillared mansions to leaky, unpainted shacks.

It may seem that homes, as manifestations of wealth, are inseparable from it as status symbols. This is not entirely the case, however. As the prime visible signs of affluence, homes reflect many characteristics of their owners apart from their actual financial standing. They tend to function as symbols also of their owners' tastes, their ideals, and their "breeding." Consider the difference between a flashy, rawly new, and tasteless house and a quietly elegant and traditional old house. Both may be of equal value and their owners may be equally wealthy, but the two homes are vastly different in status-conferring effect. Consider, too, the difference between a tasteful and elegant apartment in a fashionable part of a big city and a large but poorly designed and decorated house in another section. Such contrasts suggest that homes function as symbols of status in ways not always determined by their actual cash value.

Education. The average amount of education acquired in the United States is now about 10½ grades. Thus a high school graduate has above-average education. A college graduate is in the highest 10 per cent of the population in education received. Only about one-half of those who begin college finish. The levels of education are rising, just as dollar income is changing: in the not-too-distant future a high school education will be average, and there will be a larger percentage of college graduates. But there is no prospect for an end to the existence of the educational hierarchy itself.

This is important here because the amount of education a person has had is a status factor in itself. Thus, when a student goes off to college he is marked as capable and ambitious. At college he is associated with an institution and with activities which have favorable public standing. The diplomas and degrees which are formal recognition of his achievement there further enhance his prestige. A person gets considerable standing from being a college graduate, more from winning a master's degree, and still more from obtaining a doctor's degree.

Associations and activities. Status is also indicated by the degree and intimacy of a person's associations with people of prestige and power—the "people who count."

Being active in clubs—exclusive country clubs, for instance—contributes to one's status, as does being a member or, especially, an elder, deacon, or trustee of the church most attended by prominent people. Prestige is also acquired by sponsoring charity drives, being an alumni representative of a highly respected college or university, and being on state and national boards and committees.

Participation in politics, too, often confers status, though there are many distinguishable levels involved, from that of a precinct "boss" to that of a man quietly powerful in a national party. Here again concomitant circumstances are important. The very rich often profess condescension for the politician, but honor the long-time United States senator or the rich contributor to national campaigns. On socioeconomic levels II and III, political power is almost always a source of extra status.

At the opposite end of the socioeconomic scale, in so far as associations are concerned, are persons who show very little if any leadership and little cooperative activity. They seldom belong to organizations; their limited social lives tend to find expression in the saloon and on the street. In short, they are largely social isolates in the community, except for their incidental out-of-home contacts.

Between these extremes are persons who take part in social activity in unions, churches, political clubs, vocational organizations such as the Farm Bureau, social organizations such as fraternal orders, "service clubs" like Kiwanis, and special-interest groups such as flying clubs and sewing circles. However, there are members in some or all of these organizations who belong to the top socioeconomic level. Within their own circles, these persons are as active as the "best people." Usually, however, their associations and activities have little prestige value outside their own circles.

Other Status Factors. In addition to positive workings of these basic factors, other special factors and conditions tend to enhance status.

First are certain personal accomplishments. When a member of the family has held or holds a high political position—say as a judge, state senator, or congressman—he contributes to his own and his family's status; and high military rank or state or national office in professional or fraternal organizations has a similar effect. Being a top athlete, a good musician or painter, or an author or actor of some fame earns respect for an individual and brightens the family halo. Actually, any achievement that excites hero worship or admiration (and sometimes jealousy) gives a person and his family higher position in the socioeconomic scale than they would otherwise have.

Second are certain kinds of family background. Prestige accompanies being descended of a family which was in this country in the Revolutionary period; and there is even more prestige if the family line goes back as far as Plymouth Rock or the seventeenth-century Virginia colony. Being foreign-born generally does not give prestige, but can do so if a family is related to the royalty or otherwise very distinguished personages of some foreign country.

Another special factor that is usually of some importance is the kind of marriage a person makes. When a man marries a girl from a family considerably higher or lower on the socioeconomic scale than he is, he naturally triggers changes in his own standing. The changes are probably even more pronounced for the girl, since the man's vocation, his financial status, his education, and his attitudes are likely to set the pattern for the new family more decisively than the girl's. In either case the marriage serves as a force which often changes the important facts which give status to the parties involved. Hence marriage is a traditionally powerful force in social mobility.

Interrelationships of Status Factors. It is true that a person can be wealthy and not be college-educated or a community leader; nor will he necessarily live in the most admired section of town. To take a very different example, there are people of the lowest classes whose lineage in this country is as long as that of some of the "best" families. But as stated at the outset of this discussion and as we have even had to indicate in considering them separately, the factors of status are interrelated; more specifically, a low standing in one factor tends to cause a low standing in another, and a high standing in one tends to cause a high standing in another. How does this work?

The big, elegant houses located in the most luxurious residential section of town obviously can be purchased and maintained only by people of large job incomes or private wealth or both; in contrast, the badly deteriorated slum houses are occupied only by those whose poverty drives them there.

As another example, education qualifies a person to earn more money; indeed, vocational pay is highly dependent on education (see Table 17). Some lowly paid vocations—unskilled work, for example—require no education or preparation; and some mechanical work, again poorly paid, is so simplified that a person can begin in the morning and be competent before his first day is over. The well-paid professions, on the other hand, generally require many years of preparation; doctors and lawyers, for example, are usually twenty-five years of age or more before they begin to practice. Other vocations generally range between these extremes in amount of formal preparation needed. Some require graduation from high school, some a college degree. Many vocations require a license or certificate which is granted for specific amounts of training and demonstrations of adequate competence. Usually, a person's vocational recompense, as well as overall vocational status, reflects the amount of training or education he has had.

It is not implied that there is a perfect relationship between education

Table 17   Per Cent Distribution of Incomes in the United States according to Education of Head of Family

Years of Schooling Completed	Income		
	Under $5,000	$5,000–$9,999	$10,000 and over
Elementary (8 years only)	59	35	6
High school	38	52	10
College (4 or more years)	16	52	32

Source: *National Education Association Research Bulletin,* 38:115, December, 1960; based on data in U.S. Bureau of the Census, *Current Population Reports, Income of Families and Persons in the United States 1958,* ser. P-60, no. 33, Jan. 15, 1960, Table 8, p. 24.

and income. There are, for example, people with special, high-level talents who have not had much formal schooling but who do have substantial incomes. Furthermore, there will always be some people with great creative minds who bypass the university campus on their fast route to fame.

⚫ Reflect and Review

Bill is in the eighth grade. He has an IQ of 135, and his academic record is good; in fact, his teachers are well aware of the fact that he has a good mind. Both his father and his mother have a sixth-grade education. His father is a day laborer and is always in debt. They live in a small house in the poorest part of town.

Jim, who also is in the eighth grade, has an IQ of about 125 and also has a good academic record. Both his parents are college graduates, as are his grandparents. Jim's father owns and very successfully operates the biggest store in town. He is a high civic leader, also. The family lives in one of the largest and best-maintained old houses in the community.

Who is probably more of a leader in class, Bill or Jim? Discuss this in relation to the status factors working in both the boys' families.

What are the relative prospects for Bill and Jim to go to college?

Suppose that Bill does go to college, becomes a lawyer, marries a college classmate, and goes to a city in another state to practice. He attains success as a lawyer and then as a politician: he is elected a congressman. What is his socioeconomic status, and what are the prospects for the status of his children?

A STRUCTURE OF SOCIOECONOMIC CLASSES

In terms of the primary conditions and characteristics that determine socioeconomic position—vocation, income and wealth, home and its location, education, activities and associations—let us, then, outline and discuss the American class structure. Vocation will be used as the initial identifying status factor, because it is the most clear-cut and briefly definable element in the composition of each class. It should be remembered, however, that there are always other conditions that reinforce or alter to some degree the classification that vocation implies. Since there are hundreds of vocations and jobs, those given for the classes must necessarily be grouped in general illustrative categories.

The analysis which follows is by no means the only one that can be made of America's society. It does, however, represent a composite of the status factors which are valid for grouping people into socioeconomic classes. In one kind of classification, six classes—upper-upper, lower-upper, upper-middle, lower-middle, upper-lower, and lower-lower—are used, but this method tends to magnify relatively insignificant differences at the expense of more important and decisive similarities between classes. Conversely, to use fewer classes— say three, as is often done—would not enable us to make enough functional distinction. To be avoided is the use of the categories of upper, middle, and lower classes in the outmoded traditional senses. (Some modern analyses merely present disguised adaptations of this nineteenth-century system.) The "upper class" is generally represented in such a view as a minute, aristocratic group of the *crème de la crème,* while the "middle class" is represented as taking in almost all "bourgeois" groups from the petty storekeeper to the great industrial baron and from the bottom to the top of the professions. The "lower class" is the proletariat, the subsistence laborers. The economic and political events of this century have shifted this pattern so sharply that it is no longer useful as an anatomy of society. The aristocracy has shrunk, along with the poverty-stricken laboring class, and the "middle class" has risen abruptly in affluence, number, and power. Such a shift in class lines and proportions calls for a system of analysis that reflects the current facts better than the doctrine of the "three estates" does. Therefore, the following categories are intended to reflect conditions verifiable by statistics and objective observation of the facts of the modern American distribution of power and prestige among class groups.

Class I. Members of the professions; proprietors, executives, and managers of large businesses; big landowners and operators. These are the top vocational groups. The professions include lawyers, physicians, engineers, and professors. Owners of the community's largest stores, the leading bankers, and the top executives in factories also rate this top class, as do the large-scale ranchers and farmers. Holding these positions does not, however, guarantee Class I socioeconomic status, because each person should also be evaluated in terms of wealth, home and location, education, and community activities. Some whose professions would place them in this class actually should be assigned to Class II because they do not qualify in terms of these other conditions.

Class II. Semiprofessional persons; owners of good, but not the top, businesses; officials other than top officials in banks, factories, and large firms; holders of important government positions; sales managers and top salesmen; and top farmers. The members of this class have good incomes and better-than-average homes, are well educated, and are often community leaders, but do not excel enough in all these regards to qualify as top members of the community. They include many whose incomes may equal or exceed those of Class I members, but they lack the degree of prestige, power, and independence that would put them in Class I. Such lower-level professional groups as teachers, dentists, and certified public accountants are usually found in Class II. Often they are in subordinate, though important, jobs where they take orders from members of Class I.

Class III. Clerks and other white-collar workers; proprietors of small, average-income businesses; skilled laborers; foremen in factories; salesmen; farmers and most prosperous tenant farmers. This is the middle class in terms not only of vocation but also of wealth, home and location, education, and community associations.

Class IV. Semiskilled workers; factory workers; operators of small, marginal businesses; tenant farmers; marginal farmers. The members of this class tend to be below average in wealth, quality and location of their homes, education, and community associations. Included are such people as the less skilled construction workers; the assembly-line workers; the operators of small restaurants, taverns, and small groceries; barbers; and watchmen.

Class V. Unskilled laborers; cleaning women and housemaids; transient farm hands and other transient workers. In this, the lowest class, we find those without a trade or any special skills. They generally do not have steady jobs but take work when they get it. Many families in this class are known to social workers because of their occasional or regular need for financial aid.

A family can be classified socioeconomically by giving the head of the household a percentile rank in the various status factors, starting with vocation, and then taking an average of these rankings.

In general, a shift of no more than one class from vocation-indicated class will take place when vocation and the other status factors are taken into account collectively. Even the occupations listed for each class, however, do not determine precisely where a family fits. For example, a young physician may belong in Class II now; but later, as an established leading doctor of his community, he may belong in Class I.

Community Variations: How Many in Each Class? We have defined the classes in terms of several standards and determinants of class. Such criteria are, of course, absolute; a person who has all the characteristics of Class I, for example, could be considered to be in that class no matter how many other members of Class I live in his community.

A natural question arises, however, about the distribution of classes in terms of proportions. In general, Class I, for example, makes up about 7 per cent of the population, but this figure refers to the total national population.

It is rather misleading to attempt to transfer these percentages to any single community. A wealthy metropolitan suburb, for example, may have no residents who belong in Class V; it would be confusing to insist that the bottom 10 per cent, say, of this community's population be regarded as parallel, in any significant sense, with the bottom 10 per cent of a poverty-stricken "depressed" area.

Nevertheless, it is undeniable that the composition of an individual community affects the relative influence of each class within it. In a community with a tiny or nonexistent group who qualify for Class I, for example, the influence and prestige of Class II members are correspondingly higher.

The age, size, and industrial development of a community influence its internal socioeconomic organization. For instance, some towns are only about fifty years old, and some are over three hundred. In the new communities, class organization tends not to be very rigid, but in old communities some old families have clear-cut and fairly inflexible status priority over the new. Or again, in a little hamlet, even a young doctor and his family may virtually be the whole of Class I, while in the city of New York they would conceivably never reach this class. Finally, what makes for particular status in a rural area differs significantly from what makes for particular status where there are factories, warehouses, harbors, airports, and several railroads.

Thus, the famous analyses of Middletown, Yankee City, Elmtown, Jonesville, Deep South, and Plainville—all real towns which have been given fictitious names—have shown that there are variations among the characteristics that distinguish each class in all these places.

In a largely residential community situated close to a large city, usually many of the residents are professional men and business executives, and in such a community there are high percentages in Classes I and II. Usually, an old harbor city that has had factories and plants for many years has a large number of laborers and slightly higher vocational types. Here there are large percentages in Classes III, IV, and V. But the following percentage ranges, suggested by all the available evidence, probably represent the distribution of families by class in the average American community:

Class	I	II	III	IV	V
Percentage	5–10	15–20	30–35	25–30	10–15

According to this distribution about one-fourth are in the two highest classes, about one-third in the middle class, and about two-fifths in the two lowest classes. This distribution, it will be noted, puts more families below the middle class than above. In addition, since families in the lower classes are, as a rule, the largest in our communities, the percentage of people in the lower classes is even higher than the percentage of families; and the percentage of families in the upper classes is higher than the percentage of people in those classes because upper-class families tend to be smaller than average.

Why Do People Fall into Classes? Descriptions of the socioeconomic structure often imply that families are in the lower classes because they are victims of social discrimination and injustice and that, conversely, members of the upper classes have their positions only because of inherited wealth and the indulgence of society.

Unfortunately, too often this is accurate. Factors beyond the individual's control—race, inheritance, opportunity—too frequently make his status all but inevitable. Yet this deterministic view of status is sometimes overemphasized. Too often it is forgotten that there is mobility in the socioeconomic scale, that people do take different levels in it because of their own qualifications, and that status is thus often an accurate reflection of genuine worth. Let us use education to illustrate this.

The average amount of education acquired in the United States is now about 10½ grades, and this average is rising. There is, however, no prospect for an end to the existence of the educational hierarchy itself. Socioeconomic status is sometimes quickly improved through education. The sons of poor workingmen do sometimes graduate from high school, go to universities, and become lawyers and doctors and thus members of the top socioeconomic class. On the other hand, the son or daughter of an upper-class family can quickly lose status by dropping out of high school, taking courses in dancing and dramatic arts, for example, but drifting about doing little or nothing.

Moreover, though some students from low-status families drop out for causes beyond their control and some scions of high-status families get a higher education just through family backing, the students of all classes who continue to high educational levels are generally the most intelligent, ambitious, and industrious. The exceptions are the young creative and talented individuals who are eager to proceed at their own pace and begrudge spending time in the formal classroom.

Thus, in so far as education is concerned, the position a person takes in the socioeconomic hierarchy is, in large part, a merit rating. This is true, furthermore, of most of the other primary status factors. Some people do inherit wealth, but a person does not inherit a profession and rarely inherits a high position in commerce. It is true that a son sometimes follows his father as head of a family business; but if the son does not have the ability to succeed and the willingness to work hard, both the son and the business soon fail. Likewise, moral neglect can be followed by a sharp drop in the level of associations a person is able to maintain, to say nothing of his job. For example, if a member of the upper class becomes a narcotic addict or chronic alcoholic, he is likely to lose his old club memberships, and even friends, very quickly.

In general, then, usually people are in Classes I and II because they are intelligent, hard-working, able to deal well with people, responsible, and moral. Generally, too, people in Classes III and IV are there because they have average intelligence and average social skills; their ambitions and their morals are usually solid and conventional. The people in Class V have little to offer except unskilled hands for the menial work of the community, and absenteeism is sometimes high because of family problems and various discouragements. Social relationships are simple and primitive; few members of this class know how to act in social situations outside their own circle. Their intellectual level is below average; they read very little. Many of them have low moral standards.

The processes of living sift out and classify people according to their various merits; and the socioeconomic scale, not infallibly but without large errors, reflects this. A person takes a position on the socioeconomic scale largely according to how he succeeds with tasks he is required to do and how successfully be utilizes his opportunities.

Here, again, as in so many areas of sociological and psychological study, the subject of the relative influences of heredity and environment is an issue. The above remarks are not meant to minimize the part that environmental influences play in determining a person's social class and that of his children. Their role is great. But in a society so relatively fluid as ours, the innate qualities of a person determine his lot to a greater extent than they do in a more rigidly stratified society. We should be reluctant to make sweeping generalizations about the causes of social classifications, but neither should we ignore the facts of our own society's tendency to let the able rise above the less able.

◐ *Reflect and Review*

Paul G., an engineer with a master's degree, earns $15,000 a year and owns a modern, comfortable home in one of the best residential districts in his city of 30,000 people. He belongs to a number of clubs and organizations, in which he does his share of work. He is identified with a number of community projects. It is clear that he is in the top 5 per cent in his city in vocation, wealth, home, education, and associations.

Alvin N. is a young high school graduate with a $4,100 per year income. A shipping clerk, he lives in an average house in a rather shabby section. He does not exercise any community leadership, and his affiliations are limited largely to a church in his community.

Into which socioeconomic classifications would you place these two individuals?

Which appears to fall on the border line of two classes? Might it be possible to state his grouping more accurately if we knew his attitudes and his general prestige?

Paul G. has a son who is not very capable and who dropped out of college during the second semester. The son then joined an uncle in one of the city's leading businesses and got along fairly well. When his uncle died, however, and the responsibility for running the business became his, almost immediately the firm started to lose money; and it failed within a few years. Unemployed and without a reserve of funds, for his father believes he should "sink or swim" on his own, the son has become an alcoholic and his wife has left him. What is his socioeconomic classification? Why?

Alvin N. has a cousin who is an assistant chemist with a large pharmaceutical company in Chicago. He has a master's degree in chemistry and a salary of $10,000 a year. His characteristics seem to place him in Class II. Suppose he moved to Alvin's town of 30,000 as the head chemist in a small fertilizer factory, at the same salary as he made in Chicago. Would his class status change? Would his relative standing in the community change? How?

THE TEACHER AND SOCIOECONOMIC CLASS

Socioeconomic distinctions in the adult world concern the teacher because they carry over into the school, even into the individual classroom. But before we consider how this happens and what it means to the working teacher, let us see from what personal socioeconomic standpoint our teachers as a group approach their work in this and all its other aspects.

Status of the Teacher. The socioeconomic status of the educational profession should give its members reasonable personal and professional pride. Studies on the status of various vocations give teachers fairly good positions in the prestige scale. Of course, there is a prestige range in the educational profession—from the important professor and author, famous university president, or superintendent of a very large city school system down to the twenty-year-old girl who is teaching in a small, isolated, rural school. But all have a better-than-average status, with the possible exception of rural-school teachers, whose status is perhaps just average.

The socioeconomic status of teachers is held down by the comparatively low pay which they receive. It hurts teachers' status when it can be said, in some schools, that the custodian has a higher salary than some of the teachers. Nevertheless, the situation is favorable for many teachers. Many have attractive homes, travel in the summer, and in general enjoy a reasonably good standard of living.

Most teachers, moreover, having at least a bachelor's degree, tend to marry well-educated and thus generally high-status persons. Women teachers almost invariably marry men of high socioeconomic status—doctors, dentists, bankers, lawyers, successful businessmen, and prosperous farmers. They seldom marry carpenters; section hands; day laborers; or skilled, semiskilled, and unskilled workers. Teachers are also held in high esteem—better than their pay would ordinarily indicate—by people in the high socioeconomic levels, though snobbish upper-class people occasionally regard teachers as additional servants taking care of their children. Thus parents in the higher socioeconomic levels are usually satisfied if their daughters become teachers, and if their sons or daughters become college or university professors they are generally quite well pleased. Members of the middle or lower socioeconomic classes who become teachers improve their prestige level.

The large majority of the teachers come from the socioeconomic classes II and III, some from Class I. The number of teachers from Classes IV and V is small because very few young men and women from these classes go to college. In the larger cities, however, where colleges are close at hand, larger-than-usual proportions of teachers with Class IV and Class V backgrounds are found.

Many teachers have the outlooks and sympathies typical of Class III—which means that they have the attitudes of people in the skilled trades, of average farmers, or of small businessmen. But teachers more often tend to develop the attitudes of Classes I and II, because of their educational level and the fact that they deal largely with adults of the higher socioeconomic classes—for instance, with school-board members, who are generally upper-class. Teachers, in short, usually regard themselves as members of the top two classes and tend to have the values and attitudes of these classes. The question of values and attitudes was largely ignored in our definition of social classes because they furnish a far less tangible criterion for definition than do such matters as income and vocation. Nevertheless, the general attitudes and conceptions of value of each class are highly significant. Not only are they more basic than some of the other, more external, characteristics; they are more pervasive in their effects upon behavior and mobility between classes. Moreover, since we have said that teachers often reflect upper-class attitudes, it is important that we see exactly what these attitudes are and how they differ from lower-class attitudes. For our purposes here, we may temporarily group Classes I and II as one unit and Classes IV and V as another and may regard Class III as an intermediate group.

The following characteristics are generalized from a number of studies of socioeconomic classes and the reported attitudes and emotional problems of school children.

Classes I and II hold strongest to the values traditionally called (confusingly, for our purposes) the "middle-class virtues." They include belief in the virtues of thrift, cleanliness, education, and hard work and respect for capitalistic achievement and for property. Sexual morality and marital fidelity are respected, promiscuity and divorce frowned upon. Within the family, a spirit of democracy is regarded as desirable; corporal punishment of children is practiced less than in Classes III, IV, and V, as Nancy Bayley and E. S. Shaefer have shown [Bayley and Shaefer, 1960]. Most important, perhaps, for the schools is the fact that formal education is almost universally regarded as desirable, in sharp contrast to the frequent apathy or even hostility to it shown by Class V. Conformity to the rituals of the social code—involving dress, etiquette, and language—is stressed. Like members of all classes, members of Classes I and II tend to look down on the members of classes below them, though this attitude usually does not manifest itself in overt snobbishness.

Class III members occupy a position midway between the two extremes of the social range; hence their attitudes are similar in some ways to those of Classes I and II and in some ways to those of Classes IV and V. They, too, tend to respect the capitalistic virtues of thrift and hard work and often are more rigid in their moral views than are members of the top two classes. Education is less highly valued, though it is often aspired to by Class III members who have ambitions of rising to Class I or II. The sharpest contrast, perhaps, between Class III and Classes I and II is in the relatively greater inclination of Class III for ostentations, or self-publicizing display. Sharing many of the ideals and attitudes of Classes I and II but often lacking the economic power to reach those classes, they try to reinforce their positions by buying cars, clothes, and other material goods that identify them with upper-class groups. This pressure tends to be accompanied by many of the psychological effects of "keeping up a front."

Classes IV and V differ greatly in attitudes, perhaps much more than Classes I and II, which we have also grouped together. The members of Class IV tend to look down on the members of Class V, who lack the initiative to make their own way as Class IV members have done. In both classes, less emphasis is placed upon the upper-class morality than upon the virtues, for a man, of being a good provider and, for a women, of being a good wife. A. J. Ferreira has shown, however, that women in the last weeks of pregnancy tend to have more fears and anxieties if they are from the lower socioeconomic classes than if they are from the higher ones [Ferreira, 1960]. Apparently, lack of education and knowledge leads to insecurity about the problems of marriage and motherhood. Education is not highly regarded, and the number of school dropouts from Class V is much greater than that from Class III. This lack of enthusiasm for education is shared by Class IV persons, but their apathy extends also to the "middle-class" virtues of economic success and to "middle-class" standards of morality. In Class V rates of illegitimate births, crime, family desertion, and divorce are high; such lapses are not widely condemned. Resentment of the four classes above them is common; having no one to look down on, the Class V member expends his class feeling in hostility toward those whose lot is better than his.

It should be reemphasized that these generalizations are far from universally applicable. Class V certainly has no monopoly on immorality, nor is everyone in Class V hostile to upper-class values. In every class except the top one, there are members who aspire to upward mobility in the class structure and who therefore try to adopt the values and attitudes of the class above them. Moreover, we should avoid the pitfall of automatically labeling upper-class attitudes as "good" and lower-class ones as "bad." Each class has its characteristic weaknesses, and many sins are shared by individuals from widely different places in society. Moreover, many of the more unpleasant attitudes of Class V are understandable hostile reactions, even if futile ones, to their inferior positions in life.

These various attitudes reflect the psychological impacts of social class distinctions. The teacher who looks at Class IV and Class V children through Class II eyes will not understand that many of the seemingly illogical reactions of his students are really logical in terms of their own experiences and attitudes. And many of their worries and their problems are directly related to their class backgrounds.

J. V. Mitchell has made a study of the relation of scores on a personality test to socioeconomic status [Mitchell, 1957]. He has found that, at the fifth- and seventh-grade levels, a significantly higher proportion of lower-class children than higher-class children showed evidence of having problems like these:

Economic worries

Feelings of rejection or persecution, along with consequent aggressive tendencies

Feelings of inferiority

Psychosomatic complaints or nervous symptoms

Unfulfilled desires for increased independence

Unfulfilled desires for new experiences

Troublesome anxiety reactions

The effects of such class-grounded psychological conditions upon the school will be discussed in more detail in the remainder of this chapter.

Status and the Student's Mind. As pointed out in this chapter, adults fit into different socioeconomic classes largely because of their worth as individuals, including intellectual worth. But also, as stated earlier, the hereditary endowments which a child receives from his parents generally correspond to the class to which the parents belong. For instance, children born to upper-class parents generally inherit their superior mental equipment.

Thus is explained the fact, stated in Chapter 7, that the children in schools situated in the best residential districts have, on the average, considerably higher mental capacity than the children in schools situated in slum sections. But what, more specifically, are the facts of this matter?

The many studies that have been made of the relationship between intelligence quotients of children and their family socioeconomic status have, when correlated, revealed the following pattern of average IQs for each socioeconomic class:

Class	I	II	III	IV	V
IQ	115	110	100	90	85

(This pattern is devised on the basis of extensive data that were accumulated over the years.) Thus the average IQs of Class I and Class V children are in the bright and the dull classification, respectively. The children of Classes II, III, and IV have average IQs at the top, middle, and bottom of the normal classification, respectively.

There is a sizable range above and below these averages in all classes. Thus, there are a few very high IQs in Class V and, in rare instances, very low IQs in Class I. This means that a teacher can expect bright children from all socioeconomic classes, but most from the top classes; and dull children from all classes, but most from the lowest classes.

Some educators and psychologists feel that the test-demonstrated superiority of the upper classes and inferiority of the lower classes are due not to any real difference in mental capacities but rather to the intelligence tests themselves. It has been claimed that the content of the usual intelligence tests—vocabulary, reading, and number items—is not fair to the lower classes because of their inferior cultural backgrounds; and the claims have been followed by attempts to develop "culture-free" tests in order to prove the point.

Chief among these opponents of the tests commonly in use have been

K. Eells, A. Davis, R. J. Havighurst, V. E. Herrick, and R. Tyler, who published a book-length examination of the "cultural bias" in current IQ tests [Eells et al., 1951]. They agree that many items in intelligence tests (and all items in some tests) presuppose familiarity with material most likely to have been encountered by white, urban, middle- or upper-class children and thus are biased in favor of such children. For example, one test asks a question which requires familiarity with the meaning of "sonata." Children from upper-class homes where classical music is more likely to be heard will probably do better with such a question than children from poor homes.

Davis and Eells followed up their study with the construction of a test which they hoped was "culture-free", The Davis-Eells Games. This test asks elementary school children to answer questions about pictures which require no reading and, presumably, no special cultural background. Questions are read to the subject by the examiner. Critics have pointed out that even this test requires that children hear and understand the questions about the picture and thus is highly verbal and correspondingly discriminatory toward children with primarily nonverbal intelligence. The major difficulty with this and other such culture-free tests, however, is that so far little evidence has been collected to show that such tests measure learning capacity or intelligence satisfactorily. It is by no means certain, of course, that any existing test really measures with any degree of precision what a psychologist means by intelligence, but the "culture-free" tests have not yet achieved the degree of dependability that several other "intelligence" tests have.

Thus, the best evidence still indicates significant differences between the average intelligence of the upper and lower socioeconomic classes.

In a larger context, the opposition to current IQ tests on the grounds of cultural bias is part of a general opposition to IQ tests and their application that has persisted for years. Much of this opposition is directed primarily against abuses of the testing devices and thus the criticism is really against the users of the test and not their use. There is an undeniable tendency for some teachers to regard IQs as measures of personal worth and as accurate predictors of success or failure. Some even use the scores to justify teaching results which are actually the product of their own incompetence. Much of the debate over IQ tests would be avoided if everyone regarded them as what they are: tests of very important mental abilities and not tests of motivation, character, and health.

In some communities the interclass IQ range may not be quite so large as 30 points; but the IQs of children of the lower socioeconomic classes tend to be always under average, the IQs of children of the upper classes tend to be above average, and those of children of the middle class are about average.

School Progress and the Student's Future. It takes an IQ of over 100 to make really good progress in the present-day grade school, an IQ of over 105 to do so in high school. Accordingly, it will be found that the children of the upper classes progress further in school than children of the lower classes. And even apart from comparative standards, many children of the lower classes are poorly equipped mentally to progress far in school; for many of them, school is a program of difficult problems which causes frustrations.

School progress, of course, depends on the industry and the personality as well as the mental capacity of the student. But here again, students from the upper classes tend to excel, generally possessing superior ambition and work habits as well as better emotional health and thus ability to relate well to others.

In these areas both heredity and environment seem to favor upper-class children. There is, however, yet another influence on school progress that clearly reflects the environmental superiority of upper-class homes—the attitude of the home toward school, this often has a profound effect on a child.

Upper-class parents usually try to help their children progress in school. If a child comes home with a discouraging report card or seems to be faltering in his personal relationships, his parents will come to his support. The father or mother may go to the teacher for help in such matters, for instance. Furthermore, the relatively intellectual atmosphere of most higher-class homes complements the formal education of the school.

The situation for school children from lower-class families is frequently the opposite. The parents usually have so many social and economic problems of their own that they are not disposed to help their children with their school problems; and even if they want to, they often do not know how. Thus, as a group, lower-class parents have so many inhibitions about talking to the teacher that they rarely do so. Finally, low social level and absence of intellectual interests in the usual low-class home have a negative day-to-day effect on the educational development of its children.

These attitudes and the socioeconomic facts underlying them are especially well illustrated by the long-range educational and other plans of the youth of the various classes.

Children of Classes I and II are expected almost as a matter of course to finish college, and the sons and daughters of the Class I families usually go to colleges and universities with long-established reputations of a high order, some of them after attendance at private college-preparatory schools. The boys usually plan to enter business or one of the professions. The girls plan to marry young men in these or comparable vocations. These educational and vocational plans are fostered by the parents, who, of course, furnish the money for their carrying out. Only when a child from one of these two classes happens to have meager mental equipment for doing adequate high school work or when some other inescapable barrier exists does the family give up the expectation that all their children will go to college in preparation for a high-status job.

In Classes IV and V, parents' thinking about the future for the children rarely includes college, much less professional education. The parents, who in most cases have had little education, may even wonder whether or not a high school education is worthwhile. Thus they tend to feel that their sons might as well quit school and obtain jobs as soon as the law allows. It is generally taken for granted that the girls will marry when they are seventeen or eighteen, and the parents often urge them also to get jobs first. The boys and girls themselves often do not like school and so, though they usually have no clear-cut vocational ambitions, quit before finishing high school in order to seek employment. Many of the boys escape from their frustrating situations by enlisting in the military service.

Again, the financial reality underlies the attitude. For the parents, there is a strong need to be relieved of the burden of supporting the youth. For the children, the immediate need and desire for money of their own overwhelms any desire to stay in school and postpone the day when they will earn it. It sometimes happens, however, that a poor environment serves to motivate the children toward education. Having felt inferior because of the social and economic insecurity of that environment, some Class IV and V youth with strong ego needs are driven by what seems to be an irresistible ambition to get a good education and go on to a good job.

In Class III, there is a wide range of educational and vocational interest. The members of this middle class tend to regard graduation from high school as part of the family pattern. In addition, quite a few of the children have high capacities, and the parents often believe in higher education as a means of improving their status. The thinking often is, "I did not get much of an education, but John and Jane are bright, and I'm going to see that they go to college." Then the children are quite likely to go to college, particularly if one is located near their homes. In such cases the children tend to be motivated like the rare lower-class youth who is determined to be educated. Indeed, it is sometimes observed that both middle- and lower-class youth have stronger drives and work harder in college, as well as on the job, than their contemporaries from the upper classes. Still, there are many in Class III who have neither the capacity nor the ambition to progress far up the educational ladder, and their pattern of dropping out and going to work is like that of the ordinary run of the lower classes. The major differences are that not so many of this middle class drop out and that they are likely to obtain better jobs.

The high school courses taken by youth from the different classes correspond, of course, with class patterns of vocational ambitions. The upper classes usually take college-preparatory courses; the lower classes are likely to take industrial, vocational, and commercial courses; the Class III youth will divide, one electing to study Latin, French, and geometry, another to concentrate on such courses as woodworking, typing, and home economics.

Social Relationships in the School. From grade school to college homecoming, social activities have a great influence on the thinking and feelings of the student in the present-day school. In the modern classroom, cooperative group work sets the stage for active and continuous personal relationships; and in situations involving personal relationships, students are happy when well accepted by others but unhappy when neglected or rejected. Thus in the social life of the school the advantages of the upper classes and disadvantages of the lower classes may be even greater than those in academic matters, for the upper classes generally enjoy much more social success at school.

Because of their generally higher intelligence and social skills, the reigning groups of students in the social world of the school are from Classes I and II. When students are asked to indicate their choices of workmates and playmates on sociometric questionnaires, for instance, those in the two highest classes, with very few exceptions, choose each other. Children in the lower classes may choose friends two classes above theirs, but such choices are seldom reciprocated. Dating follows the same general pattern. Girls and boys of the high socioeconomic classes tend to date each other and, when they do cross class lines, seldom go down more than one class. Boys of the top classes will occasionally date girls two and three classes below theirs, but often to exploit those girls rather than to develop a permanent interest in them.

Thus at any social occasion, be it a formal dance or just lunch in the cafeteria, the children from upper-class homes group together. But why do the lower-class students not join them and thus begin to break the social barriers?

The answer is, of course, that some do. Almost every school has a few children from Class IV or even Class V homes who are accepted into Class I and II cliques. A girl who is unusually pretty and who is ambitious enough to adopt the external characteristics of the Class I and II girls sometimes gains entrance to these inner circles. A boy who has made a good showing as an athlete often wins acceptance, too, if he has the desire and the ability to accept upper-class values and attitudes to a great enough extent that his socioeconomic background is overlooked. Sometimes such exceptional instances of temporary upward mobility become permanent, for instance, when a girl from Class IV or V wins a scholarship or marries a boy from Class I or II or when a Class V athletic star extends his fame in college by means of an athletic grant-in-aid.

Strong forces work against such extreme mobility, however. Often class lines are blurred in certain activities when similar values and needs are involved, as in school projects or church activities, only to become clearly defined again when other activities are involved—such as expensive private dances or "exclusive" parties. Parents, too, exert a force that keeps many superficial class overlappings from becoming permanent. They may not object to their son's dating a poor girl a few times but may attempt to intervene if there appears to be a prospect of marriage. A frequent spirit of democracy or *noblesse oblige* may lead them to tolerate or even welcome occasional superficial crossings of class boundaries, but this spirit is often overcome by self-interest when serious issues are involved.

Such overt manifestations of class feeling are perhaps less frequent and less important than the matter of community of interests, which is the foundation of social cliques. Children with similar backgrounds have similar interests and common experiences; hence they tend to form cliques. Sometimes such a clique becomes an active force in maintaining and reinforcing class boundaries, as when an exclusive girls' club prescribes who shall date whom or when a group of lower-class boys make their resentment against other groups their main reason for becoming a "gang." Such cliques on every socioeconomic level tend to rigidify the class structure further.

Also, the children from the lower classes, because they are made to feel inferior by their home situations, their clothes, their lack of spending money, the low marks they get in school, and, finally, their "out-group" situation, eventually limit their social aspirations accordingly. Many of them come to say, in psychological self-defense, that they do not like school parties and that there is not any one worth being friends with in school. The fact that many lower-class youth of high school age have dropped out of school further weakens the social situation in school for students from the lower socioeconomic classes who have not, and encourages them to find their friends and social experiences outside of school. The upper-class students, then, backed by their own well-organized social clubs and friendship groups and admired from afar and thus voted for by students from the lower classes, consistently hold many more positions than their proportionate share in school classes and organizations. The students of the lower socioeconomic classes rarely hold such positions; indeed, they are usually not active at all in the school organizations.

☙ *Reflect and Review*

Living in a predominantly Class I and II section of a town of 80,000 people was a family of seven. The father was a park attendant, so the family lived upstairs in one of the park service buildings. The town was the location of a large university, and the five children attended the university laboratory school. Mary (IQ 112) was in the third grade; Tommy and Johnny, twins (IQs 110 and 118), were in the fifth grade; Bob (IQ 128) was in the seventh grade; and Mildred (IQ 105) was in the tenth grade.

The father had had an eighth-grade education; the mother had quit school in the eleventh grade to get married. The father's income at the park was low and the children were rather plainly dressed, although their mother kept them clean. Most of the children who attended the school were children of the university faculty and of the generally Class I and II families who lived in the vicinity of the university. These five children all made average or better grades in school (Bob was second in his class), though they participated little in extracurricular activities. Mildred had a part-time job in a drugstore after school; and Bob helped his father at the park, picking up trash, etc. They seldom saw any of their classmates after school hours on a social basis.

What kinds of problems would you expect these five children to have to contend with in school?

Do you think these children would be better off in a school with a higher proportion of students from their own socioeconomic class.

What would ordinarily be the psychological effects on these children of being in this community and attending the college school? How might their teachers minimize the more undesirable effects?

What Can the Teacher Do? The teacher cannot relieve the lower classes of their poverty, he cannot make the children from these classes the social equals of those from the upper classes, and perhaps he cannot make the lower-class children as interested in schooling as those from the upper classes. But the teacher can study the socioeconomic forces of his community, particularly as expressed in the outlooks of his students' parents and the other adults of the community. Then he can set out to manage his class so that children from the lower socioeconomic classes will enjoy participating in both the schoolwork and the social life of the school.

The teacher, in trying to minimize the undesirable psychological and educational effects of the class system, can direct his attention toward three objects: himself, his students, and the school itself.

First of all, the teacher should be aware of the socioeconomic pressures which affect him as well as his students. He should analyze his own status—his background, his values, and his aspirations—and try to identify the social forces which are at work upon him. He should realize that he himself has a place in society and that the values and preconceptions which seem self-evident to him may not seem so to his students. He should guard against unconsciously adopting the social coloring of his environment merely because he is a part of it. This does not mean that he should not retain attitudes and conceptions that he objectively believes to be valid; but he should distinguish between an attitude which is reasonable and one which is merely symbolic of social status. Most especially, he should guard against unconsciously favoring those students of his own class or of a higher class; he can help avoid this by continually checking his grading and his treatment of students against objective standards (anonymous grading, records of conferences, etc.).

Second, the teacher should inform himself about the social background of each student and ask himself how he can make this background an asset rather than a liability. Socially homogeneous cliques will form and there will be a certain amount of condescension and hostility; but these undesirable conditions can be kept to a minimum if the teacher sets a tone of absolute democracy, recognition of merit wherever it is found, and complete fairness in administering both praise and blame. Moreover, social situations can be guided within the school in such a way that all can participate on as equal a basis as possible. There are many demands for money in the schools today, for example, and the lower classes often lack the money for a school sweater, a fare on a football bus, or a dance ticket. More universal participation in social events can be attained if the teacher tries to avoid such demands that separate the rich from the poor. The formal dance can be a "sock hop," the student council can raise money to buy sweaters for all who earn them, and the senior trip can be a short, inexpensive one.

Should the teacher be frank with his students about class distinctions, or should he try to conceal the fact that he is aware of them at all? Some teachers freely discuss class differences with their students when activities which raise social problems come up; others believe that the students are most comfortable if the teacher appears to ignore class distinctions. There is no clear answer to this question. Certainly knowledge is a powerful weapon, and many students can profit as much from having class differences brought to their attention as teachers can. On the other hand, class feeling often may be accentuated rather than lessened if the teacher appears to be a crusader who interprets everything in terms of class. Probably the best answer is that the teacher should vary his approach, depending on the student and the activity involved. Sometimes the forthright approach is best, sometimes the more diplomatic one.

What of the teachers' relationship with parents and community adults on matters where social class conflicts are involved? The teachers' tendency to adopt the ideas and values of Classes I and II is, in part, a response to community pressure upon them; the community, or a portion of it, expects the teachers to serve the interests of the top two classes. Sometimes this tacit pressure becomes overt, when parents attempt to obtain for their children the special privileges which they feel are due them. Fortunately such situations are relatively rare, particularly in larger systems, but they can sometimes have serious consequences, even the teacher's loss of his job.

Then too it must be recognized that the parents in Classes I and II are more articulate in marking demands on the school. The school-board members and the officers in the parent-teacher association are largely from these classes and see the needs of the students mainly through their own eyes. Parents from the lower classes seldom confer with the teachers and therefore fail to make their wants known. Furthermore, the lower-class people are not very dynamic about using the school for advancing their interests. The upper classes are. Again, the teacher should use diplomacy and his knowledge of human motivations and class values to avert difficulty, if possible, but he must not lose his integrity while maintaining fairness and justice.

Third, the teacher should direct his efforts to minimize class factors in education toward the school itself. Teachers have great influence in setting practices and policies of dealing with students. Their ideal should be a school which is aimed at meeting the needs of all the students, of whatever class they may be. A school which serves all the students should not be one in which all activities and all academic work are oriented around the needs and aspirations of the upper classes, but should be one where the Class V student who aspires to the modest but honorable life of a skilled laborer can receive as much help and encouragement as the Class I boy who aspires to follow his father in the law profession.

Such a school should make every effort to encourage the lower-class students to remain in school. Even the bright children from the poorer classes often fail to capitalize on their capacities by dropping out of school too soon.

Signs of this should be watched for, especially with the brightest lower-class students and especially as the times approach when dropouts are most frequent—at age sixteen (the usual compulsory-attendance age limit), after the eighth grade when there is a four-year high school, after the ninth grade when there is a three-year high school, and, of course, after high school.

When a wavering student is recognized, serious efforts should be made to keep him in school. Perhaps there is one subject difficulty that can be lessened; perhaps the student's social life can be bettered; perhaps his parents can be persuaded to give moral (if not financial) support to his further education—and he can at least get through high school.

Finally, there are many scholarships available, and they will do more good for the best of the lower-class students than for anyone else. If a school staff can help its bright, lower-socioeconomic-class students to win some of these and thus get through college, it deserves to rejoice in the accomplishment.

SUMMARY

School children come from homes which differ widely in the size and value of the houses, the income and education of their parents, the vocation of the father, and the general standing of the family.

The socioeconomic status of children's homes influences them in many ways and has much to do with their success or failure in school.

Socioeconomic status is determined by several major factors:

1. *Vocation.* Its power, importance, abilities required, pay, and, in general, its prestige.

2. *Income and wealth.* High income and wealth contribute to high status, and low financial status characterizes low family status.

3. *Home and Its Environment.* Big, luxurious homes situated in the best residential district are associated with high socioeconomic status, and small, run-down living quarters are associated with low status. There are all degrees of homes between these extremes.

4. *Education.* The highly educated person has higher status, and the poorly educated has lower status.

5. *Associations and activities.* A person's community life—his activities and associations—influences his status. Prominence in church, club, and community activities enhances a person's status and nonparticipation tends to make one a nonentity.

In addition to these major determinants of socioeconomic status, a number of particular conditions and factors also contribute some to status, such as special abilities and a touch of fame, important relatives, long lineage in this country, and an upgrading marriage (a photographer marries a princess).

Like most features and manifestations of human characteristics and behavior, these factors tend to be related and contribute to each other.

On the basis of the criteria given, it is useful to put the top 5 to 10 per cent of the families in Class I, the highest class; the next lower 15 to 20 per cent in Class II; about 30 to 35 per cent in Class III, the middle class; some 25 to 30 per cent in Class IV; and 10 to 15 per cent in Class V, the lowest class. Communities, areas, and sections differ greatly in their socioeconomic composition; and their distribution of classes varies from this standard, which is given as a general guide.

Mobility upward or downward depends in large part on the extent to which a person's behavior is effective, which in turn depends on intelligence, industry, ethical behavior, and other desirable characteristics. The processes of living test everyone, and a person's socioeconomic status is determined largely by how successfully he meets his tasks. The school plays a large role in preparing the students for taking a socioeconomic position in life.

There is a fairly wide range of socioeconomic standing among teachers, but on the whole they have a Class II standing. Because school-board members tend to be from Classes I and II and the segment of the public which works with the schools tends to be of the same classes, the teachers have upper-class orientation.

Such values as education, good position, cleanliness, good morals, and industriousness are exemplified and appreciated most by people of Class I and correspondingly less down the socioeconomic scale to Class V, the unskilled and desultory workers, who have least appreciation for such values.

Children of the lower socioeconomic classes experience less democracy in the home, are dealt with more punitively, have more money troubles, feel more inadequate, have more illnesses, and feel more frustrated than children of the higher classes.

On the average, pupils from Class I have IQs 25 to 30 points higher than the IQs of Class V children.

Progress in school is facilitated more for upper-class children than for lower-class children because of generally higher mental capacities and the support given by the home. Children of upper-class parents are expected to finish college, while children from the lower classes may be expected to drop out of school even before finishing high school and to get a job. Usually, the upper-class children take college-preparatory courses, while lower-class children are likely to take industrial, vocational, and commercial courses.

The lower classes are handicapped in school not only academically but also socially, where they painfully feel their inferiorities. The teacher's awareness of the effects of socioeconomic status on the child alerts him to the needs of underprivileged children and may lead him to try to minimize the injurious effects of the inequalities resulting from low socioeconomic status. Students of the lower socioeconomic classes need to be encouraged both educationally and socially, and the teachers can work to make the schools as democratic as possible.

SUGGESTED READING

Carlson, R. O.: "Variation and Myth in the Social Status of Teachers," *Journal of Educational Sociology*, 35:104–118, 1961. This article shows that teachers have family backgrounds varying considerably in social status and also that teachers have various socioeconomic classifications according to their individual situations.

Groff, P. J.: "Social Status of Teachers," *Journal of Educational Sociology*, 36:20–25, 1962. Groff shows how high school and elementary school teachers rank occupationally. Various ideas about status are presented.

Reissman, Leonard: *Class in American Society*, The Free Press of Glencoe, New York, 1959. This book contains an extensive discussion of socioeconomic classes in the United States and will reward the reader who wishes to enlarge his knowledge in this field.

PART III
MENTAL HEALTH AND BEHAVIOR

CHAPTER 10
OUR NEEDS
AND SATISFYING THEM

The better a teacher understands the dynamics of behavior, the sounder basis he has for dealing effectively with his students—for easing their course of learning and generally helping them toward successful mature lives.

What are these universal forces? How does the teacher have to deal with them? To what developmental processes do they commit the individual?

To these questions we shall turn our attention in this chapter. And finally, we shall consider why it happens that—for reasons inside or outside himself—the normal human being sometimes fails in his relation to these forces, as well as the consequences of such failure.

HUMAN NEEDS, DRIVES, AND MOTIVES

A need is a lack of something which is useful, desired, and perhaps essential. The lack produces disequilibrium, or imbalance, in the individual. This imbalance is characterized by tension and brings about movement toward a goal, the achievement of which reduces the tension and, of course, ends the lack. If a need is not satisfied reasonably well, a person will be unhappy in proportion to the importance to him of that need. From the moment of birth on, needs demand the attention of all human beings, who sometimes can ignore them only at the peril of endangering health or even life itself. The needs, moreover, are ever-changing; each stage of development—indeed, each moment of life—presents its own. A need is physiological when it involves the body, psychological when it involves feelings and thoughts, and social when it involves interpersonal relations.

A drive or urge is the force in the individual which impels him to the action required to satisfy a need or needs. Our drives are the mainsprings of action, as it were.

A motive is a thought or feeling that works as a prevailing drive to prompt a person to follow one course of action rather than another over a period of time. Motivation is evident when attention and increased energy are directed toward satisfying various needs.

There are no experimental methods for isolating human needs, but the following criteria are useful for recognizing them and seeing how they produce the dynamics of human behavior.

The *personal goals* most people have in common. If we observe where people's interests center and what they seem to be seeking, we can get valuable hints about their underlying needs. When people form a long line to buy something, it is likely that whatever they are seeking is intimately connected with some common need.

The *institutions and facilities* people provide for themselves. Evidence of human needs is furnished by homes and hospitals, schools and stores, theaters, telephone offices, factories, and farms. Every day the newspapers carry evidence of what happens when people lack satisfactory social institutions to satisfy their needs. They often turn to violent ways of releasing the tension built up by their needs; we find underdeveloped countries frequently ready for uprisings and revolution.

The large and small *human events* that most people are offended by, soothed by, frightened by, or overjoyed by. These matters also display basic human needs to the careful observer. The radio broadcast that people stop their cars on the highway to listen to has profound meaning for them.

Such observations have led to no standard list of human needs; practically every writer on human behavior uses his own system of naming them. Yet the concept of needs remains a simple and useful one because this difference in terminology does not indicate any real disagreement over the concept of needs. The only real difference in most lists of needs, except for terminology, is in the emphasis that each author puts on each need.

Here, then, are the needs (and resulting drives and motives) generally believed to be the major bases of human behavior. They are set forth and explained with an orientation to the problems of the teacher and student.

Physiological Needs: The Drive to Live. A person has a need for food when he is hungry, water when he is thirsty, rest when he is tired, sleep when he is sleepy, clothing when he is cold, and medical care when he is ill or injured. Yet we seldom stop to realize how large a part of our living is involved with eating, drinking, resting, sleeping, and adjusting to the temperature, and how important it is to be well and physically whole. Usually it is only when supplies of food and drink are low, when we go a long time without rest or sleep, or when the temperature is extremely high or low that we acutely understand how important such things are to us. Then we are generally quick to respond with fear because such conditions are threats to our well-being and, in the last analysis, to our lives. When we know our lives are threatened, as when we are seriously ill, we are terribly afraid because we do not want to die. Except for the few who have been badly defeated by life, everyone wants to stay alive.

This strong desire has been called the "instinct" of self-preservation. But the word instinct, if used in connection with human behavior, would wrongly imply that a complex act could be performed by a person without his imitating or learning it. Behavior which is instinctive is performed immediately and thus without taking the time to observe and then imitate or learn it. Hardly any human behavior fits this description. The strong desire to stay alive may be called, instead, a drive which springs from and responds to the intricate complex of our physiological needs. Many of the comforts and pleasant feelings of life are obtained from satisfying the physical needs—through food and drink, sleep, elimination, relief of pain, and a soothing climate. Pleasant effects are reinforcing. Thus, a person learns to satisfy his physical requirements and becomes highly motivated to do so as they are recurrent and persistent.

Finally, certain thoughts and feelings spur people to make long-range decisions designed to maintain good physical health and thereby to avoid pain, the handicaps of being restricted in activities, and the danger of early death; these thoughts and feelings comprise the motive to live. Note, for example, the present-day concern about cigarette smoking and the highly motivated research for determining its effect on human health and length of life.

But perhaps the two most striking (as well as closely interrelated) examples of our concern for staying alive today involve the very air we breathe and the threat of a third world war. Many millions of persons who once would not have been very conscious of the air and of our breathing are now concerned, some even distraught, about the contamination of the air by the fallout from atomic explosives. The affairs of the great and small nations are constantly permeated by world concern over the fact that war machines equipped with atomic explosives are so powerful that their use might take a million lives where only a thousand were taken before.

The drive, or urge, to preserve life is at the root of these concerns, which in turn produce the motives for action of many sorts—from the construction of fallout shelters to peace marches. Contrariwise, many people are, in a sense, motivated to nonaction by taking the point of view that just because another war would be so terribly destructive of life and property, we shall not have a war.

Children are well urged to keep clean in order to avoid infection, to eat good food in order to feel better and live longer, and to avoid bad habits that may threaten their health; indeed, one of the strong appeals of health and physical education is that it offers hope of freedom from illness and pain and a chance for prolongation of life.

A Sense of Personal Worth. The need for self-esteem or a sense of personal worth—including its negative aspect, the need to avoid the feeling of inadequacy, or inferiority—is probably the strongest psychological need. Indeed, it is probably at the core of more human behavior than any other need, with the possible exception of the physiological needs.

In a word, each of us is a very important person to himself. This means that a significant portion of our behavior is driven or motivated by our egos—ourselves as conceived, identified, and considered by ourselves. More specifically, we act in accordance with the expected effect of the action on our feeling of importance or lack of it.

Ego drives show themselves in the cradle when the baby wants attention and, if attention is given someone else in his presence, he will cry or kick in order to receive it. School children show ego motives when they work well in order to have their work displayed on the wall and to be praised for it. Likewise, self-satisfaction and pride are gained from accomplishment— achieving what one sets out to do—because it is satisfying to us and the enhancement of self-esteem in such instances does not depend on recognition from others. All through life, people have the urge to seek rewards, recognition, and prizes. The strong motive to have prestige causes a person to do things which will maintain or enhance his reputation all through childhood and adulthood. Thus many seek to be leaders of whatever enterprises they engage in because leadership has ego value. Jealousy and other traits we shall consider in detail later are often motivated by a real or imagined condition of inadequacy.

How can the teacher, as well as the school in general, capitalize on this strong need for self-esteem, that is, make it serve the educational process? The strongest appeal is made to the students' need for this sense of personal worth when there is an honestly constructive atmosphere in the schoolroom, for a feeling of worth cannot be obtained fraudulently; rather, it must be obtained through the achievement and improvement which such an atmosphere encourages. For this reason if for no other, the school and its teachers should direct all efforts toward creating such a positive atmosphere.

Some of these efforts will involve simply-carried-out teacher practices; when a student tries especially hard, has an especially good idea, or makes an extra contribution to a group project, the teacher should be alert to award recognition through special mention or praise. Some of these efforts will entail school planning. A curriculum varied enough to ensure success for students of different mental levels and interests help them all to feel adequate. Relatedly, one of the important functions of the school can be to hold groups or classes in how to improve social skills and solve personal problems. The topics of these discussions can include such matters as making a good appearance, improving speech habits, and overcoming idiosyncrasies that hamper personal relationships. Students usually welcome such groups or classes, provided that they are conducted in a manner that appeals to the students, that is, in an ego-building—not a patronizing—manner.

A student may also be helped in such matters individually, of course, by school counselors and teachers. Private discussions geared toward helping him make a better self-evaluation and see solutions to his problems can build up his confidence in himself and so quickly help him on the way to improving his own estimate of his worth.

Social Contacts. Friendships, marriages, and social activities, as well as occupations, are approached and engaged in, to a considerable degree, in accordance with their influence on our feelings of worth. A child's ego, or self-concept, which is a basic feature of his personality, is shaped first by the family and then by his experiences with peer and adult groups. Having good, loyal friends and companions makes him feel confident socially. But this is not enough to explain our need for other persons. Everyone yearns to be accepted by his fellows and is very much concerned about what others think of him also because he deeply and simply needs close friendship, love, and social relationships in peer groups.

This social need, which produces the drive to be in a circle of friends, an audience, a crowd, or any other group, is called *gregariousness.* Children are gregarious in desiring to be members of a gang or "bunch"; to be left out is very distressing, not only for ego reasons. Likewise, people of all ages are motivated to join fraternities, clubs, unions, and churches at least partly because of the basic need for social participation.

During summer vacations many students—through jobs, visiting relatives, or attending camps—have experiences which enhance their confidence and ego concept; they feel needed, have new social experiences, and widen their friendships. Some students who remain at home have few companions and spend their time aimlessly. Such limited experiences narrow their outlooks and may even affect their personalities adversely.

The uses of fellowship in the school years are various. Thus the members of school-age peer groups depend upon each other for enjoyment, often for help with their schoolwork, and for all sorts of knowledge outside the school framework—knowledge of styles, games, social customs, and so forth. Such peer groups teach their members to be cooperative, to be trustworthy, and to adapt to each other. They even, paradoxically, may teach their members to exercise feelings of independence, to avoid unthinking conformity. Finally (and this is true for every period of life), when a person is alone too much, he may dwell morbidly on his troubles. In the presence of friends, he acquires a healthful mental content: interesting and satisfying experiences to think about.

The school, then, has a responsibility to provide a social atmosphere where fellowship can flourish for its own sake and for the sake of its general contributions to human development. How can this best be done?

At a school which is failing to teach its students social skills, some of the following symptoms of this failure may be evident during any recess:

Some children stand around the grounds and building in small, listless groups.

Some children are isolated, standing here and there alone looking bored.

Some children run about aimlessly, in and out of the school building.

Some children write and carve their initials on walls and deface school property in other ways.

By contrast, the sight at recess of a school where social skills are well taught is full of reflections not only of respect for the surroundings but also of fellowship. Groups are gay and active at play; the few lone students are usually on their way to join their fellows in purposeful activities.

This simple example makes an important point: the school must teach social skills in order to help satisfy individuals' ego needs *and* in order to foster the basic forms of social exchange and thus of good fellowship. This, of course, can be done not only directly but also through socialized classroom activities and a rich program of sports, parties, school government, forensics, drama, journalism, and comparable activities. To take one example, a well-run program of physical education should provide not only that young people play together under supervision but also that they learn to decide what games to play, discuss how to play them, choose teams, play with sportsmanship, and, in general, learn to adjust to group situations.

From the many socializing experiences, students will learn the skills of getting acquainted with people, of being more supportive of their associates, of being patient, and of redirecting feelings of anger and jealousy. They will learn to be respectful and appreciative of others and to overcome excessive self-centeredness.

Activity and Excitement. Another major need is that for activity and excitement. More concretely, each person needs the stimulation—involved in work, play, and entertainment—of physical action, oral expression, and sensory experience. We basically need to move; to speak, sing, and shout; and to see, hear, touch, taste, and smell. An inactive organ is the locale of illness, and a human being who lives a sluggish and dull life may become physically and emotionally limited.

The romping and running of young children and their related inability to be still for more than a short time illustrate beautifully the drive that springs from this need. If a mature athlete accompanies a preschool child and does what the child does for a few hours, the athlete is almost bound to come to the conclusion that duplicating the young one's tremendous physical activity is a grueling regime.

In adulthood the physical-action phase of this need decreases, but the basic need persists. People thus have drives that cause them to spend almost limitless amounts of money for motion pictures, concerts, the theater, ball games, horse racing, and so forth—all in the pursuit of activity and excitement. Sometimes we seek such variety just to prevent monotony and boredom, which follow close upon the lack of activity and excitement. Also, we want to talk with people, sing with them, play card games with them. Of course, we still crave to be up and doing; we want to dance, to be on the move (walking or riding), to keep playing some active games.

The typical school of our grandparents' day generally tried to repress this craving for activity, with the result that students seemed always to be annoying their teachers with minor restless behavior, and would often break out into dramatic pranks and mischief.

The fact that youth, especially young children, cannot be repressed satisfactorily is now better recognized by educators. This is one reason why the typical modern school fosters informal games, organized athletics, drama, parties, and so forth, which are enjoyed by students of all ages and grades. Yet teachers are inclined to judge their effectiveness by the extent of their own performance, for example, by the amount of information they present when talking to a class.

A sounder criterion of good teaching is the intensity and extensiveness of the activity of the students. If verbal teaching is reasonably interesting, students will pay attention; but if what they are doing stimulates them, they are going to be more completely absorbed in their lessons. The teacher's tendency to do all the performing is consistent with his urge to be doing, but he should redirect that urge so his students' need for activity will be satisfied.

Because being active is so strong a need in childhood, children should not be expected to sit rigidly in their seats for long periods. The schedule can be organized so they will work in groups, do handwork, discuss their work, play educational games, and work at the blackboard.

Sitting still is not so hard on adolescents, but they, as well as children, should be guided by their teachers into educational activities which will satisfy their basic need for stimulation. Thus the use of films, slides, the radio, the phonograph, television, laboratory demonstrations in science, and teaching machines both satisfies natural needs and contributes to effective learning.

Freedom. Freedom is basic to fulfillment of all these other needs. For instance, a person feels less worthy and is able to have fewer pleasant experiences with others when he is restrained by undue external control. Thus the need for freedom is itself an important, though often neglected, one.

The drive for freedom begins early in life. When an infant is held firmly so that he cannot move, he will cry and struggle to be free. He resists restraint.

At this stage of life the drive for freedom is practically synonymous with the drive for activity, or, more specifically, physical action. Later, like the drive for activity, it becomes more subtle. Thus neither the older child nor the adult wants license—freedom without control and law. Each wants a freedom that allows him to live ethically the best kind of life he is able to live. In school, children want the right to do their own thinking and to express themselves freely. They abhor rules and regulations whose purpose they do not understand. On the other hand, a school where freedom becomes disorder is not satisfying to students or to teachers. Such upsetting conditions interfere with the freedom of both teachers and students.

The need to have freedom under good laws and regulations of one's own making is satisfied in the school by student participation in school government. Obviously, children in the lower grades are hardly capable of self-government, but simple expression of their ideas gives them the feeling of sharing the management of the class rather than of being regimented. Beginning in the third and fourth grades, however, pupils can hold meetings to conduct business and establish rules and regulations.

The teacher's need to control his students directly will decline if he gives the students increasing responsibility in managing their individual and group affairs and gives them help in doing so. By the time students reach college, and even before, they are competent to participate in the activities of governing bodies. They will probably be more concerned, because of their experiences, with problems of human freedom. More specifically, they may be interested in academic freedom for both students and faculty: the right to express one's ideas, to be independent intellectually, and to be tolerant of conflicting ideas.

● *Reflect and Review*

A successful businessman in his middle sixties was commenting on his high school experiences and prefaced his remark by the statement, "We had a good high school even according to modern standards.

"I was on the baseball team all four years, and on the basketball and football teams for three. I was in two plays a year and on the debate team. There were opportunities to join a chorus or a glee club, the band and the orchestra. The school published a little paper every other week and an annual. These gave those who wanted to write and report something a chance to do it. About every month there was a school-sponsored party or social occasion of some kind in which most of the students participated.

"As you can see, there was a lot going on in our high school. We did many things together and had fun and excitement."

What needs did these high school experiences satisfy?

What useful abilities and healthful attitudes is this man likely to have gained from his experiences?

What are your speculations about why he did not mention the subjects he took and the teaching he experienced?

Sex. Through most of life, human beings experience sex feelings. Children of practically all ages experience such feelings, though they are much stronger after puberty. There are great individual differences in the strength of these feelings, but the need and resulting urge to have sex experience dominate much human behavior. Sex is a basic element of love and controls many human relationships.

In most schools boys and girls from kindergarten through college work and play together. In the school, then, there are many opportunities to develop wholesome relationships between the sexes—to help boys and girls get accustomed to each other. The teacher can recognize the importance of boy-girl relationships and realize that behind some of them at least is a fundamental biological urge. Teachers and counselors should be sympathetic and understanding; then the students will more readily come to them with their problems involving sex as well as other personal problems. Teachers then will have an opportunity to instruct and advise students about misconceptions and ideas which need to be harmonized with the realities of life.

But beyond this, because sex is so important an aspect of life, the more alert schools offer sex education to their students. Experience has shown that if students are acquainted with the facts about sex—its physiology, psychology, and sociology—ignorance and morbid curiosity will be largely overcome and better behavior will result.

Much of our knowledge of these matters comes from the great importance given sex in psychology and psychiatry during this century. The work of Freud, especially, has put forth the view that sex not only has the dominant role in human behavior but is primarily responsible for happiness or unhappiness. Indeed, Freud found a sexual problem at the bottom of nearly every hysteria, neurosis, psychosis, and personality disorder. He regarded the sex urge, or libido, as the dominant life force which, if badly managed, would lead to serious maladjustment.

As they have influenced many other fields of learning, Freudian and Neo-Freudian ideas have influenced education, where their greatest effect has probably been to increase the teacher's consciousness of the importance of sex in the lives of his students. This increased consciousness and a resultant increased freedom of discussion of the subject have had a largely beneficial effect on the study of educational techniques and their application, though a modern teacher need not have the extreme Freudian point of view in order to have an awareness of sexual factors in school situations. The earlier work of Havelock Ellis and the more recent research of Kinsey, Terman, and others have given a fairly sound body of facts on which one can draw for giving valid advice.

In short, the modern educator, with his background of knowledge of the physiological, psychological, and sociological aspects of sex, is able to help his students deal with the many puzzling and sometimes distressing manifestations of this important drive.

The Interrelationships of Needs. Together, these various needs, each with its resulting drives and motives, make up the force of the life stream. Indeed, without these basic needs life could not exist. In other words, if we tried to conceive and define human beings existing without needs, we should find ourselves speaking not even of most uninteresting subhuman creatures but of inorganic matter.

Nor is very much gained by dwelling at length on the question of whether we inherit these needs, drives, and motives or acquire them from our culture. They emerge from both nature and nurture, with the physiological needs seemingly more in harmony with nature and the social and psychological needs more the outgrowth of our culture.

Rather, it is more important to understand, how the various needs, drives, and motives explain human behavior. This can be done more realistically if we understand the strong interrelation and interdependence of the needs themselves.

If one need is satisfied, others are likely to be satisfied too. People work and save to have the means for acquiring food, shelter, clothing, and other necessities. By thus building up his economic situation, a person gains prestige that satisfies his need for a feeling of personal worth. His self-esteem opens opportunities for him to satisfy his needs for companionship and sex. Knowing other people well leads to stimulating activities beyond those implicit in working to survive, to achieve a good name.

Actually, the school and its curriculum are designed to help the students and the teachers satisfy their needs. It is desirable, therefore, that both

The Interplay of Our Drives

Our drives move us as individuals toward an interrelated satisfaction of all our basic needs—for health, for mental achievement, for happy interpersonal relations, and so on. At the level of group motivation, there is further complexity. Sometimes group activities satisfy one shared need or set of needs. At other times group activities satisfy different needs of different individuals, and the group continues to exist as long as the drives of its individuals work in complementary fashion.

In two of the situations presented, the need for physical well-being is being satisfied in an important way. In which is it more likely that a conscious drive for its satisfaction is at work? Does any picture suggest the presence of a drive in one person for interpersonal relationship that is complementary to an obvious similar drive of another person or persons? If so, explain the dynamics of needs and drives as you perceive them in this picture.

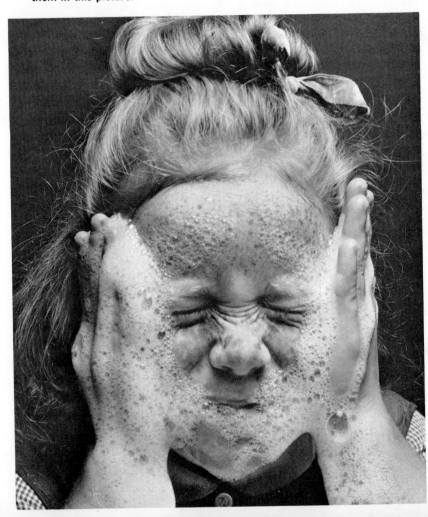

2

3

4

5

1   Courtesy of Eljer Division.
2   Courtesy of the Mannes College of Music.
3   Courtesy of American Youth Hostels, Inc.
4   Courtesy of American Youth Hostels, Inc.
5   Courtesy of Bell Telephone System.

groups be aware of what the needs are, their interrelationships, and how they can be fulfilled. This can be achieved in large part through developmental experiences which enable a person to gain competence in his developmental tasks.

☯ *Reflect and Review*

It is homecoming. Old graduates are back, and colorful decorations enliven the high school building. The stadium is beginning to fill up; the goalposts are wrapped in the colors of both teams. In some ways, it is the high point of the school year.

Cora is not going to the game. Conrad, whom she likes very much, asked her to go, but she has been ill and feels very tired. Conrad is disappointed, but is going on to the game with other friends, Linda and Luke.

These three form a happy group as they walk along. Conrad, who is very shy and because of money problems has been thinking of quitting school, begins to feel inspired to finish high school and perhaps to try to go on to college. He is encouraged by Linda and Luke, who have good friends in school, like their work and their teachers, and are looking forward to going to college, though both will have to support themselves partially while doing so.

Behind these three walk Joe and Jane. Joe has been caught cheating and is ashamed, and his parents nearly kept him home. Jane is upset when she sees several members of a neighborhood clique to which she wants to, but does not, belong. Joe and Jane's afternoon is beginning unhappily. But just as they get to their seats, Jane's brother Bill comes onto the field to captain the team. She feels a surge of pride and so is able to turn her attention to being good company for Joe and enjoying the game.

What need is the game serving for all these persons, except one? Whom does the game not help? What need is this person having to give complete attention to, instead of going to the game, and what other need satisfactions are being held in abeyance because of this? Who is satisfying the prime need of the day most directly and simply?

How are the satisfactions of some of the students helping some of the others toward need fulfillment? What needs are centrally involved in this human assistance? Discuss.

DEVELOPMENTAL TASKS

> When I was a child, I spoke as a child, I understood as a child, I thought as a child: but when I became a man, I put away childish things.
>
> *The Holy Bible,* I Corinthians 13:11

Our needs prevail; throughout life we face the effort to satisfy them. But there are various ways of doing so according to age and stage of development. Thus the meeting of needs throughout life depends on successful development and so suggests the concept of developmental tasks.

This concept provides a way of defining human development in terms of the particular behavior patterns which must be mastered by a person at different stages in his life. A developmental task is a task which arises at a certain point in the life sequence. If the individual performs the task successfully, he is likely to satisfy his needs and to be successful with later tasks. If, however, he does not perform it successfully, he is likely to fail with his needs and to experience difficulty with later tasks.

The idea of developmental tasks cuts across several fields: psychology, biology, sociology, even ethics and religion. In other words, a developmental task may involve any aspect of human development. But there are three main ways in which developmental tasks arise. The first involves physical maturation. The second involves the individual's relationship with the society of which he is a member. The third involves an individual's relationship with himself. The parallel to our three kinds of needs is obvious, of course.

Most developmental tasks involve more than one of these areas; and, like our needs, the tasks are all closely interrelated, with the result that "tasks" is almost too narrow a word to suggest accurately the range and complexity of the developmental requirements and experiences. Yet the concept is useful because certain tasks are of primary concern at certain stages in development.

Let us, then, list some of the chief developmental tasks which arise at each period in the life span of an average person, keeping in mind, of course, that the process of development is dynamic, so that compartmentalization of the life sequence in "periods" is a useful act of abstraction—not a complete reflection of real life, which knows no such clear boundaries.

In early childhood, from birth to about age six, the child is confronted by the following tasks:

To learn to eat solid foods
To learn to crawl and, eventually, to walk
To learn the use of simple objects and enough about the physical world to avoid injury, for example, that moving objects may hurt him
To learn to understand and then to speak words
To learn bowel and bladder control
To learn to make simple judgments about right and wrong and to regulate his behavior according to those judgments

In later childhood, from about age six to about age twelve, the child is confronted by new tasks and by variations on earlier ones:

To learn to dress himself and to keep his body fairly clean

To learn certain fundamental intellectual skills: reading, writing, and arithmetic

To begin to learn how to work well

To begin to learn how to use money well

To learn to get along reasonably well with others of his own age and with older and younger people

To improve his sense of right and wrong and learn to control his behavior more consistently in accordance with it

To learn various play and game skills

Adolescence, from about age twelve to about age eighteen, presents the individual with these tasks:

To make preparations for an occupation that will give him economic independence

To develop further both his intellect and his ethical sense

To begin to achieve a more reciprocal relationship with parents, teachers, and other adults

To learn to achieve desirable relationships with the opposite sex

To develop further his game and social interests

The long period of early and middle adulthood, roughly the years between eighteen and fifty, presents the individual with these other developmental tasks:

To learn to assume financial responsibility

To find a desirable social group, gain membership in it, and learn to function as a mature member of society in his city, his nation, and the world

To select a mate, marry, and rear a family

To learn to adjust to the changes in his body that middle age brings

Although we tend to think of development as taking place earlier in life, a person's final period of life—old age—involves developmental tasks, too. These are:

To learn to adjust to decreasing physical strength, more illness, and to the death of peers, including his spouse

To learn to adjust to the personal problems of retirement, including much-changed daily routine and reduced income

To offset the normally declining status in life by seeking a satisfactory role through hobbies, public service, and social activities

The interrelation of the tasks of the various periods of life can be simply demonstrated. Choosing a marriage partner and learning to live happily with him or her, for example, is a developmental task that we assigned to early adulthood. This process can be completed successfully, however, only if the person has learned successfully at early stages of development to deal with other people in general—his own family, his classmates, and his neighbors. But we can illustrate this further and see how a person who is successful with his developmental tasks is also satisfying many of his needs. This need satisfaction provides fundamental motivation for succeeding with developmental tasks. We shall take up one by one some of the developmental tasks which are typical of childhood and adolescence, the school years with which we are primarily concerned.

Dealing with Food. Shortly after birth a child begins to take nourishment; and from then on food and eating become, and must remain, a regular part of life. If a child does not acquire a healthful interest in food, he may suffer emotionally, as well as physically, all his life; for instance, finicky appetites of young children often lead to parental overconcern, and it is not unusual that this reinforces the child's unhealthful eating pattern.

As a child grows into youth he must acquire taste for a variety of foods and must learn what constitutes a good and healthful diet. All through life there are the persistent problems of obtaining food and of preparing and eating it healthfully. Much is contributed, in turn, to the satisfaction of social as well as physiological needs. In adulthood, good eating and drinking practices increasingly contribute to fellowship, as mealtime more and more becomes a time of relaxation and conversation and an important activity basis for social festivity—from the social coffee break at work to the ceremonial meals of the marriage day.

Clothes and Dressing. The mother dresses the infant so he will be attractive and comfortable; but when the young child has grown to a stage where he has adequate physical skills, he has to learn to dress himself. Then, as children enter the teens, they begin to select and buy their own clothes; and from then on, all people find that clothes demand considerable attention and concern.

Again, the needs satisfied extend beyond the physiological—in this case, the need for body protection. For example, not to be retarded in learning to dress oneself is sometimes vital to a child's needed feelings of self-esteem. Teen-agers' dealings with clothes are often a matter of controversy between them and their parents, so that dressing is a matter where youth's need for independence is involved. Finally, all through life it is not a simple matter to dress well and to be well groomed at reasonable cost, but that is something that people need to learn. To illustrate this negatively, overdressing, having a great excess of clothes, and being ostentatiously indifferent to clothes all indicate and feed a sense of social inferiority.

Dealing with the Objects around Us. Through life we deal with objects, most of which are designed to serve us. Toys, clothes, tools, furniture, books, automobiles, and many other kinds of material property fill our immediate environment. Sometimes it seems that people always have something in their hands with which they are working or playing.

The individual faces a large developmental task in learning to control all these things. First, they must be used efficiently, for with good care they will last much longer and give more pleasant service while they last than otherwise. Nor is ego satisfaction absent from taking care of possessions. In school the child who uses a book long and often and keeps it in good condition is likely to get a small feeling of pride that the other child who, in the same time, has made his an old-looking book cannot have.

Secondly, though we are in less danger from animals than our ancestors were, the modern world of kinetic tools and vehicles and other machines furnishes constant threats to our safety. The child, then, must learn to live with but protect himself from electric power saws, automobiles, airplanes, and all the other pieces of tremendously useful but fast and dangerous equipment we have; for today accidents from these things are one of the principal causes of injury and death among children, youth, and young and middle-aged adults.

Language and Communication. We have seen earlier how a child, born into a world of words, gradually learns to understand them and to use them to communicate. Thus begins the accomplishment of a complex developmental task that formally extends through the period of a person's schooling.

During much of his life, whatever his situation, the individual is being called upon to take a course in language, in a sense; for communication is a basic process, profoundly affecting success with other developmental tasks and, relatedly, the satisfaction of many needs.

The manner, as well as content, of speech of family members contributes to family fellowship and morale. Also, in speaking to others in social and vocational contexts, not only what a person says but also how he says it —accurately and appropriately or otherwise—has favorable or unfavorable need-related effects both on his listeners and on himself. Finally, acceptance or rejection by others often depends very much on the impression given by one's written words. This is true not only of our personal and social relationships but of the business and professional world also, where the development and maintenance of good working organization cannot be achieved without effective written and oral communications.

One's Share of the World's Work. One child can go about his day's activities, from getting up in the morning to going to bed at night, with dispatch and with little delay or misspent motion; another wastes time here and fritters it away there, unsure whether he should do this or that or plainly indifferent much of the time. The latter child is flirting with a lifetime of failure, for the person who reaches adulthood without being able to work and work well has failed in a crucial developmental task. Though preparing for a permanent job is usually a task of adolescence, the child's work habits are vital matters in his development from a very young age; in adulthood succeeding at one's work is a major objective.

Research has shown repeatedly that boys and girls who were not good workers in school are generally not good workers as adults on the job and that youth with high IQs who do not live up to their promise in school generally fail, also, when they are responsible for making their own livings. Thus one's work methods contribute to or penalize development over long periods of time.

The needs most clearly dependent on good work practices are the physiological needs, dependent as they are on economic sufficiency, and the needs for a sense of personal worth and for activity.

Money and Its Management. A child is not very old before he has an opportunity to play with coins; and he soon learns that coins can be exchanged for candy, toys, and other things that he wants. He sees mother and father take coins and green bills from their purses and buy food and clothing. He hears his parents talk about money and not infrequently quarrel about it, and he soon senses that money is something to be concerned about. He learns that papa works and that he is paid for working. Some children unhappily learn that when papa does not have a job he is not earning money, and that this means the family may have to do without some of the things they are accustomed to having.

As we have suggested before, one of the important developmental tasks of children is to acquire a well-balanced concept about money and its values and to learn how to deal effectively with it. Whether they are given nothing or a small allowance or have an estate or trust fund, children should master these three basic phases of money problems: how to earn, how to spend wisely, and how to invest and save. Most basically it is well for them to learn that money, like so many other things in life, exists for man and not man for it. For instance, they must find the middle ground between excessive thrift and spending their money as fast as they get it, or even spending much more than they have and thereby going into calamitous debt.

The pervasive importance of this developmental task is illustrated by the fact that an adult's way of handling money is both cause and sign of how his needs, beginning with the physiological ones, are satisfied. The person who handles his needs well generally handles his money matters well too and thereby contributes to even better need satisfaction. The person whose needs are not satisfied generally handles his money affairs poorly; this, in turn, contributes to greater need failure.

Social Skills. Another of the major developmental tasks is to learn to accept others and to acquire the qualities—understanding, friendliness, patience, and unselfishness—that will promote being accepted by them—first the members of one's family, then playmates, and so on.

These various characteristics are developed largely through social experiences a person has in the first two decades of life, especially play and recreation involving the participation of a few or many people. Thus an important part of accomplishing this task is to develop the sensorimotor skills needed for play from childhood and early youth through normal play activities. With this development, the desire for play experience generally increases, so that games and play become a better and better means for social development. Nor does this process essentially stop with physical maturity; until late adulthood, a person faces the desirability of acquiring recreational skills, though the needed skills gradually become less physical.

An individual's effectiveness in this area is largely dependent on his continuing performance of a sequence of developmental tasks such as learning play and social skills, which begins in childhood. The rewards, in terms of needs satisfied, include fellowship, self-esteem, and, of course, activity.

Seeing Oneself and the World Realistically. We have no definite knowledge of the age when a young child becomes aware of himself as a particular person, but we do know that awareness of self develops as the child gets the powers to perceive the people and things in his environment. At this stage, he begins also to sense his relationship to his environment and to experience his identity. Then on the basis of his experiences—his successes and failures, what he is told, and how he is treated—he begins to broaden this perception of himself and his environment and their relationship.

To learn to do these things well—that is, to learn to think objectively and clearly about the inside world (oneself) and the outside world (one's environment)—is one of the major developmental tasks, vital to the satisfaction of all needs; for actually, a person can understand and deal with himself effectively only in terms of his environment and vice versa.

People fail here in two important ways. Some decide any issue subjectively, that is, on the basis of what they want or how they feel about it, rather than on the basis of facts. Especially in the realm of personal relationships, we are disposed to see things as we think they are, rather than as they are; it is quite common for people to be in error over how others feel toward them and thus be uncertain in interpersonal dealings. Secondly, some people do not know how to solve a problem because they have not learned how to gather facts and use them logically. As previously suggested, one of the weaknesses of our education is that it too often trains students merely to memorize factual material and show in recitation and examination that they have done so, rather than to assimilate what they are taught by analyzing it, reasoning about its validity, and testing its relationship with other material. But how can both kinds of failure, which are sometimes combined in an individual, be prevented? In the first place, a wide variety of stimulating experiences is the basic means for getting accurate perceptions of oneself and of others, so that an individual should "walk into" as many situations as possible; that is, he should make it a point to get about a good deal. Reading is a helpful form of this, of course, but too much vicarious experience through reading may distort one's sense of reality, and extensive reading should be balanced with a rich variety of actual experiences.

Beyond this, children and young adults must acquire experience in problem solving—in evaluating the issues involved in problems and in making the choices that resolve them. Problems come up constantly from early childhood. By definition they require solution in themselves, and the child or youth who learns to make his own decisions about them has experiences that tend to give him a productive mind rather than one which merely reproduces. Also, the tendency to be wrongly subjective is decreased by the activity of reasoning.

Developing a Conscience. A psychologically and socially mature person has healthy standards of right and wrong which he observes with little disturbance. In order to achieve this, a child growing up should acquire a reasonable sensitivity to right and wrong—in other words, develop his conscience—from the behavior of the people he observes, from what he is told, and from what he experiences out of his own behavior.

Such development of values and ideals of behavior is often not easy. Thus a child raised in an extremely puritanical atmosphere may conform to it to the extent that he becomes a moral perfectionist, oversensitive about right and wrong, with his conscience too near the surface and too quickly involved. On the other hand, he may rebel and become too indifferent to right and wrong. Such a person's conscience is not sensitive enough to keep him and those involved with him out of trouble. Again, a middle course should be steered toward a conscience which gives reliable guidance for living a healthy, wholesome life. A person should learn that guilt feelings, those painful signs of the conscience at work, may develop from either actual or imagined wrongdoing. Behavior is often imagined as seriously wrong when actually it is quite innocent. A truly mature conscience, however, will prevent much real wrongdoing.

This distinction between real and fancied guilt can give direction and meaning to existence if it is applied to one's own behavior. The individual not only should realize that what he does brings corresponding results but also should assume responsibility for thinking through his behavior and planning it so it will be best for others and himself. The needs of himself and others for self-esteem, fellowship, and freedom will thus be satisfied.

● Reflect and Review

James showed early signs of becoming a problem student. From the first year he went to school, he stayed in bed so long that he did not have time to sit down and eat his breakfast. Instead, he would eat it on the run while getting ready for school. He had to hunt for his school supplies every morning, frequently left some at home, and still was almost always tardy.

When James was in the third grade, his teachers began to be seriously puzzled and troubled by his behavior. He participated only perfunctorily in class activities, he did his lessons poorly and incompletely, and he was absent at least one day a week without any clear reason.

These difficulties continued and intensified in the following grades, and when James was in the sixth grade, word reached the school that he was known in his neighborhood as a boy who roamed around late at night.

James's homelife was unhappy; for instance, he and his father quarreled a good deal about his allowance, which was supposed to last him a week but was always gone in two days. As the years went by, he became more and more quiet at school, and he did not care for games or sports. Those who observed him in his neighborhood said that he was becoming more and more "peculiar."

In what developmental tasks has James failed? What does his disordered development over the years illustrate about the interrelationships of developmental tasks? How, in his case?

What self-image do you suppose James has of himself? Explain.

Suppose James's father was able to convince him to try to improve in one way. What do you think the father's choice of an improvement area should be? How might this affect James in other activities?

FRUSTRATION

Frustration is the thwarting, or blockage, of a person's efforts to satisfy a need, or needs, in a certain way. It is present when someone tries hard, is thwarted, and then tries harder but still to no avail. It can then bring on dangerous feelings of discouragement.

Often the difficulty is that the goals are poorly chosen. Thus the child who wants to be the leader in every game chooses a goal too high for almost anyone; the youth from a poor family who wants to be given enough spending money to satisfy his every whim sets his sights too high for anyone in his socioeconomic position; and the inferior college student who plans for a very difficult professional career takes a direction which is wrong for him. Each of these persons is virtually bound to experience some degree of painful frustration. How will they react? Reaction to frustration usually takes one of the following forms.

Some *submit*; that is, they subdue themselves to accept humbly and meekly the yoke of their frustration. They adjust to a lower aspirational level and tolerate their lot in life until such time as aspiration rises again above present possibilities, if it does. A school child making low marks may passively accept the probability of retardation and go along quietly from day to day.

There are those who *become hostile* toward the conditions that frustrate them *and aggressive* toward society in general. Thus such persons typically "take out" their frustration on someone not directly involved in its cause. The boss glares at his wife when she pays a visit to the office to tell him she has bought a fur coat he feels they cannot afford, but he fumes at his secretaries after she leaves.

Some individuals set out with determination to *overcome the conditions* which frustrate them. This is the opposite of submission and is a better alternative to hostility and generalized aggression. Instead of becoming hostile, a person works hard to overcome poverty, a disordered home or social life, or whatever other handicaps he faces. He is stimulated and thus improved by frustrating conditions and often does rise far above them in a practical sense; that is, he does overcome the blockage and in doing so becomes strong and successful.

Some *avoid* the conditions that frustrate them. The unhappy little boy runs away from home; the unsuccessful candidate for club president quits the club after the election. But some of these then *substitute* new situations. The boy who runs away can usually only go back, but the thwarted candidate may form a new club. In the same way, a person who does not have the intellectual capacity for a university engineering degree may become an electrician or a railroad engineer.

Sometimes the substitute activity may be more satisfying than the original activity would have been even if there had been no frustrating conditions; and sometimes the original activity can be maintained in a casual but rewarding fashion, as when a person cannot financially afford to be a musician professionally but can play his beloved instrument avocationally.

Redirecting of socially or personally inacceptable or unsatisfactory interests and energies into acceptable activities is often termed *sublimation*. Teachers who have not married and thus satisfied the want of having children of their own but who gain equivalent satisfaction from teaching and helping the children of others are said to have sublimated their maternal interests and energies. Writing, music, painting or sculpturing, and even nonartistic hobbies are used by others to sublimate drives of many kinds. There is even a theory that if young men and women are very active in sports and physical work, frustrated sex drives will be sublimated, though actually there probably is, strictly speaking, only partial sublimation of the sex drive.

Directly overcoming frustration and substitution are generally the most personally and socially positive of these reactions, the former more useful in cases of preventable outside thwarting, the latter more so where a lack of capacity or an unpreventable outside blockage is involved.

Of course, some persons depressed by failure and disappointment take none of these ways of overcoming frustration but merely brood over their troubles. Surely this is one of the worst things to do because it only makes the tensions that come from frustrations worse.

In school, diversions such as recesses during the school day help to keep students from falling into this reaction to frustration. But more basically, one of the principal reasons that schools have, or should have, a wide variety of subjects and activities is to give students an opportunity to substitute for frustrating work the work which they can do successfully. In other words, when we stress that the student should experience success, we are saying that he should not be frustrated unduly in the school. He should learn to work assiduously to overcome frustration directly, but if he fails and fails, his efforts should be redirected so that he can be rewarded with satisfactory achievement.

Table 18 lists some specific frustrations and suggests ways of dealing with them in the classroom. Observe the nature of the frustration—internal, external, or both—and the nature of the adjustment to it. You may wish to criticize the solution and suggest something else.

Let us stress, however, that it is neither possible nor, indeed, desirable to control a child's school environment so that he will succeed always and immediately. Apart from the fact that a child who has been indifferent in effort does not deserve success, it is inevitable that all through life, everyone will have some failures. A person should learn this at an early age so that failures will not have harmful effects.

One way a teacher can foster this is by encouraging his students to acknowledge failure and talk it over with him in a matter-of-fact way. When this is done, consideration should be given to the reasons for the failure and to what can be done to prevent its repetition. This will make of failure a

Table 18   Specific Frustrations and Suggested Ways of Dealing with Them

Frustration	What to Do about It
Learns slowly because of underaverage learning capacity. Work is hard for him.	Promote him annually. Praise his successes and encourage him to work on those things he can do best. Direct him into vocational training and subsequent vocation that is most suitable for him.
Does not have the abilities to make the athletic teams.	Help him to be student manager or assistant of some kind, so he will be with the team when it practices and when it plays. He may compensate by being a high-ranking student or participating in the musical, dramatic, debating, or other activities.
Is not well liked and not accepted by others.	Teacher and student can cooperate on a program of improvement—good grooming, good manners, being helpful, becoming "you" rather than "I" oriented, and modest participation in activities.
Is raised in poverty and is short of money and what it buys. Is mentally capable of being on the honor roll.	Can be taught to utilize what he has and not to complain about his poverty. When old enough he can take various jobs to earn money for his needs. He can try to be a good student and can work his way through college.
Thinks he has top capacity and wants to be a great singer. Top potential is for being soloist in a typical church choir.	Should be taught that only a very few have the natural talent for becoming great singers. Should learn to accept himself as becoming as good a singer as he can and to sing for enjoyment.

learning situation rather than a source of continuing frustration and possibly some unhappy reaction to it. However, it is essential that the teacher provide a humane atmosphere for such discussion, or he will void the chance of bringing about the improvement being discussed; there will be a new, shared failure, instead.

If such discussions are well conducted, they can lead to better self-understanding for the failing student. They can help him to perceive what he can do and cannot do and to accept his limitations. He can then plan his work so he will have fewer failures. The teacher, of course, must follow through with careful observation of the results of discussion in all cases, and in some instances, where there is so much unavoidable failure that the student is not prepared to handle it alone, the teacher should guide him so that he will have enough successful experience and consequent satisfaction to offset his failure.

In general, life should be neither too hard nor too easy. If it is too hard, continued defeat results in a feeling of uselessness; if too easy, enthusiasm is dulled and efforts become languid and aimless. An occasional hard tussle with a problem that one cannot solve without help can be very stimulating.

SUMMARY

Drives are forces caused by human needs; the management and satisfaction of needs and drives result in good adjustment and mental health.

Needs produce an imbalance which the individual tries to correct by responding to the requirements which develop. Needs may be regarded as physiological, psychological, and social. All are more or less related.

Motives are dominant ideas and feelings that direct our energies into one course of action rather than another in order to satisfy a need.

The criteria for judging human needs are: common purposes of people; facilities which people develop to serve their needs; and experiences, which people respond to either favorably or unfavorably.

People's behavior stems from various highly related needs, which may be summarized as follows:

1. The physiological needs for comfort and the avoidance of pain and for food, drink, air, healthful temperatures, and healthful bodily processes; the motives for economic security, for healthful living, and for staying alive

2. The psychological need for a good self-image for personal worth and high status

3. The social need for companionship—the fellowship of others

4. The physiological and social need for interesting activities, fun, and excitement

5. The need for individual freedom to satisfy one's own requirements within a range that does not infringe on the freedom of others to do the same

In the evaluation of his past experiences, a person tends to treasure those which provided him with many stimulating and happy activities in a social atmosphere.

The sex drive has a physiological and social-psychological base. It needs to be understood and managed according to the cultural and ethical standards of the individual's society.

The various needs constitute an organismic, dynamic structure; generally, the fulfillment of one need tends to satisfy others also.

There are particular developmental tasks and abilities characteristic of each period in the life sequence. Success with those tasks enables a person to achieve self-actualization and good social adjustment. If he fails to acquire the developmental abilities at the appropriate time, he will be handicapped in dealing with subsequent developmental tasks.

In a general way the developmental abilities needed center on taking care of one's bodily needs and on dealing with a world of things and people, on becoming economically competent, and on acquiring the intellectual and physical skills that are regarded as constituting an education.

People are frustrated when they are thwarted in reaching their goals. There are various degrees of frustration and various ways of responding to it.

Some accept frustration; for others frustration leads to aggression. There are those who overcome the obstructions of life that thwart them. It is not unusual to avoid or get away from one's frustrations; nor is it unusual to make substitutions or redirect interests and activities.

Frustrations can be reduced if goals are chosen which are consistent with people's abilities and interests. People can learn to understand what they are capable of doing.

SUGGESTED READING

Hart, Hazel: "Developmental Patterns in Learning," *Teachers College Journal*, 32:146–148, 1961. Shows that children have developmental levels and stresses the function of appropriate learning in terms of their phases of growth and development.

Maslow, A. H.: "Some Basic Propositions of a Growth and Self-actualization Psychology," *Perceiving, Behaving, Becoming*, 1962 Yearbook of the Association for Supervision and Curriculum Development, National Education Association, Washington, D.C., chap. 4, pp. 34–49. Explains the effective development of the individual according to his potential. Such development depends in large part on satisfying his needs. The role of frustrations is discussed as well as behavior which contributes to the individual's development.

Super, D. E.: "Structure of Work Values in Relation to Status, Achievement, Interests and Adjustment," *Journal of Applied Psychology*, 46:231–239, 1962. Contains many ideas about values and needs. A work-value inventory serves to amplify a number of related concepts in these areas.

Symonds, Percival M.: "What Education Has to Learn from Psychology," *Teachers College Record*, 56:277–285, 1955. A discussion of needs and motivations. A number of human needs and strivings are presented and discussed.

CHAPTER 11
THE NATURE OF
MENTAL HEALTH

The teacher should realize that if the students he faces daily prove to be typical of the population as a whole, at least 1 out of every 20 of them will at some time be in a mental hospital. Another 1 out of 20 will probably be treated for mental disturbances, though not maladjusted enough to go to a hospital. The remaining 9 out of 10 in the average class neither do nor will have problems so serious as to require such attention but do or will have at times personal problems that make them seriously unhappy. Of course, the mental health of these 9 out of 10 is a matter of degree. A few get along in the world exceptionally well; most are fairly successful in their environment; and a few behave in such disordered ways that it is necessary for them to have medical treatment.

In the discussion that follows, attention will be centered on the emotions of this range of normal people rather than on the extreme forms of maladjustment that need psychiatric help or hospitalization; we have mentioned the frequency of more serious illness simply in order to underscore the significance of having healthy emotions and the consequent responsibility of the school for helping its students with their developmental tasks. Also, we shall find the emotional problems of our normal group so varied in seriousness that the word "normal" must be taken rather broadly.

Youth, of course, is often thought of as a carefree, sunlit time, and so it should be. But the teacher who has worked with a troubled child—one really wracked by fears and doubts—knows all too well that even childhood is not always happy.

ANXIETY: ITS EMERGENCE AND OUR RESPONSES

Emotion-laden behavior often occurs as a response to anxiety, which is aroused in this way: Fears and conflicts and their attendant worries grow out of actual or foreseen frustrations of efforts to satisfy our needs, exercise our drives, or fulfill our motives. Then, if the situation does not improve, anxiety emerges—a state of mind characterized by tension and fear and worry, sometimes over specific objects, sometimes generalized and vague as to object, but with several related needs involved. Anxiety may be defined in many ways, but for our present purpose, it is probably best to think of it as a generalized feeling of apprehension, of discontent, and of distress. The fact that it ultimately stems from specific frustrations and failures does not mean that its cause is often apparent; as an underground stream sometimes springs up in an unexpected place, far from its headwaters, so anxiety may appear sometimes to be motiveless, because its sources are remote and complex.

Anxiety evokes as many different reactions as there are people involved in a situation. One person will enter a protective shell, another will become aggressive, and a third will distract himself from doubts and fears by building upon his anxiety as an oyster builds a pearl around an irritating grain of sand. Yet, as even these examples suggest, there are broad patterns of reactions to anxiety, which can show us how our emotions are involved in ultimate need satisfaction or frustration.

We shall discuss these in terms of childhood and adulthood. But first, let us establish the main subjects of young people's normal worries—the points of departure for anxiety reactions in the student years.

Simply because students of different ages have different outlooks and experiences, their worries differ. For example, college students obviously worry more about jobs than do grade school children.

The following items are selected as a sample from the 42 questions on the children's form of the Taylor Manifest Anxiety Scale [Castaneta et al., 1956]. Manifest (or apparent) anxiety of the subject is calculated by totaling the number of "yes" responses. These items provide an accurate (though incomplete) list of some symptoms of childhood anxiety.

It is hard for me to keep my mind on anything.
I get nervous when someone watches me work.
I feel I have to be best in everything.
Others seem to do everything easier than I can.
I have trouble making up my mind.
I worry about what people will say to me.
I get angry easily.
I have to go to the toilet more than most people.
My feelings get hurt easily.
I worry about doing the right things.
I am afraid of the dark.
It is hard for me to keep my mind on my schoolwork.

Table 19 shows some of the principal objects of persistent fear reported by

Table 19   Fears of College Students

Situation Feared	Number of Times Mentioned by All Subjects
Insecurity	64
Illness	47
Failure	46
Disapproval by others	42
Loss of friends and relatives by death	32
Unhappy marriage	31
Frustration (being unable to do as desired)	30
Unhappiness	20
Poverty	18
Death	15

Source: Lynde C. Steckle, *Problems of Human Adjustment,* Harper & Row, Publishers, Incorporated, New York, 1957, p. 19.

a group of college students. For younger students, the relative frequency of some of the fears (poverty and loss of friends by death, for example) would probably change, but other fears seem fairly universal for all age groups.

There are certain similarities in the anxieties of almost all students (see Figure 16). In summary:

1. They worry about being successful in their studies—getting to school on time, mastering their lessons, obtaining good report cards.

2. They are anxious about their relationships with their teachers, parents, brothers, sisters, and fellows. Because of a craving to feel that they are loved, appreciated, and wanted by others, they fear being scolded by their teachers and parents, are troubled by quarrels with their brothers and sisters, and dread losing a friend.

3. When a child gets old enough to be conscious of it, he worries about socioeconomic status. He is concerned about his father's job and about having a nice home and money to buy good enough clothes that he will look as well as other children do.

4. Though worry about health is not one of the worst troubles of young people, it can be an important one. If they do not sleep so well as they should, have problem appetites, have cavities and irregularities in their teeth, or weigh too much or too little, they are troubled.

Young people also often become much concerned about the health of their mothers and fathers; it is not uncommon for them to worry when they see their parents suffering from pain or illness, especially when the possibility of death is involved. Some schoolchildren even worry seriously about their own death, though death is usually very remote for them. This may be considered a normal worry although not one of the more common ones.

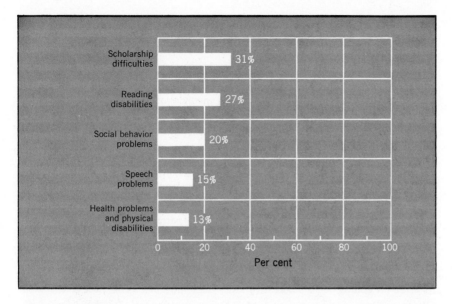

Figure 16 Problems of elementary school children *Problems of schoolwork, personal relations, speech, and health sometimes trouble even elementary schoolchildren. (These figures are derived from a study of 1,270 pupils from grades 1 to 8. Based on data from T. L. Torgerson,* Studying Children, *The Dryden Press, Inc., New York, 1947, p. 45.*

But what can the teacher do about such manifest worries while they are still only the harbingers of deep distress? How can the storm be headed off? We shall discuss below some of the ways that human beings react to specific frustrations and to generalized anxiety; we shall also indicate some of the ways that the teacher can help his students overcome their fears and anxieties. We can, however, anticipate this discussion with a few generalizations about techniques that a teacher can use to identify and help those students with potential mental health problems.

There are three steps in dealing with mental health problems. First, the problem must be identified; then it must be intelligently analyzed; and finally, something must be done about it. Many of the methods for accomplishing each step are time-honored, commonsense techniques; others make use of newer and more formal procedures.

The problem of locating mental health problems is essentially one of gathering information. The teacher who is conscious of mental health problems naturally is on the lookout for signs of disturbance in his students. He observes each child's behavior not only in class but also, as far as possible, on the playground and in other nonclassroom situations. This kind of careful, but informal, observation is merely a conscious extension of the natural curiosity most teachers feel about their students; it is, of course, augmented by informal, friendly chats with the children and, occasionally, with their parents. Also available to the teacher as sources of data on his students' behavior are the observations of other teachers, the cumulative records, and other standard record material. Sometimes the teacher may further augment these facilities by keeping "anecdotal records"—informal records of possibly significant incidents involving each child. A more formal record is the "case study," a record formed by the collection and organization of all the available material on the child for study and analysis. From such records and observations, the teacher can often spot sources of anxiety and distress in his students' situations.

A newer technique for locating and defining trouble spots of mental health involves the use of projective and expressive methods. A person naturally tends to see the world in terms of his own personality and to project his own values and concerns into the things he sees or creates. Therefore teachers sometimes study students' drawings or stories to locate seemingly persistent themes or concerns. Sometimes they ask students to provide an ending for a suggestive story beginning or to complete a sentence. These endings are then studied for signs of excessive anxiety or hostility.

Such projective techniques use the same principles as the Rorschach or ink-blot test and the Thematic Apperception Test, TAT, which can be used only by experts. The Rorschach test calls for the subjects' interpretations of ambiguous ink-blots, and the TAT requires that the subjects interpret emotionally suggestive pictures. The responses are studied in order to locate trouble areas. The teacher, of course, cannot employ these more elaborate tests, but he can use the same principles advantageously in his own observations; provided he is careful to avoid dogmatism and overinterpretation.

In Chapter 3, we have described the use of sociometric techniques in studying children's social relationships. Such techniques are also useful in collecting data on anxious children.

Once information has been collected and analyzed, there remains the problem of treating the difficulty. The teacher, of course, cannot be expected to be a psychiatrist, but he can do much to alleviate minor (though sometimes potentially serious) anxieties. Some of the techniques for locating mental health problems also have therapeutic value, since one of the most important steps in overcoming a problem is to isolate it and to understand it. Often when a child is led to project his fears and problems into a drawing or a story, they become clearer to him and sometimes he can overcome them himself. In casual conversations, too, sometimes he gains perspective on his problems and sees how to solve them. Also, when he enacts a role in a psychodrama or a sociodrama, he can see himself more objectively; some of the solutions to problems encountered in the role playing may be consciously or unconsciously transferred to his real experience.

Perhaps more common, however, as a means of aiding troubled children than any of these special techniques is direct counseling. Counseling may be of two kinds: directive and nondirective. In directive counseling, the counselor controls the interview and makes direct suggestions for overcoming problems under consideration. In nondirective counseling, on the other hand, the counselor functions mainly as a sympathetic audience, merely supporting the troubled person and often repeating and reflecting the subject's statements; the assumption here is that the subject should be allowed to work out his own solutions. Both these types of counseling are widely employed in clinics and mental health centers by psychologists and psychiatrists; the teacher may adopt some of their techniques, however, for his own use. Most teacher-student conferences use a combination of these techniques; the teacher does not push or lecture, but rather listens sympathetically and occasionally offers a quiet suggestion.

It should be emphasized that the teacher should never carry any of his efforts to such an extent that he arouses the resentment of his students. Students are likely to regard too inquisitive a teacher as a "prier" or a "meddler" and to look upon him with suspicion. Neither should the teacher try so hard to be sympathetic that he encourages excessive emotionalism. A conference should not drain the teacher or the student emotionally, though it may touch on sensitive subjects. An attitude of calm sympathy and friendly, but not meddlesome, interest is best.

Another warning concerns attempting to deal with serious maladjustments without professional help. If a child appears to have mental problems that go beyond minor worries and frustrations, the teacher should enlist the aid of the school psychologist or counselor rather than attempt therapy himself.

Probably the teacher's best way of helping his students to improve their mental health is to provide a class atmosphere in which they can find healthful challenges and opportunities for developing their best assets, as well as an atmosphere free from unnecessary threats and fears. Such an atmosphere may do much to help the student overcome his difficulties outside the classroom, as well.

Let us turn now to several important distinguishable psychological mechanisms by which persons respond to anxiety.

We shall find that the anxiety content of these mechanisms varies considerably; and, in order to see the mechanisms whole, as it were, we shall include mention of situations in which anxiety may play a minor part or even be uninvolved. But increasingly—for we shall generally work from less to more serious mechanisms—anxiety will be central in the responses.

Daydreaming. When the teacher called on him, the boy was startled, seemed confused, groped a bit, and then asked to have the question repeated. He had been in another world, a world of his own making, a dreamworld.

When the real world is so difficult that we are discouraged by defeat, we sometimes seek refuge in a dreamworld where we fancy ourselves as being what we want to be. The weak and timid fancy themselves strong and manly, the poor dream of riches, and the person who enjoys little success has himself adored for his great triumphs. A person's weaknesses are overcome; his environment is suddenly most satisfying.

A boy who likes to think of himself as a baseball pitcher is frustrated because he is not one of the two regular pitchers for the high school team. Although the team is a relatively weak one, about all the pitching this boy does is when he pitches for batting practice. He has developed an excessive windup and goes through various attention-getting antics while pitching. He likes to think of himself as headed for the major leagues to become a big star. His behavior is probably a carry-over from his long periods of fantasy when he dreams that he is a sensational pitcher performing in the nation's biggest ball parks, throwing and batting his team to victory in game after game. He dreams of himself as dreaded by the opposing teams, as being cheered by the roaring fans, featured in the baseball news and appearing frequently on television.

But entrance into the dreamworld is not limited to persons whose developmental tasks are too difficult for them and consequently distasteful. Bright persons often run from the stress of monotony by spending time in a world of their own making. Having vivid imaginations, they can build for themselves very lively dreamworlds, and many of them do so. In other words, anxiety and resultant daydreams may result from lack of challenge as well as from excessive demands.

The dreamworld develops when imaginations are stimulated and inhibitions are removed. Many imaginative tales transport their reader into glorious and happy situations. Motion pictures encourage people to identify themselves with the hero and heroine and thus experience loveliness, romance, wealth, distinction, and conquest. Sometimes adults use alcohol to "lose" their troubles and feelings of inferiority in a pleasant fantasy mist.

In an experiment, certain themes were found to occur in the fantasies of 40 adolescents, as shown in Table 20. The fantasies were responses to requests to tell a story suggested by each of 42 specially prepared pictures. Themes of the fantasies were classified and correlated with the students' personalities as judged by teacher ratings, standard tests, and other devices. The experimenters found that the themes of the fantasies bore close relationships to the subjects' personalities, though they were usually highly symbolic and difficult to interpret.

A little pleasant daydreaming may not be harmful, but habitual retreat from reality is bad. Much time is spent, and when the person who has

Table 20 Environmental Themes in the Fantasies of 40 Junior and Senior High School Students

Categories	Occurrences		
	Total	Boys	Girls
Family relationships	40	20	20
Economics	38	20	18
Punishment	33	18	15
Separation; rejection	32	18	14
Accidents; illness; injury	28	14	14
School	28	15	13
Social; gangs	21	9	12
Place of residence	17	8	9
Appearance	13	3	10
Strangeness; unusualness	12	8	4
Discussion; advice	10	7	3
Age	10	5	5
Gossip	8	5	3
Entertainment	7	3	4
Work	7	3	4
Night	4	2	2
Food; eating	4	3	1
Mail; writing	4	2	2

Source: P. M. Symonds, *Adolescent Fantasy*, Columbia University Press, New York, 1949, p. 81.

expanded his ego in fantasy gets back to the real world, he is less competent to face it than before because it has moved on while he was away.

The teacher should try to identify his daydreamers, those students who are "absent though present." Then he should look most seriously for the personal conditions that cause daydreaming. What failures or disappointments is the daydreamer experiencing, and why is he not getting a sense of his own worth in reality? Then, after such careful study is made of the student, special effort should be exerted to arouse his interest in the vital real events around him and in his own work.

Since the daydreamer may be of any capacity but is probably either too dull or too bright for his work, his is a case which clearly imposes on the teacher the responsibility of adapting the work to the individual student.

Negativism, A Kind of Imperviousness. Negativism involves a person's being particularly unreceptive to reasonable suggestions about himself and habitually unmoved by the wishes and needs of others. In a word, negativism is a state of being consistently against rather than for. Such an attitude is generally developed as an unconscious defense against a world which the individual finds frustrating. Being thwarted or experiencing some important failures, he develops a kind of anxiety which he conceals behind a façade of negativism.

The simplest form of negativism is evident when a child says, "No, no!" when asked to come into the house and take off his raincoat. He is being slightly more negative when the response is opposite to the requested one—when on being asked not to go into the living room, he goes there though he had planned to go to the kitchen.

Youth and adults show negativism when they are habitually quick to sense how others stand on a matter and then stubbornly take the opposite side. Five minutes after arriving, they see that others are enjoying a party, so they begin to find it rather dull or even become hostile toward it; and the first complaint is inevitably followed by several others.

Another manifestation of negativism is unreasoning opposition to anything new or different—modern furniture, nonobjective paintings, the new style in automobiles, advanced farming practices—anything different from what one is accustomed to. Sometimes the expression of such negativism is short-lived: the person learns to understand the new and thus to appreciate it. But usually the closed minds of people who are prey to this kind of negativism keep them from the necessary learning about new things.

Why are people negativistic?

From the child who puts a "no" fence around himself to the adult whose contrariness is so subtly expressed it is hard to detect, the negativist is generally trying to assert himself. He gets a spurious feeling of worth from doing so; he either enhances his ego or protects it. But another motive for negativism is to keep things as they are. Change is disturbing, and negativism is a rather simple way of trying to protect oneself from its threats and problems. Yet change inevitably comes, so negativism actually only prevents a person from maturing emotionally and socially in order to meet it well.

The teacher generally gains little by constantly engaging in a battle of wills with a strongly negativistic student, though this is often the temptation. Whenever possible, the teacher should avoid situations in which the negative-minded student must be forced to submit to authority. Rather, he should try to arouse enthusiasm and affirmative responses in the student by discovering and helping him to develop his particular abilities. Often it is best to avoid giving the negative student a clear-cut choice between an approved and an unapproved course of action. Instead, it can be treated as a matter of course that he will cooperate with the class. When overt hostility does appear, the teacher is probably wisest to ignore it and calmly and firmly go on with the planned activity. A young student, particularly, often loses his negativism when he finds it is socially ineffective.

Conflict, Decision Making, and Procrastination. The young woman who is in a ferment over a proposal—she is losing sleep over the problem; she wants to get married but is not sure she wants to marry this young man—is having a conflict.

So is the ten-year-old who wants to study after supper (for he is not satisfied with his marks) but has been asked to join the "gang" down at the usual corner. In both individuals, one set of ideas fights another, and neither seems to dominate and prevail; there is a cross fire of desires.

Conflict over important decisions is normal. But some people experience difficulties over them for seemingly interminable lengths of time; and some have trouble making decisions over matters that are ordinarily routine—whether to ask a certain girl for a date, what lesson to study, and so on. Anxiety may be one of the predisposing causes of conflict, and then conflict may make a person more anxious.

This is procrastination; and procrastination is both symptom and cause of personal ineffectiveness. Thus, persons who procrastinate are often those who are uncertain because they feel inadequate. Not having confidence in themselves, they hardly know how to begin any action, and they also fear its consequences. So this or that action is postponed. But the tasks of life remain to be done and present themselves almost continuously to annoy the person who postponed them and the consequent cluttering up of activities develops emotional tensions that produce greater ineffectiveness.

Much conflict centers around right or wrong. Conflict is evident when someone wavers in making a decision involving ethical standards. For example, a pupil knows that the teacher keeps some change in her desk. On the one hand, he would like to have that money; on the other, he knows that it is wrong to steal and that he will suffer disgrace and punishment if caught. These thoughts, and conflicting thoughts they are, he churns back and forth in his mind, suffering a good deal in the process.

To avoid conflict and procrastination, a person should learn to face issues and conflicts and make decisions promptly. "Passing the buck" to others or letting problems accumulate in one's own mind serves to store up trouble. A person should not make snap judgments, which are little better than guesses, but should think the problem through and then decide and act. After a decision is made, it is usually best not to dwell much on the reasons for it, for this can be a form of denying, in effect, that a decision has been made at all. Some decisions are certain to be poor ones, but there will be fewer of these if a person is not made mentally ineffective by continued cross-firing of his feelings and wants. When a poor decision is made, a person should not allow himself to be defeated by it, but should move on to new problems and analyze his past mistakes only with a view to profiting from them. Of course, when there is a tendency toward behavior inconsistent with high ideals and right, it is to be hoped that conflict will set in especially quickly to check it.

But how are such habits to be developed?

To begin with, when the home and the school environment are friendly and relaxed, children are unlikely to develop conflicts over everyday matters of concern. In a severe and tense environment, on the other hand, children tend to get the feeling that many actually minor matters are of the utmost importance; thus they soon learn to confront problems with "Shall I, shan't I"; "If I do, if I don't"; "What will happen if I do this, if I do that"; and so on. In other words, imposed tensions tend to produce conflicts; and conflicts, in turn, produce more stress. Also, parents and teachers should permit children, from an early age, to make many of their own decisions. In most instances they should not scold them if they make what seem poor ones but should let them learn by observing the consequences.

Finally, and ideally, a child should be helped not to "let his anchor drag" or dissipate his energy in several directions, so that he will have his full energy for well-coordinated efforts. If attractive incentives are set up for him, if his motives are well channeled, and if he is assisted in developing needed skills, his volitional powers will be increased and procrastination reduced.

To handle procrastination in such positive ways should remain the first thought and effort of the teacher, certainly, for children can thus be trained to develop better work habits, and good work habits lead to improved achievement, which, in turn, is a stimulus to more effective work.

The realization that illness offers temporary haven from one's problems often leads to illness in order to avoid them. When a student stays home "sick in bed" each morning there is an examination in mathematics but usually "gets well" by noon, he is malingering. Malingering is a rather special form of procrastination because, unlike many others, it can have certain immediate gratifications. Thus a convincingly pretending "sick" child gains the sympathetic attention of his parents and friends, and the doctor may be called to attend him. Now he is a special center of attention, and his feeling of worth may be temporarily increased.

A teacher should study carefully a child who gets sick when the work is hard and unpleasant. For instance, a child may have headaches and vomiting spells at such times. Such a child should be given a thorough physical examination so that if anything is wrong physically, it can be remedied. It may be found, however, that the child is perfectly well but is making a play for attention and at the same time attempting to avoid tasks and duties that he does not like.

Through procrastination and malingering, a child or adult is avoiding what is distasteful, sometimes because the work is too hard and sometimes because he has not developed effective work habits. In many instances the person's feelings of uncertainty and concern about his accomplishments inhibit his efforts and render him much less effective. As with all aspects of poor mental health which lower a person's effectiveness, the problem is how to overcome procrastination and malingering. Specifically, what can the teacher do to help his pupils?

Actually, there is no clear-cut way of overcoming these difficulties. It helps, however, if the person who procrastinates and malingers has a clear understanding of his difficulty. As with most if not all difficulties, it may help if teachers and pupils talk over these problems. Improved self-perceptions do not ensure improved behavior, but understanding is generally a desirable part of any remedial program. A second point is that the student needs to be highly motivated so his drive to work will be strong. If only certain tasks cause a pupil to malinger while he does others avidly, then it may be desirable to omit the distasteful tasks, at least temporarily. A child can be motivated by being recognized and praised for his achievements. A helpful, friendly atmosphere which reduces a child's overconcern about his work may help to release his energies for working effectively.

☯ Reflect and Review

Frances, fifteen years old and a sophomore in high school, is rather unattractive because she is overweight. Her father is a skilled laborer who has an average income; Frances' home life is chaotic because of trouble between her father and her mother, who have been separated twice for short periods of time. She has a poor self-image and makes slightly below average grades in school though her IQ is average.

Frances characteristically has a hard time making minor decisions. Sometimes her homework goes undone because she has spent the evening trying to decide whether to do it first or postpone it until after some other minor chore is done. Similarly, when she is allowed to choose between questions on an examination, Frances is troubled by the thought that she may be selecting the wrong questions. She wastes time and energy rereading the questions over and over. Soon she cannot think clearly. So when she turns to the chosen questions, she makes many poor decisions and frets over them long after they have been made.

Do you see a connection between Frances' difficulty in decision making, her procrastination, and her personal situation? Explain.

How might Frances be helped to overcome her difficulties in making decisions? What would you do, if you were her teacher?

Rationalization. A high school girl hoped a certain boy would ask her to go to a party with him. But he asked another girl. The young woman said, "I wouldn't go with him if he was the last boy on earth. He isn't at all interesting, and I could never like him the least bit."

She was rationalizing; she gave an explanation that might appear reasonable and convincing but that actually was untrue (see Figure 17).

Rationalizing is the process of saving face—protecting our self-esteem—by giving feasible but untrue excuses. Also, it involves self-deception. When a person is rationalizing, he does not feel that he is lying; in other words, a deliberate lie is not rationalizing.

When they heard her story, the young woman's more perceptive friends thought, "Sour grapes!" This is the colloquial term for her form of rationalization; it comes from Aesop's fable about the fox who, when he could not reach the grapes he jumped and jumped for, called them sour and thus implied he did not want them. Sour grapes are in evidence also when, as is not uncommon, mediocre students make the generally false remark, "Good marks are unimportant because the persons who are most successful in life were poor students in school."

"Oh, it will come out all right," says another student who is getting poor marks. "I'll pass anyway." Similarly, a boy who is not promoted says, "This is probably all for the best; now I can cover the ground more thoroughly." In both instances the boys are careless and indifferent, so that their failures are entirely their own fault. This form of rationalization is colloquially called either "Pollyanna," from the novel *Pollyanna,* whose heroine regards everything from an ultraoptimistic point of view, or "sweet lemon," because a sweet response is made to a sour situation.

The Pollyanna rationalization for failures which are the result of indifference and lack of effort is a cover for weak character. On the other hand thinking of failure as a blessing in disguise is helpful, and not pollyannaish, if it spurs one to do his best the next time. Nor is a Pollyanna rationalization at work in wholesome resignation, even if it has an optimistic tone, when nothing more can be done, as in the case of death or unavoidable failure.

It is not unusual that noble, self-effacing statements and expressions of high ideals underlying one's own behavior are actually rationalizations. Such a mechanism might be called the "holier-than-thou" reaction. When one youth says he is glad that another beat him out for a position on the team because the chosen one will enjoy the experiences he will have, or when a girl says that she thinks she will drop out of school because she wants to help her parents, it is well to look for the true motive behind the remark. Ascribing high standards to one's feelings or behavior is often an attempt to enhance one's sense of personal worth.

When one student says to another, "I'd learn that stuff in algebra if the

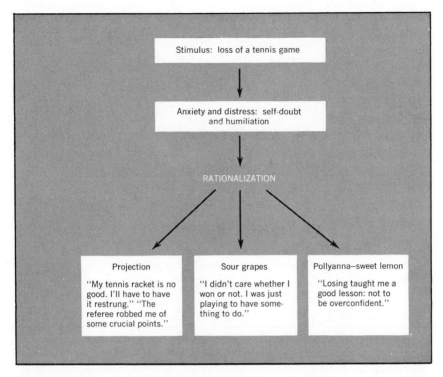

Figure 17 The mechanism of rationalization *This diagram shows how the mechanism of rationalization might be used as a defense against the frustration of losing a tennis game. First comes the distressing event, then the feelings of distress and unhappiness. The subject tries to overcome these by one or more of the rationalizations shown.*

teacher could only explain it," it is quite possible he is right. But if the fault is the student's and he is blaming the teacher in order to excuse himself, he is indulging in a form of rationalization known as projection, in which a person blames someone or something outside himself for a fault of his own.

Sometimes this is done in order to maintain the feeling of self-esteem. A truant may say he does not go to school because his clothes are not good enough when the fact is that he can have good enough clothes if he wants to. He is projecting the difficulty on the lack of clothes and the blame on his parents principally in order to stay happily out of school.

An often very subtle aspect of projection is the ascribing to another of one's own faults and weaknesses. If a person says that so-and-so cannot be trusted any further than you can see him, he may unwittingly be attributing to so-and-so his own untrustworthiness because this makes him feel more worthy and may help to take negative attention off himself.

Any rationalizing individual could be using his time trying to live more effectively by improving himself; and virtually every rationalizer deceives himself more than he deceives others. But projection is one of the most destructive psychological narcotics, because it is very common (both among individuals and among nations) and it seems to explain and excuse wrong behavior especially satisfactorily. Among the evasive mechanisms described in this chapter, the practice of projection is unexcelled for making a person fail to see things, including himself, as they really are. Hence it especially prevents a person from remedying his own weaknesses, from seeing his true goals and reaching them.

Rationalization is self-deception that keeps one from dealing well with truth and fact and so makes him hurt himself and sometimes others. Therefore a teacher is well advised to lead his students at suitable times to discuss the value both of being realistic with oneself and of telling the truth, even under conditions of personal stress. It should be stated and demonstrated by discussed examples that rationalization, like counterfeit coin, does not ring true—does not meet the requirements of genuine exchange in human relationships. Finally, ways and means of avoiding rationalization—again, even under conditions of personal stress—should be presented and discussed.

Not being confident of his status and feeling anxious about it, a person tries to soften his anxiety by blaming this and that for his troubles and by ascribing to others his own faults. Actually the basic cure for using the projection form of rationalization, as well as for using other mechanisms, is to achieve true worth. If a person is reasonably well satisfied with himself, perceives himself correctly, and understands the corrosive effect of rationalizations, he will probably face his problem more realistically. It is for this and other reasons that we emphasize the need for a student's experiencing successes and for gaining an understanding of why he behaves as he does.

Compensation. A very weak student, especially if he becomes retarded, is soon recognized by his fellows. Then he is likely to turn to mischief. He may get some sense of importance from the notice he attracts when the teacher is obliged to halt class in order to quell his mischievousness. He may even begin to feel superior, especially if and when his schoolmates begin to talk of him as a fellow who "isn't afraid of anybody." Through troublemaking, such a youth is compensating for failure to gain the recognition of doing his duties as a student.

A little fellow may affect a walk that suggests a strutting cock, apparently to give the impression of being snappy and alert. He is quick, often without cause, to sense unfavorable criticism and to defend himself against it. Although he does not realize it, he is compensating for a feeling of inadequacy caused by his small size.

The bully is usually compensating for some feeling of inadequacy. He may feel inadequate because of his home background, or because he is not doing well in school, or because he feels he is not liked by his fellows and does not "belong." Consequently he tries to acquire a feeling of worth, even superiority, by lording it over others. Likewise, persons who have an air of aloofness—those who are haughty, proud, or snobbish—are likely to be compensating for feelings of inferiority, trying to give the impression of being superior. Usually, of course, the person who is really superior does not put on airs, is easy to talk with, is interested in the other person and shows it, and rarely says much about himself.

What each of these compensating individuals does to attract attention to himself and to give an impression of his importance may be called a "plus gesture," and other forms of compensation have characteristic plus gestures also.

Thus unnaturally loud talking and laughing or pretending to be very busy ("I'd like to go out with you, but I'm working on something pretty important right now," says a boy who is not) can conceal excessive shyness. To boast and brag a lot is a plus gesture for covering a sense of personal inadequacy which some learn fairly early in life and continue as long as they live. Such children often tell favorable things about themselves that are not true. Some, for instance, may depict themselves in the role of hero or heroine when relating experiences that have actually been quite ordinary. Others, learning fairly early that important ancestors are valuable assets, repeatedly refer to a rich uncle; a grandfather who was a dashing cavalry officer; or an aunt who played on Broadway. Or they flatter the ego by easy, offhand references to names of important people they know, or claim to know. This is called name-dropping.

There is a good kind of compensation, however, from which plus gestures are characteristically absent, in which a person exploits his best qualities in order to minimize his poorest.

A student who would like to be a good athlete may have experiences which teach him that he does not have much athletic capacity. This tends to make him feel inferior, but, fortunately, he is capable of doing well in his school subjects. He works hard on his lessons and builds a very good scholastic record. He is thus compensating for an inadequacy in athletics by being an exceptionally good student and thereby proving his worth. Or, a girl who is plain and is unhappy over it can, in addition to trying to be attractive by good grooming, develop pleasing ways of dealing with people, alertness for making situations attractive and comfortable, and competence in such activities as sewing, cooking, dancing, and sports. All this represents good compensation because it brings about effective behavior.

If carried too far, however, good compensation can become overcompensation, that is, can continue to an unhealthful extreme.

For example, a person who has a poor physical start in life builds up his health and becomes an outstanding athlete. This is a fine achievement, but he does not stop there. He dramatizes physical strength and vigor by engaging in dangerous hunts, exposing himself to the extreme rigors of the outdoors, boxing, wrestling, and even trying his hand at a rodeo. He has made a passion of physical fitness at the cost of emotional ease and perhaps, ironically, of his long-term physical health.

The situation of the person who overcompensates is complicated, moreover, by the fact that overcompensation is generally aggressive behavior which is frequently a less effective way of handling his original problem than is withdrawal. It is hard to explain to the super athlete that his behavior is unhealthful, for he realizes that without the measure of status that his prowess brings him, unsatisfactory as it may be, he would be hopelessly disregarded socially; and it is harder to make him realize that such social recognition as he may achieve could be more lasting if he spent some of his efforts trying to deal with others in a healthful way.

But these dangers of overcompensation aside, a person should not compensate for a weakness that can be overcome; instead, he should direct attention to overcoming it. A person grows stronger in the process of overcoming his weaknesses, and then a weakness may even become a strength. Of course, the activity of directly overcoming a weakness should not be carried to the point of resembling, and having the ill effects of, overcompensation.

Therefore, a teacher should first try to show his students how to overcome their weaknesses. If a child is not in good physical condition, the teacher should enlist the help of the school nurse and the teacher of health and physical education or whoever is available and competent; if a child is a poor student, the teacher should help him to learn how to study effectively, and so forth. Then, if it is clear that compensation is necessary, the teacher should turn his efforts toward guiding the child into the form of compensatory activity best suited for him as an individual.

Repression and Suppression. Feelings of failure, defeat, guilt, shame, and despair not only hurt us directly but also lessen our self-esteem. We therefore seek to get rid of these and comparable feelings and the thoughts connected with them; to help save our egos and to feel more comfortable generally, we repress such feelings—unconsciously push them out of mind. Repression, then, is an unconscious forgetting of threatening experiences because of a real desire not to remember them.

According to now generally accepted theories of repression, this is unhealthful because, although we have seemingly forgotten the painful feelings and thoughts, they tend to disorder our thinking and behavior. Just as a person may have something unknown wrong with some organ of the body that causes him to feel languid, so he can unconsciously harbor mental content which may fetter him in one way or another.

Suppression is the holding secret of one's painful feelings and thoughts; here the individual consciously conceals from others. He is keenly aware of the troubling experiences he has had but is trying to protect himself by saying nothing about them. Suppression, like repression, can be harmful; suppressed material may be compared to slivers of shrapnel which one knows about but leaves in the body, where they develop sensitive areas and even cause infection and illness. Suppression tends to maintain an unhealthy emotional state. Thus, both repression and suppression load a person with troubles.

Of course, a person may also be suppressed by another person, as when parents rule their children sternly and inflexibly, telling them altogether too often what they must and must not do and so keeping them from behaving in a healthful way. This kind of suppression, more exactly called suppressive management, also twists its recipient emotionally, developing many tensions that break out in unsocial and antisocial behavior.

One may repress or suppress the memory or anticipation of failure at work, dissatisfaction with school, loss of friends, rejection in love, or any other seriously unfavorable experience, as well as desires the fulfillment of which might result in punishment, in shame, or in the lowering of status and self-esteem.

For example, a boy has been shunted aside and subtly rejected by his parents, who are very fond of his brother. Their action, of course, is a form of suppressive management. The rejected boy is not too clear about what his parents are actually doing—is not aware of the rejection in the sense of having clear and articulate memories of actual occurrences—and he represses his feelings and thoughts about these unpleasant experiences. Because he has these repressions in his unconscious, he is generally clouded emotionally, his perception of himself is distorted, and his behavior is disordered. In time he develops a clear antagonism for his brother and a confused dislike for his parents which later crystallizes into a definite hostility for them.

A case of suppression would be that of a boy who is conscious of having stolen but keeps it a secret. His secret is a sensitive spot in his emotional body; when stealing is mentioned, he feels uncomfortable and on the defensive. His many associations to his hidden act rouse painful and harmful emotions.

One likely outcome of repression and suppression is overinhibition. An overinhibited person is too restrained; that is, he seems to have internal brakes when he should be expressing himself. He seems to be too reluctant, blocked, or uncertain to engage in well-managed activities.

Secondly, suppression and repression are frequently causes of, as well as responses to, anxiety; for the concealed or forgotten emotions tend to reemerge as the generalized fear or overconcern that characterizes anxiety. By its very nature of fearfulness, anxiety confuses a person and renders him ineffective in dealing with his problems, thus making him appear inhibited.

What needs to be done by the repressing or suppressing individual and, in this case particularly, by those with whom he deals?

Just as it is painful to pull out a sliver, so it is painful to discuss truthfully an unhappy experience. But there are occasions when, in order to ease pain and to save ego value, a person must acknowledge the experience that seems to reduce that ego. Thus a good way to get some relief from the pain of suppression is to discuss the troubling feelings and ideas with someone who is so competent in counseling that full confidence can be reposed in him or her.

Dealing with repression is more difficult because the individual is unconscious of what he has repressed. Personality may be seriously disturbed because of it, especially if the unhappy experiences involved occurred many years before. Yet one of the fundamental principles of psychoanalysis is to get the patient to speak freely and try to recall unhappy experiences, even childhood experiences, that may have wounded the personality and may still be affecting it; for getting them into the open makes rejuvenation of the personality possible. It is only important to realize that the techniques for dealing with repression have to be even more careful than those used with suppression. The doctor who tries to cure a mysterious ill in a body organ usually has to use more subtle methods than he who removes a sliver from the flesh.

The function of the teacher in this area, then, varies with the case. In dealing with suppressed feelings produced by unhappy circumstances in or out of the schoolroom, a teacher can be a trusted confidante—allow his students to unburden themselves, as we say, and thus rid themselves of their troubles. This is one of the chief values of a good teacher-conducted guidance and counseling program in a school. But, teachers should avoid prying into their pupils' personal problems; teachers should not be busybodies. Also, teachers should always be careful to recognize the presence of suppression and, especially, repression problems that require specialized help; when these are evident, such help should be sought promptly.

Anger and Temper. Getting angry served a vital purpose in the earlier development of man; for the greater energy called forth by the emotion of rage, or anger, was often needed for survival in a rudimentary world. If this disposed primitive man to kill, it was often kill or be killed.

In our present world (setting aside the horrible topic of modern war), the legitimate uses of anger are much more limited. It still may, and does at times, dispose man to kill, but civilization has made this much less justifiable, especially if the victim be human; for it is now rarely necessary to kill or be killed. Today's anger tends to have a morbid effect, and not on the other person so much as on the person who is angry, because the world is not organized for its use. The emotionalism of anger often blocks the sound and rational thinking so needed in our complex world, so that many bad mistakes are made by persons who are angry—mistakes they often regret afterward.

Yet no matter how effectively we try to manage our affairs, we do become angry once in a while; so we face the problem of managing our anger so that it does not "burn us up," as is commonly said. It is because we deeply care and are justifiably concerned that we get angry.

A person who is angry usually should not "hold it in" but rather should "blow off steam" healthfully, by turning to diverting physical or mental activity; and he should also study conditions that irritate him, so that he can take sane steps to right them if they are wrong, to adjust to them if they are right. He should not, when minimized by insult or blocked from getting what he wants, indulge in that childish behavior aptly called "losing one's temper."

Finally, it is important to be willing to deal with the anger of others. Unfortunately, a flash of anger, or fear of it, sometimes diverts discussion from a topic about which a person is sensitive. We keep in mind, "Don't mention that to so-and-so because he'll get angry." The sensitivity is based on some difficulty which should be discussed but is not, so the soreness continues. On the face of it, such avoidance works ill. What is needed, rather, is forthrightness to face, though not angrily, the anger of others.

When little children are refused something such as a toy or a cookie, they sometimes lie down on the floor and go into a tantrum, holding their breath and kicking in an attempt to get their way. The teacher, especially the kindergarten or primary teacher, may encounter tantrums of this kind in his pupils. The best procedure is to pay no attention to the child. He is "acting up," and as a performer he wants an audience; without one he will soon terminate his act. He will not injure himself, the tantrum will dissipate itself, and he will learn that he gets neither attention nor his own way through such methods. He is likely to give up having temper tantrums when he learns that they are futile.

Though older children have few tantrums, the above way to handle them is actually an example of the best general principle for teachers who wish to deal well with their students' and their own tempers and, indeed, anger. Teachers must learn to be calm when conditions are most provoking. The room may be too warm, the supervisor may have just paid a visit, the children may be restless, their minds may seem most sluggish, and the teacher may be tired. It is all too easy at such times to scold and be sarcastic and angry. This should never be done. When a teacher feels that his emotional temperature is reaching the fever point, he should call a halt temporarily—tell a story, take up different work, or perhaps walk down the hall to the water fountain for a cool drink.

A person is likely to have better control of his emotions if he admits that he experienced them. "Yes, I certainly was burned up over it" or "I certainly was scared." Then the next time he seems to have more understanding in dealing with frustrations and threats which provoke emotional responses.

☻ *Reflect and Review*

Study the following descriptions of people's various reactions to anxiety and see whether you can identify and describe as specifically as possible the psychological mechanisms which are being used in each case.

1. Jane can always give a good reason for her behavior, though it often brings failure in satisfying her own purposes and trouble with other persons. According to Jane, there usually was something noble in what she was trying to do; she is also very likely to put the blame here and there—everywhere but at her own doorstep—for her difficulties.

2. Bill has a way of keeping his problems to himself, and some of his difficulties do disappear and are forgotten, or so it seems. But Bill is sensitive and on the defensive when problems of ethics—cheating on exams and the like—enter the conversation of his peers.

3. Sid, a sixth-grader, is not doing very well in school, though his sister, an eighth-grader, is one of the best students in her class. Sid is beginning to take the role of leader among the boys in his class who regularly give the teacher trouble. These boys admire him for his bravado.

4. Marie either reluctantly accepts suggestions or becomes mildly antagonistic to them. She resists all new ideas and modes of behavior. She is even likely to take a stand against her whole group of friends when they are trying to reach a decision which involves no radical change in their ways of doing things.

5. Hank, a gentle, quiet teen-ager, has not read the books on the reading list of his literature class, but always has a book in his lap during class meetings. Last week it was a book his class read 3 years ago; the week before it was a picture book on airplanes. His teacher often sees him reading, but just as often sees him gazing out the window at the clouds.

6. "If you say that word once more, I'll throw *another* book at you."

"I guess I'm just not cut out for music: Miss Jones has told me I just don't have quite enough talent. I believe I can be a good dentist, though, and dentistry interests me, too. I like using my hands in my work."

"I want to make the first team; I'm on the second team now. I got a late start and so I'm not in as good a physical shape as I should be, but now I'm working hard and in a couple of weeks I'll be caught up. If I don't make the first team this season, I expect to next year."

7. Gayle is vaguely troubled by events at home. His father never seems to be there, and his mother will not tell him why. Then, when he goes to school, he behaves as if under continuous stress and strain. Though he says everything is all right with him, he seems continuously concerned about many little day-to-day problems, the sort that never used to bother him, and is reluctant to do his studying and chat with his friends.

THE PROBLEMS OF MENTAL HEALTH

Many of these mechanisms of behavior have elements of escape and of defense, both processes involved in much human behavior. An escape, or avoidance, mechanism is a means of getting away from the difficulties of personal responsibility and into a state that is more comfortable than anxious. A defense, or protective, mechanism is designed to protect its user from unpleasantness without his having to take his attention from the scene of his activity.

Daydreaming is usually described as an escape mechanism, because the daydreaming individual is trying essentially to get away.

Rationalization seems generally to be defensive, in that an attempt is made to excuse or glorify what actually is a personal fault or difficulty and thereby protect the rationalizer's status. Negative compensation and over-compensation are defensive, too, as an attempt is made to cover up a weakness through an activity which it is hoped will be accepted or admired and thus to protect one's status.

When a person represses his painful feelings and ideas he gets them out of the way, which is, in effect, an escape from them (though, as we have seen, not a complete one). When he suppresses, he does not seek to escape them but rather to defend himself from their potentially painful consequences.

There is a defensive aspect of negativism also. Sometimes the stubbornness, the irrational opposition, and the lack of willingness to cooperate constitute protection from attempting to do what may reveal a person's inabilities—a defensive wall around personal weaknesses. Procrastination involves, primarily, escape from responsibility. Anger is not necessarily escape or defense, of course, but in its worst expressions can be either or both.

Thus we see that the concepts of defense and escape are useful keys to many patterns of behavior; these concepts explain what happens when anxiety and the other emotions it triggers lead us to act in ways that thwart us in developmental experiences and thus in need satisfaction. Useful as it is to evaluate various behavior mechanisms as escape or defense, it is sometimes very difficult to classify the behavior as one or the other.

We have also seen, however, that in most cases the inner cause of anxiety that, in turn, causes escape and defense behavior is the individual's feeling of inferiority. In order to differentiate the generally troubled person, then, we must describe the responses to such feelings.

The following behavior gives evidence of strong inferiority feelings:

Is very sensitive to personal remarks and criticism

Is critical of others

Interprets statements and events in terms of self; is highly self-referent and egocentric

Is often jealous

Is highly susceptible and responsive to flattery

Is alone more than normal

Avoids competition or responds ineffectively to it

Exhibits compensatory behavior; sometimes shows a very strong achievement drive

Nearly every individual is occasionally plagued by feelings of inferiority without great harm to himself. But when an individual's self-image is reduced to a state where he broods very often on, say, an embarrassing social incident, a physical detraction, or a failure to solve a personal intellectual problem, his self-concept suffers generally; that is, all his ego-related feelings become distorted, and he is likely to behave in ways that give evidence of a damaged personality.

A person may have such feelings for two basic reasons: He actually is inferior, or he has been treated in a way that makes him feel inferior. Thus the child who is poorly equipped—physically, mentally, or socially—typically learns that he cannot do what most children do well, and his nervous system registers the result of this knowledge rather accurately in feelings of inferiority. Also, being rejected, neglected, scolded, or minimized can make a child feel inadequate even though he has capacity enough to get along very well and so feel confident.

Prevailing feelings of inferiority are strongly dynamic and can have favorable aspects when a person who feels inferior works hard to achieve success. The sources of many strong drives to progress vocationally and to be recognized for good public service are to be found in feelings of inferiority, and such drives do not tend to disorder a person unless they are accompanied by so much rigidity that the efforts they inspire are carried to the extreme of overcompensation.

But prevailing feelings of inferiority, whether they result in good hard work or not, do often cause a person to have a restricted outlook. Having developed from his own difficult—even threatening—experiences, they often lead a person to more of the same and thus to a state in which many people, objects, situations, and tasks are seen not as they are but through the distorting lens, as it were, of extreme self-involvement.

Good mental health, most basically, is an opposite state—a state in which feelings of inferiority either do not prevail or have been and are being used to stimulate individual achievement without destroying objective and full relationship between oneself and the world.

This means that the mentally healthy individual has been able, by general success with his developmental tasks, to make his way through the experience of whatever anxiety he has known with these responses:

He has characteristically kept his attention and effort directed toward the ongoing activities he is involved in; that is, he does not habitually daydream or procrastinate, and he has not become dominated by repressed feelings about his experience.

He has found it unnecessary to deny in important ways the facts of his life and the state of his world; he is not predominantly negativistic, nor does he often defend himself from the truth by not recognizing it (rationalization) or not acknowledging it (suppression).

He has accepted his share of misfortune and tries to use his experience of it in personally and socially positive ways.

He is self-possessed and does not have his anger aroused except in the face of morally perceived injustice.

More positively, and more obviously related to developmental tasks, the mentally healthy person:

Deals well with the material objects of life—food, clothes, other objects—and with words.

Works and lives with others well.

Not only accepts himself as he is—with wholesome humility, incidentally—but works for personal improvement.

Has convictions on what is good or bad, right or wrong, and works consistently but not fanatically for what he thinks is good.

It is vital to realize that in thus describing the mentally healthy person we have defined the person most likely to satisfy his important needs. But it is also vital to realize that all the above mentioned characteristics are probably both causes and effects of mental health and need satisfaction; and it is very difficult to tell, in any complex human situation, where causes end and effects begin. Thus, when we deal with real persons, who, as we have said, always fall at least a little short of the virtual ideal just described, stimulation to achieve any of these characteristics may cause others to begin to emerge.

This is why motivated and conscious practice of healthful behavior will help in improving one's own mental health. It is also a principal reason why the teacher can have impressive success in improving the mental health of his students. The problems, however, are profound.

Origins of Emotional Difficulties. The origins of many mental health problems reach far back into the years of greatest dependency—the months in the cradle, the toddling stage, and the preschool years in general; for the foundations of his emotional patterns are being laid before a child has developed much of his mental and physical power. As stated earlier, heredity seems to be involved here, and it is even possible that prenatal environment influences emotional stability. But it is crystal-clear that the home environment during the first years of life can be emotionally decisive. For example: Some parents are so overconcerned about their children's welfare that they overprotect them; that is, they keep them from having normal experiences. They tend to keep their children from playing with other children, especially if the playing is vigorous. When their children have a dispute with others and come home crying, such parents typically take their side whether they are right or wrong. In addition, overprotected children usually have few, if any, duties to perform; rather, they are pampered and overindulged.

Such children are insulated from the facing of developmental tasks, as it were, so that their infancy is prolonged unduly—they become overdependent on their parents.

It is quite probable that the parents' frustrations and their lack of confidence are projected on the children in such cases. Where the mother is centrally involved, "momism," the popular oversentimentalizing of mothers, is thought to allow overprotective mothers to unconsciously deny their children emotional emancipation. At any rate, the children never learn to stand alone; they never become emotionally mature.

Comparison of the schoolwork habits and social adjustment of children from homes in which the children are babied or pushed and homes in which they are not produces startling results. In a study (see Table 21) by B. W. Hattwick and M. Stowell of 146 children from kindergarten through the first six grades in Winnetka, Illinois, a close relationship with the parents was maintained, extensive records were kept, and the work habits of the children were evaluated by teacher ratings as good or poor [Hattwick and Stowell, 1936]. It was found that 80 per cent of the babied, or overprotected, children had poor work habits, and thus poor records. They worked carelessly and

Table 21 Relation of Work Habits to Overattentiveness of Parents

Group	Number	Work Habits, Per Cent	
		Good	Poor
Children babied	51	20	80
Children pushed	22	18	82
Children from well-adjusted homes	73	77	23

Source: Adapted from B. W. Hattwick and M. Stowell, "The Relation of Parental Over-attentiveness to Children's Work-Habits and Social Adjustments in Kindergarten and the First Six Grades of School," *Journal of Educational Research*, 30:172, 1936.

irregularly, and their progress was slow. Of the children who were pushed, 82 per cent had poor work habits. With children from normal homes the situation was almost exactly the opposite: 77 per cent had good work habits and thus good records. The children were also evaluated for the effectiveness of their social adjustment, and about the same differences were found between the babied and pushed, and the more wisely treated children.

As these data show, the home contributes significantly to the state of the work habits and social maturity of the child.

Dealing with the Problems of Mental Health. It is comparatively easy to describe a child as, say, shy, high-strung, overconcerned, deficient in good work habits, and tending to be a chronic rationalizer. It is more difficult to explain why this child behaves as he does, and the most difficult problem of all is to better appreciably his mental health and thus his behavior. Indeed, the literature on mental health and child behavior deeply impresses any sensitive reader with the amount of work necessary to do so in some cases and with the frequently discouraging results. However, about twenty per cent of schoolchildren are maladjusted, that is, need special help in this area. Any amount of improvement for even a few of them is rewarding, and in many instances the results are very encouraging.

For many reasons, it is difficult to make favorable changes in any child who is maladjusted; and, of course, the more serious the maladjustment, the harder it is to make changes. For instance, if a child has high scholastic ability but has been a problem case in school for a long time because of dreaming, indifference, poor work habits and resulting low achievement, and misbehavior—or a combination of some of these—the teacher will find it very hard to bring about much change, especially if the child has progressed as far as the fifth or sixth grade and such characteristics are strongly in evidence.

Also, the school is only one factor in the maladjusted child's situation and often the only one which can be geared to his readjustment. Over the years, the home tends to remain much the same, the child continues to have the same companions and rather consistent interests; and, significantly, he must continue to have the same fundamental nervous system, glands, and senses. In most cases, some combination of these factors has built up his maladjustment; this combination continues to operate pretty much as it has, still affecting him and so making it hard for the school to effect many favorable changes.

The teacher must soberly recognize all this in approaching problems growing out of poor mental health and behavior among his students. Then, he must set out to deal with each problem case objectively; and even when he encounters frustration along the way, relationships will not be strained if anger is withheld and no personal dislike or resentment is developed toward troubled students, although such students are often disagreeable and exasperating.

Indeed, the problem of successfully helping maladjusted schoolchildren is not at all insurmountable. In schools where the teachers are conscious of and intelligent about their students' personality difficulties, most of them are successfully overcome. In one school where a specialist was employed to guide the teachers in trying to solve the pupils' personality problems, the specialist was not needed after a relatively short time because of the teachers' effectiveness. The teachers cooperated with the troubled children's parents and, by controlling the conditions at school, experienced great success in solving personality problems. The reason that much more is not accomplished in this field lies in the failure of the average school faculty to be keenly conscious of such difficulties and then knowledgeable enough about mental health to solve them.

◐ Reflect and Review

Mary J., fifteen and a high school sophomore, is bright and can use her brightness well: She is one of the highest-ranking students in her class. In addition, she has other endowments that constitute an advantage in getting along with people. Just slightly over average height and generally good to look at, she has the kind of hair that poets rhapsodize over.

Yet, Mary is stiff and ill at ease with people and so has no close friends. People who try to befriend her find that she seems burdened with worries and frustrations which she will not discuss. It is known that as a small child she was pampered and spoiled by her mother and shown little attention by her father, but people do not think much about this in considering Mary; this, after all, was a long time ago. She just seems to be one of those people who are happy and outgoing as babies (which she was) but never get along well after starting school.

It seems likely that Mary is trying to escape feelings rooted in her past. If this is so, what further facts about her present situation would have to be learned to tell whether she is also using a defense mechanism?

Do you think that a teacher who tried to help Mary improve her adjustment would have a relatively easy time? Why?

THE MUTUALITY OF PHYSICAL AND MENTAL HEALTH

Students of that complex and in many ways mysterious organism, the human being, are constantly reminded that the concept of a mind-body dichotomy is unsound—that the mind and the body are too closely related to admit of sharply divided consideration. And so it is that no treatment of mental health can be complete without some attention to physical health as well.

Occasionally there is a newspaper item about a teacher who has taught 40 years without missing a class because of illness. Such spectacular physical health is likely to be accompanied by good mental health, each contributing to the other. For less fortunate persons, constitutional weaknesses, pains, and illness are conducive to poor mental health just as unsuccessful emotional function is conducive to poor physical health.

The effects of physical health on mental health are designated by the term somatopsychic, the obvious opposite of the term psychosomatic, which refers to effects of mental on physical health.

In many instances of mind-and-body illness, it is difficult to distinguish between these reciprocal effects, that is, to say the body is hurting the mind (somatopsychic), or the mind is hurting the body (psychosomatic). But the terms do fit generally recognizable human experiences which it will be useful, for discussion purposes, to differentiate.

Psychosomatic Effects. From the experience of psychologists we know that above and beyond other effects, the unhealthful emotional reactions that quarreling, overprotective, highly dominant, unaffectionate, or tense parents induce in their children may persist and be converted into physical illness during childhood, youth, or adulthood. From everyday experience we know how sick and tired we feel when we have been through even a short period of sharp emotional stress.

Anxieties, grief, bitterness, rage, and so on can so change the chemistry of the body as to develop a composition of gastric juices which will consume the tissues of the stomach and cause a sore, or ulcer. In comparable manner, the following rather common psychosomatic effects[1] can be produced:

Lesser digestive disorders—"nervous stomach," vomiting
Intestinal disorders—diarrhea, constipation
Genitourinary troubles—diseases of the prostate gland or of the female organs
Hypertension—high blood pressure, heart trouble
Migraine headaches, dizziness
Chronic fatigue
Skin diseases—eczema, hives
Respiratory disorders—bronchial asthma, sinus trouble, allergies
Arthritis, rheumatism

In short, one can hardly overestimate the effect that emotional conditions can have on the health. Indeed, the one really distinguishing characteristic of people who live to be very old seems to be that they are relatively free from the tensions that accompany anxiety and related emotional ills.

Table 22 lists six common maladies which may be psychosomatic in origin, notes whether women or men suffer from each more frequently, and describes the typical psychological state of the subject in each case.

Physique as It Affects Feelings. A person's very physical size and shape can influence his mental health. Thus, if a boy or man is large, well proportioned, and well muscled, his personality is likely to be affected favorably. He may, of course, use this advantage to be overaggressive, but it is more probable that he will gain a wholesome feeling of personal confidence and social ease; and the same is true of girls and women of attractive physique.

On the other hand, being an extreme deviate in physical appearance—a person who is very short, very tall, very fat, or very thin—can predispose one toward personality problems, as the following example shows.

A child who finds others of his age group bigger and stronger, and thus hard to play with, often seeks the company of younger children who are his own size but too young to further his total development. Or he may isolate himself and seek his satisfactions solely in his studies, in which he may try passionately to surpass his fellows, or in music. This means, of course, that he will be most often with adults, when he is with people at all. A child who is mostly with adults tends to feel docile and inferior, simply because they are so much larger. Or, as we saw in discussing compensation, he may become "cocky."

---

[1] Psychosomatic fatigue will be discussed in detail as a learning problem in Chapter 13.

Table 22 Typical Psychosomatic Patterns

Illness	Incidence	Typical Background
High blood pressure	Much more common among females	Ambivalence toward dominant, over-protective mother and repressed hostility toward those on whom individual currently feels dependent
Migraine	Much more common among females	Perfectionistic tendencies combined with high intelligence, underlying insecurity, rigid conscience, and critical attitude toward others. If plans upset, individual reacts with intense but suppressed anger and anxiety
Peptic ulcers	Much more common among males	Chronic anxiety, hostility, or resentment. Often high level of aspiration and aggressiveness with underlying feelings of dependency and inadequacy
Bronchial asthma	Somewhat more common among males	Repressed emotional tension resulting from overdependency and fear of loss of support
Skin disorders	Somewhat more common among males	Immaturity, with ambivalent feelings toward those on whom individual is dependent; repressed hostility evidently directed against self. Frequently associated with feelings of helplessness, exhibitionistic tendencies, and sexual problems
Obesity	Sex ratio equal in childhood; later more common among men	Lifelong pattern of overeating, apparently as a compensatory mechanism providing some pleasure and relief from tension and frustration in other life areas

Source: James C. Coleman, *Personality Dynamics and Effective Behavior*, Scott, Foresman and Company, Chicago, 1960, p. 244.

The young woman who is nearly 6 feet tall (the average height of women is about 5 feet 5 inches) may become very self-conscious and shy and, possibly feeling that being tall reduces matrimonial opportunities, may stoop in order to lessen her height, when what she should do for her physical health *and* her mental health and social well-being is stand erect, stately, and handsome.

The slender or underweight adolescent boy—the youth who is "leggy" and whose arms, too, seem long and dangling—may suffer emotionally from his resulting awkwardness. Thus, though adolescents are often very capable athletes, in social situations where they feel self-conscious about expressing their new sexual interests, adolescents may trip or stumble, become "tangled up in their feet," withdraw awkwardly, and feel extreme pain.

Lastly, the very fat child may have personality difficulties springing from constant drain of a variety of physical difficulties—from difficulty in getting into his school seat to not being alert on the playground.

Serious Physical Ills and the Mind. Not all persons with these abnormalities have unhealthy personalities; and even when one of these deviations accompanies severe emotional problems, it is not necessarily their cause. For example, to attribute Napoleon's aggressive desire to conquer all Europe to the fact that he was so short and therefore sought to demonstrate to the world that he was a most powerful man is probably carrying an idea too far. The Napoleonic era, like the personalities of individual human beings, had complex and manifold roots in the past, in the pressures of the times, and in the potentialities of the human organism. But sickness and organic weakness in themselves invariably constitute a basis for maladjustment.

A sick person is deprived of his freedom to live normally; and as a result, his sickness tends very basically to undermine his mental health, as is simply evidenced by the fact that though some ill people are cheerful, morbidness is more often their lot. Persons who are afflicted with many colds, have poor digestions, or have very little physical energy have trouble in getting along with people and thus are prone to social maladjustment directly because of weakness. Sick persons tend to become overconcerned with self. At the same time, their pains and weaknesses make them feel inadequate. They therefore tend to become sensitive and irritable and to expect to be pampered because they are not so strong as others. This bad mental health, in turn, makes it more difficult for them to contend with the physical rigors of life.

The same basic process occurs with those persons known as the handicapped (see Table 23): those who suffer from limited vision, poor hearing, speech disorders, cerebral palsy, epilepsy, crippled limbs, or some other such organic and functional ill. But the handicapped are even more predisposed to feel inferior and therefore to withdraw and, especially, to indulge in self-pity.

Some physically handicapped children, like some mentally handicapped children, are served best in special classes with a teacher who, appreciating the problems of the handicapped, makes them feel accepted, helps them to accept themselves, and is trained to guide them well both socially and educationally. Such classes are advisable for those whose handicaps are severe enough to impair seriously their ability to carry out normal class projects, even when the work is modified for them. Such children are likely to find normal class routine a series of troubling frustrations and continuous reminders of their defects.

If such extreme cases are moved into special classes, however, there still

Table 23 Estimates of Exceptional School-age Children Who Will Need Special Education

Handicap	Estimate of Prevalence, Per Cent	Estimated Number of Exceptional Children
Blind	0.033	16,192
Partially seeing	0.06	29,441
Deaf	0.075	36,801
Hard of hearing	0.5	245,340
Speech impaired	3.5	1,717,380
Crippled	1.0	490,680
Special health problems	1.0	490,680
Emotionally disturbed or socially maladjusted	2.0	981,360
Gifted	2.0	981,360
Mentally retarded	2.3	1,128,564
Total	12.5	6,117,798

Source: Adapted from table furnished by the Department of Health, Education, and Welfare, U.S. Office of Education, 1963.

remains a large number of children with less serious defects who, with sympathetic help, can carry on most of the class activities satisfactorily. Such children probably should remain in regular classes; segregation in special classes would make even more difficult the process of adjustment to life in a world of normal people which they will eventually face.

Often the teacher is the first to identify a minor defect, and this is an important part of his responsibility toward the physically handicapped. A child who has shown the symptoms of limited vision—persistent squinting, headaches, reading difficulties—may be sent to the school doctor for eye tests. Or the child with poor hearing may be similarly helped.

When the teacher becomes aware of a physical defect of a student, he has at least two areas of responsibility in giving the child special help. First, he should try to see that the opportunities for learning are just as great for this child as for his more normal classmates. This may involve special techniques of teaching for such subjects as reading and physical education. The teacher should be sure that the child with a vision problem can see the blackboard clearly, that the child with a hearing problem is seated where he can hear what is being said, and that the child with a speech difficulty is called upon to recite only when he can avoid embarrassment and frustration.

It is also important that handicapped children not be left out of activities in which they can participate to some degree. The crippled boy need not sit idly on the sidelines during physical education class; he can be given an activity which he can carry out, preferably along with some of his friends, and thus learn that his defect does not totally bar him from the world of normal people. Many activities may need to be adapted to the needs of the handicapped in this way. The child with a cleft palate cannot debate, but he can keep the time for the debaters.

The second area of responsibility for the teacher in connection with the handicapped is in helping them make a social adjustment. Often children feel uncomfortable around a handicapped classmate and either avoid him or otherwise set him apart by an overfriendly and sentimental attitude toward him. Such tendencies can be minimized if the teacher so arranges the class that the handicapped child can take a useful and legitimate part in it. Neither the handicapped student nor his classmates should be continually reminded of his defect by his attempts to adjust to an impossible situation. Most of the devices for helping the defective child learn will also help him to make his vital social adjustment.

The Educator's Role. We have, then, many distinguishable kinds of psychosomatic and somatopsychic effects. But we often also have a round of effects becoming further causes. How can the educator act to halt this process in an early stage?

When anyone, be he child, youth, or adult, has distress of any kind, from poor appetite to serious pains, he needs a good physical examination. Perhaps medical care, even with drugs or surgery, is needed; perhaps being told that nothing is physically wrong is enough; perhaps a new mode of living that involves less hurry and worrisome work and more pleasure is advisable. But in all cases a first step in achieving good mental health is to set out to attain good physical health, or to be sure one has it.

Schools with adequate physical health services help give their students good mental as well as physical health; thus the teacher needs to be able to see quickly a manifest physical disturbance in a student and then, quite simply, to do what he can to get that student to a doctor. After this, the teacher, in all his dealings with the student, must take into account his physical condition for as long as it remains an important negative factor in his classroom adjustment.

● Reflect and Review

When Miss Evans began teaching in her seventh-grade class one fall, she found that one of her students was Dorothea, a girl with a livid, red birthmark which spread over half her face. All the other students in class were kind to her but seemed embarrassed by her disfigured appearance and generally avoided her, except for two girls who went out of their way to include her in conversations, generally without much response from Dorothea. Dorothea was a slightly-below-average student, although her records indicated that she had an above-average IQ. She spent much of her time in class looking out the window and seemed extremely embarrassed when called upon to recite. On one occasion, early in the school year, Miss Evans called upon Dorothea to answer a question. The child jumped slightly when she heard her name and, after a long pause, said "I don't know," in a voice that seemed close to tears.

How might Miss Evans help Dorothea overcome her emotional problem? Consider extracurricular as well as class activities.

Should Miss Evans discuss Dorothea's problem with her directly? If you think she should, what circumstances would be required and what should be done first?

Do you think that an interview with the school psychologist (if there is one) might help Miss Evans decide what to do?

SUMMARY

About five per cent of the people at some time or another become so seriously sick emotionally that they are hospitalized, and about another five per cent will be treated by a psychiatrist although not hospitalized. Of the rest, most will have some mental health problems and quite a few will be troubled and handicapped by them.

Anxiety is a basic difficulty and is characterized by generalized fear, excessive concern, and uncertainty. Anxiety is usually present in the various manifestations of maladjustment.

Children are concerned most about their relationships with people—members of their families, their peers, and their teachers. They are also concerned about succeeding in school and in their play activities. Personal attractiveness and good health are serious problems for a considerable number of children.

Anxiousness or overconcern can be contended with by treating children so they are not harassed and unduly troubled and by discussing the flimsy bases of most worries.

Excessive daydreaming or fantasy is an escape from the frustrations and unfulfillments of life by imagining successful experiences, superiority, and high status. It is a symptom of stunted personal development and failure.

Negativism shows itself in people of all ages in various degrees of subtlety. Some of its manifestations are noncooperativeness, nonacceptance, and unreasonable opposition to suggestions and new methods. It reflects a protective rigidity that has developed to ensure more safety in a threatening world.

One of the best evidences of good mental health is clear thinking and crisp, dynamic work habits. The opposite of this is to be found in conflict and procrastination. Conflict consists in indecision about opposing ideas and courses of action which continues unduly long and becomes highly emotionalized because of the failure to make a decision. Procrastination results from failure to decide what to do and from delay in taking action.

Rationalization is a common mechanism which consists of apparently reasonable explanations and statements motivated by the need to save face or to enhance the ego. Phases of rationalization are sour grapes, Pollyanna, and projection.

Compensation is motivated by weakness and consists in behavior intended to gain favorable recognition and worth as an offset to an inferiority. Some compensating behavior is constructive, while some is not. Overcompensation is carrying the process too far.

Suppression is consciously holding a thought secret, and repression is unconsciously pushing it into oblivion. The thought is unpleasant and therefore threatening, so a person is motivated to hide it. It is believed that repression and suppression undermine one's mental health.

Anger develops when one is frustrated, minimized, or unsuccessful in getting his way. Generally, getting angry is ineffective; and before reaching the explosion point, one should withdraw from the people he would offend by his temper.

Various mechanisms are classified as protective, or defensive, and as avoidance, or escape. Some are used to maintain or build up one's status and some to get away from difficulties that threaten and lessen one's importance.

Teachers can help their pupils by being kind and not threatening, by explaining to students that it is best to deal with their problems realistically and helping them do so. When the teacher sets the situations so the students are successful and happy, he contributes greatly to their emotional health. He must be perceptive of unhealthful symptoms and try to prevent serious developments.

A poor self-image and feelings of inferiority reflect a difficult and serious condition that leads to much unhealthful behavior. Sometimes they serve as strong motives for achieving success and ascendancy.

A person in good mental health has a well-integrated personality which shows itself in effective behavior. More specifically, he has confidence in himself, is relatively free of protective and escape mechanisms, lives ethically, works effectively, gets along well with people, and in general satisfies his needs.

A person's emotional health is developed by his experiences, beginning at birth and probably before. An infant who develops in a healthful emotional climate will have good mental health; while a child who is continuously insulted by neglect, rejection, and hostility will have poor mental health. Overconcern and babying by parents have strong negative effects also.

It is very difficult for teachers to transform their students from poor to good emotional health because of long-established habits, because the home environment generally remains the same, and because the child continues with the same bodily structures. Still, the teacher can provide a good school environment which stimulates the child favorably as long as he is there. For maximum effectiveness in dealing with students in poor mental health, the teacher should withhold any anger he may feel toward them.

Good physical health contributes to good mental health and vice versa. It is estimated that a large share of people's physical ills are caused by anxieties, conflicts, morbid mental content, and tensions of various kinds.

The attractiveness of one's physique has various mental effects. A good physique usually has favorable effects, and a poor physique or a crippled body has negative effects. Handicaps predispose a person to emotional maladjustment.

A teacher who has sound knowledge of mental health and understands its positive and negative manifestations is equipped to interpret the dynamics of his pupils' behavior. Of first importance in the management of all children is patience and kindness. All pupils, the troubled ones particularly, need the teacher as a friend. Feeling the teacher's friendliness nourishes the pupil's ego and gives him the support he needs.

Pupils also need to have satisfying activities. There is probably more therapy in successful thinking, working, and playing than in the most highly professionalized procedures. So if the knowledgeable teacher stimulates and guides pupils so they will be excited by many activities, he contributes greatly to their mental health.

SUGGESTED READING

Bernard, Harold W.: *Mental Hygiene for Classroom Teachers,* 2d ed., McGraw-Hill Book Company, Inc., New York, 1961. A comprehensive discussion of the mental health of both the pupil and the teacher, with much useful information on how the teacher can help the pupils and also how the teacher can maintain or improve his own health.

Konopka, Gisela: "*A Healthy Group Life-Social Group Work's Contribution to Mental Health,*" *Mental Hygiene,* 45:327–335, 1961. Contains criteria and discussion of mental health. Evidences of effective mental and emotional adjustment in terms of social relationships are set forth. Do not be disturbed or disordered by the title of this excellent discussion.

Lazarus, Richard S.: *Adjustment and Personality,* McGraw-Hill Book Company, Inc., New York, 1961. Emphasis on personality—its theories and characteristics. Considerable treatment of mental health and adjustment.

CHAPTER 12
ATTITUDES
AND BEHAVIOR

A person's mental health is expressed in his behavior through the intermediary, as it were, of his attitudes.

As he develops, every human being is trained and unconsciously conditioned by the forces around him to take certain attitudes toward certain subjects; and, of course, students bring theirs with them when they enter a classroom.

This is the most important immediate factor deciding how effective learning is to be. If a student has a favorable attitude toward a school subject, he may amaze the teacher with an ability to learn it that outstrips what might have been expected of him. If, on the other hand, he has a negative attitude toward the subject, he may so strongly resist learning that the teacher's efforts, no matter how thorough and ingenious, are futile. Or, if a student has been led to feel that he is superior to people of other races or that poetry is for girls and "sissies," it will be hard for him to accept the biological and artistic facts that contradict these ideas.

The study of attitudes is therefore necessary for a teacher who expects to understand why his efforts are sometimes so well rewarded and sometimes so seemingly hopeless.

But, as the last of the above examples suggests, there is a second important consideration here: the influence the teacher has on the way his students feel about things beyond the classroom door; for when they leave him, they have altered their social attitudes to a great or small degree, sometimes in a desirable direction, sometimes in an undesirable one.

If these changes are not to be purely fortuitous, the teacher should think carefully about the effect of his teaching—including, very basically, the effect of his own attitudes upon his students' attitudes.

The nature of attitudes and the effect of the educational process on them are the first main subjects of this chapter. Then we shall consider behavior—in school and beyond school—as influenced by attitudes. Finally, we shall discuss the responsibility of the teacher for dealing with school behavior.

WHAT ATTITUDES ARE

An attitude is a particular feeling about something. It therefore involves a tendency to behave in a certain way in situations which involve that something, whether person, idea, or object. It is partially rational and partially emotional and is acquired, not inherent, in an individual.

Let us illustrate this definition with a particular attitude, patriotism. A patriotic person has a favorable feeling toward his own country. Therefore he is predisposed to act and express himself in certain ways when his country is involved: He will tend to be quick to defend the country when it is disparaged and will tend to approve of its actions and to disapprove of the actions of its opponents. His feeling is partly rational and partly emotional: He may be able to give very good reasons for supporting his country, but their basis is partly beneath conscious reasoning. This patriotic feeling, also, has been acquired; he was not born with enthusiasm for this particular country.

Our illustration suggests another characteristic of attitudes: They have varying degrees of intensity. A person may be fanatically devoted to his country, only mildly inclined to support it, or between these positions.

Attitudes may be desirable or undesirable, depending on the subject and the degree of reason involved. Most of us would agree that moderate patriotism is a commendable quality, while blind support of a government solely because it is a person's own government is dangerous and foolish. On the other hand, most of us would also agree that any degree of race hatred is undesirable. Race hatred is a form of prejudice; and the person who is prejudiced on a certain subject is one whose attitudes toward it are unreasonable—indeed, so strongly colored by emotion that he can have contradictory beliefs without noticing their contradictions. A person, for example, who is prejudiced against Negroes may attack them as dirty and careless but say that their proper place is in the role of kitchen and nursery servants. His emotional attitude blinds him to the contradictions in these two statements.

Attitudes obviously are also related to opinions, but they are by no means the same. An opinion characteristically has a greater basis in reason than an attitude and has a lower emotional content; the person who holds an opinion is likely to be able to defend it more rationally than the person who holds an attitude. Indeed, opinions may best be defined as tentative answers to questions about which there is not enough factual information to reach a completely logical conclusion. Such beliefs are necessary and very useful so long as they are not confused with beliefs wholly based on fact.

Tastes may be defined as attitudes directed toward one thing of a kind. For example, taste is involved when a person says he likes or dislikes a particular poem, say *The Faery Queen*. He is revealing a general attitude if he says he likes or dislikes the poetry of Spenser or poetry as a whole. If he says that poetry has an important part or an unimportant part in human life, he is expressing one aspect of his set of values or (if he is positively inclined) ideals.

Though there are often inconsistencies among the attitudes of an individual, they are often positively related. A person who is conservative in politics tends to be conservative in religion, too. He whose attitude toward a whole race is unfavorable is likely to be prejudiced toward other kinds of minority groups, also.

The Prime Attitude-shaping Forces. Like all characteristics of human beings, attitudes are formed by many influences at work simultaneously. They are developed in complex ways, so that it is often impossible to trace all the roots of a particular attitude. Take antagonistic prejudice, for example. Such prejudice, in contrast to opposition based on fact and evidence, is formed

Table 24   Percentages of Subjects Saying That Certain Intellectually and Socially Desirable Traits Distinguish the Research Scientist

Research Scientist Is *More*	Than the Average		
	Businessman	Engineer	Lawyer
Intellectual	70	70	26
Logical	61	52	26
Orderly	70	48	48
Persistent	70	91	30
Precise	87	39	78
Studious	91	78	43
Thorough	96	65	39
Research Scientist Is *Less*	Than the Average		
	Businessman	Engineer	Lawyer
Charming	70	34	83
Friendly	65	39	57
Humorous	61	39	70
Poised	52	30	74
Self-confident	35	48	61

Source: A. W. Bendig and Peter T. Hountras, "College Student Stereotypes of the Personality Traits of Research Scientists," *Journal of Educational Psychology*, 49:313, 1958.

without taking care to judge fairly, sometimes from frequently hearing various derogatory stereotypes. If a child hears over and over, in his home, expression of ill will toward people of certain religions or certain nationalities, he is likely to acquire the attitude behind the expression. Parents have great prestige in the eyes of young children, who are not sufficiently developed to question the validity of their parents' viewpoints; so without having any experience with the people toward whom the parents are unfriendly, the child may come to dislike them. But sometimes, for obscure reasons having to do with his difficulties with his parents, a child will not take on their prejudiced hatreds; and sometimes prejudice will appear newly and suddenly in an adult.

☯   *Consider the Data*

Based on Table 24

A. W. Bendig and Peter T. Hountras asked 138 college preeducation students to compare four occupations as to the degree to which members of those occupations would possess each of 60 personality traits [Bendig and Hountras, 1958]. The most significant results are presented in Table 24. They showed that the students had a stereotyped conception of the research scientist. Note that the students conceived of him as being very high in the first seven traits, the intellectual traits but low in several of the social traits. The engineer was conceived of as lower than the scientist in personal traits, while the businessman was thought of as being relatively low in intellectual abilities.

What forces in our culture might have contributed to the formation of this stereotype? Think of the stock character of the scientist as he appears in popular fiction, movies, and television.

Might the conception of the scientist have been different if the subjects had been science majors rather than preeducation students? Why or why not?

Do you, to any extent, have a similarly stereotyped conception of these occupations? If so, try to analyze the sources of it in your experiences.

If a person has a satisfying *experience,* he will develop a favorable attitude toward the situation in which he had that experience. If, on the other hand, he has an unsatisfying experience, his attitude toward the situation involved in that experience will be unfavorable.

John K. Coster studied the attitudes toward school of 878 high school students from three income levels: high, middle, and low [Coster, 1959]. More specifically, the levels were differentiated by comparison of home equipment (bathrooms, refrigerators, automobiles, etc.) and by whether or not the children were given private lessons in drama, art, dancing, and music.

The students were given a test which enabled them to express one of five attitudes toward school, ranging from very favorable to very unfavorable. The results of the test strongly showed that the students from families at the highest level had the most favorable attitude, those from the lowest-level families the most unfavorable. Students from middle-income families were also between the two extremes in attitude toward school.

The unfavorable attitudes of the lowest-level pupils were apparently the result of their school experiences—particularly, the experiences of being less popular and thus less happy and of receiving poorer school marks and finding they had less academic and social potential than the children of the higher levels. Experience, then, frequently shapes attitudes.

A person's attitudes are also influenced greatly by his *position relative to others* in the wide ranges of physical, mental, and social abilities and status. This influence is ubiquitous because in comparing abilities and status, people of all ages constantly find that some are better than they, others are about the same, and still others are inferior to them.

When we thus perceive our personal relativity, a high position in whatever scale we are concerned with gives satisfaction and a generalized attitude of appreciation for the causes of the high position. A low position results in frustration, with a consequent attitude of hostility toward the perceived causes of the low position. At all levels, attitudes of jealousy and opposition toward those who are "higher up" are not unusual. We tend to dislike those whose superiority makes us feel less able or more lowly placed. On the other hand, we tend to take the attitude that we should not associate with those who are inferior for fear they will in some way bring us down to their level.

In the relationships of the people of different races and nationalities, the matter of superiority and inferiority clearly influences attitudes. For example, in the highly emotionalized issue of segregation in the United States, most Negroes resent their established position of inferiority, and most white men feel gratified by their established position of superiority. With desegregation, a certain number of the Negroes will take positions above a certain number of the whites—a change some Negroes have a fervent attitude for and one which some whites have a fearful attitude against. So the Negroes have been and are being kept in "their" sections of the communities, in their own schools and churches, and apart from free vocational opportunities; but they have been and are fighting for desegregation.

The attitude of racial prejudice involved here, it should be noted, is primarily ascribable to the whites. But in general, prejudice also develops easily in frustrated and troubled people who feel themselves low in status. They are disposed to be prejudiced toward the well-to-do, toward those who hold political power, toward whoever is above them. Then, by critical and contemptuous remarks, such a person often tries to take a superior role;

prejudice often becomes his ladder for trying to ascend, when he fears he cannot ascend through legitimate, competitive effort.

The impoverished student whose attitude toward school is unfavorable because his experiences there have been unpleasant and the person who hates another race because of his relative position to it have both formed attitudes also partly based on their *personal, or ego, involvement*. But ego involvement can be considered separately as a third major force which shapes attitudes because, indeed, a person's attitude toward anything often depends primarily upon how his ego is involved with it.

Thus a person is likely to have a favorable attitude toward what he himself has and does. His children, possessions, associates, religion, racial group, and country tend to evoke positive attitudes; while those of his neighbor, which are not in the least inferior, leave him indifferent. A person may feel that his car is best merely because he bought it and that his church is superior because he is a member. Teachers favor teachers, marines favor marines, scouts favor scouts, and Democrats favor Democrats.

Also, the more one is involved, the more one is favorably disposed, as a rule. If a person puts time and money into an organization, he feels special loyalty to it; and the students who are active academically, athletically, and socially will have a stronger loyalty to their school than those who are passive.

The negative aspects of this phenomenon are also apparent. The strange and the foreign are often distrusted and disliked as much as the familiar is loved as is evidenced by derogatory names for foreigners which disfigure our colloquial language, such as "Spik," "Dago," and "Bohunk." Further evidence is furnished by the ghettos into which foreign elements of the population of our large cities are often forced by social and economic pressures.

◕ Reflect and Review

Since he was a small child, Don has been easily offended; he has often felt that people have been unkind to him. Relatedly, he has come to keep very careful tabs on who ranks higher than he does in various skills and who ranks lower; and in choosing opponents in games, he tries to play against those whom he can beat. Also, he frequently finds fault with those who are superior and rarely praises anyone except for some really inconsequential performance. When a classmate behaves awkwardly and the students laugh at him, Don laughs loudest and longest.

What basic attitude-shaping force is central in the day-to-day formation of Don's attitudes toward his peers?

Does Don seem to display the attitudes of a person of high status or those of a person of low status? Explain.

THE SCHOOL AND ATTITUDES

Attitudes are of deep concern to schools in a totalitarian society. Such schools devote much of their time to cultivating certain favorable and unquestioning feelings toward the forces in power in the state. But what of attitudes in the school in a nontotalitarian society? What responsibilities concerning the attitudes of its students should the school assume?

Obviously the frustrated and unhappy student should be helped to develop a more favorable attitude toward his school experiences. Attitudes are important in school in a much larger sense than this, however; for certain broad attitudes are basic to becoming a well-educated person—respect for truth and its pursuit, tolerance, and love of freedom, for example—and it is the clear duty of our schools to educate our children well.

How effective are our schools in developing such desirable attitudes in their students? Does the educated person tend to be more objective and liberal-minded as a result of his school experiences? How effective is education in erasing prejudice?

These are some of the questions with which we shall now concern ourselves, drawing our observations from the teen-age period.

As groundwork, let us examine first some central social attitudes of teen-agers in our society and then the important specific influences on the attitudes of teen-agers (as well as other students) toward school subjects, the area in which the teacher's concern with student attitudes begins.

It would be interesting to survey the studies which have been made of the development of attitudes in childhood, and such studies will be referred to from time to time as we examine briefly adolescent attitudes. But we shall confine ourselves mainly to teen-age attitudes, since they are the direct basis of adult attitudes. They have been more thoroughly studied and are generally more broadly social in character than childhood attitudes are. Still, sight should not be lost of childhood attitudes and how teen-age attitudes develop from them.

The Social Attitudes of Teen-agers. On the whole, the attitudes of high school students—consistent with their ambitions to make successes of their lives—are integrative rather than hostile. W. H. Boyer found that about 84 per cent of a group he studied were satisfied with school and that 64 per cent, or nearly two out of three, had what they termed very satisfactory relationships with their parents [Boyer, 1959].

In general, high school students want to maintain good relationships with their parents. Also, though they resist being kept in a childhood status and sometimes say that they cannot discuss their problems with their parents, they go to their mothers and fathers for help and advice more often than to anyone else.

The attitudes of teen-agers in general toward authority do vary greatly, however, from an almost slavish respect for rules and regulations to strong antipathy toward them. This, as might be expected, is especially clear when the relationship of family socioeconomic status and adolescent attitudes toward authority is studied. Such research has, moreover, shown important boy-girl differences in attitudes.

Elias Tuma and Norman Livson studied the attitudes toward authority in home, school, and peer groups of 48 adolescents in relation to the socioeconomic status of the subjects [Tuma and Livson, 1960]. The adolescents were fourteen-, fifteen-, and sixteen-year-olds. These two men found that there was a strong negative correlation between degree of conformity and socioeconomic status among the boys; in other words, the lower the socioeconomic status, the more hostile toward authority the boy was. Other factors were also closely related to attitudes toward authority, particularly parental aspirations and physical maturity of the adolescent. The mother's attitude toward education was also clearly reflected in the adolescent attitudes. toward

Another interesting conclusion was the fact that girls did not reflect the same tendencies as boys to be more rebellious in the lower socioeconomic levels. One reason for this may be the fact that our society seems to demand more conformity and "respectability" from girls than from boys. Acquiring prestige through independence and nonconformity is seldom effective for girls, though it may often be for boys.

Why were the upper-class boys more ready to accept authority than the lower-class boys were? There are probably several reasons. One is that society's rules are usually formulated by the upper socioeconomic classes and thus reflect the interests of those classes. On the adolescent level, the lower-class boys had probably been trained by unpleasant and humiliating experiences to fear and dislike authority, to a much greater degree than the relatively more successful upper-class boys had.

We have noted before that attitudes tend to come in "clusters," being determined by broad patterns of experience and background. The Tuma-Livson study shows how an excessively rebellious attitude toward authority is correlated with frustrations which have social and economic bases. Similarly, excessively docile and authority-accepting attitudes probably have their roots in frustrations and anxieties also. Else Frenkel-Brunswik and Joan Havel studied a group of 1,500 children between the ages of eleven and sixteen in order to discover what other traits accompanied prejudiced and unprejudiced attitudes [Frenkel-Brunswik and Havel, 1953]. On the basis of their reactions to slogans dealing with race prejudice and social attitudes, the children were divided into subgroups, one consisting of the 25 per cent most highly prejudiced, another consisting of the 25 per cent least prejudiced.

These investigators found that the prejudiced children tended to be conservative, self-oriented, and mentally rigid. They tended to place an excessively high premium on money, manners, order, social approval, and cleanliness, and to advocate harsh punishment for those who broke rules or defied authority. They tended also to see their parents as symbols of power rather than of love.

The unprejudiced children, on the other hand, tended to be less self-centered and authoritarian. They viewed the world more objectively and more liberally. Love and compassion were valued more than money or power; this attitude was reflected in their attitudes toward their parents, who were viewed as symbols of love rather than of authority.

In general, such studies as Frenkel-Brunswik and Havel's imply that the clusters of attitudes which accompany prejudice must be dealt with together if prejudice is to be lessened. The school should, then, presumably attempt to help its students toward good general mental health if it aspires to attack the roots of specific prejudices. In extreme cases such as these researchers report, psychotherapy might be required. Milder prejudices might respond, however, to a general atmosphere of tolerance and kindness.

Specific Influences on Attitudes toward School Subjects. A student who says "I just hate math but I like history" generally does better in history to begin with, and keeps on liking it better because his experiences with it are successful. There are, of course, exceptions. Some students who have been very successful in English, for example, dislike the subject. But attitudes toward schoolwork, like attitudes toward other work, usually are positively bound up with one's experiences in doing it. However, the reasons for individual preference for one school subject over another are more complex than this.

Thomas Poffenberger and Donald Norton studied the attitude toward mathematics of 390 high school students (see Exhibit 14). They concluded that home attitudes, success in the subject, and the teacher all play important roles in determining attitudes toward a particular subject, in this case mathematics.

In general it can be accepted almost as a maxim that success or failure has more influence than anything else in developing positive or negative attitudes toward schoolwork. Also, family and teacher attitudes seem to be more favorable when there is more success than when there is less; in other words, the influences reinforce each other.

Exhibit 14   Factors in the formation of attitudes toward mathematics

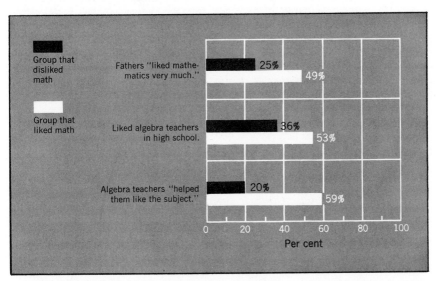

Group that disliked math

Group that liked math

Fathers "liked mathematics very much." — 25% / 49%

Liked algebra teachers in high school. — 36% / 53%

Algebra teachers "helped them like the subject." — 20% / 59%

Per cent

The graph represents a sampling of data from a study of 390 entering freshmen at the University of California in 1955. Sixty-eight students reported that they liked mathematics "very much"; seventy-five reported that they disliked it "very much." Eleven significant differences between the backgrounds of the two groups were discovered, of which the graph shows three. Other significant differences included parents' grade expectations in math, parents' encouragement in math, and experience with arithmetic in elementary school. (Based on data in Thomas Poffenberger and Donald Norton, "Factors in the Formation of Attitudes toward Mathematics," *Journal of Educational Research*, 52:171–176, 1959.)

Effects of Education on Attitudes. We have dealt at some length with the way attitudes are held and retained and have mentioned some important attitudes of adolescents: their attitudes toward races and social groups and toward their schoolwork. We have also mentioned the fact that since attitudes have their primary basis in experiences, they tend to come in clusters and to reinforce each other.

What are the implications of these observations for the teacher? Do important things happen to the attitudes of students as a result of the program of courses they take? Do some tend to become more conservative and others more liberal politically as a result of their studies? Also, do educational experiences develop in the learner more desirable direct attitudes toward people and their problems? For instance, do those who study educational psychology and teaching methods acquire a more sympathetic and helpful attitude toward their own students than they had before this study experience?

Numerous studies of such changes have been made, usually in the following way. An attitude test is given to a class at the beginning and then at the end of a course. A control group does not take the course but is given the attitude test at the same time as the class. Comparison of the beginning and end scores of class and control group enables the experimenter to come to conclusions about attitude changes caused by the course.

It has frequently been found in this way that such attitude changes do occur. For example, teacher attitude scales given to college students preparing to teach have been known to reveal substantial changes in attitude, with the prospective teachers becoming more sympathetic toward the student and his personal welfare, evidently as a result of their study.

Yet not all the research has shown course-based changes in attitude. Thus, sometimes the students in courses dealing with social problems do not change their attitudes toward crime and delinquency, racial groups, and war in what the course would seem to indicate as the desirable direction; and students who are not in courses dealing with social problems sometimes change their attitudes toward those problems in the same way as the course students. For example, J. C. Logey found that students who were taught nothing about dealing with the criminal liberalized their attitudes on the subject as much as students who studied the criminal and his treatment [Logey, 1956]. Of course, it is possible in cases like this that the teacher or the content of the course leaves the students uninterested or, conceivably, that manners and prejudices of the teacher or dullness of the textbook influences them unfavorably, or even that course content (say, especially, in a psychology class) disturbs students enough to impede attitude changes by stimulating defensive rigidity.

To turn to the longer run in the educational process, studies of the same college students as freshmen and as seniors show that there is a change in attitudes during the college years. This is what Harold Webster found, for instance, when he studied college girls' attitudes [Webster, 1958]. Using a 72-item scale, he learned that in religion they became less orthodox: The percentage who believed in the Bible as the word of God, in the future coming of Christ, and the value of prayer went down during the college years. In general, the college students also became more democratic and less authoritarian—more in favor of individual freedom and less in favor of regimentation (see Exhibit 15). Relatedly, other studies have shown that students generally move to the left politically during college.

Walter T. Plant found that what he called ethnocentrism went down during students' college careers [Plant, 1958]. He designated groups to which his tested students belonged as their in-groups and those to which they did not belong as their out-groups. Those who supported their own groups but showed negative attitudes toward out-groups were said to be ethnocentric.

Plant's attitude scale showed significant decline in ethnocentrism, or prejudice toward out-groups, for both sexes, with the college girls showing a greater decline than college boys, incidentally.

We are not sure, however, that this desirable change resulted even in this long run from learning experiences in college. It is possible that such improvement results simply from the maturing that takes place during the four college years. Noncollege youth of the same age need to be tested too, to see how they change; use of such noncollege controls would permit stronger deductions on how education modifies prejudicial attitudes.

Finally, the issue of attitude changes as related to the time involved in

Exhibit 15   Changes in attitudes during four years of college

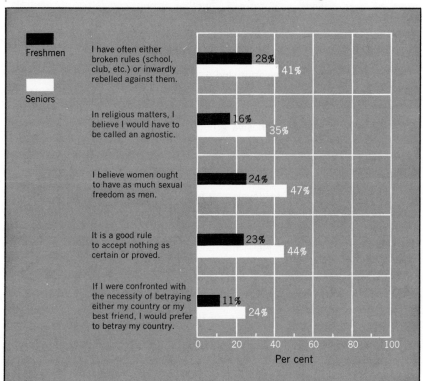

This chart shows the changes in percentage of students responding "yes" to the five questions listed after four years of college. In each case the top bar represents the percentage as freshmen, the bottom bar the percentage as seniors. The five questions are only samples from 123 questions asked; they reflect certain of the experiment's important conclusions, for example, that college led students to develop attitudes that were more unconventional, more inquiring, and more liberal. (Based on data in Harold Webster, "Changes in Attitude during College," *Journal of Educational Psychology,* 49:109–117, 1958.)

the educational process is not simple, as can be illustrated by K. M. Miller and J. B. Briggs's study of short-time changes in the attitudes of fifteen-year-old American boys toward Americans, Chinese, Dutch, English, Germans, and other races and nationalities [Miller and Briggs, 1958]. An attitude scale was given to the boys before, immediately after, and then several weeks after they had taken part in a short discussion of the various racial and national groups. The boys showed greater tolerance and appreciation for the different peoples as the immediate result of the discussion about them; and the retest several weeks later showed that the change was fairly stable.

Of special interest in this case is the way the boys were organized into discussion groups. They were grouped on the basis of a sociometric test in which they indicated their best friends and those whom they rejected. A group of best friends was formed. Another group consisted of neutrals; that is, there were no boys who chose each other as friends and none who were rejected by the others. Would the friendly group discuss freely and enthusiastically and produce a cordial atmosphere that would be conducive to the development of appreciation and tolerance? Would the group of "neither friends nor foes" be restrained and therefore ineffective in its discussion? The facts turned out to be that the neutral group showed as much reduction in prejudice as the highly cohesive group; in other words, the relative cohesiveness of the groups did not seem to influence the change in attitude.

In short, it is hard to anticipate what will happen to the broad social attitudes of students as a result of the courses they take. Teaching may be theoretically favorable to developing a liberal or tolerant outlook and still not do so. The teacher may condition the students negatively by a personality that stimulates hostility or ill will; or some other influence—events in the community itself, for example—may counteract the good "side effects" of teaching. How can the teacher make the most of his opportunities to lessen undesirable attitudes among his students?

We have already commented upon the healthful effects of a good classroom atmosphere. In an environment of friendly order and supportive interest, prejudices tend to lessen almost spontaneously. We have noted that the threatened and intimidated person is often also the prejudiced one. The teacher cannot remove the experiences that originally embedded an undesirable attitude in a student's mind, but he can help to create a school environment in which that attitude cannot easily flourish.

Second, the teacher can help overcome prejudices by direct precept. He can explain the real bases of prejudice to his students, providing cogent examples of the way prejudices are formed. As with all mental health problems, illumination and understanding are two of the simplest and best therapies. He need not preach or exhort, but he can help his students acquire the habit of looking for the facts and objectively examining a problem. Few prejudices can survive the light of intelligence and objectivity. To return to race prejudice as an example, the teacher can encourage the prejudiced student to look up the biological and sociological facts about so-called "racial superiority." Some students will reject them at first, but some will begin the process of reexamination of their beliefs.

Third, and perhaps most important, the teacher can provide a good example himself of good mental health. The teacher who presents an example to his students of confidence, kindness, and reasonableness will do much to encourage the same qualities in those whom he teaches. In this fact lies much of the responsibility of the teacher. The teacher influences his students vastly; he should try his best to make that influence a good one. No amount of preaching will overcome the bad effects on a student of a teacher who exhibits irrational dislikes and prejudices; conversely, the teacher who provides an opposite example can do much to counteract undesirable pressures from outside the school.

The example of prejudice is, of course, paramount in importance. One of the advantages claimed for the American school is that it brings together the sons and daughters of all the people to play and work together. Out of these experiences, prejudice should lessen and good mental health correspondingly increase. But in order to make this happen, the teacher and the school must be aware of the problem of prejudice in society in general and in school in particular and must do their best to counteract the effects of this moral disease.

☯ *Reflect and Review*

Here are some short descriptions of various attitude-reflecting situations. Study the situations and answer the related questions, to the best of your ability.

Pete, who lives in the poorest section of town, is not very popular with the other students in school. Also, having an IQ of 90, he has gotten only average or lower marks in his courses. What general attitude toward school is Pete likely to have? Suppose in one of his social science classes the subject of better wages and living conditions for the poor should come up. What is Pete's attitude on this topic likely to be? Suppose, further, that Pete got into a quarrel on this subject with a banker's son, and the teacher, a usually mild-mannered man, stepped in to keep the peace. If a fight had developed, who would be most likely to strike first?

Angie comes from a cultured home, and her parents expect to send her to college next year. She thinks she will major in history, which she likes and has done well in. She is a bit troubled, though; her history teacher this year has made the subject seem quite dull, and she has not studied very much.

What seems to be the most stable influence on Angie's attitude toward history? What influence seems to be changing and thus affecting her "set" toward the subject?

In a highly Scandinavian community in North Dakota, a father who had been born in Norway consistently indoctrinated his son and daughter against the Swedes. He told them in various ways that Swedes were selfish, tricky, and not to be trusted. The children loved their father and listened whenever he talked. What attitudes do you suppose the son and daughter had toward the Swedes when they became adult? Suppose the son and daughter went through college in a neighboring state where there were also many Scandinavians. How do you think their attitudes might change? Whose would probably change most?

SCHOOL BEHAVIOR AND ATTITUDES

One of the best lessons that can be learned by the student of the human being is that few of his characteristics exist in any kind of isolation; almost always we find that a particular trait is part of a pattern, or configuration, of traits. Thus the teacher regularly finds that certain students cause almost all the discipline problems while others are consistently well-behaved and courteous.

But just to say that the one group has a "bad" and the other a "good" behavior pattern is still to beg the question basically involved: What makes the students behave so differently?

The answer involves patterns on a deeper level. The sullen, rebellious, rowdy boy; the shy, withdrawn, troubled girl; and the happy, well-adjusted child *all* have complex reasons for their behavior that seem good to them. In other words, school behavior, like all other behavior, is firmly rooted in, and can only be understood in terms of, patterns of attitudes and other characteristics.

For the teacher, such understanding is, of course, immediately practical. However, in so far as the teacher has a chance to guide his students into more healthful patterns of behavior, such understanding is also of long-range moral significance.

The Relative Seriousness of Behavior Problems. How relatively serious are the various kinds of misbehavior in terms of effects on self and on others? Let us begin our consideration of this important problem by turning to E. K. Wickman's pioneer study, which heightened interest in it and so led to much more research [Wickman, 1928]. Wickman asked 395 teachers and 63 mental hygienists to rate the seriousness of various kinds of behavior and behavior-related characteristics of fifth- and sixth-grade children, ages ten to thirteen—the hygienists in terms of their effect on the development of the individual, the teachers according to how they affected the management of the classroom and school.

The hygienists (34 psychologists and 29 psychiatrists) were persons who worked in child-guidance clinics, psychiatric hospitals, mental-hygiene clinics, courts, welfare bureaus, and personal-adjustment services in colleges and universities; and in the group of teachers there was also a wide range of professional experiences out of which to interpret behavior.

The following misbehavior and characteristics were considered most serious:

Unsocialness or withdrawal	Prevailing fear of persons and situations
Cruelty and bullying	Stealing
General depression	Tendency to give up effort easily
Resentfulness	Unreliability
Suspiciousness	Overcriticalness of others
Nervousness	Physical cowardice

Some misbehavior and traits that the teachers thought serious the hygienists did not think very significant: masturbation, heterosexual activity, obscene acts and talk, untruthfulness, and destructiveness.

Subsequent and more recent studies indicate a change in the attitudes of teachers, and an important general phenomenon begins to emerge here, namely, that though teachers find overt troublesome behavior more serious than hygienists do, many teachers now also consider as serious the relatively subtle forms of misbehavior expressed above which are symptomatic of an unhealthy personality and inimical to personal development.

Cruelty and stealing provide individual exceptions to this general rule in that they *are* strongly outgoing behavior which is strongly disapproved of besides usually being signs of deep distress. But the rest of the above items largely signify introversions of unwholesome emotions that prevent good personal development and so handicap one very seriously in getting along with people (and, of course, are evidences of past failure to do so). The items are usually expressed, as here, in terms of qualities because the behavior they produce is not so easy to detect and explain as the more overt and troublesome behavior; thus the teacher must be on the lookout for these serious symptoms and, in turn, causes of poor mental health to provide himself with the chance of trying to set up remedial influences. Yet it can be very important that he do so, and sometimes very important that he do so quickly. For instance, withdrawing behavior is often related to depression and suspiciousness, so that a shy child is apt to be wary even of well-intentioned treatment and hard to reach with friendliness. But shyness has been called— with validity at times—a time bomb, the implication being that after a period of quietness the shy person may break out in violent behavior.

The phenomena that were considered least important by the raters of the Wickman study were:

Whispering	Interrupting
Disorderliness	Thoughtlessness
Restlessness	Tardiness
Inattention	Smoking
Profanity	Slovenliness

These terms categorize acts which, while often annoying, are not symptomatic of very bad mental health and do not have a very adverse effect on the growth and development of personality. These acts are not saturated with unwholesome inward feelings, as are withdrawal, depression, and other behavioral traits considered most serious by both teachers and hygienists. In general, moreover, not all of them constitute misbehavior with all teachers and in all schools. Thus, in some elementary school classrooms the teachers demand that the pupils not whisper; but in others, where the pupils work together, talking and exchanging ideas, whispering is not a problem. A teacher is concerned about behavior that disturbs the class as he has decided or been instructed to run it in order to guide the children effectively.

Yet there has probably been, in recent years, a tendency to underrate the seriousness of overt misbehavior and, by the way, teachers' and school administrators' knowledge of behavior. Thus troublesome behavior can become so serious that it interferes with the development of good learning situations for all the students, which the members of any school staff must concern themselves with maintaining. Also, the staff in the present-day school is generally intelligent and sympathetic, giving the individual student more patient help than he ever will receive after he leaves school. If undesirable behavior persists under such favorable conditions, the prognosis for adulthood with its more demanding and competitive tasks is that of inadequacy leading to failure. For example, the noisily misbehaving high school student who quits school to take a job typically shows indifference to the scheduled work hours and disrespect for the work process in general and "the boss" in particular, to the point that it becomes necessary to discharge him.

Finally, even seemingly petty overt misbehavior may, because of deep and persistent roots, present serious problems. Thus impertinence and rudeness to teachers—which teachers surveyed by the National Education Association have named as the most frequent type of classroom misbehavior—can be smoothly overcome by teaching and training if they are due simply to a lack of good manners, but impertinence and rudeness resulting from serious frustration are more difficult to remedy.

We have, then, a complex problem in just trying to see the real and crucial distinctions between serious and trivial misbehavior and the attitudes behind both—a problem that, in any one case, only time will completely resolve.

The teacher, of course, cannot simply wait for time to resolve his specific behavior-problem situations. But the teacher can learn a great deal about the dynamics of his students' patterns of attitudes and behavior, and thus about how to deal with his students by studying what the future (especially when unsuccessful) of other students with known similar patterns of attitudes and behavior has turned out to be.

We shall, therefore, now consider two contrasting categories of ill-fated misbehavers—the typical juvenile delinquent, one of the clear-cut problem individuals in our society, and the little band of Korea turncoats who surprised and shocked us not many years ago.

The Background and Bases of Delinquency. If a youth can live the first 20 years of his life without coming to the official attention of a court of law for serious infractions, the likelihood that he will ever do so is fairly small. Today, only about fifteen per cent of those arrested for the first time are over twenty-one years of age; about sixty per cent are between thirteen and twenty years of age; and about twenty-five per cent are twelve or under, reflecting the current trend for delinquent behavior to appear at earlier ages which undoubtedly accounts for the alarming overall increases in delinquency. When antisocial behavior shows up after the age of twenty, moreover, it usually turns out that some signs of it were evident during childhood and the teens. In this respect, delinquency is like genius, incidentally.

Adolescence—the time when, as the statistics show, most delinquency still comes to the fore—we have described as a period when the individual is seeking his independence. But, as we have suggested in various ways, adolescence is, more exactly, a period when there are gradual shifts of dependencies—from parents and all they provide to friends and recreation, a job and fellow workers, and then a life mate and a home of one's own.

Success in adulthood is almost always preceded by success in these developmental experiences of childhood and youth, and thus the delinquent is a classic type of person who is not headed for a successful adulthood. For, instead of having started well to develop successful personal relationships and accept work responsibilities, the delinquent has become antisocial in an active sense. He has made the anti-authority attitudes earlier ascribed to many boys from families of low socioeconomic status the basis of his behavior—a way of life.

He does, indeed, usually come from one of the lower classes, and so has usually had more than his share of environmentally caused bitterness and pain. But he differs from many other lower-class boys in being dominated by the hostile-aggressive reaction to frustration, rather than seeking to overcome it in socially legitimate ways.

But what, more specifically, are the characteristics and conditions which tend to underlie delinquency? An understanding of the bases of delinquency helps us understand delinquent behavior and the less serious misbehavior of the delinquency-prone. Patterns are the same; the difference is in degree.

The typical delinquent, or delinquent-to-be:

In terms of his environment

1. Comes from a family in a low socioeconomic class whose home is situated in a poor district.

2. Has had to move about a great deal and has attended several schools.

3. Is usually not loved and appreciated at home, which is usually a place of dissension, distrust, and often parental drunkenness—a broken home in effect if not actually.

4. Does not take part in respectably organized sports or group play, but rather belongs to a gang in which he tries to satisfy his need for status by doing whatever he feels will make him known as smart, brave, and tough.

In terms of the school

1. Dislikes its routine, requirements, and restrictions, and skips school often.

2. Fails to do his work, gets low marks, fails in his subjects, and so is retarded.

3. Has few friends in school and participates only a little, if at all, in the school's extracurricular activities.

4. Does not have definite educational and vocational plans.

In terms of himself

1. Is often mesomorphic in body type—solidly built and well proportioned.

2. Is not generally industrious—rather, loves workless adventure and excitement.

3. Has underaverage mental capacity—an IQ between 80 and 90.

4. Is stubborn, impulsive, aggressive, bad-tempered, and destructive, but claims to know very well what is right and wrong and is very sensitive about "his rights."

Let it be stressed, however, that not all these descriptive items apply to every delinquent or future delinquent. For instance, a few have high IQs and some have IQs under 80, and a few come from the higher socioeconomic levels. But the above factors do constitute the typical roots of delinquency.

The Backgrounds of the Korea "Turncoats." Following the Korean War, 21 American prisoners (and 1 British prisoner who will not be considered here) chose to live in Communist China, a country characterized by overpopulation, poverty, and extreme government control of the individual destiny, rather than return to their own relatively roomy, prosperous, and free United States.[1]

By intensively interviewing their teachers, pastors, friends, parents, neighbors, and employers, Virginia Pasley discovered the following striking data on the backgrounds of these 21 soldiers: 19 felt that they were unloved and unwanted by their fathers (or stepfathers—16 were from broken homes); 18 were reared in poverty; 18 did not participate in sports or other school activities, and 17 did not finish high school; 16 were average or below average in IQ; 16 could be described as withdrawn but, significantly, more as "lone colts" than "lone wolves," because they were not robber or killer types—only 3 of the 21 had been in difficulty with juvenile authorities, and then the trouble was minor [Pasley, 1955].

This strange prevailing pattern of these boys' social relationships was apparent to the persons interviewed, who consistently would make this sort of characterization of individual boys:[2]

"He was bitter."
"He was a strange one."
"He never smiled."
"We couldn't touch him."
"He was quiet and shy."
"He liked to go off and be alone."
"He had no friends."
"He was bull headed."
"He was silent, hardly ever said a word."
"He seemed unhappy."
"He was a dreamer."

As suggested by these descriptions and the IQ and school-career patterns, most of the 21 did not like school, and so their attendance was poor and they did poorly in their work. Then 20 of the 21 volunteered for the service (only one was conscripted!), clearly, it would seem, both in the hope of escaping from their unhappy environmental situations, failures, and loneliness and in the hope of a better life in the army.

These unhappy backgrounds, Pasley found, led these 21 boys, when captured and then offered repatriation, to feel that they had nothing to go back to, and so made them susceptible to their captors' highly embellished promises of a good life under communism.

When Pasley interviewed teachers of the boys, a significant pattern emerged. Almost all the teachers remembered the boys who had been in their classes, but most admitted that they had been unsuccessful in trying

[1] In 1955, three asked for and received permission to leave China and return home.
[2] From Virginia Pasley, *21 Stayed*, Farrar, Straus & Company, Inc., New York, 1955. By permission.

to help them. The typical pattern was that of a shy, troubled boy whose emotional problems prevented him from doing satisfactory schoolwork. (Only 5 of the 21 had low IQs; 5 others had IQs above the average.)

One boy's teacher said, "He had quite a few emotional problems to solve. It was apparent that he had a chip on his shoulder and, from things he said in class, that he didn't get along with his stepfather. He was extremely insecure and rather than try to make friends he just withdrew from the other boys in the class." The same boy's principal said, "He was a boy who was hard to know. At times he was easy to talk to and would cooperate. At other times he was silent and resentful—suspicious."

The teacher of another boy commented on his extreme tendency to daydream. He spent most of his time in school listlessly looking out the window. "You couldn't tell whether or not he was a good loser," said the teacher, "he just accepted it."

Another had four much brighter sisters with whom he felt he had to compete. His teacher said, "Clarence had to work hard for every grade he got and he did work hard. Too hard. He was overanxious to get his lesson right and was on the verge of tears when he didn't."

What could their teachers have done to avert the fate of these boys? Most had tried to help them, but had failed. Special clinical treatment had been recommended in several cases but had not been received, because of lack of facilities or some other reason. The evidence seems to indicate that most of the boys had such deep-seated emotional problems that ordinary teacher help would have been inadequate. In a few cases, no teacher had even been aware of the boys' problems.

What separates this group from the average group of juvenile delinquents? The pattern of chaotic family backgrounds and personal frustration is similar, but these boys had stayed out of major trouble at least long enough to get in the Army. There is no single answer. Perhaps the central difference is one of opportunity. Or perhaps (as seems likely) most of the "turncoats" found an outlet for their troubles in the false security of the Communist system, whereas they had been better prepared to withstand the temptations of crime, through some sort of parental or school training. Communism provided a basis of security which was—in that particular environment at least—free from the guilt associations of crime. Emotionally and personally, they resembled, as a group, the typical juvenile delinquent very closely, however.

The issue of communism is only incidental here, however. Though the sad case of these boys could easily be used to show that Communists set out to give Americans who are maladjusted an opportunity to rationalize their failures and to feel important, the significance of this case for us is rather what it reveals about the potentialities for delinquency and serious maladjustment in our midst.

Thus the findings reveal that much was seriously wrong with these 21 boys' homes, schools, and communities; otherwise they would not have repudiated what they had had when faced with the flimsy promises of their captors.

⬤ *Reflect and Review*

Jim, ten years old, gives his teacher much concern. He is antagonistic and obstinate. He reads poorly, neglects to do his lessons, and does not voluntarily participate in the games and play of his grade.

Jim's father is an unskilled laborer with low income. Father and son quarrel frequently, and Jim feels that his father dislikes him. Jim's mother and father fight, too, and the mother shows few signs that she either accepts or rejects Jim.

Jim seems to have just one friend, with whom he skips school frequently, sneaks into movies, and spends time around the railroad yards. They amuse a gang of hoboes, among whom Jim is gaining a reputation as "a strange kid." Jim has a good throwing arm and loves to throw a stone or iron missile through a window or against a wall that he can chip or dent. He shows off this ability at the yards, but never glances at the watching hoboes.

Jim seems to be on a borderline between juvenile delinquency and complete social isolation. What characteristics of both patterns is he displaying?

What do you think Jim's future will be? Why?

A CONSTRUCTIVE APPROACH TO CLASSROOM DISCIPLINE

An additional valuable, though often disappointing, bit of knowledge that the study of delinquency and other forms of social isolation can provide the teacher with is the fact that by the time a youth is well on his way along one of these wrong roads it is usually too late for a teacher to help him. This is valuable to know because it emphasizes the importance of handling day-to-day problems of behavior *now*. How is the teacher to do this best, and to what kind of a classroom situation are the proper procedures closely related? Let us begin the answer by considering how teachers actually deal with behavior problems among their students.

When Frank Slobetz investigated the methods of elementary school teachers, he discovered the following pattern of treatment of such problem situations: About thirty per cent of the teachers' responses to misbehavior or related situations were punitive; about seventy per cent of the teachers' reactions excluded punishment and were constructive and remedial instead [Slobetz, 1951].

These findings are roughly typical of our schools. Most teachers do not try to improve their students' behavior by resorting to pain and penalty. Instead, they sympathetically try to understand the student, and patiently work to change his point of view and to bring about conditions which will influence his behavior wholesomely.

This is encouraging, for the purpose of school discipline is to create such conditions, which are most conducive to the intellectual and social development of the student; in other words, good discipline is not an end in itself.

We shall therefore give attention to constructive ways of bringing about a healthful classroom climate; and since a constructive approach to classroom discipline involves continuous positive teacher behavior designed to prevent as well as correct student misbehavior, we shall refer both to situations which involve misbehavior and to situations which do not. Relatedly, the list of ideas to be presented will unify simple techniques of the moment and more general recommendations embodying basic psychological principles, some of which have been discussed in various earlier contexts.

1. The teacher should learn the names of the students as soon as possible and be sure of their pronunciation. This will be hastened if he studies the names of his students before he meets them. Knowing students by name helps the teacher in developing a good rapport with them as individuals and thereby a better general social atmosphere.

2. The teacher should begin teaching when the students are ready and willing to pay attention. He should wait a short time until they have settled down and, if necessary, make a pleasant comment to those whose attention is wanted.

3. The teacher should know what he wants to do and how to do it and should then teach with confidence and enthusiasm.

4. The teacher should change activities before interest begins to drag. He should keep the class busy and the work or play moving.

5. The teacher should use as a guide the principle that rewards are much more effective than punishments. Praise and commendation are more effective than scolding and reproof, freedom and expression than restraint and suppression, prizes than penalties; in general, the positive is more effective than the negative.

6. The teacher should be tolerant and patient. There is danger in being too quick to make an issue of some surface misbehavior which may blow over and never occur again. This does not mean, of course, that the teacher should overlook the danger of allowing serious trouble to develop.

7. The teacher should avoid an issue with a student in front of a class— should avoid exclaiming, say, "We'll hold up the class until you tell!" or "You apologize now, or I'll keep you in this room until you do!" Tempers get hotter and embarrassments are the rule when ultimatums and sharp warnings fly.

8. A student should not be allowed to become a hero because he stood

up against the teacher. This can be avoided in part if problems involving one student centrally are handled privately.

9. The teacher should carry out routine tasks involving classroom mechanics efficiently. For example, the passing out of books and papers, if done awkwardly, may stir up disorder and confusion.

10. The teacher should use supplementary materials and equipment such as reference books, globes, maps, motion pictures, teaching machines, and other teaching aids efficiently and at the appropriate times.

11. The teacher should always be ready to help the individual student. He should be patient in his explanations and friendly in his manner, thus making the student feel that the teacher thinks he is important and that he is wanted.

All the preceding suggestions are useful for both the experienced and the beginning teacher, but in addition, to help himself over the first few minutes, hours, and days:

1. The beginning teacher should not approach his first classes in an over-friendly, too easygoing manner; conversely, he should not meet them in an overserious and suspicious manner which gives the impression that he is looking for trouble.

2. The beginning teacher should know especially thoroughly the subject matter of the initial lessons and the various points he expects to stress and should plan his procedures very carefully.

3. The beginning teacher should give directions and assignments most fully and clearly so as not to let any misunderstanding develop.

4. The beginning teacher should be especially careful not to allow tendencies to disorder to develop; therefore, when deliberate misbehavior becomes evident, he should be quick to deal with it firmly, but in a friendly manner that will not overemphasize the situation.

These suggestions, which, as a whole, stress that the teacher should not regard the problems of child behavior as solved if he merely maintains order, are a practical corollary of the fact that good mental health and corresponding attitudes and behavior are based on emotional states and thus spring from much deeper sources than external order and discipline.

Conversely, the kind of quiet that results from rigorous, compulsive vigilance on the part of a teacher is often conducive to poor mental health; by acting as both foreman and policeman the teacher maintains order but suppresses his students in doing so, with the following unhappy results.

Their overt behavior in the classroom may not immediately become disturbing, but they will not have learned the independence, initiative, honesty, and self-control that would make them able to conduct themselves without supervision. Also, feeling frustrated by the apparent affront to their self-esteem, they will have little feeling for group welfare, so that rebellious and hostile behavior will eventually appear.

This, of course, brings us back to the authoritarian and the democratic teacher, whose contrasting class management we considered much earlier in relation to student social development. Now let us reexamine these types in order to see the basic interplay between their mental health, attitudes, and behavior and those of their students.

The authoritarian teacher typically does not know his subject matter well and is not sure of himself in other ways, and his authoritarian method is a compensation for these weaknesses. Consciously or unconsciously he becomes arbitrary and authoritarian in order to gain a control over the situation that he would not have in an atmosphere where curiosity and inquiry were encouraged. By his dictatorial methods he acquires a feeling of ascendancy, sometimes with overtones of self-dramatization. This is not good for the students, and it seldom if ever yields true self-esteem or other satisfaction to the teacher.

The democratic teacher typically has a thorough understanding of his subject and is free of crucial feelings of inadequacy. Consequently, he does not have to operate behind defense methods with his students and so gives them much liberty of thought and action. Also, he can act as their friend and helper; that is, he can work cooperatively with them on projects. If unforeseen problems develop, teacher and students can set about as investigators to find the answers, which is as it should be. Indeed, the good teacher likes to see new problems come to the front, so that he can help his students develop experimental situations. This does not mean that control and guidance are abandoned beyond very simple rules of order but rather that they are used with the purpose of stimulating the student to increase the variety of his independent responses.

As a result, the students are controlled not by the dominating, coercive force of their teacher but largely by the situation and developments of the classroom.

More deeply, in a democratic, cooperative atmosphere the students are not under the pressures that bring on anxiety and fear and so are free to be friendly and conscious of group welfare as well as show personal initiative. Then, when emotional troubles do occur, the students possess more self-control and patience in working them out than they have in authoritarian situations. Democratic classroom atmosphere, finally, is symbolic of the kind of freedom all persons need. Some form of student government is in evidence, but more important than this form of democracy is the spirit. Every individual is important, teacher and students alike, and there is much self-initiated participation, so that students in effect share positive responsibility for the discipline in the classroom. Nor does this mean that the democratic teacher is less responsible himself than the authoritarian teacher, for to maintain this lively atmosphere, he has to be more skillful and have much more human understanding.

We have emphasized specific action in these remarks on the teacher, but, as we have reiterated again and again in this chapter, behavior is a reflection of basic values and attitudes. When D. G. Ryans studied two groups of teachers who were ranked "high" and "low" in effectiveness (see Table 25), he found that the "high" group were outgoing in personality, positive and affirmative in their attitudes toward others, and confident and assured in their attitudes toward themselves [Ryans, 1959]. The "low" group, in contrast, was aloof, negative, and personally insecure. The teacher who would influence his students favorably should examine his own attitudes, for often they will be adopted, to a greater or lesser extent, by his students.

Previously in this chapter, the schools of a democratic society with those of a totalitarian society were contrasted briefly. The qualities of the authoritarian teacher—dogmatism, coercion, and hostility—reflect, in small, the qualities of the totalitarian society. The qualities of the democratic teacher, on the other hand—generosity, genuine personal concern, and liberalism—mirror

Table 25   Some Correlates of Teacher Behavior*

"High" Group	"Low" Group
1. Tends to judge others generously	1. Is from older age groups
2. Indicates strong interest in reading	2. Tends to be critical of others
3. Indicates strong interest in the arts	3. Values orderliness and "practical" things most highly
4. Participated in high school and college social groups	4. Prefers activities which do not involve much social contact
5. Is thought well of by students	5. Is not thought of well by students
6. Prefers nondirective classroom procedures	6. Prefers authoritarian teaching techniques
7. Is superior in verbal ability	7. Is relatively low in verbal intelligence
8. Is well adjusted emotionally	8. Is less well adjusted emotionally

* D. G. Ryans studied 2,043 elementary and secondary teachers by means of trained observers and self-reports in order to discover which ones ranked high and low on three patterns of classroom behavior: Pattern X (friendly versus aloof), Pattern Y (systematic organization versus slipshod planning), and Pattern Z (stimulating teaching versus dull teaching). He then studied the personal qualities that each group had in common; some of the major results appear above.
Source: From data in D. G. Ryans, "Some Correlates of Teacher Behavior," *Educational and Psychological Measurement,* 19:9–10, 1959.

the ideals of the democratic society. It is in the example, more than in the precepts, of the democratic teacher that democratic behavior and attitudes are best preserved.

⚫ *Reflect and Review*

A young man became the principal of a small school where the students' misbehavior had interfered seriously with the school's effectiveness. The discipline had been so poor that the school had well been described as chaotic; but after the new man took over, the school was transformed into a very orderly one. The children were literally drilled into the school building and out of it, with no talking or whispering allowed; they were never permitted to enter or leave the schoolhouse informally, quietly talking to each other as people usually do. Even the activities on the playgrounds were carefully supervised. The principal or another staff member was always there with the children to make decisions and to prevent any possible confusion.

To the townspeople it appeared that the school was very well operated. "Everything is running smoothly," they said with relief. After all, there was no disobedience, and the teachers were in control.

During one recess, however, all the members of the staff were called to a meeting by the principal, and the children were left on the playground without supervision. Then they did not engage in organized games, as they always had under the usual close direction. Instead, they ran about the grounds helter-skelter, throwing things at each other, the bigger boys tossing the smaller boys on top of each other in great piles. There was complete disorganization, complete breakdown—a discipline that had seemed good went to pieces.

When the showdown later came, the students were not very honest about what had happened. Give two likely reasons for this.

Do you think the students were basically having a happy time when they were running riot? Why?

The principal displayed one very specific sign of lack of skill. What was this? What might this one event show about his mental health?

SUMMARY

One's attitudes have deep-seated roots, are integral aspects of the personality, and are both causes and effects of behavior.

Attitudes have both feeling and ideational content and tend to engender behavior consistent with those feelings and thoughts.

A prejudice is an attitude (generally one of opposition) that is not supported by sound evidence. An opinion is an estimate or point of view based on knowledge.

Attitudes develop in a number of ways:

1. From the attitudes expressed in the home, school, church, peer group, and other places.

2. From the ideas, facts, and attitudes expressed in books, movies, radio, and television.

3. From experiences, in terms of how pleasant or unpleasant they are.

4. From a person's status in relation to others, his personal relativity.

5. From self or ego involvement. This is related to item 4 but is more comprehensive.

The school has the responsibility of developing in the students good attitudes toward others, toward self, toward learning, toward right and wrong, and in general toward desirable values.

Boys from higher socioeconomic classes accept authority much more readily than do boys of the lower socioeconomic classes, who show considerable hostility toward authority. This difference does not exist among the girls of the high and low classes.

The personality pattern of prejudiced people is different from that of the unprejudiced, the former adhering more rigidly to given forms and material values.

Attitudes toward school subjects are developed largely by success or failure with those subjects. The attitudes of the home and teacher, as well as the attitudes of the student toward his parents and teachers, influence the forming of attitudes toward school subjects.

The effects of education on the attitudes of any given person are difficult to predict because the influences often have unexpected results. The reasons for this are found in the teacher, the learner himself, and the many facets of the environment that influence the learner.

In general, education seems to have the effect of developing mature attitudes and of reducing prejudice.

A teacher probably has the best influence on the attitude development of his pupils if he is personally likable and professionally competent, and if he observes problem-solving procedures and helps the student seek out the evidence.

Understanding the attitudes of students helps the teacher to understand their behavior.

Behavior should be regarded as serious if its effect is to prevent personal development and thus to render the individual maladjusted. Behavior is also serious if it interferes with and upsets the efforts of others and if it is in conflict with what the individual should be doing in order to be effective. Such behavior indicates profound disturbances and unhealthy emotions. Failing to do schoolwork, skipping school, and rudeness to the teacher are evidence of serious failure by youth and presage delinquency and an unsuccessful adulthood, in many instances.

If youth reach adulthood with no record of delinquency and in general with a good record in school, there is a strong likelihood that adulthood will be free of serious antisocial behavior. Delinquency usually appears during late childhood and especially during the teens; and in cases of initial delinquency in adulthood, usually there were symptoms during adolescence.

A delinquent usually is born into and reared in an insulting and damaging environment of his home and community; he typically does not conform to the school requirements, does not respond to its intellectual and social opportunities, has underaverage intelligence, seems incapable of systematic work, loves desultory activities, and is hostile and impulsive.

The 21 American prisoners in the Korean War who adopted Chinese Communism had been problem cases in school and had the typical background of maladjusted youth. Their premilitary history was one of many personal troubles; and they were characterized by shyness, stubbornness, bitterness, friendlessness, and unhappiness. These boys probably volunteered for military service to escape from their home and community situations and in turn chose Communism to escape even further.

Teachers need to be aware of their students' personal disorder and problem tendencies in order to try to offset the possibility of serious difficulty.

Most teachers tend to take constructive measures rather than punitive ones in response to misbehavior.

The teacher who maintains good discipline in the modern sense keeps the students busy with their learning activities and thereby prevents disorder and wasting of time. However, discipline in this sense will usually not be of much help to those relatively few students who have deep-seated personality problems.

Positive, efficient teaching, or a good offense, is the best defense. Good teachers tend to be generous with their appreciations and praise, like their students and are liked by them, and have intellectual interests.

Effective teachers bring about industry in a democratic and cooperative atmosphere and help their students in learning to initiate and sustain desirable individual and group behavior.

SUGGESTED READING

Haring, Norris G., and E. L. Phillips: *Educating Emotionally Disturbed Children,* McGraw-Hill Book Company, Inc., New York, 1962. Describes some of the characteristics of children in poor emotional health and tells of various attempts and ways to help them. Provides a good orientation to the magnitude of the problem of dealing effectively with emotionally handicapped children.

Johannesson, Ingvor: "School Differentiation and the Social Adjustment of the Pupils: A Summary of Research for the Swedish Parliamentary School Committee," *Educational Research*, 4:133–139, 1962. Shows how personal relationships and attitudes are influenced by the home, teachers, kind of school, school friends, and community environment. This is a comprehensive study carried out in Sweden. This is a socially significant study.

Phillips, E. L., Daniel N. Wiener, and Norris G. Haring: *Achievement and Mental Health*, Prentice-Hall, Inc., Englewood Cliffs, N.J., 1960. An integrative treatment of the three areas: discipline, achievement, and mental health. The relationships are handled effectively, and this book contains much practical help as well as sound, basic knowledge.

Werner, Emmy, and Elizabeth Gallistel: "Prediction of Outstanding Performance, Delinquency, and Emotional Disturbance from Childhood Evaluations," *Child Development*, 32:255–260, 1961. On the basis of an extensive study, it appears that the socioeconomic status of the family, the intelligence of the child, evidences of responsibility, and other indications of maturity predict personal success or failure. Factors that do not differentiate between outstanding and delinquent youth are also given.

PART IV
LEARNING

CHAPTER 13
THE ACTIVITY
OF LEARNING

If water is poured at a fixed rate into a bucket, it will fill up steadily and evenly. Many people tend to think learning is like this. Are they right in this view?

If learning consisted in the steady "filling up" of an essentially passive student (the bucket) with knowledge (the water), there would be a perfect correlation between study time and acquisition of knowledge. Furthermore, buckets being essentially alike, there would be little variation in the rates at which different students learn. Finally, there would be little variation in the rates at which different material is learned: a bucket may be filled as quickly with gasoline as with water.

Clearly, the analogy is extremely misleading. As we have seen repeatedly during our consideration of growth and development, individual differences, and mental health and attitudes, learning is affected by many influences, internal and external, not hinted at in the analogy.

What, then, is learning? What exactly goes on in a person's mind when he is learning something? What changes have taken place when he has learned it?

The plain truth is that we do not conclusively know; contemporary research, although illuminating, tells us that we are still far from a definitive answer to these questions. We, however, have limited understanding of the process of learning in the form of general theories, and we do know that certain ways of learning and conditions of the learner are more effective than others. Considering these topics together can tell us much about the activity of learning.

But first, let us state the essential known facts of the learning process, partly by distinguishing learning from performance.

We have learned when we are able to do something which we could not do before; moreover, learning is usually evident in fundamental behavior changes. We learn how to read, how to play a musical instrument, how to please people; but we also learn to do things in individual ways, some choosing more effective ways than others. When we do these things, our behavior has become essentially different. In this sense, learning includes improvement: We may learn to read better—with greater accuracy, fewer errors, and increased speed; when we do read better, we have learned, for our behavior has changed. Three children may learn to react to frustration; one learns to get angry, another to think and work for a solution, and another to turn away from the frustrating situation.

The amount of learning, then, is indicated both by the number of things a person can do and by the way he reacts in the learning situation.

Performance consists in doing that which has been learned; this shows what a person's learned abilities are. The professional baseball player, pianist, and typist in action are doing what they have learned and have done many times before. Performance involves previously learned responses and activities. Usually, of course, a person tries not only to perform as well as he can but also to learn, while he is performing, ways of improving his performance.

Finally, an important part of learning and performance is the development and use of our ideas. Human beings possess, to an extent no other animal does, the ability to make abstract generalizations. The acquisition and use of an idea, however, is only a more complicated example of the process we have been illustrating in extremely simple terms. We shall have much to say about the nature of abstraction and generalization, but we shall start with a consideration of theories of the basic processes that underlie all learning, from the most simple to the most complex.

THEORIES OF LEARNING

Man has always been tempted to say that certain drives are "instinctive" and that certain ideas are "innate," because when an emotion or idea has a complex and subtle origin, it is easier to say we are born with it than to trace it through the living past. But modern psychologists tend to believe that only a few drives—such as those for food, sex, and sleep—exist without being learned. As for the belief in innate ideas, John Locke, the great seventeenth-century philosopher, was in harmony with present-day thought when he stated that we are born without any ideas at all—that all ideas, from the most humble to the most exalted, are learned. The problem, then, is to discover *how* we do learn the almost infinite number of abilities that living demands of us.

The study of the processes of learning has a long and distinguished history in the Western world. Aristotle (384–322 B.C.) proposed three laws of association—those of contiguity, similarity, and contrast—which purported to explain how one idea may suggest another. In the modern era, landmarks in the study of learning were raised by men such as Locke (1632–1704), David Hartley (1714–1757), Thomas Brown (1778–1820), and, in our own time, E. L. Thorndike (1874–1949). But since we wish to stress the use of theories of learning, we shall make no attempt to summarize their historical development. Instead, we shall outline briefly the major ideas in the field today.

The two general approaches to learning in modern psychology are the associationist approach and the field-psychology approach. Various schools of psychology embrace one or the other, and there is by no means complete agreement within the groups that represent each approach—a situation further complicated by the fact that the two approaches are not mutually exclusive: Many psychologists draw upon both in their efforts to understand learning. Nevertheless, pointing out the general differences between the two approaches can illuminate the various ways in which the problems of learning can be viewed.

Association: Stimulus and Response. Many interpretations of learning—including those called *structuralism, functionalism,* and *behaviorism*—may loosely be termed associationist. American psychology has predominantly been broadly associationist and specifically behaviorist. Our present purpose, however, does not require analysis of the differences that have existed and do exist among these associationist approaches, especially since the chief differences have been partially resolved. In general, then, according to the association theory, learning takes place through the establishment of a connection between a stimulus and a response. One way of establishing a connection is through conditioning. For example, in his famous experiment, Pavlov conditioned dogs to salivate when a bell was rung by establishing a connection between the ringing of the bell and the appearance of available food. A simpler way is a direct connection such as the word papa with the adult who is the father.

Learning through association goes far beyond the establishment of simple physiological and verbal responses, however. Emotions and ideas, even very abstract ideas, may be acquired in the same way. Thus a young woman may like to wear blue because, her party dresses and traveling suits having traditionally been blue, she associates blue with festiveness. An individual may have learned to regard people with certain facial characteristics with suspicion because someone with these features once painfully tricked him. Words themselves are learned by associating them with the object or action they name or describe.

The associated or conditioned response is illustrated by the following diagram:

$$S_1 \longrightarrow R_1$$
$$S_2 \longrightarrow R_2$$
$$S_1 + S_2 \longrightarrow R_2$$
$$S_1 \longrightarrow R_2$$

To spell this out, Stimulus 1 (S_1) brings on Response 1 (R_1), and Stimulus 2 (S_2) brings on Response 2 (R_2, the conditioned response). But if S_1 and S_2 occur together to evoke R_2, S_1 will eventually come to evoke R_2, even when S_2 is withdrawn.

Another example, in terms of the young woman who favors blue, is this: S_1 is the color blue in clothes, and R_1 is putting them on just like any other clothes. S_2 is invitations to parties and chances to travel, and R_2 is the happiness such opportunities bring. $S_1 + S_2$ is the (conditioned) donning of blue for such festive occasions, which eventually causes blue clothes themselves (S_1) to evoke a happy feeling (R_2).

Similarly, children who have authoritative and domineering parents may regard all adults ($S_1 + S_2$) as stern figures and react to them shyly, submissively, or with hostility (R_2). A great deal of exposure to kind and sympathetic adults is necessary before such feelings can be overcome and the feeling that adults in general may be not such bad people after all can be established. This example, of course, underscores the large amount of work sometimes involved in reconditioning.

S_1 (adults in general) $\longrightarrow R_1$ (usual responses)
S_2 (overstrict parents) $\longrightarrow R_2$ (shyness, submissiveness, hostility)
$S_1 + S_2$ (all adults) $\longrightarrow R_2$ (shyness, submissiveness, hostility)
S_1 (adults in general) $\longrightarrow R_2$ (shyness, submissiveness, hostility)

This shows how children are conditioned to respond to adults by the behavior of their parents. In the same way, when children have been well treated by adults they will learn to respond accordingly to them.

As these illustrations suggest, any kind of learning can involve stimulus—response patterns that are not simple. But the learning of ideas sometimes involves especially complex patterns of previously acquired stimulus-response connections. Consider, for example, the number of stimulus-response relationships that might be involved in learning to work a complicated problem in algebra. First there are the simple numerical and arithmetical skills that must have been acquired through learning the correct responses to earlier stimuli. Then there is a buildup of tension directed toward finding the correct way to work the particular problem, which is released when the answer, or response, is produced.

Furthermore, stimuli and responses become linked in complex ways in actual learning. In our example, the desire to work the problem correctly has furnished a stimulus, and the pleasure in knowing the work has been done correctly has provided a response. This response will be associated with the stimulus the next time a similar problem is encountered, in addition to the complex of motives that made up the stimulus for the first problem. Thus, to say that there is a connection *between* a stimulus and a response is often misleading. It is usually better to use the word among when the stimuli and responses are many and varied in a total learning situation.

Two questions suggested by the association theory form the basis of most of the work done by psychologists who deal with it: First, what is necessary for the formation of a stimulus-response connection? Second, what determines the strength of the connection?

The answers to these questions involve the laws of association, which state that connections will be formed between two psychological processes if they occur simultaneously or in immediate succession (the concept of contiguity) and that a new stimulus will evoke a response like that evoked by some similar stimulus in the past (the concept of assimilation). But the conditions that influence the formation and strength of stimulus-response relationships also include the frequency with which a stimulus appears, its duration and liveliness, the presence or absence of alternative responses, constitutional differences, and previous habits and experiences.

In essence, then, learning by association is influenced not only by the frequency and strength of the stimulus but also by the capacity and background of the learner.

These generalized statements, of course, suggest other questions of a practical nature: How much and how frequently should a student study? What kind of good do drill and other kinds of practice do? How can we fit the stimulus (the material to be learned) to the previous learning of the student? These are questions which we shall consider later in this chapter.

Field Theories of Learning: The Gestalt Approach. The other major source of theories of learning is field psychology, which, in general, emphasizes perception in the learning process rather than response. Response is considered to be the sign that learning has taken place, not an integral part of the process. Field-psychology learning theories, then, emphasize not the stimulus-response sequence, but the context, or field (thus the name), in which the stimulus occurs and the insight derived when the relationship between stimulus and context is seen by the learner.

Although there are other schools of field psychology, the one which is best known and most influential, particularly in America, is gestalt psychology, which is to a large extent the development of a group of German psychologists, several of whom settled in America.

As we have seen, it is possible to explain fairly complex processes of learning in terms of association, but the explanation tends to become rather labored as the complexity of the learning task increases. Gestalt psychology claims to avoid this in several ways.

Gestalt psychology holds—to quote one of its most famous principles— that "the whole is greater than the sum of its parts," that is, that what is learned is greater than the sum of the individual stimulus-response patterns which have gone into it.

We can illustrate this point of disagreement with the associationists by considering the question: How does a child develop the concept of "dog"? Concept, here, is the perception of certain similarities. After a child has seen a cocker spaniel and a collie and learned that these are dogs, he may see a German shepherd and understand that this, too, is a dog, because certain perceived similarities in the three animals make for the concept of "dog." An associationist psychologist would say that the child has "generalized" a number of responses. The gestalt psychologist would agree that a number of stimulus-response patterns have been present, but he would say that the concept has been developed not just by generalizing but by grasping the grouping of stimuli and organizing these perceptions to make the concept "dog."

This simple example does not, of course, deal fully with the two theories, but it does illustrate the point that they differ chiefly in emphasis. Proponents of both would agree that learning consists in perceiving, responding, and generalizing, but they would disagree as to the relative importance of each element and as to the *way* in which understanding comes about.

But the strength of gestalt psychology lies chiefly in its clarification of the phenomenon of insight and its relationship to the formation of concepts. Learning, according to the gestaltists, is determined by the *pattern*, or *configuration*, or *gestalt*, of the stimuli. The interrelationship of the stimuli elements in the field—how they shape up as a whole—determines the character of the perceptual field. The perceptual field will be shifted or changed according to the rearrangement, or emergence of new patterns, of the stimuli. The changes in pattern can then result in new learning, including the sudden sensing of an idea or the acquiring of a solution in a flash, which is called *insight* by the gestaltists. For example, a person may be working a problem in arithmetic or a puzzle and make no progress until the solution comes all at once, so to speak. This is sometimes referred to as the "Eureka" experience.

Contrasted with the gestalt insight is the associationists' trial-and-error concept. According to this theory, the learner tries this and that until he hits on the right answer. In the one case a learner works until the elements of a situation are perceived in the right pattern and he gets the answer by sudden insight. In the other he tries until he hits upon the response.

Gestalt vocabulary generally reflects the idea that the learner reacts to a pattern, or more fully, that the whole of a situation, rather than its separate parts, determines the perceptions of the learner, the whole being considered the meaningful organization of the parts. *Closure,* for example, is used to describe the completion by the mind of a partial, or incomplete, pattern. Thus, if an outline of a house, human figure, or baseball field has a part missing, the mind "closes it"—this is the process of closure—by supplying the missing part. The mind also has "closed" because a pattern of thought has been completed, a situation has been effectively organized, a solution worked out, or a discovery made. Figure 18 gives some additional examples of the organization of a visual field into independent units.

Gestalt psychologists have caused educators, as well as other psychologists, to conceive of the problem of learning in more comprehensive terms. It has become clear that the general principles of gestalt psychology can be applied to teaching by organizing subject matter and activities into larger units or, in gestalt terms, meaningful wholes. Indeed, education is tending nowadays to use gestalt-derived ideas to a considerable extent, particularly in the teaching of reading. In the organization of the curriculum and the related teaching, the gestaltists see as most fundamental the integrated and organismic plan of presenting and studying the material. In the area of personality, the gestalt concepts are especially applicable because of the holistic and organismic structure of personality. They emphasize the pattern of all the abilities, characteristics, and manifestations of a person.

☯ *Reflect and Review*

One night a father brought home a child's book about numbers to his three-year-old son. After supper, they sat down to look at it. On succeeding pages of the book were pictures of two apples, two cats, two elephants, and two bananas. The child quickly learned to say "two" when his father pointed to the pictures; but when, on a later page, he saw three monkeys, he said "two" again. The father demonstrated the difference between groups of two and groups of three on his fingers and by reference to the pictures and to various objects in the room. Finally, the child grasped the conception of the number 2 and went around the house counting up to 2 and pointing to various objects—books, lamps, shoes, etc.

What would an associationist psychologist find interesting in this instance of

THE ACTIVITY OF LEARNING

learning? Can you reduce the learning to a pattern of stimulus and response? What would a gestalt psychologist emphasize? In what way was organization of the visual field important to the learning?

MAKING STUDY AND PRACTICE MORE EFFECTIVE

If the state of learning theory today is of more interest to us than its history, of more immediate concern still is how we, as students and teachers, can make learning take place more effectively. Every student wishes he could learn more quickly and easily, and every teacher wishes he could give his students a magic formula to do so.

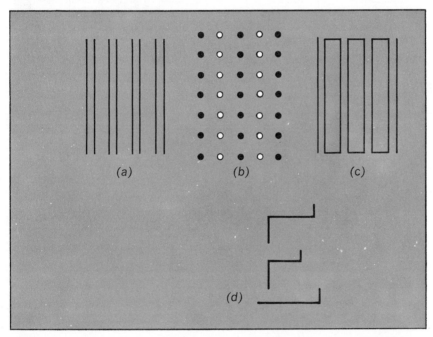

Figure 18 Gestalt laws of organization of a field *These are some of the factors which gestalt psychology identifies as those that organize a visual field into independent units. In what groups do you see each of the points, circles, and lines?*
  The figure illustrates: (a) the law of proximity. Elements close to each other tend to be seen in groups. (b) The law of similarity. With proximity equal, the rows are perceived as vertical because similar elements tend to be seen in groups. (c) The law of closed forms. Because some of the lines in (c) have been connected, we see different lines in groups. (d) The law of experience. If the viewer has experience with the Latin alphabet, he sees the three disconnected lines as a letter "E."
  Other gestalt laws are those of "good" contour and common destiny and of common movement. (Figures adapted from David Katz, Gestalt Psychology, *tr. Robert Tyson, The Ronald Press, Inc., New York, 1950, pp. 24–29.)*

There is no such formula, of course. But we are not without knowledge of some of the major factors which influence the efficiency of study and practice.

Learning by Wholes or Parts. What is the best way to memorize lines for a role in a play? Is it better to memorize each line individually, not going on to the next line until the previous one is thoroughly learned; or is it better to read a whole scene over and over, learning all the lines simultaneously? If the learning task is more complex than a simple job of memorization—for example, if one is studying history—is it better to divide a historical period into subperiods and study each one thoroughly, or to treat the material as interrelated units of topics and range freely over a wider area of time?

Both cases state the problem of part versus whole learning, and in both cases the best solution lies in compromise; indeed, a combination of the two methods, used appropriately, is better generally than either of them used inflexibly. But even when this is known, the problem of learning by parts or by wholes persistently reoccurs in class and individual study because it is hard to determine the right combination of methods. Therefore, let us identify the virtues of each method separately.

One advantage of the whole method is that it helps the learner to understand better the logical sequence of parts. When one is learning lines in a play, the whole method enables him to fix the flow of lines in his memory better. Also, when the play—or chapter, or poem, or problem—has a strong pattern of closely related parts, the whole method is consistent with the cohesive nature of the material; even if the material is loosely unified, the whole method moves toward good organization.

These examples all, of course, suggest one of the great values of the whole method: making a task a *meaningful* whole. This value is especially clear in the long run of time. A student can be oriented to a long-range learning problem in its entirety and so enabled to learn better by comprehending the main principles involved, whether this means learning the general characteristics of the entire violin concerto he is just starting to study or knowing in September what a course will cover from then until next May. Indeed, if the whole method is to be of maximum effectiveness for both student and teacher, it must be used to develop a thorough conception of the whole, as well as the interrelationship of parts.

Correspondingly, the main disadvantage of learning by parts is that the student, in learning by rote, may not see the interrelationship of individual ideas and may therefore lose or never acquire the overall theme of what is learned. Yet the part method is very useful in certain situations. Much learning involves the mastery of facts and details. Many illogical spellings in our own immensely complicated language, for example, must be committed to memory by rote. Likewise, when a series of random numbers is to be learned—say 1, 7, 4, 2, 22, etc.—the part method is essential (though it certainly facilitates learning if the learner perceives the random character of the series). In many cases, hard concentration on unrelated details may be the only effective learning method.

As we have said, however, the usual problem in any situations other than very limited ones is to combine the methods; thus the part method is a valuable adjunct to the whole method in learning play lines. The actor may read the whole scene several times; then study each line carefully, testing himself frequently, and then go back to reading or reciting the whole scene in sequence. Similarly, the student studying history may use the part method in memorizing arbitrary bits of necessary information and also use the whole method in studying broad trends and movements over a whole period. In general, then, the efficient student and the good teacher have to be able to analyze material and decide accurately when broad surveys or close attention to particulars is called for. But the age, capacity, and motivation of the student are relevant here too. The young child does not have the mental capacity to grasp large bodies of material; the same may be true of an older student of low mental capacity or low motivation. The older, more capable, and more highly motivated student will perceive large units and comprehend their interrelated structure. Such considerations, of course, make the teacher's problems especially complex in this area.

Distribution of Study and Practice Time. Does it matter how study time is distributed? When a student is committing geometry theorems to memory, for example, should he work in half-hour periods or in longer periods of sustained concentration? Should he spread the work over four days or compress it into one afternoon?

An excellent study (see Table 26) measuring the length of time required for learning when the practice periods vary in length and frequency was conducted by C. G. Knapp and W. R. Dixon; the study was made with 66 male college seniors divided into two groups of equal athletic experience and skill [Knapp and Dixon, 1950]. The object was to learn to juggle three paddle-tennis balls until 100 consecutive catches were made. The members of one group practiced 5 minutes a day and the other group 15 minutes every other day until each subject had achieved this objective. Those in the group which practiced 5 minutes per day learned in the average time of 70 minutes, and those who practiced 15 minutes every other day learned in an average of 126 minutes. Obviously, short periods of daily practice were much more effective in this learning situation.

Table 26 Effect of Variation in Length and Frequency of Practice Periods on Time Required to Learn to Make 100 Consecutive Catches in Juggling Three Balls

Group	N	Mean Number of Minutes	Significance of the Difference*
Five-minute-daily	35	69.9	Highly significant at less than .01
Fifteen minutes every other day	31	125.8	

* See Appendix.
Source: Adapted from C. G. Knapp and W. R. Dixon, "Learning to Juggle: I. A Study to Determine the Effect of Two Different Distributions of Practice on Learning Efficiency," *Research Quarterly of the American Association for Health, Physical Education and Recreation,* 21:334, 1950.

But let us divide the elements of length and frequency in order to consider each more thoroughly.

The age and the capacity of the learner should be considered in deciding on the length of practice sessions. In piano practice, for example, young beginners have less power to sustain attention than adults do. Therefore, they may find intensive practice periods of 15 or 20 minutes very effective. An adult musician, on the other hand, motivated to achieve a high degree of artistry, may find longer periods more profitable. Long periods permit the practice of the material as a whole, whereas short periods restrict practice to bit-by-bit work or to shorter pieces.

The length of the period should also vary with the nature of the material or subject matter. Short drills, in which keen interest can be maintained, are of maximum effectiveness for teaching arithmetic combinations, reading words, and various isolated facts in other comparable subjects. For instance, it has been discovered that drills about ten minutes in length can be just as effective in teaching addition-combination and multiplication tables as drills two or three times as long.

If, on the other hand, such periods are too short, the amount of time lost in beginning and stopping may be a large proportion of the total; the learner no sooner gets well started, or "warmed up," than the time is up. More technically, the student may be cut off when the period of greatest efficiency is being reached.

In fields that by their nature are best studied through careful analysis, reflective thinking, and speculation, study periods obviously should be longer than in those where drill is appropriate. One cannot, for instance, discuss well the economic implications of the First and Second World Wars by the quick-drill method; and in problem-solving situations, the students need time to collect and present facts, to reflect on ideas, and to make applications and generalizations. Of course, even in such subjects there may sometimes be bare-data study context that calls for "short and snappy" drill periods.

What of the frequency of study periods?

The intervals between study periods should be of such a length that the learner is well rested and resumes the task of study with a maximum of interest and available skill. However, if the intervals are too long, some of the acquired skill will be forgotten, and the learner will have to "warm up" to the task again because of the loss.

Thus the tendency of a learner who wishes to improve his efficiency usually should be toward more frequent periods of learning. In general, practice or study five or more times a week is probably best; once a week is usually not often enough. Again, many factors—the nature of the material to be learned, the age and capacity of the learner, teaching methods, and motivation—should be considered.

In the last analysis, of course, the issues of practice-period length and frequency have to be considered together; together they comprise the more basic issue: massed versus distributed practice.

For example, during the Second World War, United States Army soldiers spent 8 hours a day in classes for learning various codes. What about the efficiency of such massed practice—or, in this case, learning tactics—compared with a program of distributed practice? Since time was an important factor, it might be asked whether or not the soldiers could have learned more over, say, a 30-day period if they had studied the codes 5 hours a day with four 1 hour-long intervals in which they studied something else or rested. Many other distributions of time might also have proved successful. At least, what we know about massed versus distributed practice indicates that some pattern of distributed practice would have been best and might well have been tried, since it was very important at the time to use the most efficient methods.

This example is problematic, but it clearly brings us to the general problem of cramming, which is so well known that it can be treated more definitely. Cramming is a special kind of massed practice used to replace the method of studying a reasonable amount each day. It is not a basically sound method of learning, for it hampers many sound learning processes, such as thinking reflectively, maintaining a critical attitude toward references, relating new material to old, and working in a thorough and painstaking manner. In other words, it substitutes haste for care, learning by rote for reasoning and problem solving.

The student who crams usually starts with the attitude that the material is to be acquired only temporarily. This attitude is, as a rule, regrettable in itself, but it is also a contributing factor in forgetting rapidly. Yet occasions arise when it is necessary to cram. If a person gets into a situation where he must marshal many facts for a single occasion in a hurry he must, on the face of it, cram them. For instance, a lawyer collecting evidence— although he has the legal knowledge, acquired over a long period of study— must cram, with a view of remembering for a short period only, a large number of related and isolated facts pertinent to the particular case that is at hand.

However, even such cramming is not effective unless the material learned for the moment is correlated with a solid background of general principles and specific knowledge. The lawyer must correlate all his temporarily memorized facts with legal principles and precedents which he has studied carefully. If he had to cram all the details *and* all the law involved, he could not be a very effective lawyer in any case.

The very example of necessary cramming, then, supports the principle that the best way to learn is by thorough day-by-day study.

Good Basic Study Habits. In school, the highly motivated student who always knows what the assignment is, who has the necessary books, papers, and other equipment, and who keeps up with his daily work will usually be well prepared for the final test and thus will not need to cram the whole course in a few hours.

Apart from effective use of time, there are certain ways of approaching the activity of studying that lead to better results than others (see Exhibit 16); and when a student who can do well and is regularly trying to do well is failing instead, he probably lacks knowledge of these appropriate processes.

Such a student should be sure to:

1. Read and study with the primary intention of understanding the material. This requires that he not hurry to get through; instead, sustained concentration is necessary.

2. Try to single out the ideas and principles being presented; formulate the main thought and the supporting ideas in each paragraph.

3. Reread any sections of the material that are not understood; look up unfamiliar words in the dictionary, keep a list of new words, and review them occasionally.

4. Study charts, tables, and formulas carefully; generally, they will yield much knowledge to the student who will do this rather than run over them quickly, as is often done.

5. Usually, outline and/or take notes about the material being studied in class to be integrated with what is read out of class.

6. Stop occasionally while studying and try to recall the ideas and prin-

Exhibit 16   Magnitude of gains following study-skills courses

Study	Kind of Course	Size of Gain
Barbe	Reading, vocabulary, study habits; 5 hours per week for 12 weeks	About half a letter grade
Charles	Reading, general study methods, library and term-paper skills, test-taking skills, diagnostic testing; 10-week laboratory course	0.47 letter grade (?)
Kilby	Reading	15 centile points on class distribution
McDonald	Reading	2.5 percentage points
McGinnis	Reading, general study skills; 16 weeks	0.56 point in point-hour ratio (probably half a letter grade)
Mouly	Reading; 3 hours per week for one semester	0.42 letter grade
Ranson	Reading, individual testing, study habits; varying from part of one semester to three or four semesters	0.43 letter grade
Robinson	"Remedial instruction"; 21 hours over 10 weeks	1.6 percentage points
Simpson	Counseling, reading, "other skills"	0.22 to 0.30 letter grade
Smith and Wood	Reading	0.25 letter grade
Tresselt and Richlin	Lectures on study techniques, group sessions of "free expression," plus individual sessions totaling 2–30 hours	For *some* subgroups: 2.3 to 3.3 percentage points
Willey and Thomson	Reading	0.40 letter grade
Winter	Discussion of study methods for 2 hours plus 7 hours supervised study per week	54% averaged C or better vs. 23% for controls
Wittenborn	About two-thirds reading, one-third study methods; 2 hours per week for 7 weeks	About 0.40 letter grade

This table indicates the results of 14 studies of the effectiveness of courses on how to study and the development of skills needed for study. All 14 studies were of college-level courses. Note the wide variation in content. Miss Entwisle, who compiled these data, comments that the studies vary widely in the degree to which intelligence and motivation are controlled. Gains are largest, however, for voluntary courses, in which motivation is presumably high. Although the gains in grade achievement (generally calculated over a matched control group) are small, the fact that they are uniformly positive is notable. (Adapted from Doris R. Entwisle, "Evaluations of Study-skills Courses—A Review," *Journal of Educational Research*, 53:249, 1960. Bibliographical citations for studies included are given in full by Miss Entwisle.)

ciples that have already been presented; this is both test and practice; then, skim over the material again and restudy important points that were not recalled.

7. Study a number of different sources. Different points of view add vividness to a subject which is missed when only one source is consulted.

Finally, there is probably nothing so effective as review to ensure that what has been learned will not be forgotten. Effective review can improve learning from about twenty-five to about seventy-five per cent, depending upon the number of reviews and their spacing after learning, as experiments have shown.

1. The first reviewing (and here timing enters the picture again) should usually be done a day or two after the original learning. The advantage of such timing is that it enables the student to rebuild the knowledge structure at a point when forgetting is very rapid and beyond which the material will often have to be relearned.

2. The second reviewing can take place after an interval two or three times as long as the first. Two reviews thus spaced generally improve retention more than 50 per cent.

3. The value of reviewing can be increased if the material is related to other fields of knowledge. In reviewing history, for example, the influence of geography and economics on historical events can help cast these events in a multidimensional light. This can provide an integrated "core" of what might otherwise be random pieces of learning.

☯ Reflect and Review

Esther, George, and Polly are all faced with important specific learning problems. Tony wants to learn how to juggle three balls. He has no deadline to meet and wants to use a comfortable but effective procedure. George is going to take a test on the Revolutionary period in American history in 3 days. George feels that he has kept up fairly well on the daily assignments. However, he wants to review thoroughly and do as well on the test as possible. Polly, an amateur actress in the local Little Theatre, has been cast in a long leading role for the next play. The director has asked that the cast know their lines at the end of 2 weeks, so Polly must begin memorizing now.

Would you recommend that these three students approach their learning tasks differently? Or would the same process of learning work for all three? Why? Consider particularly the use of the whole method or the part method or combinations of the whole-and-part idea, the distribution of study time, and the length of the learning periods.

INTERNAL AND EXTERNAL CONDITIONS THAT INFLUENCE LEARNING

Imagine a student trying to study English grammar while his eyes burn from lack of sleep, while a trip-hammer clatters in the street outside or the temperature soars to 100 degrees, or while his pulse quickens from stimulants or lags from depressants. Clearly, both internal and external conditions, as well as learning methods and study habits, influence the learner's efficiency.

Many questions suggest themselves in connection with this topic. Is a teacher justified in saying "My students are so worn out by 2:30 that I can't accomplish a thing after that"? Is a student justified in saying "I can study only when I have complete quiet" or "I need coffee to help me study for my final exam tomorrow"?

Let us consider the effects on learning efficiency of fatigue, discomfort, and stimulants and depressants.

Actual Fatigue versus a Feeling of Fatigue. Actual fatigue has set in when no matter how hard a person tries, his learning or performance is declining; its cause is toxins which develop in the body because of the expenditure of energy.

Actual fatigue is sometimes called mental or physical, but usually, actual physical and mental fatigue are not independent of each other. In reading, for example, the mind is in use, but so are the eyes, which make hundreds of movements and get tired, thus reducing the efficiency of reading. Also, the reader usually holds the book and maintains a fairly constant body position; consequently, various body muscles get tired, dull pains are felt, and efficiency is further reduced.

As a whole, surveys that have used arithmetic, memory, and other tests to determine the efficiency of children through the school day have shown an overall small increase in efficiency from the beginning until midmorning of the school day. More specifically, though the results hardly warrant charting a precise course of efficiency, such surveys have shown clearly a general tendency for efficiency to increase slightly during the first half of the morning and to be maintained at an even level until the last hour of the school day, when a slight decline sets in. The first and last hours of the school day are thus shown to be the least efficient.

The fact that changes in basic efficiency during the school day are slight—and particularly the fact that the decline in students' true learning capacity in the afternoon is slight—strongly indicates that actual fatigue is not an important factor in the decline in learning that takes place. In a practical sense, the teacher *does* have to contend with considerably decreasing efficiency on the part of his students and on the part of himself also. In the typical schoolroom the teacher not only finds it a good deal harder to interest students as dismissal time nears but also finds it harder to maintain his own alertness and interest toward the end of the school day.

What causes this, if not actual fatigue?

Often we feel fatigued but actually are not; in many situations, how we feel is not a true indication of our energy reserves. A bowler may say he is so tired he can hardly pull on his bowling shoes, then start the evening with a strike, forget his tiredness, and bowl avidly all evening. Children may seem tired in class but then forget their supposed fatigue when an interesting movie is shown. Or a feeling of fatigue may cause older students to be less efficient, unless the circumstances of the schoolroom impel them to work at top efficiency: If they are placed in a test situation at the end of the day, they perform about as well as at any other time.

But, to develop this last example, the usual control during the school day is not so rigorous as that of a test situation; as the day passes, a mind-set or mental expectation develops for after-school activities, and the student experiences lagging interest, restlessness, and a feeling of tiredness resulting directly from all this. This feeling, incidentally, seems to be accelerated in the individual by the drop in classroom morale that occurs because everyone is having the same experiences.

The teacher's solution to this eminently practical problem lies in arranging his program so that the students will be willing to work more zealously during the last hour when it seems harder to concentrate and will thereby offset the usual letdown.

This necessitates not lessening the amount of work in the school day but getting it away from the sameness that causes a sense of monotony. When the work is unvaried and thus uninteresting, the student gets bored. Different courses call for different activities; if the schedule is arranged with a view to varying the activities, boredom and the feeling of fatigue will be minimized and efficiency increased.

This procedure involves not just the last hour but the whole day, for the feeling of fatigue characteristic of the last hour can pervade a classroom at any time. Thus, during the whole school day, subjects that involve merely reading and reciting should be alternated with those which involve some physical activity.

But the context extends even further: The problem of sameness and boredom is not limited to the program of a single day; rather, it applies day after day. A student wearies of doing the same things every day. Scheduling the tasks and activities to achieve variety during the day helps avoid monotony, but new interests also, need to be aroused periodically throughout the school year.

There are, of course, many variations on this theme. If a student is poorly adjusted to schoolwork because he has not the ability for it or because the teacher is too severe a taskmaster, he may react by feeling tired or lack-adaisical, as teachers, seeing the results of the feeling, are inclined to call it. If the student is overstimulated by too much activity and too many sensory impacts in the form of television programs, music, or noise, he may also feel fatigued.

Also, an exceptionally enthusiastic teacher occasionally overstimulates whole groups of his students in such a way as to produce a feeling of fatigue. (Because in some instances this is so, one psychologist has suggested, rather facetiously, that it might be desirable for students to have one dull, uninteresting teacher during the day. Then they would pay only indifferent attention, their minds would wander aimlessly, and they would have a period of needed rest.)

Finally, at all ages, serious problems attributed to actual physical and mental fatigue are often due to such other causes as fear, repressions, anger, and the like, all of which have emotion at their core. For example, when a student is working hard at the end of a course to avoid failing, or even when a housewife is preparing a big dinner, emotions typically cause much more wear and tear than the physical and mental fatigue induced by the activity.

The important business of dealing with such feelings of fatigue and the problems they engender should not, however, blind us to the presence of chronic actual fatigue. If, after rest, recreation, or a night's sleep, a person still usually feels tired, there may be something basically wrong. In other words, chronically felt fatigue is a danger signal.

A person may be chronically fatigued because he is ill or just because he is poorly nourished. His diet may be too starchy and sugary, or deficient in vitamins and minerals, or both. Or it may be too light: The Iowa Breakfast Studies have shown that the omission of breakfast results in a loss of energy and efficiency. Thus a student who has not had a breakfast at all or has had just a hasty bite or two will be fatigued and, as a result, restless and distracted by discomfort the latter part of the morning.

Fatigue is also caused by physical work because the activity of the muscles produces fatigue toxins. It is difficult, however, to fatigue a nerve. Even if it is stimulated again and again, its efficiency decreases very little. Furthermore, while researches have definitely identified the fatigue toxins resulting from muscular work, they have not clearly identified any resulting from the activity of nerve tissues. It is possible, however, that fatigue toxins affect the connections of the nerves, or the synapses, and thus do reduce mental efficiency.

The nature of the school routine makes it improbable that many children will be physically fatigued in class, but when special circumstances such as poor parental control or getting up very early in the morning to work make fatigue a problem for a particular student, the teacher should be ready to adjust the routine accordingly.

In the classroom, as elsewhere, sleepiness is the most obvious symptom of fatigue. Another important one, of course, is lack of attention. Thus, it takes energy to attend to the proceedings of a class; and if a child is fatigued, he will tend to avoid expending that energy. He may become worried, tense, and fretful, and he may cry easily. Fumbling with objects, as well as other acts displaying poor motor coordination, is also a symptom of fatigue.

A student should not be scolded for prevailing evidence of fatigue, for this is likely to make him worse rather than better. Careful observation supplemented by direct discussion, sympathetic in tone, is the best initial step to take for finding out why he is tired. The home and school should cooperate in this exploratory procedure, which may lead to fairly simple plans by which the student may be considerably helped.

Most basically, however, the child, like anyone else suffering from what may be chronic actual fatigue or may be an intense psychosomatic feeling of fatigue, needs a thorough physical examination.

The Schoolroom: Comfort and Efficiency. From industry we learn that comfort affects achievement. For example, A. T. Poffenberger, when he studied factory output, heat, and ventilation, found that in unventilated factories the output during the hottest weeks averaged 14.5 per cent less than that in the coldest weeks, while in ventilated factories the output dropped only 8 per cent [Poffenberger, 1942, p. 170]. Conceivably, if the factories had been cooled to comfortable temperatures, there would have been no decline in output.

An early study by E. L. Thorndike and others showed that for a period of 4 hours a day on 5 consecutive days a group of adults did as well on tests involving mental multiplication and finding words opposite in meaning to a given list of words when the temperature was 86 degrees and the humidity 80 per cent as did a group in ideal temperature and humidity [Thorndike et al., 1916]. It is quite probable, however, that over a long period an uncomfortable thermal environment in a usual classroom rather than an experimental situation will affect the learning and general behavior adversely. We do not have any recent studies showing clearly how temperature and humidity affect the activities of students. There is a growing body of evidence from the business and industrial world that morale is improved by good temperature and humidity control, that productivity is increased, and that absenteeism and turnover are lessened. A student or adult worker cannot be highly efficient when he is under the strain and distraction of uncomfortable temperatures. Apart from consideration of accomplishments, comfortable temperatures and humidity are a sufficient objective in themselves.

The levels of comfort in temperatures and humidity depend on the season of the year and the activity of those in a given situation. On a hot summer day when the outside temperature is over 90 degrees, a room temperature of 78 degrees with some movement of the air will be comfortable. A room temperature of 78 degrees in winter is uncomfortably warm. In a gymnasium or playroom a temperature of about 60 degrees is comfortable, for light physical activity a temperature of about 66 degrees is pleasant, but for sedentary situations a temperature of about 72 degrees is comfortable. Dress, too, is a factor which determines what temperatures are comfortable. When the children are on the floor some of the time, as in kindergarten, a temperature of 75 degrees may be advisable. Ideally the humidity should be 40 to 50, but a range from 30 to 60 is satisfactory. The teacher who is conscious of thermal comfort will try to keep his pupils and himself in a pleasant thermal environment.

Also central among external conditions are light and noise. If a student has to squint or blink because of too strong or badly directed light, or if he is disturbed by thunderous or shrieking noises, he cannot work efficiently: the unnecessary strain drains energy that should go into his learning.

But these are examples of very bad conditions, indeed. What has been determined about the best?

Lighting in the classroom should be uniform; any shadows or direct sunlight in the room will have a fatiguing effect. Lighting should also be of adequate intensity; more specifically, window shades and artificial lighting are properly adjusted when the light intensity is about 15 foot-candles (the light provided by 15 candles 1 foot away from the book or paper being studied).

The sound of a busy classroom is not disturbing. However, outside noises, such as the sirens of ambulances and fire trucks and the screeching of brakes, can upset the students; some become satisfactorily inured, but others are continuously disturbed if such sounds prevail. When extreme noise makes it hard to conduct class, it is best to wait until the disturbance subsides.

Drugs and Learning Efficiency. It is not likely that teachers will try to improve their students' mental efficiency by chemical means. However, man is continuously in search of some food, drink, or drug that will increase and sharpen mental powers and processes, and children have been involved in such efforts. A number of years ago it was reported that some physicians were using glutamic acid, an extract from wheat germ, in efforts to increase the mental capacity of growing children and that they had achieved, it seemed, small to substantial increases in IQ with all the children taking it. The theory advanced to explain this purported increase in IQ was that the glutamic acid promoted overall growth and thereby improved the neurological structures.

Careful analysis has cast doubt on the validity of these reported results, and no subsequent evidence has supported them. Therefore, we must state that we are no further along in the use of food, drink, or drug to create human mental gold, as it were, than we ever have been.

But are there any harmless drugs or stimulants that can temporarily increase a person's learning power? This is an important question to teachers; for some students, as well as other people, use alcoholic and non-alcoholic beverages, tobacco, or drugs because they feel they can thus be stimulated or relaxed. They may feel refreshed from the caffeine in a cup of tea or coffee or in certain soda-fountain drinks. They may feel stimulated physically and mentally from whiskey, wine, or beer. They may smoke cigarettes when under stress as a means of relieving their tensions. They may periodically take "energizers" to quicken their physical and mental processes, or "tranquilizers" for just the opposite reason, to be toned down.

Elementary school students are further from the problems of the effects of chemicals on personal development and learning ability than high school and college students, but they do have some experience with coffee, tea, cola drinks, and tobacco. Therefore, when questions are raised about possible effects (especially ill effects) of drugs and stimulants on students—and such questions often are raised—all teachers should know the answers.

Stimulant Drugs: Light and Heavy. The most common and probably the most harmless stimulant drug is caffeine, of which tea and coffee contain 2 or 3 grains per cup. What is its effect?

Various amounts of caffeine have different effects on physical abilities, it has been found. For instance, doses not exceeding 3 grains increase the speed of typists, and their accuracy is not impaired; but doses between 3 and 6 grains both reduce speed and impair accuracy.

Small doses of caffeine, such as obtained from a cup of coffee, also stimulate the mental processes, the effect here becoming noticeable about an hour after the dose is taken and persisting for several hours. Large doses persist even longer. The period of stimulation from a small dose is apparently followed by no period of inefficiency; the period of stimulation from a large dose, however, is followed by a period in which efficiency drops below normal.

One or two cups of coffee increases the pulse rate about 5 to 10 per cent and the blood pressure about 5 per cent. Memory and the ability to add figures are both slightly improved, lending support to the generally accepted findings that caffeine stimulates the higher mental processes.

Relatedly, the evidence also indicates that caffeine reduces boredom and sleepiness and tends to increase attentiveness and "peppiness."

Thus caffeine used moderately seems to do its adult user no harm, as a rule. But let us now consider some drugs of which this cannot be said.

During the past decade there has been a large increase in the use of highly stimulating drugs to keep awake and give oneself energy—drugs with such slang names as "bennies," "thrill pills," "speedballs," and "pep pills." These drugs once contained benzedrine sulfate. This was followed by the amphetamines, of which Dexedrine is one.

All these drugs overcome sleepiness and produce a feeling of well-being in most people right after they are taken. Also, they temporarily improve mental functions and sensorimotor abilities. But they all have aftereffects— and some of them may have serious aftereffects—because, essentially, they do not give new energy; instead, they have the effect of "whipping a tired horse," as it were.

Thus "pep pills" are sometimes taken by college students, particularly when they are cramming for examinations and must stay awake to study for longer hours, and they are effective for that purpose. But they have such physiological aftereffects as headache, fatigue, insomnia, and poor circulation, and these conditions sometimes become so severe that consequent illnesses and blackouts require hospitalization.

In essence, then, the use of strong drugs to increase mental and physical powers results, in the end, in lowered efficiency. They may give a person who is depressed or apparently without energy a temporary feeling of exhilaration or renewed liveliness or may help a person drive an automobile all night. But it is a sound rule that there are no chemical methods for supplementing the energies of normally healthy people. Stimulants or depressants may promise to do so, but eventually exact a high penalty from the person who believes the promise. In most cases he would do much better to ask himself, how can I avoid or change this situation that makes me seem to need this outside help?

Tobacco. Teachers of adolescent students frequently hear them say that smoking a cigarette is a good way to ease tensions. The prevalence of faculty smoking rooms in new school buildings indicates, too, that many teachers find a cigarette relaxing after a wearing class. Is there any truth to this? What are the effects of tobacco on the mind and body?

Studies have repeatedly revealed that grade school boys who smoke receive lower marks than do boys who do not smoke, and this has been interpreted to indicate that smoking affects the interest and learning ability of these boys so much that their scholarship suffers appreciably.

This interpretation would be justified if the smoker and nonsmoker were the same in every respect except for the smoking habit, but this is not the case. Schoolboys who are nonsmokers generally have higher IQs, come from better homes, and show fewer behavior-problem tendencies; in other words, the smokers and nonsmokers differ in the related factors that most basically influence scholarship. Therefore, the difference in school achievement would not seem to be attributable to the use of tobacco—an argument that is confirmed by the fact that in high school there is less difference between the scholarship of smokers and nonsmokers and in college there is even less difference.

Smoking does have a negative effect on mental and physical efficiency, but the effect is a very small one. On the other hand, any benefits in the form of "relaxation" come from the symbolic value of smoking, not from its chemical effects.

Alcohol. The reputation of alcohol is somewhat different from that of tobacco. No one who has seen the staggering and heard the incoherent speech of an intoxicated man would argue that large intakes of alcohol improve efficiency. Some people, however, assert that a small amount of alcohol stimulates their mental and physical processes; a drink is sometimes referred to as a "pick-me-up."

This is wrong. Alcohol is actually a depressant rather than a stimulant. Any stimulation felt after drinking alcohol is strictly illusory and comes from its tendency to relax a person and weaken his inhibitions. Relatedly, any amount of alcohol interferes with mental and physical efficiency to some extent, for most people. For example, H. L. Hollingsworth tested a number of subjects for mental ability, steadiness, and coordination under various circumstances: when they did no drinking, when they drank a considerable amount of water, when they drank beer that contained no alcohol, when they drank about three bottles of 2.75 beer, when they drank six to nine bottles of 2.75 beer, and when they ate a heavy meal [Hollingsworth, 1924]. The eating and drinking were done at noon on a number of days, and tests were made during the morning and the afternoon periods. Then results of the afternoon tests were compared with those of the morning tests.

The experiment showed a close correlation between alcohol consumption and loss of efficiency, particularly in the area of steadiness. In general, losses in efficiency varied between 5 and 15 per cent, according to the amount of alcohol consumed. Toward four o'clock, the end of the afternoon period, the subjects began to regain efficiency because the effect of the alcohol was wearing off.

It was also discovered in the experiment that individual resistance to the effects of alcohol varied according to ability; in general, those of the highest mental and physical abilities were influenced least by alcohol. It appeared, too, that efficiency could be better maintained if the subject was highly motivated and tried to fight off the effects of the alcohol. In other words, if a subject did not "let go," the injurious effects were much less marked.

Buttressed by others as it is, the Hollingsworth experiment shows clearly that gains in efficiency from alcohol are nonexistent and that, on the contrary, even a small amount of alcohol may perceptibly decrease performance.

Body Chemistry. While we are considering chemical intake and its effects on the feelings and mental efficiency we ought to consider the biochemistry of the individual. Mental development and brain function involve the body chemistry—the hormones, the vitamins, the enzymes, and many others. Thus in turn the endocrine glands such as the thyroid and the pituitary are involved because of the hormones they secrete and the influence they have on the chemical balance of the body. People differ greatly in their biochemistry, which in turn accounts in part for differences in mental competence and personality.

Probably the simplest example of chemical effects on human development is the case of the cretin who becomes greatly stunted in his development because of thyroid malfunction which results in a deficiency of thyroxin. Some cretins respond to artificial supplements of thyroxin with greatly improved physical growth and accompanying improvement in learning capacity. Some cretins do not respond very well to the thyroxin treatment, thus indicating that there probably is another chemical disorder also which is not known.

If there is malfunction of other endocrine glands so the hormone supply is either in shortage, in surplus, or in wrong combinations, the human suffers both physically and mentally. Inadequate or disordered enzyme function has the same effect as does vitamin deficiency. The necessity of having the right sugar supply and of its being controlled is evident in the case of diabetes. Insulin treatment is needed, and if it is not received, many diabetics will go into a coma and die.

Special mention should be made of oxygen. The brain, for example, makes great demand on the oxygen supply. Although the brain constitutes only about two per cent of the total body weight, it uses about twenty-five per cent of the oxygen consumed by the body. This indicates that a very large free-flowing supply of blood is needed to provide oxygen and irrigate the brain thoroughly.

The blood supply is restricted when the arteries harden and the openings become smaller. This reduction of blood supply is not common for young people but occurs more frequently in middle and especially in older age. The brain deteriorates when this happens, and, correspondingly, learning capacity declines.

Of significance to all ages is the effect of the emotions on body chemistry and vice versa. We are particularly interested in chemistry and learning. If a child is under stress and unhappy, his learning is affected adversely. Clearly, his motivation will be greatly reduced. The emphasis in today's education on the need for happy children and youth in school probably has a sound basis in the relation of the emotions to body chemistry and the effect of both on learning.

In this connection it can be stated, because of its relation to learning efficiency, that poor mental health and serious mental illness often have their genesis in the body chemistry. In other words, if a person's body chemistry is normal, he probably will not be mentally ill. In terms of all this, it is conceivable that learning effectiveness is influenced greatly by the chemistry of the body.

☯ Reflect and Review

In an experiment on mental fatigue and the effects of changing tasks, Miss Arai devoted 11 consecutive hours for several days to the strenuous mental arithmetic of memorizing four-place numbers and then finding their product mentally. After 11 hours, it took her about twice as long to get an answer, and the amount of error was slightly higher. Her efficiency at the end of 11 hours was thus about fifty per cent of what it was at the beginning of the period.

At the end of each 11-hour period of mental multiplication, Miss Arai also memorized 40 German words. She was about three-fourths as efficient in memorizing German after 11 hours of mental multiplication as she was when she memorized the words under ordinary circumstances, that is, without first spending 11 hours in mental multiplication. Thus, her loss of efficiency in memorizing words after doing 11 hours of arithmetic was 25 per cent.

What accounted for the difference in loss of efficiency between the two tasks?

Does this experiment indicate that schoolwork induces little actual mental fatigue?

How might a teacher capitalize on the principle demonstrated by this experiment?

SUMMARY

Learning is not a filling-up process; correspondingly, teaching is not a pouring-in procedure. Learning is a change in responding that involves abilities, emotions, attitudes, and all other behavior that results from the activity of the learner.

Performance consists basically in doing or repeating what one has already learned.

Learning by association, in one of its simplest forms, is indicated by associating a name with a person or object. Such association is termed associated response.

In the case of the conditioned response, S_1 brings on R_2 when it is associated with S_2, which normally brings on R_2. Thus a child who has not been disturbed by darkness can be conditioned to fear the dark if his mother, when putting the child to bed, shows fear of the dark. The child has learned to associate fear with darkness where formerly he had reacted in a simple adaptive way.

In the field or gestalt theories of learning, the emphasis is on the perception of the field or pattern of the stimuli—the concept of the whole unit or problem.

The sudden perception of relationship or organization of elements in a situation which leads to comprehension or solution of a problem is termed insight.

The gestaltists hold that the mind completes or closes a concept, pattern, or problem by supplying the missing parts; this is called closure.

Gestalt psychology strengthens the trend in modern education to correlate, integrate, and unify bodies of knowledge. It encourages teaching to abandon the memorization of isolated facts and to deal instead with comprehensive structures of meanings.

The practice of studying parts or wholes is influenced by a number of factors: the difficulty of the material, the degree of its meaningfulness, the capacity or maturity of the learner, and the way it logically divides into meaningful parts. Also, a combination of part and whole methods is probably the best way to learn most material.

It has been demonstrated many times that distributing one's work into several periods results in more learning than does devoting the same amount of time to a single long period. In general, the ambitious learner will do best if he distributes his study time throughout the day and also throughout the week, but the total time devoted to one's learning activity should be substantial. Cramming will help the learner to acquire quickly various materials that serve a temporary use.

Good study methods are essentially thorough, painstaking work procedures. They include the careful study and understanding of all the printed material, as well as going over it by keeping notes and recalling the content both by self-recitation and by review.

Conditions within and without the learner influence his learning either positively or negatively. Fatigue of the eyes from sustained reading and of the muscles from continued sitting reduces learning efficiency. Ordinarily the usual student does not suffer from fatigue during the school day. The basic problem is usually not actual fatigue but a drop in interest because of monotony and letdown in anticipation of dismissal. Still, there are children who do suffer from chronic fatigue because of emotional problems, faulty nutrition, and too little sleep; they are therefore not utilizing fully their school experiences.

A schoolroom should be comfortable, so as not to drain the student's energy from his school activities. Distracting noises, weak or overbright light, and uncomfortable temperatures are the usual negative conditions that need correction.

People take pills and drink beverages to help them emotionally and mentally. In general, there is a net loss from such use, with the possible exception of a moderate intake of caffeine as found in coffee and tea. There is hope of finding a chemical that will increase the mental growth of children, but to date the results are not encouraging. Body chemistry clearly is involved in the development of and in maintaining normal physical and mental growth, and has definite influence on the capacity to learn.

SUGGESTED READING

Burton, William H.: *The Guidance of Learning Activities*, 3d ed., Appleton-Century-Crofts, Inc., New York, 1962. A practical treatment of learning in school situations. Covers a wide range of topics, and the reader will find a discussion of most concepts that are relevant to teaching and learning effectively.

Clement, Stanley L.: "Seven Principles of Learning," *Clearing House*, 36:23–26, 1961. Clement presents a number of learning concepts and suggests specific ways of helping students to learn. This article is sound and practical.

Travers, Robert M. W.: *Essentials of Learning*, The Macmillan Company, New York, 1963. Discusses and explains many of the basic topics in learning. Useful for obtaining additional explanations of learning concepts. Orientation is toward education.

CHAPTER 14
MOTIVATION AND
REINFORCEMENT

Suppose that a student wants very much to make a good grade on a test in history to raise his status in the eyes of others as well as himself. He studies thoroughly for it, makes an A, is inwardly delighted, and is praised by others. He then begins to think about the next test and determines to make an A on it too.

Suppose, alternatively, that a man has been embarrassed over the years because all his friends ride horses and he cannot. One day, after someone has made fun of him about this, he makes a date for a riding lesson. He goes to it, but is painfully thrown from his horse. He will think twice before he gets in the saddle again.

These situations exemplify an essential fact about the process of learning. The learner becomes motivated to learn something in order to fulfill one or more of his goals. After motivation comes the activity of learning, leading to either success or failure. He who succeeds associates gratification with his particular learning activity and therefore the learning is strengthened; he who fails associates a lack of gratification and therefore the learning is weakened. In other words, success and the pleasure that comes with it constitute positive reinforcement; failure and attendant displeasure constitute negative reinforcement.

Thus the three basic steps in the learning process are motivation, activity (which we discussed on its own terms in Chapter 13), and reinforcement. It can be put this way: We want something, we do something, and we get something.

This description, of course, fails to state several things about the learning process. First, many other mental and emotional factors complicate the pattern in any actual learning situation. Second, usually activity is inseparably linked to the other steps; and also, as our opening examples have suggested, steps 1 and 3 actually overlap in most learning. That is, success and failure in learning compound themselves, because they not only reinforce—positively or negatively—one piece of learning but also determine the motivation for the next learning.

THE ANATOMY OF MOTIVATION

When a person wants to learn something, he does it much more effectively than when he does not want to or is indifferent. This is clear when, for example, we see children mechanically and perfunctorily go through the motions of studying without learning very much, because they have little interest or have an active disinterest in what they are studying and thus have little motivation for learning it. But what are some of the factors that influence people to be eager for, indifferent to, or disposed against learning?

Willingness and Set. In learning, as elsewhere, motivation is fundamentally dependent on an individual's needs and drives. They produce willingness to learn, in general. But further, these needs and drives, acting in specific combination, focus the willingness. When a person wants to learn a thing, other activities do not attract his efforts. Instead, there is a buildup in him of expectancy and then tension, which comprise a set for learning this one thing. This causes a mobilization of energy, which is expended when the particular learning is accomplished. When the effort is successful, the tension is relieved also; failure or inability to act generally brings frustration, because the tension is not released.

Readiness. If the effort is to be successful, the person must be not only willing and set but also ready to perform the learning task in question, and readiness requires certain capacities and abilities. Thus a student is ready for reading, arithmetic, baseball, or bowling only when his capacities and abilities are adequate for it; the higher the capacities and abilities, the greater the readiness. On the other other hand—and this completes the definition of readiness—the capacities and abilities may advance so much that the learning activity becomes so easy as to be boring and therefore not challenging. For example, when a child is ready to read, he should be taught; if learning to read is delayed too long, he may be less motivated than he was when he was first ready.

Aspiration Level. Aspiration level involves both the difficulty of the learning tasks a person is willing to undertake and the amount of work he is willing to try to do on them in a given time. In short, aspiration level defines the specific learning goals a person sets for himself.

Aspiration level itself is defined fairly consistently by capacity and ability and, relatedly, by previous success or failure (see Exhibit 17). In general, there is a tendency to select work that by these standards is appropriately hard—not too easy, not too difficult. Success or failure is the more dynamic element here because of strong ego involvement, success being accompanied by the glow of a sense of personal worth and failure causing feelings of inadequacy.

Thus, for the single lesson, for the individual day, for the term's work, or for a career, the student's aspiration level is particularly influenced by successes and failures, as is confirmed by the following generalized findings of numerous experiments on how students' relate to learning goals:

1. In general, what a student plans to do and does to educate himself is fairly likely to provide success, being based on sound knowledge of his

Exhibit 17 Goal-setting for a reading task: discrepancy between goal set and previous achievement

	−5	0	+5	+10	+15	+20
Success group			+	+++ +++ +++ +	+	
Failure group	+	+ +	+ +	+ + + + +	+	+

Amount of discrepancy

Pauline Sears studied the aspiration levels set by 36 children between the ages of nine and twelve; 12 of the children had experienced success in reading and arithmetic, 12 had experienced failure in both subjects, and 12 had experienced success in reading but failure in arithmetic (this last group is omitted from the table). The children were asked to perform a series of timed reading and arithmetic tasks, each time being told their speed in seconds on the last task and then being asked to estimate their speed on the next task. It was found (see table) that the group which had experienced consistent success in these subjects generally set their goals just a little higher than their last score. The group which had experienced consistent failure, on the other hand, tended to set erratic and unrealistic goals for themselves. The scale on the bottom of the table represents a measure of discrepancy between performance on one task and the goal set for the next task. Each cross represents one subject's goal-setting. Note that the success group's goals are clustered just above their last performance, while the failure group's goals are scattered above and below the realistic range.

In a later phase of the experiment, Dr. Sears induced experimental feelings of success and failure into each group by telling them that they were doing well or poorly. She found that all groups tended, when they felt they were succeeding, to set more realistic goals, and when they felt they were failing, to set erratic goals. (Adapted from Pauline S. Sears, "Levels of Aspiration in Academically Successful and Unsuccessful Children," *Journal of Abnormal and Social Psychology*, 35:511, 1940.)

capacities and abilities. Weak students tend to take courses in which they can succeed; excellent students tend to select studies appropriate to their better minds.

2. The experience of success with tasks usually results in raising the level of aspiration. If a student has succeeded in doing nine problems in a given time, he is likely to be prompted to say, "I think that I'll try 10 this time"; that is, his success encourages him to try harder, to keep "going and growing." In this connection, a large success usually results in a large increase in aspiration level, a small success in a small increase.

3. Failure usually leads to three kinds of reactions in the choosing of goals:

a. Avoiding the situation which has led to failure. As we have seen, those who do poorly in school drop out much more often than those who are successful.

b. Lowering the aspiration level. The student who has aspired for A's but gotten C's learns from experience to accept C's, becomes pleasantly surprised by an occasional B, and no longer expects an A.

c. Maintaining levels of aspiration inconsistent with failure: raising the goals or keeping them the same. Here we have the students who do only fair work in their courses but have high vocational ambitions. Aware that many colleagues do better work than they, they still aspire to professions which require a high standard of school success which they simply cannot meet.

Leonard Worell has even found that realistic aspiration levels are valid predictors of school success [Worell, 1959]. In a study of 421 liberal arts college students, he compared aspiration levels, as determined by answers on a questionnaire, with previous academic records and present performance. He found that students who set realistic goals for themselves, in terms of their past work, tended to be successful academically, while those who set unrealistic goals tended to be less successful.

Incidentally, goals are generally most motivating when they *are* set by those who must reach them. For instance, it has been discovered that one of the best ways of motivating factory workers is to let them have a hand in setting production quotas and that when they are consulted about the hiring of new personnel, they generally make good recommendations and then are motivated to help the new men succeed. Likewise, in the school, if the students have a voice in deciding on learning tasks, they will be more highly motivated to reach the goals set than if the planning has been completely done by the teacher. Indeed, this is the essential value of having students share responsibility in decision making in school.

Attitudes. People's attitudes toward learning situations—their feelings for or feelings against them—affect learning correspondingly. This is because attitudes are a basic component of motivation. More specifically, being in a situation which he likes motivates the learner to do what is necessary to sustain that situation, that is, to learn; being in a situation he finds unpleasant disposes him not to learn.

But social attitudes also affect motivation in this way: There are many areas, such as politics and religion, in which the reception of ideas and facts is toned by an individual's social attitudes; the mind works selectively, and a person is more receptive to information that supports his point of view and less receptive to that which is opposed to it. In short, we are motivated by our attitudes to learn and remember that which confirms them. This is important in education because many topics come up, and must come up, in school in which students and teachers are thus emotionally involved.

Anxiety. At present there is much interest in the idea that anxiety positively affects learning. Importantly, some writers seem to regard anxiety as a synonym for the strong concern associated with working hard to learn. In this way they tend to make anxiety an element of motivation. Is this valid?

It is true, of course, that when one is working hard to learn, he is in a state of pressure and tension because of the concentration of energy required for this activity. But this is not anxiety in the true sense, for, as we have seen, anxiety actually is a state of pervasive fearfulness and overconcern. As such, anxiety is not conducive to effective learning; rather, it usually interferes with learning, diffusing the energy which must be channeled through strong motivation if learning is to be effective. Thus anxious students are not task-oriented; indeed, they have interfering interests that prevent them from developing drive for doing their learning tasks at all or that make them tend to be erratic in their goals and in their efforts to reach their goals. Also, unlike the temporary tension associated with normal concern to get the work done, anxiety, with its core of general fear, is not dispelled by the learning effort.

In addition, since rigidity is an important part of anxiety, anxious students lack the flexibility and facility needed not only in imaginative and creative thinking but also in reasoning, as is demonstrated by findings that anxious students sometimes do better than nonanxious students in simple mechanical performances but regularly do less well in complex problem solving.

The anxious learner therefore is in the situation of striving to dispel painful tension—the result of his nagging fear—and at the same time having his efforts frustrated by the very tension which he seeks to dispel. The symptoms of rigidity and diffuse efforts reflect this contradiction; they stem from the fact that the learner is being asked to dispel tension by means that are continually weakened by his own anxiety and uncertainty.

Finally, fearful and rigid as they are, anxious students have poor personal relationships with their fellows and with their teachers. This is an especially important fact in today's classroom, where group activities based on the emotionally uninhibited communications that flow from good personal relationships are used to motivate much learning.

◑ *Reflect and Review*

What is called the stereotyped mind tends to think in definite categories—yes or no, all or none, this is so and this is not—while the nonstereotyped mind tends to be receptive to rich, varying, and even conflicting concepts. R. E. Egner and A. J. Obelsky studied these contrasting mentalities and their relation to learning in the following way: They tested a group of 218 college students with an inventory of 100 "beliefs," of which 60 were expressions of stereotypes and 40 were neutral or mildly liberal expressions of belief [Egner and Obelsky, 1957]. A sample stereotyped belief was "Any man can find a job if he really wants to work," and a sample liberal belief was "Science will eventually explain the origin of life." Each subject had four choices of response: strong or mild agreement or strong or mild disagreement. Agreement with the stereotypes was taken to be an indication of a tendency toward a stereotyped personality, as was disagreement with the neutral expressions. The results of the test provided the basis for a classification of the 218 students along a scale of stereotypy. The students' positions on this scale were then correlated with their school records in particular subject areas.

It was found that both groups—stereotyped and nonstereotyped—had the same average intellectual capacity, but there the similarities ended. The nonstereotyped students succeeded in the humanities and social sciences more than the stereotyped students, while the stereotyped students tended to excel in mathematics and the natural sciences. The researchers report that other similar studies have revealed that stereotyped students frequently are dissatisfied with classes which are not "practical," in which the teaching is not authoritarian, and in which final and definite answers to all questions are not provided. In contrast, nonstereotyped students tend to prefer classes which involve considerable flexibility of outlook and in which the teaching is not authoritarian.

The questions involved stereotypes on all subjects—religion, politics, business, etc. Do you think it likely that a person who revealed stereotyped thinking in one area would also reveal it in others? On the basis of what you have learned about psychology, can you say why?

Which group do you suppose was more anxiety-ridden? Why? Relatedly, which group would be more likely to include a great creative mathematician in the making?

INCREASING MOTIVATION IN THE CLASSROOM

We have said that motivation depends basically upon the presence of one or more of the human needs and drives. But the teacher can do much to *make* the schoolwork involve the students' needs and drives. Indeed, one of the fundamental duties of any teacher is thus to develop in students both readiness and willingness to learn their lessons. How are these duties to be done?

Let us begin the answer with a simple but basic example. An assignment develops in students a favorable set toward the learning involved if it raises interesting questions and makes new materials attractive. Thus a teacher who is thoughtful in his assignments implicitly or explicitly asks such questions and relates them to the new materials.

The project method of teaching, of course, carries this approach to motivation to its logical conclusion. Instead of formally taking up a topic, the teacher aims to bring about a learning situation in which it will naturally be explored in order to complete a project or solve a problem. If the students have such a motive, they tend to develop a set for the new topic and also to sustain it especially well. For example, in learning to write letters, young pupils may actually write real letters to real people rather than perfunctory letters for handing to the teacher. If the children are maintaining a flower bed and feel the need of specific information, they may write to agricultural bureaus for bulletins and reports. If they are studying world geography, they may exchange letters with boys and girls in other countries. Under such circumstances children achieve and keep set for writing correctly and interestingly in a way not provided by routine letter-writing assignments.

After such techniques have been consistently used in several learning situations, of course, the students tend to develop a stronger general motivation for learning itself. Individual learning activities have been pleasant and reinforcing; therefore new learning situations are more likely to be welcomed and attacked with strong motivation.

What are some of the more complicated aspects of increasing motivation in the classroom?

Feedback: Knowing the Results. Basketball players frequently glance at the scoreboard during a game so they will know just what the score is. This feedback—the incoming knowledge of how they are doing—keeps up the interest of the players and motivates them to improve their performances. Similarly, in the classroom, if the student knows how he is doing, he will work harder and more intelligently (see Exhibit 18). If the spelling-test words are corrected and he learns how many he got right and how many and what kind of mistakes he made, he will be more interested in correcting his misspellings and so improve his spelling scores. But let us consider knowledge of results in more detail.

Soldiers customarily practice their marksmanship on rifle ranges by firing at targets so far away that it is impossible to see where the bullet hits. Therefore, men placed in pits behind a barricade and below the targets hold up colored markers after each shot to indicate where it entered the target. This enables the marksman to improve more rapidly than he would if he did not get such feedback or got it only at the end of the firing session.

Such a procedure is generally a better stimulus to effective learning than only casual or occasional feedback. First, telling the learner the kind of error he has made helps show him how to correct his mistake and thus speeds learning more than just telling him that he failed. Secondly, it is better to tell the learner his results immediately after each attempt than to delay telling him until after a group of attempts.

A considerable body of experimental evidence verifies these two generizations. For example, J. L. Elwell and G. C. Grindley confirmed both when they tested the ability of two groups of subjects to keep a beam of light, controlled by a mechanism which required the use of both hands, centered on a target [Elwell and Grindley, 1938–1939]. One group was given information about its success as it learned the task; the other was told nothing of its

Exhibit 18   The effect of allowing pupils to inspect their corrected test papers

Material Studied	Condition	Number of Students	Mean Score, First Testing	Mean Score, Second Testing	Difference
A	Papers inspected	125	21.46	25.16	5.15; highly significant
A	Papers not inspected	125	21.50	20.01	
B	Papers inspected	125	21.27	25.01	4.62; highly significant
B	Papers not inspected	125	21.83	20.39	

L. Plowman and J. B. Stroud conducted an experiment with 250 eleventh-grade students which involved typical classroom problems and materials. The material studied was on bookmaking and was part of an English class. Two objective tests were administered to all 250 students; each test was given twice. Each time half the students received their papers back the next day with correct answers marked; the other half did not. The groups were reversed for the second test, the students were not told they would be retested, and practice effects were controlled by reversing the sequence of the two conditions for each group. As the results above show, the students did substantially better on the second test when they were allowed to inspect their corrected papers on the first test. (Adapted from L. Plowman and J. B. Stroud, "Effect of Informing Pupils of the Correctness of Their Responses to Objective Test Questions," *Journal of Educational Research*, 36:19, 1942.)

own progress. The first group learned the task fairly rapidly; the second made no improvement at all. Furthermore, when knowledge of results was later withheld from the first group, the skill deteriorated—it actually fell below the initial level.

The truth of the second generalization—that precise knowledge of results is more effective than general knowledge—was also illustrated by B. Reynolds and J. A. Adams, who asked experimental subjects to hold a stylus on a target set on a moving disc similar to a phonograph record [Reynolds and Adams, 1953]. All subjects could see whether they were succeeding or not, but one group also heard a clicking sound when they were on the target; this additional feedback led to a clear superiority for this group.

Competition versus Cooperation. Athletics, as we know, is based on rivalry, both individual and group. But in conventional school subjects, also, rivalry appears in one form or another. Indeed, the life of the typical school includes many kinds of contests in which rivalry becomes keen and tense. Students compete against each other to obtain higher scores in examinations and higher marks on report cards. The old-style spelling bee is competitive—side against side and individual against individual to see who will be the lone survivor. Even in everyday spelling lessons the individual child strives to obtain the highest mark. Contests in debate, declamation, and music bring out the spirit of sharp rivalry.

But in at least this last area, there is a trend away from all this today. Because the rivalries in contests have become so acute that hard feeling has developed, the use of contests to stimulate achievement (and thus learning, of course) is not so common as it used to be. The statewide debate, dramatic, and musical contests of yore are being transformed into noncompetitive festivals and clinics which give the participants an opportunity to display their abilities in the friendly atmosphere of constructive criticism. The spirit thus developed is less the spirit to win and more the spirit to learn by receiving help and guidance.

Are we going in the right direction? J. B. Maller tested the speed of 814 children in correctly solving simple arithmetic problems under four conditions [Maller, 1929]. He first tested the children without providing any particular motivation, to determine what their unspurred accomplishment would be. He then tested them after they were told that the high individual scorer would receive a prize, thus setting up an atmosphere of individual competition. Third, the children were divided into classes, and a prize for the best class was offered; the children did not even write their own names on their papers, but instead wrote the name of their class. Last, the children were given a choice of working for themselves or for a group.

The results, shown below, indicate that individual competition produced the most success, with group or class cooperation next. As might be expected, the unmotivated work produced the lowest results.

	Unmotivated (Practice)	Self-motivated (Competition)	Group-motivated (Cooperation)
Average score	41.2	46.3	43.6
Gain over no motivation	. . . .	5.1	2.3

Source: Adapted from J. B. Maller, "Cooperation and Competition: An Experimental Study in Motivation," *Contributions to Education*, 384, Teachers College, Columbia University, New York, 1929.

Also, students tended to prefer to work for themselves rather than for the group. When they were given the choice, about seventy-four per cent chose to work for themselves, about twenty-six per cent for the group. It would be wrong, however, to suppose that individual competition usually produces the best learning and performance. In the first place, various types of learners differ. Thus E. B. Hurlock has found experimentally that younger children and duller children respond better to group rivalry than older and brighter children [Hurlock, 1927–1928]. Moreover, there is variation by types of task. For instance, A. Mintz has found that in a task which requires the exercise of care, restraint, and cooperation, a spirit of rivalry may actually impair learning and performance [Mintz, 1951]. He asked 26 groups of experimental subjects to remove cones, before they got wet, tied to strings in a bottle in which water was gradually rising. The bottle neck and the cones were of such a size that only one could be removed at a time; thus cooperation between partners was required. One group was to receive individual money rewards or pay penalties for their efforts, another group was asked only to cooperate in removing the cones. The achievement of the cooperative group was spectacularly better than that of the competitors in this task, which required careful cooperative work. In an experiment by Marvin Shaw (see Exhibit 19) the cooperative subjects also did best, with individual performers next, and competitive subjects last.

Finally, competition may sometimes have unpleasant effects upon behavior. In another competition-cooperation experiment, C. B. Stendler, D. Damrin, and A. C. Haines had three groups of seven-year-old children—each group made up of eight children—paint two murals apiece [Stendler et al., 1951]. Group prizes were offered for one mural and individual prizes were offered for the other. In other words, in one case the situation was cooperative; in the other, it was competitive. The observers then noted the behavior of the children under each condition. In the competitive situation, the children engaged in much more negative behavior—hostile talk, refusal to share materials, boastfulness—than in the cooperative situation (see Table 27).

M. M. Grossack conducted a study of the effects of cooperation and competition upon the behavior of small groups by having 18 groups of five subjects each solve a rather complex problem in psychology [Grossack, 1954]. The subjects in each group were seated in a room facing the wall so they could not see each other and were required to solve the problem by passing notes back and forth. In each group, varying motivations of cooperation or competition were provided for each person by distributing different instructions to them. Some were told that they would be scored individually, some were told they would be scored as a group.

He found that the subjects motivated by cooperation showed much more "cohesive behavior" (relevant notes, attempts to influence other members of

Exhibit 19 Cooperation, competition, and individual performance on a tracking task

		Males			Females		
		Coop.	Comp.	Ind.	Coop.	Comp.	Ind.
Time on target, seconds	Mean	10.11	6.75	9.45	8.60	6.86	7.40
	SD	0.93	2.52	1.35	1.47	1.53	2.08
Ratings of satisfaction	Mean	7.0	7.3	7.0	5.5	7.9	5.5
	SD	1.4	1.6	1.4	0.9	0.9	0.5
Ratings of task interest	Mean	8.0	7.8	7.4	5.6	7.3	7.0
	SD	1.4	1.1	0.7	1.7	1.6	0.5

Marvin Shaw set up an experiment designed to test relative performance and relative satisfaction of subjects performing a task under cooperative, competitive, and individual conditions. Ten subjects were tested under each condition. They were asked to keep a rotating arrow on a rotating target by means of a guiding wheel. In the cooperative situation, control of the arrow passed back and forth between two wheels, one operated by the subject and the other by an assistant. The two participants could succeed best by cooperating. In the competitive situation, the subject was supposed to keep the arrow on a white target by competing with the other subject, who tried to keep it on a red target. In the individual situation, the subject worked alone.

The results (see above) showed that the cooperative subjects did best and the competitive subjects did worst, with individual performances in between. Competitive subjects enjoyed the task most, however. The experimenter speculated that the fact that the subjects were college students who customarily found pleasure in competition might have been reflected in this difference. He also concluded, from his observations of the subjects' behavior, that the competitive subjects were the most highly motivated, but that their very enthusiasm made their performances more erratic and less efficient. (Adapted from Marvin E. Shaw, "Some Motivational Factors in Cooperation and Competition," *Journal of Personality*, 26:160, 1958.)

Table 27 Behavior Patterns Recorded in Group- and Individual-reward
Painting Situations for Three Second-grade Groups

| Group | Motivation | Percentages of Positive or Negative Actions | |
		Positive	Negative
1	Group rewards	58	42
	Individual rewards	43	57
2	Group rewards	81	19
	Individual rewards	42	58
3	Group rewards	80	20
	Individual rewards	56	44

Source: Adapted from Celia B. Stendler, D. Damrin, and A. C. Haines, "Studies in Cooperation and Competition: I. The Effects of Working for Group and Individual Rewards on the Social Climate of Children's Groups," *Journal of Genetic Psychology*, 79:189, 1951.

the group, pressure to conform) than did the competitive subjects. He also found some indication of greater tension among the competitive subjects and found that the motivation of each subject tended to determine what kind of behavior they expected from each other. Competitive subjects expected the others to be competitive; cooperative subjects expected the others to be cooperative.

The problem of whether competition or cooperation furnishes the best atmosphere for learning is, then, fairly complex. An intensely competitive atmosphere may lead to harmful emotional effects as well as failure to learn the frequently valuable techniques of cooperation. A too-placid atmosphere of pressureless cooperation, on the other hand, may fail to stimulate certain students to achievement. It seems, an atmosphere in which students sometimes compete in a friendly, sportsmanlike way and sometimes join in spirited teamwork is most emotionally healthful and educationally effective.

Incentives. A motive is intrinsic, or within a person; it is closely integrated with his activities, persistent, and prevailing. An incentive is extrinsic to a person, or outside of him; it is an intangible honor or tangible reward to be won, for particular accomplishment. An incentive should thus cause a student to focus his energies on the task at hand; it should help him keep clearly in mind the study goal and his real need to learn.

All people have the same basic motives, though in various degrees of strength, but incentives for one person may not be incentives for another. Devices used to stimulate kindergarten children will not appeal to high school students; there are similarities in the recognition given the achievement of old and young, but the incentives for children have to be much more visible. Incentives must also vary greatly with learners' capacities, abilities, and motivation. Prizes, scholarships, and high marks can appeal only to the few who have a good chance of achieving these honors. But there should be incentives for children of all degrees of capacity and throughout the wide range of general and special abilities and interests—music, athletics, drama, industrial arts, and other areas of activity.

Most schools, of course, try to provide a wide range of incentives. Still, there are some pupils who are not "reached." Why not?

For one thing, aspiration levels may not be consistent with capacities; a few of high capacity seem to be satisfied with little, and some of low capacities have goals which are much too high. Both types need direction toward appropriate incentives, the more capable so that they will "raise their sights" and the less capable so that they will lower theirs. But the more general problem is that the incentive is too often made the end rather than the means, with the consequence that the approach to the tasks at hand is not made with deep-rooted interest. Instead, students work just for the prize, school mark, praise, or whatever the incentive happens to be.

This is very wrong because the basic purpose of incentives is not to increase the effort devoted to incentives themselves but to heighten the interest in the tasks at hand. The incentive is basically not effective if the student ceases to work when the badge, certificate, mark, or other reward has been received.

Therefore, though incentives are usually evaluated according to the achievement of the students, which is a good criterion, they should also be evaluated in terms of the resultant feelings and attitudes. Goodwill ought to result from the use of incentives. If rivalry is used, does it result in sharp practices and hard feeling? Also, if prizes are used to give distinction, do they lead to jealousy, selfishness, and excessive individualism? In other words, the morale that is developed must be taken into account along with achievement. We know that students in coercive and high-pressure situations may achieve well even though their morale is not good, but if the incentives stimulate good morale, such achievement can be increased.

Most basically, incentives are usually potent in terms of their bearing on feelings of personal worth. If they make a person feel that he is appreciated, respected, and wanted, then his efforts will be directed toward maintaining and even enhancing that status. If they depreciate him, he is likely not to care very much and so make indifferent efforts.

Thus, when a person works for a prize, it is doubtful that the material value of the prize lures the student to his highest achievement. Except when the prize is worth a large amount—and even then not in all instances—the desire is not only to have the prize but also to gain the distinction of winning it; the feeling of personal worth gained from social recognition is about as fundamental an incentive as the prize itself.

This, as well as other related facts about incentives, was demonstrated by Clarence L. Leuba in the following way [Leuba, 1930]. Thirty-five children of a fifth-grade class were tested with problems involving multiplying numbers of two digits for 7 weeks on Mondays, Wednesdays, and Fridays. Their usual achievement was first established by ascertaining the number of problems done without incentives. Then the children worked for 5-cent chocolate bars and for captaincy of the class and other ranking in the class: The person with the highest score was announced as captain, and the rankings of all other persons were written on the blackboard next to their names. Finally, achievement was tested when there was a combination of the two kinds of incentives. The results follow:

	No In-centive	Prize of Chocolate Bar	Captaincy and Ranking	Combined Incentives
Mean score	23.6	35.9	34.6	38.9
Gain over no incentive		12.3	11.0	15.3

Source: Adapted from Clarence L. Leuba, "A Preliminary Experiment to Qualify an Incentive and Its Effects," *Journal of Abnormal and Social Psychology*, 25:275–288, 1930.

Obviously, when the pupils were spurred by incentives, their achievement increased considerably, as most experimenters have found to be the case. It is also clear that intangible honor was almost as strong an incentive as material reward and that a combination of incentives proved to be most effective. Incidentally, the pupils in the lowest quarter made the highest percentage of gain.

☯ Reflect and Review

Early one fall afternoon a few years ago, there was an eclipse of the sun, visible in many parts of the land. In one particular school at least and possibly in thousands of others, an elementary school teacher had difficulty in teaching because the children were distracted by the approach of the eclipse.

The teacher being very concerned that the class complete its reading assignment for the day would not deviate from his routine enough to explain how the eclipse shut out the light from the sun and caused darkness. At the end of the day the teacher complained that he had found it so hard to keep the children's attention on their work that he was exhausted.

On the teacher's desk was his own well-read copy of Mark Twain's *A Connecticut Yankee in King Arthur's Court*, in which an eclipse of the sun figures crucially and delightfully. What does this suggest to you the teacher might have done to increase the pupils' motivation for reading?

How might the teacher have explained and illustrated an eclipse?

Should the teacher caution the children about the dangers of looking at the eclipse?

When the pictures of the eclipse became available, what use could the teacher have made of them to interest the students in several topics?

THE NATURE OF REINFORCEMENT

Positive and negative reinforcement—the strengthening of learning which is accompanied by satisfying results and the weakening of learning which is accompanied by unpleasant feelings—determine to a large extent which of a person's many responses survive to become abilities and habits. This process begins with the resolution of the tension in any one learning experience. Successful learning reduces the tension involved in accomplishing it, and the satisfaction which comes just from the release of tension positively reinforces, or strengthens, the learning. Failure, on the other hand, fails to reduce that tension, and the frustration which follows negatively reinforces, or weakens, the learning.

Here, motivation and reinforcement differ, but in the long continuation of learning experiences, reinforcement and motivation are, as previously stated, inseparable. Feelings which positively or negatively reinforce one piece of learning serve to motivate the learner when a similar situation arises. Much of what has been said about motivation, therefore, applies to reinforcement as well.

Positive Reinforcement. Let us examine positive reinforcement—that brought about by success and the fruits of success—through reviewing some of the important experimental work that has been done on it.

Bonnie B. Tyler tested the effect of encouragement and praise and of discouragement and disparagement with 120 subjects whom she asked to predict the order in which lights arranged in a row were flashed on [Tyler, 1958]. The subjects were divided into four groups; one group was encouraged on each trial, another was discouraged on each trial, another was inconsistently treated, and the last received no comments. There was a training, or practice, period in which no comments were made by the examiner; then, in the test period, each subject indicated what light he thought would be flashed next. At the end of the training period, the subject was given a hint as to the pattern followed in flashing the lights. His task was, first, to predict which light would be flashed next in each trial, and, second, to describe the general pattern of the sequences. After each trial, he learned whether his prediction had been right or wrong.

During the test, members of one group were encouraged and praised. When a member made the right response, the examiner would say, "Good!" and encouraging words such as "You are doing fine."

Opposite treatment was accorded the members of a second group. The examiner used such statements as "Wrong again!" "You are not doing very well" and, for correct responses, "It is about time you got one right" and "That was just luck."

To the members of a third group, inconsistently treated, the examiner alternately made remarks similar to those used for the other two groups.

To summarize the results briefly, a significantly larger number of encouraged and praised learners than of discouraged and disparaged learners solved the problems. Furthermore, the former arrived at their answers significantly faster. Those who were both encouraged and discouraged did better than the discouraged group but did not do so well as those who were encouraged.

M. J. Steigman and H. W. Stevenson have shown how rewards not only encourage learning but also develop better feelings among the learners [Steigman and Stevenson, 1960]. In this experiment, 36 children who were slightly under five years old were divided into two groups and given 12 learning tasks which consisted of three experimental games using pictures, card and nursery school games, and a size-discrimination problem involving blocks and marbles. The members of one group were given 10 prizes—marbles and little trinkets— and the other children were given only 2 prizes after they did each of the 12 tasks.

The children who received 10 rewards for doing the 12 tasks enjoyed them and "took them in their stride." The other children were upset: They became aggressive toward the examiner or tried to withdraw. They showed they were very glad to get a marble but also that they felt frustrated.

In subsequent problems where the rewards were dispensed equally, the children of the group which had been more highly rewarded previously did better; the previous experience of reward maintained its favorable influence in the subsequent learning experiences.

E. B. Page tested the effects of praise on 2,139 students in 74 classrooms by comparing the achievement in their school subjects when there was no comment, when the instructor praised freely and spontaneously, and when the instructor made specified comments [Page, 1958]. The experiment was conducted through one school term. The free, spontaneous praise consisted of whatever encouraging or favorable comments came to the mind of the instructor. The comments that were specified consisted of the following statements:

"Excellent! Keep it up."
"Good work. Keep at it."
"Perhaps try to do still better."
"Let's bring this up."
"Let's raise this grade!"

The instructor chose words that seemed most appropriate to the degree of success the student was having in his work.

The test scores were lowest for those who received no comment. Those commended and encouraged by the established comments related to each student's specific work were significantly higher in achievement than the unpraised group. But the highest-scoring group was the one praised by spontaneous words originating with the instructor.

Some confirmation of this conclusion about the importance of rather intangible personality factors in the administration of either praise or blame is provided by the study of Herman O. Schmidt [Schmidt, 1941]. He studied the performance of 574 subjects (seventh-grade to college levels) on a code substitution test under varying conditions of praise and blame. He found that some groups did best when praised, some when blamed. The greatest variations in achievement, however, seemed to be related to the tester himself. Schmidt concluded that the teacher should avoid intense stimulation of students by either praise or blame.

In these experiments, the following truths are evident. The first is simply that both praise and reward tend to improve learning and thus clearly constitute positive reinforcement, in contradistinction, usually, to scolding and deprivation. Secondly, positive reinforcement has a favorable effect not only on learning but also on the mental health of the learner. Finally, praise contributes more toward positive reinforcement when it is spontaneous and sincere, reflecting genuine concern on the part of the instructor.

Negative Reinforcement. In two of the studies we have been considering, reward was shown to be more effective than punishment in improving learning; imposition of displeasure with his work tended to negatively reinforce the student's learning—to weaken it or even, as is sometimes said, to extinguish it.

Here this process seemed to have bad results. But can it be well used educationally? For example, can a student's feelings of annoyance associated with an incorrect solution to a problem effectively and helpfully erase the incorrect answers?

Society in general has tried to do this. Our legal and penal system is, to a large extent, based on the principle of negative reinforcement. A motorist is not rewarded for stopping for a red light; he is punished if he drives through it. A thief is imprisoned, partly on the theory that he should be removed from society for its safety, but also partly on the theory that incarceration will encourage him to mend his ways. In both cases, society implicitly says it is trying to weaken the learning that led to the transgression.

Then social conflict emerges. Some say that many of society's beliefs on this point are psychologically unsound and that alterations should be made in the direction of substituting rehabilitation, which is based on application of positive reinforcement, for punishment. Others answer that, although the system has its weaknesses, practicality demands that lawbreakers be restrained forcibly from their crimes and that they do learn to do better. We cannot hope to solve this social problem here. We can, however, consider some of its implications for our school systems.

It is generally thought that poor students can sometimes be made to improve their work if they are scolded or threatened with failure or punished in some other way. But that this hope is largely futile is suggested by the experimental evidence which we have presented. Moreover, other experiments have confirmed that negative reinforcement not only is poor as a teaching device but is also unfortunate in its effects on the mental health of students, which sometimes go far beyond the immediate learning situation.

Some evidence, however, indicates that negative reinforcement may have a certain limited usefulness. Reproof and other forms of punishment have effects that are often more immediate than those of positive reinforcement. Negative reinforcement may tell a person what he should not do but not what he should do; however, this is not always an inappropriate lesson to learn: The motorist who drives past a red light is likely to avoid doing it again if he is fined. In short, unrewarded or punished responses are usually extinguished.

Clearly, then, the issue of positive versus negative reinforcement in the classroom is a complex one for the teacher.

Let us illustrate one way in which this is so. Some investigators have suggested that blame may work better with some people than praise does; more specifically, the factors of introversion and extroversion have been called important to the relative effectiveness of such positive and negative reinforcement.

G. G. Thompson and C. W. Hunnicutt tested this idea in an experiment with 124 fifth-grade children [Thompson and Hunnicutt, 1944]. The children were first given an introversion-extroversion test and, on the basis of the scores, were classified as introverts or extroverts. They were then given a cancellation test; they were instructed to draw a line through all the 7s found in rows of Arabic numbers from 0 to 9 printed in random order. This is not a difficult or complex task, so that simple attention and effort determine to a large extent the scores attained.

Praise and blame were distributed by the examiners, who printed P (for poor) or G (for good) at the top of the test paper after one complete test. Both extroverts and introverts, on successive tests, received blame, praise, and no comment at all. The test was administered six times in all, but the trial times were so short (30 seconds) that fatigue and practice effects were minimized.

The results showed that, for the group as a whole, both blame and praise increased achievement. As we have observed, blame often goads a person to try harder, particularly in the short run. But the most interesting result was the observation that blame was far more effective for the extroverts than praise was and, conversely, praise was much more effective for the introverts than blame was. The highest scores, as a matter of fact, were made by blamed extroverts and praised introverts. Had the extroverted people received more praise, become more used to it, and so responded less favorably to it? Had the introverts been found fault with more, so that they were stimulated by praise but not by blame?

These experimental results and the very questions they raise suggest that the teacher should use blame and praise discriminatingly in terms of the individual child. Probably the more sensitive, retiring child who "lives in his own world" will usually respond favorably to praise; it will improve his achievement and do him good emotionally. The extroverted child, the one who is forward and aggressive, will probably be improved by being blamed; at least the teacher can be relatively quick to make him feel responsible for doing better, it appears. Yet blame and reproof should not be used with an extrovert to the point that the child feels that the teacher is "picking on him"; that is bad for any child. In short, the teacher should recognize the differential effect of praise and blame on students and adapt his methods accordingly.

OVERACHIEVERS AND UNDERACHIEVERS

The underachieving student is he whose achievement is clearly lower than what would be expected from one of his learning capacity. Thus a gifted student is an underachiever when his achievement test scores are only average, as is a student of average learning capacity with failing or even low marks. The overachiever, as also indicated earlier, is he whose achievement is clearly above the level that ordinarily can be expected from one of his learning capacity—the dull student whose achievement is about average for his class, or the student with average capacity whose achievement is considerably higher than average. Finally, the student who is at the top of his class in capacity is an overachiever when he does better than the average of students of similar capacity.

In strict terms of educational systems, overachievers are those whose group ranking in achievement (tests and school marks) is clearly and consistently higher than their ranking in general aptitude and general intelligence tests, with an opposite relationship between the two kinds of standards prevailing for the underachievers. Of course, special achievements and breadth of achievement—the spread through various fields of accomplishment—may also be taken into account in judging a student's achievement status. Clearly, there is a crucial difference in long-range learning processes here, which detailed examination of these contrasting types of students will clarify (see Exhibit 20). Such examination will show the long-range workings not only of activity but of motivation and reinforcement in learning.

Exhibit 20   Characteristics of achieving and underachieving high school boys of high intellectual ability

Achievers	Underachievers
1. Greatest aptitude and interest in mathematics and science	1. Greatest aptitude and interest in mechanical and artistic areas
2. Main personal problems: future, college and vocational choices	2. Main personal problems: present, scholastic difficulties
3. Families' socioeconomic status relatively high	3. Families' socioeconomic status relatively low
4. Liked mathematics best of school subjects, English least	4. Liked sciences best, foreign languages least
5. Liked school	5. Disliked school
6. Much participation in out-of-school activities	6. Little participation in out-of-school activities
7. Viewed college as preparatory to specialization in graduate school	7. Viewed college as direct vocational preparation

The above data were gathered by Edward Frankel in a study of 100 seventeen-year-old boys with high IQs, half of whom were achievers, the other half underachievers. The bias in favor of mathematics and science on the part of the achievers might be attributable in part to the setting of the study: a large New York high school which specializes in a scientific program. (Based on data in Edward Frankel, "A Comparative Study of Achieving and Underachieving High School Boys of High Intellectual Ability," *Journal of Educational Research*, 53:172–80, 1960.)

Analysis of many research studies on the subject of overachievers and underachievers indicates that habit patterns, underlying personality structure, and environmental factors are responsible in large part for their relationships to achievement and capacity.

Compared with the underachiever, in terms of learning habit patterns the overachiever typically:

Studies more regularly at the same time and places.

Gets to work with less procrastination.

Spends considerably more time in study.

Concentrates more and yields less to distractions.

Has better school attendance.

In terms of personality structure, and thus of mental health, the overachiever ordinarily:

Has a greater need for achievement, which is felt and intellectually perceived.

Has more singularity of purpose: will consistently substitute hard work for immediate pleasures.

Accepts self with much more confidence and faith and relatedly is much freer of emotional cramp or anxiety.

Is both more self-sufficient and more flexible.

Is less inclined to rationalize his failures.

Is more responsible and cooperative in his personal relationships and so is a better leader and gets along better with authority figures.

Likes school better and is clearer in his educational and vocational objectives.

The emotions, which largely tone the personality structure, are the motivating forces which direct the use of one's energies. That a healthy emotional condition is conducive to consistent and continuing learning effectiveness is shown in the accomplishments of the overachiever; on the other hand, poor mental health lowers efficiency, as is shown by the failures of the underachiever. Though it has been held by some writers that personal maladjustment serves as a strong drive for achievement and though it is true that, in some instances, people are motivated by feelings of inadequacy, it is far more often true that good mental health contributes to good achievement, which in turn improves the personality. Unhealthy feelings typically function to inhibit and restrain effort, and the resulting lack of success accentuates the unhealthy feelings even more. Thus good mental health is basic to the kind of behavior that results in effective learning.

Finally, in terms of environmental conditions:

Overachievers are usually from the higher socioeconomic levels and under-achievers from the lower socioeconomic levels.

The homes of overachievers are likely to be more stable, and there is usually better child-parent integration; thus, parents of overachievers more typically intervene in their children's behalf when they consider it desirable.

Overachievers usually come from homes which are intellectually oriented and so take a positive, supporting attitude toward education; underachievers, from homes in which this is not true.

Schools with sound educational traditions, high general morale, and good teaching produce more overachievers than do schools which lack these assets. Thus, when a student can enhance his ego in his school by saying "I haven't cracked a book for a month" or is influenced by school atmosphere to believe that the C and D students "go furthest in the world," the morale of the school is low, high scholastic achievement will not get much encouragement, and there will be relatively few overachievers.

The community, which is a composite of its families, also sets standards which make for overachievement or underachievement. If it puts the highest values on athletic teams, marching bands, and high-stepping, plume-hatted majorettes, the environment will be conducive to underachievement. On the other hand, if high-ranking students are featured in the local newspaper and if the people of the community are quick to applaud in other ways the students who have made the best use of their educational aptitudes, then the potentiality for overachievement will be good.

These three factors in achievement—habit patterns, personality structure, and environmental factors—are closely interrelated, of course, and so function reciprocally, both immediately and in the long run. The neat divisions into which we are theoretically able to separate human motivations are therefore seldom clear in actual cases of individual human beings. A person may be strongly motivated to accomplish a task by his desire for reward or by his desire for self-esteem, but other factors may influence the results of these motivations when they are translated into actual achievement. A student may wish intensely to make the debate team. In the process of trying to achieve this ambition, however, he is either helped or hindered by his habits. If he has to overcome bad habits of study and concentration, a stumbling block is in his path. Both the original motivation and the habits are intimately bound up, too, with his personality structure. His desire for a place on the debate team indicates that he experiences a tension that can be relieved by such success; but if his mental health is such that he cannot work efficiently, his goal is further off. And finally, motivation, habits, and personality affect and are affected by environmental factors. If the would-be debater comes from a socioeconomic group in which his ambition is regarded as odd, or if his environment has conditioned him in speech habits that would be a defect in his debating skill, he has a further obstacle to hurdle.

These comments are not intended to blur the distinctions which have been made between concepts; they are merely a reminder that motivation and achievement and all their manifestations constitute highly complicated and intricately related behavior. They are capable of appearing in many guises when they are traced in the infinitely complex individual human being.

● *Reflect and Review*

Following are several short descriptions of behavior and results of it. In each case, do you think the results would tend to positively reinforce or to extinguish the behavior? Also, in cases 4, 5, and 6, do you think the student would be likely to be an achiever or an underachiever on the basis of the one behavioral clue given?

1. Some three-year-old children show off at a family reunion with giggly and rowdy remarks and antics. Some parents respond with beaming smiles, others ignore the children, and others show disapproval.

2. Mel makes a rude remark to the teacher; the teacher makes Mel stay after school.

3. A high school pitcher tries out a curve ball he has been practicing. Only one hit is made on his curve ball during the game.

4. Jake dislikes school; he frequently makes crude, humorous remarks about the teacher and the class routine under his breath to the boys who sit near him. They laugh and regard Jake as a wit.

5. After practicing on his trumpet solo for 3 months, Gordon wins a "superior" rating at the state music festival.

6. Jill is very much interested in chemistry and has done her first three reports in chemistry class more thoroughly and carefully than she was required to. Her teacher, however, returns them without comment except for an "s" (satisfactory) marked on each one.

SUMMARY

The basic processes of learning involve motivation, activity, and reinforcement.

A learner is motivated for a given task when, because of willingness, his energies are set for doing it.

A learner is ready for certain learnings when he is able and willing, and that is the time when they should be undertaken.

Aspiration level is defined in terms of the difficulty of the task the learner chooses to do. In general, a person chooses goals consistent with his capacities, but choice is influenced by success or failure. Success generally causes a reasonable increase in the choice of goal level. Failure generally causes a consistent lowering of the goal levels, but sometimes it may erratically change or not change.

Realistic goals facilitate learning, and the learner needs opportunities to set his goals both individually and through group action.

Studies have shown that we acquire more readily those ideas that we agree with, because we have a set for them.

Anxiety is a personal condition that interferes with learning and should not be confused with the normal concern which the motivated learner has for getting his work done.

It seems that stereotyped minds do better in mathematics and science, where procedures and answers are precise, while nonstereotyped minds favor the humanities and social studies, where there is more elasticity of thought.

In general, learners are motivated when they do something that is real and meaningful to them.

Feedback is a very effective way of motivating learners by providing them with general and specific information on their achievements. They need to know about their status and progress as well as their specific successes and errors.

The effectiveness of competition and cooperation varies with the learner, the task, and the objectives. Some situations are individually competitive, some are competitive and cooperative, and some are cooperative. All may be conducive to effective learning. It is desirable to learn to work both competitively and cooperatively, as effective learning and living require both.

Incentives are prizes, honors, and other rewards which a person works to obtain and which give satisfaction when obtained. If an incentive is to motivate the learner, it must satisfy a need. Generally, incentives in school cause students to direct their energy toward worthy goals and achieve much more than they would without incentives.

Positive reinforcement is the strengthening of a response; because that response was successful and gave satisfaction, it was rewarded positively.

In turn, positive reinforcement encourages the learner to attempt more responses. When learners are praised or rewarded in various ways, they achieve more than those who are not rewarded.

Negative reinforcement consists in no reward or in various degrees of negative reactions to a response, ranging from the word "wrong" to the threat of capital punishment. Capital punishment, of course, makes sure that all undesirable responses have been extinguished.

The effectiveness of both positive and negative reinforcement is influenced greatly by the feelings they develop, such as pride, indifference, and hostility. When positive and negative reinforcement develop a desire to maintain or enhance one's worth and status, the learner will be highly motivated to improve.

As compared with underachievers, overachievers tend to work more hours and with greater concentration, have greater need for achievement and are more responsible, and come from intellectual and achievement-oriented homes and communities.

SUGGESTED READING

Symonds, Percival M.: "What Education Has to Learn from Psychology II. Reward," *Teachers College Record,* 57:15–25, 1955, "III. Punishment," *Teachers College Record,* 57:449–462, 1956. In these two articles, Symonds discusses positive and negative reinforcement. Points out the effectiveness (or lack of effectiveness) of both and makes helpful applications to human situations.

Waimon, Morton D.: "Feedback in Classroom: A Study of Corrective Teacher Responses," *Journal of Experimental Education,* 30:355–359, 1962. An analysis of the actual behavior of teachers in response to the degree of readiness of the pupils. This is an attempt to analyze the nature of classroom behavior in relation to learning.

Young, Paul T.: *Motivation and Emotion,* John Wiley & Sons, Inc., New York, 1961. A comprehensive treatment of human behavior with emphasis on the emotional elements in the dynamics of motivation. An excellent treatment that will challenge the superior student.

CHAPTER 15
THE COURSE
OF LEARNING
AND FORGETTING

The rate of learning is affected by the age, capacity, and motivation of the learner, by the conditions under which the learning takes place, and by the nature of the material itself. In other words, the three basic factors in learning are the learner, the process, and the material. Consequently, learning sometimes proceeds slowly and sometimes seems instantaneous.

However, the same factors affect the degree of retention—the memory of the learned material—and the rate at which forgetting takes place. For instance, it is not necessarily true that 6 months after we have learned something, we have forgotten exactly half of what we shall have forgotten in a year. Such a simple example only hints at the almost infinite variations to which the rates of both learning and forgetting are subject. These variations the teacher sees continuously. Within the same music class, he observes one boy who can play simple melodies on a trumpet within a week after he picks it up and another boy who cannot play the same exercises until he has studied for several weeks. A third boy may progress very rapidly at first and then not show any perceptible improvement for several months. Or, the teacher frequently hears remarks like these: "I dug and dug until I got discouraged; then it seemed like everything fell into place." "I studied Latin for two years, and then six months after I quit, I couldn't even read the mottos on the coats of arms in my history book."

To understand what such events and statements mean and then to use this understanding to help his students is an important part of the teacher's job. This chapter, therefore, is concerned directly with the course of learning and forgetting: how it goes and how it may be altered.

VARIATIONS IN THE PROGRESS OF LEARNING

Progress in learning varies greatly among individuals as well as among kinds of learning; and this is as true during the preschool and elementary school years as it is in later stages of life. For any individual, moreover, there are usually great variations in efficiency in learning, even day by day. Nevertheless, certain broad characteristics of the general course of learning may be distinguished.

First, learning may take place either with a slow initial start or with a rapid initial start. With the former, little is apparently gained at the beginning of learning. The typical progress of an adult learning a difficult foreign language is this: For a period of weeks and sometimes months, a few words are learned, but little ability to read from the printed page is developed. Then there is a rapid measurable increase in ability. Much human learning takes such a course, beginning at any early age. Thus, for nearly a year after birth, there is apparently little approach to walking ability, although of course the development of the physical structure involved in walking is taking place. Then, after a child begins to walk, his ability increases rapidly. There is, for the average child, no apparent learning of words until about twelve months of age; then his acquisition of usable and used words begins and increases rapidly. Similarly, in later life, not only learning an unfamiliar language but also learning hard problems in mathematics, learning to play the piano, and acquiring many other complex skills and abilities seem to defy learning attempts for a time. (Some generalized curves of learning are shown in Figure 19.)

With rapid initial start, on the other hand, improvement is manifestly rapid from the beginning of learning effort. The contrast with slow initial start is not so complete as it might seem, however; for when learning appears to move rapidly from the beginning, the slow initial phases of learning have in reality been overcome by previous learning.

For example, we bring to the problem of learning to skate all the other sensorimotor skills that we have acquired in learning to stand, walk, and even run. In the same way, when a person starts to learn algebra after having studied arithmetic a number of years or when he approaches geography and history after having had several years of reading experience, initial progress is rapid because of allied experiences. Actually, we rarely start any learning task which does not to a small extent, at least, involve some ability acquired from previous learning.

This fact, of course, brings us face to face with the problem of essential difference between slow and rapid initial start. What is it, generally, if not the difference between usable previous skill and no usable previous skill?

It would seem that the basic difference might be a matter of degree of

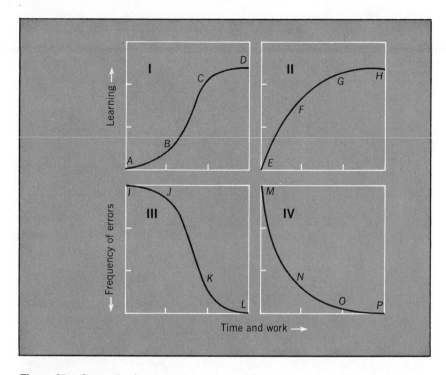

Figure 19 Generalized curves of learning *The curves in I and II indicate learning by increasing scores; the curves in III and IV indicate learning by decreasing the number of errors. In I and III the slow starts (A to B and I to J) are followed by rapid learning (B to C and J to K), which levels out at or near its limits (C to D and K to L).*

In II and IV fast starts (E to F and M to N) are followed by a more perceptible slowing down (F to G and N to O), which approaches the limits (G to H and O to P).

usability of previous learning. But other explanations are made also. One explanation for slow start is that the learner must develop insight into problems. An explanation for rapid progress from the beginning is that some tasks or problems strike the learner as intriguing when first attacked. On the other hand, the learner may not be so interested in the beginning as he becomes later when he increases his efficiency; in the acquisition of many of our abilities, it is first necessary to go through much discouraging work before the development of facility stimulates us to work with zest. In short, there seems to be no one simple answer.

Periods of no visible learning progress, preceded and followed by improvement, are called plateaus. Such are the periods when the second-grader does not improve in his reading, when the brilliant piano student's playing seems arrested, and when the gymnast is not able to increase the variety of feats on the parallel bars. Plateaus may last days, weeks, or months. Then comes a spurt in achievement which takes the learner on to new ventures. These plateaus, or periods of no gain, begin unpredictably, and their termination is just as unpredictable; but, let us reemphasize, they do end. They should not be confused with the limit beyond which one is not able to progress, which will be discussed later.

What are the causes of these puzzling periods?

One of the causes of the plateau is fatigue; another, and probably the more important of the two, is boredom. If the learner becomes perfunctory or falls into a mechanical routine, and so enters a plateau, he is quite likely to be doing so out of boredom.

The plateau also may be a period when the learner is acquiring a higher form of response. In other words, a learner may be on a plateau because the learning methods he is using have carried him as far as he can go and they, indeed, restrict further progress. The idea here is that while on the plateau the learner is acquiring better techniques, and at the end of the plateau he emerges from a simpler and less effective form of learning response to one that is more complex and efficient. In reading, for example, the pupil may be on a plateau when he is learning to combine the phonetic parts into words or the words into phrases and then swing upward from the plateau when he has "finally learned," that is, when he has succeeded in making the larger combinations. In arithmetic the same things may happen as the learner becomes able to add several numbers at a time rather than one number to the next, that to the next, and so on. A person who has long used the simple one-finger "hunt-and-peck" system of typewriting may experience a plateau in trying to learn the touch system, which involves all fingers and requires that the typist not look at the keys. Here performance may even be poorer for a while so that after the period of practice, which is the plateau, skill will appear to have suddenly reached a higher level. In a higher context, a person may be on a plateau in the levels of his thinking until he can generalize his facts as principles and, in turn, apply the principles to specific situations.

Finally, however, all learning must slow down and then stop; that is, it must approach and ultimately reach a period of no improvement. No one can continue to improve indefinitely in any given function. A person can take up a new school subject or attempt to acquire a new athletic skill, and he will improve, but ultimately he will reach a *limit* which he cannot surpass. A student, no matter how bright and hardworking, reaches at some time the limit of his ability to compute arithmetically. The typist reaches a point where, no matter how agile his fingers and how hard he tries, he cannot type more rapidly. The musician reaches a point where he does not improve; he can learn new pieces, but the quality of his playing does not become better. And this is true with all our learning; there are always limits beyond which we cannot go.

The flow of these characteristics, which forms the course of learning, may be plotted on a graph and represented as a learning curve (see Exhibit 21). Such curves, of course, may represent growth in one or in many abilities over a long or a short period of time; they may be smoothed, or generalized, or they may be executed in such detail as to display actual day-to-day variations in learning efficiency. Learning curves, moreover, may represent group, as well as individual, learning progress and may also show just a part of the overall course of learning we have been discussing in broad terms. Two contrasting examples of the many things that can be depicted by learning curves

Exhibit 21   Production of a new taxicab driver

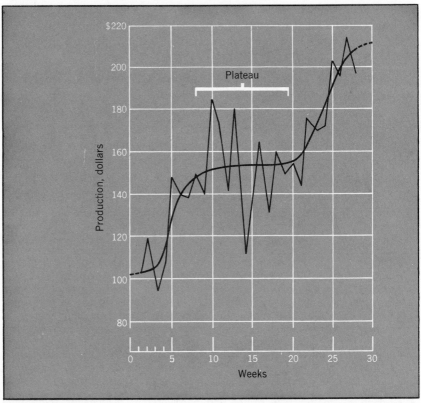

The graph shows the progress made by a new taxicab driver during his first 28 weeks of employment, in terms of the amount of money he brought in. It will be observed that there is an initial period of rapid learning, a plateau period, and then a period of fast improvement. It is evident, too, that there are wide variations from week to week. These wide fluctuations are typical of many learning curves. The smooth line is an average line and shows the general trend. [E. E. Ghiselli and C. W. Brown, *Personnel and Industrial Psychology*, 2d ed., McGraw-Hill Book Company, Inc., New York, 1955, p. 385.]

are an individual's acquisition of vocabulary from birth to old age and the course of learning in all subjects among a group of eighth-grade students in the month of November.

The Limits of Learning Explored. The range of forms of learning, from the simple to the complex, is often referred to as *hierarchical organization*. The simpler is transformed into the more complex, which, in turn, becomes reorganized in still more complex and effective forms. Hierarchical organization is reflected in a sequential arrangement of subject matter, as in mathematics, the content of which ranges from the simplest addition to the most complicated equations of Einstein. As this example suggests, material can progressively become so complex that only a few can comprehend it. Thus the hierarchical organization is symbolized by the subject-matter levels beyond which various learners cannot go. Those with little capacity in any complex field go hardly beyond the simplest levels; a few are capable of the highest reaches. In less complex fields, the rate of learning eventually slows down partly because of the decreasing possible improvement that remains. At the beginning, all is in front, so to speak; but as the learner progresses, the amount of material to be learned diminishes.

But we can best deepen our understanding of the limits of learning by exploring them more fully in terms of the learner himself.

When the sensorimotor skills are involved, it is easy to see that there are individual limits of learning. It is quite apparent that in typing or tennis a person will eventually reach a limit of improvement. For all, there is a limit in the facility with which the eyes can move in the case of reading, the legs in running, and the speech organs in speaking. In all such cases, moreover, it is easy to understand this *physiological limit*.

It is not so easy to understand limits in the learning of abstract materials; it would seem possible for all people to continue throughout life acquiring more words, increasing their fund of historical and geographical knowledge, improving their abilities in mathematics, and so on. However, an equilibrium is reached when the amount acquired equals the amount forgotten or lost, and then the limit of improvement has been reached. This is the *theoretical limit*.

As we have indicated, these limits of learning, both physiological and theoretical, vary from person to person. But just as importantly, a person very seldom reaches either limit. Each person ordinarily stays at a level below, which may be called the *practical level*.

The distance from the practical level to the theoretical or physiological limit varies according to the person and according to the kind of skill or material learned, but in any difficult learning task the limit is reached only when a person is so highly motivated that he expends all the energy he possesses in learning what he is trying to master. Children preparing for an important spelling contest with intensive drills are usually learning at their limits, whereas those who are routinely studying words are far from theirs.

Here, however, a subtler differentiation enters the picture. When high school students cram for their examinations, their learning rate is at a maximum: They are, in this case, at their theoretical limits. But, in the end, the amount that they have learned does not even approach fulfillment of their capacity. Comparably, a child may, on a particular day, be doing his very best in silent reading but may not have reached the limits of speed and comprehension of which he is capable. Thus it is well to distinguish learning at maximum for a short period and the consistent long-term approach to one's limit; and we do this by defining the level a person reaches by efficient work habits—by the best long-term management of time and effort—as the *optimum level*. This is usually between the practical level and the theoretical or physiological limit.

The Teacher's Use of These Concepts. How do such concepts as the initial start, the rate of improvement, plateaus and their duration, levels, and limits—which help us characterize the course of learning generally—become of practical use to the teacher?

First of all, it is desirable both for individual students and for a class as a whole to have as rapid a start as possible when new work is taken up; and, if the teacher himself knows what he is going to do in a new learning area and how to do it, such a good beginning is more likely. Correspondingly, students will make more rapid progress from the start if they are ready for the tasks to be undertaken; and this readiness, as indicated before, results from adequate capacity and preparatory experiences. Thus it can be said that the purpose of readiness programs in reading and arithmetic is to develop the pupils to a stage of readiness which enables them to make rapid and satisfying progress from the beginning. The teacher, then, must see to it that his class as a whole is ready for each new area of learning when it is to be entered, which may entail group preparation or special attention to certain individuals who seem likely to hold the class back, or both.

The rate of improvement after the start must also be consistently watched both with the whole group and with the individual student. A student may be arrested in his progress because the work is too complex for him (this might be called a problem point in the hierarchical organization). At this time the teacher can be of great help by observing carefully the student's recitations, written work, and examinations so as to detect the parts of the work that give him trouble. In addition, the teacher can encourage all his students to ask questions and to bring their special problems to his attention so that he can help them with the parts that are blocking their progress. As in many situations, a block in the progress of learning may be like a tangle in a skein of yarn; when it is untangled, the winding of the yarn into a ball can continue rapidly until another tangle has to be loosened.

Especially, the teacher should watch his students in order to detect bad study habits that may lead to lack of interest, a sequence that often occurs, For instance, in reading such habits as moving the lips, moving the eyes back and forth often over the same lines, and reading slowly should be looked for. Then a remedial program for the student should be begun, to liberate him from his fault and thus free him to move ahead.

Of course, a student may be on a plateau, not just entrapped by a bad habit, when his motivation apparently dies down—when he seems not to try very hard and to feel there is no point to it. What should the teacher do then?

This question is hard to answer but is very important, for at such a time a student actually loses ground in his learning in some ways.

Certainly, whenever students seem aimless or without motive, the teacher should point out the advantages of engaging in various activities and of seriously studying the subject matter in which apparently they have no interest. Thus one of the purposes of guidance and counseling is to show the students that both the general activities and the scholastic programs of the school offer many excellent opportunities for learning. But the teacher must also follow through on such attempts to show students the reason for what they are attempting to do, and by helping them to do it.

One way of accomplishing this is by direct help. To take a simple example, multiplication may show improvement when the grade school teacher helps his pupils out of their specific difficulties in carrying. Likewise, an athletic coach can demonstrate to the golfer a new way to hold the club; and the dramatic director can suggest a new way to overcome the difficulty of the big scene. It is essential, of course, to follow such helps with encouragement to practice the new technique, for this is frequently necessary to bring about improvement.

Advanced music and drama students, for example—and even performers—take lessons from the leading teachers with the hope of acquiring some techniques and abilities which will improve their performance. Business and the professions seek—through coaching, lessons, and research—various methods that will enable them to work more effectively. It is through reorganization, as well as integration of new and old information and skills, that learners improve their responses and get off their plateaus or dead levels of performance. Furthermore, it is important to encourage the learner to experiment with self-chosen different methods until he finds one that extricates him from the plateau.

But the best recommendation that can be made for overcoming plateaus is for the learner to cease practice when he has lost interest or seems stale and unable to make progress. He can take a few days off or turn to a different task. We all know that in the long run we progress most if we take time out from our work. Most people rest at least one day a week and during the year have vacations, partly so that they can return to work more efficient than before. Similarly, plateaus can be left behind more quickly in learning tasks of even narrow scope if the learner discontinues efforts to learn when he is in a period of no improvement. When he comes back to the task, certain inhibitory factors or poor techniques may have dropped out. Time for rest as well as time for practice is a useful part of any learning program.

The teacher's—and, indeed, the school's—function here is to provide a flexible learning atmosphere which allows for diversion from particularized effort at the appropriate times. It was mentioned previously that when a new method is used or an experiment is conducted, students and teachers respond with an enthusiasm that usually brings about improved learning. Similarly, if teachers vary their methods, they will keep the pupils from becoming bored. So projects, excursions, student-centered methods, and independent work supplemented with audiovisual aids and teaching machines will help to maintain the students' interest; and any procedure that departs from the usual school monotonies will lessen the no-progress periods.

Finally, it is doubtful that a student should ever be keyed up for long to a point where he reaches his theoretical or, as the case may be, physiological limit of learning. For short time periods, a student may devote his maximum efforts to learning. But he spends six or more hours every school day learning and obviously cannot be buoyed up to a maximum efficiency for all of that time. Even musicians, actresses, surgeons, golf players, and lecturers have to be at maximum efficiency only occasionally, and this is essentially when they are performing rather than learning.

Apart from this analogy, however, if students worked to maintain for long a learning level designed to keep them at their theoretical and physiological limits, they would endanger their mental health. Rather, learning should be maintained at what we have called the optimum level—the level reflecting good long-term management of time and effort.

Many students—and teachers too, of course—have a practical level much below this; and they should be motivated to greater efficiency. Some, on the other hand, strain themselves by attempting too much learning; and they should adjust downward to an optimum level.

In short, by keeping the students interested and working at optimum levels, the teacher can best help their curves of learning swing upward. Further-more, by maintaining his own effort at an optimum level, the teacher can best maintain awareness of learning problems and do the best work in solv-ing them from day to day and over the long pull.

In Chapter 5, we developed the topic of the personal and professional growth of teachers. It is appropriate now to recall the relationship of that development to the responses of the students. Teachers who are popular with their students because of their personal qualities and professional com-petence have good effects on them. Consequently, anything the teacher does that stimulates his own enthusiasm and enhances his own development will tend to do the same for the students.

☯ *Reflect and Review*

In an experiment on trial-and-error learning, John Dollard and Neal E. Miller hid a piece of candy under the center book on the bottom shelf of a 4-foot bookcase and then asked a six-year-old girl to find it [Dollard and Miller, 1951]. The bookcase was full of books which were all similar in color and shape, so the girl had no clear way of discriminating between the right book and the others, even after she had found the candy one time. There were 10 trials, each following the other immediately. Following is a paraphrase of the experimenters' record of her progress in learning:

First trial: The girl, on being told the candy was hidden under one of the books, began to look under the books at random. She moved some books on the top shelf, then some from the lower shelf; then looked under some maga-zines on the top shelf, then under the same books on the top shelf, then under a book on the table; and finally began to remove more books from the bottom shelf. After moving 37 books, she found the candy; she took 210 seconds to find it.

Second trial: she went directly to the bookcase and began to remove books from the lower shelf. After 86 seconds, she found the candy under the twelfth book.

Third trial: She went to the correct place almost immediately and found the candy after 11 seconds under the second book she picked up.

Fourth trial: She went to one end of the shelf and moved 15 books before finding the candy. She took 86 seconds.

Fifth through tenth trials: Her scores improved steadily until, on the ninth trial, she went immediately to the correct book; she repeated her success on the tenth trial. She took three seconds on the ninth trial, only two seconds on the tenth trial.

What generalization can be made on trial-and-error learning?
What would a curve of this six-year-old girl's learning progress look like?

Plot such a curve on a graph, naming the abscissa and ordinate, and identifying the phases of the curve.

What factor or factors may have influenced her to do more poorly on the fourth trial than on the third trial?

MEMORY: REMEMBERING AND FORGETTING

There is a theory that nothing is actually forgotten, that all that has been learned is actually stored in the memory, as it were, and can be recalled if the right association can be made or certain inhibitions can be removed. The evidence for this theory lies partly in the fact that people in a coma or under hypnosis have recalled experiences which had long been apparently forgotten. Also, psychoanalysts hold that a patient, through free association, can dig out of his unconscious mind experiences and ideas which have been repressed for years.

This evidence, however, is essentially of limited recall under very specific conditions; it is poor grounds for believing that all learning is in a kind of storage and that there actually is no forgetting. Besides, as we experience life normally, relatively little of all learning is retained. We can recognize only a small proportion of all the people and things we have seen, recall only a few of the stories we have read, and remember only a few poems we have memorized.

Nor is this forgetting undesirable; we should not clutter our minds with all the trifles of our experiences. Even if we could remember every transitory detail of our past life without confusion, would such remembering serve a useful purpose?

Yet a basic problem of education is to determine both what should be learned and how it can be retained; for while the learner tends to forget what he has no need to remember and retain what he has need for, he still forgets much that it would be desirable to remember.

The Course of Forgetting. When a teacher tries to recall a name involved in even a relatively recent course, he often finds that what he thought he knew so well has now vanished. If a student who has studied a foreign language tries to read a few sentences in the language a year or so after stopping, he often finds that some words are completely incomprehensible to him.

Research has, to a large extent, confirmed the prevalence of such discouraging events. The many studies that have been made of retention by college students show, when taken together, that loss of knowledge through forgetting generally varies from about one-half to as much as two-thirds of individual subject content after one year. But how does this forgetting proceed?

The course of forgetting takes a definite general trend: It is most rapid at first and then slows down. Again, many studies have shown that as much as one-half of nonsense syllables memorized well enough to be repeated are forgotten within a few hours; after the first day, forgetting tends to be much slower; after 15 days have passed, one-third to one-half of what was known is generally retained; at the end of a month, only about one-fourth is retained, as a rule.

Turning from experiments with nonsense materials to studies related to actual school subjects, we find the typical curve of forgetting repeated. For the members of one grade school history class, it followed this course: At the end of the class, average knowledge of subject matter was about 69 per cent. Four months later retention was about 58 per cent; then forgetting became less rapid; and 16 months later the students still retained 48 per cent of the subject matter. Students in a college botany class retained about 68 per cent of the content at the end of the course. Retention dropped sharply to about 36 per cent 4 months later; and only about 18 per cent of what they had learned was still remembered 16 months later. But forgetting then leveled off, and 28 months later the students had forgotten little of this 18 per cent. Classes in high school chemistry, college zoology, and college psychology have shown substantially the same pattern of sharp decline in retention, followed by more gradual decline and then leveling off.

But notice that actual percentages of subject material retained differed widely, ranging in the detailed cases alone from 48 per cent retained after 16 months to only 18 per cent. Why is this?

The detailed cases, one from a grade school and one from a college class, reflect the fact that retention is usually found to be higher for younger students. This would seem explicable by the fact that classes on the lower levels typically contain rather basic materials which are used in subsequent courses and hence are, in a sense, reviewed. College courses tend to be more sophisticated and more separate in content; a college student is not likely to use any of the material he learned in botany class, for example, in subsequent classes in English, history, geology, or ROTC.

But the point to be emphasized here is that several variables are involved: the nature of the material; its future use (and thus the experience following learning) and the age, capacity, and general motivation of the learners.

These and other more subtle variables are virtually always involved, moreover, in defining the course of forgetting; and since this is our primary aim here, we shall not seek an exact answer to the preceding particular question; rather, we shall explore the various general factors of retention. As we do so, we shall find that retention may be increased; while learning sometimes seems to be a process of taking three steps forward and two steps back, the application of certain principles may mean that only one step backward need be taken.

Experience Following Learning: Proactive Interference. Does the past interfere with the present? More specifically, do the lessons of a month ago in arithmetic interfere with the learning of geography today? Interference of past learning with present learning and retention is *proactive interference* or *inhibition*. Why should there be proactive effects which make learning more difficult and thereby hinder additional learning? This explanation is to be found in such terms as disruption, distortion, obliteration, complication, and increased difficulty. When one list of words, numbers, or nonsense syllables is followed by another, the total combination or pattern is complicated and disrupted, thereby making learning more difficult and also reducing retention.

But as we have pointed out, school learning today does not parallel the memorizing of lists of numbers or nonsense syllables, as is the case in so many laboratory experiments. Rote learning is not characteristic of modern education with its emphasis on meaning, understanding, and problem solving. The evidence indicates that, for the typical school subject matter, previous learning facilitates and reinforces learning rather than hindering it. As discussed previously, relating and correlating knowledge into larger and more meaningful patterns or units avoids interference and promotes understanding and retention. The study of the proactive effects of learning meaningful material by D. P. Ausubel and Elias Blake, Jr. (Exhibit 22) shows an increase in learning rather than a decrease [Ausubel and Blake, 1958].

Exhibit 22   A study of the proactive effects of learning meaningful material

Program of Learning to Test Proactive Interference

Group	Material Studied		
	First Day		After 48 Hours
Experimental	Opiate addiction (1,400 words)*	Christianity (1,700 words)	Comparison of Buddhism and Christianity (2,100 words)†
Control A	Opiate addiction (1,400 words)*	Christianity (1,700 words)	Buddhism (1,700 words)†
Control B	Opiate addiction (1,400 words)*		Buddhism (1,700 words)†

* Retention tested after 2 days.
† Retention tested after 12 days.

Differences between Means of Experimental and Control Groups in Retention of Buddhism Material

Group	N	Mean	Significance
Experimental Control A	49	7.88 7.41	Difference between means is too small to be significant.
Experimental Control B	19	7.78 4.89	Difference between means is large enough to be highly significant. Level of less than .001.
Control A Control B	21	6.39 6.16	Difference between means is too small to be significant.

In an experiment involving 156 college students, D. P. Ausubel and Elias Blake, Jr., aimed to measure proactive effects of previous learning.

All 156 students first studied a 1,400-word essay on the history of opiate addiction for 22 minutes and were told, with the purpose of motivating them to learn and to remember as much as they could of the passage, that they would be tested on it 2 days later. The scores obtained by this first testing two days after the study of opiate addiction were used as a basis for matching the members of the three groups so they would be equal in average ability to remember. Following this part of the experiment, the experimental group and control group A were given an essay of 1,700 words on Christianity. Then 48 hours later the experimental group studied for 25 minutes a 2,100-word essay comparing Buddhism and Christianity (and including the material of the 1,700-word essay on Christianity) and were told that they would be tested 12 days later. Both control groups then studied an essay of 1,700 words on Buddhism and were told that they would be tested 12 days later. Twelve days later, as announced, they were all tested on Buddhism; and following that test, they were tested on the passage on Christianity.

The students were divided into three groups, equally matched on the basis of their demonstrated learning ability as indicated by the test of retention of the material in the 1,400-word passage of opiate addiction. The two control groups studied an essay of 1,700 words on Buddhism, and control group A studied a 1,700-word essay on Christianity 18 hours before studying the Buddhism essay. Control group B did not study the essay on Christianity. The experimental group studied a 2,100-word essay on Buddhism which contained the material of the 1,700-word Christianity essay plus additional material showing their similarities and differences.

Comparisons of the matched experimental and control groups as given in the second table indicate that the knowledge of Buddhism by the experimental group is slightly, but not significantly, higher than that of control group A but significantly higher than that of control group B. Control groups A and B are about equal.

These results show clearly that there is no proactive interference, for if there were, control group B would score highest on Buddhism knowledge, as it has no previous learning to reduce that knowledge. The experimental group scores highest and still it has the interactive learning—Christianity and also the Christianity as part of the Buddhism-Christianity passage. No practice interference was evident, and the studying of the 2,100-word passage comparing Buddhism and Christianity facilitated learning and retention. [David P. Ausubel and Elias Blake, Jr., "Proactive Inhibition in the Forgetting of Meaningful School Material," *Journal of Educational Research*, 52:145–149, 1958.]

The results of the experiment bring up a point about how to handle the meaningful material of difficult topics or subjects. It was found that learning is enhanced by comparing two bodies of material and observing similarities and differences. So it seems that the learning of meaningful material does not reduce remembering of other meaningful subject matter that has been learned but actually improves it. In the case of nonsense syllables and word tests (rote learning), experimental work does indicate that interference takes place, but those findings do not apply to the usual school learnings.

Experience Following Learning: Retroactive Effects. The experience of the learner after the period of learning is an omnipresent factor in the retention of learned material. A period of sleep, for example, tends to retard forgetting, for few stimuli play on the mind during sleep to demand attention and crowd out the material learned.

When long time spans are involved, moreover, experience may affect the retention of large bodies of material. Thus, by testing children before and after summer vacation, some investigators have discovered considerable loss of knowledge. On the other hand, one group of eighth- and ninth-grade pupils has been shown to have made minor gains in vocabulary, language ability, history, civics, geography, and literature and to have lost a considerable amount only in arithmetical computation, the more mechanical phase of arithmetic.

But what happens when interactive effects centrally involve other learning?

Retention may be negatively affected when one piece of learning follows another.

First, the second piece of learning may decrease the memory of the first. If a child learns a story about spacemen and then a story about cowboys, he may remember less of the spaceman story than he would if he had not been told the cowboy story. In retelling the first story, he may make some of its spacemen into cowboys. This effect is called *retroactive inhibition* or, sometimes, *retroactive interference*.

On the other hand, the child may remember the second (cowboy) story less well because he has previously learned the story about spacemen and may, in telling the second story, have some of the cowboys make trips to outer space. This is *proactive inhibition*. (The opposition of the retroactive and proactive inhibition can be clarified by noting that "retroactive" means "acting back upon" and "proactive" means "acting forward.") The interference with previous learning by subsequent learning, which thereby reduces the retention of the previous learning, is a retroactive effect. When subsequent learning interferes with previous learning and the retention of the previous learning is thereby reduced, this is retroactive interference.

Retroactive inhibition was being implied when a former president of Stanford University, David Starr Jordan, who had long been a great ichthyologist (scholar of fish), said that when he learned the name of a student, he forgot the name of a fish. If Dr. Jordan had said that he found himself addressing his students by the names of fish, he would have been acknowledging the working of proactive inhibition or interference.

Experimentation on retroactive inhibition has demonstrated negative learning effects. But much of this experimentation has involved nonsense syllables and word lists. Such material is not like most of the material which is learned in or out of school. Furthermore, the way nonsense materials and word lists are learned in experimental situations is not typical of learning in or out of school. For these reasons, as was pointed out before, it is not safe to draw conclusions about retroactive inhibition for typical learning from the usual laboratory experiments on the subject. D. P. Ausubel, L. C. Robbins, and Elias Blake, Jr., have carried out an experiment (see Exhibit 23) with meaningful material, however, the findings of which are highly significant [Ausubel et al., 1957a].

This investigation certainly indicates that retroactive inhibition does not take place in learning meaningful materials if material studied in sequence is interrelated, compared, or unified. Thus it supports the idea that the relating of present material to formerly learned material will improve the retention of both materials. The interactive effects are thus reinforcing and not interfering. Thus the current trend in education away from compartmentalization of subject matter and courses and toward larger units and the core curriculum seems a sound procedure for improving retention.

An isolated fact is relatively meaningless; if the same fact is thoroughly understood and its implications—its relation to other facts—are made clear, it becomes much more meaningful. A literature teacher who wants his students to remember the dates of a poet's life will have much better success if he relates the dates to other events and shows how they place the poet in a certain era.

This brings us to the closely interrelated subjects of the nature and the use of learned material and retention.

What the Material Is, How It Is Used, and Retention. Discussion of memory logically leads to a consideration of differential retention. We have had evidence for many years that nonsense syllables are forgotten very rapidly, word lists less rapidly, and facts and ideas or knowledge that is organized meaningfully are forgotten still less rapidly. Those who concern themselves with effective teaching and learning advocate that the students be guided into educational settings which cause them to generalize, interpret, and make

Exhibit 23   Retroactive effects on learning by subsequent learning

Group	First Learning	Subsequent Learning	Per Cent of First Learning Retained
Experimental	Studied essay on Buddhism	Studied essay on Buddhism and Christianity	107.7
Control A	Same	Restudied Buddhism	105.1
Control B	Same	Studied essay on Christianity	82.3
Control C	Same	No interpolated learning	84.0

In this experiment 188 college students first learned meaningful material, and were tested on it. Then additional meaningful material was learned, and the learners were tested to discover how much of the first learning was retained. More specifically, an experimental group and three control groups first studied and were tested on a 1,700-word passage on Buddhism. Then the experimental group studied a 2,100-word essay in which Buddhism and Christianity were compared. Control group A spent this second study period restudying the passage on Buddhism; control group B studied a 1,700-word essay on Christianity; and control group C did not study. Then all groups were tested again on the Buddhism passages. Finally the first and second test scores within each group were compared, in order to determine how much of the first learning was retained after the second learning. The results are given in the table.

The results clearly indicate that subsequent learning can go beyond 100 per cent of the first-tested retention to strengthen previous learning. This was true for the experimental group, who studied an essay which dealt with new material (Christianity) related to formerly learned material (Buddhism). This was also true, to a slightly lesser degree, for control group A, who restudied formerly learned material. By contrast, control group B, which completely switched subjects following the first learning, retained less than 100 per cent of first learning—even slightly less than control group C, which did not have any interpolated learning. (Whatever control group B learned about Christianity was an extra dividend in total learning, however, since it retained nearly as much as control group C did from the study of Buddhism.) [Based on data in David P. Ausubel, L. C. Robbins, and Elias Blake, Jr., "Retroactive Inhibition and Facilitation in the Learning of School Materials," *Journal of Educational Psychology*, 48:334–343, 1957.]

applications in terms of principles. The emphasis, then, is on problem solving rather than on memorizing the words of the teacher and of the book. Consequently, there has been considerable interest in testing the retention of facts and principles and the ability to interpret and apply them. The findings indicate rather consistently that "bare" facts such as names, dates, and formulas are retained least, that meaningful knowledge is retained better, and that principles and their interpretation and application are remembered best of all. Furthermore, well-organized material is retained better than unstructured material.

A recent study by William P. McDougall tends to support previous findings to the effect that abilities to interpret and to apply are retained best, but the results do indicate that specific knowledge can also be retained well if it is handled in a comprehensive manner in the teaching and testing (see Exhibit 24).

B. H. Cohen and W. A. Bousfield have found a direct correlation between retention and the degree to which the learner organizes and classifies the material into meaningful patterns [Cohen and Bousfield, 1956]. College students were asked to learn and then recall a list of 40 words arranged in a random order. Those who had grouped the words into categories or classes during learning recalled them much better than those who had learned them at random.

These results have been corroborated by other experiments which have tested learning and remembering when the learning is by fact, or rote, and when it is by systematic organization, or principle. For example, in an ingenious and significant study, R. H. Fargus and R. J. Schwartz tested stu-

Exhibit 24 Percentage of items correct at pretest, end test, and retest

	Knowledge, Per Cent	Translation, Per Cent	Interpretation, Extrapolation, Per Cent
Pretest	49.6	50.2	49.2
End test	64.8	62.4	60.2
Retest	60.6	59.5	57.9
Per cent of gain retained	72.6	73.4	79.2

In a college class in educational psychology, the students were tested at the beginning of the course before they had done any studying (pretest), then at the end of the course (end test), and then again after four months to learn how much was retained. The topics covered in the course were learning and evaluation (tests and measurements).

The above table gives the information about differential learning and retention. It will be observed that the students scored surprisingly high on the pretest, showing that they had considerable knowledge and ability in dealing with the concepts of the course before taking it. The differences in the retention are not large, but the interpretive abilities were retained a little better than knowledge. The good retention of knowledge, even though not so high as the other retention, indicates that in the teaching and testing, emphasis was on meaning rather than on bare, isolated facts which require rote memorizing. In the report of this research, several test items were included and it was evident that the tests were designed in terms of the broader concepts of knowledge. [Adapted from William P. McDougall, "Differential Retention of Course Outcomes in Educational Psychology," *Journal of Educational Psychology,* 49:53–60, 1958.]

dents' learning and remembering of symbols which represented the letters of the alphabet [Fargus and Schwartz, 1957]. Here is the list of symbols:

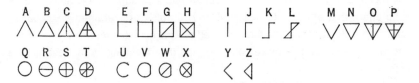

Notice that a regular principle underlies the symbols. The regular alphabet is divided into groups of four letters each. The symbol for the first letter of each group consists of a simplified version of that letter. For each following symbol in each group, one more line is added to the initial symbol.

The subjects were divided into three groups. One was shown the principle, another was told that there was a principle but not what it was, and the third was given the symbols in a garbled order that concealed the principle and was told to memorize them.

Speed of learning was measured for all three groups. A week later, all subjects were retested for recall, transfer, and problem solving. The transfer test consisted in asking the subjects to translate a passage using a different but similar set of symbols (one which had five letters in each group). The problem-solving test consisted in asking them to translate a passage using a set of symbols differing markedly from the original set (alphabet groups were represented by numbers, as were positions in groups, B thus being "2").

The results showed that the two groups which knew about the principle learned the code about twice as quickly as the group which memorized it by rote. Furthermore, their recall of it was much higher, and their scores on the transfer and problem-solving tests were about three times as high.

These last two experiments are most important because they indicate that the power to apply principles is lost less rapidly than the knowledge of terms and thus help explain why the teacher should not limit his teaching to drilling on bare facts, or even principles, but should enrich these by relating them to live situations. And all the experiments just cited indicate that the current deprecation of formal structuring of content in teaching may be too extreme. For example, current opponents of the teaching of formal grammar may be correct in believing that grammar is best approached when it is actually needed in writing and speaking, but grammatical principles probably should be learned a little later in the student's development, to facilitate recall of the structure of grammar he needs in writing.

All this discussion of the characteristics of learned material as related to retention, as well as the earlier discussion showing that some later learning strengthens recall of previously learned material, suggests the importance in retention of the degree to which the learning is not just usable but also used. In a study made by Sister M. Florence L. Lahey of the retention of algebra, for example, it has been discovered that after a year there was about a nineteen per cent loss in knowledge of fundamental operations but an increase of 10.5 per cent in problem-solving ability [Lahey, 1941]. The fact that all the students in the experiment took geometry the year after studying algebra accounted in no small part for the small decline in ability to do the fundamental operations and the increase in ability to solve problems. The training in geometry utilized the abilities that had been acquired in algebra the year before. The students applied their knowledge of algebra to geometry.

Retention is invariably increased if the learned material is used; but use may take either of two forms—*symbolic review* or *reimpression.* In their geometry class, the students mentioned above doubtless used symbolic review. That is, over the year they at various times found it helpful to attempt to recall material learned in algebra to think back over what they had learned. Reimpression consists in actually going over learned material again, as in the case of a French student who, after the course is over, continues to study the language every day. Such a student will obviously recall more French after a year has elapsed than the student who never again speaks or writes the language. The number of reviews, their duration, and their spacing in time are all relevant in determining their effectiveness, of course.

The evidence on the amount forgotten may seem discouraging, but there is an aspect to the learning-forgetting cycle that is not so discouraging. This is the rapidity and effectiveness of relearning. If one needs to review and relearn knowledge that has been forgotten, he often can do so in a relatively short time. Subject matter which is rich in connections with other knowledge is relearned quickly. This is encouraging educationally, as a learner can enlarge his body of knowledge by a quick review of previously learned material.

Relearning of verbatim material is not so rapid; but this is not very relevant to education, as most learning is not of that kind. In today's schools, the teachers encourage conceptualization, reasoning, and the comprehending of meanings. Facts and skills are acquired as part of these intellectual processes and learning verbatim or by sheer memorizing belongs largely to the school of another age. For the kind of knowledge that is usually acquired, relearning is quick because of a reciprocal reinforcement of restored and retained knowledge.

Overlearning is extra-thorough learning, or, more exactly, learning beyond the stage where the material has first been learned. Thus it is, in a sense, midway between learning and review. If a child has learned the multiplication tables so that he can repeat them without error, he may be said to have learned them. Continued study of them may be described as overlearning the combinations. Up to a certain extent, time spent in overlearning is profitably used. This matter of extra time and effort for more thorough learning leads to the question of optimum amounts. As in most situations, too little fails to reach the best rewards and too much is wasteful. There is no rule; but, in general, 50 per cent more time devoted to overlearning is a good investment for strengthening the learning and increasing retention. If, for example, an hour is needed to learn a poem, then up to a half-hour—or 50 per cent more time—can well be used to overlearn it. Indeed, overlearning often moves a learner toward having a firm grasp of a subject rather than a faint hold, because it prevents much forgetting, as has been experimentally shown in various ways (see Exhibit 25).

Overlearning is generally thought of as resulting from additional repetition and practice. Drill and sheer repetition are effective in many learning situations. The school, promotes thorough learning by additional use in a new setting. By integrating and correlating material from several subjects, formerly learned material is brought into new situations. Problem solving calls for new uses of old learnings. Comparisons are made to bring out similarities and differences. This may be considered incidental review, but in effect it produces overlearning by additional use of learned material. This formerly learned material is not drilled formally but becomes involved in various ways. This is probably the most effective way of learning thoroughly. Multiple use of this sort, as when a student experiences the same words in several contexts, is conducive to thorough learning and does not necessitate formal repetition. This kind of thorough or over learning is highly desirable.

The Learner Himself and Retention. Just as the learner's own characteristics influence his learning, so do they affect his retention of what he has learned. The most important of these characteristics are his capacity, his determination to remember, and his attitudes toward the material.

It might be thought that the more knowledge a person has, the more he will forget; but studies of the relationship between mental capacity, amount learned, and retention have shown that this is not the case. High-capacity—and thus knowledgeable—learners have been shown to retain much more of what they have learned than low-capacity—and thus relatively slow—learners.

There seem to be several reasons for this. First, those who are more capable understand better what they learn and therefore learn it more thoroughly. Secondly, the more capable tend to be expansive in their intellectual activities and other interests. Consequently, they learn much that is interrelated;

Exhibit 25   The effect of overlearning on fact recall after three different intervals of time

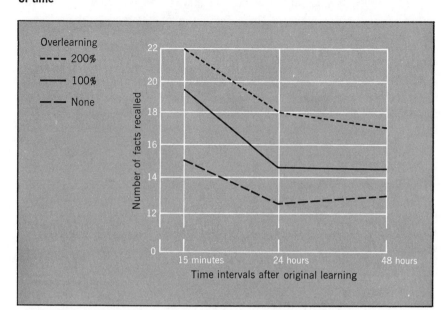

The retention of 27 subjects who ranged in age from twenty to thirty-six years was tested. The subjects listened to the reading and rereading of a fictitious passage of 230 words which contained 22 historical and geographical facts, such as names, dates, populations, and farm products (oats and potatoes). They were then questioned on the 22 facts. The members of one group correctly recalled each of the 22 facts once; it was considered that the facts had been learned. The members of another group correctly recalled the facts twice, or on repetition; this was considered 100 per cent overlearning. The members of the remaining group recalled the facts three times, or two repetitions; this was considered 200 per cent overlearning. The retention tests given after various intervals indicated that the group with the most overlearning recalled most facts and the group with no overlearning recalled fewest. [Thomas F. Gilbert, "Overlearning and the Retention of Meaningful Prose," *Journal of General Psychology*, 56:281–289, 1957. Figure is on page 286.]

their associations among the parts of this wider learning then tend to retard forgetting of what is learned.

John R. Smeltz made a study of the relationship between intelligence and retention of high school chemistry by 180 students [Smeltz, 1956]. They were tested at the beginning of the year's course, at its end to test achievement, and then a year later to test retention. He found a correlation of .51 between achievement and intelligence, which is typical of that relationship. The correlation between achievement and retention was .70, showing a rather high relationship between the amount that is learned and the amount that is retained.

The retention test in chemistry was given a year after the course was concluded, and it was discovered that the students as a whole retained an average of 68 per cent of the material. There was not much difference in the retention of facts, theories, and meanings. Such good retention indicates that the facts were taught not in rote, or isolated fashion but rather as functioning parts of an organic whole.

Sometimes it seems that the slow learner remembers some things very well. The reason is that the facts and concepts which he learns are not difficult and have been much overlearned by having been drilled and reviewed many times in relation with other learning. The dull generally do not cover so wide a range as the more capable and go over a more restricted amount of material much more frequently.

To turn to the learner's determination to remember, it is fairly well established that when a student has a strong intention to learn, he learns better than he does when his approach is more passive. However, it is also generally accepted that when the learner has a strong intention to remember, he remembers better than when he does not particularly care to do so. Various experiments have indicated that learning, with the set to retain, results in higher retention than learning without any intention of remembering. The experimental work of M. N. Thisted and H. H. Remmers has even indicated that an intention to remember something for a specific length of time has a definite effect [Thisted and Remmers, 1932]. They found that if a subject learned something with the intention of retaining it for only one day, his retention at the end of 2 weeks was lower than that of the learner who determined to remember for the 2-week period.

D. P. Ausubel, S. H. Schopoont, and L. Cukier also have refined our knowledge of intention to remember through experimentation [Ausubel et al., 1957b]. They read a 1,400-word passage on narcotic addiction to college students and tested them to ascertain how much they had learned of it. Then one group of students was told that it would be tested again in 2 weeks; the other group was not told. When the two groups were tested 2 weeks later, it was found that each group remembered the same amount. The particular indication was that if intention to remember is to result in more retention for later testing, the learner should know before he begins to learn something that he will be tested at a later date. The general indication was that motivation should be strengthened at the time of, rather than after, learning if retention is to be improved.

The course of learning and the course of forgetting thus are intimately related. This suggests that remembering is a functioning part of the learning process: If we learn more, we retain more, and this in turn improves our learning. But also, and literally at the same time, the intent to remember results in more learning and therefore better retention.

☯ Reflect and Review

In the eighth grade, a student had an arithmetic course; in the ninth grade, algebra; in his sophomore year, geometry; and in his junior year, trigonometry. Then in college he majored in mathematics. Is it likely that his college courses helped or hurt his memory of his high school courses? Is it likely that his high school courses helped him in his college courses? Why?

Teachers year after year learn the names of the students in their classes. Is learning the names of the students in one class likely to reduce the memory for the names of students in previous classes and vice versa?

A given teacher who has taught for 30 years remembers the names of all the students he had in his first class but not of those in his other classes. Why?

One student studied Latin, French, and Italian within a span of 4 years. Another student studied German, Russian, and Chinese within the same span. Which student experienced more proactive interference and which experienced more retroactive interference?

A history teacher repeatedly introduced economic and sociological interpretation in teaching the history of the United States. He also brought in psychological concepts about the needs and motives of the people. His examinations emphasized these various relationships, and he dealt with names, dates, and places only as needed. Is this sound in terms of learning and retaining?

Finally, experiments have shown specifically that the learner's favorable or unfavorable attitudes both toward his own experiences and toward study materials may have decided influences not only on learning but also on retention.

In the first area—that of personal experience—L. I. O'Kelly and L. C. Steckle had college students, on their return from their Christmas vacations, report their pleasant and unpleasant vacation experiences [O'Kelly and Steckle, 1940]. Sixty-two per cent of the experiences were pleasant, and thirty-seven per cent were unpleasant—a ratio of almost 2 to 1. Ten weeks later, 48 per cent of the pleasant experiences were recalled and 40 per cent of the unpleasant, suggesting better retention of the pleasant than the unpleasant. Yet when the experiences were rated for intensity, it was found that the essential point of difference in recall ability was that experiences of high intensity were recalled most and those of low intensity were recalled least. The difference in the recall of pleasant and unpleasant experiences was incidental; the important difference was in the acuteness of the experience and the corresponding intensity of feeling.

This is generally true; that which is personally toned with feeling is remembered better than that which is neutral, or has no feeling tone. There seems to be a difference in recall, however, based on whether what is to be recalled is an experience of the person recalling it, or is someone else's experience, or consists of emotionally colored words and ideas. It is likely that, for emotionalized material not out of our own experiences, we tend primarily to remember the pleasant better than the unpleasant.

This last point seems to be confirmed in the second of the above areas of the effect of attitude on the learner's retention—the area of study materials. Two experiments have demonstrated it by using the highly emotional topic of Communism for material in testing retention. J. M. Levine and G. Murphy had two groups of college students—one pro-Communist, the other anti-Communist—read material on Soviet Russia and then tested the students' retention of the material [Levine and Murphy, 1943]. R. B. Garber also had students read a passage on Russia and then tested retention [Garber, 1955]. In both cases, the students retained many more of the ideas with which they agreed than of those with which they disagreed.

Over a period of several decades there have been a number of experiments designed to test the retention of the pleasant or the unpleasant, the favorable or the unfavorable, the likable or the dislikable, the threatening or the unthreatening, and the ego-building or the ego-damaging. The results are fairly consistent, even though the differences are not large, in showing that the favorable and nonthreatening material is remembered better than the disagreeable and disliked. This is true on the average, but there are individuals who remember one kind of material as well as another and even some who tend to remember the unpleasant better than they remember the pleasant. Differential retention is probably related to the personality pattern of the learner. The ones who are well balanced and feel safe and sure will probably not react negatively to unpleasant material and will remember it as well as the pleasant. Learners who are sensitive to threat are disposed to remember the ego-nourishing concepts and events, and the persons with self-pitying or masochistic tendencies will probably remember better the threatening material.

I. N. Korner devised an ingenious experiment to test the retention of both supportive and damaging ideas [Korner, 1950]. This research involved 98 college students who were divided into experimental and control groups. On the basis of 18 starting sentences they wrote 18 short stories by continuing with three or four sentences. Each story was given a three-word title. The students were told that in these short stories they projected their personalities and that the stories would be rated by three experts to determine their balance or unbalance. These judges marked 6 of the 18 with a plus sign to indicate good balance; 6 were marked with a minus sign to indicate poor balance or adjustment; and 6 were not marked.

It was hypothesized that the short stories with the minus marks would be disturbing. It is disrupting to one's self-image to be told that one is maladjusted, and certainly such ideas are disagreeable. A plus sign indicating a well-balanced personality is very pleasing and gratifying. No mark is considered as being neutral.

The subjects learned the 18 titles, as indicated by the ability to recall all 18 of them without error. Then after 4 days they were asked to recall the titles again, and a comparison of the number of plus and minus titles indicated the differential recall of those with which there was supportive self-involvement and those with which the self-involvement was disturbing. During the experiment it was observed that many of the subjects were disturbed by the minus mark on their stories. It should also be noted that the ratings were not real ratings but merely marks divided among the 18 titles.

In short, there were more minus than plus titles forgotten, the respective totals being 117 and 81. The difference between these values is significant at the 1 per cent level. This finding is consistent with the results of other experiments in this area of retention and forgetting.

These facts raise a question of why there is this differential retention. A theory advanced by Korner and others is that we have a tendency to repress threatening, ego-damaging material. People do not want to feel guilty, shamed, or reduced in status and therefore wish to remove from their awareness any mental content that has such effects. They reject such ideas through repression. Some of the subjects had difficulty in learning some titles which to them were negatively emotionalized and commented to the effect that they did not understand why these titles gave them so much trouble. Thus it seems that the positive and negative feelings that the learner has for ideas and concepts influence the facility with which they are learned and also how well they are retained.

Of course, as suggested in our original discussion of attitudes, emotionally neutral material may often become emotionally loaded through classroom associations; thus material which has been learned in a hostile, dogmatic threatening atmosphere is likely to become associated with unpleasant feelings; and, on the other hand, material learned in a friendly atmosphere tends to have pleasant associations. Accordingly, as experiments have shown, material learned in a pleasant atmosphere is recalled better than material learned in an unpleasant one.

The findings on remembering pleasant and unpleasant materials do not lead to very definite conclusions. In general, it seems that pleasant words and pleasant experiences are remembered a little more than the unpleasant. There is a complication in this connection, and that is the intensity of the pleasantness and the unpleasantness. It seems that we remember better the more emotionally toned experiences or ideas, whether pleasant or unpleasant. And it is very difficult to judge the intensity of feeling.

It seems that remembering the agreeable or disagreeable may be related to the personality of the learner. For example, it may be found that the more optimistic individuals tend to remember better the agreeable and pleasant, while the pessimistic or more negative individuals remember the unpleasant better.

At this point it is well to recall the theory of repression. Disagreeable ideas and experiences that are threatening to a person, as many of them are, may be forgotten through the process of repression. If this pushing of disagreeable mental content into oblivion does take place, then there will be relatively more recall of the pleasant.

This leads to pointing out that remembering, as well as all phases of learning, should be interpreted in terms of needs and motives. We are motivated to learn and remember that which is satisfying. We try to avoid that which is not. Still, children, youth, and adults have personal experiences and dealings with ideational material which they do not like. There are many topics of a political, economic, social, and religious nature, for example, that are controversial and emotionally toned. We do tend to learn and remember what we like and reject that which we do not favor. Our intellects tend to be motivational and selective, and feelings are strong elements in the dynamics of learning and forgetting.

In regard to the teacher, pupils, and classroom, the research indicates that a good emotional classroom climate is conducive to learning but a neutral, dead, and colorless classroom climate is not conducive to learning. The research suggests that students who have a personable and enthusiastic teacher will develop a feeling about their studies which will facilitate effective learning. Neutral and colorless teachers tend to leave the students cold and indifferent about their work. Without a good feeling for learning, the students accomplish less. Other teachers develop much feeling in their students but in the direction of anger, disappointment, and resentment. Such unfavorably emotionalized situations linger in the students' memory. They may remember few events that took place during the school year with a neutral teacher, but they will remember many incidents that took place in the classroom of a maladjusted teacher who stirs up unhappy feelings in his students. But instructionally, such teachers are rarely effective in stimulating the learning and increasing the retention of the school curriculum. In short, then, the good teacher permeates the learning of his students with wholesome feelings and thereby strengthens that learning.

✐ Reflect and Review

The topic of multiplying fractions is to be taken up in a sixth-grade arithmetic class. The teacher takes a great deal of time explaining the process, making sure that each student understands it. He uses the students' own experiences as background material for his problems. Despite the fact that several of the students are very slow to grasp the process, the teacher does not become impatient, and at one point in the discussion tells a little joke which eases the tension and makes everyone laugh. Then, when everyone in class seems to understand the process and has worked several problems, a period of drill begins. The next day, when he is talking about how to divide fractions, the teacher contrasts the process to multiplication of fractions and shows how the two processes differ.

The teacher has made use of what principles to increase retention? How, in each case, has he done this? Particularly, how did he move toward evoking positive attitudes toward the work?

The teacher had the class drill after they had worked several sample problems. Would you have other drill sessions on both multiplying and dividing fractions? Where, in the course of learning, should they come?

SUMMARY

In trying to understand the progress made in learning and the losses of forgetting it is helpful to think (1) of the learner and his characteristics, (2) of the task or problem and its characteristics, and (3) of the methods and processes of learning.

In much that is learned, the progress at first is slow because the task is difficult for the learner and he does not have the prerequisite abilities which enable him to progress rapidly. Initial progress is fast when the learner does have such abilities or when the learning is very easy. The teacher aims to develop the readiness of his pupils for their learnings so they make encouraging progress from the start.

A plateau is a period of temporary arrest of progress caused by fatigue, boredom, lack of interest and motivation, or failure of presently used methods to provide additional progress. When these negative factors are replaced by positive ones, the learner assumes a new phase of progress.

Limits are reached beyond which the learner cannot go no matter how hard and well he tries. These are the learner's ultimate, physiological, or theoretical limits. The term "physiological limit" applies particularly to physical activities such as typing, piano playing, and athletics. Still it must be remembered that there is a physical element in all responses.

The levels on which learners actually function are known as their practical levels. If the learner is indifferent in his efforts, his level is low; but if he is efficient, his level is very high and may be regarded as an optimum level. No one can continue for long at his physiological or ultimate limit.

The teacher can make use of these concepts by selecting subject matter and preparing the students so they will make fairly rapid and rewarding starts, by stimulating his students' progress, and by preventing them from stagnating. He can keep the students interested by keeping them aware of their progress, and he can help them over difficult places when they need it. He can also apply these same concepts to his own living and learning.

Like the course of learning, the course of forgetting has several definable characteristics. It can be best understood by reference to the learner; to the nature of the material; and to the experiences before, during, and after learning.

One element that affects remembering or forgetting is the learning of other material before or after something is learned. The effects that two learning tasks have on each other are called "interactive" effects.

Proactive inhibition or interference takes place when previous learning interferes with subsequent learning.

Retroactive interference takes place when subsequent learning interferes with retention of previous learning.

The evidence is rather clear that in learning lists of words, numbers, and nonsense syllables, there is proactive as well as retroactive interference.

In the case of meaningful material which may be related, compared, and unified or, in general, associated, there is reinforcement rather than interference.

Meaningfulness, organization, and good problem-solving procedures facilitate retention. Retention of nonsense material learned by rote is poorest of all.

Use or application retards forgetting and increases retention.

Overlearning is learning beyond the point of first retention by more repetition or by use.

In general, the more capable learners both learn and retain more.

Intention to remember, in order to be effective, must be manifested at the time of learning. Such intention has little effect on retention after the learning.

There is a positive substantial correlation between the amount retained and the amount learned.

We tend to learn and remember better that which is pleasant and agreeable. Emotional conditions do influence learning, and students are most effective in a pleasant and rewarding atmosphere.

SUGGESTED READING

Fitzgerald, Donald, and David P. Ausubel: "Cognitive versus Affective Factors in the Learning and Retention of Controversial Material," *Journal of Educational Psychology*, 54:73–84, 1963. Fitzgerald and Ausubel interpret their experimental results as indicating that cognitive or intellectual factors are at work rather than feeling or affective ones in influencing learning and retention of a passage of the War between the States, which was characterized by the Southern point of view. This article is rich in learning concepts.

Levinger, George, and James Clark: "Emotional Factors in the Forgetting of Word Associations," *Journal of Abnormal and Social Psychology*, 62:99–105, 1961. This carefully conducted experiment indicates that more word responses to emotional words are forgotten than the word responses to neutral words. In the discussion, a number of significant concepts are set forth.

Postman, Leo: "Retention as a Function of Degree of Overlearning," *Science*, 135:666–667, 1962. This article shows the value of overlearning and particularly its value for the retention of difficult items. Helpful discussion supplements a neat experiment.

Symonds, Percival M.: "What Education Has to Learn from Psychology. VI. Emotion and Learning," *Teachers College Record*, 60:9–22, 1958. This article brings out many concepts on how feelings influence learning. The influence of anxiety is discussed at length.

CHAPTER 16
TRANSFER
AND EFFECTIVE LEARNING

Transfer, the process by which something learned in one situation is used in another, is absolutely essential if education is to be effective. For a striking example, if grammar had to be learned separately in every context where language is used—writing grammatically in geography class, writing grammatically in arithmetic class, speaking grammatically at home, and so forth—the task would be Herculean, and so it would never be done or would be done to the extreme detriment of other phases of education and general development. But transfer cannot be passively relied upon in education, as is seen daily when we encounter students who do such things as study grammar and write and speak grammatically in English class and then write and speak ungrammatically in other classes and outside of school.

The primary purpose of this chapter, then, is to explain this process of transfer—what it is in fuller terms, how it takes place, and how it can be brought about.

But all this will lead us to define and discuss also the equally important phenomenon of mental discipline, which is closely related to and, indeed, has often been equated with transfer, but which is not the same.

THE CONCEPTS OF TRANSFER

Transfer is evident when we learn or behave better or worse in a situation as a consequence of what we have learned in another situation. Being more effective in situation B because of what we have learned in situation A indicates positive transfer; being less effective in situation B because of what we have learned in A indicates negative transfer. There is also a condition known as compartmentalization, in which there is no transfer. As the term indicates, compartmentalization is, in essence, a separation; one learned thing does not transfer to bolster or to hamper a person in a later situation. The left hand is seemingly unaware of what the right hand has done, and vice versa. The term compartmentalization has its background in the fields of mental and emotional health, where it has been used to describe areas of inconsistent and contradictory behavior without transfer and conflict. Compartmentalization also may involve ideas and ideals. Conceivably, compartmentalization develops as a protection against the disturbance that would develop if there were transfer of inconsistent knowledge and behavior.

Other relevant terms we have already encountered are proactive and retroactive interference and proactive and retroactive reinforcement (see Chapter 15). In terms of transfer, interference is negative transfer, and reinforcement is positive transfer.

For the most part, however, we shall discuss positive transfer, which we shall hereafter simply call transfer, in three of its most educationally important categories:

1. *Transfer of knowledge.* There is positive transfer when the facts, principles, and meanings acquired in one learning situation improve learning or behavior in another. When knowledge of mathematics helps a person grasp chemistry, or knowledge of geometry helps him appreciate figures in art, or knowledge of psychology helps him understand literature, we have examples of transfer of knowledge to learning. And when a person's knowledge of moral principles results in his behavior's being more ethical, there is transfer of knowledge to behavior.

2. *Transfer of techniques.* There is also transfer of learned ways of doing things. Such techniques may, of course, be largely sensorimotor, as in sports and mechanical activities; or abstract and symbolic, as in language study, problem solving, and scientific research. Both kinds of techniques may transfer. Thus knowing how to play baseball may help a person in football, experience with carpenter's tools may help him in using the tools of a plumber, the methods developed in studying French may help him in studying German, and solving a research problem experimentally in the laboratory may help him solve a personal problem in an objective way. All are examples of transfer of techniques.

3. *Transfer of ideals and attitudes.* There is transfer of an ideal, for example, when it is applied in various situations. A person may express certain ideals and attitudes about right and wrong, and transfer is evident when his behavior is influenced correspondingly. A person may express deep sympathy for the poor people who are submerged by a low standard of living and may argue for an ideal society in which all people will have economic security. Still, he may actually do nothing for the poor and may, when he hires temporary workers, pay them the lowest possible wage and complain that they are lazy. He fails to apply his attitudes to actual behavior. Similarly, a person may fail to transfer an attitude from one area of activity

to another. A secretary may be extremely meticulous, for example, in her office work, but be disorderly and chaotic in her housekeeping at home. The ideal of neatness is not transferred from one activity to the other, in this case. There is transfer of attitudes and ideals when the mental and emotional content is manifested in behavior consistent with that content. When a person's behavior is out of harmony with his ideals and attitudes, then he is failing to transfer these ideals to his behavior.

But how does transfer take place?

HOW TRANSFER OCCURS: THE EXPERIMENTAL BACKGROUND

Two theories are commonly advanced to explain transfer—the theory of *identical elements* and the theory of *generalization*. According to the theory of identical elements, there is transfer from one situation to another to the extent that the same elements, or components, are found in the different situations. There is transfer (of knowledge) from algebra to geometry to the extent that some elements of geometry occur also in algebra—symbols, equations, and proportions, for example. There is transfer (of technique) from baseball to football to the extent that there are common components such as running, throwing, catching, and general bodily agility. In comparative terms, there is more transfer from reading to spelling than from reading to playing baseball because, while the processes are far from the same, in reading and spelling there are centrally important identical elements, which is not true of reading and playing baseball. For the same reason, there is more transfer from geography to history than from geography to penmanship, and there is more transfer from arithmetic to algebra than from art to algebra.

According to the theory of generalization, transfer occurs when a person learns a principle or idea in one situation and then is able to apply it in another situation. More specifically, the learner learns a concept in the first situation, sees that the concept can contribute to the understanding of the second situation (the beginning of transfer), and applies the concept to it.

A little reflection will make it clear that these theories do not contradict each other but are complementary. Transfer may take place by means of both processes in the same learning situation. Let us take as an example a good baseball player who is learning to play golf. The identical or similar elements in baseball and golf—the similarity between the use of the bat and the club, the importance in both of a carefully controlled body position, and the general fact that both involve a controlled striking of a ball—will help him learn golf more quickly. But many of these elements are not exactly the same in baseball and golf. Therefore he will learn more quickly if he can generalize his baseball experience and apply it to golf. If he is having trouble with holding the club properly, he may remember the slow process of trial and error he went through in learning to bat and may try some of the same experimentation with his golf stroke. Thus, even in the respects in which holding a bat and a club differ, his baseball experience may help him. If he does not generalize, on the other hand, and obstinately holds the club just as he holds a bat, negative transfer or proactive interference takes place.

The theory of generalization was set forth at the beginning of this century by the distinguished psychologist and educator C. H. Judd, who tested the ability of boys to hit a target placed under water [Judd, 1908]. Some of the boys had studied the principles of refraction of light—how it shifts direction when it leaves one light-transmitting substance and enters another, and how this makes objects appear to be where they are not. They had learned why an oar in water does not seem straight to the rower and why a fish in the water is farther under the surface than it seems to the fisherman on the bank. Others had not been given such instruction. The purpose of the experiment was to determine whether or not the boys who had studied the refraction of light could hit a target under water better than the boys who had not.

It was discovered that when the target was 1 foot below the surface of the water, there was no significant difference in the abilities of the two groups, but that when the target was raised to within 4 inches of the water's surface, the boys who had been taught the refraction were able to adjust better than the others.

Hitting a target 12 inches under water is considerably harder than hitting one 4 inches under, for it is harder to estimate a "correction" of aim based on refraction principles for the greater depth and also to overcome the resistance of the water; and at 12 inches, these difficulties apparently offset the transfer of the principles which the one group had learned. Once these difficulties were lessened, however, this group was able to generalize its knowledge of light refraction, developed by experience with the greater depth, by applying it to a new situation, it was concluded.

G. Hendrickson and W. H. Schroeder further developed the essentials of the Judd experiment with three groups of eighth-grade boys who shot with a BB gun at a bull's-eye type of target submerged in water at depths of 6 and 2 inches [Hendrickson and Schroeder, 1941]. Groups A and B were told about refraction, but group B was given more explanation than group A. Group C, the control group, was given no information about refraction.

The results were essentially these:

1. Group B made the best score at both depths.
2. Group C made the poorest score at both depths.
3. Group B's superiority over group A was proportional to the difference in the amount of instruction given these two groups.

These experiments tested ability to apply knowledge learned in one situation to another situation; but transfer of technique through generalization has also been tested. Thus M. C. Barlow, using as subjects mostly seventh- and eighth-graders, sought to discover whether—and if so, how much—the power to interpret *Aesop's Fables* was improved by special practice in reasoning and behavior analysis in the following way [Barlow, 1937].

The subjects were tested at the beginning of the experiment on the ability to interpret 15 fables. One, for example, was the tale of a widow who doubled the amount she fed her hen, expecting two eggs a day; the best interpretation was that "figures are not always facts." Then an experimental group had four lessons in reasoning by analogy (boy is to girl as man is to _____), four in reasoning by induction (from particular to general) and by deduction (from general to particular), and four in analyzing behavior situations. In the lessons the students discussed the material and explained how they arrived at their conclusions. A control group did not have this practice. Then all the students were retested and the tests compared.

The net gain of the experimental group's ability to interpret the fables was 64 per cent—clear evidence that techniques of reasoning transfer to improve ability in reasoning with materials other than those used originally to teach the techniques.

In another study—similar to Barlow's in that transfer of technique, not of knowledge, was centrally involved—transfer as a consequence of practice in outlining and summarizing has been obtained with seventh- to twelfth-grade students in an actual schoolroom situation.

In this study, by Rachel Salisbury, an experimental group was given 30 specially prepared bodies of material to be outlined and summarized [Salisbury, 1934]. The practice consisted in picking out the main points, arranging them in logical order, and observing the "next steps" in thought; also included was some practice in preparing outlines for the students' own compositions. A control group was not given this practice, and consequently the differences in the changes of abilities of the two groups could be attributed to transfer of the practiced techniques. This was measured by administering to both groups, before and after the practice period, a test of general mental ability; a reading examination; a reasoning test; and an achievement test in American history, civics, and general science. Finally, a comparison of the test scores was made to determine the extent to which the practiced techniques might have been applied to the second mental, reading, reasoning, and achievement tests and so improved the abilities measured by these tests.

The results indicate that important transfer occurred: The practice group showed improvement in all tests. The improvement in the mental-ability test was not large enough to be attributable without doubt to the special practice;

but this reflects the fact that it is most difficult to influence the scores on a test consisting of various kinds of exercises, so that to expect improvement in a general mental-ability test would be setting up a very high criterion for transfer, indeed. The improvement in reading, on the other hand, was expressed with critical ratios ranging from 4.7 for the seventh grade to 6.6 for the twelfth grade. Critical ratios this high leave no doubt that the differences are due not to chance but to the actual effects being measured—in this case, the practice effects. Also, the reasoning and achievement test results displayed differences in ability large enough to represent significant transfer.

In summary, it was concluded that "The mental skills involved in outlining and summarizing, described herein as the processes of logical organization, transfer to produce improvement in general thinking or reasoning ability, as tested by problems not related to the specific school curriculum."

In this experiment, while the ability to obtain meaning from printed paragraphs increased, the speed of reading decreased—a case of negative transfer; but this decrease was more than offset by the fact that the practice of studiously outlining a selection resulted in more careful, as well as slower, reading—all of which brings us to a currently very important educational area where the power and refinement of the process of transfer of technique are well illustrated.

There has been a great deal of interest in the past decade in learning to read faster—a task that is complicated by the need to maintain or even improve comprehension. But also, speed of reading is affected by the nature of the material read—whether prose is technical and difficult or nontechnical and written in a simple, easy style, for instance.

If we analyze the problem in terms of transfer theory, we can see that what is involved is primarily a question of transfer of technique. If a person learns a reading technique with one kind of material, can he transfer that technique to another kind of material? On the one hand, we should look for identical elements; there are, of course, many in two tasks which both consist in reading. On the other hand, we should look for the elements in the two tasks which are different in order to avoid negative transfer. Reading complex material may require more stops for mental organization and review than reading a simple narrative, for example.

All this leads to the question whether improved speed and comprehension in reading one kind of material results in similar improvement in reading another. Is there such transfer of practiced reading technique?

In an experiment conducted by M. Schwartz, a preflight group in the United States Navy had 17.5 hours of training in reading nontechnical material which was not difficult, and then was tested on ability to read technical material in the fields of engineering, physics, and chemistry [Schwartz, 1957].

The results were striking. As a group, these young men gained 104 per cent in speed of reading technical material. There was a decrease of about six per cent in comprehension; but since speed more than doubled, the amount comprehended in a given time nearly doubled.

◑   *Reflect and Review*

A most unusual example of transfer was reported by Eunice Winn, a teacher in a Kentucky high school, when she told how a youth overcame the bad temper he often displayed on the basketball court. In learning to do geometry problems, the student concluded that order and consistency helped and so that extraneous facts and ideas hindered the process of getting the correct answer to a problem. As a result of this experience in geometry, he perceived that there were also order and consistency in basketball and that his outbursts of anger on the court were an extraneous factor which disturbed this order and consistency and so made his basketball playing less effective. He then applied these ideas concretely to his playing and decreased greatly his involvement in angry disputes during games.

Eunice Winn also told of a girl who was doing well in her sewing class but was doing poorly in history. She was able to comprehend the rather complicated printed directions for sewing dresses but had trouble comprehending what she read in history. Her sewing teacher explained to her that her ability to interpret the sewing directions showed that she was a good reader, so that she should also be able to understand her history lessons. The sewing and history teachers then joined forces to show the girl how she might apply study methods which had proved successful in sewing to the study of history. The student soon learned that she was capable of understanding and doing the assignments in history, and her work improved greatly: Instead of failing, she achieved C and B standing.

Which theory of transfer explains the first case and which the second? Describe each step of these two events in theoretical terms.

Did one of the two students experience a more complicated transfer process than the other? Explain your answer.

The first transfer case is especially unusual because geometry and basketball would normally be quite separate as activities. What is the theoretical term for this state of relationship?

HOW TO ACHIEVE TRANSFER

Having seen, in various special contexts, how transfer occurs, let us approach the vital question of how we should learn in order to achieve the considerable transfer that is necessary for effective education. This, of course, is a question with large ramifications, for in its broadest terms the issue is how we can make as wide use of all that we learn as possible. Let us, however, begin our discussion of this issue in the simple and clearly defined terms of the individual school subject. Specifically, let us consider the question of the effects of studying particular subjects on mental abilities.

Transfer and Specific Subjects. Two experiments have been conducted with the purpose of determining whether the abilities measured by intelligence tests—the general abilities to use words, numbers, and other symbols, and to deal with spatial relationships—are affected by the subjects taken in high school and, if so, by one subject more than another.

In both experiments, one by E. L. Thorndike and one by A. G. Wesman, students were given intelligence tests at the beginning of the school year and divided into groups according to their scores [Thorndike, 1924; Wesman, 1945]. (Similarity in other important respects was also a grouping factor.) Then the lists of subjects taken by the students in each group were studied in order to find programs of study which were the same except for one subject and thus to form experimental subgroups. At the end of the year, all the students were again given intelligence tests, and the scores were compared with beginning scores. Thus the absolute and relative effects of given subjects on the abstract intelligence of the bright, the average, and the dull could be measured. For example, if a subgroup of bright students whose courses for the year were English, algebra, sociology, and Latin and a comparable sub-group who studied English, algebra, sociology, and economics showed an overall difference in ability in the intelligence tests taken at the end of the school year, this difference could be attributed to difference between the trans-fer effects of Latin and economics; if, say, those studying economics scored higher in the end tests than the Latin students, then it might be inferred that economics had greater transfer value than Latin. The effects of subjects on specific abilities shown by the various parts of the intelligence tests were similarly determined. Following is an outline of the essential conclusions of these two studies:

1. The study of particular subjects did not consistently improve the sum of abilities reflected by the intelligence-test scores.

2. Particular subjects had no consistent effects on those sections of the intelligence tests they might have been expected to affect importantly. For example, the apparent effect of language courses was sometimes to increase the scores on the verbal tests and sometimes to lower them; likewise, the seeming effect of mathematics courses was sometimes to increase the scores on the numerical tests, but in some instances these scores became lower.

3. There was no consistent relationship between amount of improvement in subject-matter knowledge and improvement in intelligence-test scores.

4. There was a little more transfer for bright students than for dull, apart from the fact, important in itself, that bright students learned a great deal about subjects they did not take in school from their outside reading and other experiences.

5. There was a little greater apparent transfer for students who took the largest load of courses; these students were the brightest students, however, and this is a factor that must be considered as well as the extra work.

The studies indicate, then, that there is no more transfer to general mental ability from one subject than from another and that, indeed, specific school subjects do not have important effects on mental abilities at all. These findings, incidentally, are especially pertinent at the present time when the schools are being criticized on the ground that too few students are taking the "solid and substantial subjects" in order to achieve excellence; for on the basis of this evidence, we can say definitely that there are no preferred subjects for their transfer value, though the richer mental experiences obtained from studying a greater variety of subjects appear to facilitate transfer, so that it seems desirable for a student to take as full a program of subjects as he can reasonably carry.

A reference here back to the Salisbury experiment in which practice in outlining and summarizing led to improvements in performance in other areas may be useful for comparison. Salisbury was working with a technique which could be applied to any body of material—that of organizing and ordering a series of facts. Thorndike and Wesman, on the other hand, were working with complete courses separated by differences in subject matter, and they evaluated the effects of individual school subjects on the mental-test abilities of the students taking those subjects.

But what is the significance of the other aspects of these findings—the suggestions that (1) most transfer occurs for the bright and that (2) experience, including but also extending beyond the experience of a wide curriculum, facilitates transfer? For instance, in the earlier-cited Barlow experiment on effects of thinking practice on ability to interpret fables, the more intelligent half of the trained subjects transferred 30 per cent more than the less intelligent half. Also, it is generally true that experience facilitates transfer. Thus, an experiment was devised to test whether the study of science causes a scientific attitude to supplant superstitions and other emotional biases in controlling thinking in various life situations.

It was discovered that some subjects with considerable knowledge of science could not apply it to life situations, and also that those who applied their learning most rationally—those for whom the transfer was greatest—were those students of high intelligence who had the most experience in situations embracing the scientific fact studied.

Transfer and Capacity and Experience. It is a well-established fact that capacity is a prime factor in transfer. Practically all the experiments in this area indicate that the transfer values of learning vary according to the mental capacity of the learners—that the bright not only learn more but also transfer more than the average and that the average similarly profit more than the dull.

These two factors, then, are more central to the problem of furthering transfer than are particular courses of subject matter.

Teaching must stimulate each student to use all his capacity, whatever it is, in learning. But since we have dealt with this need earlier, we shall here focus on the experience factor in encouraging transfer, beginning with the crucial moment-to-moment and hour-to-hour experiences of teaching and learning any subject.

The Theories of Transfer as Guides. Not surprisingly, teaching furthers transfer especially well when the teacher directly stimulates the processes set forth in the two previously discussed theories of transfer—the recognition of identical elements and the generalization of learned concepts. Thus the teacher should consciously provide a basis for transfer by looking for identical elements in learning situations that follow one another and helping the students see them; for apart from the specific relationships being considered, the experience in detecting similarities between situations will mean that more transfer will take place for the students.

The Latin teacher, for example, can build up in students a consciousness of and thus an ability to see the identical elements in Latin and English by pointing out how certain English words are derived from the Latin and then encouraging the students to look for more. This may be done in various ways. One of the more interesting is through the analysis of words in some of the more formal statements that appear in newspapers. The number of English words that have Latin origins in some of the speeches recorded in our newspapers is surprisingly large, and the use of newspapers introduces an element of worldly experience into the classroom. But however it is done, most, if not all, investigations indicate that more gain is made in the comprehension of English words when teachers of Latin devote some time to the analysis of English words. In terms of the theory of identical elements, transfer is furthered when the teacher helps his students perceive the similar words (or word parts) in Latin and English and gives them practice in transferring their knowledge of the former language to the learning of the latter.

This does not apply only to Latin, of course. In social studies, the biological and physical sciences, mathematics, the languages, the arts, and the vocational subjects—within each of the fields and between the fields—there are similarities which the student needs to perceive. There are, for example, applications of mathematics to home economics, physical education, and industrial arts. And good teaching guides the students to understand such relationships wherever they occur.

Being able to develop and apply a concept—which is, of course, to transfer through generalization—is also desirable in most, if not all, subjects. For example, in history it is useful for students to learn that in countries where poverty, ignorance, and injustice prevail, there exists a strong potential for unrest and revolution; in geometry, students' progress depends importantly on their being led to draw generalizations about lines and angles; and for psychology to be most meaningful, the teacher's orientation must be toward encouraging full understanding and use of the widely applicable ideas about motivation, needs, and so forth that lie in the subject matter.

But the teacher's work in stimulating such transfer through generalization is more complicated than his job of fostering the recognition of identical elements in two learning situations. Why?

A principle or idea can be taught in three basic ways. The teacher can state and then explain it; he can actively lead the students in discovering it, giving strong hints and/or cues as they proceed; or he can provide only data suggesting the existence of the concept and then allow the students to discover it for themselves. But the choice of method to be used in developing a concept influences the amount of transfer attained. Specifically, the research on this topic indicates that students not only learn and comprehend a concept better when they discover it for themselves but also are more effective in transferring it. This, of course, is a very basic value.

It seems, then, that the teacher generally should try to give minimal direct help in leading students to discover and formulate a concept. Then, when students have reached the generalization, they can be guided to transfer it to various situations.

The earlier parts of this procedure, particularly, impose responsibilities on the teacher that are not easy. To set the stage for development of the concept requires especially careful, even subtle use of subject matter; and once this is done, the teacher can be tempted to lead the students directly to the concept. But if care and restraint are habitually used here, the students will develop a strong and prevailing set for transfer; and the results will point up the fact that teaching which encourages reasoning, discovery, and application is more effective than teaching which encourages merely the mechanical acquisition and memorizing of facts and principles.

But we have been discussing ideals; and unfortunately it must be said that the high opportunities for furthering transfer—of concepts and of identical elements, too—are often, in fact, missed by educators.

Thus history is often taught as a conglomeration of battles, coronations, treaties, births, and various other events strung together largely by dates, when it should be a vast story of the past, comprehensively describing and explaining the varied forces that caused the people in its pages to behave as they did—human psychology, religions, sociology, economics, geography, and others. History should help us understand people, interpret their behavior, and even predict what they will do under given circumstances. In other words, history treated so broadly and richly can be viewed as the roots of the present; we can learn to trace present situations back into the past and thus interpret the present more profoundly. But we cannot expect "date and name" history thus to transfer, in the broadest sense of the word, to the present day and help students interpret the social, economic, and other current problems. Such history is merely a rattling of the dead bones of the past and, as such, cannot stimulate students to achieve the lively orientation to the field that is essential for good transfer. Instead, intellectual vitality is taken away by the essential artificiality of the data and their presentation.

Such artificial teaching, as we have indicated, is all too common in our schools, though it would have to be described somewhat differently for each learning area. Accordingly, vitality disappears from learning to such an extent that disheartened observers have sometimes been prompted to make such statements as "School is a place where pebbles are polished and diamonds are dimmed."

Learning through Vital Experiences. In the last analysis, of course, it is not enough just to read and read about a subject and talk and talk about it, no matter how well these things are directed and done, for this is vicarious experience that must eventually become barren and anemic. Thus we end with the agriculturist who has written on farm management but cannot manage a farm; the thoroughly schooled psychiatrist who has been around in the world so little that he cannot distinguish his patients' reality problems from their symptoms; and the well-read man of whatever vocation who thinks he has solutions for every one of his town's, his country's, and even the world's ills but is a failure in handling his own affairs and more of a failure when he joins a civic committee. All these people are well equipped with ideas but fail in practice. Their "mental" learning should have been integrated with vital practical experiences. Indeed, any learner needs to face reality directly—have a wealth of worldly experiences—and, by so doing, to establish rich patterns of transfer of whatever he learns in or out of books.

This value is seen especially clearly in the many great Americans who have solved their educational problems through coping with the struggles of life rather than in formal situations in the schoolroom. Until this century, the great Americans had little formal schooling. Think, for example, of Benjamin Franklin in science, government, diplomacy, and general citizenship and of Thomas Edison in science and invention. Consider, also, Henry Ford as manufacturer and industrialist and Mark Twain as writer. We do not know, of course, how great these men and other self-educated men of similar stature would have become had they had the schooling which some could not afford but from which most chose to escape; but their biographies and contributions to our society make it clear, at least, that nearly all managed to educate themselves extremely well through experiences and the circumstances of life, their efforts being highly motivated by their needs.

Such learning, possessing a core of reality that cannot be provided in the classroom, has personal implications and external ramifications that stimulate transfer tremendously.

But the school can—and many schools today do—support out-of-classroom activities that provide such experiences during students' school careers.

Thus many schools encourage their students to have outside, part-time jobs. Also, excursions—which, with the school bus as standard equipment in many schools, are becoming an increasing part of the school program—are being used to take students to places of interest and educational value. Some trips take a week or more, and the children have educational as well as social experiences that give an important link between school life and the world's reality.

Finally, on the higher level where the student is having to prepare to end his school career, a few colleges and high schools have courses in business, commerce, engineering, and teacher training which provide that students alternate their time between the classroom and the job. Thus the students get a chance to transfer their academic learning to actual performance. Again transfer is facilitated, and so a growth of all-round effectiveness is achieved.

☯ Reflect and Review

A little more than four decades ago, a college student took a course in history called The Modern World, which included the seventeenth, eighteenth, nineteenth, and twentieth centuries. He had just lived through the First World War, was intensely interested in the world-stirring events that had taken place, and hoped to obtain a basis for understanding them. He was greatly disappointed. The course consisted in superficial recitation—first by lecturer and then by students—of events anchored to their dates; and before the great events of the twentieth century were reached, the course ended. It was just as well, thought the originally eager young man.

If this course had reached the twentieth century, it most probably would have been more interesting to the student. Why, in terms of transfer-stimulating factors? In spite of what?

How might the consideration of earlier wars have helped this student's understanding of the First World War? How might the course have been organized and conducted to develop such understanding? Answer in terms of discussed teaching procedures.

DISCIPLINING THE MIND

The term "mental discipline" has been used as a polemic term for so long that its meaning has become obscured. Traditionally, it refers to the false belief that the mind, like a muscle, can be strengthened by exercise. Therefore, goes the argument, a person develops "mental power" by studying difficult subjects and solving hard problems. In this sense, mental discipline is a false conception. The mind is not analogous to a muscle in this respect; and while it may become more capable, it does not become so through mental calisthenics.

On the other hand, there is a legitimate sense in which the term may be used. A person's mind may become "disciplined" if he trains himself to think habitually in an orderly, logical way and to attack problems methodically and critically. Thus W. B. Kolesnik[1] describes mental discipline as

> . . . the quest for ways and means of developing habits of orderly thought, of logical reasoning, of accuracy in weighing evidence, of suspending judgment until sufficient evidence has been gathered and analyzed, of critically examining claims before they are accepted, of persistence in the face of intellectual difficulty, and of precision in formulating and communicating thoughts.

Defined thus, the development of disciplined minds is clearly one of the most important goals of education. And therefore much attention has been directed toward the discovery of ways to achieve such a goal.

We have chosen to discuss mental discipline in connection with transfer because the two concepts are often confused. This is particularly true in debates over the primacy of certain subjects in the curriculum. The traditional "mental disciplinarian" may defend the teaching of grammar, for example, because it "trains the student to think well." His opponent may favor eliminating grammar from the curriculum because he knows that no particular subject is better than any other in teaching a person to think well (see discussions of the Thorndike-Wesman studies cited earlier in this chapter). However, a third

[1] W. B. Kolesnik, "Mental Discipline and the Modern Curriculum," *Peabody Journal of Education*, 35:300–301, 1958.

possibility exists: Grammar may contain elements which will transfer to a great many other subjects and thus facilitate later learning. Thus a certain subject may be very valuable to later learning not because it has "toughened the mind" but because it has elements readily transferable to other subjects.

Apart from transfer, however, we also need to direct our attention to the real problem of mental discipline—how students can be helped to think in an orderly and purposeful way. As the Salisbury experiment cited above showed, it is possible to develop methods of approach useful in many fields. This is mental discipline in the best sense, but it can be achieved only when we drop our traditional confusion between such problem-solving techniques and certain specific bodies of subject matter.

Learning and Mental Discipline. Very little teaching today has mental discipline as its primary purpose; educators have turned their attention to the selection of overall subject matter that is actually used by people and specific problems that are true to life.

Thus, spelling texts used to contain as a rule about twenty-five thousand words, many of which seldom or never were normally written or read by either children or adults. Now such obscure words are omitted from the spelling lists. Letters written by adults and children, as well as children's school compositions and other written work, are examined to discover the words most frequently used and most frequently misspelled. These are then selected and classified by school grade, largely according to difficulty. Clearly, if no mental disciplinary values are gained from learning to spell words we shall seldom (if ever) write or meet in our reading, it is much more to the point to learn to spell the words we do or shall use. For the same basic reason, certain kinds of obscure arithmetic problems once thought to have value in training the mind to reason logically have been discarded in favor of more realistic problems.

But the general trend being discussed here sometimes tends more to impose a change of teaching mode than of subject matter, which the case of grammar will illustrate. A few decades ago it was almost universally believed that parsing sentences and elaborately diagramming them to indicate the various parts of speech developed the general ability to think logically, sharpened the faculty of making fine distinctions accurately, and increased the power of attention—and that these disciplinary values, as well as the grammatical knowledge acquired, transferred to speech and composition.

Now, however, it appears that these claims for such formal study of grammar may have been greatly exaggerated. Many contend such study does not result in written composition and speech at all commensurate with the time spent on it, that the above disciplinary values are not even developed, and even that negative results sometimes occur. Thus, they say that the practice of laboriously analyzing sentences grammatically develops habits that cause a person to read less fluently. It is doubtful, then, that grammar should be taught in this formal style. But does this indicate that it should not be taught as a separate subject at all? The question is vital because, as stated in our introduction to the problem of transfer, grammar cannot be taught anew in every context in which it is used.

Most development usually results in the use of better English. More specifically, grammar can best serve as a tool for understanding English when it is used to explain incorrect and correct expressions.

Grammar, then, should be taught as an integral part of composition, public speaking, and other courses devoted to the improvement of the students' writing and speaking, and should be taught in a way which the following example will clarify.

Studies have been made to determine the most common grammatical errors by observing, recording, and rating those which children make in their speech and in their writing. The teacher can use such data to increase his awareness of the errors that should be watched and listened for. Then, when an error is directly at hand, the teacher can not only point out the correction but also set forth the grammatical principle or principles covering the specific error to serve as a reason for correcting it and to prevent its recurrence. Thus, when a student asks, "Will the boy who usually sits between Bill and I be in class today, Miss Smith?" the teacher can first say that the phrase should be "between Bill and me" and then point out that a preposition should be followed by the objective rather than the subjective case of the pronoun. The error here, incidentally, is one of the most common.

A person is usually unconscious of the error he is making, so the first step is that he be aware of his mistake. Awareness is strengthened when the right form is known. The right form is then used consciously and, with its continued use, should become automatic.

A difficulty in employing grammar in this way lies in the fact that very young children cannot as a rule understand grammatical principles; but the very difficulty illustrates the validity of the manner of teaching here recommended. Thus children acquire their language from their environment.

If they hear good language, they come to school speaking correctly; if they hear defective language, their speech reflects that experience. Of course, when lower-grade pupils are taught correct forms without being given the reasons for them, some improvement occurs; but they persist in most of their errors until they become grammar-grade pupils and thus are old enough to be given explanations of the principles of grammar.

Defining the Teacher's Role. With the decline of belief that mental discipline can be furthered directly through teaching certain preferred kinds of subject matter and through certain "disciplinary" modes of teaching, is the teacher relieved of responsibility for building the mental discipline of his students? Obviously not. Disciplinary values do result from the kind of teaching provided in the school. Thus, on the one hand the teacher's procedures may train students to keep attention on their work even when it is difficult, prepare their lessons carefully, and express themselves eagerly and fully; on the other hand, what the teacher does may develop carelessness, inability to concentrate, and indifference. The teacher, then, should interpret his work occasionally in terms of its effect on these related qualities and habits that characterize good and poor scholarship, as in his students, and in so doing will do well to keep the following considerations in mind.

The disciplinary values students receive in different school situations vary according to the always interrelated control and motivation that exist in these situations.

Thus, if work plans are indefinite and disorder and confusion characterize most class activities, the students will tend to develop poor work habits and otherwise become uncertain and ineffective in dealing with school situations.

But if there is overstrict control, students may do their work diligently and according to a fixed and repetitive pattern, seemingly well, and yet really only go through the form of lesson getting. Here again, good habits of scholarship and related disciplinary values are not established, for the students compelled by teacher-student authority relationship to study according to a fixed and repetitive pattern develop no true motive for learning; little if any propelling interest is generated. Then when the compulsion of the teacher is removed, the students do not manifest the habits of good scholarship.

Sadly, much of our formal educational work is of this lockstep type, and so the graduates of our schools carry on too little independent study. Thus they illustrate the general truth that formal repetitive processes directed from the outside do not result in the establishment of controlling aims and dominant habits which would cause the processes to be continued voluntarily. In this regard, in school and out, there is often not just discontinuance of, but real reaction to, vigorously controlled formal behavior. Thus many young men prepare regularly for military inspection by having their shoes shined, their clothes pressed and spotless—everything in order; then when they get out of service and are free of such strictly enforced requirements, they bask in the luxury of dressing informally (often the word "sloppily" is accurate) and of keeping their possessions in a disorder that can hardly be equaled by junk shops.

But even if we achieve a proper balance of control and curiosity-inspiring procedures and thus educate children so that they acquire the mental dis-cipline for solving their school problems, we cannot be sure that they will attack other problems as well or that the discipline acquired in school will carry over, that is, transfer into adult life. Usually there are some such present applications, and carry-over for habits and characteristics acquired in school in childhood is both pervasive and stubborn; that is, it tends to spread and persist a long time. These effects, of course, are to be desired, stimulated, and looked for; thus it is important for a teacher to know that some students are well controlled in school but not in other situations.

Even if there is no transfer, however, good training for the school situa-tion is important in itself. A common aberration in our thinking is to con-ceive of discipline as intended for a situation outside school or for a time different from the present, when actually, the need to develop interests and good habits for the situation at hand should govern the teacher more than concern for the student's out-of-school life or future.

Reflect and Review

A professor of law who had some control over law school admissions stated that he preferred not students who had studied sociology, political science, and economics but those who had taken a considerable number of courses in mathematics. "They can think more clearly," he said, "and can solve the legal problems that confront a law student." This professor did not say that the knowledge acquired in mathematics helped in the study of law, only that the mental discipline obtained from the study of mathematics functioned in it. There is a twofold fallacy in this thinking. What is it?

Suppose that only the brightest 10 per cent of high school students took typing classes. Would it be likely that these students would experience a high degree of later success in professions? Would it be reasonable to attribute this success to their training in typing?

SUMMARY

We learn by transfer when we apply or use in a given situation that which we have learned in another. This is positive transfer, but there is negative transfer also. This occurs when that which we have learned in one situation interferes with learning or performance in another. In some situations there is neither positive nor negative transfer.

Transfer generally involves knowledge, techniques, or attitudes and ideals. According to one explanation of transfer, a learner profits in a situation to the extent that that situation is similar to previous situations. This is known as the theory of identical elements. Perceiving the similarities facilitates the transfer.

Another form of transfer is the application of a principle or concept to a situation which results in more effective responses. This is explained by the theory of generalization, which implies that a principle is generalized when it can be applied to various situations.

Experiments have demonstrated that transfer varies in general according to the number of similar components, and also according to the degree that principles are applied in other situations and thereby increase learning in the new situation.

Experimental evidence indicates that no particular subject increases mental-test abilities more than another subject. Bright students tend to experience a little more transfer in this respect than do dull students.

In general, mental capacity is a basic factor in transfer, and the bright students are capable of considerably more transfer than are the slow learners.

In order to increase the amount of transfer, the teacher needs to guide the students to look for similarities in various situations and also to encourage them to apply the concepts and principles which are developed in class.

The teacher will help the students make more useful generalizations if he guides them to develop concepts and principles rather than telling them what they are.

Teaching which emphasizes the memorizing of dates, names, events, and other specific knowledge provides poor intellectual equipment for transfer.

Much of the vitality in learning is to be found in the wide application of comprehensive meanings, which is essentially transfer according to the principle of generalization.

Transfer can be brought about when a student is given actual experiences in practical situations where he will have an opportunity to apply the theoretical and abstract ideas he acquires in class.

The purpose of mental discipline is to produce minds which have learned to be curious, which can concentrate and persist for long periods, which are accurate and discriminating, which are good problem solvers, and which draw conclusions on the basis of dependable evidence. In short, the well-disciplined mind is scholarly and scientific.

Mental discipline is not the same as transfer, although the good qualities of a well-disciplined mind facilitate transfer in all situations where effective thinking is needed.

No specific courses discipline the mind more than others, and school subjects are not selected today with mental discipline as an objective as they were in the last century. For example, grammar is studied not to discipline the mind but as a means for speaking and writing correct and more effective English. The crucial problem with grammar is to bring about transfer to the students' spoken and written English.

Still, mental discipline is an objective of the school, as evidenced by its concern over problem solving, study skills, ability to work both independently and cooperatively, retention of learning, creativeness, and generally effective use of capacities.

Teaching which motivates and interests the students and thereby develops in them the habits of good scholarship is achieving good disciplinary values.

SUGGESTED READING

Falk, Doris F.: "Learning of Chemical Equations; Meaningful versus Mechanical Methods," *Science Education*, 46:37–42, 1962. Shows how meaningful teaching of chemical equations by emphasis on organization, relationships, and understanding resulted in acquiring more knowledge and achieving more transfer than mechanical learning of equations through drill and rote learning.

Muuss, R. E.: "Transfer Effect of a Learning Program in Social Causality on an Understanding of Physical Causality," *Journal of Experimental Education*, 29:231–247, March, 1961. Demonstrates transfer, as indicated in the title, of understanding social causality to understanding physical causality. This article contains many ideas about thinking and transfer.

Symonds, Percival M.: "What Education Has to Learn from Psychology. VII. Transfer and Formal Discipline," *Teachers College Record*, 61:30–45, 1959. Shows how the formalism of the old school was ineffective but indicates that transfer and mental discipline as conceived today are worthy objectives which can be achieved through effective experiences.

CHAPTER 17
MODERN METHODS
OF TEACHING AND THE
PROMOTION OF LEARNING

Over the years a gradual evolution in educational procedures is always taking place. But in our era, the exponents of progressive education, founded in this country by John Dewey, have introduced especially strong changes in teaching methods—changes designed to replace academic formalism with more lifelike learning situations, and in a few schools the effects have been radical. Such effects, sometimes real but sometimes imagined, have stirred critics to impassioned attacks on the schools. The schools are accused of ignoring the traditional "three R's" in favor of bland, spineless amusements and of betraying the trust the American people have put in them by delivering the control of the classroom into the hands of the delighted but irresponsible students.

We have referred in various contexts to several of the changes wrought by the newer education and, in doing so, have suggested that such accusations are extreme and ordinarily groundless. Now we shall seek to support this suggestion by unified consideration of the elements of modern education in the light of the experimental evidence for its effectiveness in learning and in such learning-related areas as attitudes and social development. We shall not, however, fail to consider the negative and the complicating factors involved in the modern techniques of teaching; and thus it will become clear that the major purpose in discussing them is not to argue for their supreme effectiveness, but to show that they have enlarged our concepts of learning and in doing so have provided the educator with additional means for stimulating it.

Both the traditional and the newer education are concerned that the students learn the subject matter. It is said of the traditional teachers that they teach the subject and therefore are subject-matter-centered, while the teachers using recently developed procedures teach the students. Similar antitheses are implied by these terms: authoritarian or democratic, teacher-centered or student-centered, and teacher-directed or self-directed. The traditional school concentrates on subject matter and the passing of examinations. The newer methods do not neglect knowledge, but they are designed also for the personal and social development of the learner. The advocates of the newer methods claim also that the intellectual development of the students experiencing those methods is more functional and effective.

THE PROJECT METHOD OF TEACHING

How shall our students be taught in order to achieve the best education possible?

The traditional answer is through a logically arranged, hierarchical sequence of steps, each with its quota of assigned textbook reading, recitation, lectures, and examinations. A more contemporary answer is that they shall be taught through doing; they shall carry out certain interest-arousing projects demanding certain skills and information, which they shall thus learn when they need to and when they are highly motivated to learn them. This is the project, or activity, method of teaching, and it is one of the cornerstones of modern education.

The essence of the traditional method of teaching is first, systematization and then, formality. The work program is carefully structured into definite courses, or subjects, with a specific and very regular time and place for each. This program is then diligently followed in the assigned lessons and lectures, and the recitations and examinations are considered very important. Drill and review are also stressed.

As all this implies, the teacher is conspicuously in control, and the work typically focuses on the content of textbooks. But some of the terms most frequently used to describe the objectives and outcomes of traditional teaching may say most about the learning atmosphere it imposes: *systematic study, thoroughness, competition, mastery, habit,* and *accuracy.*

The project method of teaching lays aside the highly formal structure of traditional teaching in order to stress activities that appeal to the students' natural interest. During the course of the school day, the students not only study conventionally but also engage in projects as another way of acquiring the knowledge and skills that are acquired systematically in formal study. Some projects are carried out entirely in the classroom, while others lead in and out of it.

The students are encouraged to help their teacher plan the work; they make suggestions and help make decisions on the class program. Thus the teacher is in control but not conspicuously so, attempting to guide and help rather than dictate. The textbook is not of central importance, and the terminology of the newer methods is a far cry from that of the traditional: *interest, purpose, initiative, planning, cooperation, attitude, learning in a natural situation,* and *learning psychologically rather than logically* exemplify the terms employed.

Those who attack the project method claim that the children it educates do not acquire the fundamental skills and knowledge that almost everyone agrees are essential, or at least that the results are largely hit-or-miss, because too much of the control is left to students. It is contended that students are not capable of planning their own work; consequently, the work they do plan usually is indefinite and often chaotic. Also, these critics—who, of course, favor the more formal type of teaching—say that students' own interests are two immature for such responsibility, so that even when the work has a clear direction, it is likely to be a bad one.

The sponsors of the project method hold that their students learn as much subject matter as others, probably even more than others, and that they gain many intangible values not acquired in the traditional schoolroom. Thus they claim that the drills and reviews, questions and answers, and so forth of the traditional school keep many students from learning effectively at all and tinge everyone's learning with artificiality. Then they go on to say that when a child learns through activities instead, he acquires his skills and knowledge in a natural situation, so that the work of the schools becomes real and lively and thus basically meaningful to him.

But what does the record show? What, more specifically, is done in project-method teaching, and what are the results?

The Ellsworth Collings Experiment. One of the pioneer attempts to demonstrate that teaching by means of interesting and purposeful projects could be effective was the extensive Collings experiment, carried out in Missouri [Collings, 1926]. Three rural schools were included. One, known as the *experimental school,* had an enrollment of 41; the others, known as the *control schools,* had enrollments of 29 and 31, respectively. Over a period of 4 years the project method predominated in the experimental school; in the control schools the traditional methods prevailed.

The schools were typical rural schools of eight grades in the same county with the same kind of farms in each of these school districts. At the beginning of the experiment the children of the experimental and control schools were tested in reading, handwriting, spelling, and arithmetic and found to be equal in their abilities. This was to be expected, as the districts had had the same kind of schools, and the people of those districts were farmers of the same socioeconomic levels. With two control schools, the comparisons are more dependable than if only one school had been used.

In the experimental school the day was devoted to four types of projects— story, hand, play, and excursion. In the investigator's words:[1]

> Play projects represent those experiences in which the purpose is to engage in such group activities as games, folk dancing, dramatization, or social parties. Excursion projects involve purposeful study of problems connected with environments and activities of people. Story projects include purposes to enjoy the story in its various forms—oral, song, picture, phonograph, or piano. Hand projects represent purposes to express ideas in concrete form—to make a rabbit trap, to prepare cocoa for the school luncheon, or to grow cantaloupes.

The teachers in the experimental school tried to develop and combine these various kind of projects naturally, or, more specifically, out of actual experiences. For example, the children of the nine- to eleven-year-old group studied the causes of frequent typhoid fever in the home of Mr. Smith, one of the residents of the school district, and did so in these ways: They made visits to the Smith home, obtained and read bulletins, calculated costs for window screens and flytraps, made the flytraps themselves, and prepared reports to Mr. Smith; and finally, they made real recommendations to Mr. Smith on how to avoid typhoid fever.

Thus, as a part of their motivated activity, they received training in oral and written English (especially the latter, for they had to do considerable reading and writing), arithmetic, manual arts, and sanitation and hygiene. Also, because they studied a real problem which aroused their human concern, the students developed definite positive attitudes toward hygienic and sanitary living.

But many projects grew out of these students' immediate environment— projects in which they sought to learn such various things as how Mr. Long made molasses, how the dandelions they saw daily spread so rapidly, how tomatoes were canned at the local factory, reporting and discussing what was to be seen at the big circus and at a trial in a juvenile court, and how the county agent tested soil. Then at the end of the experiment, these students and those in the control schools and the parents of both groups were compared to determine the effectiveness of all this. The essential results follow:

The students of the experimental school had been expected to learn as much subject matter from their projects as the students of the control schools learned from traditional teaching. But when all were tested in penmanship, composition, spelling, American history, geography, reading, and

[1] Ellsworth Collings, *An Experiment with a Project Curriculum*, The Macmillan Company, New York, 1926, p. 48.

the four fundamental processes in arithmetic, the achievement of the students in the experimental school was shown to be 138.1 per cent of that of the control-school students, indicating (with due allowance for the ever-present danger of some error in expressing relative achievement by means of percentages) a definite superiority in knowledge and skills of the children taught by the project method. Apparently, in order to answer the real questions involved in their projects, the project-method youngsters studied in the various subject-matter fields extensively enough to achieve better than those who studied only the "next lesson."

In addition, the attitudes of both students and parents toward the schools were investigated. Those of the students were evaluated by calculating figures on attendance, including tardiness and truancy, frequency of corporal punishment, and graduation from the eighth grade and high school entrance. In all these items, distinct superiority characterized the experimental-school students; for example, 85 per cent of them graduated from the eighth grade, whereas only 10 per cent of the control-school students did so. The parents' attitudes were judged by numbers of visits to the school, frequency of use of school equipment and school library, attendance at annual school meetings, support of a higher tax rate for teachers' salaries, and votes for establishment of a rural high school. Again, in all items, the experimental-school parents appeared decidedly more interested in and supportive of the school; for example, the increase in the number of parents visiting school during the experiment was 90 per cent in the experimental school as against some 5 per cent in the control schools.

It should be noted that when the effectiveness of any educational program is tested, favorable results are usually obtained because the experiment stimulates increased efforts for the program on the part of teachers and their supervisors: The experiment takes on the character of a campaign to make the program effective.

Nevertheless, the results of this experiment were strong enough to indicate that regardless of such zealousness, excellent results can be achieved when students are motivated through interesting projects—that methods which depart from the traditional do not necessarily result in poor education but actually can bring about considerable improvement over formal teaching methods.

Of course, Collings' now-famous experiment demonstrates this for the lower grade levels only. Can the project method also be effective at the higher levels?

The Thirty High Schools. An experiment was conducted by 30 high schools that broke away from the traditional to adopt in various degrees the project method [Aikin, 1942]. The basic objectives of these high schools, which became known as the 30 progressive high schools, were to help their students:

1. Acquire fundamental knowledge, skill, and habits.
2. Develop good work habits.
3. Learn to think independently.
4. Acquire cultural appreciation and interests.
5. Adjust socially.
6. Be emotionally stable.
7. Be physically healthy.
8. Discover and develop a vocational objective.

These are, of course, worthy objectives and much more comprehensive than the single objective of imparting information.

The experimental high schools participating in the study were both public and private, large and small, and located in various sections of the United States. The schools did not all follow the same plan; instead, they made their own changes, which differed considerably among the schools. Some changed a great deal and others only a moderate amount. All got away from the traditional organization, which is usually characterized by a given number of specific subjects and credits and by the textbook–question-and-answer procedure.

Barriers between subjects were broken, subject matter was integrated, and teachers and students shared the responsibility of developing areas of study. Students were encouraged to work on large problems both independently and cooperatively, and research, problem-solving, and experience procedures were encouraged. Teachers in their planning and in the development of their philosophy adopted the guidance concept and worked to promote the emotional and social development of their students. Consideration was given to individual vocational and career needs. Students studied themselves in terms of their abilities and interests. In some schools, enrichment was provided for the gifted students in the form of additional study and activities. In general, the aim was to give students intellectual and personal experiences that would satisfy the aforementioned objectives.

Sometimes science and mathematics were combined; also, English and the social studies were integrated. In connection with social studies the students in one class examined the newspapers to discover examples of propaganda. Students visited farms, factories, museums, libraries, and various government agencies. They supplemented these visits with penetrating investigation and study about them. The students were encouraged to find more and more knowledge on a subject and to do sustained and reflective thinking on that subject. They learned that a great deal of time must be spent in the library, finding and assimilating that knowledge.

How did the students of these schools fare?

One of the major tests made of the effectiveness of the experimental program in the progressive high schools was the collection of evidence on how well their students did in college.

A total of 1,475 graduates of the Thirty Schools were matched with 1,475 students from traditional schools for comparison of their effectiveness in college. Matching was made on the basis of sex, age, race, scholastic aptitude scores, and their home background.

In one sense, the results were pleasingly ironic. Many colleges which regularly required certain prescribed courses for entrance had waived such requirements for students from these experimental schools. It turned out to be well for the colleges that they had, for these students got slightly higher marks, all in all, than students of equal intelligence from the traditional high schools. But of greater significance was the finding that, when a group of students was selected for capacity to do independent work, 75 per cent were students educated in the experimental high schools.

Also, the experimental students were generally described as knowing how to search for facts and tending to base their beliefs on them—evidence of good mental discipline; and they were described not as "grinds" but rather as more dynamic than students educated in the traditional way. Unfortunately but not too surprisingly, students from the experimental schools were handicapped in some instances by these very virtues—specifically, when their well-disciplined and adventurous minds collided with narrow teaching methods in college. For instance, a student would discover that desire to relate his wide independent reading to his history course did not fit the plans of his professor, who "wants me to take notes and give back to him what he has said," and this would tend to upset his good study habits.

Finally, research into the extracurricular activities of the college students revealed that here also the experimental students excelled over traditionally educated youth. The former were more interested in social problems and politics, had fuller social lives, and exercised more leadership on campus in all fields except athletics.

The experience of the Thirty Schools made its contribution by breaking away from the traditional, stereotyped kind of teaching and by promoting the more organic, functional, and need-satisfying kind of education. It also demonstrated that the usual college entrance requirement of a given number of specified credits is not necessarily the best basis for admission but that the mental capacity of the student, his work habits, and a zest for learning are more fundamental for having rewarding experiences in college. Thus another contribution of this research was to loosen the control which the usual college requirements have over the high schools.

General Effectiveness and Applicability. Many other experiments have also demonstrated that students can be taught effectively by means of the guided experiences provided by the project method and thus, necessarily, that subject matter does not have to be presented in a logical, hierarchical order in order to be learned.

Furthermore, the evidence indicates that the psychological strength of the project method is to be found where its supporters claim it is—in superior motivation for learning. In other words, it appears to be basically true that when the student is not told what he must do but instead is given an opportunity to sense a lifelike purpose in what he is doing, the problems become more real to him and consequently he is more highly motivated than he is in the traditional classroom where he has only to systematically pursue assigned lessons in textbooks.

The educational strength of any teaching method is finally defined, of course, by the results. But here again, it has been demonstrated repeatedly that when the project-method teacher capitalizes well on students' needs and related interests so that they do become highly motivated, they usually learn quickly even if they have not had what are traditionally considered the previous learning steps or if the logical sequence of the steps has not been observed. This very basic fact, incidentally, is gradually bringing about a liberation from systematic, step-by-step schooling, with the interesting result that today's classroom procedures parallel more and more the way adults learn. For adults study what they need and so are highly motivated to study. Young mothers study child care; many if not most adults keep records and work out their income taxes; when a family builds a house, its members study house plans and calculate costs; many men and women study to be more competent in their vocations, and so forth.

Thus it seems clear that project teaching should be encouraged. The teacher should not slavishly try to do all his teaching by means of projects, but he should be aware of their great value in helping students learn.

Yet he should also be aware that the task of putting the more modern methods into action necessarily involves the following complexities.

The Dynamics of Learning Groups. The very definition of the project method of teaching tells us that when it is used, students work together and thus learn collectively as well as individually, so that application of the project method must be based on sound understanding of the dynamics of group work per se. Thus it is often asked whether a greater amount of subject matter is learned through group or through individual work.

This particular question is, of course, very general, and so it can only be very generally answered by saying that students learn more through group work in some situations and more through individual work in others; also, some students are basically more responsive to group methods than others are. Yet research has established the following pros and cons of group learning which can serve as useful, if still general, guidelines for the teacher.

In judging the learning of a group, the accomplishment of each person must be evaluated as well as, and in relation to, the accomplishment of the group as a unit. In the first place, the learning of a group taken as a unit is likely to be largely the product of the best members of the group and thus higher than the average learning of the individual members. When a group reaches a correct solution to an experiment in physics, for example, it is likely that the solution was worked out largely by one or two leading members of the group with a little help from others and that not every member of the group knows that solution. Even if all do know the solution, it is still likely that the process of reaching it is not thoroughly understood by one or more members of the group. Secondly, the work of a group may not equal the work of which the best members of the group are capable; there is a tendency for group work to regress toward the average work of the individual members. Thus the best members of a physics class may be held back in their well-directed efforts by the relative slowness of the others' progress.

On the other hand, in group work there can be a pooling of information, ideas, and reasoning, so that the group will have more facts, suggestions, interpretations, and criticisms to use than will individuals working alone. This is clearly favorable to the increase of learning. This at least lessens the danger that the bright will be held back and often means that those who have less to contribute gain more from group work than from working alone, in which case they would not be aware of many ideas and facts that would be presented in a group. On the other hand, a group often fails to reach the right answer to a learning problem because a superficially more plausible but wrong answer is supported by enthusiastic members of the group who are very convincing in their strongly but wrongly motivated support of it.

There is, then, a complex balance of the positive and the negative in group learning as considered in direct terms of results. But the balance can also be seen in the motivational dynamics that contribute so importantly to these results. Thus a decision reached by a group is, in effect, a commitment and so serves as a strong motive. The members of the group, because they have had a part in making the decision, have become self-involved and so have a strong personal interest in supporting that decision. Such strong motivation is generally a desirable educational objective, which is why it is very desirable that students help plan, that is, decide about, their work.

But what kind of grouping works best for learning?

It is sometimes recommended that students who are mutual choices on sociometric questionnaires be put in the same learning group, the assumption being that good friends working together will be highly effective. This has not always proved to be the case, however. Indeed, some groups are more effective if they are not very cohesive socially. Thus, in one study in which opposed groups were each allowed to ask 20 questions for finding out what something was, the groups that were less cohesive socially identified the thing with fewer questions than the more cohesive groups [Phillips, 1956].

The reason for such events generally appears to be that when a group is too homogeneous socially, it does not have so strong an achievement motive as a group in which there is less friendship.

☯ *Reflect and Review*

Alvin Zander and Elmer Van Egmond studied the interpersonal behavior of 230 second-graders and 188 fifth-graders who were divided into small groups to work on various problems of interest to children of those ages [Zander and Van Egmond, 1958]. The teachers then rated the pupils for their social influence and the pupils rated each other for their ability to do schoolwork, for attractiveness, and for ability to influence others.

Following is a selection of the number of interesting findings obtained.

There was a low positive correlation between intelligence and social power—specifically, .20 for the boys and .28 for the girls. In other words, measured mental capacity in itself did not appear to be a large factor in the social influence of individuals in this situation.

Boys of high intelligence who were successful in their schoolwork and personally attractive and who tended to be positive and forward in their approaches to others had social power. Intelligent and attractive girls had social power; that is, good scholarship and personal forwardness seemed less socially important for bright and attractive girls. However, attractive girls who had low intelligence but did their schoolwork acceptably did have social power.

Boys made more classwork suggestions than girls and generally tried more often to influence others. Excepting those who were personally attractive, boys of low intelligence had low social power. Also, these boys tended to be passive in the group processes, seemingly to protect themselves from the unsuccessful results their personal inadequacy would produce if they were active. However, when these boys did express themselves, they were more demanding and more positive in their comments, apparently to try to compensate for low effectiveness in the group.

Suppose that you as a teacher had a number of these children as a student-centered learning group and that they were so selected as to reflect these findings accurately.

Describe a way in which the low correlations here between intelligence and social power might affect group dynamics in such a way as to hamper learning.

In general, would it seem wise to give more attention to the average boys' or to the average girls' participation in the group? Explain.

Which of the categories of boys described above would have to be most carefully considered in developing projects? How might this be done?

STUDENT-CENTERED TEACHING

The successful teacher is no longer on a height, pumping knowledge at high pressure into passive receptacles. The new methods have changed all this. He is no longer Sir Oracle, perhaps unconsciously by his very manner antagonizing minds to whose level he cannot possibly descend, but he is a senior student anxious to help his juniors. When a simple, earnest spirit animates a college, there is no appreciable interval between the teacher and the taught—both are in the same class, the one more advanced than the other. So animated the student feels that he has joined a family whose honor is his honor, whose welfare is his own and whose interests would be his first consideration.

So wrote Sir William Osler (1849–1919), Canadian physician, teacher, and medical author.

Today's education is trying to develop, in our grade and high schools, as well as colleges, the situation described by the distinguished Dr. Osler, on the theory that better learning will result. To explain:

The traditional highly structured classroom is typically described as teacher-centered, or teacher-directed, and authoritarian, or autocratic, because the complete responsibility for determining the work to be done and the control of actual class procedures are solely the teacher's. In contrast, the more modern classroom is called student-centered and democratic because of the much greater degree to which students participate in planning and directing the classwork. We have touched on this contrast in discussing the project method of teaching, which, to be fully carried out, demands an approach to student centering. Now for purposes of emphasis, we shall describe the extreme of student centering: the class run almost entirely by the students.

The students plan the activities, direct the discussion to each other, and make the decisions about class matters as the class proceeds. Basically, the teacher is on the sidelines as an observer; he does not ordinarily come forward to make contributions or even to correct the students' errors and misunderstandings. If and when the students turn to him for guidance, however, the teacher does give his help—by explaining and thus easing a difficulty, suggesting a reference, or in some other way leading the students to find again their lost direction.

This extreme of student centering is not often reached, of course, but is sometimes closely approached; and to the extent that this happens, the old idea that the teacher's principal function is to impart knowledge to the student gives way to the teacher's being a member of a democratic group devoted to learning. What are the learning results?

At the outset, modern education is somewhat justified in this change by the established fact that the best source of learning is often not what the teacher says but what the student does. This is quite clear at the higher learning levels where a basic part of what the student does includes his reading in journals and books chosen as the best efforts of scholars in the various fields of learning. Our examination of experimental evidence on the project method, moreover, has shown us implicitly that even in the lower grades, appropriate degrees of student-centered methods can be effective— that pupils can be guided into methods of independent cooperative work much earlier than one might think they were ready for it.

It must not be assumed that student-centered classes are self-generating— that they just start automatically, develop their own momentum, and keep carrying on. Obviously, the teacher at the beginning orients the students to the contents of the course, suggests some books in the subjects being studied, and, in general, gets them off to a good start. Throughout the course, the teacher will be consulted occasionally and then can give the guidance which the students need. Student-centered classes are not completely self-directed, although self-direction is one of the main values of this kind of education.

But let us, for a more thorough view, turn to further evidence which will help us evaluate student-centered teaching in terms of its capacity to impart information, the intellectual processes it engenders, how it appeals to individuals of various mental and personal qualities, and its effect on personality.

Achievement and Student Preferences. Experiments to determine the relative subject-matter achievement of teacher-centered and student-centered classes have not consistently favored one kind or the other. Thus, some experiments indicate that teacher-centered methods result in a greater acquisition of facts than student-centered methods, and some do not.

An important difference between the results of the two methods has been shown, however, in terms of intellectual processes stimulated. Thus the evidence indicates that the nondirective element in student-centered classes gives students better insights into causes and effects. For example, when one group of psychology students saw a movie depicting personal problems, subsequent discussion revealed that the students with experience in student-centered classes had better perception of the depicted situation and comprehended the motives and behavior dynamics of the characters better than the students from teacher-centered classes. Also, students from classes in which they have planned, made decisions, and discussed freely have usually been judged as having learned, out of their practice in evaluating facts and analyzing problems, to think more independently and—not unrelatedly, as we shall see later—to have better problem-solving methods.

The courses in which the methods have been tested, it should be noted, are reading courses such as psychology, philosophy, and education; and the tested students have been college students whose habits of study were rather firmly established—which leaves us with the possibilities that in such highly specialized or technical courses as language, science, and mathematics and also in lower-level courses, group-centered work would not yield so favorable test results as would classes in which the teacher regularly gives the students careful explanations of processes and principles. Yet the fact that student-centered methods of teaching have been shown at all to cause the students to gain clearer understanding of situations, to do more independent thinking, and to be better problem solvers makes the outcomes of student-centered procedures very significant—validation in part at least of the principle that the responsibility for an education should be put on the students' mental shoulders. There is, of course, a wide range of personal reactions to both methods of teaching being discussed here; regardless of which method prevails in it, a class that stirs one student to enthusiastic effort will leave another indifferent, passive, and convinced that the class is a waste of time. This range of preference, moreover, must be taken into account in dealing with the problem of achievement through the two methods. A learning situation that a student likes is a more wholesome situation intellectually for him than one he dislikes. (In speaking of a disliked situation we are not referring to hard work that ends in very satisfying achievement, but to a situation that from start to finish consistently displeases the student.)

Thus it has been found that students who in general are comfortable with authority figures and like to be told what to do favor the teacher-centered classes, in which specific work assignments are laid out for them, and also work best in these classes. Relatedly, such students tend to be frustrated by any changes which upset their habit patterns and to be especially troubled when they are in a situation where they must plan their own work and make decisions.

On the other hand, some students—including those with initiative, creativeness, and high desire to achieve—have been found to like and intellectually flourish under student-centered teaching. The interest of these students is heightened by participation in the discussions, by helping plan the activities, and by carrying on independent study; and they willingly assume the responsibility that goes with the freedom to do their work in their own way that is provided by student-centered classes.

The polarities here are not so simple as all this might suggest, however. For instance, most students, including many who basically prefer student-centered teaching, like and do well in teacher-centered classes when they like and respect the teacher. There are sometimes students in student-centered classes who feel that they are not acquiring so much factual information as they would in traditional teacher-centered classes but who, when they are tested, turn out to have achievement ratings as high as those of students at their level who are being taught in the traditional way.

The evidence on student preferences, then, leads to the conclusion that our schools should provide both kinds of teaching and classroom procedures so as to give all the students the learning experiences best suited to them as individuals. But beyond this, it appears that just as a person should eat a variety of foods in order to nourish the body well, the individual student (in many cases at least) will be nourished better intellectually by a variety of student-centered and teacher-centered learning experiences.

There is, however, one important qualification to this general conclusion.

The Psychological Effects of Authoritarian and of Democratic Classes. It has been found in a number of scientific investigations that when dealt with autocratically, students typically respond—in individually determined degrees and combinations—with anxiety, tenseness, hostility, aggression, vacillation, lifeless submission, indifference, egocentricity, or self-centeredness. These reactions, moreover, have been found to extend into the relations between members of classes, creating or at least tending to create a lack of group unity and prevailing ill will and conflict.

Scientific observation of democratic classes, on the other hand, has revealed these prevailing student responses: enthusiasm, spontaneity, work initiative, cooperativeness, mutual respect, and friendliness. Not surprisingly, these socially integrative reactions have been found to result in friendly interpersonal relationships among students and between teachers and students, as well as good balance between closeness and independence in work and play.

We have, of course, touched on the contrast displayed by these findings earlier in discussing behavior in general. Now let us examine the implications here, and especially the negative implications of authoritarian treatment, for learning.

At the higher grade levels, the above psychological effects of authoritarian, or autocratic, treatment—which by definition generally prevails in teacher-centered classes—are often overcome by the relatively strong personality structures that the older students have developed. The students have built-in reactions, defenses, and positive modes of coping, as it were. But what of the lower grade levels?

Ralph K. White and Ronald Lippitt experimentally observed two groups of ten-year-old boys, one in an authoritarian and one in a democratic situation, with such very striking results as these [White and Lippitt, 1961].

In one comparison, thirty times as much hostility was observed in the authoritarian as in the democratic group. Nineteen out of twenty boys liked the democratic leader better than the authoritarian leader, it was found. In the authoritarian group 73 per cent of the oral expression, or language behavior, was self-involved or subjective, while in the democratic group self-involvement in oral expression was 31 per cent, definitely less than half as great. This means, of course, that objective expression—language behavior dealing with matters outside the individual—prevailed in the democratic group but not in the authoritarian group.

All these findings are significant for learning, but since the last findings are especially so, and since this might easily be overlooked, let us concentrate on them.

The degree of self-involvement in language behavior generally reflects the degree of egocentricity, or self-centeredness, functioning in a person in the situation that calls forth the behavior.

The work of White and Lippitt, then, suggests strongly that autocratic treatment makes relatively impressionable younger students more self-centered.

This is very important generally because egocentricity is one of the most basic negative factors in mental health; thus the adult who converses largely about himself and whose language behavior, even when he speaks of an outside subject, is characterized by almost continuous self-reference is not very mature socially or emotionally. This is very important in specific regard to learning because here we are shown the autocratic climate causing young people to feel under threat and thus driving them in upon themselves—making the ego a self-protective focus of their interest and verbal expression—so that they become in an important sense unavailable for direct learning about the world outside of themselves.

This effect, of course, is emphasized by the contrast with the overall effect of democratic methods, under which, instead of being a threat to the individual, the climate supports him. Thus, when the procedures are student-centered, the need for egocentricity is less, so that thoughts and verbal behavior tend to be free to be directed toward others and the learning problems that concern the group.

Not all authoritarian teachers antagonize their pupils. Many of them are friendly and helpful and are truly liked by their students, who are glad to do the work which authoritarian teachers assign to them. Neither are all democratic teachers kindly and patient. Not all of them have warm personalities and are popular with their students. Picturing the authoritarian teacher as an offensive despot and the democratic teacher as a friendly helper who subtly motivates the students to high levels of achievement is not consonant with the characteristics of these two types of teachers.

It should be added, too, that the authoritarian teacher in the White-Lippitt study was probably an extreme case. Personal offensiveness quite beyond the effects of any particular method probably accounted for these results, which are more extreme than could generally be expected—which brings us to one more consideration important to a full comparative evaluation of teacher-centered and student-centered procedures.

Basic to the question of reactions stimulated by the teacher's methods is always, and at all grade levels, the true merit of the teacher; for a teacher who is highly respected and appreciated by his students is likely to be effective whether his methods are teacher-centered or student-centered, and a teacher is typically regarded this way when he has a large body of knowledge which he deals with interestingly; manages the classwork efficiently and keeps good order; and is friendly, helpful, and respectful toward his students. Also, if a teacher is humble enough to admit his errors, and shows that he too is sincerely in search of knowledge, the students will tend to be cooperative rather than antagonistic.

Thus Hugh Hartshorne and M. A. May, who experimentally tested students from various kinds of classes to discover how much they would lie, cheat, and steal, found that the extent of dishonesty seemed to be less a function of the teachers' varying methods than of the varying degrees of respect and appreciation the teachers had won out of such personal qualities [Hartshorne and May, 1928]. This example, of course, is not directly related to learning; it simply indicates that when students have a high regard for a teacher, there is likely to be a good social climate in the classroom. But it is just this kind of identification and class social climate that created good learning morale.

☯ *Reflect and Review*

It would be difficult to label Miss Edwards's classes as either "teacher-centered" or "student-centered." It is true that she is autocratic in the sense that she determines just what the students should study and makes assignments and examines the students regularly, giving her students little or no voice in these matters. On the other hand, what she says in class is regularly interesting to her students, and all of them look on her as a friend because she is always pleasant, kindly, and fair. She also has a good sense of humor which she shares with her class, and none of her students is ever made afraid to speak up in her class with a question or a comment. She grades rigidly, but she tries very hard to see that each student is really well prepared for her tests.

From this description, would you say that Miss Edwards is an effective or an ineffective teacher? Discuss.

Imagine a teacher who is the reverse of Miss Edwards—democratic in methods, but offensive personally. How would such a teacher compare with Miss Edwards in the results of his teaching?

What do the reactions of her students to Miss Edwards suggest about the relative importance of personality and teaching methods in determining the quality of a teacher's work? Explain.

MODERN WAYS OF DEALING WITH THE MATERIALS OF LEARNING

Our discussion has primarily stressed the human dynamics of the newer trends in education, and so we have only rather summarily referred to the importance of the new teaching methods in their relation to subject matter. Now let us redress this balance by considering three topics which by their very nature focus on the educator's use of the materials of learning.

As we do so, the following point should be kept in mind.

We have said that traditional teaching relies heavily on a logical, hierarchical presentation of subject matter, and that the newer education tends to depart from such structuring. This departure, however, should not be taken as basically a journey into illogicality; rather, it is an effort to replace traditional logicality based on a formalistic scheme of education with a use of logic that more closely relies on the needs and motivation of the student for its impetus and force.

Methods of Problem Solving. The study of problem solving is simply the study of how to attack a problem—any problem—soundly and thoroughly and thus with some assurance that the solution produced will be the best one possible. The following sequence of steps in problem solving, then, is by no means the only possible procedure, but rather is one example of modern techniques:

1. The student should first be encouraged to state the problem. He should learn that the best way of defining a problem is to form it in a clear sentence which gets down to its hard core.

2. He should next reflect on the problem. This should enable him both

to bring his previous experiences to bear on it and to decide what new knowledge will be necessary to solve it.

3. Next, the student should collect material that may comprise this new knowledge. He should read all the relevant reference material he can find and, if appropriate, should make direct observations and interview individuals or groups that can help him. He should, of course, make notes along the way. This process should continue until it fails to produce any new facts or ideas.

4. He should then organize and condense the notes he has taken while collecting material, discarding the irrelevant in order to set his evidence out in clear view.

5. Next, the student should correlate and evaluate this evidence; and if at this point it becomes clear that his knowledge provides clues, but not a solution to the problem, he will need to search for still more material to be integrated into his study.

6. Finally, he should solve the problem in terms of all the evidence that has been collected. By the time he starts this final step the student should be so familiar with his subject that the lines of evidence are clear to him; and when he completes it he should be able to see clearly the nature of the solution and how satisfactory it is.

Of course, any mature person realizes that many problems are incapable of final solution at our present state of knowledge; and if such is the case with our student's problem, he should present and justify his solution as only the best possible at the moment in terms of all the evidence. The lines for future investigation, moreover, should be clear to him and set forth with his tentative solution.

Other problems require different approaches. These are mathematics, science, and puzzle-like problems which are solved by trying one course of action after another until the solution seemingly pops out from one's efforts. Persistent and varied attacks on such problems usually bring success. Sometimes it may help during a long wrestle with a problem to stop and reflect about "what have I done, what has been wrong, and what probably is the right procedure?"

Problem-solving processes have profound meaning for education. Our schools are often criticized on the grounds that their students do not learn to think and so develop the practice of expressing ideas without knowing the evidence for them. If this is ever so—and indeed, it sometimes is—it is because students are not motivated to think and do not have well-directed practice in thinking. On the other hand, if students are intelligently provided with problems to solve and are made able to attack them according to some procedure resembling that just outlined, they will think and, almost certainly, think well. In fact, sound and systematic thinking essentially is good problem solving. This leaves us, however, with the basic need of finding the ways and means of teaching problem solving that will best establish the desirable problem-solving abilities.

Again the reader must be warned that solving problems is not necessarily achieved by observing a series of steps such as these set forth here. There is little more educational merit in the formalism of problem solving than in the formalism that characterized teaching at the turn of the century.

The teacher can help the students most if he and the students cooperatively describe and define the problem; if they discuss where to look for study materials; and—after the students have studied and assembled their evidence—if he helps them draw conclusions and then conducts class discussions in which these conclusions are analyzed and tested in terms of the evidence. While the students are learning how to attack problems, some guidance of this kind can save much trial-and-error learning.

Some students need help in attacking a problem because they do not know how to identify the ideas involved. Others will not persist and work at the problem until they reach a solution. Others are hampered by excessive emotional involvement; they fail to appreciate that problem solving is an objective, orderly process. The teacher can help all these students best by supporting them but not prescribing exact steps to follow.

During class discussion, the leadership of the teacher and his consciousness of the need for using good-reasoning, problem-solving processes will influence the students to contribute materially to the understanding of the subject under discussion. In many classrooms the students speak out with the most irrelevant and superficial comments because they have learned that they will be rewarded for participating. The teacher who sets a higher standard will pull the students up to better levels of handling facts, principles, and theories.

When teaching is rigid (as is likely to be the case with traditional teaching) and there is a problem to solve, students take steps prescribed and outlined by the teacher to arrive at their solutions. When teaching is flexible (as is likely when student-centered methods are being used), the teacher encourages the students to do their own thinking and so to arrive at their own solutions in their own ways.

This contrast, moreover, leads directly to the most basic question about the teaching of problem solving: Is it desirable that students learn one or various methods of solving a problem? Let us turn to the experimental evidence for our answer. W. I. Ackerman and H. Levin taught one group of sixth-grade children to use two ways of solving problems and another group of sixth-grade children to use only one way [Ackerman and Levin, 1958]. The

problems involved three different-sized water jars. To solve each one the children had to measure out a given volume of water, pouring it from one jar to another so that they came out with the required amount. The children did not work with actual jars and water but with cards having pictures of jars and a number on each picture showing the capacity of the jar. On the side of each jar was a number indicating the amount of water to end up with (the solution of the problem) by pouring in and out of the jars. The problems called for holding number or jar capacities in mind and working out the right sequences of addition and subtraction.

After this training period each child was given water-jar problems, all of which had to be solved by new methods except one, which was to be solved by the method that had been practiced. Then followed 13 jigsaw-puzzle problems in which pieces were to be put together to make figures. Some were to be solved according to a fixed pattern and others by any of several other methods.

The findings consistently favored the group of children who had experienced two methods of finding the solutions to the water-jar problems. They did better in the testing period on both the water-jar problems and the jigsaw-puzzle problems. Furthermore, the pupils who learned alternative procedures stayed with the problems longer—an apparent result of greater confidence in being able to get the right answer through the use of different methods.

This study by Ackerman and Levin tells us that when the method of problem solving is cut-and-dried, students will be handicapped in two ways— that limiting problem solving to a single, set method leads to relatively poor results in solving the problem at hand and, importantly, in transferring knowledge to other problems. On the other hand, we are shown that practice in alternative methods results in relatively good problem-solving abilities.

Thus it is highly desirable that the problem-solving methods be taught flexibly. The area of problem solving well exemplifies the general truth that teaching which is exploratory, which throws up varied possibilities, and which looks for answers in original ways gives students more fruitful experiences than teaching that is continuously saying, in effect, "This is the one and only way."

The Core Curriculum. It has become widely accepted that the compartmentalization of subjects is, in many instances, artificial—that much knowledge that lies separated in specific subjects is so closely related that it should be brought together; and this idea has led to the development of the core curriculum. The core curriculum combines and treats as a unit the subject matter from a number of subjects that are ordinarily taught separately. The "class periods" consequently become longer, sometimes as long as

The Broadening Horizons of Education

Modern education aims at giving the learner mastery of basic facts, skills, and ideas, developing his problem-solving methods, involving him in cooperative group behavior, and furthering his all-round personal development. These four cardinal objectives are realized by bringing the school into closer relationship and resemblance to the outside world.

Each of these scenes reflects a means of furthering at least one of the named objectives. To which one or two objectives is each scene most clearly related? Is modern technology more closely involved in the building of problem-solving methods when young people use teaching machines or when they meet with distinguished older persons on television? Of all the situations pictured, which best reflects the modern psychological theory that personal development is furthered by reducing the compartmentalization of activity?

1

2

3

4

1   Courtesy of Hunter College High School.
2   Courtesy of *Youth Wants To Know*.
3   Courtesy of Graflex, Inc.
4   From Barclay-Champion, *Teen Guide to Homemaking*, McGraw-Hill Book Company, New York.
5   Courtesy of the Metropolitan Museum of Art, photo by Lew Merrim.

5

three traditional periods, and are referred to as blocks of time. Subjects usually combined are English and the social studies. Other subjects that may be "cored" are mathematics and science.

Beyond this principal objective of breaking down the barriers between subjects, however, there are other modern elements in the core-curriculum program. Thus emphasis is placed on learning to do critical thinking and problem solving, with the stress placed on broad life problems. Also, the vocabulary used to explain the core curriculum has much in common with the vocabulary used in describing the project type of teaching. An illustration of both these interrelated resemblances is the fact that the core curriculum is sometimes spoken of as "democratic education for a democratic people."

Even though the name core curriculum suggests that the "core" emphasizes combining and organization of subject matter into larger units and doubling or tripling the length of the usual class period, actually core teaching goes far beyond that and stresses many of the same values as nontraditional teaching, which is designated as democratic, student-centered, progressive, and project- and learning-centered. In other words, the core method seems to be directly in the lineage of John Dewey's concepts and clearly not in the perspective of the traditional, authoritarian kind of education. So actually when the core teaching is discussed, the terms and concepts have much in common with the more modern procedures that have been discussed.

For example, the following are some of the procedures and objectives of core teaching, in addition to unification of courses:

Student-teacher planning and cooperative work

Creative, experimental, problem-solving procedures

Learning from many sources: extensive reading in references, textbooks, and current material; field trips, audiovisual experiences, listening to special speakers, and doing original research

Encouragement of critical and evaluative thinking

Development of work skills and habits and the ability to do sustained independent work

Development of the powers of self-direction and individual responsibility

Satisfying the interests and meeting the needs of the individual students

It is evident that these are the objectives emphasized by the various schools of modern education whose concern is with the intellectual, personal, social, and volitional development of students. By integrating various subjects and using larger blocks of time and by using more democratic, pupil-centered procedures, attempts are made to achieve these objectives.

A considerable number of studies have been made to test the effectiveness of the core method of teaching. No table can be presented which accurately represents these findings, because they are not consistent. This is understandable, as not only the method is being tested. Most influential of all is probably the teacher. Also affecting the results is the availability of teaching materials. It is possible that there was only a nominal use of the core method in some instances, and the teaching was actually pretty much as before. The effectiveness of the teacher is especially significant, as some teachers will have poor results whatever method they use, while others always teach well. Some are good with one method but not with another. So when interpreting the results, the variables other than the core method should at least be acknowledged.

The following is an evaluation of a summary of the results of core teaching:

1. The core students in general know the subject as well as or a little better than do traditionally taught students, but in some experiments the latter achieved a little higher.

2. The core students tend to develop better educational skills or study habits, as indicated by more extensive and independent study.

3. Core students have more experience in working with others and tend to be more self-confident, have better personal relationships, and develop leadership. They tend to have better morale.

4. Core students seem to be better prepared for college because of the work and social experiences described above. They also have received better guidance.

5. In general, core students seem better satisfied with their experiences than do other students.

Not all students profited more from core teaching, but the preponderance of evidence supports the five categories of values as given. It is clear that good results have been obtained from core teaching.

The Benezet Experiment. One of the most fascinating experiments in the literature of education is that describing the rather abysmal failure of a group of students to comprehend arithmetic, the postponement of its formal study until the seventh grade, and what happened as a result. This experiment was not scientific in the usual sense, for it did not have precisely measurable control- and experimental-group procedures. Nevertheless, it is so thought-provoking that it is worth detailed consideration.

L. P. Benezet was a superintendent of a New Hampshire school, and during his visits to the classrooms he had an opportunity to observe the recitations of the students [Benezet, 1936]. He was disturbed by the large number of failures in the first grade because of arithmetic. Also, he was appalled by the answers that eighth-grade students gave to his questions on the subject.

A stenographer recorded the replies; to a question about fractions, some were as follows:

> "The smaller number in fractions is always the largest."
> "If the numerators are both the same, and denominators one is smaller than one, that one that is the smaller is the larger."
> "The denominator that is smallest is the larger."
> "If you have two fractions and the one fraction has the smallest number at the bottom, it is cut into pieces, and one has more pieces. If the two fractions are equal, the bottom number was smaller than what the other one in the other fraction. The smallest one has the largest number of pieces— would have the smallest number of pieces, but they would be larger than what the ones that were cut into more pieces."

It is evident that the students were trying to use the words of explanations which they had heard and read but which they did not understand, and so were coming forth with strange and empty verbalizations, the likes of which are not unusual in formal classrooms, incidentally.

As a consequence of these experiences, Benezet, in certain classes, "abandoned all formal instruction in arithmetic below the seventh grade and concentrated on teaching the children to read, to reason and recite—'my new three R's.'" The time that had been used in teaching arithmetic was utilized in reading, reporting, and reciting. Students were encouraged to tell stories in their own words and also to be interpretive and imaginative. Emphasis was also placed on reasoning and problem solving.

In the first six grades there was some informal arithmetic, designed to give students quantitative concepts and to stimulate sound and accurate quantitative thinking—realistic rather than mechanical comprehension. In the first grade, the pupils learned the numbers up to 100 as well as such comparative terms as many and few, more and less, tall and short, and higher and lower. In the second grade the comparatives were continued, but pupils also learned how to tell time, what page numbers mean, the values of coins, and such simple measures as the pint and quart. The fourth grade did considerable estimating of dimensions in terms of inches, feet, and yards and of distances in terms of miles.

Two interesting kinds of checks were made of resulting progress.

First, the experimental classes and the conventional classes matched by grade level were asked, after the experiment was well under way, to put down what they were inspired to write when a picture of a polar bear on a small iceberg was hung before them. It was Benezet's theory that early formal arithmetic stifled the power of expression and so typically caused pupils to make unimaginative statements.

He found that in the classes in which the arithmetic was informal the pupils were distinctly superior in their use of adjectives. They characteristically used such words as *magnificent, awe-inspiring, unique,* and *majestic,* whereas the students in the classrooms where the arithmetic was formal tended to use such words as *nice* and *pretty.*

Later—specifically, 5 years after the program began—the formal and informal classes were given this problem: A wooden pole is stuck in the mud of a pond; one-half of the pole is in the mud, two-thirds of the rest is in the water, and 1 foot is sticking out in the air; how long is the pole?

In the traditional classrooms the answers were as incoherent as those quoted above; the students themselves were stuck in the mud, as it were. On the other hand, the students in the classes where formal arithmetic was postponed to the upper grades figured out the answers without any difficulty; and when the answers of 5 years before were read to them, they shouted with laughter.

It can be argued, of course, that since neither these testing activities nor the procedures that led to them involved carefully controlled measurements, these apparent results are very dubious, and this is true in a strict experimental sense. Nevertheless, this empirical phase of the study had considerable value, if only because of the ideas that it brought forth and emphasized. For this experiment does focus our attention on the effects of rigid, mechanical, and routine teaching versus flexible, organic, and functional methods.

A comparison was made of the arithmetic accomplishment of the students who were taught arithmetic in the traditional way, beginning in the third grade, with the experimental pupils who started their formal arithmetic at the beginning of the sixth grade. Comparisons were made at the end of the sixth grade, and the experimental students with 1 year of arithmetic did essentially as well on tests as those who had had arithmetic during grades 3 through 6. Maturity plus experiences in logical and effective expression quickly brought achievement up to the level of those who had several years more teaching when they probably were not educationally mature enough to understand the import of much of what they were taught.

❂ *Reflect and Review*

A graduate engineer ran into trouble when he helped his ten-year-old son with his arithmetic problems. He and his son would solve each problem cooperatively and get the right answer, and the son would achieve good understanding of what had been done. Still, his teacher would mark him down because the method she taught had not been observed in detail and so he had not put down the solution step by step according to this method. The boy became frustrated and the father exasperated. He exclaimed, "She seems more concerned with a rigid procedure than with arithmetical understanding."

Educationally, who had the sounder point of view, the teacher or the father? Explain.

What might be gained by letting pupils explain their own unique methods of arriving at a solution?

Do you think this teacher would have favored introduction of the core curriculum in her school? Why?

Do you think this boy needed an arithmetic program such as the Benezet experiment? Why?

TEAM TEACHING

When a number of teachers plan and teach a course cooperatively, we have team teaching. It is an attempt by teachers to pool their talents and resources and also to capitalize on the special abilities of the individual members of the team. With good team teaching it may be assumed that the "whole is larger than the sum of its parts."

It has been found from the experience of several hundred schools that have tried or are trying team teaching that when teachers work together, strong motives and efforts develop. In the first place, each teacher wants to perform as well as he can so he will gain the respect of his teammates. The individual teacher will be encouraged to prepare more carefully, and he is discouraged from spending excessive time on his pet areas or from digressing from the work at hand.

A team is more likely to use various assets such as autoinstructors (teaching machines), television, films, museums, resource people, and a large selection of books. When a larger number of teachers and pupils are involved, the teachers will feel the responsibility to utilize the various teaching devices and aids.

Teachers have special interests and talents. One of a team might be especially interested in providing the resources which have just been mentioned and in managing their use. Some teachers are especially effective in teaching large groups, while others are excellent with small groups, in conferences, or in directing individual study.

In team teaching there is a place for nonprofessional help to take care of routine details. Student assistants or special clerks are able to do this work, which will relieve the teachers so they can spend their time on the professional aspects of teaching.

The vitality of team teaching can be brought out by describing the team teaching by Ivan Bodine, E. M. Hollister, and Harry Sackett, three high school teachers who cooperated in teaching a course called American Problems [Bodine et al., 1962]. The teaming up for a course had the effect of encouraging them to plan and work and of committing them to give as good a course as they were able.

Each had a different field of specialization. One had college majors in geography and history; one had specialized in sociology and economics; and the third had special training and experience in psychology, dramatics, and speech.

In planning the course in American Problems these three high school teachers examined all the textbooks and also set up a special library of 250 books for the course. In addition, they organized the course into seven units. All this indicates extensive and careful planning.

In the teaching, each assumed leadership when his specialty was needed. Various procedures were used, so various talents were needed. There were over 300 high school students taking the course, and these were in three tracks or groupings: the honor students, the college preparatory, and the terminal. A number of methods were used: lectures, exhibits, discussions, demonstrations, tape recordings, films, dramatizations, debates, interviews of students, and utilization of current newspapers, books, and radio and television programs. It is evident that the members of the teaching team had many opportunities to use their special abilities.

In both the teaching and the examinations, emphasis was on problem solving. The students were guided to understand the basic procedures in solving a problem, and the tests were designed to encourage logical analysis and critical thinking.

In this team teaching no control group was used with which to make comparisons. There have been a few comparisons, and they indicate what most evaluations of various new methods of teaching show: The results in general are satisfactory, but in some cases the traditional methods work out better. As was explained before, there are differences in the results of all kinds of teaching because of the teacher, particularly, but because of other factors too, so no method will be consistently superior to others.

SUMMARY

Teaching methods vary greatly according to what the teachers do, the educational materials that are used, and what the students do.

Much of today's education is formal but not so rigid as the traditional education practiced at the beginning of this century. For several decades many schools have experimented with ways of improving education by appealing to the students' normal interests and thereby making the school situation much less artificial than it was.

The newer education is concerned about the students' learning the subject matter but also about their acquiring good working habits and developing well personally.

The project method of teaching has the students engage in activities and undertake real problems which require them to read, write, and calculate. Thereby it is expected that they will learn more than they will by the traditional methods.

The project activity method is less formal and more cooperative than the traditional method and depends on many sources rather than on the teacher and textbook.

The Collings experiment was a pioneer experiment for testing the project method. The setting consisted of one experimental rural school and two comparable control schools. Achievement tests revealed that children learned 138.1 per cent as much by the project as by the traditional method.

In the experimental school, there was much better attendance, a much larger percentage graduated from the eighth grade, and the parents manifested much more interest in the school.

The study referred to as the Thirty Schools was also an attempt to overcome the artificialities of the traditional high school by combining subjects and by searching out information in factories, libraries, museums, and other places. Students were encouraged to work independently in large areas of knowledge.

When 1,475 graduates of these 30 high schools were compared with 1,475 matched graduates of the typical high schools, it was discovered that graduates from the experimental schools were more capable of doing independent work, were more active in campus affairs, and showed more leadership. In achievement or college marks they were a little higher.

These results indicate that colleges need not prescribe specific high school subjects as a requirement for college entrance.

In group work the students have the opportunity to pool their resources; consequently, group achievement is usually high. The brightest students contribute most to group work. Brightest students tend to learn more when they work alone, but the achievement of the group is usually more than that of the poorer students, who nevertheless seem to be helped by group work.

Socially cohesive groups do not always work better than noncohesive groups, and the cohesiveness of a group is not always strengthened by group work.

Generally, students of high intelligence who earn good marks in their subjects, who are personally attractive, and who are reasonably forward have most social power.

In student-centered teaching, most responsibility for learning lies with the students, and the teacher is a guide and helper who gets the work started and stands by to help when called upon.

The general results of student-centered teaching have been favorable. The academic achievements of the students have been favorable, as has been their personal development. Students who like to be independent favor student-centered teaching, and those who are dependent on authority figures like teacher-centered classes better.

Rigid, unsympathetic, authoritarian teachers tend to drive the students into a defensive position that is conducive to egocentric behavior. Such teachers are disliked by their students.

Pleasant, democratic teachers are liked by their students and have favorable personal effects on them.

Many authoritarian teachers are generous with their students although they exercise definite control of the school procedures. Such teachers are liked by their students, while teachers who are democratic educationally may not be likable in their personal relations. A fundamental issue is whether or not the students like and respect their teachers rather than whether their methods are democratic or authoritarian.

In learning to solve problems, students should not be guided formally through a set of steps. In general, they should understand and state the problem clearly, decide on how to obtain evidence for solving it, do the searching for the needed knowledge and collect all possible evidence, analyze the collected material in terms of the problem, and then offer the solutions to the problem.

Through many experiences in solving problems, a student learns to think more effectively. Students who learn more than one way of solving problems become better problem solvers than those who learn only one way.

The core-curriculum method involves the organization of subject matter into larger areas with a view to developing more comprehensive understanding. In addition, the teaching methods are also more comprehensive and have much in common with the project, student-centered, and more democratic methods of teaching. As is true of most modern education, the core-curriculum method proves to be effective when given a trial by competent teachers.

The Benezet experiment indicates that formal, mechanical repetition does not result in learning and that children should be helped in their maturing by having meaningful experiences which they can assimilate. Some schoolwork normally given in the lower grades can be postponed until the children are older, and in a short time their achievement will be as high as that of those of the same age who have studied the subject for several years. It is also evident that students can be helped to be more creative.

Team teaching enables a large group of students to benefit from the specialized abilities and interests of their teachers. Also, teachers are more motivated when they work as a team, because of their cooperative and competitive efforts. Under team teaching, teachers can be relieved of routine duties by secretarial and clerical help. Team teaching usually results in a more modern and comprehensive approach to learning than does traditional teaching, and there is some evidence that good intellectual and personal effects are achieved.

SUGGESTED READING

Beach, L. R.: "Sociability and Academic Achievement in Various Types of Learning Situations," *Journal of Educational Psychology*, 51:208–212, 1960. Four methods of teaching and learning were used: lecture, discussion, autonomous small groups, and independent study. Students were evaluated according to their sociableness, and achievement was determined according to the four different methods and the sociability of the students.

Fischler, A. S.: "Use of Team Teaching in the Elementary School," *School Science and Mathematics*, 62:281–288, 1962. Indicates how to do team teaching and discusses the values that occur from cooperative teamwork.

Wiest, W. M., L. W. Porter, and E. E. Ghiselli: "Relationship between Individual Proficiency and Team Performance and Efficiency," *Journal of Applied Psychology*, 45:435–440, 1961. Sets forth a number of valuable ideas about individual and group performance and learning. Also presents an experiment and discusses the effects of the poorest and best individuals on group performances as well as the sum of the individual's performance.

CHAPTER 18
EVALUATING AND REPORTING
STUDENT LEARNING

Teachers and students share a common dislike for examinations and marks, which often seem to distract attention from the true purpose of the school—learning and development. The teacher is likely to feel that he is inadequate to categorize neatly the complex human beings he has been teaching, and the student is likely to feel that he is on trial and being cross-examined by a hostile prosecutor.

These points of view have some validity. Certainly there are serious weaknesses in present-day systems of testing and marking; and radical changes may be needed. However, even the present examination and marking system may be well used or abused. Accordingly, the good teacher tries to make tests and marks devices for learning, not tools for coercion.

In this final chapter, we shall discuss ways to do this, as well as the part parent-teacher and teacher-student conferences may play in minimizing the deficiencies of our current system of tests and marks by eliminating the report card.

USES OF THE EXAMINATION

The formal examination of learning, whether long or short, specific or expansive, is a classroom instrument for measuring proficiency or, more specifically, achievement in school subjects; and its value is generally analyzed from this point of view. But the examination of learning may be more than this; it may operate in three further ways to shape the nature of the education a person receives.

First, the examination may be used often for *diagnostic instructional purposes,* that is, to help the student discover his strengths and weaknesses. To fulfill this objective, an examination should be given with the understanding that no marks will be based on it; it will thus be clear that the test is intended not to coerce the student to work, but solely to promote his education.

Secondly, the examination may be used to *organize and integrate knowledge and thought*. It can be devised to cover the largest possible body of knowledge from various areas of learning. More specifically, it can require the student to focus information from many areas on each given test problem. This will encourage him to bring his ideas as well as facts out of isolation. Such an examination will thus help the student see the interrelationships of the various areas of learning.

Finally, the examination may be used to indicate the quality of the student's scholarship in order to *guide the student in a practical way* in his school and later career. As such a guide, the examination should not be used too often, however, as is explained by the following caution about all examinations.

If the examination is used as a whip to make the student do his work, he will be trained to work for examination results. When a student asks the teacher, "Shall we need to know this for the test?" or "What has this got to do with the entrance examination?" we have evidence that the examination has this sort of control over the student. It is true that students and teacher should not as a regular practice stray far off into the remotely illustrative or speculative so that such questions tend to pop up, but a system of examinations that holds them to a very narrow course is not good educationally.

But let us consider the three most important specific kinds of examinations of learning and see how they relate to all these purposes and this danger.

The Essay or Free-answer Examination. The essay examination is any test in which the student answers questions by constructing written answers using his own choice of detail and phraseology within the limits imposed by the questions. Such answers may range in length from a single sentence to several pages. The procedure is capable of some adaptation to grade level and subject matter.

The major advantage claimed for the essay examination (or, as it is sometimes called, the free-answer or subjective examination) is that the student, required to organize his materials and write them as logically and completely as he is able, learns to exercise judgment in drawing from his fund of information, to evaluate the relative importance of the chosen facts and his ideas, and to use originality in setting them forth.

The essay test is also called the free-response test. Actually it is not that, because the student should be clearly told what he is to do. Beyond that, however, he is free to use his initiative in recalling and setting forth his facts and ideas. The essay test is a free-response test in contrast to the objective test, which is completely structured.

Any activity that thus gives play to the powers of judgment and association and to individual initiative and imagination is very sound educationally. But ordinarily, the essay examination is not used in a manner that achieves such fine training.

In the first place, the student is not encouraged to exercise his initiative by presenting his own interpretations and bringing in supplementary, although not immediately related, facts. In the second place, the student is too hurried. He does not have time to weigh facts and organize them carefully. The student therefore writes as rapidly as he can, putting down the answers that he thinks the teacher wants; and from the standpoints of both composition and content, the examination papers are generally not good.

Another criticism of the essay or free-response test is that it is hard to grade accurately. It is almost impossible to arrive at a reliable mark for a test or theme, and furthermore such exercises take an inordinate amount of the teacher's time to read.

Still, it must not be assumed that because the essay examination does not always produce the desired results, these results cannot be obtained. Certainly if teachers set out to realize the virtues that are attributed to the essay examination, they could come much closer to doing so.

The criticism about the unreliability of the mark assigned a student's paper becomes, however, less important with the diminishing emphasis on marking and on report cards. Themes, examinations, and written work will come to a better instructional purpose than that of determining marks. The papers will be evaluated by the teacher, but with the purpose of helping the student correct his errors and supply the learning in the areas where he was deficient. When a student has difficulty in understanding why his discussion of a question is not a superior one, he should read the answers of those students who have written the best papers. With the help of the teacher and by general discussion and by mutual criticism and help, the students can base much of their improvement on the written work which has been appraised by the teacher and returned to them.

The teacher should formulate the questions so that the student is asked to interpret a wide variety of facts. But he should also encourage the student to make simple, direct, and accurate presentation of facts and ideas. In addition, since haste and carelessness cause students to write badly composed examinations, they should be given more time than is usual for the composition of their answers. Then the teacher should reward clear answers of the more meaningful type with praise and higher marks taking care not to let disagreement with any student's viewpoint make him unfair.

If these things are done, better essay examinations will be written because the examinations, which theoretically are based on the whole rather than the part method of teaching, really will stimulate students to reflect broadly on facts and ideas and to deal with them more comprehensively. In other words, the examination really will organize and integrate the student's knowledge and thought.

The essay examination may also be useful in diagnosing the learning strengths and weaknesses of students. The student should be encouraged to study his corrected papers carefully; he will benefit from the reinforcement of his successes and from the opportunity to correct his specific errors and to fill the gaps in his learning. Still more diagnostic value will be gained from the examination if the teacher goes over the returned papers with the students and helps them to see their shortcomings and their strong points. This, indeed, is the best way to carry diagnosis by the use of the essay examination to the point where it will strongly motivate the student.

The Objective or Short-answer Examination. This is the structured examination in which the student picks out the best answers (multiple-choice test) or indicates whether a statement is true or false (true-false test). Matching items are sometimes used. These are called recognition tests, because the student is directed to recognize the right answer in the case of the multiple-choice test or to recognize true or false statements in the case of the true-false test. In the completion test, the student is asked to write the correct word, number, or phrase in a blank and thereby make the sentence correct. This is a recall test. The multiple-choice items are those most frequently used in objective tests.

The objective examination handicaps the bluffer in two ways.

He cannot interpret a question loosely and write about just the aspects of it he knows; for the objective test, by posing very specific questions and limiting the number of possible answers, does not permit this kind of evasion.

Also, the objective test can cover the material of a study area more completely than the subjective test can. Because of the many items in the objective test, no large section of subject matter is omitted, and questions can be included which approach the material from many different angles. The bluffer cannot complain that some parts of his preparation were not even touched by the test.

The objective examination, therefore, is an excellent device for testing the extent of a student's knowledge of the factual elements in a subject and its vocabulary—a far better test of these things than the typical essay examination. In short, it may be said that the objective examination is a reliable measure of the student's achievement in gaining information.

Furthermore, the precise form of objective-test items makes it possible for the test to be precisely, easily, and rapidly scored—even by a machine.

Finally, the scoring is free of subjective influences. The score that a student obtains on an objective test straightforwardly indicates to him how much he knows on the test subject and also has a definite meaning in terms of the scores of other students in the class, which were determined on the same basis. Thus the student is likely to feel that he has been marked fairly. The instructor, too, can feel confident of the fairness of his marking standards, since he knows that he cannot be influenced by the good, bad, or even neutral feelings that may exist between himself and the student.

However, the objective test, as now generally made, is deficient in several important respects.

Usually limited to the more factual elements of a course, it necessarily stresses definitions and quantitative materials. This is not a disadvantage if the examination is limited to information that is significant; but unfortunately, it often includes details the educational value of which almost anyone would question. (This, of course, is the primary fault of the person who devises the particular test.)

Also, if questions to which no one incontrovertible answer exists were included among the precisely answerable questions, they would not only confuse the students but would also confuse the scoring; for instance, debatable answers cannot be satisfactorily picked up by a scoring key made to fit over examination-blank answer columns. Consequently, the questions are limited to those over which no disagreement can arise about the answer. Therefore, some of the best material in literature, history, sociology, and many other subjects must be excluded because it is speculative and hypothetical.

Relatedly, the usual objective examination does not lead the student to do independent and creative thinking. The features that discourage the poor student from bluffing also tend to prevent the good student from organizing facts and expressing points of view; and so the examination does not provide an opportunity for, much less encourage, original intellectual explorations.

The good, as well as the poor, student, then, tends to study in the following manner: He adjusts his studying to the examination question that he anticipates. In class, he listens to the teacher largely to note phrases or facts that later may appear in an examination, and these he writes down. In reading, he attends only to what he thinks will be called for, and so becomes a hunter for strategic fragments of material. He does not try to coordinate these fragments in a pattern, for this will not help him in his test. Instead, he tries to memorize in a short time many informational bits: cramming has been accentuated, not reduced, by the objective test. Then, just before the examination, he frequently gathers together with other students who have done likewise, and they "try each other out" on the facts that each thinks will be useful.

How well aware students are that they do this sort of thing has been experimentally shown. In an investigation of the effect of the type of examination on students' methods of preparation and efficiency in learning, Herbert M. Silvey discovered that over 80 per cent were conscious of preparing differently for essay and objective tests [Silvey, 1951]. Nearly all students (95 per cent) wanted to know whether the examination would be objective or essay. They knew that for true-false and multiple-choice tests they placed emphasis on rote memorizing of more or less isolated details and that in preparation for essay tests, they emphasized the organization and summarizing of material. But why do students so behave?

Experience and research indicate that the rote memorizers are self-defeating even in terms of the tests, for the results indicated that a method of study emphasizing integration of material results in a better command of the test subject as tested by both essay and objective types of examination. But it is possible for the rote learners to prepare quickly for an objective test, and students know this and so set out for, in a sense, very practical reasons to become "bit pickers" rather than reasoners, inquirers, and thus real learners.

All this points up the dangers lying in the control that examinations in general—but objective examinations in particular—come to exercise over educational methods and procedures at all levels, from elementary grades through graduate school. But these dangers become even clearer when the broad use of the same examinations is considered. For example, if examinations which emphasize limited, scrappy details are given all over a state under the auspices of the state board of education or similar sponsorship, they may tend to harm both the study habits of many students and the methods of many teachers. They may cause the teachers to narrow their teaching to relentless drill and the students to learn innumerable bits of information by rote in order to store up answers for prospective questions. In short, examinations may control the objectives of the school and restrict the educational processes, rather than stimulate originality and creativeness.

These evils are not necessarily inherent in the objective examination, how-ever, any more than the deficiencies attributed to the essay examination are inherent in it. It may be best to use objective tests primarily for subjects which are quantitative and simply descriptive in nature rather than for those which involve a good deal of evaluation and speculation. But if teachers decide to devise their objective test items so that they stress analysis, evalua-tion, judgment, and original reactions, many of them can succeed in doing so. However, the task is a very difficult one—a fact that, indeed, goes far to account for the makeup and stress on memory of most present objective tests.

These comments, of course, are not intended to minimize the value of facts; we must learn many of them. Facts, however, are not very valuable if they stand alone: They have to be imbedded in principles to contribute most to understanding. It is probably best to use the objective test, then, primarily as a way of measuring mastery of definable facts and concepts and thus discovering areas in which further study needs to be done. It should be supplemented, however, by essay tests and discussions in which the facts are organized in a larger context.

Standardized Achievement Tests. Standardized achievement tests are tests carefully constructed to measure mastery of fairly large bodies of material and to compare the individual student's achievement with that of average students of similar age and grade level.

Carefully devised standardized achievement tests, given once a year, will adequately determine the achievement status of individual students. Such annual examinations, which require several hours to take, will indeed, serve as a better index to what the students have learned than all the marks on his report cards. Thus they (or, alternatively, good teacher-made comprehensive examinations) are a prime tool for long-term guidance of the student. Generally, students with the highest scores or marks in junior high school will earn the highest marks in senior high school; the same is true for those who have average and low scores or marks. The same relationships exist for senior high school and college.

Although marks are valuable in indicating the intellectual abilities and study practices of a student, the scores on comprehensive achievement tests are almost as valuable for predicting future academic success. A pupil's standing on such tests predicts what he will do in his future schooling almost as accurately as the composite of his school marks.

A good standardized achievement test is constructed to include a thorough sampling of the material in a variety of school subjects—history, geography, arithmetic, reading, algebra, and others. Then, in a preliminary form, the test is given to selected students of the various grades—who, as groups, represent average abilities—in order to obtain norms, or standards. More specifically, norms are established for the various grades in each of the subjects in grade, junior high, and senior high schools. For example, the average score of the originally tested third-graders would be made the reading-test norm for that grade. Thus a teacher can compare the average score of his class with the norms to determine whether or not his class measures up to the established achievement standards for the grade; and similarly, the grade status of individual students can be found from the norms.

Achievement-test norms are also established for ages, in the same way they are established for grades: Preliminary tests are given to age groups chosen for representative or average ability in the various subjects. Of course, in order that the norms may be accurate, those to whom the test is given must be carefully chosen. Thus, apart from subject proficiency, if too many bright or too many dull children are chosen, the age norm on a test will be too high or too low. Ideally, each age group should have an average IQ of 100.

By means of age norms, it can be discovered whether or not a student is "at age" in achievement in his various subjects and, if not, the number of years that he is above or below his age. For example, average achievement of nine-year-olds in arithmetic determines the arithmetic age of nine; but nine-year-old students may vary greatly in arithmetic achievement, so that we have nine-year-olds with arithmetic ages ranging from six to thirteen. Indeed, the range may be even greater.

A student has an arithmetic age, a reading age, a history age, and so forth, the inclusions being determined by the particular achievement-test sections; and each of these ages is technically called his achievement age (AA) in the specific subject. His average for all the test subjects is expressed as his educational age (EA). In other words, a student's general educational achievement—his composite achievement in the several tested subjects—determines his EA.

This EA is to general ability in school subjects as mental age (MA) is to general mental capacity. Like MA, the EA may be equal to chronological age (CA) or may be less or higher. The relationship of EA to CA is expressed as the educational quotient (EQ); more specifically, EQ is found by dividing EA by CA and multiplying by 100. Again there is a parallel to the measurement of general mental capacity, for EQ plays a similar part here to that of intelligence quotient (IQ), which, as we have seen, expresses the relationship of MA to CA:

$$IQ = \frac{MA}{CA} \times 100 \qquad and \qquad EQ = \frac{EA}{CA} \times 100$$

(The purpose of the 100 in the formula is to get rid of the decimal point. Thus the EQ, like the IQs, which in strict ratio terms are 0.90, 1.00, and 1.10, are expressed as 90, 100, and 110.)

A child whose EA and CA are equal has an EQ of 100, which is average; for example, a boy ten years old whose achievement is equal to the average for ten-year-olds has an EQ of 100. The EQ of a student twelve years old who has an EA of nine is 75 or, nine-twelfths as high as the average. An eight-year-old with an EA of ten has an EQ of 125, or ten-eighths of the average.

Achievement quotients (AQs) can also be calculated, of course, for the student in each of the school subjects covered by a test. Here the formula would be

$$AQ = \frac{AA}{CA} \times 100$$

Thus, if a student is 11 years, 7 months old and has a history age of 13 years, 2 months, he has a history quotient of 114. (Note that here—as, indeed, in most actual cases—the compared ages include months.)

The educational quotient may seem in part a confirmation of a student's intelligence quotient. Normally, EQ and IQ correspond fairly closely. For example, if both quotients of a student are uniformly very high, there is satisfactory evidence of very high capacities and abilities.

Large discrepancies for any individual should be checked by retesting; and if a student is clearly lower in his educational quotient, he is probably not studying enough. It will be found that some achieve high in terms of their capacities. Such evidence of relative achievement is very helpful in evaluating and guiding a student.

☯ *Reflect and Review*

Here are achievement ages and achievement quotients for John, a fourth-grader 9 years and 4 months old.

Subject	AA	AQ
Reading	12 years, 2 months	130
Arithmetic	9 years, 9 months	104
History	13 years, 3 months	142
Geography	12 years, 6 months	134
Spelling	9 years, 6 months	102

What other information about John's mental abilities and school progress would help in deciding how he might be guided in his future school work? How, specifically, would the following information illuminate the achievement figures given above: IQ, school marks, teacher's evaluation, John's attitudes toward different subjects?

Do you see any significant relationships between the AQs given above? In what subjects will John probably be best in high school and college?

THE PROBLEM OF MARKS

Ask several teachers how they mark and you will receive many different answers.

Some will say that they mark on the basis of absolute achievement only. Such teachers are guided by the principle that a mark in a subject should represent competence in that subject and nothing else. So when they give marks, they try to be governed solely by the results of examinations and, in some cases, formal recitations which actually are tests. Such teachers try very hard, in marking students, not to be at all influenced by their personal likes and dislikes of the students in their classrooms.

At the other extreme are the teachers who will say they take attitude, effort, and progress into account. Such teachers tend to treat achievement purely on an individual basis. Thus, if a student changes his position in a class from low to above-average, he will get a higher mark than a student who has consistently held a higher position. Also, such teachers will mark down a student if he is late, misses class, or presents some other discipline problem.

Between these extreme points of view are many gradations, of course; obviously, many marking standards exist. Moreover, in the rigors of teaching practice, few if any can follow their standards completely, so that it is doubly difficult to understand what marks actually mean by considering them solely in relation to the teacher.

The idea of marking "according to the curve" is still prevalent and has been an issue in American education for over 40 years. Technically, marking according to the curve would result in the following percentage distribution of marks, or something close to it:

A	B	C	D	F
7	24	38	24	7

Actually, not many teachers observe this distribution: Most of them tend to give more higher marks and fewer low ones.

Even though "the curve" is not observed statistically, still the idea of distributing the marks on a relative basis is a sound one. The scores or values which the students have earned in a given subject can be arranged according to size from the highest to the lowest. Then the teacher can divide the ranked group into parts according to some general standard of the school and assign the A's, B's, etc., accordingly. The marks in a subject should represent the students' standing or achievement in the subject. Ranking of the students according to their measured abilities gives a sound basis for assigning the marks.

When students are marked on a relative basis, the marks indicate the relative level of achievement in a subject, but the students of low capacity are condemned to receive the lowest marks while the highest marks go to the bright, hard-working students. To overcome this condition, which limits the A's to only a few of the students, a plan for marking on an individual basis is frequently proposed.

According to this plan, the student is marked on the extent to which he achieves in terms of his capacity. Thereby the student of high mental capacity who does not work hard and therefore is a nonachiever will be given a low mark while a student of low capacity who is a high achiever will be given a high mark, though in terms of actual achievement the bright student will probably be much higher than the dull student. To a great degree, then, the student is marked on effort or on his study habits.

The purpose of such a system is to encourage the student to utilize fully his capacities. This is a worthy purpose, but there are so many drawbacks to the system that it is doubtful that such a purpose can be achieved. In the first place, it is very difficult—almost impossible, in fact—for the teacher to judge accurately the extent to which a student is trying. Two factors are involved—the capacity of the learner and his achievement—and it is very frustrating to relate those two. Judging capacity is complicated by the fact that both mental age and IQ are involved. Furthermore, the dull older child usually has had more years of schooling than the bright younger child and therefore may seem to be relatively more competent. All these complications make it almost impossible to mark on achievement in terms of capacity to achieve.

Furthermore, marks determined on this basis do not reflect the student's ability in the subject and may be very misleading. A dull student with an A will be much less competent in a subject than a bright student who gets a D because he impresses the teacher that he studies too little.

The school should encourage good study habits and make hard, effective workers out of its students. So if it wants to mark the students separately on effort or study habits it can do so rather than give them marks in a subject according to how hard they seem to work on it. It might be added that giving a separate mark for study habits will probably do little good. It is better for the teacher in the classroom to put the students in situations where they are stimulated to work hard. Furthermore, the teacher has many opportunities to encourage the student and praise him for his efforts.

Personal Characteristics of Students and Their Marks. We have known for a long time that, on the whole, girls get higher marks than boys but boys get higher scores on comprehensive achievement tests than girls. The explanation seems to be that (1) girls' penmanship is better, (2) girls do their work more painstakingly and promptly, (3) girls cause less disturbance, and (4) most teachers are women who probably favor their own sex. On the average, girls appear to be more conforming and as a result please the teachers more than the boys do; they therefore get better marks, even though, on the average, they attain less knowledge of subject matter.

Relatedly, when E. G. Kelley made an analysis of students whose standings on comprehensive examinations were above their school marks, equal to their school marks, and below their school marks, respectively, he found that those whose standings on the examinations were higher than their school marks were the best readers and had the highest general mental ability and that those who received marks which surpassed their standing on the tests were as a group insecure, relatively rigid, compulsive, and conforming [Kelley, 1958]. Thus again it is suggested that less independent students are more congenial to teachers and therefore are evaluated a little higher than their actual achievement warrants. As a result, the usual educational atmosphere does not sufficiently encourage the more independent students.

Kelley's study tends, then, to confirm the relationship between the tendency of girls to conform more than boys and their tendency to receive higher marks. But his evidence that marks are a partial reflection of personal attitudes as well as objective achievement should not be viewed as a condemnation of marks. In so far as a certain amount of surrender of individuality is necessary in any social activity, it is understandable that the student who conforms to the expectations of the school in most cases will receive higher marks than the troublesome individualist.

In the school situation there is much work to be done; to do it, a student must deny himself the luxury of aimlessness. He must be willing to integrate his purposes and set out to work effectively; he must also have a good learning capacity. A person with such willingness and such capacity usually enjoys better-than-average marks in school and also is very likely to be successful when he leaves school for the jobs of his adult life, the reason being that the requirements for both good marks and later success are basically these two qualities combined.

This is illustrated negatively by those few among Terman's gifted children who by middle age had compiled job records far poorer than the rest of these very bright persons. Examination of their school records showed that instead of having superior marks, as most of the gifted children did, those whose jobs were below their capacity also had school marks below their capacity—generally, only average and poorer marks. In school they had lacked control and concentration of effort for getting the work done just as they lacked those qualities during their adult years. Along the way, because their school marks were lower, they tended, as a group, not to graduate from college and do the advanced academic and professional study that led their peers further.

But the record is also very clear on the positive relationship of marks and industry in school to success in post-school life. Our straight-A valedictorians and salutatorians furnish far more than their proportion of success in political, professional, and industrial positions. Many members of Phi Beta Kappa (in which the principal requirement for membership is superior scholarship as evidenced by marks) are not last heard of when their election to membership is announced in the college paper. They generally have considerably more than average success in the world, and a considerable number distinguish themselves highly. J. W. Tilton has reported that the highest tenth in college marks furnishes twice as many starred (highly distinguished) men of science as the other nine-tenths; and three times as many of those elected to the National Academy, a still higher recognition, are in the upper tenth in scholarship as are in the other nine-tenths [Tilton, 1951]. And virtually all such persons are real workers, as well as bright. Finally, the arbiters of worldly success are not unaware of the relationship we have been discussing. When representatives of the most successful law firms, medical clinics, and industrial corporations visit a university campus to select the spring graduates to whom they will offer positions, they typically favor students with the highest marks who also have a record of successful participation in student affairs—a record which indicates social maturity.

Marks, then, do have considerable and important validity for the student in indicating how well he will do in the next grade or, when he finishes school, how well he will do in his vocation. But they have serious drawbacks too. How are these facts to be resolved for the educational betterment of our youth?

We shall conclude this chapter with a discussion of a possible alternative to the report-card phase of the present system of tests and marks. But—since marks themselves are clearly with us for the foreseeable future—we shall first discuss how the present marking practices may be best applied and improved.

Policies of Marking. There appear to be five major objections to the marking systems used in conventional schools at present.

1. For the student, marks sometimes become the end—the major purpose of education—rather than a means. The student working for marks tends to be uninterested in what he actually learns. Instead, he studies his teachers, tries to gain their favor, and otherwise develops tactics designed to give him the best marks possible. Thus he asks, "Will we be marked on this?" and works on it only if the answer is yes or maybe. Some capable students will select easy courses with the purpose of getting a high mark when their needs would be served better by other courses. Relatedly, the marking system, by emphasizing the mark itself as a desirable or undesirable label, indirectly encourages cheating. Under a system which simply shifted attention away from the race for grades to the delights of learning, the student would have no incentive to cheat; he could clearly see that cheating would keep him from his main educational business—learning.

2. The great differences in capacities make the competition for marks very unfair, and this competition is not good for the emotional life of the

dull, the average, or the bright. If the teacher gives marks on the basis of achievement, it is impossible for the dullest students to get good marks. The higher marks will always go to the bright children, for whom marks are not an incentive because they can get good marks without working up to capacity; the dull students, on the other hand, are recurringly or even permanently discouraged by the marks they receive. For the teachers to give the slow-learning child who works hard higher marks than his achievement warrants is not satisfactory either, since they do not tell the truth about the achievement of the low-capacity student and sometimes irritate brighter students and their parents.

3. Teachers do differ in their evaluations and thus marking of students' work. For example, one teacher will mark as a failure an examination which another teacher will think is quite good; this has happened, surprisingly, in all kinds of subjects, from English and history to such supposedly objective subjects as mathematics and physics. Again, the teacher in the fourth grade may be an easy marker who gives many A's; but the next year, the teacher in the fifth grade may be a hard marker who gives very few A's indeed.

4. Traditional marks stir up antagonisms among teachers, parents, and students. This continuous marking of students' work and the practice of using report cards probably creates more unpleasantness in teaching than does anything else. The egos of both parents and children become involved in school marks so that the report card can easily provoke hostility. The teacher, then, has to think of how the marks he gives may antagonize his students and their parents. The mark thus gets in the way of a friendly relationship devoted to the growth and development of the student.

5. Marking the students takes an excessive amount of time. One of the often justified complaints of teachers is that they have to spend too large a proportion of their time on clerical details; and keeping a record of pupils' marks and then preparing report cards adds to this burden, which takes away from real teaching activities.

Much trouble can be avoided if the teachers of a school or school system thrash out and agree on a percentage distribution of marks that can be used as a general guide. For example, the grade and high school teachers of a city could agree on the following distribution:

A	B	C	D	F
15	25	45	15	Seldom, only in special cases.

Then, if they go ahead to actually distribute their marks according to the chosen pattern—or, at least, reasonably adhere to it—variations should not be large from classroom to classroom and from grade to grade. Such a clear-cut standard will therefore help avoid the difficulty with parents that arises when the students are given much better or, especially, much poorer marks than they were given the previous year or years. There will be, of course, certain individual classes which warrant considerable deviation from any such standard, such as classes which have an unusually large proportion of exceptionally bright and ambitious students. When a teacher joins a teaching staff, he should inquire about the marking standards and practices of the school and then distribute his marks in reasonable conformity with the practices of his colleagues.

In addition to the problem of distributing the marks is the problem of unreliability of individual marks, be it the marking of the individual theme, a drawing, or an examination paper. There really is no satisfactory way of improving very much the reliability of marking written material, as the subjective element cannot be eliminated. Careful grading of written work according to standards developed by the faculty will improve reliability, but the difficulty can be obviated largely if the written work is graded and comments made with the purpose of teaching the student rather than to give him a mark.

The other side effects of our marking system, such as the students' chief concern being to get a good or passing mark rather than really learning the subject, and the ill will that marking develops, can be overcome only by doing away with the present system of marking and report cards and meeting the students' needs for achieving optimum growth and development. This has been alluded to on previous pages and will be discussed more fully later.

In summary, the principal objectives of the school can be expressed most simply as the achievement of the optimum development of the students, physically, mentally, socially, and emotionally. The usual examinations are mental or cognitive in nature. Some report cards provide places for checking the progress that is made in the other areas of development or for making comments. In the permanent records of the school, there are usually recorded several appraisals of the volitional and personal progress of the pupils, along with the usual extensive records of achievement in the school subjects.

Marks and examinations, ideally, should be based on the major purposes of the school. In the intellectual or cognitive areas, the examinations should be so devised that they stimulate imaginative—creative abilities, the critical and evaluative processes, and the practice of transfer rather than just listing facts and recording the words of the book. In other words, examinations and reporting should stimulate the productive mental processes rather than the reproductive ones.

In the other areas, the school's activities should be conducive to effective student development. Still, the school needs to be aware of the fact that it is not necessarily fostering the character and the emotional, social, and physical development of the pupil by giving him a mark periodically in those areas of development. What the student needs is the guidance and experience which will cause him to develop most effectively.

⚫ *Reflect and Review*

Thirteen-year-old Stephen has an IQ of 152. He has made nearly all A's on his report cards ever since he started school, and is the outstanding student in his eighth-grade class. He learns quickly and retains what he has learned. His teacher, however, does not believe Stephen is being encouraged by his education to develop as fully as he is able to. Furthermore, the teacher has noticed that the boy is generally satisfied to maintain a position just above the rest of the class and seems to have no desire to forge ahead to a level approximating that of which he is capable. This is true; although Stephen is not conceited, he naturally realizes that his capacities are high and that he does not need to exert himself to maintain his A average.

Everett, who is the same age as Stephen and in the same grade, has an IQ of 92. He finds it difficult to do the work required of him, and although he has a C average, he is frequently worried by the prospect of getting a failing mark. He is, indeed, extremely conscious of grades; for instance, he envies Stephen's ease in maintaining his high average. Everett is a hard worker and studies efficiently, but he is sometimes tempted to follow the example of some of his classmates and cheat to win grades.

What does the grading system at these two boys' school seem to emphasize? What is the evidence of this in both of the above vignettes?

Suppose the grading system were changed to emphasize effort almost completely. What do you think would be the effects on the habits of learning of Stephen and Everett, respectively? Do you think the change would be good or bad for each, all things considered? Why?

CONFERENCES WITH PARENTS AND STUDENTS

Imagine a doctor sending a child or adolescent he has just examined home with a card on which is recorded

Lungs	A
Stomach	C
Tonsils	B
Kidneys	B
Heart	C+
Thyroid	A—
Eyes	D
Ears	B

Of course, a doctor makes case records. But he does not thrust them in abbreviated form into the hands of the young patient and consider the case closed until the next examination or until the parents phone and ask what to do, say, about their son's or daughter's vision. Instead, the doctor characteristically makes a point of talking to the parents, with the purpose of learning more about his patient and of gaining their cooperation in helping him with his health problems.

A similar procedure would seem reasonable for a school to change over to, and some schools have thus substituted parent-teacher conferences for the report card, but there is not a strong trend in that direction. Why?

There seem to be two principal obvious reasons:

1. Parents are accustomed to marks as a means of judging the academic standing of their children.

2. It is difficult, practically, for the father to arrange to meet with the teacher. But more basically, parents tend to shift to the school the responsibility for rearing their children. Then, when the marks come home, they may look at them and summarily blame or praise the child or show indifference; or, in some instances, the parents may use the partial knowledge of the marks to worsen the relationships of teacher and student by projecting the blame unfairly on the teacher. In either case, teachers often feel, in turn, that the home is expecting too much of the school.

Such situations indicate that there should be closer cooperation between teachers and parents, and, indeed, parent-teacher conferences might become more common if school administrators and teachers tried more consistently to influence parents to accept the conferences.

Conducting the Conference with Parents. The parent-teacher conference can awaken the parents to their responsibilities and then help them toward a more intelligent understanding of what they might do to further the development of their children. This does not mean that the school then will have less responsibility, but rather that the school and home as a partnership will cooperate in understanding the student, his needs, and what to do about providing good developmental experiences for him.

Yet it is not easy to conduct a fruitful parent-teacher conference. As we have suggested, parents are often more inclined to want their child graded than to get information that will help them understand him; therefore they may be on the defensive about the whole idea; or they may be overprotective of their child or put forth some other distorted point of view in discussing him with the teacher. The teacher may be on the defensive for any number of reasons, too, and so have difficulty in discussing a child with his parents. Indeed, the feelings of worth of teacher and parents are usually threatened to some extent at the beginning of a conference, and egos often get in the way.

The teacher, then, must initially work to establish good rapport. He may begin by telling the parents of some pleasant experience he has had with their child—if possible, a little story which will show how "their boy" or "their girl" is interested in school or has done something creditable there. A few friendly, complimentary words seldom fail to disarm the parents and elicit their cooperation. Then the teacher will be able to proceed to explain the progress that the child is making much more easily. If their Johnny has been a troublemaker, it is even more desirable to start off in a friendly manner.

The child's progress in the following areas should be discussed with the parents:

General mental development and achievement in the various school subjects

Social and emotional development

Physical development: general health and physical abilities, including athletic skills

Special interests and capacities in art, music, dramatics, public speaking, debate, and mechanical pursuits

Parents are usually most concerned, however, about how their children are "learning," meaning how they are doing in their subjects. Learning is usually not associated with social and personal matters, even though learning is actually as applicable to these as it is to subject matter. Thus the teacher should have, and be ready to bring out first, records of the student's achievement in the various subjects, expressed as achievement ages and achievement quotients, and records of other teachers' experiences with the achievement of the student. Of course the teacher should also have records of the student's intelligence quotient and mental age, so that he can explain how the student is doing in terms of his own capacity.

All these data the teacher should have reviewed before the conference; but he should not be highly quantitative in his descriptions of the data at the conference. For instance, to say "John has a reading age of 10 years and 6 months and a reading quotient of 112" would ordinarily be a mistake; most parents do not have the specialized training for understanding such technical terms. It is most satisfactory, rather, to inform the parents in general terms how a child is doing in relation to his capacity, as well as his relative standing in his class, if the parents ask for this also.

On the matter of the student's mental capacity, the teacher again may prevent misunderstanding by not being too precise or definite. In the first place, when the child is in the lower grades the teacher should be very conservative in telling the parents about their child's IQ at all because usually he does not have adequate evidence; as stated earlier, it takes annual testing, or testing every other year, over a period of several years to determine IQ clearly. Thus the teacher can best take care of the parental desire for IQ information by describing in a general way the child's brightness as evidenced by the progress he is making in reading and arithmetic. When enough intelligence tests have been given over the years, it becomes satisfactory and even desirable for the teacher to tell the parent that the child's IQ is under average, average, a little above average, or considerably above average. But the teacher still should not, in most cases, quote definite figures such as 96, 113, or 145, because the parents can be misled by them.

The crucial point about this area of conference discussion, indeed, is continuation. Thus, parents who have conferences with their child's teachers every year after the child starts school will tend to develop, without delving into precise numerical details, a good understanding of their child's capacity and of the progress he has made, and thus a realistic attitude toward his potentialities for subject-matter achievement. This should make it increasingly possible for the teacher to gear the discussion to specific ways in which he and the parents can cooperate to help the child if necessary and to encourage him if he is doing well.

Let us consider one other conference area: social and emotional development of the child.

As previously indicated, many parents are not aware of how today's schools try to give students experiences that will make them become healthy and effective social beings, just as many parents are not aware of their own responsibility for helping their child develop emotionally and socially. Thus, when the teacher directs conference discussion to a mutual consideration of the student's personal and social success and failures, in order to find out what the home and school can do to guide him into maturing social experiences, there may be a recurrence of the ego-threat difficulties of parents at the very beginning of the conference. Also, and not unrelatedly, there will be deeper problems which will especially require tact. For instance, it may be known to the teacher that a child's social difficulty is caused largely by the continuous quarreling of his parents. But the teacher cannot say to the mother and father, "Your troubles are causing the shyness and withdrawal of your son; you had better mend your ways and have a happy home for him." Yet the teacher may tactfully help awaken such a consciousness in the parents by talking thoroughly though carefully about ways in which their home—just as if it were a happier-than-average home—might provide good social outlets for the now-miserable child.

Teachers have usually had training in school health and are usually observant of the health of their students. For example, if they have become suspicious of the eyesight, the food habits, the energy level, or other physical conditions of the child, they can bring the matter up with the parents, who may then wish to have their family doctor check on the suspected condition.

In general, the teacher should mention matters that involve the child's welfare in a spirit of helpfulness. These matters should include special talents also. It happens that when the special talents and interests which students have are encouraged they sometimes develop into very successful careers.

Cooperation between home and school as democracy in action is carried even further by including the student in the conference. This is not an extensive practice but has been tried, with all the participants being satisfied. When the student is present, he often profits from the discussion about his progress and development. Furthermore, he can contribute to the understanding of both the teacher and his parents about what his needs are and what he is trying to do to satisfy them. Inasmuch at the student and his advancement are the subject of the conference, he can gain most by being present, it seems. Students appreciate the opportunity of "having their say." Experience has indicated, however, that pupils below the fourth grade are too immature for participating effectively in teacher-parent-pupil conferences.

Letters to the Parents. In some schools the teachers write letters to the parents at various intervals and try to describe the educational and personal progress which their children are making. The letters also contain suggestions about what the home and school can do to help the child with any particular problem he may have. These letters are another attempt to get away from the traditional report cards and provide ideas and information that will contribute more to the child's development than a listing of marks on a report card.

If letters are written periodically, they tend to become monotonous and fail to say anything individual and helpful. When a teacher writes 30 or 40 letters, he is greatly taxed to write something that is particularly applicable to a given student. The letters soon reach the point of diminishing returns. Furthermore, it is an inordinately trying task to write so many letters every 6 weeks or so. Conceivably a letter, like the teacher-parent conference, should be an annual event or should be employed when a special situation makes it desirable. It was found, in the case of conferences, that when they were held several times a year, the number of parents participating was high for the first conferences but fell off rapidly with subsequent conferences. Interest in letters seems to follow the same trend.

Student-Teacher Conferences. There should also be planned regular conferences with students in the same areas as those described for the parent-teacher conference: progress in subject matter and mental development;

social and emotional development; physical development; and special interests and activities. Also, the same ideas for conducting the conferences generally apply—notably, those concerned with overcoming defensiveness and establishing good rapport, as well as refraining from giving too specific information on such items as intelligence and achievement quotients. One special point of procedure, however, applies especially to the student-teacher conference.

The teacher should not make the conference a preaching session in which he bluntly analyzes the student's faults and virtues and tells him what to do. Instead, the student should be encouraged to talk about himself, his problems, and his ambitions.

Two important interrelated events will usually take place as a result:

1. The student, just by doing the talking, will get various useful perceptions of his capacities, interest, and personal qualities.

2. The teacher will get much information useful for discovering what can be done to help the student.

Such student-teacher conferences along with the teacher-parent conferences, which may also include the student, lessen the need of having the traditional report cards. Thereby, the weaknesses of the marking and report-card system will be done away with. The information conveyed by the report card can be handled much better in conferences. Evaluation can be merged with guidance in the conference situation, thereby giving the student the help he needs.

If the student seems unable to evaluate himself correctly, the teacher may make suggestions or guide his thought among the described experiences in such a way as to help the student see himself more accurately; and actually, out of such active guidance the teacher should understand the student even better also. Such student-teacher conferences can develop into very pleasant, as well as personally valuable, experiences for the student if the purpose is not to pass judgment on the student but to guide him toward optimum growth and development.

● *Reflect and Review*

A father, alarmed by a series of report cards studded with D's, said to the high school principal of a typical small-town high school at a luncheon club meeting that he wanted him to keep his boys out of the pool hall. The principal replied that he was glad to have his boys in high school and that he would cooperate as much as he could in helping them, but that in out-of-school matters such as the boys' staying out of the pool hall, the responsibility would have to be the father's and not his own.

How does this very social situation suggest that there are needs for parent-teacher conferences and that they are not so difficult to hold as is often said?

Suppose that this school instituted a program of one conference each year between the teachers and parents. How would this principal and the parents have to adjust their points of view about the school's and the home's function in order to make the program fully successful?

What areas would have to be explored together before a program for these boys could be worked out?

SUMMARY

The question should be raised about the role of school marks in today's schools. Conceivably, school marks and report cards distort the teaching and also cause the students to concern themselves about the marks they receive and not about their learning and development.

Examinations are used to evaluate the student's knowledge in a subject and provide evidence for determining his marks.

Examinations will facilitate the student's learning when they are used diagnostically to discover his learning needs, to stimulate him to organize and integrate his knowledge, and to provide information about his intellectual and educational abilities which can be used for guiding him educationally and vocationally.

The essay or free-answer examination, if fully utilized, brings out the student's originality and interpretative abilities rather than mechanical answers in terms of barren facts.

Most of the negative criticism of the free-answer test is that teachers vary greatly in grading it. However, when the emphasis is shifted from marks to learning—before, during, and after it is taken—this objection no longer applies.

A student needs plenty of time so that his essay examinations can become a good experience in careful thinking and composition.

The objective or short-answer test is a structured test which generally calls for recognizing the best answer or indicating whether or not an answer is right or wrong. It is a good test of knowledge, and it can be constructed so it will require a high order of reasoning. Often, however, short-answer tests encourage the rote memorization of bare and often insignificant facts. Usually the objective test does not promote speculative and imaginative thinking.

Objective tests yield objective scores which indicate reliably the student's relative achievement in the course, provided the test is well constructed. Generally, the more comprehensively a student studies, as contrasted with rote memorizing, the better he will do on both short-answer and free-answer tests.

Tests that are used throughout a whole school system or statewide may tend to limit the teaching to direct preparation for those tests and thereby exclude both broader and more penetrating teaching.

Standardized achievement tests are objective in nature and are designed to indicate the students' achievement in the different school subjects. They are developed to yield age and grade norms.

Educational ages divided by chronological ages multiplied by 100 yield educational quotients, which indicate subject-matter achievement in terms of age. A student may be above, at, or below his age in achievement.

In marking students, different teachers take into account a number of things such as improvement, attitude, effort, behavior, and achievement. As a general rule, the mark should represent a student's competence in the subject. By ranking the students according to achievement and then assigning the marks according to standing, much injustice will be eliminated.

Girls usually get better marks than the boys even though boys tend to score a little higher on comprehensive, objective achievement tests. Students whose school marks are better than their standings on such achievement tests tend to be insecure and conforming, while those whose examination standings are above their marks are students of the highest mental-test and reading-test abilities.

A student's school marks provide a fairly good index to his industry and mental capacity. Thus the level of a student's marks is prognostic of success in adult life.

There are several objections to the usual marking systems: Teachers' individual marks are unreliable; students maneuver to get as good a mark as they can rather than learn as much as they can; marks develop much unpleasantness which is inimical to learning; in many instances bright students get high marks too easily and the low-endowed students are in the dismal position of never being able to get good marks; and marking takes an excessive amount of time—time which could be used for helping students. The objections to the marking system can be reduced by establishing reasonable standards of marking for all teachers, by giving more high marks and fewer failing ones, but most of all by doing away with the traditional marking and report-card system.

Parent-teacher conferences would become a more widely accepted practice if the school apprised the parents of the purposes and values of such conferences and then managed them efficiently. If, in a nonthreatening way, the teacher gave the parents information about the educational and personal development of their children and manifested a desire to learn from the parents, conferences would usually turn into a joint enterprise of home and school for bringing about the development of their children. Teachers should be equipped with solid data about the educational capacities and achievements of their students as well as their health, attitudes, and social behavior. Out of such conferences should evolve more effective ways of handling the students, both in school and at home. Having the child or teen-ager present at the conference usually has enlarged the bases of understanding and created more cooperation.

Writing letters to parents may be useful in some cases but if done regularly may fail to give any additional information and will be burdensome to the teacher.

Teachers and students need to have regular conferences in which they try to help each other be more effective in bringing about more successful experiences. In such conferences the student can be encouraged to evaluate himself and make recommendations for his own improvement. Mutual understanding will develop in many instances that will improve individual and school morale.

SUGGESTED READING

Ahmann, Stanley J., and Marvin D. Glock: *Evaluating Pupil Growth,* 2d ed., Allyn and Bacon, Inc., Boston, 1963. Extensive discussion of the topics taken up in this chapter. Excellent coverage of the problems dealing with the evaluation of pupil learning.

Doak, E. D.: "Grading: A Deterrent to Learning," *Clearing House,* 37:245–248, 1962. Points out how the need for school marks detours the student from the major objective, which is his learning and development. Plans for overcoming the ill effects of working for marks are set forth.

Muessig, Raymond H.: "How Do I Grade Thee? Let Me Count the Ways," *Clearing House,* 36:414–416, 1962. A teacher of English points out the different ingredients that can go into a mark and the impossibilities of accurately combining or averaging them. There are quantitative and qualitative, objective and subjective features that make accurate marking impossible.

APPENDIX

GENERAL EXPLANATIONS OF THE STATISTICAL TERMS USED IN THIS TEXT

THE AVERAGES

The three commonly used averages are the mean, the median, and the mode. The mean, also called the arithmetical average, is the average to which we are most accustomed. It is the average that we learned to calculate in grade school by adding up a group of numbers and dividing by their number. Thus we may calculate, for example, the average age, the average height, and the average spelling score for the pupils of a grade. Such means can be calculated when the scores or values and the number of them are known. The mean is the most important and most used average.

The median is a value, number, or point that divides the scores or values into two equal parts when they are arranged according to size from the highest to the lowest. In other words, the upper half of the scores is above the median and the lower half of the scores is below the median. Actually, then, the median is the midpoint and is an average of location or position.

The mode is the score or value of a group of scores that is the most frequent. If, in a spelling class, more pupils obtain a score of 100 than any other score, then 100 is the mode; if more women of a group are wearing red dresses than any other color, then red is the mode; if more people order beef than any other meat, then beef is the modal choice; and if more children start school at age six than at any other age, then six is the modal starting age.

The averages are generalized values, summaries or values that are most typical or usual. In distributions of scores, the averages are usually found where the scores are most concentrated; in other words, the averages usually have a central position.

PERCENTILE POSITIONS

Percentiles are points or values that indicate position or ranking in terms of per cent. Specifically, a percentile indicates the percentage of a group which is below a given point. Thus if a student has a percentile standing or rank of 86, then 86 per cent of the group are below that value. Similarly, percentiles of 15, 18, 52, 74, 99, or any other percentile indicate respectively the percentage below the points they represent. The median always is the 50th percentile. Percentiles are also called centiles.

DESCRIBING THE SPREAD OR VARIABILITY OF VALUES

One of the most striking features of human performance, abilities, and characteristics is their great differences. There is a great spread in all human qualities and behavior. These differences are discussed in several chapters.

The most useful statistical values for describing distributions are the standard deviation and the range. Of these two, the standard deviation is much more valuable and is the basic measure of variability. The standard deviation is based on the deviation of each score or value from the mean of the values.

The standard deviation, when used to describe the spread of the scores of a group, indicates how heterogeneous it is. When the standard deviation is very small the group is less heterogeneous and thus more homogeneous; and, obviously, when the standard deviation of a group is large, it is the opposite. Inasmuch as children are grouped into grades or sections for instructional purposes, it is useful to find how homogeneous or heterogeneous the groups are by finding their standard deviations for intelligence quotients, mental ages, achievement scores, height, weight, or any other measurements that may be considered important. Groups may be compared on the basis of their standard deviations in order to check on the extent of their variability.

A standard deviation may be defined as a distance above and below the mean of a normal or nearly normal distribution that includes about two-thirds of the cases (68.27 per cent).

It may also be used to give the location of any score of the distribution. For example, students whose scores are one and two standard deviations below the mean have percentile ranks or standings of about 16 and 2, respectively. The mean in a balanced or symmetrical distribution has a percentile standing of 50, and one and two standard deviations above the mean have percentile standings of approximately 84 and 98, respectively. By the use of tables, the percentile ranking for any standard-deviation position can be found readily.

The range is the spread from the lowest to the highest score. For example, the range in IQ is the difference between the highest and the lowest; and the range in height, the difference between the tallest and the shortest. If the highest mental age in a class is 12 years and 10 months and the lowest is 7 years and 2 months, then the range in mental age is 5 years and 8 months.

The range is an interesting value, but it does not have the statistical importance that the standard deviation has.

SIGNIFICANCE OF THE DIFFERENCE

This term is so frequently used in psychology and education that its general meaning should be understood by every student of these fields. Its more exact meaning will have to be learned by special study and instruction. When the difference between the averages of two groups is found, the question is asked: Is the difference large enough to be significant? In other words, it may be asked whether or not similar differences will be found if corresponding groups are compared under similar conditions a great number of times. If, with repetition, a difference was found between groups, and the same group was superior each time, then we may be sure that the difference is a true and significant one.

Obviously, it is impossible to repeat an experiment a large enough number of times to discover whether or not one group or the groups of the same characteristics are always superior and thus to determine that the difference first obtained is a true one. For example, one may be testing the effectiveness of a method of teaching reading by comparing it with other methods through actually trying the various methods on groups of pupils of similar initial ability and capacity. It would be impossible to repeat the experiment indefinitely to see whether or not the differences obtained were consistent and thus real ones. Instead, statistical procedures are applied to the averages of the groups to determine whether the differences are true ones or are due to chance factors. The results of the statistical analysis thus indicate the certainty with which we can conclude that a difference will occur under similar circumstances.

In other words, the largeness of the difference is tested. Thus, when it is said that the difference between two groups, as determined by comparing their averages, is significant, this means that the difference has been tested and found to be a real one and not one due to chance or accidental factors. Then reliance can be placed on the value of the method, influence, or factor being tested.

The extent to which one can be confident that the difference is a true one is called confidence level. We speak of a confidence level of .15, .12, .05, .03, .01, .001., or <.001. Suppose we say that the confidence level is .01. This indicates that the chances of the difference being a true one are ninety-nine times out of a hundred, but there is one chance in a hundred that it is not. A confidence level of <.001 is a very high one, because there is less than 1 chance in 1,000 that the difference could have happened by chance and therefore is not a true difference. Thus one can be almost completely confident that the difference is caused by the method, capacities, or whatever it is that is being tested. It will be observed that the smaller the confidence level is numerically, the greater the probability is that the difference is a true one.

CORRELATION

Correlation means relationship. In educational and psychological publications there are frequent uses of the concept of correlation. It is especially valuable to know how various abilities and characteristics correlate. It is because of our knowledge of these correlations that we can deal with students more intelligently.

Correlations are expressed as coefficients which range from 0 to ± 1.00. When the correlation is 0, there is no correlation between the scores. When the correlation is $+1.00$, then a perfect positive correlation exists; and when the correlation is -1.00, then a perfect negative relationship prevails between the scores.

In the explanation of correlation there are a number of concepts that should be understood:

1. There are two measurements or scores for each person. These are referred to as the variables.

2. Think of these scores or variables in terms of size, and think of them from the highest to the lowest.

3. If the highest score of one variable is paired with the highest of the other, the second highest with the second highest, the third highest with the third highest, and so on to the lowest, which is paired with the lowest, then the correlation is 1.00 (when the correlation is positive, the + sign is usually omitted).

4. If the highest score is paired with the lowest, the second highest is paired with the second lowest, and so on to the lowest, which is paired with the highest, then there is a consistent inverse relationship between the scores and the correlation is expressed by a coefficient of -1.00.

5. There may be no trend in the

relationships as just described in items 3 and 4. High scores may be associated with high, average, or low scores; average scores may be paired with high, average, or low scores; and low scores with high, average, or low ones. In other words, the relationships are as if caused by chance. In such cases, the correlation is zero or approximately so.

Few correlations are perfect but usually range between 0 and ±1.00. They are usually expressed in such coefficients as .22, .35, .48, .56, .61, .74, .87, and .90. When the correlations are negative a minus sign is used, as in the coefficient of −.54.

When most of the pairs of values tend to be correspondingly high, average, or low, the correlation tends to be high positive. As this relationship becomes less and less, the correlations become lower also. In negative correlations, the relationships are inverse; as the number of inverse pairs goes down, the correlation does also.

The degree of correlation corresponds to the amount of likeness in the position of the pairs according to size if the correlation is positive, or the amount of unlikeness in the position of the pairs if the correlation is negative.

A coefficient of .90 indicates a very high correlation; correlations of .40 to .60 are moderate, and correlations of 0 to .20 are very low. In a correlation of .90 the members of each pair take the same relative position, with few exceptions. When the correlation is .40 to .60, the number of exceptions is much larger; and when the correlations are just a little higher than zero, there is very little consistent relationship in the scores of each pair.

The degree of correlation does not correspond directly with the size of the correlation. In other words, an increase from .05 to .15 is not so much as from .85 to .95, the latter increase being much larger. Similarly, .40 is not twice .20 in degree of correlation, nor is .80 twice .40. Actually, in terms of correlation .80 is considerably more than twice .40. This is correlationally speaking and not arithmetically.

To illustrate further, let us deal with a correlation of .50 between IQ and school marks for a large group of sixth-grade children. This is about the typical correlation between these variables. What does this correlation mean in a general way? It means that of those who are above the average in IQ, about two-thirds will also be above the average in their school marks, but one-third will be below the average. Of the students with IQs below the average, two-thirds will have marks below the average and one-third of them above. When the correlations are higher, the proportions taking the same relative position in both variables are higher too; and when the correlations are lower, the proportions taking the same relative position are also lower. These statements apply to plus correlations.

In the case of identical twins, the measurements of height correlate about .95. What does this mean? It means that pairs of identical twins are very nearly equal in height. There are only a few exceptions; and when the pairs of identical twins do differ in height, the differences are generally very small.

There are special techniques for calculating the various statistics which have been described. The purpose of the discussion here is only to present the meanings of statistical terms which are used in the text. If the student wants to learn how to calculate the various statistical measures, he should consult textbooks in statistics or take a course in statistics.

REFERENCES

Ackerman, W. I., and H. Levin: "Effects of Training in Alternative Solutions on Subsequent Problem Solving," *Journal of Educational Psychology,* 49:239–244, 1958.

Aikin, W. W.: *The Story of the Eight Year Study,* Harper & Row, Publishers, Incorporated, New York, 1942.

Ausubel, David P., and Elias Blake, Jr.: "Proactive Inhibition in the Forgetting of Meaningful School Material," *Journal of Educational Research,* 52:145–149, 1958.

———, L. C. Robbins, and Elias Blake, Jr.: "Retroactive Inhibition and Facilitation in the Learning of School Materials," *Journal of Educational Psychology,* 48:334–343, 1957*a*.

———, S. H. Schopoont, and L. Cukier: "Influence of Intention on the Retention of School Materials," *Journal of Educational Psychology,* 48:87–92, 1957*b*.

Barlow, M. C.: "Transfer of Training in Reasoning," *Journal of Educational Psychology,* 28:122–128, 1937.

Barry, H., M. K. Bacon, and I. L. Child: "A Cross-cultural Survey of Some Sex Differences in Socialization," *Journal of Abnormal and Social Psychology,* 55:327–332, 1957.

Bayley, Nancy: "Growth Curves of Height and Weight by Age for Boys and Girls, Scaled according to Physical Maturity," *Journal of Pediatrics,* 48:187–194, 1956*a*.

———: "Individual Patterns of Development," *Child Development,* 27:45–74, 1956*b*.

———, and E. S. Shaefer: "Relationship between Socioeconomic Variables and the Behavior of Mothers toward Young Children," *Journal of Genetic Psychology,* 96:61–77, 1960.

Bendig, A. W., and Peter T. Hountras: "College Student Stereotypes of the Personality Traits of Research Scientists," *Journal of Educational Psychology,* 49:309–314, 1958.

Benezet, L. P.: "The Story of an Experiment," *Journal of the National Education Association,* 24:241–244, 301–303, 1935; 25:7–8, 1936.

Bloom, B. S.: "The 1955 Normative Study of the Tests of General Educational Development," *School Review,* 64:110–124, 1956.

Bodine, Ivan, E. M. Hollister, and Harry Sackett: "A Contribution to Team Teaching," *Bulletin of the National Association of Secondary School Principals,* 46:111–117, 1962.

Boyd, Edith: *Outline of Physical Growth and Development,* Burgess Publishing Company, Minneapolis, 1941.

Boyer, W. H.: "Survey of Attitudes, Opinions and Objectives of High School Students in the Milwaukee Area," *Journal of Educational Sociology,* 32:344–348, 1959.

Brumbaugh, Florence: "What Is an I.Q.?" *Journal of Experimental Education,* 23:359–363, 1955.

Cannon, K. L.: "Stability of Sociometric Scores of High School Students," *Journal of Educational Research,* 52:43–48, 1958.

Castaneta, Alfred, Boyd R. McCandless, and David S. Paterno: "The Children's Form of the Manifest Anxiety Scale," *Child Development,* 27:317–326, 1956.

Clark, Willis W.: "Boys and Girls—Are There Significant Ability and Achievement Differences," *Phi Delta Kappan,* 41:73–76, 1959.

Coffield, W. H., and Paul Blommers: "Effects of Non-promotion on Educational Achievement in the Elementary School," *Journal of Educational Psychology,* 47:235–250, 1956.

Cohen, B. H., and W. A. Bousfield: "The Effect of a Dual-level Stimulus-word list on the Occurrence of the Clustering in Recall," *Journal of General Psychology,* 55:51–58, 1956.

Coleman, James C.: *Personality Dynamics and Effective Behavior,* Scott, Foresman and Company, Chicago, 1960.

Collings, Ellsworth: *An Experiment with a Project Curriculum,* The Macmillan Company, New York, 1926.

Coster, John K.: "Some Characteristics of High School Pupils from Three Income Groups," *Journal of Educational Psychology,* 50:55–62, 1959.

Dollard, John, and Neal E Miller: *Personality and Psychotherapy,* McGraw-Hill Book Company, Inc., New York, 1950.

Drews, Elizabeth M.: "The Effectiveness of Homogeneous and Heterogeneous Ability Grouping in Ninth Grade English Classes with Slow, Average, and Superior Students," *Newsletter, American Psychological Association,* No. 1, 1960–61, p. 14.

Dunlap, J. M.: "Gifted Children in an Enriched Program," *Exceptional Children,* 21:135–137, 1955.

Eells, K., A. Davis, R. J. Havighurst, V. E. Herrick, and R. Tyler: *Intelligence and Cultural Differences,* The University of Chicago Press, Chicago, 1951.

Egner, R. E., and A. J. Obelsky: "Significance of Stereotyped Conditions for Education," *Journal of Higher Education,* 28:329–336, 1957.

Elwell, J. L., and G. C. Grindley: "The Effect of Knowledge of Results on Learning and Performance," *British Journal of Psychology,* 29:39–54, 1938–39.

Entwisle, Doris R.: "Evaluations of Study-skills Courses—A Review," *Journal of Educational Research,* 53:243–251, 1960.

Fargus, R. H., and R. J. Schwartz: "Efficient Retention and Transfer as Affected by Learning Methods," *Journal of Psychology,* 43:135–139, 1957.

Faust, Margaret S.: "Developmental Maturity as a Determinant in Prestige of Adolescent Girls," *Child Development,* 31:173–184, 1960.

Ferreira, A. J.: "The Pregnant Woman's Emotional Attitude and Its Reflection on the Newborn," *American Journal of Orthopsychiatry,* 30:553–561, 1960.

Flesher, Marie A., and S. L. Pressey: "War Time Accelerates Ten Years After," *Journal of Educational Psychology,* 46:228–238, 1955.

Frankel, Edward: "A Comparative Study of Achieving and Underachieving High School Boys of High Intellectual Ability," *Journal of Educational Research,* 53:172–180, 1960.

Frenkel-Brunswik, Else, and Joan Havel: "Prejudice in the Interviews of Children: I. Attitudes toward Minority Groups," *Pedagogical Seminary,* 82:91–136, 1953.

Gallagher, J. J.: "Social Status of Children Related to Intelligence, Propinquity and Social Perception," *Elementary School Journal,* 58:225–231, 1958.

Garber, R. B.: "Influence of Cognitive and Affective Factors in Learning and Retaining Attitudinal Material," *Journal of Abnormal and Social Psychology,* 51:384–389, 1955.

Ghiselli, E. E., and C. W. Brown, *Personnel and Industrial Psychology*, 2d ed., McGraw-Hill Book Company, Inc., New York, 1955, p. 385.

Gilbert, Thomas F.: "Overlearning and the Retention of Meaningful Prose," *Journal of General Psychology*, 56:281–289, 1957.

Goodlad, J. I.: "Some Effects of Promotion and Non-promotion upon the Social and Personal Adjustment of Children," *Journal of Experimental Education*, 22:301–328, 1954.

Gordon, Hugh: *Mental and Scholastic Tests among Retarded Children*, Educational Pamphlet 44, Board of Education, London, 1923.

Gowan, J. C.: "Summary of the Intensive Study of Twenty Highly Selected Elementary Woman Teachers," *Journal of Experimental Education*, 26:115–124, 1957.

Gronlund, N. E., and W. S. Holmlund: "Value of Elementary School Sociometric Status Scores for Predicting Pupils' Adjustment in High School," *Educational Administration and Supervision*, 44:255–260, 1958.

Grossack, M. M.: "Some Effects of Cooperation and Competition upon Small Group Behavior," *Journal of Abnormal and Social Psychology*, 49:341–348, 1954.

Hartshorne, Hugh, and M. A. May: *Studies in the Nature of Character*, The Macmillan Company, New York, 1928.

Hattwick, B. W., and M. Stowell: "The Relation of Parental Over-attentiveness to Children's Work-Habits and Social Adjustments in Kindergarten and the First Six Grades in School," *Journal of Educational Research*, 30:169–176, 1936.

Heber, R. F.: "The Relation of Intelligence and Physical Maturity to Social Status of Children," *Journal of Educational Psychology*, 47:158–162, 1956.

Heist, Paul: "Diversity in College Characteristics, *Journal of Educational Sociology*, 33:279–291, 1960.

Hendrickson, G., and W. H. Schroeder: "Transfer of Training in Learning to Hit a Submerged Target," *Journal of Educational Psychology*, 32:205–213, 1941.

Hilden, A. H.: "Longitudinal Study of Intellectual Development," *Journal of Psychology*, 28:187–214, 1949.

Hildreth, Gertrude: *Educating Gifted Children*, Harper & Row, Publishers, Incorporated, New York, 1952.

Holland, J. L.: "Creative and Academic Performance among Talented Adolescents," *Journal of Educational Psychology*, 52:136–147, 1961.

Hollingworth, H. L.: "The Influence of Alcohol," *Journal of Abnormal and Social Psychology*, 18:204–237, 311–333, 1923, 1924.

Hurlock, E. B.: "The Use of Group Rivalry as an Incentive," *Journal of Abnormal and Social Psychology*, 22:278–290, 1927–1928.

Jones, Daisy Marvel: An Experiment in Adaptation to Individual Differences," *Journal of Educational Psychology*, 39:257–272, 1948.

Jones, Mary: "Later Careers of Boys Who Were Early or Late Maturing," *Child Development*, 28:113–128, 1957.

———, and Nancy Bayley: "Physical Maturing among Boys as Related to Behavior," *Journal of Educational Psychology*, 41:129–148, 1950.

Judd, C. H.: "The Relation of Special Training to General Intelligence," *Educational Review*, 36:28–42, 1908.

Kadis, Asyra L.: "Analytic Group Work with Teachers," *National Association of Women, Deans and Counselors Journal*, 23:78–81, 1960.

Kelley, E. G.: "Study of Consistent Discrepancies between Instructor Grades and Term-end Examinations,"

Journal of Educational Psychology, 49:328–334, 1958.

Keys, Noel: "The Value of Group Test I.Q.'s for Prediction of Progress beyond High School," *Journal of Educational Psychology,* 31:81–93, 1940.

Knapp, C. G., and W. R. Dixon: "Learning to Juggle: I. A Study to Determine the Effect of Two Different Distributions of Practice on Learning Efficiency," *Research Quarterly of the American Association for Health, Physical Education and Recreation,* 21:331–336, 1950.

Kolesnik, W. B.: *Mental Discipline in Modern Education,* The University of Wisconsin Press, Madison, Wis., 1958.

Korner, I. N.: "Experimental Investigation of Some Aspects of the Problem of Repression: Repressive Forgetting," *Contributions to Education,* 970, Teachers College, Columbia University, New York, 1950.

Lahey, Sister M. Florence L.: "Permanence of Retention of First Year Algebra," *Journal of Educational Psychology,* 32:401–413, 1941.

Learned, W. S., and B. D. K. Wood: *The Student and His Knowledge,* Carnegie Foundation for the Advancement of Teaching, Bulletin No. 29, 1938.

Leuba, Clarence J.: "A Preliminary Experiment to Quantify an Incentive and Its Effects," *Journal of Abnormal and Social Psychology,* 25:275–288, 1930.

Levine, J. M., and G. Murphy: "The Learning and Forgetting of Controversial Material," *Journal of Abnormal and Social Psychology,* 38:507–517, 1943.

Levy, D. M.: "Infants Earliest Memory of Inoculation: A Contribution to Public Health Procedures," *Journal of Genetic Psychology,* 96:3–46, 1960.

Liddle, Gordon: "Overlap among Desirable and Undesirable Characteristics in Gifted Children," *Journal of Educational Psychology,* 49:219–228, 1958.

Logey, J. C.: "Does Teaching Change Students' Attitudes," *Journal of Educational Research,* 50:307–311, 1956.

McDougall, William P.: "Differential Retention of Course Outcomes in Educational Psychology," *Journal of Educational Psychology,* 49:53–60, 1958.

McElwee, Edna W.: "A Comparison of the Personality Traits of 300 Accelerated, Normal, and Retarded Children," *Journal of Educational Research,* 26:31–34, 1932.

Maller, J. B.: "Cooperation and Competition: An Experimental Study in Motivation," *Contributions to Education,* 384, Teachers College, Columbia University, New York, 1929.

Maslow, A. H., and W. Zimmerman: "College Teaching Ability, Scholarly Activity and Personality," *Journal of Educational Psychology,* 47:185–189, 1956.

Meltger, H.: "Individual Differences in Forgetting Pleasant and Unpleasant Experiences," *Journal of Educational Psychology,* 21:399–409, 1930.

Meredith, H. V., Dale B. Harris (ed.): *The Concept of Development,* The University of Minnesota Press, Minneapolis, 1957, pp. 114–121.

———: "The Rhythm of Physical Growth," *University of Iowa Studies,* XI (3), Iowa City, 1935.

Miller, K. M., and J. B. Briggs: "Attitude Change through Undirected Group Discussion," *Journal of Educational Psychology,* 49:224–228, 1958.

Mintz, A.: "Non-adaptive Group Behavior," *Journal of Abnormal and Social Psychology,* 46:150–159, 1951.

Mitchell, J. V.: "The Identification

of Items in the California Test of Personality that Differentiate between Subjects of High and Low Socio-economic Status of the Fifth and Seventh Grade Levels," *Journal of Educational Research,* 51:241–250, 1957.

Mitchell, Virginia: "An Analysis of the Grade Expectancies and the Actual Achievement of Fourth, Fifth and Sixth Grade Pupils," *Teachers College Journal,* 31:21–22, 1959.

Moore, J. E.: "Annoying Habits of High School Teachers," *Peabody Journal of Education,* 18:161–165, 1940.

Mueller, Karl: "Success of Elementary Students Admitted to Public Schools under the Requirements of the Nebraska Program of Early Entrance," unpublished Ph.D. dissertation, University of Nebraska, 1955; cited in D. A. Worcester, *The Education of Children of Above-average Mentality,* University of Nebraska Press, Lincoln, Nebr., 1955, pp. 21–28.

National Education Association, *Fostering Mental Health in Our Schools,* Yearbook of the Association for Supervision and Curriculum Development, Washington, D.C., 1950.

Neilon, Patricia: "Shirley's Babies after Fifteen Years; a Personality Study," *Journal of Genetic Psychology,* 73:175–186, 1948.

Newman, Horatio H., Frank N. Freeman, and Karl J. Holzinger: *Twins: A Study of Heredity and Environment,* The University of Chicago Press, Chicago, 1937.

Oak-Bruce, Laura: What Do We Know for Sure? *Childhood Education,* 24:312–321, 1948.

O'Kelly, L. I., and L. C. Steckle: "The Forgetting of Pleasant and Unpleasant Experiences," *American Journal of Psychology,* 53:432–434, 1940.

Olander, H. T., and H. M. Kleyle: Difference in Personal and Professional Characteristics of a Selected Group of Elementary Teachers with Contrasting Success Records," *Educational Administration and Supervision,* 45:191–198, 1959.

Page, E. B.: "Teacher Comments and Student Performance: A Seventy-four Classroom Experiment in School Motivation," *Journal of Educational Psychology,* 49:173–181, 1958.

Pasley, Virginia: *21 Stayed,* Farrar, Straus & Company, Inc., New York, 1955.

Pauk, Walter J.: "Are Present Reading Tests Valid for Girls and Boys?" *Journal of Educational Research,* 53:279–280, 1960.

Phillips, Beeman N.: "Effect of Cohesion and Intelligence on Problem Solving Efficiency of Small Face to Face Groups in Cooperative and Competitive Situations," *Journal of Educational Research,* 50:127–132, 1956.

Phillips, W. S., and J. E. Green: "A Preliminary Study of the Relationship of Age, Hobbies and Civil Status to Neuroticism among Women Teachers," *Journal of Educational Psychology,* 30:440–444, 1939.

Plant, Walter T.: "Changes in Ethnocentrism Associated with a Four-year College Education," *Journal of Educational Psychology,* 49:162–165, 1958.

Plowman, L., and J. B. Stroud: "Effect of Informing Pupils of the Correctness of Their Responses to Objective Test Questions," *Journal of Educational Research,* 36:16–20, 1942.

Poffenberger, A. T.: *Principles of Applied Psychology,* Appleton-Century-Crofts Company, Inc., New York, 1942.

Poffenberger, Thomas, and Donald Norton: "Factors in the Formation of Attitudes toward Mathematics," *Journal of Educational Research,* 52:171–176, 1959.

Provus, Malcolm M.: "Ability Grouping in Arithmetic," *Elementary School Journal,* 60:391–398, 1960.

Reynolds, B., and J. A. Adams: "Motor Performance as a Function of Click Reinforcement," *Journal of Experimental Psychology*, 45:315–320, 1953.

Rowe, F. A.: "Should Junior High Schools Have Highly Organized Competitive Athletics?" *School Activities*, 22:96–99, 129–130, 1950.

Ryans, D. G.: *Characteristics of Teachers*, American Council on Education, Washington, D.C., 1960.

———: "Some Correlates of Teacher Behavior," *Educational and Psychological Measurement*, 19:9–10, 1959.

Salisbury, Rachel: "A Study of the Transfer Effects of the Training in Logical Organization," *Journal of Educational Research*, 28:241–254, 1934.

Sarason, Irwin G.: "Test Anxiety, General Anxiety and Intellectual Performance," *Journal of Consulting Psychology*, 21:485–490, 1957.

Schmidt, Herman O.: "The Effects of Praise and Blame as Incentives to Learning," *Psychological Monographs*, 53(240):1–56, 1941.

Schwartz, M.: "Transfer of Reading Training from Non-technical to Technical Material," *Journal of Educational Psychology*, 48:498–504, 1957.

Sears, Pauline S.: "Levels of Aspiration in Academically Successful and Unsuccessful Children," *Journal of Abnormal and Social Psychology*, 35:498–536, 1940.

Shaw, Marvin E.: "Some Motivational Factors in Cooperation and Competition," *Journal of Personality*, 26:155–169, 1958.

Shields, James: "Twins Brought Up Apart," *The Eugenics Review*, 50:115–123, 1958.

Shuttleworth, F. K.: *The Physical and Mental Growth of Girls and Boys Age Six to Nineteen in Relation to Age of Maximum Growth*, Society for Research in Child Development, National Research Council, Washington, D.C., 1939.

Silvey, Herbert M.: "Student Reaction to the Objective and Essay Test," *School and Society*, 73:377–378, 1951.

Simmons, K.: *The Brush Foundation of Child Growth and Development. II. Physical Growth and Development*, Monograph IX (1), Society for Research in Child Development, National Research Council, Washington, D.C., 1944.

Slobetz, Frank: "How Elementary School Teachers Meet Selected School Situations," *Journal of Educational Psychology*, 42:339–356, 1951.

Smeltz, John R.: "Retention of Learning in High School Chemistry," *Science Teacher*, 23:285–305, 1956.

Sommer, Robert: "Sex Differences in the Retention of Quantitative Information," *Journal of Educational Psychology*, 49:187–192, 1958.

Sontag, Lester W., Charles T. Baker, and Virginia L. Nelson: *Mental Growth and Personality Development: A Longitudinal Study*, Monograph XXIII (2), Society for Research in Child Development, National Research Council, Washington, D.C., 1958, pp. 57–81.

Steckle, Lynde C.: *Problems of Human Adjustment*, Harper & Row, Publishers, Incorporated, New York, 1957.

Steigman, M. J., and H. W. Stevenson: "Effect of Pretraining Reinforcement Schedules on Children's Learning," *Child Development*, 31:53–58, 1960.

Stendler, Celia B., D. Damrin, and A. C. Haines: "Studies in Cooperation and Competition: I. The Effects of Working for Group and Individual Rewards on the Social Climate of Children's Groups," *Journal of Genetic Psychology*, 79:173–197, 1951.

———, and Norman Young: "The

Impact of Beginning First Grade upon Socialization as Reported by Mothers," *Child Development,* 21:241–260, 1950.

Stewart, Naomi: "AGCT Scores of Army Personnel Grouped by Occupation," *Occupations,* 26:5–51, 1947.

Stinson, P. J., and Mildred M. Morrison: "Sex Differences among High School Seniors," *Journal of Educational Research,* 53:103–108, 1959.

Stuart, H. C.: *Healthy Childhood,* Appleton-Century-Crofts, Inc., New York, 1933.

Symonds, Percival M.: *Adolescent Fantasy,* Columbia University Press, New York, 1949.

Tanner, J. M.: *Growth at Adolescence,* 2d ed., Charles C Thomas, Publisher, Springfield, Ill., 1962.

Terman, Lewis M., and Maud A. Merrill: *Stanford-Binet Intelligence Scale; Manual for the Third Revision, Form L-M,* Houghton Mifflin Company, Boston, 1960.

———, and Melita H. Oden: *Genetic Studies of Genius,* vol. V, *The Gifted Group at Mid-life,* Stanford University Press, Stanford, Calif., 1959.

———, and L. E. Tyler: "Psychological Sex Differences," in Carmichael, L. (ed.): *Manual of Child Psychology,* John Wiley & Sons, Inc., New York, 1954, pp. 1064–1114.

Thisted, M. N., and H. H. Remmers: "The Effect of Temporal Set on Learning," *Journal of Applied Psychology,* 16:257–268, 1932.

Thompson, G. G., and C. W. Hunnicutt: "The Effect of Repeated Praise or Blame on the Work Achievement of Introverts and Extroverts," *Journal of Educational Psychology,* 35:257–266, 1944.

Thorndike, E. L.: "Mental Discipline in High School Studies," *Journal of Educational Psychology,* 15:1–22, 83–98, 1924.

———, W. A. McCall, and J. C.

Chapman: "Ventilation in Relation to Mental Work," *Contributions to Education,* 78, Teachers College, Columbia University, New York, 1916.

Tilton, J. W.: *Educational Psychology of Learning,* The Macmillan Company, New York, 1951.

Torgerson, T. L.: *Studying Children,* Holt, Rinehart and Winston, Inc., New York, 1947.

Tryon, R. C.: "Individual Differences," in F. A. Moss (ed.): *Comparative Psychology,* Prentice-Hall, Inc., Englewood Cliffs, N.J., 1934.

Tuddenton, R. D., and M. M. Snyder: "The Physical Growth of California Boys and Girls from Birth to Eighteen Years," University of California Publications in *Child Development,* 1:183–364, 1954.

Tuma, Elias, and Norman Livson: "Family Socioeconomic Status and Adolescent Attitudes to Authority," *Child Development,* 31:387–399, 1960.

Tyler, Bonnie B.: "Expectancy for Eventual Success as a Factor in Problem Solving Behavior," *Journal of Educational Psychology,* 49:166–172, 1958.

Vernon, Philip E.: "Education and the Psychology of Individual Differences," *Harvard Educational Review,* 28:91–104, 1958.

Vickers, V. S., and H. C. Stuart: "Anthropometry in Pediatricians Office; Norms for Selected Body Measurements Based on Studies of Children of North European Stock," *Journal of Pediatrics,* 22:155–170, 1943.

Wallis, Ruth: "How Children Grow: An Anthropometric Study of Points of Private School Children from Two to Eight Years of Age," *University of Iowa Studies in Child Welfare,* V(1), 1931.

Webster, Harold: "Changes in Attitude during College," *Journal of Edu-*

cational Psychology, 49:109–117, 1958.

Wesman, A. G.: "A Study of Transfer of Training from High School Subjects to Intelligence," Journal of Educational Research, 39:254–264, 1945.

White, Ralph K., and Ronald Lippitt: Autocracy and Democracy, Harper & Row, Publishers, Incorporated, New York, 1961.

Whittle, H. Douglas: "Effects of Elementary School Physical Education upon Aspects of Physical, Motor and Personality Development," Research Quarterly of the American Association for Health, Physical Education and Recreation, 32:249–260, 1961.

Wickman, E. K.: Children's Behavior and Teachers' Attitudes, The Commonwealth Fund, New York, 1928.

Wilson, C. Robert: "The Unedu-cated: How We Have Neglected the Bright Child," Atlantic Monthly, 195:60–62, 1955.

Wolfson, I. N.: "Follow up Studies of 92 Male and 131 Female Patients Who Were Discharged from the Newark State School in 1946," American Journal of Mental Deficiency, 61:224–238, 1956.

Worcester, D. A.: The Education of Children of Above-average Mentality, University of Nebraska Press, Lincoln, Nebr., 1955.

Worell, Leonard: "Level of Aspiration and Academic Success," Journal of Educational Psychology 50:47–54, 1959.

Zander, Alvin, and Elmer Van Egmond: "Relationship of Intelligence and Social Power to the Interpersonal Behavior of Children," Journal of Educational Psychology, 49:257–268, 1958.

INDEX

Date Due

0.